The King Arthur Baking Company

All-Purpose Baker's Companion

THE ALL-PURPOSE
BAKER'S COMPANION

Countryman Press

An Imprint of W. W. Norton & Company
Independent Publishers Since 1923

All food photography and styling by Liz Neily, unless otherwise noted:
Crunchy Cornmeal Waffles by Posie Brien, Croissants de Boulanger by Erica Allen,
and Black and White Cookies by Shilpa Iyer.

Previous edition published under the title *The King Arthur Flour Baker's Companion:
The All-Purpose Baking Cookbook*

For information about permission to reproduce selections from this book, write to
Permissions, The Countryman Press, 500 Fifth Avenue, New York, NY 10110

For information about special discounts for bulk purchases, please contact
W. W. Norton Special Sales at specialsales@wwnorton.com or 800-233-4830

Manufacturing by RR Donnelley Asia
Production manager: Devon Zahn
Prepress production director: Joe Lops
Art director: Allison Chi
Production editor: Jess Murphy

Library of Congress Cataloging-in-Publication Data

Names: King Arthur Baking Company, author, issuing body.
Title: The all-purpose baker's companion / King Arthur Baking Company.
Other titles: King Arthur Baking Company all-purpose baker's companion
Description: New York : The Countryman Press, a division of W.W. Norton & Company, [2021] |
    "Previous edition published under the title The King Arthur Flour baker's companion: the all-
    purpose baking cookbook"—Colophon.
Identifiers: LCCN 2020053669 | ISBN 9781682686171 (hardcover) | ISBN 9781682686188 (epub)
Subjects: LCSH: Baking. | LCGFT: Cookbooks.
Classification: LCC TX765 .K55 2021 | DDC 641.81/5—dc23
LC record available at https://lccn.loc.gov/2020053669

Countryman Press
www.countrymanpress.com

An imprint of W. W. Norton & Company, Inc.
500 Fifth Avenue, New York, NY 10110
www.wwnorton.com

10 9 8 7 6 5 4 3 2 1

Contents

Introduction

We bake. Baking brings us joy and a sense of accomplishment. We choose to bake even though nearly anything we might ever want to eat is available ready-made, and often can be delivered to us at the click of a button. We find pleasure in baking a birthday cake and taking the time to frost and decorate it. To nurture a sourdough starter for bread. To tinker with a cookie dough recipe until it's perfect. Why do we do it?

Because baking is an expression of love and care—a way to nourish those around us, and a way to ground ourselves in the tangible act of creating something real. And it's personal: When you bake, you can tailor a recipe to your own tastes. Do you like fudgy brownies with a shiny crust or cakey ones with a hint of espresso? Do you want less salt or more? Do you like your coffeecake less sweet or loaded with extra streusel? Your chocolate chip cookies crunchy or chewy? When you bake, it's all up to you.

But what if you never learned to bake? Or you have learned, but aren't totally satisfied with the results? You may not have had a grandmother gently guiding your hands as you rolled out your first pie crust—and even if you did, perhaps you've forgotten most of what she showed you. That's where *The All-Purpose Baker's Companion* comes in. In this book, you'll find the recipes and solid, reliable information that you need to become a top-notch baker, one who makes the lightest and most tender pancakes, the richest chocolate cake, and an apple pie that'll bring people to tears. You'll make oatmeal cookies better than any you've ever tasted, and your yeast breads will rival those of the local bakery.

Let this book be your guide as you walk a path followed by so many from around the world for thousands of years. You're a link in a limitless line of bakers: the sticky bun recipe you pass along to your children today will continue to be shared long after you're gone. And the guiding hand you place atop a friend's as she kneads her first batch of bread dough will in turn be placed atop another's someday. We here at King Arthur take our responsibility to bakers seriously; as America's oldest flour company, founded in 1790, we are committed to both preserving a treasured baking heritage and helping to forge its future.

This cookbook is an integral part of that preservation. In the years since its first publication, it has become an essential piece of so many kitchens. In 2019, we set out on a mission to bring a new, updated version of this beloved cookbook to bakers everywhere. We sought to preserve the incredible voice and knowledge that has made the original cookbook so beloved. We listened to the stories of readers who have cherished the recipes within these pages—recipes that are touchstones of family traditions, important memories, and more. We wanted to respect those traditions, while ensuring that every recipe holds up to the test of time. We've grown as a company and we've applied the lessons of the past decades to this book, polishing and perfecting each word. You'll find that we've added some favorite new recipes and new information for bakers on topics like whole grain and gluten-free baking. We hope you find it as useful as generations of bakers have before you, and that it becomes a delicious part of the fabric of your life for the years ahead.

THE BAKERS OF KING ARTHUR BAKING COMPANY

A Note on Measuring

Butter the size of an egg? A cup of flour or 100 grams of sugar? Measuring is one of those things we don't think about until we're slightly stymied, or until we open a British cookbook, or perhaps one from Europe, or maybe our grandmother's. There are, of course, a number of systems for measuring, some pretty out of date, some unique to the United States, and one that's pretty universal. Measuring has always been somewhat of an interpretive business.

But measuring goes beyond the devices you use to determine how much of what goes into a recipe. Thermometers, both in your drawer and in your oven, are measuring devices. So is your timer, and the thermostat in your kitchen. So is a barometer, hygrometer, and altimeter. When you're aware that bread rises quicker when the barometer is falling (it's good to bake on a rainy day), that flour "shrinks" in the winter because it's dry so you may need less of it (flour absorbs or sheds moisture depending on humidity), or that you'll need less yeast and baking powder if you live at 8,000 feet, you'll begin to understand all the variables you need to consider when you bake. You may find that you can make something successfully at home, time after time, but take the same recipe and try it in another kitchen with other equipment and you may have a very different result. Measuring cups and spoons, scales, humidity, altitude, and temperature all have an impact on the results of your efforts.

Our System of Measuring

Our American system of weights and measures was based originally on the British system, but they have developed differently from one another in the past two centuries. Although in 1959, English-speaking scientists agreed to use the metric system for scientific and technological purposes, that's been of little use to bakers.

In the early 1800s, Americans began to substitute volume measurements for weight, probably because a "teacup" or an "egg" as bases for measurement were easier to come by than an accurate scale, especially on the trail west. A "knob" of butter, "butter the size of an egg," even "alum the size of a cherry," are measurements that are sprinkled through old cookbooks. In earlier times, "receipts" for baked goods were based on these fairly rough ingredient guidelines that led to very individualized results. Baking success was dependent on an accumulation of experience.

Today we try to re-create recipes accurately, without eliminating an individual's touch. Just as your speech has a personality of its own, so should your baking. But as we try to become more accurate, our tradition of volume measuring can leave us short because volume measurements are prone to wide variations (a "cup" of flour can weigh anywhere between 110 and 155 grams, and the measuring cups themselves can legally vary up to 12%). Measuring by weight is much more consistent and accurate.

Measuring Flour

At King Arthur Baking Company, we've held a long debate about what a "cup" of flour weighs. In the past, for simplicity's sake, we called it 113 grams. You can, in fact, create a 113-gram cup of flour by sifting the flour first. The sifting process incorporates a lot of air into the flour, which is the first source of leavening. Scooping flour, which can produce a much heavier cup (up to 155 grams), will obviously contain less air and more flour. You can also fluff up flour in your flour bag, sprinkle it gently into your measuring cup, scrape the top with a straight edge, and get close to 113 grams, but you probably will get a little bit more.

Thus, in recent years we've changed preferred weight for a cup of flour is 120 grams, and that's what we've used throughout the book. This is closer to the standard weight that bakers use. It makes calculating total grams a little more difficult, but in all of the recipes we've done the calculating for you. This discussion would be much easier if we'd stop relying on measuring cups and start using the scale. But since the old volume system of measurement is still pretty standard, we're using it along with weight measurements.

Measuring Devices

- Our first plea is that you buy and use a scale (see Tools, page 541).
- For volume or weight measuring, have on hand a couple of sets of measuring

spoons. It's easier to measure small amounts—a teaspoon, a tablespoon—with spoons even if you have a scale. There are some sets available that measure from ⅛ teaspoon through ½ to 1 tablespoon. There are also sets containing odd sizes. It's useful to have more than one set (see Tools, page 539).

- Have two kinds of measuring cups, one that measures flush at the top edge for dry ingredients and one that has a lip at the top for liquids. There are some liquid measures available that also have metric measurements on one side. These can be useful when using cookbooks from other parts of the world.

- Other important measuring devices are thermometers and timers (see Tools, pages 540 and 542). Because ovens have their own personalities, a thermometer that helps you know what's going on inside is important. Oven temperatures can vary considerably, as can oven thermostats, which drive how long your oven "cools" before the heating element kicks in again. Thermometers can also measure the temperature of a dough, batters, syrups, and finished goods.

- Even with the most accurate of measurements, such variables as humidity, altitude, the fat content of the milk you use, and the mineral content of your water all are going to affect your baking. Ultimately your eyes and hands, when they have had enough experience, will make many of your measuring decisions.

Measuring Hints

Make sure that you know what you're supposed to be measuring, for example, 1 pound of apples, chopped, or 1 pound of chopped apple. The former is apples weighed before they've been chopped—with skins and cores. The latter is peeled, cored, chopped apple.

Measuring by Volume

- When measuring flour by volume, fluff up the flour, sprinkle into your dry-cup measure (the one that measures exactly a cup at the top), and scrape off the excess with a straight edge (a metal flour scoop with a straight edge allows you to scoop and sweep with one hand). This will get you approximately 120 grams. (See illustrations on page xii.)

- When measuring other dry ingredients such as sugar by volume, overfill your dry-cup measure and scrape off the excess with a straight edge.

- Measure light or dark brown sugar by packing it into your measuring cup.

- To measure a solid fat (butter, shortening, or lard) in a measuring cup, use one that is significantly larger than the amount you want to measure. For example, to measure 1 cup of butter, fill a 2-cup liquid measure up to the 1-cup mark with cold water. Push butter into the water until the water reaches the 2-cup mark, which will give you 1 cup of butter. Drain the fat thoroughly. Alternatively, use a measuring cup specifically designed for measuring sticky substances (see Tools, page 540).

①

Stir the flour to fluff it up . . .

②

. . . sprinkle it into the measuring cup . . .

③

. . . and sweep off the excess with the straight edge of the scoop.

- If you need to measure a liquid sweetener or peanut butter, spray the inside of your measuring cup lightly with a vegetable oil spray first. That will make it easier to get the sweetener out of the cup. (If the recipe calls for vegetable oil or other liquid fat, just measure that in the cup before you measure the sweetener; you'll get the same result.)

Measuring by Weight

Weighing ingredients is a more accurate way of determining amounts than measuring by volume. When it comes to volume measurements, there are many variables that can affect actual amounts. Measuring cups and spoons can vary significantly, as we've discovered over and over in our test kitchen. Cooks everywhere use varying techniques, and one person's idea of "full" or "packed" is usually different from the next person's.

Ingredient weights can also vary significantly. Flour weighs less in some climates, where the air is drier, than it does in others, where it's humid. It also varies from summer to winter. Raisins from an opened box that have been in the pantry or refrigerator for months won't weigh as much as fresh ones. Vegetables and berries can have a wide range of water contents, so they may weigh different amounts at any given time. You get the idea.

This chart gives average weights for commonly used amounts given in recipes. It can help you plan your shopping, as well as being handy if you want to convert recipes to significantly larger amounts.

Ingredient Weight Chart

INGREDIENT	VOLUME	GRAMS	OUNCES
All-Purpose Flour	1 cup	120	4¼
Almond Flour	1 cup	96	3⅜
Almond Meal	1 cup	84	3
Almond Paste (packed)	1 cup	259	9⅛
Almonds (sliced)	½ cup	43	1½
Almonds (slivered)	½ cup	57	2
Almonds, whole (unblanched)	1 cup	142	5
Amaranth Flour	1 cup	103	3⅝
Apples (dried, diced)	1 cup	85	3
Apples (peeled, sliced)	1 cup	113	4
Applesauce	1 cup	255	9
Apricots (dried, diced)	½ cup	64	2¼
Artisan Bread Flour	1 cup	120	4¼
Baker's Fruit Blend	1 cup	128	4½
Baker's Special Sugar (super-fine sugar, castor sugar)	1 cup	190	6¾
Baking Powder	1 teaspoon	4	
Baking Soda	½ teaspoon	3	
Bananas (mashed)	1 cup	227	8
Barley (cooked)	1 cup	215	7⅝
Barley (pearled)	1 cup	213	7½
Barley Flakes	½ cup	46	1⅝
Barley Flour	1 cup	85	3
Basil Pesto	2 tablespoons	28	1
Bell Peppers (fresh)	1 cup	142	5
Berries (frozen)	1 cup	142	5
Blueberries (dried)	1 cup	156	5½
Blueberries (fresh)	1 cup	170	6
Blueberry Juice	1 cup	241	8½
Boiled Cider	¼ cup	85	3
Bran Cereal	1 cup	60	2⅛
Bread Crumbs (dried)	¼ cup	28	1
Bread Crumbs (fresh)	¼ cup	21	¾
Bread Crumbs (Panko)	¼ cup	50	1¾
Bread Flour	1 cup	120	4¼
Brown Rice (cooked)	1 cup	170	6
Brown Rice Flour	1 cup	128	4½

INGREDIENT	VOLUME	GRAMS	OUNCES
Brown Sugar (dark or light, packed)	1 cup	213	7½
Buckwheat (whole)	1 cup	170	6
Buckwheat Flour	1 cup	120	4¼
Bulgar	1 cup	152	5⅜
Butter	8 tablespoons (½ cup)	113	4
Buttermilk	1 cup	227	8
Cake Enhancer	2 tablespoons	14	½
Candied Peel	½ cup	85	3
Caramel (14 to 16 individual pieces, 1″ squares)	½ cup	142	5
Caramel Bits (chopped Heath or toffee)	1 cup	156	5½
Caraway Seeds	2 tablespoons	18	⅝
Carrots (cooked and puréed)	½ cup	128	4½
Carrots (diced)	1 cup	142	5
Carrots (grated)	1 cup	99	3½
Cashews (chopped)	1 cup	113	4
Cashews (whole)	1 cup	113	4
Celery (diced)	1 cup	142	5
Cheese (feta)	½ cup	57	2
Cheese (grated cheddar, jack, mozzarella or Swiss)	1 cup	113	4
Cheese (grated Parmesan)	½ cup	50	1¾
Cheese (ricotta)	1 cup	227	8
Cherries (candied)	¼ cup	50	1¾
Cherries (dried)	½ cup	71	2½
Cherries (frozen)	1 cup	113	4
Chickpea Flour	1 cup	85	3
Chives (fresh)	½ cup	21	¾
Chocolate (chopped)	1 cup	170	6
Chocolate Chips	1 cup	170	6
Cinnamon Sugar	¼ cup	50	1¾
Cocoa (unsweetened)	½ cup	42	1½
Coconut (sweetened, shredded)	1 cup	85	3
Coconut (unsweetened, large flakes)	1 cup	60	2⅛
Coconut (unsweetened, shredded)	1 cup	113	4
Coconut Flour	1 cup	128	4½

INGREDIENT	VOLUME	GRAMS	OUNCES
Coconut Milk Powder	½ cup	57	2
Coconut Oil	½ cup	113	4
Confectioners' Sugar (unsifted)	2 cups	227	8
Cookie Crumbs	1 cup	85	3
Corn (popped)	4 cups	21	¾
Corn Syrup	1 cup	312	11
Cornmeal (whole)	1 cup	138	4⅞
Cornmeal (yellow, Quaker)	1 cup	156	5½
Cornstarch	¼ cup	28	1
Cracked Wheat	1 cup	149	5¼
Cranberries (dried)	½ cup	57	2
Cranberries (fresh or frozen)	1 cup	99	3½
Cream (heavy cream, light cream, or half-and-half)	1 cup	227	8
Cream Cheese	1 cup	227	8
Crystallized Ginger	½ cup	92	3¼
Currants	1 cup	142	5
Dates (chopped)	1 cup	149	5¼
Demerara Sugar	1 cup	220	7¾
Dried Blueberry Powder	¼ cup	28	1
Dried Buttermilk Powder	2 tablespoons	25	⅞
Dried Milk (Baker's Special Dried Milk)	¼ cup	35	1¼
Dried Nonfat Milk (powdered)	¼ cup	21	¾
Dried Potato Flakes (instant mashed potatoes)	½ cup	43	1½
Dried Whole Milk (powdered)	½ cup	50	1¾
Durum Flour	1 cup	124	4⅜
Easy Roll Dough Improver	2 tablespoons	18	⅝
Egg (fresh)	1 large	50	1¾
Egg White (fresh)	1 large	35	1¼
Egg Whites (dried)	2 tablespoons	11	⅜
Egg Yolk (fresh)	1 large	14	½
Espresso Powder	1 tablespoon	7	¼
Figs (dried, chopped)	1 cup	149	5¼
First Clear Flour	1 cup	106	3¾
Flax Meal	½ cup	50	1¾
Flaxseed	¼ cup	35	1¼

INGREDIENT	VOLUME	GRAMS	OUNCES
Garlic (cloves, in skin for roasting)	1 large head	113	4
Garlic (minced)	2 tablespoons	28	1
Garlic (peeled and sliced)	1 cup	149	5¼
Ginger (fresh, sliced)	¼ cup	57	2
Gluten-Free All-Purpose Baking Mix	1 cup	120	4¼
Gluten-Free All-Purpose Flour	1 cup	156	5½
Graham Cracker Crumbs (boxed)	1 cup	99	3½
Graham Crackers (crushed)	1 cup	142	5
Granola	1 cup	113	4
Grape-Nuts	½ cup	57	2
Harvest Grains Blend	½ cup	74	2⅝
Hazelnut Flour	1 cup	89	3⅛
Hazelnut Praline Paste	½ cup	156	5½
Hazelnut Spread	½ cup	160	5⅝
Hazelnuts (whole)	1 cup	142	5
Hi-Maize Natural Fiber	¼ cup	32	1⅛
High-Gluten Flour	1 cup	120	4¼
Honey	1 tablespoon	21	¾
Instant ClearJel	1 tablespoon	11	⅜
Jam or Preserves	¼ cup	85	3
Jammy Bits	1 cup	184	6½
Key Lime Juice	1 cup	227	8
Lard	½ cup	113	4
Leeks (diced)	1 cup	92	3¼
Lemon Juice Powder	2 tablespoons	18	⅝
Lime Juice Powder	2 tablespoons	18	⅝
Macadamia Nuts (whole)	1 cup	149	5¼
Malt Syrup	2 tablespoons	43	1½
Malted Milk Powder	¼ cup	35	1¼
Malted Wheat Flakes	½ cup	64	2¼
Maple Sugar	½ cup	78	2¾
Maple Syrup	½ cup	156	5½
Marshmallow Fluff	1 cup	128	4½
Marshmallows (mini)	1 cup	43	1½
Marzipan	1 cup	290	10⅛
Mashed Potatoes	1 cup	213	7½
Mayonnaise	½ cup	113	4

INGREDIENT	VOLUME	GRAMS	OUNCES
Meringue Powder	¼ cup	43	1½
Milk (evaporated)	½ cup	113	4
Milk (fresh)	1 cup	227	8
Millet (whole)	½ cup	103	3⅝
Mini Chocolate Chips	1 cup	177	6¼
Molasses	¼ cup	85	3
Mushrooms (sliced)	1 cup	78	2¾
Non-Diastatic Malt Powder	2 tablespoons	18	⅝
Oat Bran	½ cup	53	1⅞
Oat Flour	1 cup	92	3¼
Old-Fashioned Rolled Oats	1 cup	99	3½
Olive Oil	¼ cup	50	1¾
Olives (sliced)	1 cup	142	5
Onions (fresh, diced)	1 cup	142	5
Pastry Flour	1 cup	106	3¾
Peaches (peeled and diced)	1 cup	170	6
Peanut Butter	½ cup	135	4¾
Peanuts (whole, shelled)	1 cup	142	5
Pears (peeled and diced)	1 cup	163	5¾
Pecan Meal	1 cup	80	2¾
Pecans (diced)	½ cup	57	2
Pie Filling Enhancer	¼ cup	46	1⅝
Pine Nuts	½ cup	71	2½
Pineapple (dried)	½ cup	71	2½
Pineapple (fresh or canned, diced)	1 cup	170	6
Pistachios (shelled)	½ cup	60	2⅛
Pistachio Paste	¼ cup	78	2¾
Polenta (coarse ground cornmeal)	1 cup	163	5¾
Poppy Seeds	2 tablespoons	18	⅝
Potato Flour	¼ cup	46	1⅝
Potato Starch	1 cup	152	5⅜
Pumpernickel Flour	1 cup	106	3¾
Pumpkin (canned)	1 cup	227	8
Quick Cooking Oats	1 cup	89	3⅛
Quinoa (cooked)	1 cup	184	6½
Quinoa (whole)	1 cup	177	6¼
Quinoa Flour	1 cup	110	3⅞
Raisins (loose)	1 cup	149	5¼
Raisins (packed)	½ cup	85	3

INGREDIENT	VOLUME	GRAMS	OUNCES
Raspberries (fresh)	1 cup	120	4¼
Rhubarb (sliced, ½″ slices)	1 cup	120	4¼
Rice (long grain, dry)	½ cup	99	3½
Rice Flour (white)	1 cup	142	5
Rice Krispies	1 cup	28	1
Rye Chops	1 cup	120	4¼
Rye Flakes	1 cup	124	4⅜
Rye Flour	1 cup	103	3⅝
Rye Flour Blend	1 cup	106	3¾
Salt (kosher, Diamond Crystal)	1 tablespoon	8	
Salt (kosher, Morton's)	1 tablespoon	16	
Salt (table)	1 tablespoon	18	
Scallions (sliced)	1 cup	64	2¼
Self-Rising Flour	1 cup	113	4
Semolina Flour	1 cup	163	5¾
Sesame Seeds	½ cup	71	2½
Shallots (peeled and sliced)	1 cup	156	5½
Six-Grain Blend	1 cup	128	4½
Sorghum Flour	1 cup	138	4⅞
Sour Cream	1 cup	227	8
Sourdough Starter	1 cup	227 to 241	8 to 8½
Soy Flour	¼ cup	35	1¼
Spelt Flour	1 cup	99	3½
Sprouted Wheat Flour	1 cup	113	4
Steel Cut Oats (cooked)	1 cup	255	9
Steel Cut Oats (raw)	½ cup	99	2⅞
Strawberries (fresh sliced)	1 cup	167	5⅞
Sugar (granulated white)	1 cup	198	7
Sun-Dried Tomatoes (dry pack)	1 cup	170	6
Sunflower Seeds	¼ cup	35	1¼
Sweetened Condensed Milk	¼ cup	78	2¾
Tahini Paste	½ cup	128	4½
Tapioca Starch or Flour	1 cup	113	4
Tapioca (quick cooking)	2 tablespoons	21	¾
Teff Flour	1 cup	135	4¾
Toasted Almond Flour	1 cup	96	3⅜
Toffee Chunks	1 cup	156	5½
Tubinado Sugar (raw)	1 cup	180	6⅜

INGREDIENT	VOLUME	GRAMS	OUNCES
Unbleached Cake Flour	1 cup	120	4¼
Vanilla Extract	1 tablespoon	14	½
Vegetable Oil	1 cup	198	7
Vegetable Shortening	¼ cup	46	1⅝
Vermont Cheese Powder	½ cup	57	2
Vital Wheat Gluten	2 tablespoons	18	⅝
Walnuts (chopped)	1 cup	113	4
Walnuts (whole)	½ cup	64	2¼
Water	1 cup	227	8
Wheat Berries (red)	1 cup	184	6½
Wheat Bran	½ cup	32	1⅛
Wheat Germ	¼ cup	28	1
White Chocolate Chips	1 cup	170	6
White Rye Flour	1 cup	106	3¾
White Whole Wheat Flour	1 cup	113	4
Whole Wheat Flour (premium 100%)	1 cup	113	4
Whole Wheat Pastry Flour/ Graham Flour	1 cup	96	3⅜
Yeast (instant)	2¼ teaspoons	7	¼
Yogurt	1 cup	227	8
Zucchini (shredded)	1 cup	142 to 170	5 to 6

- A number of scales are available for a variety of prices (see Tools, page 541). You'll want a scale with a "tare" function so you can add ingredients to your bowl, zero out what you've just weighed, and add and accurately weigh the next ingredient.
- Get to know your scale. Make sure it will accommodate both the weight of your ingredients and the weight of the container. Lightweight mixing bowls are a good choice for weight measurement.

A TRANSLATION OF OLD-FASHIONED AMERICAN MEASUREMENTS

We shouldn't give up our old measurements entirely. There's too much history and sentiment tied up in them. "Butter the size of a walnut" stirs a chord that "28.35g butter" just can't. But where there are no walnuts, we need the other measurement as well.

Butter the size of a walnut (or a "lump") = 2 tablespoons

Butter the size of an egg = ¼ cup

Coffee cup = 1 cup

Dash = ⅛ teaspoon

Dessert spoon = 1½ teaspoons

60 drops = 1 teaspoon

Gill = ½ cup

Pinch = ⅟₁₆ or ⅛ teaspoon

Salt spoon = ¼ teaspoon

Teacup = ¾ cup

Tin cup = 1 cup

Tumblerful = 2 cups

Wineglass = ½ gill or ¼ cup

USING COOKBOOKS FROM OUTSIDE THE UNITED STATES

With the exception of the other English-speaking nations, cookbooks are written with metric measurements. Should you run into a metric cookbook, here are some conversions of our basic measurements, which are difficult to translate exactly. Small amounts will not make much difference, so metric amounts are usually rounded. (You use milliliters [ml] when speaking of liquids, and grams [g] when speaking of solids.) For baking purposes, a gram is the same as a milliliter.

1 teaspoon = 5 ml/g

1 tablespoon = 15 ml/g

1 ounce = 28.35 (or 30) ml/g

1 cup = 227 (or 230) ml/g

1 pound = 450 ml/g

2.2 pounds = 1 kilogram

And should you be faced with an overseas oven, here are some temperature conversions from Fahrenheit to centigrade, with the gas marks, used in some countries, as well.

225°F = 100°C or Gas Mark ¼

250°F = 130°C or Gas Mark ½

275°F = 140°C or Gas Mark 1

300°F = 150°C or Gas Mark 2

325°F = 170°C or Gas Mark 3

350°F = 180°C or Gas Mark 4

375°F = 190°C or Gas Mark 5

400°F = 200°C or Gas Mark 6

425°F = 220°C or Gas Mark 7

450°F = 230°C or Gas Mark 8

475°F = 240°C or Gas Mark 9

High-Altitude Baking

The higher the altitude, the lower the air pressure. While this is an excellent environment for training athletes, it's a difficult one for baking. Baking depends on the specific interactions of several kinds of ingredients, including flour, leavening, fats, and liquid; throw in the wild card of atmospheric pressure and all bets are off if you've been used to baking at sea level. To complicate things further, individual microclimates vary greatly in the mountains, so the adjustment that works for you may not work for your neighbor down (or up) the road.

If you're baking at an elevation of 3,000 feet or greater, this chart is meant as a starting point, to help you convert recipes. Different types of baked goods need different adjustments; some suggestions follow. It may take a few tries to get results you're happy with; if possible, try to adjust only one ingredient at a time so you can isolate the effect it has. Be sure to keep notes on what you've done, and try the smaller adjustments first when a range is given.

Leavening

When using baking powder and baking soda, the chart on page xxii can help you adjust amounts. When making a recipe that calls for both baking powder and baking soda plus an acidic ingredient, such as buttermilk or sour cream, try switching to all baking powder, and using regular milk in place of the acidic ingredient.

WHAT TO CHANGE	HOW TO CHANGE IT	WHY
OVEN TEMPERATURE	Increase 15°F to 25°F; use the smaller increase when making chocolate or delicate cakes.	Since leavening and evaporation proceed more quickly, the idea is to use a higher temperature to "set" the structure of baked goods before they over-expand and dry out, or rise too quickly and then collapse.
BAKING TIME	Decrease by 5 to 8 minutes per 30 minutes of baking time.	Baking at higher temperatures means products are done sooner.
SUGAR	Decrease by 1 tablespoon per cup.	Increased evaporation also increases concentration of sugar, which can weaken the structure of what you're baking.
LIQUID	Increase by 1 to 2 tablespoons at 3,000 feet. Increase by 1½ teaspoons for each additional 1,000 feet over 3,000. You can also use extra eggs as part of this liquid in recipes with a tender crumb, like muffins and cakes.	Extra liquid keeps products from drying out at higher baking temperatures and accelerated evaporation rates.
FLOUR	At 3,500 feet, add 1 tablespoon per recipe. For each additional 1,500 feet, add 1 more tablespoon. In quick bread and muffin recipes, flour with a higher protein content may yield better results.	Additional flour helps to strengthen the structure of baked goods.

HIGH-ALTITUDE CHANGES

BAKING POWDER OR BAKING SODA IN ORIGINAL RECIPE	3,000 TO 5,000 FEET	5,000 TO 6,500 FEET	ABOVE 6,500 FEET
1 teaspoon	⅞	¾	½
1½ teaspoons	1¼	1	¾
2 teaspoons	1½	1¼	1
2½ teaspoons	1¾	1½	1¼
3 teaspoons	2	1½	1¼
3½ teaspoons	2½	2	1½
4 teaspoons	2½	2	1½

CAKES: To increase liquids, use extra eggs; if only part of an egg is needed, use the white.

COOKIES, CRACKERS, AND PIE CRUSTS: These baked goods won't be dramatically affected; they will usually need extra water to help the dough come together.

FRIED DOUGHS: Lower the frying temperature by 3°F for every 1,000 feet above 3,000 feet, and increase cooking times.

QUICK BREADS: No additional adjustments are necessary other than those suggested in the tables.

YEAST BREADS: Decrease the amount of yeast in the recipe by 25%, and make water and flour adjustments as necessary to get a dough with the correct texture. Make sure your bowl has plenty of room for the dough to rise.

Since rising times are much shorter at higher altitudes, and the dough won't have sufficient time to develop its optimum flavor with one rise, you have a number of options to improve the flavor:

- Give the dough one extra rise by deflating it and letting it rise an additional time before forming it.
- Try covering the dough and placing it in the refrigerator for its first rise to slow the action of the yeast and give the dough more time to develop.
- If you have sourdough starter, use some of it for some of the liquid in the recipe. Make a sponge by mixing the yeast and liquid in the recipe with 1 to 2 cups (120g to 240g) of the flour. Cover and let the sponge work for a few hours in the refrigerator, until it becomes bubbly and rises, then continue with the recipe.

CHAPTER ONE

Breakfasts

"WAKE UP AND SMELL THE COFFEE!" Often tossed out as a good-natured nudge to dreamers, in reality the phrase could be a siren's song to start the day.

Is there anything so satisfying as gradually surfacing from the depths of sleep to the soft light of day and catching a whiff of brewing coffee? Someone has been up ahead of you; coffee is made, and if you close your eyes and snuggle into the blankets just a bit longer, breakfast might be made, too.

The simplest breakfast of all is just a bowl of cold cereal or steaming hot oatmeal topped with fruit. But there's an entire world of breakfast beyond the quick and practical.

You can break out the griddle, the mixing bowl, the flour, buttermilk, and eggs. You can spend some time gently whisking pancake batter, seeing it suddenly become creamy and smooth, watching it spread into a perfect round when it hits the griddle with a sharp sizzle, seeing it bubble, smelling the cakes—this is a pleasurable way to begin a morning.

Pancakes are only the start. There are waffles and French toast too, of course. And being bread bakers, we've found many interesting breads to soak in a milk-and-egg bath and sauté in butter. When we're feeling even more ambitious, and have actually planned ahead, we might make crêpes, filling them with spinach and cheese when a hearty breakfast is in order, or cheese blintzes with fresh berries on top if we're in the mood for something sweet and fruity.

Pancakes

Griddle cake or fry cake, flannel cake, flapjack, or hoe cake, the pancake—flour, milk, butter, a touch of leavening, and eggs, stirred together and cooked on a griddle—has long been a morning staple. An old tradition in England, where Pancake Tuesday is celebrated the day before Lent begins, and in Holland, where buckwheat is the grain of choice, pancakes take many forms around the world. Using everyday ingredients, easy to stir together and cook, pancakes are a wonderful go-to for both weekdays and weekends alike.

WHY SHOULD PANCAKE BATTER REST BEFORE USING IT?

Pancakes (like muffins) rely on both fat and gentle handling for their tenderness. Once flour is combined with a liquid, it forms a network of proteins that, if handled roughly (e.g., beaten vigorously) will become tough by bonding together. This toughness will evidence itself in a tendency to become rubbery. When making pancake batter, whisk together the dry ingredients, whisk together the wet ingredients in a separate bowl, then gently combine the two, stirring just until everything is moistened. Let the batter rest for 5 to 10 minutes, to allow the leavening to start working and to let the flour start absorbing the liquid. If you have the time, refrigerate the batter for an hour or so, which allows any lumps of flour to slowly dissolve and makes for a more fluffy, flavorful batter. When you're ready to cook the pancakes, give the batter a quick stir and you're good to go. (In recipes where you beat the egg whites separately and add them at the end, don't beat and add them until the end of the batter's resting period.) For ultra-tender pancakes or waffles, try using pastry flour.

SIMPLY PERFECT PANCAKES

SIXTEEN 3″ PANCAKES

The name says it all: This is the go-to recipe to keep on hand for the ultimate pancake. To give them their subtle sweetness, you can use regular granulated sugar or malt powder. Malt is what sweetens most commercial pancake mixes and the pancakes you'll find in many restaurants, diners, and hotels. If you're after that typical "diner" taste, try malt instead of sugar.

2 large eggs

1¼ cups (285g) milk

2 teaspoons vanilla extract (optional)

3 tablespoons (39g) butter, melted, or
   vegetable oil

1½ cups (180g) unbleached all-
   purpose flour

¾ teaspoon salt

2 teaspoons baking powder

2 tablespoons (25g) sugar or ¼ cup
   (35g) malted milk powder

Beat the eggs, milk, and vanilla until light and foamy, about 3 minutes at the high speed of a stand or hand mixer. Stir in the butter.

Whisk the dry ingredients together to evenly distribute the salt, baking powder, and sugar or malted milk powder. Gently and quickly mix into the egg/milk mixture. Let the batter relax while the griddle is heating (or overnight in the refrigerator). The batter will thicken slightly while resting.

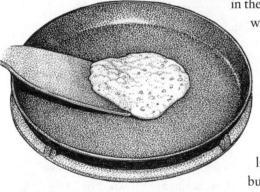

The pancake is ready to turn when the edges begin to look dry and bubbles form and start to break.

Grease and preheat the griddle. The griddle is ready if a drop of water will skitter across the surface, evaporating immediately; if you have an electric griddle, set the temperature between 325°F and 350°F. Drop ¼ cupfuls of batter onto the lightly greased griddle. Cook on one side until bubbles begin to form and break, then turn the pancakes and cook the other side until brown. Turn over only once. Serve immediately.

NOTE: To make waffles, reduce the milk to 1 cup and 2 tablespoons, and increase the butter or oil to 5 tablespoons.

NUTRITION INFORMATION PER SERVING: **4 pancakes, 104g**

199 cal | 7g fat | 6g protein | 24g complex carbohydrates | 4g sugar | 1g dietary fiber | 19mg cholesterol | 450mg sodium

BUTTERMILK PANCAKES

FOURTEEN TO SIXTEEN 4″ PANCAKES

Light and fluffy, these classic buttermilk pancakes are eager to soak up the pools of melted butter and maple syrup required of the breakfast of (y)our dreams. The batter couldn't be simpler to make—and if you're like us, you'll pop a pan of bacon into the oven to be ready as soon as the first batch of pancakes comes off the griddle.

2 cups (240g) unbleached all-purpose flour

3 tablespoons (35g) sugar

1 teaspoon baking powder

1 teaspoon baking soda

½ teaspoon salt

1 large egg

2 cups (454g) buttermilk

2 tablespoons (28g) butter, melted, or vegetable oil

1½ teaspoons vanilla extract (optional)

In a large bowl, whisk together the flour, sugar, baking powder, baking soda, and salt.

In a separate bowl or large measuring cup, whisk together the egg, buttermilk, melted butter or oil, and vanilla.

Pour the wet ingredients into the dry ingredients, stirring to combine. Stir until the mixture is fairly smooth; some small lumps are OK.

Allow the batter to rest, uncovered, for 15 minutes.

While the batter is resting, heat a large skillet over medium heat or preheat a griddle to 350°F, until the surface is hot enough for a droplet of water to skitter across it. Lightly grease the pan with butter or vegetable oil.

Spoon the batter, ¼ cup at a time, onto the hot surface; a scone and muffin scoop works well here.

Cook pancakes on the first side until bubbles form on the tops and the bottoms are brown, about 1 to 2 minutes. Flip and cook until the bottoms are brown, 1 to 2 minutes longer.

Serve immediately.

Leftover pancakes can be frozen the same day they're made and reheated in a 250°F oven.

NUTRITION INFORMATION PER SERVING: 3 pancakes, 123g

226 cal | 6g fat | 8g protein | 36g complex carbohydrates | 9g sugar | 1g dietary fiber | 41mg cholesterol | 493mg sodium

GLUTEN-FREE PANCAKES OR WAFFLES

SIXTEEN 4″ PANCAKES OR 10 FULL-SIZE WAFFLES

An easy route to pancakes and waffles for all! Designed to yield the same wonderful texture and flavor as conventional recipes, this one relies on gluten-free all-purpose flour to make buttery, fluffy pancakes or crisp, golden waffles. If you like extra-fluffy pancakes, allow the batter to rest for 15 minutes at room temperature before cooking.

2 large eggs

4 tablespoons (57g) butter, melted, or vegetable oil (add 2 additional tablespoons [28g] butter or oil to make waffles)

2 cups (454g) milk

1 teaspoon vanilla extract

2⅓ cups (347g) gluten-free all-purpose flour

¼ cup (50g) buttermilk powder (optional)

2 tablespoons (25g) sugar

1½ teaspoons baking powder

¾ teaspoon salt

¾ teaspoon xanthan gum

Whisk together the eggs, melted butter or oil, milk, and vanilla.

In a separate bowl, whisk together the dry ingredients. Stir in the egg mixture.

TO MAKE THE PANCAKES: Preheat the griddle to medium (350°F), greasing it lightly. Scoop the batter by ¼ cupfuls onto the griddle.

Cook pancakes for 1 to 2 minutes, until the tops lose their shine and bottoms are golden brown. Flip and cook for 1 to 2 minutes on the other side.

Serve hot, with butter and syrup.

TO MAKE THE WAFFLES: Prepare the batter as directed, adding the extra fat; this will help make the waffles crisp. To cook, follow the directions that come with your waffle iron.

NUTRITION INFORMATION PER SERVING: 4 pancakes, 241g
374 cal | 3g fat | 8g protein | 71g complex carbohydrates | 7g sugar | 2g dietary fiber | 106mg cholesterol | 648mg sodium

ZEPHYR PANCAKES

TWENTY-FOUR 3½″ PANCAKES

These pancakes hail from the Midwest and are a true celebration of what dairy can do. They're incredibly light and tender and literally melt in your mouth.

2 cups (240g) unbleached all-purpose flour

2½ tablespoons (35g) sugar

1½ teaspoons baking powder

1 teaspoon baking soda

½ teaspoon salt

3 large egg yolks

1¼ cups (284g) cream

1¼ cups (284g) buttermilk

2 tablespoons (28g) butter, melted

1 teaspoon vanilla extract (optional)

In a medium bowl, whisk together the flour, sugar, baking powder, baking soda, and salt. In a separate bowl, whisk together the egg yolks, cream, buttermilk, melted butter, and vanilla, if using. Whisk the wet ingredients into the dry, just until combined—it's OK if there are a few lumps.

Preheat and lightly grease a heavy skillet or griddle. Scoop the batter onto the griddle with a ¼ cup measure or a large spoon. Make sure the heat is slightly less than medium. The pancakes will puff up very high. When the first side is golden brown and the edges start to look dry, turn pancakes over to finish cooking the second side. Remove the pancakes from the griddle and keep them in a warm serving dish until you have enough to feed everyone.

NUTRITION INFORMATION PER SERVING: 3 pancakes, 88g
227 cal | 14g fat | 4g protein | 18g complex carbohydrates | 3g sugar | 1g dietary fiber | 104mg cholesterol | 223mg sodium

---

AN EASY WAY TO SCOOP OUT PANCAKE BATTER

For nice, round, evenly sized pancakes, use a scoop to portion the batter from bowl to griddle. A muffin scoop holding about ¼ cup of batter will make a familiar 3″ to 4″ pancake.

GINGERBREAD PANCAKES

TWELVE 3½″ PANCAKES

These pancakes are a nice shortcut to enjoying warm gingerbread in minutes. All the things that team well with gingerbread make sense with these pancakes: warm applesauce, sliced peaches, or warm custard sauce. Naturally, some lightly sweetened whipped cream will only enhance this recipe.

1 cup (120g) unbleached all-purpose flour

¼ cup (39g) yellow cornmeal

2 tablespoons (25g) sugar

½ teaspoon cinnamon

¾ teaspoon ginger

⅛ teaspoon cloves

½ teaspoon salt

1 teaspoon baking powder

½ teaspoon baking soda

¼ cup (46g) chopped crystallized ginger (optional)

2 tablespoons (27g) vegetable oil

¼ cup (85g) molasses

1 cup (227g) buttermilk

1 large egg, lightly beaten

In a large bowl, whisk together the flour, cornmeal, sugar, spices, salt, baking powder, baking soda, and the crystallized ginger, if using. In a separate bowl, mix together the oil, molasses, buttermilk, and egg. Add liquids to dry ingredients all at once, stirring until just combined.

Preheat a griddle and lightly grease it. Drop the batter, ¼ cup at a time, to make a 3½″ pancake. Cook until the edges look dry and some of the bubbles that come to the surface break. Turn the pancakes over to finish cooking, then remove them from griddle to a warm serving dish.

NUTRITION INFORMATION PER SERVING: **3 pancakes, 147g**

324 cal | 9g fat | 7g protein | 31g complex carbohydrates | 23g sugar | 2g dietary fiber | 55mg cholesterol | 623mg sodium

RICOTTA SOUFFLÉ PANCAKES

TWENTY-FOUR 3½″ PANCAKES

We love to make these light, eggy pancakes when berries are in season, as they're especially good garnished with fresh strawberries or blueberries. The pancakes are unusually airy and lofty, thanks to the addition of beaten egg whites. It's worth the extra step—their ethereal texture sets them apart from all other pancakes.

3 large eggs, separated

1½ cups (340g) buttermilk

3 tablespoons (38g) sugar

1 cup (227g) ricotta cheese

1½ cups (180g) unbleached all-
    purpose flour

1 teaspoon baking soda

1 teaspoon baking powder

1 tablespoon (6g) lemon zest

¼ teaspoon nutmeg

½ teaspoon salt

In a medium bowl, beat together the egg yolks, buttermilk, sugar, and ricotta cheese. In a separate bowl, whisk together the flour, baking soda, baking powder, lemon zest, nutmeg, and salt. In a third bowl, beat the egg whites until stiff but not dry. Mix the dry ingredients into the buttermilk mixture with a few quick strokes. A few lumps remaining are OK. Fold in the egg whites.

Heat a lightly greased griddle or skillet over medium heat until hot enough to evaporate a drop of water immediately. Drop the batter by ¼ cupfuls onto the heated griddle. Cook for about 2½ minutes on the first side; bubbles should rise and burst on the first side before you flip the pancakes. Cook for about 1 minute on the second side. They should be a very light golden brown when finished. The pancakes may be made a day ahead, cooled on a rack, then wrapped tightly and refrigerated. To reheat, preheat the oven to 375°F, place the pancakes on a lightly greased baking sheet, and heat for 5 minutes.

NUTRITION INFORMATION PER SERVING: 3 pancakes, 193g

314 cal | 8g fat | 15g protein | 25g complex carbohydrates | 20g sugar | 1g dietary fiber | 115mg cholesterol | 648mg sodium

LEMON PUFF PANCAKE

ONE 9″ PANCAKE

This is one of those magical recipes that's much easier than it appears at first glance. A rather unattractive flour, milk, and egg batter is poured into a pan, and 20 minutes later emerges as a giant golden puff, awaiting a final anointing of lemon juice and sugar. It's delicious; it's easy; and who cares if it settles back a bit from its glorious oven-fresh heights as it cools? Part popover, part crêpe, part pancake, it combines the best aspects of all three.

2 tablespoons (28g) butter, divided

⅓ cup (40g) unbleached all-purpose flour

heaping ⅛ teaspoon salt

1 teaspoon granulated sugar

¼ cup (57g) milk

½ teaspoon vanilla extract

2 large eggs

1 tablespoon (14g) freshly squeezed lemon juice

confectioners' sugar

Preheat the oven to 425°F. Lightly grease a 9″ cast iron skillet, or 8″ round cake pan. The size of the pan matters here, so measure carefully. Too small, it'll overflow. Too large, it won't puff as high.

Melt 1 tablespoon of the butter in the skillet or cake pan.

Whisk together the flour, salt, and sugar.

In a separate bowl, whisk together the milk, vanilla, and eggs.

Add the liquid ingredients to the dry ingredients, whisking until fairly smooth; a few small lumps are OK. Melt the remaining tablespoon of butter, stir it into the batter, and pour the batter into the pan.

Bake the pancake for 15 to 20 minutes, or until it's puffed and golden, with deeper brown patches.

Remove it from the oven, and sprinkle with the lemon juice, then the sugar. Serve immediately.

NUTRITION INFORMATION PER SERVING: 2 pancakes, 129g
295 cal | 17g fat | 10g protein | 16g complex carbohydrates | 11g sugar | 1g dietary fiber | 218mg cholesterol | 86mg sodium

WELSH CAKES

FIFTY 3½″ CAKES

These cakes are a cross between a pancake and a baking powder biscuit, but much richer and sweeter. Sturdy enough to be eaten out of hand, they can be served plain, sprinkled with sugar, or spread with butter and smothered in jam. In addition, they're excellent the next day, warmed in the toaster. Be sure to use currants rather than raisins, which are too large for these thin cakes.

3 cups (360g) unbleached all-purpose flour

1 cup (198g) sugar

2 teaspoons baking powder

½ teaspoon nutmeg

¼ teaspoon salt

16 tablespoons (226g) unsalted butter, cut into pieces

¾ cup (108g) currants

2 eggs beaten with enough milk to yield ¾ cup (170g) liquid

In a medium bowl, sift together the flour, sugar, baking powder, nutmeg, and salt. Cut in the butter until the mixture is a coarse, even consistency. Add the currants, and then the egg and milk. Stir until the mixture forms a soft dough.

Divide the dough in half and, working with one half at a time (keep the other half covered and refrigerated), roll the dough into a circle ¼″ thick. Using a biscuit cutter or other small (2½″ to 3½″) round cutter, cut circles of dough.

Heat an ungreased skillet over medium heat (an electric frying pan, set at 325°F, works well, too). Fry the cakes for about 2 minutes on the first side, and an additional 1½ minutes on the second, or until both sides are golden brown. As with pancakes, you'll have to adjust the heat if you find the cakes are browned on the outside before they're thoroughly cooked in the middle. Repeat with the remaining dough. Keep the cakes warm in a 200°F oven until ready to serve.

NUTRITION INFORMATION PER SERVING: 2 cakes, 43g

166 cal | 5g fat | 2g protein | 14g complex carbohydrates | 8g sugar | 1g dietary fiber | 38mg cholesterol | 68mg sodium

HOMEMADE WHOLE GRAIN PANCAKE MIX

10 CUPS DRY MIX (ENOUGH FOR 50 TO 80 PANCAKES)

Just shy of 90% whole grain, these pancakes are absolutely delicious—sweet and nutty with the taste of oats and wheat. Keeping a batch of this homemade dry mix on hand means that you're never far from a stack of warm pancakes made entirely from scratch.

MIX

3½ cups (347g) rolled oats

4 cups (454g) white whole wheat flour

1 cup (120g) unbleached all-
purpose flour

3 tablespoons (43g) sugar

3 tablespoons (36g) baking powder

1 tablespoon (18g) salt

1 tablespoon (18g) baking soda

1 cup (198g) vegetable oil

PANCAKES

1 cup (120g to 135g) homemade mix

1 cup (227g) buttermilk

1 large egg

TO MAKE THE MIX: Grind the oats in a food processor until they're finely chopped, but not in a powder.

Put the oats, flours, and all other dry ingredients into a mixer with a paddle. Mix on slow speed and drizzle the vegetable oil into the bowl slowly while the mixer is running.

Store in an airtight container for up to two weeks at room temperature, or indefinitely in the refrigerator or freezer.

TO MAKE A BATCH OF PANCAKES (5 TO 8, DEPENDING ON SIZE): Whisk together 1 cup of mix, 1 cup of buttermilk, and 1 large egg. Don't worry if it seems thin at first: the oats will soak up the milk, and the mix will thicken a bit as it stands.

Let the batter stand for at least 20 minutes before cooking.

Heat a lightly greased griddle to 350°F (if you've got a griddle with a temperature setting; if not, medium-hot will do).

Drop the batter onto it ¼ cup at a time (a jumbo cookie scoop works well here) to make a 4˝ diameter pancake.

When the edges look dry and bubbles come to the surface without breaking, turn the pancake over to finish cooking on the second side, which will take about 2 minutes.

NUTRITION INFORMATION PER SERVING: 1 pancake, 56g

110 cal | 5g fat | 4g protein | 9g complex carbohydrates | 3g sugar | 3g dietary fiber | 30mg cholesterol | 260mg sodium

BLINI

These buckwheat pancakes are traditionally Russian and meant to be eaten at the pre-Lenten feast known as Maslenitsa, or "butter week" (which comes from the Russian word *maslo*, meaning butter). No meat was allowed during this week, thus the relish with which they consumed dairy products and fish, preferably caviar—which you'll often see as a topping for blini along with sour cream. You can serve them any way you like, although good suggestions include melted butter, smoked salmon, capers, or jam for a sweet option.

SPONGE

1⅓ cups (159g) buckwheat flour

1½ cups (340g) warm water

2 tablespoons (11g) Baker's Special Dry Milk or ⅓ cup (28g) nonfat dry milk

1½ teaspoons instant yeast

BATTER

2 large eggs, separated

½ cup (113g) milk

1 teaspoon sugar

½ teaspoon salt

4 tablespoons (½ stick, 57g) butter, melted

TO MAKE THE SPONGE: Mix all the ingredients together in a medium bowl, cover, and set aside. Depending on how much sour flavor you like in your blini, the sponge can ripen for a few hours, all day, or overnight, so plan ahead when preparing it. The more time you give it, the more tang you'll taste.

TO MAKE THE BATTER: Beat the egg yolks until light, then beat in the milk, sugar, and salt.

Blend the batter into the sponge and let it rest for 30 to 45 minutes. Set aside the egg whites and let them warm to room temperature.

Just before you're ready to cook the blini, whisk the melted butter into the batter. Beat the egg whites until they form medium peaks and fold them into the batter. Use a heavy, well-seasoned cast iron griddle, if you have one. If not, use any heavy frying pan or griddle. Heat the pan over low to medium heat and wipe it with butter. (You shouldn't need to grease the pan again once you start cooking.)

Pour 2 to 3 tablespoons batter onto the griddle for each blini. They should be about 4″ in diameter. Cook them as you would pancakes, until bubbles appear that break and don't fill in. Flip over and cook until lightly browned. These can be stacked on a warm plate in a warm oven until serving.

NUTRITION INFORMATION PER SERVING: 1 blini, ungarnished, 38g

66 cal | 2.7g fat | 3g protein | 8g complex carbohydrates | 0g sugar | 1g dietary fiber | 29mg cholesterol | 86mg sodium

Waffles

Waffles are a step up from pancakes in looks, but often are essentially the same recipe in a different form. They take specialized equipment to produce—an iron—and generally look as if they take more effort, even if they really don't. There are two basic styles of waffle: the relatively flat, baking powder–leavened waffle that's usually shaped in squares, rounds, or hearts; and Belgian-style, a thicker, more deeply indented square waffle, often made with yeast. Belgian waffles are often seen accompanied by whipped cream and strawberries along with maple syrup and butter.

PANCAKES VS. WAFFLES

The major difference between most pancake and waffle batters is that waffles need to have more fat in them than pancakes. Waffles without sufficient fat will remain somewhat flabby even when toasted to a dark brown; they also have a tendency to stick to the waffle iron. Pancakes are also more tolerant of having extras thrown in—a handful of blueberries, some cornmeal, slices of banana or strawberry. Waffles are usually prepared plain, with any additions served on top or alongside, because "add-ins" often prevent them from becoming crisp. Also, the ins and outs of the waffle grid are prone to stick to a slice of peach or a nugget of crystallized ginger.

Waffles weren't always a breakfast food, and they haven't always been served with a sweet topping. In the 1930s, waffle suppers consisting of waffles with a savory topping—most often creamed chicken—were standard entertainment. Lately fried chicken has taken the place of honor for this savory waffle combination.

Waffles elevate any meal—consider how you could even serve chocolate pecan waffles with ice cream and hot fudge sauce for a memorable dessert. Still, there are few breakfasts so satisfying as a crunchy yet tender waffle, butter melting into its crevices and gilded with syrup.

HELP! MY WAFFLES STICK TO THE IRON!

What a pain: digging stuck-on waffles out of the grids of your waffle iron. To avoid this particular challenge, make sure there's some fat in the batter; fat not only will make waffles crisp on the outside and soft within, it will also help them separate from the iron.

Before spooning batter into the iron, make sure it's thoroughly greased with vegetable oil or melted shortening applied with a pastry brush, or with nonstick vegetable oil spray. Finally, when the steaming slows down and you think the waffle is done, open the iron just a bit; if the waffle clings to the top grid, give it a gentle tug to see if it will let go. If not, try giving it a minute or so more in the closed iron. A waffle that's not fully baked tends to stick.

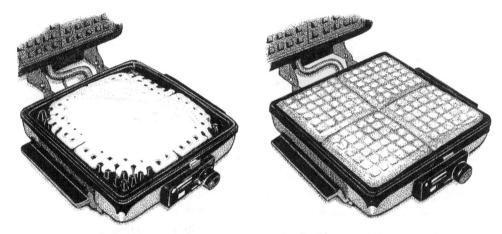

Spoon in enough waffle batter to not quite fill all of the space, as shown. The batter will fill in the empty space when the top is lowered for baking.

CLASSIC BUTTERMILK WAFFLES

ABOUT TEN 8" WAFFLES

When we think of brunch, we think of waffles. This recipe makes a plain waffle, crisp and golden, that's perfect with maple syrup and butter or berries and whipped cream. When made with pastry flour, it will be extra crispy and light as air inside. When made with all-purpose flour, the waffle has a bit more body—still light, but chewier on the inside. Waffles are best consumed as soon as they're baked, but in a pinch you can place them on a rack to cool, wrap tightly to store in the refrigerator, then reheat for 6 minutes in a 350°F oven. The optional pecan meal adds a nutty flavor.

2 large eggs

1¾ cups (398g) buttermilk

8 tablespoons (1 stick, 113g) unsalted butter, melted and cooled to room temperature

2 teaspoons vanilla extract

2 cups (212g) unbleached pastry flour or 1¾ cups (210g) unbleached all-purpose flour

2 tablespoons (25g) sugar (omit for savory waffles)

2 teaspoons baking powder

1 teaspoon baking soda

1 teaspoon salt

½ cup (40g) pecan meal (optional)

In a medium bowl, beat together the eggs, buttermilk, melted butter, and vanilla. In another bowl, whisk together the dry ingredients; combine the wet and dry ingredients just until smooth.

Spray the waffle iron with a nonstick cooking spray before preheating it. For an 8" round waffle iron, use about ⅓ cup batter. Cook for 2 to 3 minutes, until the iron stops steaming.

NUTRITION INFORMATION PER SERVING: 1 waffle, 82g
360 cal | 15g fat | 19g protein | 34g complex carbohydrates | 3g sugar | 1g dietary fiber | 110mg cholesterol | 604mg sodium

WHY BUTTERMILK?

Many of our pancake and waffle recipes call for buttermilk rather than regular milk. The reason? The acidity in buttermilk tenderizes the gluten (protein) in flour, plus it works with baking soda better than plain milk by both neutralizing the flavor of the soda at the same time it is activating it, providing wonderful leavening. If you don't have any on hand, make your own by mixing 1 cup of milk with 1 tablespoon vinegar or lemon juice and letting it sit for 10 to 15 minutes.

CRUNCHY CORNMEAL WAFFLES

ABOUT TEN 8″ WAFFLES

This recipe makes a very excellent crunchy cornmeal waffle for breakfast. We like the slight grit and texture that cornmeal adds; a stack of these doused in melted butter is pretty much perfect.

1¾ cups (398g) buttermilk

2 large eggs

5 tablespoons (71g) unsalted butter, melted and cooled, or ⅓ cup (73g) vegetable oil

1½ cups (180g) unbleached all-purpose flour

1 cup (156g) yellow cornmeal

2 tablespoons (25g) sugar

2 teaspoons baking powder

1 teaspoon baking soda

1 teaspoon salt

In a medium bowl, whisk together the buttermilk, eggs, and melted butter or oil. In a separate bowl, blend together the dry ingredients, then quickly and gently combine the wet and dry ingredients. Let the batter sit for 10 minutes to allow the cornmeal to soften.

Drop the batter by ⅔ cupfuls onto a hot waffle iron and bake until the waffle iron stops steaming.

NUTRITION INFORMATION PER SERVING: 1 waffle, 75g

266 cal | 3g fat | 18g protein | 40g complex carbohydrates | 2g sugar | 2g dietary fiber | 30mg cholesterol | 588mg sodium

FUDGE WAFFLES

TEN 8″ WAFFLES

Is it a brownie in disguise or a waffle that took a wrong turn at breakfast and ended up on the dessert table? This indulgent breakfast recipe may have an identity problem, but you won't have any problem when you serve it to your family or friends—they'll enjoy every rich bite.

2 large eggs, at room temperature

4 tablespoons (½ stick, 57g) butter, melted and cooled, or ¼ cup (50g) vegetable oil

1 teaspoon vanilla extract

1 cup (227g) buttermilk

1 cup (120g) unbleached all-purpose flour

¾ cup (149g) sugar

½ cup (42g) unsweetened cocoa

½ teaspoon baking powder

½ teaspoon baking soda

¼ teaspoon salt

¼ teaspoon nutmeg

½ cup (57g) chopped walnuts

½ cup (86g) miniature chocolate chips

In a large bowl, combine the eggs, butter or oil, and vanilla. Beat until light, about 2 minutes. Blend in buttermilk, then flour, sugar, cocoa, baking powder, baking soda, salt, and nutmeg. Gently fold in nuts and chocolate chips.

Bake waffles in a preheated, well-greased waffle iron until done (following directions for your own waffle iron). Waffles can be served immediately or wrapped tightly and served the next day. Warm them in a toaster oven if you wish.

NUTRITION INFORMATION PER SERVING: 1 waffle, 82g

243 cal | 12g fat | 5g protein | 11g complex carbohydrates | 19g sugar | 1g dietary fiber | 56mg cholesterol | 233mg sodium

POTATO WAFFLES

TEN 8″ WAFFLES

Mashed potatoes give a wonderfully tender texture and earthy flavor to these waffles. If using leftover mashed potatoes that have already been well seasoned, cut back on the salt slightly.

1½ cups (320g) riced, cooked potatoes, or leftover mashed potatoes

1 teaspoon salt

2 large eggs, separated

4 tablespoons (½ stick, 57g) butter, melted, or 3 tablespoons (37g) vegetable oil

2 cups (454g) buttermilk

1½ cups (180g) unbleached all-purpose flour

1 teaspoon baking powder

1 teaspoon baking soda

3 tablespoons minced fresh chives or scallions (optional)

6 slices bacon, cooked and crumbled (optional)

In a medium bowl, combine the potatoes, salt, egg yolks, and butter, mashing and mixing until lump-free. (A blender or food processor will do the job in a few seconds if your potatoes are very lumpy.) Beat in the buttermilk.

In a separate bowl, whisk together the flour, baking powder, baking soda, chives, and crumbled bacon. Add these dry ingredients to the liquid mixture and mix quickly just until most of the lumps are incorporated.

Beat the egg whites until stiff but not dry, then fold them into the potato/flour mixture. Bake the waffles immediately (so they remain light). Waffles may be made ahead—immediately wrap the waffles tightly when cool, then reheat in a 375°F oven for approximately 5 minutes just before serving.

NUTRITION INFORMATION PER SERVING: 1 waffle, 105g

301 cal | 7g fat | 20g protein | 39g complex carbohydrates | 0g sugar | 1g dietary fiber | 48mg cholesterol | 463mg sodium

PUMPKIN PRALINE WAFFLES

TWELVE 8″ WAFFLES

What is more warm and homey than the scent of baking pumpkin? These waffles are redolent of spices and would pair well with lightly sweetened whipped cream (but really, what wouldn't?).

1 cup (120g) unbleached all-purpose flour

1 cup (113g) whole wheat flour

2 teaspoons baking powder

½ teaspoon baking soda

1 teaspoon salt

2 teaspoons ginger

1 teaspoon cinnamon

½ teaspoon nutmeg

½ teaspoon cloves

1½ cups (341g) cooked fresh pumpkin or canned pumpkin purée

½ cup (107g) brown sugar, packed

6 tablespoons (¾ stick, 85g) unsalted butter, melted

4 large eggs, separated

2 cups (454g) buttermilk

½ cup (57g) chopped pecans

In a large bowl, combine flours, baking powder, baking soda, salt, and spices, stirring to mix. Stir in pumpkin, brown sugar, butter, and egg yolks. Add buttermilk and mix until thoroughly blended.

In a large bowl, beat the egg whites until stiff. Fold the whites into the batter and gently stir in pecans.

Scoop batter into a preheated waffle iron. Bake waffles until golden brown. Serve warm with butter and maple syrup, if you like.

NUTRITION INFORMATION PER SERVING: 1 waffle, 133g
250 cal | 12g fat | 7g protein | 22g complex carbohydrates | 9g sugar | 3g dietary fiber | 89mg cholesterol | 362mg sodium

BELGIAN-STYLE YEAST WAFFLES

ABOUT 4 BELGIAN-STYLE 7″ WAFFLES

This classic yeasted recipe produces waffles that are wonderfully crisp outside, and creamy and moist inside. Even when cooling, they retain their wonderful texture. But don't worry, their flavor is so delightful they won't spend much time on the serving plate! You can choose to prepare the batter for these waffles and cook it after an hour, but we prefer to let the batter rest overnight in the fridge, where it develops a real yeasty and rich depth of flavor. If you aren't fond of a slightly fermented, sourdough-like flavor, just add 1½ teaspoons of baking powder to the recipe (in addition to the yeast), and cook after just a 30-minute rest; don't refrigerate overnight.

1½ cups (340g) lukewarm milk

6 tablespoons (¾ stick, 85g) unsalted butter, melted

2 to 3 tablespoons (39g to 57g) maple syrup (optional)

¾ teaspoon salt

1 teaspoon vanilla extract

2 large eggs

2 cups (240g) unbleached all-purpose flour

1½ teaspoons instant yeast

Combine all the ingredients in a large bowl, leaving room for expansion; the mixture will bubble and grow.

Stir to combine; it's fine if the mixture isn't perfectly smooth.

Cover with plastic wrap and let rest at room temperature for 1 hour; the mixture will begin to bubble. You can cook the waffles at this point or refrigerate the batter overnight to cook waffles the next day.

Preheat your waffle iron. Spray with nonstick vegetable oil spray, and pour ⅔ to ¾ cup batter (or the amount recommended by the manufacturer) onto the center of the iron. Close the lid and bake for the recommended amount of time, until the waffle is golden brown, about 5 to 6 minutes on a standard 7″ Belgian-style (deep-pocket) waffle iron.

Serve immediately.

NUTRITION INFORMATION PER SERVING: 1 waffle, 213g

480 cal | 21g fat | 14g protein | 44g complex carbohydrates | 16g sugar | 2g dietary fiber | 145mg cholesterol | 520mg sodium

French Toast

French toast, true to its name, originated in France, where it is called *pain perdu* ("lost bread"), as it's made with leftover stale bread. You'll find some variation on the theme in many culinary cultures; after all, what could be a simpler combination than bread, milk, and eggs?

This is an instance of the sum being more than its parts; French toast is up there with some of the true classic comfort foods. Soft, moist bread with a thin layer of hot butter-crisped crust, just begging for an application of more butter, and syrup—we can't imagine anyone but the most curmudgeonly culinary snob not entertaining a lifelong love affair with French toast.

French toast is customarily made with plain white bread, though there are those who swear by day-old challah or whole grain breads and those who think French toast made with cinnamon raisin bread is just about as close to breakfast heaven as you can get. There are two basic methods used to prepare French toast: the typical soak and sauté or the technique of cutting the bread thicker (or layering two slices and stuffing it with a filling), laying it in a pan, pouring the soaking liquid over it, and letting it rest overnight before baking in the oven. This "French toast" is closer to a strata, but, nomenclature aside, it does taste wonderful.

Finally, did you know that you can make French toast in a waffle iron? After the bread has been soaked in egg and milk (or, even better, cream or melted vanilla ice cream), simply place the slice of bread in your square waffle iron. The result is an interesting combination of two breakfast favorites.

RICH FRENCH TOAST

12 SLICES

When we tested this recipe, it was met with universal acclaim. The difference between this and ordinary French toast is the quality of the ingredients. Start with a high-rising, white bread—be sure it's slightly stale, otherwise it will fall apart in the batter. Slice it thick; we found ⅝″ just about right. Bathe it in nutmeg- and rum-accented cream. Sauté it gently in butter then serve it on warmed plates with sifted sugar and maple syrup. Crispy on the outside, toothsome yet tender within, this is the French toast of which dreams are made.

1 tablespoon (14g) butter

1 tablespoon (12g) vegetable oil

3 large eggs

¾ cup (171g) cream

¼ teaspoon salt

¼ teaspoon nutmeg

2 teaspoons rum (optional)

1 teaspoon vanilla extract

6 slices bread, frozen and thawed or several days old

Preheat the oven to 250°F. Line a baking sheet with parchment paper or grease it generously and set aside.

Place the butter and vegetable oil in a heavy skillet and set it over medium heat.

In a small bowl, whisk together the eggs, cream, salt, nutmeg, rum, and vanilla. Stir until smooth but not foamy. Pour the batter into a shallow casserole dish large enough to hold two pieces of bread snugly.

Place two pieces of bread in the soaking dish, turn them over, and turn them over again. The entire process should take about 15 seconds; you want the bread to absorb some of the liquid but not to become thoroughly saturated.

Place the bread in the skillet and fry it for 3 minutes before turning. Turn the bread; it should be golden brown. If not, raise the burner heat slightly. Fry the bread on the second side for about 2 minutes. Again, it should be golden brown. Transfer the French toast to the baking sheet and place it in the preheated oven. Allow it to remain in the oven while you cook the remaining pieces.

When all the pieces are cooked, serve the French toast on heated plates, dusting it with confectioners' sugar, if you like.

NUTRITION INFORMATION PER SERVING: 1 slice, 87g
223 cal | 15g fat | 5g protein | 13g complex carbohydrates | 1g sugar | 1g dietary fiber | 147mg cholesterol | 249mg sodium

BANANA BREAD FRENCH TOAST

14 SLICES

Banana bread gets new life in this decadent and unique version of French toast, which works equally well for breakfast or the warm base for a scoop of vanilla ice cream as dessert. The flavors of banana and coconut are a natural together. The eggnog gives it an extra kick— because why not?

3 large eggs

1 cup (254g) eggnog or 1 cup (227g) half-and-half mixed with 2 teaspoons dark rum

½ teaspoon nutmeg

1 package (283g) shredded sweetened coconut

1 loaf (about fourteen ½″ slices) banana bread

3 tablespoons (43g) butter

Whisk together the eggs, eggnog (or half-and-half with rum), and nutmeg until smooth. Pour the batter into a shallow pan or bowl with a flat bottom. In a separate shallow dish, pour out the coconut. Slice the banana bread.

Heat the griddle to medium, until a piece of butter swirled on top of it bubbles. Put the slices of banana bread into the batter, let them sit for 30 seconds, then turn them over. You may want to have a slotted spatula handy to lift them out of the batter once they become soaked through. Let the excess batter drip off the bread, then place the bread onto the coconut. Turn over, then transfer coated bread onto griddle. Turn down the heat to medium low and let the French toast cook for 2 to 3 minutes on the first side. Turn over to finish cooking on the second side, then transfer to a heated plate or serving platter to keep warm. Serve with syrup or ice cream, as you prefer.

NUTRITION INFORMATION PER SERVING: 2 slices, without syrup, 112g

355 cal | 18g fat | 5g protein | 22g complex carbohydrates | 23g sugar | 1g dietary fiber | 89mg cholesterol | 257mg sodium

STUFFED FRENCH TOAST

12 SLICES

Stuffed French toast—a "casserole" made from layers of bread, cream cheese, and strawberry jam, moistened with egg and milk, and baked to soft yet crisp perfection—is a breakfast everyone clamors for. You can fill the French toast and make up the custard in advance, then dip and bake when you're ready to go. Spread the filling on the slice of bread about ¼″ thick, then top with the second slice of bread. Wrap and keep in the refrigerator until you're ready to bake.

BREAD

twelve ½″ thick slices white sandwich
    bread (or the bread of your choice)

FILLING

4 ounces (½ cup, 114g) cream cheese,
    softened

1 tablespoon (7g) confectioners' sugar

½ cup (170g) strawberry jam, or the jam
    or preserve of your choice

1 teaspoon vanilla extract

¼ teaspoon cinnamon

CUSTARD

8 large eggs

3 cups (681g) milk

¼ cup (50g) sugar

¾ teaspoon salt

2 teaspoons vanilla extract

freshly grated nutmeg, for topping

First, select the pan you want to use, one that best fits the size of your bread slices. (We like to use a 9″ × 13″ pan, and cut some of the slices as needed to fit the pan.) The point is to try to leave the bread as intact as possible, as lifting out and serving whole pieces is nicer than dealing with smaller pieces. Lightly grease the pan, preferably with butter.

In a small bowl, beat the cream cheese until soft, then blend in the remaining filling ingredients. Spread 6 slices of bread with the filling, top them with the remaining 6 slices, and lay these "sandwiches" in the pan, cutting to fit as necessary.

In a medium bowl, blend together the custard ingredients and pour the mixture over the bread in the pan. Let it sit for 30 minutes total, so the bread can soak up the custard.

Preheat the oven to 350°F.

Sprinkle freshly grated nutmeg atop the French toast and bake it for about 20 minutes. Turn over the pieces and bake for another 20 minutes, until the bread is puffy and lightly browned. Transfer the French toast to individual plates and serve it warm, with maple syrup, if you like.

NUTRITION INFORMATION PER SERVING: 1 stuffed French toast, 295g
451 cal | 17.7g fat | 57g complex carbohydrates | 30g sugar | 18g protein | 2g dietary fiber | 313mg cholesterol | 748mg sodium

Crêpes

Crêpes, a thinner, larger, unleavened version of pancakes, are a staple street food in Paris, where they were born. There, vendors with pushcarts and special large, flat crêpe irons make crêpes that are a full 12″ in diameter. Spread with the customer's choice of filling (ranging from simple butter and sugar to ham and cheese to hazelnut-scented chocolate), the crêpes are folded for ease of handling and eaten with gusto.

In the '50s, versions such as crêpes suzette were the star of many a flamboyant restaurant dessert finale, lit brandy adding an element of excitement to what might otherwise have been perceived as simply pancakes with orange sauce.

Happily, crêpes are easy to find now, and even easier to make at home. Fill them with meat, cheese, or scrambled eggs for a savory breakfast, or serve them blintz-style with a rich creamy cheese filling and a topping of sour cream and fruit. However you choose to serve them, they're suitable for making ahead, then assembling and heating just before serving.

PARISIAN STREET VENDOR CRÊPES

ELEVEN 10˝ CRÊPES

In Paris, they sell these delicate crêpes on the street in huge circles—big enough for a real meal and a half. You can use any size pan you like, however. Crêpe batter is a cinch to make. You just need to prepare it far enough ahead so it can sit at room temperature for an hour or so. This resting time really changes the nature of the batter and makes for a much better crêpe. You can easily cut the recipe in half, or make the whole recipe and freeze the extra crêpes for later.

2 cups (240g) unbleached all-purpose flour

½ to ¾ teaspoon salt

1½ cups (340g) milk

4 large eggs

4 tablespoons (½ stick, 57g) butter, melted but not bubbling hot

In a large bowl, combine the flour and salt. In a medium bowl, beat together the milk and eggs. Make a well in the flour mixture and pour in about half the liquid mixture. Blend well, then add the remaining liquid and stir until fairly smooth; a few lumps can remain. Stir in the butter. Cover and let sit for at least 1 hour.

The best thing to cook these crêpes in is a 10˝ cast iron pan (or, for smaller crêpes, a neat little crêpe pan). Heat the pan until it's medium hot. Wipe the bottom of the pan with a bit of butter. Pour a scant ⅓ cup of batter into the bottom of the pan, pick up the pan, and tip it in a circle so the batter covers the bottom of the pan. Cook until the bottom begins to brown and you can slide a spatula under the crêpe. Cook briefly on the other side and place on a warm plate. Cover until the remaining batter is cooked.

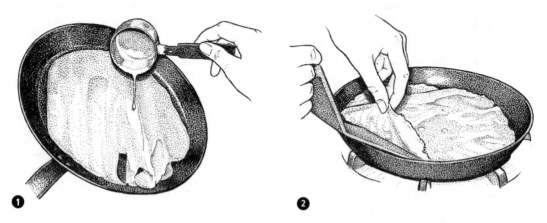

1. Tilt the pan toward yourself at a 45° angle while you pour the batter on it. Tilt the pan from side to side to finish covering the surface. **2.** The crêpe is ready to flip when the top looks dry and the edges are just beginning to curl. Don't let it take on a lot of color.

TO MAKE THE FILLING: This can be anything from sliced ham and cheese to butter sprinkled with sugar with (or without) a bit of Cointreau. A Parisian favorite is crêpes lightly smeared with chocolate hazelnut paste. After that, diced banana goes on top. The crêpes can be folded in quarters to eat on a plate, or rolled, burrito-style, for a walk-around snack.

NUTRITION INFORMATION PER SERVING: **1 crêpe with 1 tablespoon Nutella and 1 banana, 207g**
291 cal | 6g fat | 8g protein | 44g complex carbohydrates | 12g sugar | 4g dietary fiber | 81mg cholesterol | 173mg sodium

SAVORY SPINACH-FILLED CRÊPES

14 CRÊPES

Breakfast isn't always sweet, and crêpes don't have to be either. They're the perfect canvas for a savory filling. The following filling, made with spinach and mushrooms, is excellent for crêpes either rolled, folded, or used to make two crêpe cakes (see variation below).

1 tablespoon (12g) vegetable oil

4 cups (312g) sliced fresh mushrooms

1 cup (142g) peeled and chopped onions

1 cup (150g) chopped ham (optional)

3 pounds (1.36kg) fresh spinach, stemmed and chopped, or three 10-ounce packages (284g) frozen chopped spinach, thawed and drained

2 tablespoons (28g) butter

¼ cup (30g) unbleached all-purpose flour

1½ cups (340g) milk

salt and pepper to taste

3 large eggs

In a large pan, heat the oil and sauté the mushrooms, onions, and ham, if using, until the liquid has cooked off. Add the chopped spinach, stir quickly, then cover the pan and cook just until the spinach has wilted. Remove from the heat and set aside.

Melt the butter in a small saucepan. Add the flour and cook, stirring constantly, until the flour is golden. While whisking, add the milk a little at a time. Bring to a boil and cook until it's thickened; add salt and pepper to taste. Remove from the heat and cool for 15 minutes, then stir together the cream sauce, spinach mixture, and eggs. Use this mixture to fill crêpes (see page 24). You can sauté them in butter until heated through, or place in a buttered baking dish, sprinkle with grated cheese, and bake them in a preheated 350°F oven for 20 minutes.

NUTRITION INFORMATION PER SERVING: **2 crêpes, 290g**
372 cal | 19g fat | 19g protein | 32g complex carbohydrates | 4g dietary fiber | 230mg cholesterol | 749mg sodium

TO MAKE CRÊPE CAKES: Place one unrolled, unfilled crêpe in the bottom of a lightly greased 8″ or 9″ round cake pan. Fan 5 crêpes around the perimeter of the pan, allowing about a quarter of each crêpe to overlap the one next to it. Spread half the filling evenly over the crêpes and fold in the edges. Place 1 crêpe on top. Repeat with the remaining crêpes and filling in another lightly greased 8″ or 9″ round cake pan.

· Brush the top crêpe in each pan with melted butter or oil and bake the cakes in a preheated 350°F oven for 35 to 40 minutes, until the tops are slightly brown and crisp. Let the cakes sit for 10 minutes before cutting them into wedges. Serve hot.

CHEESE BLINTZES

14 BLINTZES

A thin, buttery crêpe, wrapped around a mild, smooth, ricotta- or cottage cheese–based filling, is a wonderful base for the spoonful of fruit sauce that completes this dish.

This recipe may be made ahead, either in total or in part. The crêpes may be cooked, cooled completely, then stacked, wrapped well, and either refrigerated or frozen. Stuff them one day ahead, then hold in the refrigerator overnight; or stuff and freeze for up to a month.

We offer two types of filling: a creamy ricotta filling, slightly runny when baked, and a firmer, less sweet, more traditional filling. Serve with blueberry compote (see recipe on page 28).

1 cup (227g) water	5 tablespoons (71g) unsalted butter, melted
¾ cup (171g) milk	½ teaspoon salt
3 large eggs	1½ cups (180g) unbleached all-purpose flour

In a medium bowl, whisk together everything to make a smooth batter. Place the batter in the refrigerator for 1 hour or longer, to relax the gluten.

Heat an 8″ (or slightly larger) crêpe or omelet pan until a drop of water skips across the pan. Lightly grease the pan and pour a scant ¼ cupful of batter into the middle. Tilt the pan and swirl the batter to completely coat the bottom with batter (see illustration on page 24). Cook until the crêpe is opaque and set. Transfer the crêpes, uncooked side down, to a baking sheet or rack to cool. You cook the crêpes on only one side; this is sufficient to cook them all the way through. When you stack them, stack them "uncooked" side down, so that this side will be on the outside when you roll them.

Creamy Ricotta Filling

3 ounces (¼ cup, 84g) cream cheese

1 large egg, lightly beaten

2 teaspoons lemon zest

2 teaspoons vanilla extract

¼ teaspoon salt

3 tablespoons (36g) sugar

3¾ cup (30 ounces, 851g) ricotta cheese

In a medium bowl, beat the cream cheese until soft. Add the beaten egg a bit at a time, beating until smooth after each addition and scraping the sides of the bowl often. Add the lemon zest, vanilla extract, salt, and sugar and mix until well combined. Fold in the ricotta cheese.

Traditional Filling

1¼ cups (284g) cottage cheese

2 cups (16 ounces, 454g) ricotta cheese

1 large egg

1 teaspoon vanilla extract

1 teaspoon lemon zest

2 tablespoons (25g) sugar

Place the cottage cheese and ricotta cheese in a colander lined with cheesecloth, or in a yogurt cheese maker. Let them drain for 1½ to 2 hours, pressing down lightly occasionally.

For a smoother, creamier filling, blend all the ingredients in a food processor. For a more traditional, grainier filling, simply mash the cottage cheese with a fork and stir in the remaining ingredients.

TO ASSEMBLE: Use approximately 3 rounded tablespoons filling for each 8″ crêpe. Place the filling about 2″ from the top of the crêpe, fold the sides in, fold the top down, then loosely roll the crêpe into a log.

Heat a medium frying pan and melt about 2 tablespoons of butter in it until it's sizzling. Sauté the blintzes until they're lightly browned and heated through.

Alternatively, nestle the blintzes in a buttered 9″ × 13″ pan and bake them in a preheated 350°F oven for 25 to 30 minutes or until they're thoroughly heated.

NUTRITION INFORMATION PER SERVING: **2 blintzes filled with creamy ricotta filling, 188g**
381 cal | 23g fat | 15g protein | 23g complex carbohydrates | 6g sugar | 1g dietary fiber | 184mg cholesterol | 326mg sodium

NUTRITION INFORMATION PER SERVING: **2 blintzes filled with traditional filling, 220g**
374 cal | 18g fat | 23g protein | 25g complex carbohydrates | 4g sugar | 1g dietary fiber | 171mg cholesterol | 541mg sodium

Blueberry Compote

2 CUPS

½ cup (99g) sugar

1 tablespoon (7g) cornstarch

¼ cup (57g) cold water or fruit juice

1 teaspoon lemon zest

1 teaspoon lemon juice

pinch of salt

2 cups (340g) fresh or frozen
blueberries

In a medium saucepan, whisk together the sugar, cornstarch, and cold water or fruit juice. Add the remaining ingredients, except the blueberries, then bring the mixture to a boil over medium heat, stirring constantly; this will take only a few minutes. Remove the mixture from the heat and cool it to lukewarm. Stir in the fresh or frozen blueberries just before serving.

NUTRITION INFORMATION PER SERVING: 3 tablespoons compote, 61g
85 cal | 0g fat | 0g protein | 8g complex carbohydrates | 14g sugar | 1g dietary fiber | 0mg cholesterol | 1mg sodium

---

WHY DO POPOVERS POP?

Popovers are one of the few baked goods that rise from eggs and steam rather than from a leavener or yeast. Popover batter has a larger proportion of liquid to flour than most other baked goods. It's the steam created by the liquid in the batter that raises popovers to their astounding heights.

The protein in the eggs and flour combine to form a matrix that's soft enough to expand with the steam but strong enough to contain it. We've had our most consistent results with popovers when we made them using all-purpose flour (with at least 11.7% protein), rather than a lower-protein pastry flour, which you might be inclined to use for tenderness. Popovers will expand until their crust finally hardens.

When you remove them from the oven, pierce them with the tip of a knife, so any leftover steam can escape quickly. This keeps the popovers from becoming soggy.

POPOVERS

12 POPOVERS

We like the following recipe because it's easily made, doesn't require a popover pan (although they are helpful), and makes an even dozen popovers. A teaspoon of dried mixed herbs is optional.

3 large eggs

1½ cups (340g) whole milk

scant 1½ cups (180g) unbleached all-purpose flour

½ teaspoon salt

4 tablespoons (½ stick, 57g) butter, melted

1 teaspoon dried mixed herbs (optional)

Preheat the oven to 450°F.

Place all the ingredients in a blender in the order indicated above. Blend for 30 seconds, stopping midway through to scrape down the sides of the blender. Allow the batter to rest for 15 minutes.

Thoroughly grease 12 muffin cups (or 6 popover or 12 mini-popover cups). Be sure to grease the area around the cups as well as the cups themselves. Fill the cups about two-thirds full with the batter. Bake for 20 minutes, then reduce the oven to 350°F and bake for an additional 10 minutes. Resist the urge to open the oven door at any time during this process. Remove the baked popovers from the oven, pierce the tops with a knife, and allow them to cool in the pan for 5 minutes. Then gently turn them out of the pan onto a rack. Serve warm.

NUTRITION INFORMATION PER SERVING: 1 popover, 52g

112cal | 5g fat | 4g protein | 12g complex carbohydrates | 0g sugar | 0g dietary fiber | 64mg cholesterol | 11mg sodium

Coffeecakes

Coffeecake is good anytime, but we often save it for the weekend, when you actually have the time to bake a cake and sit down to enjoy it. Open the Sunday paper and serve yourself a square of cake from the corner, where big, sweet nuggets of streusel gather and melt.

NO-FUSS COFFEECAKE

ONE 9″ × 13″ CAKE

The name of this coffeecake comes from the convenience of assembling it the day before baking. If you can't wait, by all means make and bake it right away; it's wonderful either way. Topped with nuts, cinnamon sugar, and chocolate chips, it's your ticket to a luxurious morning.

CAKE

12 tablespoons (1½ sticks, 170g) unsalted butter, softened

½ cup (107g) brown sugar, packed

1 cup (198g) granulated sugar

1 teaspoon baking powder

½ teaspoon baking soda

¾ teaspoon salt

1 teaspoon cinnamon

1 teaspoon vanilla extract

2 large eggs

2 cups (240g) unbleached all-purpose flour

1 cup (227g) sour cream or plain full-fat yogurt

TOPPING

¾ cup (160g) brown sugar, packed

¾ teaspoon cinnamon

¾ cup (85g) chopped walnuts

1 cup (170g) chocolate chips

Lightly grease a 9″ × 13″ metal pan (if using a glass or stoneware pan, add at least 10 minutes to the baking time).

TO MAKE THE CAKE: In a large bowl, beat together the butter, sugars, baking powder, baking soda, salt, cinnamon, and vanilla, mixing until smooth. Add the eggs, one at a time, mixing until each is absorbed before adding the next.

Scrape down the bowl and add the flour, alternating with the sour cream until both are incorporated. Scrape the bowl again and mix for 30 seconds more. Transfer the batter to the prepared pan and smooth the top.

TO MAKE THE TOPPING: Combine the brown sugar, cinnamon, nuts, and chips. Sprinkle over the batter. If desired, cover the pan and refrigerate overnight to bake the next morning.

If baking right away, preheat the oven to 350°F and bake for 35 to 40 minutes, or until a cake tester or toothpick inserted into the center comes out clean. If the cake was refrigerated overnight, uncover and bake for 40 to 45 minutes in a preheated 350°F oven. Remove from the oven and let cool on a rack before serving.

Store leftovers covered on the counter for up to 3 days; freeze for longer storage.

NUTRITION INFORMATION PER SERVING: 1 square, 94g

373 cal | 19g fat | 5g protein | 14g complex carbohydrates | 36g sugar | 2g dietary fiber | 56mg cholesterol | 39mg sodium

OUR FAVORITE SOUR CREAM COFFEECAKE

ONE 9½" BUNDT CAKE OR 9" SQUARE CAKE

This tender cake is both filled and topped with cinnamon sugar. Sour cream adds tenderness and flavor to any baked good, and this breakfast cake is no exception. It's called "our favorite" for good reason!

CAKE

8 tablespoons (1 stick, 113g) unsalted butter, softened

1 cup (198g) sugar

2 large eggs, at room temperature

2 cups (240g) unbleached all-purpose flour

1 teaspoon baking powder

¼ teaspoon baking soda

½ teaspoon salt

1 cup (227g) sour cream or yogurt, at room temperature

TOPPING

½ cup (99g) sugar

2 teaspoons cinnamon

2 teaspoons vanilla extract

½ cup (57g) chopped walnuts or pecans (optional)

Preheat the oven to 350°F. Grease and flour a 9½" tube pan or a 9" square pan.

TO MAKE THE CAKE: Beat together the butter, sugar, and eggs. In a separate bowl, mix together the flour, baking powder, baking soda, and salt.

Add the flour mixture to the butter mixture alternately with the sour cream or yogurt, stirring after each addition.

TO MAKE THE TOPPING: Stir together the topping ingredients until evenly crumbly.

Spread half the batter in the pan, and sprinkle with half the topping mixture. Repeat with the remaining batter and topping.

Bake the coffeecake for 30 to 40 minutes, or until a cake tester or toothpick inserted into the center comes out clean, or with just a few moist crumbs sticking to it. Glass pans may take an additional 5 to 10 minutes to bake through completely.

Remove the cake from the oven; if you've baked it in a tube pan, wait 10 minutes, loosen the edges, and carefully turn it out of the pan. Place the cake right-side up (topping up) on a plate to serve. If you've baked the cake in a 9" square pan, just serve it right from the pan. Serve the cake warm or at room temperature.

NUTRITION INFORMATION PER SERVING: 1 square, 88g

320 cal | 15g fat | 5g protein | 16g complex carbohydrates | 26g sugar | 1g dietary fiber | 60mg cholesterol | 180mg sodium

CRANBERRY ALMOND COFFEECAKE

ONE 9″ OR 10″ BUNDT CAKE

Although it's especially ideal for making use of leftover cranberry sauce on the day after Thanksgiving, this cake is a beloved part of our baking repertoire all year long. Cranberries add a nice tartness to the sweetness of the cake, as well as a beautiful jewel-toned color.

CAKE

8 tablespoons (1 stick, 113g) unsalted butter

1 cup (198g) granulated sugar

2 large eggs

1 cup (227g) buttermilk or yogurt

1 teaspoon almond extract

1 teaspoon baking powder

1 teaspoon baking soda

2 cups (240g) unbleached all-purpose flour

½ teaspoon salt

1 cup (212g) cranberry sauce (whole berry is preferable)

½ cup (43g) blanched slivered almonds, toasted

GLAZE

¾ cup (85g) confectioners' sugar

2 tablespoons (28g) milk

½ teaspoon almond extract

Preheat the oven to 350°F.

In a large bowl, cream together the butter and sugar. Beat in the eggs, buttermilk, and almond extract. In a separate bowl, mix together the baking powder, baking soda, flour, and salt. Add all at once to the wet ingredients, stirring just to blend.

Grease and flour a 9″ or 10″ tube pan. Spoon half the batter into the pan. Spread half the cranberry sauce evenly atop the batter, then spread the remaining batter over that. Top with the remaining cranberry sauce and sprinkle toasted almonds evenly over the sauce.

Bake the coffeecake for 55 minutes, or until a cake tester or toothpick inserted in the center comes out clean. Remove it from the oven and cool it in the pan for 5 minutes.

While the cake is cooling, make the glaze by whisking together all the glaze ingredients. Turn the cake out of the pan and drizzle the glaze over the warm cake. Let the cake cool completely before serving (or serve it warm if you don't mind it crumbling a bit).

NUTRITION INFORMATION PER SERVING: 1 slice, 85g

240 cal | 9g fat | 4g protein | 13g complex carbohydrates | 23g sugar | 1g dietary fiber | 43mg cholesterol | 211mg sodium

CRUMB COFFEECAKE

TWO 8″ ROUND CAKES, ONE 9″ × 13″ CAKE, OR ONE 9″ OR 10″ BUNDT CAKE

This coffeecake is the culmination of a longtime quest to recapture a certain kind of moist, pick-up-with-one-finger, clean-the-plate-coffeecake crumb. After a lot of trial and error, we discovered what was missing was a simple technique: to melt the butter before combining it with the sugar and flour. It made all the difference. This coffeecake is downright irresistible.

CRUMB

- 2½ cups (300g) unbleached all-purpose flour
- 1¼ cups (248g) granulated sugar
- ½ teaspoon salt
- 1½ teaspoons cinnamon
- 16 tablespoons (2 sticks, 226g) unsalted butter, melted
- 1 teaspoon vanilla extract
- ¾ teaspoon almond extract

CAKE

- 8 tablespoons (1 stick, 113g) unsalted butter
- 1 cup (198g) granulated sugar
- 2 large eggs
- 1 teaspoon vanilla extract
- 1 cup (227g) sour cream
- 2 cups (240g) unbleached all-purpose flour
- ½ teaspoon baking soda
- ½ teaspoon salt
- 1 teaspoon baking powder
- confectioners' sugar for dusting

Preheat the oven to 350°F. Grease your preferred cake or Bundt pan.

TO MAKE THE CRUMB: In a medium bowl, whisk together the flour, sugar, salt, and cinnamon. Melt the butter in the microwave or small saucepan and add the extracts to it. Pour the butter into the flour mixture and mix until all the butter is absorbed and you have a uniformly moistened crumb mixture. Set aside.

TO MAKE THE BATTER: In a large mixing bowl, cream the butter and sugar until light and fluffy. Add the eggs one at a time, and beat between additions. Scrape down the mixing bowl, then beat in the vanilla and sour cream. In a medium bowl, whisk the flour, baking soda, salt, and baking powder together. Add to the butter/sour cream mixture, mixing until evenly combined. Pour the batter into the greased baking pan(s). Crumble the crumb mixture over the top, until the batter is completely covered. Bake for 20 to 25 minutes for 8″ rounds, 30 to 35 minutes for a 9″ × 13″ pan, or 35 to 40 minutes for a tube pan, until a cake tester or toothpick comes out clean. Remove the cake from the oven and cool on a rack; dust with confectioners' sugar, if desired.

NUTRITION INFORMATION PER SERVING: 1 square, 58g

242 cal | 14g fat | 2g protein | 9g complex carbohydrates | 18g sugar | 0g dietary fiber | 54mg cholesterol | 154mg sodium

BLUEBERRY BUCKLE COFFEECAKE

ONE 8″ OR 9″ SQUARE OR ONE 9″ ROUND CAKE

Not actually a buckle at all, this recipe has been a classic for years: moist, easy to make, and liberally studded with juicy berries. It's the perfect way to make use of summer fruit.

STREUSEL

⅓ cup (67g) sugar

½ cup (60g) unbleached all-purpose flour

1 teaspoon cinnamon

⅛ teaspoon salt

4 tablespoons (½ stick, 57g) butter, at room temperature (at least 65°F)

CAKE

2 cups (240g) unbleached all-purpose flour

2 teaspoons baking powder

½ teaspoon salt

¾ cup (149g) sugar

4 tablespoons (½ stick, 57g) butter, softened

1 large egg, at room temperature

1 teaspoon vanilla extract

½ cup (113g) milk, at room temperature

2 cups (283g) fresh or frozen blueberries

Preheat the oven to 375°F. Lightly grease an 8″ square, 9″ square, or 9″ round cake pan. If you use an 8″ square pan or round pan, make sure it's at least 2″ deep.

TO MAKE THE STREUSEL TOPPING: In a small bowl, mix the sugar, flour, cinnamon, and salt. Cut or rub in the butter with the side of a fork, two knives, or your fingertips until it reaches a crumbly state. Set aside.

TO MAKE THE CAKE: In a medium bowl, blend the flour, baking powder, and salt together. In a large bowl, beat together the sugar, butter, egg, and vanilla.

Alternately add the milk and the flour mixture to the sugar/butter mixture, ending with flour. Add blueberries. Stir only enough to blend.

Pour the batter into the prepared pan. Sprinkle the streusel topping over the batter.

Bake the cake for 40 to 45 minutes, or until a cake tester or toothpick inserted into the center comes out clean.

Remove the cake from the oven and set it on a rack to cool for 10 minutes. Serve right from the pan, or transfer to a serving dish by loosening the sides with a knife or spatula and gently tipping the cake out into one of your hands and setting it onto the dish.

NUTRITION INFORMATION PER SERVING: 1 square, 64g

160 cal | 3.5g fat | 3g protein | 15g complex carbohydrates | 15g sugar | 1g dietary fiber | 20mg cholesterol | 160mg sodium

— CHAPTER TWO —

Quick Breads

BANANA BREAD, long a staple of bakery counters. Blueberry muffins, a classic breakfast treat. Baking powder biscuits, the perfect partner for a bowl of soup. Scones, highlighting the late afternoon tea break. What do all of these wonderful recipes have in common? They fall under the mantle of quick breads: breads leavened with baking powder, baking soda, or eggs (rather than yeast), and put immediately into the oven, rather than rising on the counter first.

They're the answer when you want baked goods in a hurry. Quick breads fall into two basic categories: batter breads and free-form shaped doughs. Batter breads, whose initial dough texture ranges from pourable to thick, are baked in a shaped pan of some kind; breads in this category include muffins, batter loaves, steamed breads and puddings, and some updated soda breads.

Quick breads made from a stiff dough—including biscuits, scones, and traditional soda breads—are usually baked on a baking sheet, after being formed by hand or cutter, or simply "dropped" from the bowl onto the pan. Drop biscuits or scones are characterized by their craggy shape and slightly moister texture.

Muffins

There's nothing quite so comfortingly familiar as a warm muffin, spread with butter or preserves, enjoyed with a cup of coffee or tea.

Muffins are versatile. You can add nuts, fruit, cinnamon, nutmeg, pumpkin pie spice, or ginger. Chopped chocolate or chocolate chips are nice, too. Savory muffins might include cheese, dried or fresh herbs, or even meat (like crumbled bacon). Just remember not to be too heavy-handed with the additions: One cup of fruit, nuts, or other addition per cup of flour is just about the outer limit of what you can add and still expect the muffin to hold together and rise. We highly recommend a muffin scoop (see Tools, page 546) to deliver your batter to the pans with minimal mess.

SIFTING DRY INGREDIENTS IN "STIR" RECIPES

There are good reasons for the dry ingredients to be sifted or whisked together before you add them to the wet ingredients. First, there's nothing quite so unappetizing as biting into a muffin or cookie and tasting a big lump of either baking powder or baking soda. Second, sifting or whisking aerates the flour, and when you add it to the wet ingredients in its aerated state, you're more likely to have a light, finished product.

BEATEN VS. STIRRED

There are two basic ways to prepare a muffin: the easy formula that barely marries the dry ingredients with the wet ingredients, and can be completed with a few simple swipes of a spoon; and a more complicated, cake-like technique that makes a more tender, finer-grained muffin.

When using the simple method of muffin preparation, the key phrase to remember is "fast and gentle." Whisk together the flour and other dry ingredients until you've created a veritable kitchen dust storm; beat the wet ingredients together until they're absolutely smooth. But once liquid meets dry—tread softly. When the protein in the flour meets liquid it forms gluten, a tough, elastic matrix of proteins whose structure traps carbon dioxide and allows bread to rise. Gluten also allows muffins to rise, but muffins don't need to rise nearly as far as bread, and their structure sets much more quickly. Thus we want to keep gluten development to a minimum when making muffins, which means mixing muffin ingredients gently and quickly once they've combined to form a batter—just barely enough to moisten the flour is sufficient. Don't worry about any small lumps as they'll disappear during baking.

The second muffin preparation method, creaming, relies on thorough beating of the butter and sugar in the recipe, which fills it with tiny air bubbles. The resulting batter makes a fine-grained, tender product, because each of those tiny air bubbles expands as it's heated during the baking process, creating a fine rather than coarse texture in the muffin. You'll find this preparation method no different than that used for cake-making.

ALL-STAR MUFFINS

16 LARGE MUFFINS

This all-purpose, basic muffin can easily be customized (see variations below). Once mixed, the batter will keep up to a week in the refrigerator. It's nice to wake up, turn on the oven, make your morning coffee, scoop two muffins, pop them in to bake, and by the time you've fetched the paper and let the dog back in, you're ready to settle down for a wonderful, warm, freshly baked breakfast.

3½ cups (420g) unbleached all-purpose or 3⅓ cup cake flour (400g)

2 teaspoons baking powder

½ teaspoon baking soda

1 teaspoon salt

8 tablespoons (1 stick, 113g) unsalted butter, at room temperature

1 cup (198g) sugar

3 large eggs

2 teaspoons vanilla extract

1 cup (227g) sour cream

Preheat the oven to 400°F and lightly grease 16 muffin cups or use paper liners.

In a medium bowl, whisk together flour, baking powder, baking soda, and salt, then set aside.

In a large bowl, cream the butter and sugar together with a hand-held or stand mixer until light and fluffy and almost white in color. Scrape down the bowl to make sure all the butter is incorporated, then add the eggs, one at a time, beating well after each addition. Add the vanilla and sour cream and mix until incorporated. Add the dry ingredients and mix on low speed just until the batter is smooth. Fill muffin cups and bake for 18 to 24 minutes, until a cake tester or toothpick inserted in the center comes out clean. Remove them from the oven, cool in the pan for 5 minutes, then remove the muffins from the pan to finish cooling on a rack. (Muffins left in the pan to cool will become tough from steaming.)

Scoop muffin batter into greased tin, filling three-quarters full.

NUTRITION INFORMATION PER SERVING: 1 muffin, 73g

274 cal | 15g fat | 4g protein | 19g complex carbohydrates | 12g sugar | 1g dietary fiber | 76mg cholesterol | 254mg sodium

VARIATIONS

APPLE CINNAMON: Peel and grate 3 to 4 tart apples, such as Granny Smiths or Jonathans. Fold into muffin batter with ¼ cup (50g) cinnamon sugar. Top muffins with more cinnamon sugar before baking, if desired.

APRICOT ALMOND: Add ½ teaspoon almond extract, 1½ cups (192g) diced apricots, and 1 cup (86g) sliced almonds to batter before baking.

APRICOT, CHERRY, CRANBERRY, DATE, RAISIN: Soak 2 cups (380g) of any of these dried fruits in ⅓ cup (75g) orange juice, water, rum, or bourbon, then fold into the muffin batter. Garnish muffin tops with chopped nuts if you like.

APPLE, BANANA, NECTARINE, PEACH, PLUM: Dice 3 cups (525g) of any of these fruits and fold into batter before baking. Garnish muffin tops with granulated sugar.

BANANA COCONUT: Add 2 diced bananas and 1½ cups (127g) shredded sweetened coconut to batter before baking.

BLUEBERRY, RASPBERRY, BLACKBERRY: Fold 3 cups (510g) berries into batter before baking; sprinkle the tops with cinnamon sugar or streusel (see Apple Streusel Muffin Tops, page 48, for streusel) before baking.

CARROT GINGER RAISIN: Add 2 cups (198g) shredded carrots, ½ cup (92g) crystallized or minced fresh ginger, and 1½ cups (225g) raisins to batter before baking.

CHERRY CHOCOLATE CHIP: Add 1¼ cups (213g) dried sweet cherries (soaked in ¾ cup (170g) liquid for 20 minutes, if they're very hard) and 1¼ cups (213g) chocolate chips to batter before baking.

DATE NUT: Add 1½ cups (225g) dates and 1½ cups (171g) pecans to the batter before baking.

MAPLE WALNUT: Add ½ cup (78g) maple sugar and 1½ to 2 cups (170g to 226g) chopped walnuts to batter before baking.

OATMEAL: Add 2 cups (198g) rolled oats to batter before baking.

PEANUT BUTTER CHOCOLATE CHIP: Add 1½ cups (405g) creamy peanut butter (it helps to soften the peanut butter in the microwave before combining it with the batter) and 1½ cups (255g) chocolate chips to batter before baking.

TOFFEE CHOCOLATE CHIP: Add a 10-ounce bag of Heath bar bits or 1½ cups (234g) of your favorite buttercrunch, chopped, and 1½ cups (255g) chocolate chips to batter before baking.

BANANA CHOCOLATE CHIP MUFFINS

12 MUFFINS

This muffin treats you to the ever-popular banana and chocolate combination, with just enough whole wheat to tip it away from cake territory and firmly into breakfast.

8 tablespoons (1 stick, 113g) unsalted butter, at room temperature

1 cup (198g) sugar

1 large egg

½ teaspoon nutmeg

½ teaspoon allspice

2 medium ripe bananas, mashed (about ¾ cup, 170g)

⅓ cup (76g) milk

1 cup (113g) white whole wheat flour or whole wheat flour

1 cup (120g) unbleached all-purpose flour

1½ teaspoons baking powder

½ teaspoon baking soda

½ teaspoon salt

¾ cup (128g) chocolate chips

1 cup (113g) chopped walnuts

Preheat the oven to 350°F.

In a medium bowl, cream together the butter and sugar until they're smooth. Scrape down the bowl, then beat in the egg, spices, banana, and milk. In a separate medium bowl, whisk together the dry ingredients, then gently stir them into the butter/sugar mixture.

Spoon the batter into 12 lightly greased muffin cups. Bake the muffins for 20 minutes, or until a cake tester or toothpick inserted in the center comes out clean. Remove from the oven, and after 10 minutes, turn them out of the pan to cool.

NUTRITION INFORMATION PER SERVING: 1 muffin, 98g

322 cal | 14g fat | 6g protein | 21g complex carbohydrates | 23g sugar | 3g dietary fiber | 31mg cholesterol | 222mg sodium

CHOCOLATE BREAKFAST MUFFINS

12 MUFFINS

Chocolate for breakfast: Why not? After all, if you were in Paris right now, you might be standing on the corner outside the local *boulangerie*, a steaming cup of *café au lait* in one hand and a fresh *pain au chocolat* in the other.

These muffins are rich and tender, high-rising, and *deeply* chocolate, both in color and flavor. They don't need to be relegated to the breakfast table; frosted with fudge-y icing, they double nicely as cupcakes.

⅔ cup (56g) unsweetened cocoa, Dutch-process or natural

1¾ cups (210g) unbleached all-purpose flour

1¼ cups (266g) light brown sugar

1 teaspoon baking powder

1 teaspoon baking soda

¾ teaspoon salt

1 cup (170g) chocolate chips

2 large eggs

1 cup (227g) milk

2 teaspoons vanilla extract

2 teaspoons vinegar

8 tablespoons (1 stick, 113g) unsalted butter, melted

Preheat the oven to 425°F.

In a large bowl, whisk together the cocoa, flour, brown sugar, baking powder, baking soda, salt, and chocolate chips. Set aside.

In a large measuring cup or medium bowl, whisk together the eggs, milk, vanilla, and vinegar. Add the wet ingredients, along with the melted butter, to the dry ingredients, stirring to blend. There's no need to beat these muffins; just make sure everything is well combined.

Scoop the batter into 12 lightly greased muffin cups. Bake the muffins for 15 to 20 minutes, or until a cake tester or toothpick inserted in the center of a muffin comes out clean (watch them closely, as they'll burn around the edges if they bake too long). Remove the muffins from the oven, and after 5 minutes remove them from the pan, allowing them to cool slightly on a rack before serving.

NUTRITION INFORMATION PER SERVING: 1 muffin, 101g
335 cal | 13.8g fat | 6g protein | 18g complex carbohydrates | 28g sugar | 3g dietary fiber | 69mg cholesterol | 273mg sodium

DOUGHNUT MUFFINS

12 LARGE MUFFINS

Our baking philosophy: simple and classic go hand in hand. These understated yet elegant muffins are high-rising with a lofty crown and delicate, cake-like texture, and a hint of nutmeg to perfume the batter. When combined with the cinnamon-sugar topping, it creates a flavor reminiscent of plain doughnuts.

MUFFINS

3 cups (360g) unbleached all-purpose flour

1 cup (198g) sugar

2½ teaspoons baking powder

1¼ teaspoons nutmeg

¾ teaspoon salt

2 large eggs

1¼ cups (284g) milk

5⅓ tablespoons (⅔ stick, 75g) unsalted butter, melted

TOPPING

¼ cup (50g) sugar

½ teaspoon cinnamon

4 tablespoons (½ stick, 57g) butter, melted

Preheat the oven to 350°F.

TO MAKE THE MUFFINS: In a large bowl, whisk together the flour, sugar, baking powder, nutmeg, and salt. Make a well in the center of the dry ingredients. In a medium bowl, beat the eggs slightly, then add the milk and melted butter, stirring constantly. Add the wet mixture to the well in the flour mixture. Stir just until evenly moistened (the batter may be lumpy). Lightly grease muffin cups. Fill cups about three-quarters full. Bake for 20 to 25 minutes, or until muffins are golden.

TO MAKE THE TOPPING: While the muffins are baking, combine sugar and cinnamon in a small, shallow bowl until evenly blended. When muffins come out of the oven, let them cool just enough so that you can pick them up. Immediately dip the tops of the hot muffins into melted butter, then into the cinnamon-sugar mixture until coated. Serve warm.

NUTRITION INFORMATION PER SERVING: 1 muffin, 93g

278 cal | 11g fat | 5g protein | 23g complex carbohydrates | 17g sugar | 1g dietary fiber | 64mg cholesterol | 187mg sodium

CLASSIC BLUEBERRY MUFFINS

12 MUFFINS

These muffins have a storied history: They're a variation on the ones served in the cafeteria at the bygone Jordan Marsh department store, which was a Boston destination for years. Tired shoppers, footsore and in need of comfort, could trek to the top of the Jordan Marsh building, there to enjoy a cup of tea and a king-size blueberry muffin as they compared purchases.

This is a cake-type muffin, very tender, sweet, and fine-grained. We use it whenever we want a more-delicate-than-usual muffin; for that reason, it's one of our favorite muffin recipes to make in miniature form. We prefer to use tiny Maine blueberries when they're available, as we find them much less prone to "leaking" and breaking during the baking process.

8 tablespoons (1 stick, 113g) unsalted butter, at room temperature

1 cup (198g) sugar

½ teaspoon salt

2 large eggs

2 teaspoons baking powder

2 cups (240g) unbleached all-purpose flour

½ cup (113g) milk

2½ cups (425g) fresh blueberries

1 teaspoon vanilla extract

2 teaspoons sugar or cinnamon sugar, for topping (optional)

Preheat the oven to 375°F. In a medium bowl, cream together the butter, sugar, and salt until light and fluffy. Add the eggs one at a time, beating well after each addition. Add the baking powder, then add the flour alternately with the milk, beating well after each addition. Mash ½ cup (85g) of the blueberries and add them to the batter. Stir in the vanilla at the end, along with the whole blueberries.

Mound the batter into 12 lightly greased or paper-lined muffin cups, filling each completely to the top (actually, over the top; the batter is thick enough that it'll hold its shape). Sprinkle with sugar or cinnamon sugar, if desired.

Bake the muffins for 30 minutes, or until a cake tester or toothpick inserted in the center of one comes out clean. Remove the muffins from the oven, and after 5 minutes remove them from the pan to cool completely on a rack, or gently flip them sideways in the pan. (Muffins left in the pan will steam, creating a tough crust.)

NUTRITION INFORMATION PER SERVING: 1 muffin, 85g

231 cal | 10g fat | 3g protein | 18g complex carbohydrates | 16g sugar | 1g dietary fiber | 59mg cholesterol | 196mg sodium

HOT CROSS MUFFINS

12 MUFFINS

These muffins offer the distinctive taste of hot cross buns in a quarter of the time it would take to make a sweetened yeast bread. Everybody wins!

MUFFINS

2 tablespoons (28g) rum or water

1 cup (149g) golden raisins

3 cups (360g) unbleached all-purpose flour

1 tablespoon (12g) baking powder

⅓ cup (66g) sugar

½ teaspoon salt

½ teaspoon cinnamon

½ teaspoon nutmeg

¼ teaspoon allspice

½ cup (85g) candied citron or mixed candied fruit (optional)

2 large eggs

1½ cups (340g) milk

8 tablespoons (1 stick, 113g) unsalted butter, melted

FROSTING

1¼ cups (142g) confectioners' sugar

2 tablespoons (14g) butter, softened

1 teaspoon vanilla extract

1 tablespoon (14g) milk or cream

Preheat the oven to 400°F.

In a small bowl, pour the rum or water over the raisins; set aside while you assemble all of the other ingredients.

In a large bowl, whisk together the flour, baking powder, sugar, salt, and spices. Make a well in the center. Add the soaked raisins and candied peel or citron (if using). Beat together the eggs and milk, add the melted butter, and add, all at once, to the dry ingredients. Stir until everything is evenly combined. Scoop into greased muffin cups, filling each three-quarters full. Bake for 20 to 25 minutes, until a cake tester or toothpick inserted in the center comes out clean. Remove from the oven and cool on a rack while you combine the frosting ingredients. When the muffins are cool, frost with a cross over the tops.

NUTRITION INFORMATION PER SERVING: 1 muffin, 115g

321 cal | 11g fat | 6g protein | 34g complex carbohydrates | 15g sugar | 1g dietary fiber | 63mg cholesterol | 240mg sodium

MORNING GLORY MUFFINS

12 LARGE OR 15 MEDIUM MUFFINS

A cross between a granola bar and a carrot cake, these beloved muffins are full of all kinds of good things to get your day started. This is a sturdy muffin that reheats well. If you have kids who can't be talked into sitting down to breakfast, send them out the door with one of these and you know they'll have a decent start to their day.

½ cup (75g) raisins

2 cups (240g) unbleached all-purpose flour

1 cup (198g) sugar

2 teaspoons baking soda

2 teaspoons cinnamon

½ teaspoon ginger

½ teaspoon salt

2 cups (198g) peeled and grated carrots

1 large tart apple (224 to 226g), grated

½ cup (43g) sweetened shredded coconut

½ cup (43g) sliced almonds or chopped walnuts

⅓ cup (47g) sunflower seeds or wheat germ (optional)

3 large eggs

⅔ cup (132g) vegetable oil

2 teaspoons vanilla extract

Preheat the oven to 375°F and lightly grease 12 muffin cups. Put the raisins in a small bowl and cover them with hot water; set aside to soak while you assemble the rest of the recipe.

In a large bowl, whisk together the flour, sugar, baking soda, spices, and salt. Add the carrots, apple, coconut, nuts, and sunflower seeds or wheat germ, if using. In a separate bowl, beat eggs, oil, and vanilla together. Add to the flour mixture and stir until evenly combined. Drain the raisins and stir into the batter. Divide the batter among the muffin cups and bake for 20 to 25 minutes, until golden brown. Remove from the oven, let cool for 5 minutes, then turn out of the pans to finish cooling.

NUTRITION INFORMATION PER SERVING: 1 large muffin, 106g

334 cal | 17g fat | 5g protein | 25g complex carbohydrates | 17g sugar | 2g dietary fiber | 53mg cholesterol | 339mg sodium

RAISIN BRAN MUFFINS

12 MUFFINS

Dark brown, moist, and sweet from the brown sugar and raisins, these muffins keep extremely well. They're packed with fiber and incredibly flavorful: a lovely way to start the day. Use either flour, or a combination; muffins made with 100% unbleached all-purpose flour will be lighter both in color and texture, but for flavor we actually prefer those made with whole wheat.

1 cup (227g) milk or buttermilk

⅓ cup (66g) vegetable oil

2 large eggs

¼ cup (85g) molasses

½ cup (107g) brown sugar

¾ cup (48g) wheat bran

½ cup (50g) rolled oats

1½ teaspoons cinnamon

½ teaspoon salt

1¼ cups (141g) whole wheat flour or unbleached all-purpose flour (150g)

1 tablespoon (12g) baking powder

½ cup (75g) raisins

In a medium bowl, whisk together the milk or buttermilk, oil, eggs, molasses, and brown sugar. Add the bran and oats. Set this mixture aside for 15 minutes to give the oats and bran a chance to absorb some of the liquid and become soft. Preheat the oven to 425°F.

Whisk the remaining dry ingredients together thoroughly, making sure there are absolutely no stray lumps of baking powder remaining. Add the dry ingredients to the wet ingredients, stirring just until blended.

Spoon the batter into 12 lightly greased or paper-lined muffin cups, filling each cup almost to the top. Bake the muffins for 14 to 18 minutes, or until they spring back when pressed lightly in the middle, and a cake tester or toothpick inserted in the center comes out clean. Remove the muffins from the oven, and after 5 minutes remove them from the pan (or gently flip them sideways) to cool completely on a rack. (Muffins left in the pan will steam, creating a tough crust.)

NUTRITION INFORMATION PER SERVING: 1 muffin, 74g

203 cal | 9g fat | 5g protein | 20g complex carbohydrates | 9g sugar | 4g dietary fiber | 38mg cholesterol | 204mg sodium

SPICED PEACH MUFFINS

16 MUFFINS

These are big, high-crowned muffins that seem to explode right out of the muffin cup. During the summer in Vermont, we make them with peaches, but they're also delightful made with blueberries, blackberries, or raspberries. This is a big recipe, but once you taste one of these, you will be happy to have more than the usual dozen on hand.

4½ cups (540g) unbleached all-purpose flour

1 teaspoon salt

4½ teaspoons baking powder

2 cups (426g) dark brown sugar

½ teaspoon allspice

½ teaspoon nutmeg

1 teaspoon cinnamon

2 large eggs

¾ cup (149g) vegetable oil

1¼ cups (284g) milk

4 peaches (454g), diced (not peeled), or 3 cups (340g) small whole berries

granulated sugar, for sprinkling

Preheat the oven to 400°F.

Combine the flour, salt, baking powder, brown sugar, allspice, nutmeg, and cinnamon in a large bowl. Whisk until brown sugar is evenly distributed and there are no lumps. In a separate bowl or large measuring cup, beat eggs, vegetable oil, and milk together, then stir into dry ingredients. Gently stir in the fruit. Grease 16 muffin cups and heap the batter into the cups; they'll be very full. Sprinkle the tops with granulated sugar. Bake for 25 to 30 minutes, or until a cake tester or toothpick comes out clean. Remove from the oven, let cool for 5 minutes on a rack, then turn out of the pans to finish cooling.

NUTRITION INFORMATION PER SERVING: 1 muffin, 130g

340 cal | 11g fat | 5g protein | 29g complex carbohydrates | 27g sugar | 2g dietary fiber | 27mg cholesterol | 298mg sodium

ZUCCHINI LEMON MUFFINS

12 MUFFINS

These muffins are light and tender, with a clean lemon flavor shining through and just a little crunch from the walnuts. Once you've made them, you won't be sorry about the over-abundance of zucchini in late summer.

2 cups (240g) unbleached all-purpose flour

½ cup (99g) sugar

1 tablespoon (12g) baking powder

1 teaspoon salt

zest of 1 lemon

½ cup (57g) chopped walnuts

½ cup (75g) raisins

2 large eggs, beaten

½ cup (113g) milk

½ cup (99g) vegetable oil

1 cup (142 to 170g) shredded zucchini, packed

Preheat the oven to 400°F.

Combine the flour, sugar, baking powder, salt, and lemon zest in a large bowl. Stir in the walnuts and raisins. In a smaller bowl (or a 2-cup liquid measure), combine the eggs, milk, and oil. Make a well in the center of the dry ingredients and add the wet ingredients. Stir just until barely combined and then gently fold in the zucchini.

Spoon the batter into a greased 12-cup muffin tin and bake for 20 to 25 minutes, or until the muffins spring back when you press them with your fingertips. Remove from the oven, let cool for 5 minutes on a rack, then turn out of the pans to finish cooling.

NUTRITION INFORMATION PER SERVING: 1 muffin, 82g

238 cal | 13g fat | 4g protein | 22g complex carbohydrates | 8g sugar | 1g dietary fiber | 32mg cholesterol | 307mg sodium

APPLE STREUSEL MUFFIN TOPS

9 MUFFIN TOPS

If you're one of those people who wants the top of the muffin, the whole top and nothing but the top, you should probably own a specialty muffin top pan: one with large shallow wells that yields just the crackly, craggy top. Truthfully though, any muffin recipe will work to make muffin tops; all you need to do is measure out ⅓ cup of your favorite muffin recipe into the greased wells of your muffin top pan. If you want to use your quarter-cup measuring cup for a scoop, that will work fine, too. These deliciously light muffin tops pair tart apples with a touch of honey, all topped off with a crunchy brown sugar streusel.

STREUSEL

½ cup (60g) unbleached all-purpose flour

6 tablespoons (84g) brown sugar, packed

pinch of salt

½ teaspoon cinnamon (optional)

½ cup (57g) chopped walnuts

3 tablespoons (21g) butter, softened

MUFFIN TOPS

2 cups (240g) unbleached all-purpose flour

1 tablespoon (12g) baking powder

½ teaspoon salt

1 cup (113g) peeled, finely chopped apples

2 large eggs

⅓ cup (111g) honey

½ cup (113g) milk

¼ cup (57g) brandy or milk

¼ cup (50g) vegetable oil

Preheat the oven to 375°F.

TO MAKE THE STREUSEL: In a small bowl, mix together the flour, brown sugar, salt, cinnamon (if using), walnuts, and butter until the mixture is crumbly. Set aside.

TO MAKE THE MUFFIN TOPS: In a large bowl, combine the flour, baking powder, and salt, then stir in the apples. In another bowl, beat together the eggs, honey, milk, brandy or milk, and vegetable oil. Gently stir the wet ingredients into the dry ingredients, mixing just until blended. Spoon muffin batter into a greased muffin top pan. Sprinkle each muffin with topping, dividing it evenly among the cups. Bake the muffins until they're golden brown, 21 to 25 minutes. Remove from the oven and let sit for 5 minutes before taking the muffins out of the pan and cooling them completely on a rack.

NUTRITION INFORMATION PER SERVING: 1 muffin top, 113g

355 cal | 16g fat | 6g protein | 27g complex carbohydrates | 18g sugar | 1g dietary fiber | 59mg cholesterol | 307mg sodium

TOASTER CORNCAKES

9 CAKES

These English muffin–size, sort-of-sweet cornbread rounds that can be split, toasted, and slathered with softened butter (they'll crumble if confronted with ice-cold butter and a strong knife) and strawberry jam.

In order to make these corncakes in their traditional shape, you must have the proper baking pan. A hamburger bun pan is ideal, as are English muffin rings or 3¾″ × 1″ shallow paper baking cups. Alternatively, you may bake this in a parchment-lined 9″ × 13″ pan, then cut the resulting flat loaf into pieces.

1½ cups (180g) unbleached all-purpose flour

¾ cup (117g) yellow cornmeal

2¼ teaspoons baking powder

¾ teaspoon salt

6 tablespoons (74g) sugar

3 large eggs

⅔ cup (151g) milk

8 tablespoons (1 stick, 113g) unsalted butter, melted

Preheat the oven to 350°F.

In a large bowl, whisk together the flour, cornmeal, baking powder, salt, and sugar. In a separate bowl, whisk the eggs and milk until thoroughly combined. (We like to use a hand blender for this type of chore.)

Pour the milk/egg mixture and the melted butter over the dry ingredients and stir just to combine; don't beat this mixture or the cakes will be tough.

Using a spoon or muffin scoop, scoop a generous ¼ cup (or scant ⅓ cup) of batter into nine 3¾″ lightly greased wells of a hamburger bun pan (or English muffin rings set on a parchment-lined baking sheet). The cups should be about half full, maybe a bit less. Wet your fingers and spread the batter to cover the bottom of the cups, smoothing the top at the same time. If you're using a 9″ × 13″ pan, grease it lightly (or line it with parchment) and spread the batter into it, smoothing the top.

Bake the cakes for about 18 minutes, or until the bottoms are golden brown but the tops aren't colored yet, or just barely beginning to color. (Since they'll be going into the toaster, you don't want them to brown too much in the oven.) Remove the cakes from the oven and let them cool for 15 to 20 minutes before removing them from the cups. If you've used a 9″ × 13″ pan, let the cake cool, then cut it into nine rectangles, each approximately 3″ wide and 4¼″ long. Split and eat warm, or cool to room temperature, split, and toast.

NUTRITION INFORMATION PER SERVING: 1 cake, 71g

255 cal | 11.9g fat | 5g protein | 24g complex carbohydrates | 8g sugar | 1g dietary fiber | 118mg cholesterol | 309mg sodium

GLUTEN-FREE CORN MUFFINS

12 MUFFINS

Here's our secret to creating moist, tender, gluten-free corn muffins: pre-soaking the cornmeal and gluten-free flour blend to soften them up before using. The difference between dry and "wet" meal or flour is dramatic: a moist, tender muffin with the tiniest hint of sweetness. They'll freeze well, so you can make a batch and take out what you need as you need it.

1¾ cups (273g) gluten-free all-purpose flour

1 cup (138g) gluten-free cornmeal

1¼ cups (283g) buttermilk or heavy cream

8 tablespoons (1 stick, 113g) unsalted butter, softened

3 tablespoons (64g) honey

1 large egg

2 teaspoons baking powder

¼ teaspoon baking soda

½ teaspoon salt

Combine the gluten-free flour and cornmeal in a large bowl.

Pour the buttermilk or cream into the bowl and stir to evenly moisten the flours. Cover and let sit for 2 to 3 hours, or in the refrigerator overnight.

When you're ready to bake, preheat the oven to 375°F. Grease the wells of a 12-cup muffin tin, or line with papers and grease the insides of the papers.

Add the butter, honey, egg, baking powder, baking soda, and salt to the moistened flours and beat at high speed for 1 to 2 minutes. This isn't like a wheat flour muffin, where you have to worry about them getting tough: the beating helps to develop the structure of these muffins.

Scoop the batter into the wells of the prepared pan and bake the muffins for 22 to 24 minutes, until they appear set; a cake tester or toothpick inserted into the center of one of the muffins in the middle of the pan should come out clean.

Remove the muffins from the oven and put the pan on a rack; transfer the muffins from the pan to a cooling rack after 5 minutes, so they don't steam. Serve warm.

NUTRITION INFORMATION PER SERVING: 1 muffin, 72g

212 cal | 9g fat | 3g protein | 25g complex carbohydrates | 6g sugar | 1g dietary fiber | 22mg cholesterol | 223mg sodium

A STICKY SITUATION

Crumbled muffins are surely not one of life's greatest tragedies, but aggravating nonetheless.

First, a nonstick muffin pan helps to prevent crumbling. Even if it's nonstick, however, we recommend greasing it lightly with shortening or a nonstick vegetable oil spray. This both protects the pan's finish and increases its effectiveness. If you're using a muffin pan that's not nonstick, grease it a bit more heavily and be thorough; cover every inch of the inside of the pan (and the top, too, in case muffins crown and mushroom over) with shortening or pan spray.

An alternative solution is to use paper muffin cups. If you can find cups labeled "parchment," use those. Regular paper or foil muffin cups are also a fine choice.

To keep muffins from becoming soggy, as well as to help them out of the pan, wait a couple of minutes after you've taken them out of the oven, then gently tip them sideways in their cups. If you pull (gently!) and the muffin doesn't budge, run a knife around the edge of the cup to help it along. If you pull, and the muffin starts to crumble, give it another 5 minutes before attempting to move it. Muffins taken out of the pan (at least partially) while they're still hot, without having had a chance to cool and harden, have less chance of sticking to the pan.

If you've baked muffins in paper, don't try to eat them right away, while they're hot; they'll probably stick to the paper. Give them a chance to cool to lukewarm, at least, before tearing into them.

So what if you've done everything right, and your muffins still stick? Muffins lower in fat, without the self-lubricating quality of their higher-fat siblings, do tend to stick; it's a fact of life. Either accept it or add a bit more fat to your recipe. The flip side to this coin is that muffins very high in fat are so delicate that they have a tendency to crumble, no matter how careful you are. So experiment with the level of fat in your muffin batter until you're pleased with the results.

Loaves

Stir it, spoon it into the pan, and bake—it's not surprising that the term "quick bread" often refers specifically to a loaf of bread that can be mixed together and popped into the oven in a matter of minutes. Banana bread, the dowager queen of quick breads; pumpkin bread, zucchini bread, lemon poppy seed, cranberry orange, date-nut—these are all familiar examples of the genre.

In fact, this is such a popular type of baking that quick bread loaves have their own special pan: the 9″ × 5″ loaf pan. While often used interchangeably with its slightly smaller sibling, the 8½″ × 4½″ loaf pan, the 9″ × 5″ pan is perfect for most quick bread recipes (while the smaller pan is the ideal size for most yeast bread recipes). Quick loaves are also a good candidate for Bundt or tube pans; a 9″ to 10″ tube pan can take the place of a loaf pan when you want a more sophisticated presentation for your quick loaf. A 12″ × 4″ × 2½″ pan is another choice; we like it because loaves take a bit less time to bake, assuring that your loaf doesn't get too brown on the outside.

CHOCOLATE COCONUT QUICK BREAD

ONE 8½″ LOAF OR ONE 8″ SQUARE CAKE

Needing no embellishment, this dense, moist, gluten-free quick bread is a perfect snack to serve with coffee. The texture is wonderfully tender and moist, and it's a simple and reliably delicious option for a gluten-free dessert if you top it with a dollop of freshly whipped cream.

½ cup (64g) coconut flour

1 teaspoon baking powder

6 tablespoons (¾ stick, 85g) unsalted butter

½ cup (43g) unsweetened Dutch-process cocoa

¾ cup (149g) sugar

½ teaspoon salt

1 teaspoon vanilla extract

6 large eggs

Preheat the oven to 350°F. Grease an 8½″ × 4½″ loaf pan or an 8″ square cake pan.

Sift together the coconut flour and baking powder, mixing to combine; set aside.

In a large, microwave-safe bowl, melt the butter with the cocoa, stirring until well blended.

Whisk the sugar, salt, vanilla, and eggs into the butter/cocoa mixture. Add the coconut flour and baking powder, whisking until smooth.

Pour the batter into the prepared pan. Let it rest for 10 minutes.

Bake the loaf or cake until set, and a cake tester or toothpick inserted into the middle comes out clean. This will take 35 to 45 minutes for the loaf pan, or 30 to 35 minutes for the square pan.

Cool the cake in the pan for 30 minutes before turning it out onto a rack to cool completely. The cake is easiest to slice when it's completely cool.

NUTRITION INFORMATION PER SERVING: 1 slice, 41g

123 cal | 4g fat | 4g protein | 3g complex carbohydrates | 10g sugar | 2g dietary fiber | 81mg cholesterol | 150mg sodium

WHOLE GRAIN BANANA BREAD

ONE 9″ LOAF

This one-bowl banana bread uses the simplest ingredients, but is incredibly moist and flavorful. While the recipe calls for a 50/50 mix of flours (all-purpose and white whole wheat), we often make it with 100% whole wheat, and honestly, no one can tell: it's that good!

BATTER

2 cups (454g) mashed banana (about 4 or 5 medium bananas)

½ cup (99g) vegetable oil

1 cup (213g) brown sugar

2 large eggs

1 teaspoon vanilla extract

1 cup (120g) unbleached all-purpose flour

1 cup (113g) white whole wheat flour

1 teaspoon baking soda

½ teaspoon baking powder

¾ teaspoon salt

1 teaspoon cinnamon

½ cup (57g) chopped walnuts, toasted if desired (optional)

TOPPING

1 tablespoon (13g) sugar

½ teaspoon cinnamon

Preheat the oven to 350°F with a rack in the center position. Lightly grease a 9″ × 5″ loaf pan; if your pan is glass or stoneware, reduce the oven temperature to 325°F.

In a large bowl, stir together the mashed banana, oil, brown sugar, eggs, and vanilla.

Mix the flours, baking soda, baking powder, salt, cinnamon, and chopped walnuts into the mixture until the batter is smooth, then scoop into the prepared pan.

TO MAKE THE TOPPING: In a small bowl, mix together the sugar and cinnamon, and sprinkle over the batter.

Bake the bread for 60 to 75 minutes, until the bread feels set on the top, and a paring knife (or other thin knife) inserted into the center comes out clean, or with just a few moist crumbs (but no wet batter). If the bread appears to be browning too quickly, tent it with aluminum foil for the final 15 to 20 minutes of baking. If baking in a glass or stoneware pan, increase the baking time by 10 to 15 minutes.

Remove the bread from the oven. Cool it in the pan for 15 minutes, then loosen the edges, and turn it out of the pan onto a rack to cool completely.

NUTRITION INFORMATION PER SERVING: 1 slice, 102g

290 cal | 13g fat | 5g protein | 18g complex carbohydrates | 24g sugar | 3g dietary fiber | 30mg cholesterol | 240mg sodium

CRANBERRY ORANGE NUT BREAD

ONE 9″ LARGE LOAF

Whoever decided that cranberries and oranges belonged together was so obviously right that we can only thank them and enjoy the results of their good judgment. The combination of the two flavors evokes brisk weather, a fire in the fireplace, and cozy mornings.

2 cups (240g) unbleached all-purpose flour

¾ cup (149g) sugar

1½ teaspoons baking powder

½ teaspoon baking soda

¾ teaspoon salt

1 orange, zested and juiced

¾ cup (170g) buttermilk, sour cream, or yogurt

1 large egg, beaten

3 tablespoons (37g) vegetable oil

1 cup (99g) roughly chopped cranberries (fresh, frozen, or dried)

½ cup (57g) chopped nuts (optional)

Preheat the oven to 350°F.

In a large bowl, whisk together the flour, sugar, baking powder, baking soda, and salt. In a medium bowl, combine the orange juice and zest, buttermilk, egg, and vegetable oil. Add the wet ingredients to the dry and mix until evenly combined. Stir in the cranberries and nuts, then pour the batter into a greased 9″ × 5″ loaf pan. Bake the bread for 55 to 65 minutes, until a cake tester or toothpick inserted in the center of the loaf comes out clean and the bread starts to pull away from the edges of the pan. Remove it from the oven and cool on a rack for 15 minutes, then turn it out of the pan to finish cooling.

NUTRITION INFORMATION PER SERVING: 1 slice, 61g

126 cal | 3g fat | 2g protein | 13g complex carbohydrates | 9g sugar | 1g dietary fiber | 14mg cholesterol | 209mg sodium

DATE-NUT BREAD

ONE 9" LARGE LOAF

You might think that we at King Arthur never stoop to buying store-bought bread. But there are some store-bought breads that we really, really like, and this is one. The Arnold Bakery used to offer a date-nut bread that was small (really a tea bread size), and so moist and gooey that it came in its own little paper cradle. It has been one of our quests to re-create this sumptuous bread, and we think we've finally succeeded.

¾ cup (168g) boiling water

1½ cups (224g) chopped dates

1 tablespoon (14g) butter

¼ cup (53g) brown sugar

¼ cup (85g) molasses

2 large eggs

1 cup (120g) unbleached all-purpose flour

1½ teaspoons baking powder

¼ teaspoon baking soda

½ teaspoon salt

1 cup (113g) chopped walnuts

Preheat the oven to 350°F.

In a medium bowl, pour water over the dates and butter. Stir and let the mixture sit until lukewarm. Purée one-third of the mixture in a food processor or blender to make a paste, then stir it back into the date mixture. (This step can be skipped, but it really adds to the gooey texture of the finished product.) Add the brown sugar, molasses, and eggs. Stir until everything is thoroughly combined.

In a separate large bowl, sift together the flour, baking powder, baking soda, and salt. Make a well in the center and pour in the date mixture. Mix until all the ingredients are combined. Pour the batter into a greased 9" × 5" loaf pan. Bake for 60 to 65 minutes; the bread is done when the top has risen and a cake tester or toothpick inserted in the center will have some dates clinging to it but no batter. You'll also see the loaf start to pull away, just slightly, from the sides of the pan. Don't overbake or you'll lose the gooey factor. Remove the bread from the oven and cool it on a rack for 10 minutes before turning it out of the pan to finish cooling.

NUTRITION INFORMATION PER SERVING: 1 small slice, 39g

107 cal | 4g fat | 2g protein | 13g complex carbohydrates | 5g sugar | 1g dietary fiber | 18mg cholesterol | 103mg sodium

EASY PUMPKIN BREAD

TWO 8½″ OR 9″ LOAVES

Whenever we bring it to gatherings, this pumpkin bread is one of the first things to disappear. Incredibly moist and packed with flavor, it can be kept as a simple pumpkin loaf, or enhanced with anything from chocolate chips to nuts to dried fruit.

1 cup (198g) vegetable oil

2⅔ cups (528g) granulated sugar

4 large eggs

one 15-ounce can (425g) pumpkin
    purée

⅔ cup (152g) water

3⅓ cups (400g) unbleached all-
    purpose flour

½ teaspoon baking powder

1 teaspoon baking soda

1½ teaspoons salt

1 teaspoon nutmeg

1 teaspoon vanilla extract

1½ cups (255g) chocolate chips
    (optional)

1 cup (113g) chopped walnuts or pecans
    (optional)

coarse white sugar, for sprinkling on top
    (optional)

Preheat the oven to 350°F. Lightly grease two 8½″ × 4½″ loaf pans (if you're making the plain version of the bread); two 9″ × 5″ loaf pans (if you're adding chocolate chips and nuts); or one of each, if you're making one plain loaf, and one loaf with chips and nuts.

In a large bowl, beat together the oil, sugar, eggs, pumpkin, and water.

Add the flour, baking powder, baking soda, salt, nutmeg, and vanilla, stirring to combine.

Mix in the chips and nuts, if you're using them. To make one loaf with chips and nuts and one loaf without, divide the batter in half. Leave one half plain, and add ¾ cup chips and ½ cup nuts to the other half.

Spoon the batter into the prepared pans. Sprinkle the tops of the loaves with coarse sugar, if desired.

Bake the bread for 60 to 80 minutes, or until a cake tester or toothpick inserted in the center of the loaf comes out clean; and that same tester inserted about ½″ into the top of the loaf doesn't encounter any totally unbaked batter.

Remove the bread from the oven and cool it on a rack. When it's completely cool, wrap it well in plastic wrap, and store it overnight before serving.

NUTRITION INFORMATION PER SERVING: 1 slice, 72g

240 cal | 12g fat | 3g protein | 11g complex carbohydrates | 22g sugar | 1g dietary fiber | 25mg cholesterol | 125mg sodium

LEMON BREAD

ONE 9″ LOAF

This bread is moist, with a bright lemon flavor. If you can't get enough of that sunny flavor, brush the top with the lemon glaze while the loaves are still warm and serve with lemon butter.

BREAD

1 cup (198g) sugar

½ cup (99g) vegetable oil

3 tablespoons (18g) lemon zest

¼ cup (58g) lemon juice

¾ cup (170g) buttermilk

2 large eggs

1½ teaspoons salt

1 tablespoon (12g) baking powder

1 tablespoon (9g) poppy seeds (optional)

2½ cups (300g) unbleached all-
purpose flour

LEMON GLAZE AND LEMON BUTTER (OPTIONAL)

½ cup (116g) lemon juice (about
2 lemons)

⅔ cup (132g) sugar

8 tablespoons (1 stick, 113g) unsalted
butter, at room temperature

¼ teaspoon salt

Preheat the oven to 350°F and grease a 9″ × 5″ loaf pan.

TO MAKE THE BREAD: In a large bowl, combine the sugar, oil, lemon zest, and lemon juice, beating until thoroughly combined. In a separate small bowl or large mixing cup, beat together the buttermilk and eggs. Combine the dry ingredients in a medium bowl and whisk together to mix evenly. Add the dry ingredients to the sugar/oil mixture alternately with the buttermilk mixture, scraping the mixing bowl at least once. When everything is incorporated, pour the batter into the prepared pan. Bake until a cake tester or toothpick inserted in the center comes out clean, 50 to 60 minutes. Remove the bread from the oven and place it on a rack.

TO MAKE THE LEMON GLAZE: Combine the lemon juice and sugar in a microwave-safe container and microwave on high for 30 seconds to dissolve the sugar. Brush half of this mixture on the bread as it cools, if desired.

TO MAKE THE LEMON BUTTER: Take the other half of the lemon glaze and heat it in a small saucepan set over medium heat. Simmer the liquid until it has a syrupy consistency. Remove from the heat and cool to room temperature. Mix the syrup with the softened butter and salt. Chill; spread on lemon bread.

NUTRITION INFORMATION PER SERVING: 1 slice, not glazed, 61g

184 cal | 8g fat | 3g protein | 14g complex carbohydrates | 12g sugar | 1g dietary fiber | 27mg cholesterol | 311mg sodium

MAPLE CORNBREAD

ONE 8″ SQUARE OR 9″ ROUND CORNBREAD

Years ago we received a message from a King Arthur customer named Carol Stevens, who sent us her favorite recipe for maple cornbread, thinking we Vermonters would love it. She was right! This dense, sturdy cornbread is just slightly sweet, with a bare hint of maple. For any Southerners who decry the use of sugar in cornbread, read no further; we confess, this is a north-of-the-Mason-Dixon-line aberration. But to those of you who don't object to sweetened cornbread, read on: We think this is just the ticket with a bowl of chili or stew.

1 cup (120g) unbleached all-purpose flour

1 cup (133g) yellow cornmeal

1 tablespoon (12g) baking powder

½ teaspoon salt

1 cup (227g) milk

¼ cup (77g) maple syrup

4 tablespoons (½ stick, 56g) butter, melted

2 large eggs

Preheat the oven to 425°F. Lightly grease an 8″ square or 9″ round baking pan.

In a medium bowl, whisk together the flour, cornmeal, baking powder, and salt until thoroughly combined. In a small bowl or a large measuring cup, whisk together the milk, maple syrup, melted butter, and eggs. Add the liquid mixture to the dry ingredients and stir just until moistened.

Pour the batter into the prepared pan and bake the cornbread for 20 to 25 minutes, until it's lightly browned and a cake tester or toothpick inserted in the center comes out clean. Remove it from the oven and serve it warm with butter and additional maple syrup, or with a main dish.

NUTRITION INFORMATION PER SERVING: 1 piece, 83g

203 cal | 7g fat | 5g protein | 23g complex carbohydrates | 6g sugar | 2g dietary fiber | 65mg cholesterol | 372mg mg sodium

HERBED BEER BREAD

ONE 9″ LOAF

Beer can't exist without yeast, and the carbonation produced by both yeast and beer is a nice touch in a quick bread. This classic recipe, with its simple list of ingredients, requires very little in the way of tools or technique. Beloved by busy bakers everywhere, the bread is moist, nicely dense and chewy, and perfect for toast and sandwiches.

2 cups (240g) unbleached all-
purpose flour

½ cup (57g) whole wheat flour

½ cup (82g) semolina

1 tablespoon (12g) baking powder

1 teaspoon salt

2 tablespoons (28g) sugar

12 ounces (336g) beer

3 tablespoons (28g) vegetable oil

¾ cup (98g) hulled sunflower seeds

1 teaspoon each dried parsley, sage,
rosemary, and thyme

Preheat the oven to 350°F and grease a 9″ × 5″ loaf pan.

In a large bowl, mix together the flours, baking powder, salt, and sugar. Add the beer and oil and stir until the batter is evenly moistened. Stir in the sunflower seeds and herbs, then pour the batter into the prepared loaf pan. Bake the bread for 45 minutes, until a cake tester or toothpick inserted in the center comes out clean. Remove it from the oven and cool it in the pan for 15 minutes on a rack. Run a dull knife around the edge of the bread and turn it out of the pan to finish cooling.

NUTRITION INFORMATION PER SERVING: 1 slice, 59g

166 cal | 7g fat | 4g protein | 20g complex carbohydrates | 2g sugar | 2g dietary fiber | 0g cholesterol | 226mg sodium

SIMPLE ZUCCHINI BREAD

ONE 8½" LOAF

Every baker should have an excellent basic zucchini bread in their collection and this is ours. It's moist, flavorful, and easy to slice, as well as being a good blank canvas for extra add-ins, such as chocolate chips, dried fruit, or toasted nuts.

¾ cup (159g) brown sugar

2 tablespoons (43g) boiled cider, or 2 tablespoons (28g) apple juice, orange juice, milk, water, or the liquid of your choice

½ cup (99g) vegetable oil

2 large eggs

1 teaspoon vanilla extract

¼ teaspoon baking powder

½ teaspoon baking soda

1 teaspoon salt

1½ teaspoons cinnamon (optional)

1¾ cups (210g) unbleached all-purpose flour

2 cups (198g) grated zucchini

¾ cup (85g) chopped walnuts, toasted until golden

¾ cup (128g) raisins or currants

Preheat the oven to 350°F. Lightly grease an 8½" × 4½" loaf pan.

In a medium bowl, beat together the brown sugar, boiled cider or other liquid, vegetable oil, eggs, and vanilla until smooth.

Whisk the baking powder, baking soda, salt, and cinnamon (if using) into the flour. Add the dry ingredients to the liquid ingredients in the bowl, stirring or beating gently until smooth.

Stir in the zucchini, walnuts, and raisins or currants.

Scoop the batter into the prepared pan, smoothing it if necessary. Sprinkle with additional brown sugar, if desired.

Bake the bread for 55 to 65 minutes, until a cake tester or toothpick inserted into the center comes out clean. The top (just under the crust) may seem a bit sticky; but as long as the toothpick doesn't reveal wet batter, it's done.

Remove the bread from the oven, and cool it in the pan for 10 minutes. Turn it out of the pan onto a rack to cool completely. For best results, don't slice until it's cool.

NUTRITION INFORMATION PER SERVING: 1 slice, 66g

230 cal | 11g fat | 4g protein | 12g complex carbohydrates | 17g sugar | 1g dietary fiber | 25mg cholesterol | 210mg sodium

ROSEMARY CHEDDAR CHEESE BREAD

TWO 8½″ LOAVES

We love the combination of rosemary and cheddar cheese, so we combined them here in a marbled quick bread. Our recipe calls for making two batters, but the extra step is well worth the effort.

ROSEMARY WHOLE WHEAT BATTER

1 large egg

1¼ cups (284g) milk

4 tablespoons (½ stick, 56g) butter, softened

1 tablespoon (12g) baking powder

1 tablespoon (3g) dried rosemary

½ teaspoon salt

2 cups (226g) whole wheat flour or white whole wheat flour (280g)

CHEDDAR CHEESE BATTER

1 large egg

1 cup (227g) milk

4 tablespoons (½ stick, 56g) butter, melted

1 tablespoon (12g) baking powder

½ teaspoon salt

¼ teaspoon cayenne

½ teaspoon freshly ground black pepper

2 cups (240g) unbleached all-purpose flour

1¼ cups (140g) grated cheddar cheese

Preheat the oven to 350°F. Grease two 8½″ × 4½″ loaf pans.

TO MAKE THE ROSEMARY BATTER: In a medium bowl, beat the egg and add the milk and softened butter. Stir well. In a large bowl, mix together the baking powder, rosemary, salt, and flour. Stir with a whisk to incorporate all the ingredients. Add the egg mixture and stir just until combined. Put half of the batter into each of the two prepared pans.

TO MAKE THE CHEESE BATTER: In a medium bowl, beat the egg, then stir in the milk and melted butter. In a large bowl, whisk together the baking powder, salt, cayenne, black pepper, and flour. Stir in the cheese, then the milk mixture, until just combined.

Pour half of the cheddar batter into each pan on top of the rosemary batter. Use a table knife and stick it, point down, all the way through the batter to the bottom of the pan. Keep the tip touching the bottom of the pan and drag the knife through the batter in curving motions until the loaf is marbled. Repeat with the second loaf.

Bake the loaves for 50 to 60 minutes, or until nicely browned and a cake tester or toothpick inserted in the middle of a loaf comes out clean. Remove from the oven and let them rest for 5 to 10 minutes before turning out onto a cooling rack.

NUTRITION INFORMATION PER SERVING: 1 slice, 55g

114 cal | 3g fat | 5g protein | 16g complex carbohydrates | 0g sugar | 2g dietary fiber | 25mg cholesterol | 264mg sodium

SAVORY CHRISTMAS BREAD

ONE 10″ LOAF

This loaf gets its name from showcasing the festive red, green, and gold colors of Christmas with sun-dried tomatoes and green pepper or chives. Though it bakes as a freestanding loaf, this easy-to-make baking powder bread handles surprisingly like a yeast bread and can even be braided if you're feeling fancy.

3 cups (360g) unbleached all-purpose flour

2 teaspoons baking powder

1 teaspoon salt

8 ounces (about 2 cups, 224g) grated provolone cheese

4 large eggs, beaten

½ cup (112g) half-and-half

3 large garlic cloves, minced

¼ cup (35g) finely chopped green pepper (or 10g fresh chives or green part of scallions)

¼ cup (42g) finely chopped sun-dried tomatoes (or drained pimientos or red bell pepper)

Preheat the oven to 350°F.

In a medium bowl, mix together the flour, baking powder, salt, and cheese. Add the beaten eggs, reserving 2 tablespoons for glazing the bread before baking. Mix in the half-and-half, garlic, and vegetables, stirring to make a soft dough.

Turn out the dough onto a well-floured surface and form it into a smooth ball. Roll the ball into a log shape about 10″ long. Place it on a greased baking sheet. Brush with the reserved beaten egg.

Bake for 30 to 35 minutes, or until the loaf is golden brown. Cool thoroughly before slicing and serving.

A SHARP TIP

Use a good-quality pair of shears to chop many kinds of herbs and vegetables. Snip parsley, chives, or other fresh herbs; use the part of the scissor blade closest to the handle to cut tougher items, such as scallions, celery stalks, or sun-dried tomatoes.

NUTRITION INFORMATION PER SERVING: 1 slice, 60g

154 cal | 5g fat | 8g protein | 18g complex carbohydrates | 0g sugar | 1g dietary fiber | 63mg cholesterol | 359mg sodium

TURNING QUICK BREAD BATTER INTO MUFFINS (AND VICE VERSA)

A typical quick bread recipe using 1½ to 2 cups of flour will fill about a dozen regular-size (about 2½″ diameter) muffin cups. Prepare the quick bread batter, grease the muffin cups, fill them to nearly full, and bake in a preheated 425°F oven for 18 to 22 minutes, or until they're puffed, set on the top, and a cake tester or toothpick inserted in the center of one comes out clean.

Or try the reverse: Take a favorite 12-muffin recipe and make it into a quick loaf. If the recipe calls for about 2 cups of flour, use a 9″ × 5″ loaf pan; for 1½ cups of flour (or less), use an 8½″ × 4½″ pan. For amounts in between, well, use your best judgment; the batter should fill the pan about two-thirds full. Bake the bread in a preheated 350°F oven for 50 to 70 minutes (although generally 55 to 60 minutes); times may vary depending on the exact amount of the batter, and the composition of any "add-ins"; juicy additions such as berries will make for a slightly longer bake.

Biscuits

Biscuits, like pie crust, seem enrobed in an aura of mystery to beginning or unconfident bakers. Both involve a few basic ingredients and a couple of key (but not difficult) steps. If you use the right ingredients and follow the directions carefully, either should be within anyone's realm of expertise.

While you can use entirely all-purpose flour for biscuits, we like using pastry flour for a tender crumb. (See page 459 for more on pastry flour.) Your key to success, as with any biscuit recipe, is using a gentle hand and a sharp cutter. By just barely coaxing the fat and flour together, then patting the dough together as lovingly and gently as you'd towel-dry a baby, you're keeping the flour's gluten from toughening as you handle it. And by cutting the biscuits with a sharp blade, you're leaving "side-walls" that will freely expand as the biscuit bakes, allowing them to rise to their full height. The edges of a biscuit, cut with a drinking glass, will be squashed down and the biscuit won't rise as well.

Serve biscuits with butter or double Devon cream; serve them with jam or jelly; slather them with lemon curd or honey or golden or cane syrup or even maple syrup. But whatever you do, serve them hot from the oven. A cold biscuit, while still good, can't hold a candle to one plucked hot from the oven, broken open to reveal a steaming interior, and topped with a pat of cold butter.

1. Cut biscuit dough with a straight-sided metal cutter. **2.** A biscuit cut with a glass won't rise as high as a biscuit cut with a metal cutter. The dull edge of the glass compresses the layers in the dough.

NEVER-FAIL BISCUITS

12 BISCUITS

Dare we call these the easiest biscuits ever? With just two ingredients, we absolutely will.

1½ cups (170g) self-rising flour
¾ cup (170g) heavy cream

Preheat the oven to 450°F, with a rack in the top third.

Mix the flour and cream until smooth and cohesive.

Scoop 28g balls of dough onto an ungreased or parchment-lined baking sheet; a tablespoon cookie scoop works well here. Leave a couple of inches between them. Not into scooping? Pat the dough ¾″ thick and cut biscuits with a cutter instead, if desired.

Brush the tops of the biscuits with cream, milk, or water; this will help them rise.

Bake the biscuits for 10 minutes, until they're light golden brown on top, and baked all the way through; break one open to make sure.

Remove the biscuits from the oven, and serve warm, or at room temperature.

NUTRITION INFORMATION PER SERVING: 1 biscuit, 28g
98 cal | 5g fat | 1g protein | 12g complex carbohydrates | 0g sugar | 0g dietary fiber | 19mg cholesterol | 184mg sodium

---

WHAT MAKES BISCUITS FLAKY?

The technique for making biscuits is quite similar to pie crust, as is the goal: a tender, flaky final product. In both cases, fat is cut into the dry ingredients, then liquid is added to make the dough cohesive. The fat is there to create tenderness, which happens two ways. First, fat coats the proteins in the flour, preventing them from forming long gluten strands, and thus creating a fine-grained texture. Second, fat acts as a temporary buffer between layers of the flour-liquid matrix; as the biscuit bakes, the fat eventually melts. But it's done its job, creating a structure in the biscuit that we perceive as flaky.

BAKING POWDER BISCUITS

12 BISCUITS

It never ceases to amaze us how just a few ingredients and a small slice of time (less than half an hour) can yield such miraculous results. These flaky biscuits are the ultimate version of the genre, and simple enough for any baker to master.

3 cups (360g) unbleached all-purpose flour

1 teaspoon salt

1 tablespoon (12g) baking powder

1 tablespoon (12g) sugar

6 tablespoons (¾ stick, 85g) unsalted butter, at room temperature

1 to 1⅛ cups (227g to 255g) cold milk or buttermilk (use whole milk for the most tender biscuits)

Preheat your oven to 425°F with a rack in the upper portion. Get out a baking sheet; there's no need to grease it. Line it with parchment if you like, for easy cleanup.

Mix together the flour, salt, baking powder, and sugar.

Work the butter into the flour mixture using your fingers, a fork or pastry blender, a stand mixer, or a food processor. Your goal is an evenly crumbly mixture (like bread crumbs).

Drizzle the smaller amount of milk evenly over the flour mixture. Mix quickly and gently for about 15 seconds, until you've made a cohesive dough. If the mixture seems dry and won't come together, don't keep working it; drizzle in enough milk—up to an additional 2 tablespoons (28g) to make it cohesive.

Place the dough on a lightly floured work surface. Pat it into a rough rectangle about ¾˝ thick. Fold it into thirds like a letter and roll gently with a floured rolling pin until the dough is ¾˝ thick again.

Cut the dough into circles with a biscuit cutter for traditional round biscuits; a 2⅜˝ cutter makes nicely sized biscuits. Or, to avoid leftover dough scraps, cut the dough into squares or diamonds with a bench knife or sharp knife.

Place the biscuits bottom side up on your prepared baking sheet; turning them over like this yields biscuits with nice, smooth tops. Brush the biscuits with milk to enhance browning.

Bake the biscuits for 15 to 20 minutes, until they're lightly browned. Remove them from the oven, and serve warm.

NUTRITION INFORMATION PER SERVING: 1 biscuit, 28g
160 cal | 4.5g fat | 4g protein | 12g complex carbohydrates | 2g sugar | 1g dietary fiber | 10mg cholesterol | 330mg sodium

FREEZING BISCUITS AND SCONES BEFORE BAKING

Here's one cool thing: For light and fluffy biscuits or scones, shape the biscuits (or scones), place them on a baking sheet, and freeze for 30 minutes or as long as a week (wrapped airtight). Baked goods that rely on the combination of flour, liquid, baking powder, and solid fat for their structure will rise slightly better when frozen. Why? Because the fat stays solid longer in the oven. Eventually the fat melts, but by that time the flour/liquid matrix has developed and set, and what you've got left is layers of bread interspersed with thin air pockets where once resided solid fat—a flaky, tender biscuit! Frozen biscuits can be put straight into the oven, but will likely need another 5 minutes baking time.

———

THE DIFFERENCE BETWEEN BISCUITS AND SCONES

Biscuits contain little or no sugar, and usually no additions of any kind. The classic baking powder biscuit is best served hot, with butter or honey, along with a meal. Scones, on the other hand, are usually sweetened; very often contain fruit, nuts, or spices; and are not generally served hot with meals, but more often alone, or with tea or coffee. So, while the basic breads may be quite similar, they take different paths as they're baked and served.

CHEDDAR AND BLACK PEPPER BISCUITS

ABOUT 25 BISCUITS

The tang of black pepper teams up with the rich flavor of cheddar cheese in these biscuits. We suggest you adjust the amount of black pepper to suit your taste—less gives you a nice warm touch; more is spicy but wonderful.

3 cups (360g) unbleached all-purpose flour

2 tablespoons (24g) baking powder

½ teaspoon baking soda

1 teaspoon salt

1 tablespoon (12g) sugar

8 tablespoons (1 stick, 113g) unsalted butter, cold

1 cup (112g) grated cheddar cheese

¾ to 2½ teaspoons coarsely ground black pepper

¾ cup (170g) buttermilk or plain yogurt

additional buttermilk or yogurt, for glaze

In a large bowl, sift together the flour, baking powder, baking soda, salt, and sugar. Cut in the butter and cheese. Stir in the black pepper. Refrigerate the dough for 30 minutes. Meanwhile preheat the oven to 400°F.

Gently stir the buttermilk into the chilled dough. Gather the mixture into a ball with your hands, and on a well-floured surface, roll or pat the dough into a 12″ × 8″ rectangle approximately ¾″ thick.

Grease a baking sheet. Using a large spatula, or a couple of spatulas, transfer the dough to the baking sheet. Use a dough scraper, bench knife, or a sharp knife to cut dough into 1½″ squares. Separate the squares slightly on the baking sheet. Brush each square with a little buttermilk or yogurt.

Bake the biscuits for 15 to 20 minutes, or until they're very lightly browned.

NUTRITION INFORMATION PER SERVING: 1 biscuit, 32g

105 cal | 5g fat | 3g protein | 11g complex carbohydrates | 1g sugar | 0g dietary fiber | 15mg cholesterol | 264mg sodium

HERBED CREAM CHEESE BISCUITS

20 BISCUITS

When it's finally warm enough in the morning to eat breakfast on the porch or deck, why not celebrate the occasion? Our R&D director Sue Gray says a favorite brunch dish of hers is these herbed biscuits with smoked salmon and scrambled eggs. "Chives are one of the first plants I harvest from my herb garden," she says. "And even though this recipe is one I can make year-round, it's one of those things that tells me summer's almost here. Just the colors on the plate—the green chives in the golden biscuits set next to the orange salmon and bright yellow eggs—are wonderful."

2½ cups (300g) unbleached all-purpose flour

1 tablespoon (12g) baking powder

1 teaspoon salt

½ teaspoon freshly ground black pepper

3 tablespoons chopped fresh chives, or 2 tablespoons dried chives

1 teaspoon dried thyme

1 cup (112g) grated sharp cheddar cheese

4 tablespoons (½ stick, 56g) butter, cold

4 ounces (112g) cream cheese, cold

¾ cup (168g) milk

Preheat the oven to 425°F. In a medium bowl, whisk together the dry ingredients, including the grated cheese, until everything is evenly distributed. Using a pastry fork or blender, your fingers or an electric mixer, cut in the butter and cream cheese, mixing until crumbly; some larger chunks of cheese and butter can remain. Pour in the milk while tossing with a fork; the dough should remain a bit crumbly but hold together when squeezed. Add an additional 1 to 2 tablespoons of milk, if needed.

Turn out the dough onto a lightly floured work surface and fold it over a few times so that you can be sure it's totally cohesive. Pat it into an 8″ square, ¾″ thick. Cut it into 2″ squares, or use a 2″ round cutter. Place the biscuits on an ungreased baking sheet.

Bake the biscuits for 16 to 18 minutes, until they're lightly browned. Serve them warm or at room temperature.

NUTRITION INFORMATION PER SERVING: 1 biscuit, 37g

99 cal | 4g fat | 4g protein | 11g complex carbohydrates | 1g sugar | 1g dietary fiber | 13mg cholesterol | 236mg sodium

SOUR CREAM RYE BISCUITS

16 BISCUITS

These pair well with any kind of hearty soup or stew. In the unlikely event you have some, reheat any leftover biscuits briefly, and use them to make ham and cheese biscuit sandwiches. We love the crunch of whole caraway seeds, but if you'd prefer less texture, pulse them in a spice grinder first.

2½ cups (300g) unbleached all-purpose flour

½ cup (56g) pumpernickel or medium rye flour

1 tablespoon (12g) baking powder

¼ teaspoon baking soda

1 teaspoon salt

1 tablespoon (9g) caraway seeds

4 tablespoons (½ stick, 56g) butter, cold

½ cup (112g) sour cream

¾ cup (168g) milk

Preheat the oven to 400°F.

In a medium bowl, whisk together the dry ingredients, including the caraway seeds. Using a pastry blender or fork, your fingers, or a mixer, cut in the butter.

Measure the sour cream into a 2-cup liquid measure and add the milk, stirring to combine. Add these liquid ingredients to the dry ingredients, stirring until everything is evenly moistened. Turn out the dough onto a lightly floured surface and fold it over a few times to make sure it's cohesive. Pat it into an 8″ square about ½″ thick.

Use a 2″ cutter to make round biscuits, or cut the dough into 2″ squares. Place the biscuits on a lightly greased baking sheet, brushing the top of each with milk (or an egg mixed with milk) to make them shiny and a deeper brown, if you like.

Bake the biscuits for 12 to 14 minutes, until lightly browned. Serve them hot or warm.

NUTRITION INFORMATION PER SERVING: 1 biscuit, 44g

119 cal | 5g fat | 3g protein | 17g complex carbohydrates | 0g sugar | 1g dietary fiber | 11mg cholesterol | 254mg sodium

Scones

Sweeter and more varied in their incarnations than biscuits, scones as we see them most often in bakeries nowadays bear little resemblance to the original, but they surely are good. Just like biscuits and muffins, scones can be embellished with just about any flavor, from fruit to chocolate, cinnamon, coffee, coconut, or ginger, from nuts and seeds to savory cheese and vegetable versions.

BASIC SCONES AND VARIATIONS

16 SCONES

The following is a basic scone recipe that's easily enhanced by the addition of different dried fruits and spices.

3 cups (360g) unbleached all-purpose flour

⅓ cup (84g) granulated sugar

¼ cup (56g) buttermilk powder

¾ teaspoon salt

1 tablespoon (12g) baking powder

¾ cup (84g to 112g) currants, raisins, apricots, or other dried fruit

2 large eggs

2 teaspoons vanilla extract

½ cup (113g) milk or buttermilk

8 tablespoons (1 stick, 113g) unsalted butter, cold

1 egg beaten with 1 teaspoon water, for topping

coarse sugar or cinnamon sugar, for topping (optional, but good)

Preheat the oven to 450°F.

In a medium bowl, whisk together all the dry ingredients, including the fruit. In a separate bowl, whisk together the eggs, vanilla, and milk. (Milk will give you a richer scone than water; buttermilk, because of its acidic interaction with the baking powder, will give you a tender, slightly higher-rising scone with a touch of tang.)

The next step, cutting in the fat, is important because this largely determines the texture of the scones. Use cold butter. (Liquid vegetable oil isn't a good choice because scones get their flaky texture from small bits of fat that separate thin layers of a flour/water matrix.) As the biscuit or scone bakes, the fat holds these dough layers apart. Finally the fat reaches its melting point and disappears into the dough—but by that time, the biscuit's structure has set into many thin layers of dough, which, in the finished product, create tenderness and flakiness. (And, in the case of butter, wonderful flavor.)

Begin with cold fat, as cold fat retains its integrity in the dough better than warm. It helps to have the fat cut into marble-size pieces before adding it to the flour. One of our favorite methods is to freeze a half-stick of butter, then grate it coarsely into the dry ingredients. Be sure there are pieces of fat that remain the size of small peas.

Next, add the liquid ingredients to the flour/fat mixture. Be careful: Too much mixing or kneading at this point will result in tough, heavy scones. Gently fold everything together until the mixture is mostly moistened; a bit of the flour may remain dry.

Turn out the dough onto a lightly floured surface and fold and gather it together until it's cohesive. Divide the dough in half and place both halves on a lightly greased or parchment-lined baking sheet. Pat each half into a 7″ circle approximately ½″ thick, then cut each circle into 8 wedges. Separate the wedges slightly, leaving about a ½″ between each at the outer edge; at the center, they'll be about ¼″ apart. Alternatively, you can pat the entire piece of dough into a rectangle and cut it into 1½″ to 2″ rounds, using a biscuit cutter, or into 1½″ to 2″ squares.

Brush the scones with the beaten egg, then sprinkle with coarse sugar or cinnamon sugar, if desired. Bake them for 7 minutes, then turn the oven off and, without opening the door, let the scones remain in the oven for an additional 8 to 10 minutes, or until they're golden brown. (It's important to bake scones on your oven's middle rack.) Remove the scones from the oven, and let them cool minimally on a rack.

Serve the scones immediately or within a few hours, for best flavor. Conveniently enough, scone dough lends itself to being made ahead, shaped, and either frozen or refrigerated overnight before baking. For scones refrigerated overnight, bake for the same amount of time; for frozen, add 2 minutes to the baking time before you turn the oven off.

NUTRITION INFORMATION PER SERVING: 1 scone, 50g

170 cal | 6g fat | 3g protein | 26g complex carbohydrates | 4g sugar | 1g dietary fiber | 17mg cholesterol | 131mg sodium

VARIATIONS

CRANBERRY ORANGE: Use cranberries as the added fruit, add 2 tablespoons (12g) orange zest or ½ teaspoon orange oil to the dough, and use orange juice for the liquid.

LEMON POPPY SEED: Add 3 tablespoons (27g) poppy seeds and ¼ to ½ teaspoon lemon oil, or 2 tablespoons (12g) lemon zest, to the dough.

GINGER CHOCOLATE CHIP: Add ¼ cup (46g) finely diced crystallized ginger and 1 teaspoon ginger to the dough along with ½ cup (85g) chocolate chips.

CINNAMON PECAN: Add ¾ cup (86g) chopped, toasted pecans to the dough, and substitute 2 teaspoons cinnamon for the vanilla.

APRICOT CREAM CHEESE SCONES

ABOUT 18 SCONES

We love the bright flavor and color of apricots in scones; cream cheese adds richness. Using unbleached pastry flour yields a final product that's more tender and delicate than most scones.

SCONES

3¼ cups (345g) unbleached pastry flour or 3 cups (360g) unbleached all-purpose flour plus ¼ cup (28g) cornstarch

½ cup (98g) granulated sugar

2½ teaspoons baking powder

½ teaspoon salt

8 ounces (224g) cream cheese, cold

8 tablespoons (1 stick, 113g) unsalted butter, cold

1 cup (126g) diced or slivered dried apricots

1 large egg

2 teaspoons vanilla extract

¼ cup (57g) milk

TOPPING

milk

coarse white sugar or pearl sugar

Preheat the oven to 425°F.

In a medium bowl, whisk together the flour, sugar, baking powder, and salt. Cut in the cream cheese and butter, using your fingers, a pastry blender, fork, or a mixer, until the mixture resembles coarse cornmeal, then stir in the apricots. In a separate bowl, whisk together the egg, vanilla, and milk.

Combine the liquid and dry ingredients and stir until the dough becomes cohesive. Don't mix and mix and mix; the more you work with the dough, the tougher it will get.

Turn out the dough onto a floured work surface and fold it over several times, until it holds together. Pat the dough into a ¾˝ thick rectangle.

Cut scones with a round cutter, gathering the scraps and re-rolling the dough. Or simply cut the dough into squares or diamonds. Brush the tops lightly with milk and sprinkle with coarse white or pearl sugar.

Place scones about 2˝ apart on an ungreased or parchment-lined baking sheet. Bake them for 8 minutes. Turn the oven off, leave the door closed, and continue to bake for 8 more minutes, until the scones are a light golden brown. Serve warm, with clotted cream and jam or raspberry curd.

NUTRITION INFORMATION PER SERVING: 1 scone, 60g

207 cal | 10g fat | 4g protein | 21g complex carbohydrates | 5g sugar | 1g dietary fiber | 40mg cholesterol | 171mg sodium

FRESH BLUEBERRY SCONES

10 SCONES

These tender, moist scones—studded with juicy blueberries—are wonderful when eaten hot, split in half, and slathered with butter. With a more delicate crumb, they're less sturdy than other scones and best enjoyed right from the oven, although they do freeze well.

SCONES

2 cups (240g) unbleached all-
    purpose flour

½ teaspoon salt

¼ cup (50g) sugar

1 tablespoon (12g) baking powder

6 tablespoons (¾ stick, 85g) unsalted
    butter, cold, cut into pieces

2 large eggs

⅓ cup (74g) plain yogurt

½ teaspoon vanilla extract

1 tablespoon (6g) lemon zest or
    ¼ teaspoon lemon oil

1 cup (170g) blueberries

TOPPING

2 tablespoons (28g) butter, melted

2 tablespoons (25g) sugar

Preheat the oven to 375°F.

Whisk the dry ingredients together in a bowl. Use your fingers to work the cold butter into the dry ingredients.

Stir the eggs, yogurt, vanilla, and lemon zest or oil together. Add to the dry ingredients and stir just until combined. Stir in the blueberries. This dough is the consistency of a wet drop-cookie dough.

Liberally flour your counter and your hands. Take the dough out of the bowl and place it on the counter. Pat it into a 1″ thick rectangle. Cut into 10 scones. Place on a well-greased or parchment-lined baking sheet.

Brush the scones with melted butter, and sprinkle with sugar. Bake for 20 minutes, or until lightly browned and a cake tester or toothpick inserted into a scone comes out dry. Cool completely on a rack.

Scones are best enjoyed fresh from the oven, or within several hours of baking.

NUTRITION INFORMATION PER SERVING: 1 scone, 80g
220 cal | 11g fat | 5g protein | 19g complex carbohydrates | 10g sugar | 1g dietary fiber | 60mg cholesterol | 260mg sodium

CREAM TEA SCONES

12 SCONES

From its humble beginning as the Scottish griddle cake, the scone has traveled beyond Scottish borders and been taken to heart by the English. Here's the prototypical cream tea scone that we've come to associate with that very British (and oh-so-civilized and restorative) of rites: afternoon tea. These scones couldn't be more basic—or more delicious.

3 cups (360g) unbleached all-purpose flour

1 tablespoon (12g) baking powder

1 teaspoon salt

¼ to ⅓ cup (50g to 67g) sugar, to taste

1 teaspoon vanilla extract

1⅓ to 1½ cups (301g to 340g) heavy cream, plus more for brushing

Preheat the oven to 425°F. Line a baking sheet with parchment paper (or not; it helps with cleanup, but isn't necessary to prevent sticking).

Whisk together the flour, baking powder, salt, and sugar.

Combine the vanilla with 1⅓ cups cream. Drizzle the liquid mixture over the dry ingredients, tossing and stirring gently all the while. Add enough cream to make a cohesive dough, using up to 3 additional tablespoons if necessary. There shouldn't be any dry flour in the bottom of the bowl, but the dough shouldn't be particularly sticky, either.

Lightly flour a clean work surface. Divide the dough in half, and gently pat each half into a 5½″ circle about ¾″ thick. Brush each circle with heavy cream.

Place the two circles of dough on the baking sheet, and cut each into 6 wedges. Pull the wedges apart a bit, leaving them in a circular pattern with about 1″ space between each wedge.

For best rising, place the pan of scones into the freezer for 15 minutes, while you preheat your oven to 425°F.

Bake the chilled scones for 14 to 15 minutes, until they're starting to brown, and they're baked all the way through, without any wet dough in the center.

Remove the scones from the oven. Serve warm, split and spread with a bit of sweet butter and jam or preserves.

NUTRITION INFORMATION PER SERVING: 1 scone, 61g

210 cal | 9g fat | 4g protein | 23g complex carbohydrates | 5g sugar | 1g dietary fiber | 30mg cholesterol | 320mg sodium

HARVEST PUMPKIN SCONES

12 SCONES

Deeply golden, these scones taste even more wonderful than they look. Cinnamon, ginger, allspice, and nutmeg spice the dough; diced crystallized ginger takes the flavor over the top.

2¾ cups (330g) unbleached all-purpose flour

⅓ cup (66g) granulated sugar

1 tablespoon (12g) baking powder

¾ teaspoon salt

1½ teaspoons pumpkin pie spice or ¾ teaspoon cinnamon plus ¼ teaspoon each ginger, nutmeg, and allspice

8 tablespoons (1 stick, 113g) unsalted butter, cold

1 cup to 2 cups (184g to 369g) diced crystallized ginger or cinnamon chips

⅔ cup (152g) pumpkin purée

2 large eggs

coarse white sugar, for topping

In a large bowl, whisk together the flour, sugar, baking powder, salt, and spices.

Work in the butter just until the mixture is unevenly crumbly; it's OK for some larger chunks of butter to remain unincorporated.

Stir in the ginger or chips.

In a medium bowl, whisk together the pumpkin and eggs until smooth.

Add the pumpkin/egg to the dry ingredients and stir until all is moistened and holds together.

Line a baking sheet with parchment; if you don't have parchment, just use it without greasing it. Sprinkle a bit of flour atop the parchment or pan.

Scrape the dough onto the floured parchment or pan, and divide it in half. Round each half into a 5″ circle. The circles should be about ¾″ thick.

Brush each circle with milk, and sprinkle with coarse sugar.

Using a knife or bench knife that you've run under cold water, slice each circle into 6 wedges.

Carefully pull the wedges away from the center to separate them just a bit; there should be about ½″ space between them, at their outer edges.

For best texture and highest rise, place the pan of scones in the freezer for 30 minutes, uncovered. While the scones are chilling, preheat the oven to 425°F.

Bake the scones for 22 to 25 minutes, or until they're golden brown and a toothpick inserted into the center of one comes out clean, with no wet crumbs. If you pull one of the scones away from the others, the edges should look baked through, not wet or doughy.

Remove the scones from the oven, and serve warm.

NUTRITION INFORMATION PER SERVING: 1 scone, 61g
270 cal | 9g fat | 4g protein | 21g complex carbohydrates | 23g sugar | 2g dietary fiber | 50mg cholesterol | 270mg sodium

NEW HAMPSHIRE MAPLE-WALNUT SCONES

16 LARGE SCONES

New Hampshire maple syrup is every bit as good as Vermont maple syrup, although it's never enjoyed the same fame (or acclaim). If you're ever visiting northern New England in the early spring—late February through March—try to stop at a sugarhouse. The hot, rich maple steam billowing from the flat sugar pans, as the maple sap slowly boils down to golden syrup, is a smell you'll never forget. This recipe comes to us courtesy of Barbara Lauterbach, cooking teacher, author, and a longtime friend of King Arthur.

3½ cups (400g) unbleached all-purpose flour

4 teaspoons baking powder

1 teaspoon salt

11 tablespoons (154g) unsalted butter, cold

1 cup (112g) finely chopped toasted walnuts

1 cup (224g) milk

½ cup (156g) maple syrup, divided

½ teaspoon maple flavoring (optional, but very good)

Preheat the oven to 425°F.

In a large bowl, combine the flour, baking powder, and salt. Cut in the butter until the mixture resembles coarse crumbs. Stir in the walnuts.

In a medium bowl, combine the milk, ⅓ cup of the maple syrup, and the maple flavoring. (You can leave out the maple flavoring if you wish, but it really adds a nice touch.) Add the wet ingredients to the dry ingredients and mix until you've formed a very soft dough.

Flour your work surface generously and scrape the dough out of the mixing bowl onto the floured surface. Divide the dough in half.

Working with one half at a time, gently pat the dough into a 7″ circle about ⅞″ thick. Transfer the circle to a parchment-lined or lightly greased baking sheet or other flat pan; it'll be very soft; if you have a giant spatula, it's the tool of choice here. Repeat with the remaining half of the dough, placing it on a separate pan.

Using a sharp bench knife or rolling pizza wheel, divide each dough circle into eight wedges. Gently separate the wedges so that they're almost touching in the center, but are spaced about 1″ apart at the edges. Pierce the tops of the scones with the tines of a fork and brush them with some of the remaining maple syrup.

Bake the scones for 15 to 18 minutes, or until they're golden brown. Remove them from the oven and brush them with any remaining maple syrup. Wait a couple of minutes, then gently separate the scones with a knife (they'll be very fragile), and carefully transfer them to a cooling rack. Serve warm or at room temperature, with jam or maple butter.

NUTRITION INFORMATION PER SERVING: 1 scone, made with half unsalted butter/half shortening, and 1% milk, 66g
224 cal | 12g fat | 4g protein | 19g complex carbohydrates | 6g sugar | 1g dietary fiber | 12mg cholesterol | 250mg sodium

PEACH NUTMEG SCONES

12 SCONES

The flavors of almond and nutmeg are the perfect supporting cast for one of summer's star ingredients: ripe peaches. Frozen sliced peaches will do in a pinch, if you're looking for an antidote to winter blahs.

SCONES

2 cups (240g) unbleached all-purpose flour or unbleached pastry flour (224g)

½ teaspoon salt

⅓ cup (64g) sugar

1 teaspoon nutmeg

1 tablespoon (12g) baking powder

6 tablespoons (¾ stick, 84g) unsalted butter, cold, cut into pieces

2 large eggs, beaten

⅓ cup (77g) plain yogurt

½ teaspoon almond extract

1 cup (170g) diced peaches (about 1 medium peach)

TOPPING

2 tablespoons (28g) butter, melted

2 tablespoons (28g) sugar

Preheat the oven to 375°F.

In a large bowl, sift the flour, salt, sugar, nutmeg, and baking powder together. Work the butter into the dry ingredients, using your fingertips or a fork or pastry blender.

In another bowl, mix the eggs, yogurt, and almond extract. Stir this into the dry ingredients. Add the peaches and stir just until mixed. This is a very sticky dough.

Liberally flour the counter and your hands. Put the dough on the counter and pat it into a 6″ × 9″ rectangle about 1″ thick. Cut the rectangle into 6 pieces and cut each small rectangle in half, forming two triangles. You'll have 12 triangles.

Place scones on a well-greased baking sheet. Brush with the melted butter and sprinkle with the sugar. Bake for 20 minutes, or until nicely browned.

NUTRITION INFORMATION PER SERVING: 1 scone, 57g

179 cal | 9g fat | 3g protein | 16g complex carbohydrates | 5g sugar | 1g dietary fiber | 58mg cholesterol | 226mg sodium

SCALLION CHEDDAR SCONES

12 SCONES

These savory wedges pair nicely with soup or salad. Cut smaller, they are a quick and easy way to serve a bite-size savory appetizer.

2 cups (240g) unbleached all-purpose flour or unbleached pastry flour (224g)

½ teaspoon salt

1 tablespoon (12g) sugar

1 tablespoon (12g) baking powder

6 tablespoons (¾ stick, 84g) unsalted butter, cold, cut into pieces

2 large eggs, beaten

⅓ cup (77g) cream or sour cream

1 tablespoon (16g) Dijon mustard

1 cup (112g) grated sharp cheddar cheese

3 to 5 scallions (56g), chopped

Preheat the oven to 375°F. Sift together the flour, salt, sugar, and baking powder. Rub in the butter with your fingers.

Mix together the eggs, cream, and mustard. Add this to the dry ingredients. Stir in the grated cheese and the scallions. Mix just until combined.

Liberally flour the counter and your hands. Pat the dough into a 6″ × 9″ rectangle, about 1″ thick. Cut the rectangle into 6 smaller rectangles, and cut each smaller rectangle into two triangles, forming 12 triangular scones. Place on a well-greased baking sheet.

Bake for 20 minutes, or until nicely browned.

NUTRITION INFORMATION PER SERVING: 1 scone, 57g

189 cal | 11g fat | 6g protein | 15g complex carbohydrates | 1g sugar | 1g dietary fiber | 64mg cholesterol | 316mg sodium

Soda Breads and Steamed Breads

Here we come to a collection of breads with their own unique culinary history. Irish soda bread is a term that encompasses everything from the simplest flour-buttermilk-salt-baking soda bread to those featuring sugar, eggs, butter, raisins, and caraway seeds. The latter make a lighter, softer, sweeter bread—more cake than bread, actually. The original Irish soda bread, known as dairy bread, was nothing more than flour, salt and buttermilk, with just a bit of leavening, baked into a round loaf in a pot hung over a peat fire. What we now think of as Irish soda bread contains additional ingredients (such as caraway seeds and currants) that would have made a native Irishman scratch his head in puzzlement, but it is the additions that combine to give this bread the flavor that we recognize as "Irish."

Steamed breads (and puddings) show up all around the world, from Chinese buns to British Christmas puddings. They're incredibly moist and run the gamut from sweet to savory.

IRISH SODA BREAD

ONE 8″ OR 9″ ROUND LOAF

"Authentic" Irish soda bread consists simply of Irish wholemeal flour (equivalent to a coarse grind of American whole wheat flour), baking soda, salt, and buttermilk. At the other end of the spectrum is Americanized Irish soda bread, a more cake-like version made with all-purpose flour and filled with raisins or currants and caraway seeds. This version is much closer to the traditional recipe than to its American cousin; we did, however, lighten and tenderize it slightly.

2½ cups (276g) Irish-style wholemeal flour	4 tablespoons (½ stick, 57g) butter, cold, cut into 8 pieces
1¼ cups (149g) bread flour	1⅓ cups (301g) buttermilk
3 tablespoons (35g) sugar	1 large egg
1 teaspoon baking soda	2 tablespoons (28g) butter, melted (optional)
¾ teaspoon salt	
⅔ cup (99g) currants or raisins	

Preheat the oven to 400°F. Lightly grease an 8″ or 9″ round cake pan.

In a medium bowl, whisk together the flours, sugar, baking soda, salt, and currants or raisins.

Using a mixer, a pastry fork or blender, or your fingers, work in the butter until it's evenly distributed and no large chunks remain.

In a small bowl (or in a measuring cup), whisk together the buttermilk and egg. Pour this mixture into the dry ingredients and mix to combine. The dough will be stiff; if it's too crumbly to squeeze together, add another tablespoon or two of buttermilk.

Knead the dough a couple of times to make sure it's holding together, then shape it into a ball. Flatten the ball slightly, and place the loaf in your pan. Use a sharp knife to cut a ½″ deep cross in the loaf.

Bake the bread for about 45 to 55 minutes, until it's golden brown and a cake tester or toothpick inserted in the center comes out clean. Remove the bread from the oven and brush the top with melted butter, if desired.

NUTRITION INFORMATION PER SERVING: **1 slice, 81g**
206 cal | 5g fat | 6g protein | 29g complex carbohydrates | 9g sugar | 3g dietary fiber | 28mg cholesterol | 285mg sodium

AMERICAN-STYLE IRISH SODA BREAD

1 LOAF

Although sweeter and more tender than traditional Irish soda bread, this Americanized version hits similar flavor notes, and is sure to please anyone who appreciates this genre.

4½ cups (540g) unbleached all-purpose flour

5 teaspoons baking powder

1½ teaspoons salt

1 teaspoon baking soda

16 tablespoons (2 sticks, 226g) unsalted butter

2 large eggs

1 cup (198g) sugar

2 cups (454g) milk

1 tablespoon (9g) caraway seeds

1½ cups (224g) raisins

Preheat the oven to 325°F.

In a large bowl, sift together the flour, baking powder, salt, and baking soda; set aside. In another large bowl, cream together the butter, eggs, and sugar until light and fluffy. Fold the dry ingredients into the wet ingredients alternately with the milk. Stir in the caraway seeds and raisins.

Spoon the batter into a greased, deep (9″ × 4″ round) cake pan or springform pan. Bake the bread for about 1½ hours, or until a tester inserted in the center comes out clean. Remove the bread from the oven and cool on a rack.

NUTRITION INFORMATION PER SERVING: **1 slice, 76g**
221 cal | 8g fat | 4g protein | 25g complex carbohydrates | 8g sugar | 1g dietary fiber | 39mg cholesterol | 305mg sodium

BOSTON BROWN BREAD

1 LOAF

This is a very classic New England recipe, often served alongside baked beans (small navy or pea beans sweetened with brown sugar or molasses, flavored with onion and mustard, and enriched with bacon or salt pork). This bread is a cylindrical, molasses-brown, raisin-studded loaf, moist and tender from its hours of steaming. Although arguably the most familiar of the steamed breads, brown bread isn't the only one (think plum pudding).

Although less common nowadays, steamed breads are a wonderful treasure for a baker to discover. They're moist and tender, usually sweet, and, when served hot from the steamer, a perfect vehicle for melting butter.

1 cup (140g) yellow cornmeal
1 cup (106g) pumpernickel
1 cup (113g) whole wheat flour
1 teaspoon baking soda
1 teaspoon salt

1 cup (149g) raisins (optional, but good)
2 cups (454g) buttermilk or plain
   yogurt
¾ cup (252g) dark molasses

Mix the cornmeal, flours, baking soda, salt, and raisins together. Combine the buttermilk and molasses and stir them into the dry ingredients.

Place the mixture in a greased 2-quart pudding mold or other tall, cylindrical heatproof container, filling it about two-thirds full. Grease the inside lid of the pudding mold as well. Secure the lid.

Place the mold in a kettle or saucepan on top of something (crinkled aluminum foil or a stainless steel steamer insert will do nicely) to keep the mold off the bottom of the pan. The kettle should be deep enough so its lid can cover the pudding mold.

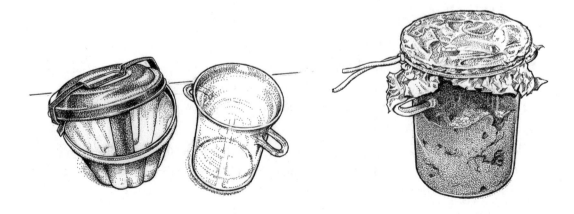

You can steam quick breads in a pudding mold with a lid, or a lab glass container, with foil tightly tied on top.

Fill the kettle with boiling water two-thirds of the way up the mold. Cover, bring the water back to a boil, then lower to a simmer. Steam for about 2 hours, adding water if necessary. Remove the mold and undo the lid. Give the bread a tap on the bottom to encourage it to slide out. Remove the bread while it is still warm and let it cool on a rack.

VARIATION

TO BAKE THE BREAD INSTEAD: Spoon the batter into a lightly greased 8½″ × 4½″ loaf pan and cover it with buttered aluminum foil. Leave room at the top of the foil for ballooning in the center, so the bread has room to expand without hitting the foil. Fasten the foil tightly to the edges of the pan so the bread will steam a bit.

Bake the bread in a 325°F oven for 1 hour. Remove the foil (the middle may be slightly sunken) and bake for an additional 10 minutes.

NUTRITION INFORMATION PER SERVING: 1 slice (without raisins), 71g
146 cal | 1g fat | 4g protein | 18g complex carbohydrates | 13g sugar | 3g dietary fiber | 1mg cholesterol | 268mg sodium

Buckles, Cobblers, and Crisps

—

THERE'S A TIME IN LATE SUMMER when the days, almost overnight, seem to change. Like climbing up one side of a mountain, reaching the peak, then starting down the other, the view is different. Goldenrod and marigolds replace the dandelions and daisies of early summer. The sun starts to slant low in the late afternoon, not after dinner. Fields that were dewy and fresh at summer's beginning hold a permanent patina of pollen and dust from a long, dry summer. Fall is coming, and our part of the earth is once again turning toward winter.

The growing season draws to a close in August and September, and it does so in a spectacular burst of color and flavor. Seize this moment! Summer is the time to enjoy peach cobbler, blueberry buckle, and cherry crisp while these fruits are at their freshest and best. The possibilities are endless for summer fruits (and year-round fruits, too!). Red plums, black plums, and purple plums;

sour pie cherries and Bing cherries; peaches, nectarines, and apricots; raspberries, blueberries, strawberries, and blackberries: all can be tucked into a pie shell, sliced onto shortcake, wrapped in a turnover, or baked into a crisp.

Living in New England, we're lucky to be familiar with the complete range of baked fruit desserts native to this region—from the common (crisps and cobblers) to the more unusual and increasingly rare (slumps, grunts, and pandowdies). All are made with fruit, sugar, flour, and butter, in different proportions and configurations. And all are good to keep in mind when it's apple-picking time, or the strawberries are ripe, or crates of low-bush blueberries, hand-raked from Maine's windswept coastal fields, are being sold alongside the road. Easy, fast, and delicious, these fruit-based desserts are a godsend to bakers who have fruit (but not time) on their hands and is looking to make something sweet.

NOT SO FAST!

Most fruit desserts—especially crisps, cobblers, and other juicier recipes—are best eaten warm but not just out of the oven; give them about 30 minutes to rest on a cooling rack. This cooling-off time gives the juices a chance to set, and will also prevent you from burning your mouth on the scalding combination of bubbling fruit juice and sugar.

Crisps and Crumbles

A crisp and a crumble are quite similar—containing toppings of sugar, butter, flour, and sometimes oats—but not the same. The names point simply to their fundamental differences. Crumble toppings contain a ratio of streusel ingredients that tend towards a more crumbly texture, whereas the blend of ingredients in a crisp topping will yield just that: a crisper result.

CLASSIC APPLE CRISP

ONE 9″ SQUARE CRISP

With all of the recipes out there, it's amazing how difficult it is to find a good, basic, go-to apple crisp. This version of apple crisp may seem daunting due to the fairly long list of ingredients, but many are optional enhancements. The base recipe is simply a filling of apples, sugar, thickener, and a touch of spice; and a topping of flour, sugar, butter, oats, and cinnamon. We like using rum or apple cider, but you can also substitute water or the liquor or juice of your choice for the liquid in the filling.

FILLING

3 pounds (1.36 kg) whole apples, enough to yield 2 pounds peeled, cored, and sliced apples (about 9 cups)

¼ cup (57g) rum or apple cider

¼ to ¾ cup (53g to 159g) brown sugar, depending on the sweetness of your apples

2 tablespoons (28g) butter, melted

2 tablespoons (43g) boiled cider (optional)

1 teaspoon cinnamon

¼ teaspoon nutmeg

¼ teaspoon ginger

3 tablespoons (21g) unbleached all-purpose flour or tapioca flour

¼ teaspoon salt

TOPPING

¾ cup (90g) unbleached all-purpose flour

½ cup (85g) quick-cooking oats

heaping ¼ teaspoon salt

⅔ cup (142g) brown sugar

1 teaspoon cinnamon

¾ teaspoon baking powder

8 tablespoons (1 stick, 113g) unsalted butter, cold, cut in pats

½ cup (57g) diced pecans or walnuts (optional)

Preheat your oven to 350°F. Grease a 9″ square cake pan, or similar-size casserole pan.

TO MAKE THE FILLING: Peel, core, and slice the apples about ¼″ thick. Toss them with the remaining filling ingredients and spread them in the pan.

TO MAKE THE TOPPING: Whisk together the flour, oats, salt, brown sugar, cinnamon, and baking powder.

Add the cold butter, working it in to make an unevenly crumbly mixture. Stir in the nuts, if using.

Spread the topping over the apples in the pan.

Set the pan on a parchment- or foil-lined baking sheet, to catch any potential drips. Bake the crisp for about 60 minutes, until it's bubbling and the top is golden brown.

Remove it from the oven, and allow it to cool for at least 20 minutes before serving. If you serve the crisp hot or warm, it may be quite soft. If you wait until it's completely cool, it'll firm up nicely.

NUTRITION INFORMATION PER SERVING: 1 piece, 130g

250 cal | 10g fat | 2g protein | 37g complex carbohydrates | 25g sugar | 2g dietary fiber | 25mg cholesterol | 55mg sodium

APPLE CRUMBLE

ONE 9″ SQUARE CRUMBLE

The warm, cinnamon-spiced apples in this dish are a perfect base for vanilla ice cream, which gradually sends vanilla-scented rivulets through the crisp, buttery streusel topping, and into the apples. Both tapioca flour and all-purpose flour will thicken the filling equally well, but tapioca flour will make the sauce in the filling clearer looking whereas all-purpose flour will make it opaque. If you like, try using pears in place of the apples.

FILLING

2 pounds (907g, about 5 medium to large) Granny Smith apples

1 pound (454g, about 2 large) McIntosh or Cortland apples

¼ cup (56g) rum or apple cider

2 tablespoons (28g) butter, melted

2 tablespoons (28g) boiled cider (optional)

¾ cup (159g) brown sugar

1 teaspoon cinnamon

¼ teaspoon nutmeg

¼ teaspoon ginger

3 tablespoons (21g) tapioca flour or unbleached all-purpose flour

¼ teaspoon salt

STREUSEL TOPPING

½ cup (60g) unbleached all-purpose flour

½ cup (49g) old-fashioned rolled oats

⅛ teaspoon salt

½ cup (106g) brown sugar

½ teaspoon cinnamon

¾ teaspoon baking powder

8 tablespoons (1 stick, 113g) unsalted butter

Preheat the oven to 350°F.

TO MAKE THE FILLING: Peel, core, and slice the apples into ¼″ thick pieces. Place them in a large bowl with the remainder of the filling ingredients and stir vigorously to combine. In the process, the apple pieces will break into smaller bits; this is fine.

Spoon the apple mixture into a lightly greased 9˝ square cake pan, or a ceramic pan of similar capacity and surface area.

TO MAKE THE TOPPING: In a medium bowl, stir together the flour, oats, salt, brown sugar, cinnamon, and baking powder. Add the butter, cutting it in with a mixer, your fingers, or a pastry blender as you would when making pie crust. Mix until crumbly; if you work it too much the mixture will clump together, so use a light touch but be thorough. Sprinkle the topping over the filling.

Bake the crumble for 1½ hours, or until it's bubbly and a deep, golden brown. Remove it from the oven and let it cool to lukewarm before serving.

NUTRITION INFORMATION PER SERVING: 1 square, 122g
208 cal | 7g fat | 1g protein | 17g complex carbohydrates | 14g sugar | 3g dietary fiber | 20mg cholesterol | 109mg sodium

DELICIOUS, DEFINED

Buckle: Streusel- and fruit-topped coffeecake. The topping after cooking has an uneven, "buckled" appearance.

Cobbler: A mixture of fruit and dough baked together. Dough can be cake or pie crust. The name comes from the occasionally lumpy look and ease of assembly; something "cobbled" together.

Crisp: Fruit baked with a topping of sugar, flour, butter, and spices. The top should shatter when pierced with a serving spoon; thus the name crisp.

Crumble: All the components of crisp topping with the addition of oats. The oats give the topping a softer, crumblier texture.

Dumplings: Fruit topped with dough and cooked, covered, as for Grunts and Slumps, or fruit wrapped in dough and baked in liquid. The dumplings are uniformly shaped, round or oval, and, when well made, are light and soft from cooking in a steamy environment.

Grunts and Slumps: Fruit cooked on the stove, topped with biscuit dough and slowly simmered. The finished dish makes grunting noises as the steam bubbles out, and the topping cooks down and slumps over the fruit.

Pandowdy: A double-crust pie with a very liquid filling that's thoroughly baked. The crust is then "dowdied" (broken up into chunks) while hot and served warm, after the pastry absorbs the fruit juices and the dish thickens.

Buckles

Coffeecake meets fruit in a buckle, which is the most cake-like of all these fruit desserts. Tradition has it that the name comes from the way the cake "buckles" as it bakes, rising around its fruit topping (which is also sinking), so that the cake finishes with a craggy top surface.

BLUEBERRY BUCKLE

ONE 9″ SQUARE OR ROUND COFFEECAKE

August is a luxuriant time of year, when all growing things are yielding the results of long days and warm nights. Flowers burst into frenetic bloom and we scramble to take in the bounty of summer produce. This rich, moist coffeecake is one of our favorite summer morning recipes, when the blueberries are ripe and abundant. It's rarely around for more than an hour out of the oven, but should you have admirable restraint, it will still be just as delicious for dessert. If, understandably, you'd like to enjoy this year-round, frozen berries will also work here.

BATTER

¾ cup (149g) sugar

4 tablespoons (½ stick, 56g) butter

1 large egg

2 cups (240g) unbleached all-purpose flour

2 teaspoons baking powder

½ teaspoon salt

¼ teaspoon cardamom (optional)

½ cup (113g) milk

1 teaspoon vanilla extract (optional)

2 cups (308g) blueberries (fresh or, if frozen, unthawed)

STREUSEL

¾ cup (149g) sugar

¾ cup (90g) unbleached all-purpose flour

1 teaspoon cinnamon

2 to 3 teaspoons lemon zest or ⅛ teaspoon lemon oil

½ teaspoon salt

5⅓ tablespoons (⅔ stick, 75g) unsalted butter, softened

Grease and flour a 9″ square or 9″ round pan and preheat the oven to 375°F.

TO MAKE THE BATTER: Cream together the sugar and butter, then add the egg and mix at medium speed for 1 minute. Whisk together the dry ingredients. Stir in the milk alternately with the dry ingredients and vanilla, scraping down the sides of the bowl. Gently fold in the blueberries. Spread the batter in the prepared pan.

TO MAKE THE STREUSEL: In a medium bowl, whisk together the sugar, flour, cinnamon, lemon zest or lemon oil, and salt. Add the butter, mixing to make medium-size crumbs. Sprinkle the streusel evenly over the batter.

Bake the buckle for 45 to 50 minutes, or until a cake tester or toothpick inserted into the center comes out clean. Remove from the oven, and cool it (in the pan) on a rack. Serve the buckle with coffee in the morning, or with whipped cream for dessert.

NUTRITION INFORMATION PER SERVING: 1 square, 72g

226 cal | 7g fat | 3g protein | 18g complex carbohydrates | 19g sugar | 1g dietary fiber | 32mg cholesterol | 204mg sodium

VARIATION

BLUEBERRY PEACH BUCKLE: This variation features one of our favorite fruit combinations: blueberries and peaches.

Prepare the batter from the preceding recipe, substituting ¼ teaspoon nutmeg for the ¼ teaspoon cardamom.

Prepare the topping from the preceding recipe, substituting ½ teaspoon almond extract for the lemon zest or oil.

Spread half the batter in the prepared pan. Layer with the peach slices. Fold the blueberries into the remaining batter and dollop it on top. Sprinkle the streusel over the batter. Bake as directed.

Grunts and Slumps

These are recipes whose name alone will bring a smile to the face of anyone familiar with traditional New England desserts—and a quizzical look from those unfamiliar with them. To understand the provenance of the terms "grunt" and "slump," it helps to picture how they're put together and cooked.

To make a slump or a grunt—the two terms are interchangeable—take a quart of berries or diced fruit, stir in some sugar and water, and put the mixture in a cast iron skillet or casserole dish that can sit on a burner. (Grunts used to be cooked in an open cast iron Dutch oven over the coals of a fire.) Then top the berries with spoonfuls of biscuit dough and let the mixture cook very slowly.

As the concoction begins to heat, bubbles slowly work their way up from the bottom of the pot to break through the biscuit dough topping. The wet snufflings you hear bear some resemblance to an animal's grunt. Once served, the dessert slumps on the plate in a sweet, juicy heap of warm biscuits. (Really, this is much more appetizing than it sounds.)

MAINE BLUEBERRY GRUNT

1 GRUNT

A blueberry is just a blueberry until you've tried freshly picked low-bush blueberries, which grow in profusion on low, scrubby bushes scattered over rather barren land in Maine and over the Northeast (although the tiny tart ones from Maine are by far the most famous). If you can find those small berries, use them—but this recipe is absolutely excellent regardless of where you get your fruit.

FRUIT

1 cup (227g) water

1 cup (198g) sugar

1 teaspoon lemon juice (if the berries aren't tart)

½ teaspoon cinnamon (optional)

1 quart (680g) blueberries

DOUGH

2 cups (240g) unbleached all-purpose flour

2 teaspoons baking powder

½ teaspoon baking soda

½ teaspoon salt

4 tablespoons (½ stick, 56g) butter

1 cup (227g) buttermilk

TO MAKE THE FRUIT: Blend the water, sugar, lemon juice (if using), and cinnamon (if using) in a skillet and stir in the blueberries. Bring to a gentle boil over low heat.

TO MAKE THE DOUGH: While the blueberries are heating, blend the dry dough ingredients together in a large bowl. Rub in the butter with your fingertips. Quickly stir in the buttermilk.

Drop the dough in blobs over the blueberry mixture. Cover and cook over low heat until the biscuit dough is done, about 15 minutes. To serve, scoop up the berries and a biscuit and invert on a plate, so that the berries fall over the biscuit. Spoon any extra berry mixture over the biscuit.

NUTRITION INFORMATION PER SERVING: ¹⁄₁₁ **skillet, 142g**

218 cal | 5g fat | 3g protein | 24g complex carbohydrates | 17g sugar | 2g dietary fiber | 13mg cholesterol | 271mg sodium

BLUEBERRY SLUMP

ONE 9″ × 13″ SLUMP

Louisa May Alcott named her home in Concord, Massachusetts, "Apple Slump," perhaps because it evoked for her the same thing that her apple slump did: warmth and comfort. This blueberry version of slump is an offspring of Apple Dumpling Slices (page 101). By adding some fat to the dumpling dough, you change its nature enough so you can bake it, rather than steam it, and produce something tender and crisp rather than tough and rubbery (which is what would happen to a "lean" dumpling dough if baked). The dumplings will continue to absorb the syrup and will taste even better the second day.

SYRUP
4 tablespoons (½ stick, 56g) butter

1 cup (224g) water

1 cup (213g) brown sugar

⅛ teaspoon allspice

⅛ teaspoon nutmeg

1 tablespoon (14g) lemon juice

DUMPLINGS
2 cups (240g) unbleached all-purpose flour

1 tablespoon (18g) baking powder

½ teaspoon salt

6 tablespoons (¾ stick, 84g) unsalted butter

¾ cup (168g) milk

FILLING
1 quart (680g) blueberries

Melt the butter in a 9″ × 13″ baking dish.

TO MAKE THE SYRUP: In a small saucepan, warm the water, brown sugar, spices, and lemon juice over low heat until the sugar dissolves.

TO MAKE THE DUMPLINGS: Put the flour, baking powder, and salt in a medium bowl and rub in the butter with your fingertips, a pastry blender, or two knives. Pour in the milk and stir together until you have a shaggy dough.

TO ASSEMBLE: Pour the blueberries into the dish. Place dollops of dumpling dough on top of the blueberries and pour the syrup over the top. Bake the slump in a preheated 350°F oven for 40 minutes, or until it's golden and bubbly. Serve warm.

NUTRITION INFORMATION PER SERVING: 1 serving, 127g

241 cal | 8g fat | 2g protein | 115g complex carbohydrates | 25g sugar | 1g dietary fiber | 22mg cholesterol | 176mg sodium

Cobblers

A cobbler, which is made of up fruit baked under (or in) a blanket of crust or cake, is a distinctly delicious dish. Its name is said to come from the phrase "to cobble," meaning to patch something together roughly; to "cobble up," put something together in a hurry; or perhaps from the fact that the combination of fruit and dough on top of the dish looks like cobblestones.

Three very different types of crust are what differentiate categories of cobblers from one another. Traditionally, a cobbler's top crust was simply thick spoonfuls of biscuit dough, similar to slumps or grunts. Later, that dough was rolled out and fitted atop the fruit; still later, pastry (pie crust) dough was placed over the fruit, making a cobbler akin to a deep-dish fruit pie without the bottom crust. More recent variations have a cake-like batter poured over the fruit (or fruit layered over the cake batter); the fruit and batter create a "marbled" effect, each remaining distinct though melded. Any way you put together a cobbler, the fruit and crust end up mixing and mingling, the fruit softening some of the crust, the crust absorbing the fruit juices.

Use your imagination to pair various fruits with different flavors in the crust. There are very few desserts as flexible as this one.

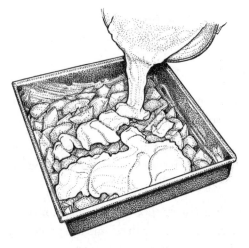

For cake-style cobbler, pour the batter over the fruit in a prepared pan.

BASIC FRUIT COBBLER

ONE 9″ SQUARE OR 11″ ROUND COBBLER

This basic recipe follows the format of fruit piled atop a cake-like batter. Note that cobbler can be made with many different fruits, alone or in combination. First a few words about measuring. This is not an exact science, because fruit is an inexact ingredient. It can vary in size, water content, sugar or acid content, and pectin; all of those have an impact on the other ingredients with which it may be combined. When we give fruit measurements, they are meant to be general guidelines. Your experience and common sense may cause you to vary both the type of fruit and the amounts, and when the result is a success, you've become a real baker.

Any fruit you'd use to make a pie is appropriate for cobbler. Berries of all sorts; stone fruits (cherries, peaches, plums, and nectarines); rhubarb; and apples and pears are all good candidates. Whichever fruit you use, it should be peeled and cored (if necessary), and cut into small bite-size pieces; berries should be hulled, but unless they're mammoth strawberries, can remain whole. Taste your fruit! If it's quite ripe and sweet, dial back the sugar. If not, use the full amount called for. You can adjust to your taste here as well. If you'd like to omit the liquor, increase the milk in the recipe to ¼ cup and use a mixture of 1 tablespoon lemon juice, 1 teaspoon vanilla extract, ½ teaspoon almond extract, and ¼ cup of water in place of the liquor.

1 cup (120g) unbleached all-purpose flour	2 tablespoons (28g) butter, softened
1 teaspoon baking powder	2 tablespoons (28g) milk
½ teaspoon salt	½ cup (112g) sherry, brandy, or bourbon
2 large eggs	3 to 4 cups fresh fruit (large fruits sliced; berries left whole)
1½ cups (297g) sugar	

Preheat the oven to 375°F. Grease a 9″ square pan (or similar-size casserole dish) or an 11″ round quiche dish.

Mix the flour, baking powder, and salt and set aside. Beat together the eggs and 1 cup of the sugar. Add butter and milk. Add the flour mixture, stirring just to combine. Pour the batter into the greased pan.

In a medium saucepan, simmer together the sherry and the remaining ½ cup of sugar for 3 to 4 minutes. Add the fruit and stir to coat with the syrup. Pour this hot fruit mixture over the batter in the pan.

Bake for 30 minutes. Serve warm with whipped cream or ice cream.

NUTRITION INFORMATION PER SERVING USING CHERRIES AS FRUIT: 1 square, 171g
273 cal | 4g fat | 4g protein | 18g complex carbohydrates | 32g sugar | 1g dietary fiber | 55mg cholesterol | 196mg sodium

PEACH AND RASPBERRY COBBLER

ONE 9″ ROUND COBBLER

This pie-crust-cobbler variation features the seductive combination of peach and raspberry; surely the great chef Georges Escoffier must have thought it so when he created the classic Peach Melba dessert for one of his favorite customers, Australian opera singer Nellie Melba. Peach Melba's got nothing on this cobbler!

CRUST

1 cup (120g) unbleached all-
    purpose flour

¼ teaspoon salt

4 tablespoons (½ stick, 56g) butter, cold

¼ cup (46g) vegetable shortening, cold

2 to 4 tablespoons (28g to 56g) ice
    water

FILLING

5 cups (12 to 13 peaches,
    4 to 4½ pounds, 1.81 to 2.04kg)
    peeled, sliced peaches

1 cup (120g) raspberries

1 teaspoon lemon juice

¾ to 1 cup (161g to 198g) sugar (to taste)

1 tablespoon (7g) cornstarch*

¼ teaspoon salt

¼ teaspoon nutmeg

2 tablespoons (28g) coarse white sugar

Preheat the oven to 425°F.

TO MAKE THE CRUST: Butter a 9″ round cake pan or pie dish. Whisk together the flour and salt in a medium bowl, or use a food processor, then cut or pulse in the butter and shortening until the mixture is coarse and crumbly. Add just enough water to form a cohesive dough (bring the dough together with your hands, or if using a food processor, pulse just enough times for the dough to form a ball in the bowl). Wrap the dough and refrigerate for 30 minutes.

TO MAKE THE FILLING: Combine the peaches, raspberries, and lemon juice in a large bowl. Mix together the sugar, cornstarch, salt, and nutmeg, and stir into the fruit. Spoon the filling into the prepared pan.

Roll out the crust to a 9″ circle and place on top of the fruit. Sprinkle with coarse sugar. Cut several vents in the top and bake the cobbler for 15 minutes. Reduce the oven heat to 350°F and bake for an additional 40 to 45 minutes, until the crust is golden and the juices are bubbling. Remove the cobbler from the oven and cool it on a rack.

* Use an extra tablespoon of cornstarch if the peaches are very juicy.

NUTRITION INFORMATION PER SERVING: 1 serving, 139g

203 cal | 5g fat | 2g protein | 20g complex carbohydrates | 18g sugar | 3g dietary fiber | 12mg cholesterol | 107mg sodium

MIXED BERRY COBBLER

ONE 9″ ROUND OR SQUARE COBBLER

A delicious mix of berries (use any you like) offsets the mildly sweet and tender biscuit topping. It's a winning combination.

FILLING

2 pounds (about 8 cups, 1.14kg) fresh or frozen berries

1 tablespoon (7g) cornstarch

1 cup (198g) granulated or brown sugar (213g)

CRUST

2⅓ cups (280g) unbleached all-purpose flour

1 tablespoon (12g) granulated sugar

1 tablespoon (12g) baking powder

¼ teaspoon salt

4 tablespoons (½ stick, 56g) butter

¾ cup (170g) buttermilk

1 large egg

Preheat the oven to 350°F. Grease a 9″ round cake pan, preferably one with 3″ sides. Or use a 9″ square pan or 2-quart casserole dish, or something that's approximately the same size. The cobbler will bubble up and spill over if you try to bake it in something smaller or less deep.

TO MAKE THE FILLING: Place the berries in the greased pan or casserole dish. Mix the cornstarch into the sugar and sprinkle over the fruit. While the sugar begins to draw the juice out of the fruit, make the dough.

TO MAKE THE CRUST: Whisk together the remaining dry ingredients in a large bowl. With your fingertips, mix in the butter until the blend looks like coarse cornmeal. In a smaller bowl, beat together the buttermilk and egg. Make a well in the dry ingredients and pour in the buttermilk/egg mixture. Quickly mix these together with a spoon; it should take about 20 seconds. The dough will be quite wet and sticky.

Turn the dough out onto a well-floured surface and knead until it's reasonably cohesive. When you've shaped the dough into a nice ball, gently roll it out until you have a circle that will roughly cover the berries. Place over the fruit and bake for about 45 minutes.

The cobbler is done when the top is lightly browned and the fruit is soft and bubbling. Remove it from the oven and let it sit for a few minutes. Serve it "right-side-up" with whipped cream or ice cream. You can attempt to flip it, but the combination of hot pan and hot fruit is a tricky, messy, and dangerous one to execute!

NUTRITION INFORMATION PER SERVING: 1 piece, 201g

315 cal | 6g fat | 5g protein | 42g complex carbohydrates | 20g sugar | 7g dietary fiber | 35mg cholesterol | 238mg sodium

APPLE PANDOWDY

ONE 9″ SQUARE PANDOWDY

Apple pandowdy is a traditional American dish dating to the early 1800s. A combination of pie and pudding, the name likely comes from the method: After an apple-based filling is baked in a crust-topped casserole dish, the baker takes a fork and "dowdies" the crust, breaking it into pieces that manage to remain crisp despite being partly immersed in the filling. (Some claim the origin of the name stems from the dish's humble, "dowdy" appearance.)

The filling is juicy; don't be surprised when you cut into the crust and find a sea of liquid. As the dish cools, the "dowdied" crust absorbs a lot of the juice, leaving you with an almost pudding-like confection. This dish is best served right from its pan.

1 recipe pie crust for double-crust 9″ pie (see page 358 for medium-flake pie crust)

7 or 8 large apples

1 cup (198g) sugar

¼ teaspoon salt

¼ teaspoon cinnamon

¼ teaspoon nutmeg

¼ cup (56g) water

½ cup (170g) molasses or maple syrup (156g)

3 tablespoons (42g) butter, cut into pats

2 tablespoons (28g) milk

Put the oven rack on its lowest rung and preheat the oven to 425°F.

Divide the pie dough into two pieces, one slightly larger than the other. Roll out the larger piece to fit into the bottom and up the sides of a casserole dish (a 9″ square pan, or equivalent, is the right size). Peel, core, and cut the apples into ¼″ slices. You should have about 9 cups. Toss the slices with ½ cup of the sugar, the salt, cinnamon, and nutmeg. Spoon apples into pie crust.

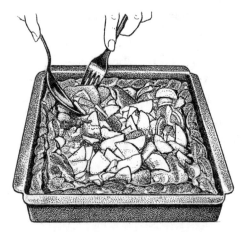

Use a fork and spoon to "dowdy" the crust for apple pandowdy.

Mix water and molasses or maple syrup and pour over apples. Dot with butter.

Roll out second piece of dough and fit it over the apple mixture. Brush the edge of the bottom crust with the milk and squeeze together the edges of the bottom and top crust, sealing them; the protein in the milk will act as glue, keeping a tight seal while the pandowdy bakes. Brush the top crust with the milk and sprinkle lightly with the remaining sugar. (This will make a brown, sugary crust.)

Bake for 45 minutes, then decrease heat to 325°F and continue to bake until the crust is well browned (the initial 45 minutes may be enough for the browning; each oven is a bit different).

Remove from the oven and cool on a rack for 5 minutes. After 5 minutes, take a knife and slash, in a random pattern, all the way through the pandowdy. With a fork and spoon, gently lift pieces of crust from the bottom and submerge pieces of the top crust; in effect, you're really messing this whole thing up. Don't get carried away; crust pieces should remain in fairly large (2″ square) chunks. Let the dish cool to warm before serving; if you serve it too hot, it will be very runny.

NUTRITION INFORMATION PER SERVING: 1 square, 149g
280 cal | 12g fat | 2g protein | 26g complex carbohydrates | 17g sugar | 2g dietary fiber | 19mg cholesterol | 225mg sodium

Dumplings

Dumplings come in both sweet and savory versions, and the two resemble one another in shape only. The sweet dumpling category comes in two styles as well: fruit that's surrounded with a pastry crust and baked (as with traditional apple dumplings); and baking powder biscuit–like dough that's simmered in a sweet sauce and often served with cream. Savory dumplings run the gamut from biscuit dumplings simmered in soup or stew to quenelles (ground meat or seafood mixed with egg and poached in salted water) to gnocchi (small rolled shapes of flour and potato, usually simmered in a savory sauce) to stuffed wontons and some types of dim sum.

The two types of dumplings we'll concentrate on are the sweet, fruit-filled pastry ones and the ones based on biscuit dough that simmer in another medium, be it sweet or savory.

BERRY DUMPLINGS

26 TO 28 DUMPLINGS

These dumplings are cooked in a delicious bath of simmering fruit, then finished with a dusting of cinnamon or confectioners' sugar. The liquid from the fruit will thicken slightly as they cook. Resist the temptation to peek under the lid: It will keep the dumplings from being as light as they should. We think these would make a very comforting breakfast on a snowy morning.

FILLING

1 quart (680g) fresh or frozen berries

1 cup (198g) sugar

1 cup (227g) water

2 tablespoons (28g) lemon juice

½ teaspoon cinnamon

DOUGH

2 cups (240g) unbleached all-purpose flour

1 teaspoon salt

¼ cup (49g) sugar

2½ teaspoons baking powder

6 tablespoons (¾ stick, 84g) unsalted butter, cold

½ cup (113g) milk or cream

1 large egg

½ teaspoon vanilla or almond extract (optional)

TO MAKE THE FILLING: Put the fruit, sugar, water, lemon juice, and cinnamon in a large skillet for which you have a lid, or a large heatproof casserole dish. Set aside.

TO MAKE THE DOUGH: In a medium bowl, whisk together the flour, salt, sugar, and baking powder. Cut the butter into pats and work the butter into the flour, using a pastry blender, mixer, or your fingers (you can also use a food processor up to this point). When thoroughly combined, the mixture should resemble uneven, coarse crumbs; don't keep working it until it's perfectly homogeneous. The tender texture of the dumplings comes from pockets of cold fat in the dough, which in the cooking process don't melt until after the dough is set, leaving butter-catching fissures in the finished dumpling.

Put the fruit over medium heat to start simmering while you mix the dough.

Measure the milk into a liquid measuring cup, add the egg and vanilla, if using, and whisk until smooth. Add this to the flour/fat mixture, and stir just until the dough is evenly mixed; it will be stiff. Drop the dough by tablespoons into the simmering fruit. Once all the dough is scooped out, put a lid on the pan and reduce the heat to low. Let the dumplings simmer for 10 to 12 minutes, until cooked all the way through. Remove from the heat immediately and spoon into bowls to serve warm. Sprinkle with cinnamon sugar or confectioners' sugar, or serve with a scoop of ice cream if you prefer.

NUTRITION INFORMATION PER SERVING: 3 dumplings, with fruit, 225g

361 cal | 12g fat | 4g protein | 33g complex carbohydrates | 27g sugar | 6g dietary fiber | 39mg cholesterol | 252mg sodium

APPLE DUMPLING SLICES

ABOUT 16 SLICES

This dish hovers somewhere between a dumpling, a sticky bun, a pie, and a cobbler; in our opinion, it combines the best aspects of each. Sweet, soft, and buttery, it's true comfort food. If you have some on hand, we love using boiled cider here; if you'd like to, then decrease the sugar and water to 1½ cups each, prepare the sugar syrup, then add ½ cup boiled cider.

10 tablespoons (1¼ sticks, 140g)
    unsalted butter, cold

2 cups (448g) water

2 cups (392g) sugar

2 cups (240g) unbleached all-
    purpose flour

1 tablespoon (12g) baking powder

½ teaspoon salt

⅓ cup (74g) milk, at room temperature

1 teaspoon cinnamon

2 cups (224g to 252g) peeled, diced
    apple

Preheat the oven to 350°F. Melt 4 tablespoons (56g) of the butter in a 9″ × 13″ baking dish; glass or ceramic is preferable. Set the dish aside.

In a medium saucepan, heat the water and sugar until the sugar melts. Meanwhile, combine the flour, baking powder, and salt with the remaining 6 tablespoons butter in a medium bowl. Rub the butter into the flour with the tips of your fingers, a pastry blender, or two knives until the mixture is crumbly. Stir in the milk and mix until the dough just comes together and leaves the sides of the bowl. Chill the dough while preparing the apples.

Turn the dough out onto a floured surface and knead it gently, until it's somewhat cohesive. Roll it gently into a 10″ × 15″ rectangle. Mix together the cinnamon and apples and spread them over the dough. Carefully roll the dough into a log, sticky-bun style, pinching the edges together to seal. It may tear, but don't worry; mend it as best you can. (It's actually better if it comes apart a bit as it bakes.)

With a bench knife or serrated knife, cut the log into 16 slices, starting in the middle and moving out toward the ends. Arrange the slices over the butter in the baking dish as artfully as possible. The

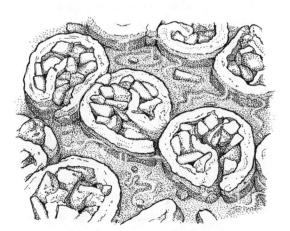

Apple dumpling slices look very wet before baking; the dough will expand to fill the spaces between them as they bake.

slices may want to fall apart, but again, not to worry. The finished product will look fine.

Pour the sugar syrup over the apple dumpling slices and place this quite-liquid conglomeration in the oven. Bake for 40 to 45 minutes. When you take the baking dish out of the oven, the biscuits will be lightly browned on top of a still-very-liquid syrup. The whole thing can surge from one end to the other very easily if you're not extremely careful as you're moving it.

Let the slices cool a bit, then serve them with syrup poured over the top. We found that by leaving this uncovered at room temperature overnight (we managed to have some left over!), the texture of the biscuits remained crisp and it was just as good the next day.

NUTRITION INFORMATION PER SERVING: 1 piece, 106g

243 cal | 9.5g fat | 1g protein | 13g complex carbohydrates | 25g sugar | 1g dietary fiber | 27mg cholesterol | 173mg sodium

BASIC SAVORY DUMPLINGS

10 TO 12 DUMPLINGS

Dumplings are a wonderful addition to any simmering soup or stew; not only do they add substance in the form of delicious, tender hunks of bread, but some of their starch leaches out into the soup as they cook, thickening it nicely. Here, we detail the method for making the dumpling itself—the rest is up to you. Use these to top any soup or stew as it cooks. Depending on how your soup or stew is seasoned, 1 tablespoon chopped parsley or chives, black pepper, or a pinch of thyme can make a flavorful addition to your dumpling dough.

1 cup (120g) unbleached all-purpose flour

¾ teaspoon salt

1½ teaspoons baking powder

2 tablespoons (28g) butter, cold

½ cup (113g) milk

Mix the flour, salt, and baking powder together in a bowl. Cut in the butter until the mixture is the texture of coarse sand. Add the milk all at once, stirring quickly and as little as possible, just until everything is moistened. Drop the dough by rounded spoonfuls into a simmering soup or stew. Cook, uncovered, for 10 minutes, then cover and simmer for 10 minutes more, or until the dumplings are cooked through.

NUTRITION INFORMATION PER SERVING: 1 large dumpling, 36g

106 cal | 4g fat | 2g protein | 15g complex carbohydrates | 0g sugar | 1g dietary fiber | 11mg cholesterol | 378mg sodium

HERBED ITALIAN DUMPLINGS

12 DUMPLINGS

These savory dumplings, redolent of Parmesan, are a wonderful addition to any broth-based soup. They are also an excellent use for that last bit of a loaf or baguette that needs to be used up before going stale, as they rely on bread crumbs for body.

2 large eggs

⅓ cup (33g) grated Parmesan cheese

1 cup (84g) soft bread crumbs

3 tablespoons (42g) butter, melted

1 teaspoon dried basil

1 teaspoon lemon zest

1 tablespoon chopped fresh parsley

1 teaspoon freshly ground black pepper

Combine all the ingredients in a bowl. With lightly greased hands, shape the mixture into 1″ balls (or use a teaspoon cookie scoop for this step). Drop about 10 dumplings at a time into a simmering broth-based soup and cook them for about 8 minutes. Remove from the broth and keep them warm while cooking the rest. Place the dumplings in soup bowls and ladle the soup over them. Serve with additional grated Parmesan, if desired.

NUTRITION INFORMATION PER SERVING: 2 dumplings, 24g

75 cal | 5g fat | 3g protein | 3g complex carbohydrates | 0g sugar | 0g dietary fiber | 15mg cholesterol | 108mg sodium

POTATO PUFF DUMPLINGS

48 DUMPLINGS

A close cousin to cream puffs (baked, they're a cross between cream puffs and biscuits), these taste like a soft potato biscuit when added to soup. Or, as we think of them, a buttery cloud of potato! If you want something really extraordinary, toss them into the deep fryer to make wonderful, golden, potato fritter-like creations.

5 tablespoons (71g) unsalted butter

½ cup (113g) milk

1 teaspoon salt

1 cup (120g) unbleached all-purpose flour

3 large eggs

1 cup (140g) mashed potato, lightly packed (2 to 3 medium potatoes, cooked and riced)

2 tablespoons chopped fresh parsley or chives

In a medium saucepan, melt the butter with the milk and add the salt. Bring the mixture to a boil, add the flour all at once, and stir until it forms a ball. Remove the pan from the heat and beat to remove some of the steam. Add the eggs one at a time, beating well after each addition, then beat in the mashed potato and parsley or chives.

Drop the dough by teaspoonfuls into boiling salted water or soup, about 15 at a time. Boil them for 5 to 6 minutes, then remove from the broth and keep them warm in the oven while cooking the remaining dumplings. Or drop them by the teaspoonful into hot, deep fat. Cook until golden brown (3 to 4 minutes), and place on a rack to drain. Finally, you may drop by the tablespoonful onto baking sheets and bake in a preheated 400°F oven for 12 to 15 minutes, or until they're a light golden brown. Each method of cooking makes a very different product—soft white boiled dumplings, crunchy fritters, or golden puffs.

NUTRITION INFORMATION PER SERVING: 2 boiled or baked puffs, 52g

128 cal | 7g fat | 3g protein | 12g complex carbohydrates | 0g sugar | 0g dietary fiber | 20mg cholesterol | 374mg sodium

Clafouti

And now, to conclude this chapter of baked goods with absolutely wonderful names, we come to clafouti, a traditional French dessert. To make it, you first place fresh fruit in a shallow layer in a wide pan (often a large pie pan or cake pan). An eggy, sweetened batter (like a cross between cake batter and pancake batter) is poured over the fruit, where it sinks to the bottom of the pan, then the entire thing is baked until the crust has risen over the fruit and begins to brown. The texture is all at once cake-like and custardy.

The best-known clafouti is made with dark sweet cherries. Peaches, apples, pears, and plums also make good clafouti. More delicate berries, such as raspberries, aren't good clafouti candidates, as they'll turn to mush before the clafouti finishes baking, but blueberries or strawberries are good options.

CHERRY CLAFOUTI

ONE 10˝ ROUND CLAFOUTI

This relatively quick and simple summer dessert is our favorite version of France's best-known clafouti. It's the sort of recipe that works equally well as a fancy dinner party finale or an easy go-to weeknight dessert.

¾ cup (90g) unbleached all-purpose flour

⅔ cup (130g) sugar

3 large eggs

1¼ cups (284g) milk

1 teaspoon almond or vanilla extract

3 cups (about 2 pounds, 480g) pitted sweet cherries

Preheat the oven to 375°F. Thoroughly grease a 10˝ round pan or ovenproof skillet.

In a medium bowl, whisk together the flour and sugar. In a smaller bowl or large measuring cup, beat the eggs until foamy. Beat in the milk and vanilla. Gradually whisk the egg mixture into the flour and sugar, stirring to smooth out any lumps.

Place the fruit in the prepared dish and pour the batter over it. Bake for 35 to 40 minutes. A cake tester inserted in the center should come out clean. Serve warm or at room temperature.

NOTE: For a more custard-like clafouti, bake in a 9˝ pan at 350°F for 40 to 45 minutes.

NUTRITION INFORMATION PER SERVING: 1 slice, 133g

162 cal | 1g fat | 5g protein | 18g complex carbohydrates | 15g sugar | 1g dietary fiber | 3mg cholesterol | 38mg sodium

PEACH OR APRICOT CLAFOUTI

8 SLICES

Clafouti recipes would traditionally call for cherries or plums from the Limousin region of France, but we decided to give peaches a go and were very happy with the results. The peaches fan nicely in the bottom of the pan, and the brown sugar gives a slightly taffy-like crust to the dish as it bakes.

3 cups (504g) sliced peaches or
  quartered fresh apricots (510g)

⅓ cup (70g) brown sugar, packed

¾ cup (90g) unbleached all-
  purpose flour

⅓ cup (66g) granulated sugar

½ teaspoon salt

3 large eggs

1¼ cups (284g) milk

¾ teaspoon almond or vanilla extract

Preheat the oven to 375°F. Thoroughly grease a 10″ round pan or ovenproof skillet. Arrange the peach slices or apricot quarters on the bottom of the pan and sprinkle evenly with the brown sugar.

In a medium bowl, whisk together the flour, sugar, and salt. In a separate smaller bowl or large mixing cup, combine the eggs, milk, and vanilla. Beat until thoroughly combined, then gradually whisk into the flour mixture, smoothing out the lumps. Pour the batter over the fruit in the prepared baking pan and bake for 35 to 40 minutes. A cake tester or toothpick inserted into the center should come out clean. Serve warm or at room temperature.

NUTRITION INFORMATION PER SERVING: 1 slice, 148g

168 cal | 2g fat | 5g protein | 17g complex carbohydrates | 15g sugar | 0g dietary fiber | 81mg cholesterol | 179mg sodium

CHAPTER FOUR

Crackers and Flatbreads

___

IF YOU HAVE ANY AFFINITY at all for a rolling pin, you can make all kinds of flatbreads, including crackers, tortillas, naan, Armenian lavash (cracker bread), and all the myriad variations of flatbread, crisp bread, and parchment bread from various cultures around the world.

If the word "bread" conjures up fears of working with yeast, don't be intimidated. We'll allay all those fears further along in this book, but for now, fear not: Most of the following recipes don't use yeast. Just flour and a do-it-yourself attitude!

Crackers

Crackers and milk. Crackers and soup. Cheese and crackers. Crackers and peanut butter. Crackers are one of the most beloved and simple snacks, and can be an excellent prelude to a more substantial meal. They pair beautifully with dips, spreads, and wine and cheese. They're exceedingly easy to make (and they're also an unusual and thoughtful gift).

The following cracker recipes range from plain (water biscuits) to more colorful (curry and ginger), but they all have one thing in common: They begin with a simple combination of flour, fat, and liquid. In fact, crackers are a lot like pie crust. They exhibit the same changes when the formula is varied: The more fat and less water, the flakier and more tender the cracker; the less fat and more water, the crisper and harder the cracker. The following recipe will familiarize you with the basics of the cracker-making process.

CRACKER-MAKING TOOLS

As we made batch after batch of crackers, we discovered a couple of tools that make the whole job incredibly easy. One is a giant spatula (see Tools, page 546), with a 10″ × 10″ blade, perfect for lifting the dough as you roll (to sprinkle more flour underneath to prevent sticking), and also ideal for transferring the unbaked crackers to the baking sheets and the baked crackers to the cooling rack. The other tool we just couldn't have done without is a rolling pizza cutter (or, for a more intricate look, a crimped pastry wheel). Using the cutter, we were able to cut 95 to 100 crackers out of a piece of rolled dough in less than 10 seconds. And we discovered a 1-liter clamp-top Mason jar is just about the perfect size to hold most batches of crackers; the rubber gasket keeps crackers nice and fresh, and a red ribbon tied around the top is all you need in the way of wrapping or decoration if you're giving the crackers as a present.

BASIC CRACKERS

ABOUT 96 CRACKERS

2 cups flour (all-purpose, pastry, whole wheat, rye, barley, or semolina)

optional flavorings (spices, herbs, extracts, seeds, and/or minced vegetables)

2 to 8 tablespoons fat (butter, vegetable shortening, or oil)

2 to 8 tablespoons liquid (water, milk, beer, yogurt, buttermilk, or sour cream)

Preheat the oven to 350°F.

Place flour in a mixing bowl. Add flavorings, if using. Cut in fat as if you were making pie crust, until the mixture forms small, even crumbs. Then quickly stir in the liquid, using only enough to hold the dough together. Too much will toughen the crackers and make them hard to roll out. Remember, the more fat you use, the less liquid you'll need.

Transfer dough to a lightly floured work surface or board. Using a heavy rolling pin and a firm hand, use a minimal number of strokes to roll the dough very thin—1/16″ to 1/8″ is the norm. The fewer strokes it takes you to roll out the dough, the more tender your crackers will be. Prick the dough all over with a fork.

1. Roll out cracker dough to 1/8″ thick. Brush with water and sprinkle with salt, if desired, then prick holes all over the dough with a fork or dough docker (pictured). **2.** Use a ruler and a pizza wheel (or sharp knife) to cut the dough into strips, then cut again into cracker shapes.

Cut the dough into 2½″ squares, rounds, or triangles.

Transfer the crackers to a parchment-lined or lightly greased baking sheet and bake for 20 to 25 minutes, until the crackers just begin to brown.

Remove the crackers from the oven and transfer them to a rack to cool. They'll become crisp as they cool. Store in an airtight container.

WHICH FLOUR SHOULD I USE?

Crackers are one of the baking world's most flexible recipes. You can make a successful cracker from just about any type of flour you choose.

Bakers usually prefer to use a medium-protein flour; this gives crackers a tender bite, with sufficient body to avoid crumbling. We find all-purpose flour (about 11.7% protein) makes a dough that's extensible enough to roll out nicely without fighting back, yet strong enough to hold together while rolling and cutting. The resulting cracker is crisp-hard. For a cracker that's crisp but more tender, try blending one part cake or pastry flour with three parts all-purpose; the price you'll pay is a bit more difficulty handling the dough. However, if you're an accomplished pie crust baker, we suggest you give this formula a try.

To make whole grain crackers, substitute a whole grain flour—rye, whole wheat, or white whole wheat (see pages 460–462)—for one-fourth to one-third of the all-purpose flour in the recipe. You won't experience any noticeable problems in handling the dough at this level of substitution, but any greater percentage of nonwhite flour will produce a crumbly or sticky dough. Crackers don't have adequate water in the dough to hydrate the bran in the whole grain flour enough so they'll hold together as well.

RICH CRACKERS

ABOUT 96 ROUND CRACKERS

We don't call these rich for nothing! Butter, egg, and cream enrich the dough, which is made just like pie crust.

2 cups (240g) unbleached all-purpose flour

1 teaspoon salt

1 teaspoon baking powder

2½ tablespoons (31g) sugar

4 tablespoons (½ stick, 56g) butter, cold

1 large egg

6 tablespoons (85g) cream

2 to 3 tablespoons (28g to 42g) butter, melted

In a large bowl, mix together flour, salt, baking powder, and sugar. Cut in the butter. In a separate bowl, use a fork to stir the egg and cream together until smooth. Add to flour/butter mixture and stir until mixture forms a loose ball. Gather in your hands and squeeze together. Pat into an oval about 1″ thick, wrap in waxed paper, and chill for 1 hour.

Preheat the oven to 425°F.

On a lightly floured surface, roll dough into a circle between ⅟₁₆″ and ⅛″ in thickness. Cut dough into rounds with a 3″ or smaller cutter. Repeat with remaining dough scraps. Unlike pie crust, this repeated rolling doesn't seem to toughen the final product. Transfer rounds to lightly greased or parchment-lined baking sheets and prick each round several times with a fork.

Bake crackers for 6 minutes. Remove pan from oven, turn crackers over, and bake an additional 5 minutes, or until crackers are lightly browned. Remove crackers from oven and brush with melted butter. Transfer to a rack to cool completely.

NUTRITION INFORMATION PER SERVING: 2 crackers, 11g

42 cal | 2g fat | 1g protein | 4g complex carbohydrates | 1g sugar | 0g dietary fiber | 12mg cholesterol | 57mg sodium

CHEESE PENNIES

ABOUT 80 PENNIES

If you're a lover of cheese crackers in any form, these homemade cheese pennies will be a revelation. A rich concoction of cheese and butter held together with a bit of flour and baked until golden brown, they're given a spicy kick with a hit of cayenne. These are very good served with drinks—nonalcoholic or otherwise.

8 ounces (2 cups, 224g) finely grated sharp cheddar or Asiago cheese

8 tablespoons (1 stick, 113g) unsalted butter

1½ cups (180g) unbleached all-purpose flour

¾ teaspoon salt

½ teaspoon dry mustard

⅛ to ¼ teaspoon cayenne

paprika (optional)

In a medium bowl, combine all the ingredients except paprika to make a cohesive dough, sprinkling in a tablespoon or so of water if the dough doesn't seem to come together. As soon as it does, turn off the mixer and gather it into a rough ball. Transfer it to a lightly floured work surface and roll it into a 16″ log about 1½″ in diameter.

Wrap the log in waxed paper or plastic wrap and chill it in the freezer for 30 minutes. (If you want to freeze it longer, make sure to remove it from the freezer about 30 minutes before you slice it into pennies.)

Preheat the oven to 400°F.

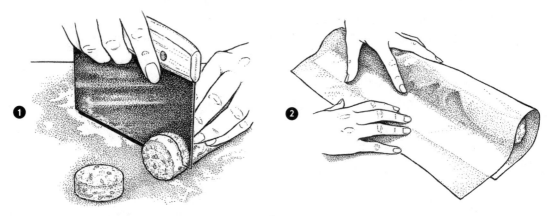

1. Chilled dough can be cut into uniform disks with the help of a bench knife. **2.** To roll dough into a log, put it on a sheet of parchment or waxed paper. Fold the paper over, and press on the top sheet. Pull the bottom sheet toward you to tighten the dough into a log shape before refrigerating.

Remove the plastic wrap or waxed paper, and, using a bench or serrated knife, slice the log crosswise into ⅛″ rounds. Place them on an ungreased or parchment-lined baking sheet, leaving only about ½″ between; they won't spread much as they bake. Sprinkle them with a bit of paprika, if desired.

Bake the cheese pennies for 12 to 14 minutes, or until they're just beginning to brown. Remove them from the oven and let cool on the pan for several minutes before transferring them to racks to cool completely.

NUTRITION INFORMATION PER SERVING: 5 pennies, 34g
150 cal | 10.2g fat | 5g protein | 8g complex carbohydrates | 0g sugar | 0g dietary fiber | 32mg cholesterol | 189mg sodium

BENNE WAFERS

36 WAFERS

These ethereally light, snapping-crisp, sweet sesame crackers are a popular favorite in South Carolina's Lowcountry and neighboring areas. These rich brown crackers have a nutty and subtly sweet flavor and an interesting texture: solid and crisp on the bottom, crunchy-light on top. They are awfully close to being a cookie.

8 tablespoons (1 stick, 113g) unsalted
    butter
1 cup (213g) light brown sugar, packed
¼ teaspoon salt
¼ teaspoon baking soda

1 teaspoon vanilla extract
1 large egg
1 cup (120g) unbleached all-
    purpose flour
1 cup (140g) toasted sesame seeds

Preheat the oven to 350°F.

In a large bowl, cream together the butter, brown sugar, salt, baking soda, vanilla, and egg. Add the flour and mix until smooth. Stir in the sesame seeds.

Drop the dough by tablespoonfuls (a tablespoon cookie scoop works well here) onto parchment-lined or lightly greased baking sheets. Bake the wafers for 8 to 9 minutes, until they're golden brown. Remove them from the oven, let cool for 1 minute on the pan, then transfer the wafers to a rack to cool completely.

NUTRITION INFORMATION PER SERVING: 1 wafer, 18g
84 cal | 5g fat | 1g protein | 3g complex carbohydrates | 6g sugar | 1g dietary fiber | 13mg cholesterol | 30mg sodium

RYE CRISPS

60 CRACKERS

The flavors of this deeply dark brown, substantial rye cracker make it a worthy base for smoked Gouda cheese and the best charcuterie you can find.

CRACKERS

1½ cups (180g) unbleached all-purpose flour

1½ cups (168g) medium rye flour or pumpernickel flour

3 tablespoons (21g) nonfat dry milk

2 teaspoons baking powder

2 teaspoons instant yeast

2 teaspoons cider vinegar

2 teaspoons salt

1 tablespoon (8g) caraway seeds or 2 teaspoons ground caraway

½ cup (77g) vegetable oil

¾ cup (168g) milk, lukewarm

1 egg, separated

EGG WASH

1 egg yolk (reserved from above)

1 tablespoon (14g) milk or water

In a medium bowl, whisk together the flours, dry milk, baking powder, and yeast. Add the vinegar, salt, caraway, and oil. The mixture will be crumbly because you're coating some of the flour with oil; this prevents some gluten from developing that would otherwise toughen the cracker unpleasantly.

In a small bowl, whisk the warmed milk and egg white together, then add this to the flour mixture. Mix, then knead the dough by hand or mixer to form a smooth ball.

Place the dough into a greased bowl, turn it to coat, and cover the bowl with plastic wrap. Let the dough rise for 1 hour, then refrigerate it for several hours, or for up to 24 hours. Don't expect a big, bread-like rise; it will just become a bit puffy, but the flavor will improve as it rests.

Turn out the dough onto a lightly greased or floured work surface. Roll it into a 14″ × 17″ rectangle, slightly less than ⅛″ thick. If the dough starts to shrink or tear, cover it and let it rest for a few minutes before continuing. Before cutting it, transfer the dough onto a piece of parchment paper or a lightly greased baking sheet. Remember, though, you'll be cutting the crackers on the pan, so place the dough only onto a pan that may be cut on, or line a nonstick pan with parchment.

Prick the dough all over with a fork.

Cut the dough into sticks or triangles using a pizza wheel, pastry cutter, or bench knife. Don't worry about separating them; they'll break apart easily along the scored lines when cool.

TO MAKE THE EGG WASH: Mix the reserved egg yolk with the tablespoon of milk or water. Brush the top of the crackers with this mixture and let them rest, covered, for 1 hour.

Preheat the oven to 375°F.

Bake the crackers for 10 minutes, then reduce the oven heat to 325°F and continue to bake for 30 to 40 minutes. The crackers should be golden brown and feel firm when pressed; you will also suddenly catch the aroma of caraway when the crackers are done.

Remove the crackers from the oven and transfer them to a rack to cool completely. Store them in airtight containers for 4 to 5 days.

NUTRITION INFORMATION PER SERVING: 5 crackers, 62g

208 cal | 11g fat | 4g protein | 24g complex carbohydrates | 0g sugar | 3g dietary fiber | 20mg cholesterol | 450mg sodium

VERMONT CHEESE CRACKERS

ABOUT 100 CRACKERS

Crisp and fantastically cheesy, these savory crackers are worlds better than any cheese cracker you've ever bought from a store. The secret ingredient is cheese powder, which blends more seamlessly into the dough than grated cheese will.

1½ cups (159g) Italian-style flour or 1½ cups (180g) unbleached all-purpose flour

½ cup (57g) Vermont cheddar cheese powder

1 teaspoon instant yeast

¼ teaspoon salt

½ teaspoon baking powder

¼ cup (50g) vegetable shortening

7 to 8 tablespoons (99g to 113g) ice water

Whisk together the flour, cheese powder, yeast, salt, and baking powder.

Add the shortening, working it in to make an unevenly crumbly mixture.

Stir and toss in enough of the ice water to make a cohesive (but not sticky) dough.

Divide the dough in half, and shape each half into a small rectangular slab.

Cover with plastic wrap and refrigerate for 30 minutes or up to a couple of hours; don't chill longer than that. Preheat the oven to 400°F.

Very lightly flour a piece of parchment, your rolling pin, and the top of the dough. Working with one piece at a time, roll the dough about 1/16˝ thick, or slightly thicker.

If you don't have parchment, roll on a lightly floured work surface or silicone rolling mat. The dough will have ragged, uneven edges; just try to make it as even as possible.

If you've used parchment, gently slide the parchment and crackers onto a baking sheet. Cut the dough into 1¼″ squares; a rolling pizza wheel works well here. Don't separate the squares. If you haven't used parchment, gently fold the rolled dough in half, pick it up, and place it on a lightly greased baking sheet, then cut it.

Prick each square with the tines of a fork.

Bake the crackers for about 8 minutes, until the ones on the outside are starting to brown around the edges. Remove them from the oven, and transfer the browned crackers to a cooling rack or piece of parchment—these outer crackers are done. Quickly and carefully pull the remaining crackers apart to separate them. Return to the oven.

Bake for an additional 3 minutes or so, or until the remaining crackers are a very light golden brown. You'll need to watch these closely at the end; don't walk away from the oven. They go from golden to dark brown very quickly.

Remove them from the oven, and cool right on the pan. When completely cool, store in an airtight container.

NUTRITION INFORMATION PER SERVING: 5 crackers, 19g

66 cal | 3g fat | 2g protein | 6g complex carbohydrates | 1g sugar | 0g dietary fiber | 3mg cholesterol | 177mg sodium

---

PUT THEM THROUGH THE WRINGER

If you have a pasta machine, many cracker doughs can be rolled out in it, from fairly thick to ultra-thin. Those made with more fat and less liquid, and/or with a lower-protein flour, may be too fragile to put through the machine's rollers. You'll need to be the judge of whether the dough you're working with is strong enough to take it. But if it is, once the pasta machine rolls out the dough in a long strip, it's very simple to cut it into square or rectangular crackers with a pizza wheel.

GOURMET SODA CRACKERS

ABOUT 45 CRACKERS

Light and crunchy, these yeasted crackers are incredibly flavorful (and comforting!) on their own but also make a nice blank canvas for other flavors such as herbs, cheese, and spices.

1½ cups (163g) Italian-style flour	1 teaspoon sugar
2 teaspoons instant yeast	6 tablespoons (85g) water
¼ teaspoon salt	2 tablespoons (28g) butter
¼ teaspoon baking soda	2 tablespoons (25g) vegetable oil
¼ teaspoon cream of tartar	flavored salt, for topping (optional)

In a large bowl, whisk together the flour, yeast, salt, baking soda, cream of tartar, and sugar. Set it aside.

Put the water, butter, and oil in a microwave-safe cup, or in a saucepan. Heat gently just to melt the butter. Remove from the heat, and cool to 120°F to 130°F. If you don't have a thermometer, this will feel hotter than lukewarm but not at all uncomfortably hot; it'll be cooler than your hottest tap water.

Add the liquid ingredients to the dry ingredients. Beat at medium, then high speed for a total of about 90 seconds, to make a soft dough.

Place the dough in a lightly greased bowl, cover it, and refrigerate overnight, or for up to 18 hours. It won't rise much; the bowl can be small.

Remove the dough from the refrigerator, and allow it to rest for about 15 minutes. Preheat the oven to 425°F.

Lightly flour a work surface (a silicone rolling mat works well here), and remove the dough from its rising bowl. It won't feel like normal yeast dough; it'll be more clay-like. Shape the dough into a 3″ × 5″ rectangular block; pre-shaping it like this will help you roll it out evenly. Roll it into a rough 13″ × 15″ rectangle; it'll be quite thin. Be sure to keep the rolling surface well floured, to avoid sticking.

Starting with a shorter side, fold the dough in three like a business letter.

Roll it out again, this time into an 11″ × 19″ rectangle, or thereabouts. The dough will shrink when you stop rolling it; your goal is to end up with a rectangle that's about 10″ × 18″.

Sprinkle the dough with your choice of salt—we like an herbed or smoked salt—and gently press it in with the rolling pin.

Using a rolling pizza wheel (easiest) or a bench knife, cut the dough into 2″ squares. (If you're using a silicone mat, cut very carefully to avoid damaging the mat. We like to use an acrylic-blade pizza wheel.)

Transfer the crackers to two lightly greased or parchment-lined baking sheets; you can put them fairly close together, as they'll shrink as they bake, rather than spread. Prick each cracker once or twice with the tines of a fork.

Bake the crackers for about 10 minutes, until they're a very light golden brown. Watch them carefully toward the end of the baking time; they can darken very quickly.

Turn off the oven and open the door completely. Leave the crackers on the oven rack; they're going to cool down right in the cooling oven, in order to preserve their crispness. Keep your eye on them for the first couple of minutes. If for some reason your oven isn't cooling off quickly, and the crackers are continuing to brown, pull the rack out partway.

When the crackers are completely cool, remove them from the oven, and wrap airtight, to preserve their crispness.

NUTRITION INFORMATION PER SERVING: 5 crackers, 36g

120 cal | 6g fat | 2g protein | 14g complex carbohydrates | 0g sugar | 1g dietary fiber | 7mg cholesterol | 330mg sodium

SMOKY CHILI CRACKERS

ABOUT 72 CRACKERS

These crackers smell deliciously of cumin as they bake, and they turn a very attractive deep golden orange. Chipotle powder gives the crackers a pleasing, smoky flavor.

1½ cups (180g) unbleached all-purpose flour

½ cup (67g) yellow or white cornmeal

1 tablespoon (8g) nonfat dry milk

1 teaspoon cumin

½ teaspoon baking soda

¾ teaspoon salt

2 teaspoons sugar

½ teaspoon chipotle powder

¼ cup (44g) vegetable shortening

1 tablespoon (17g) tomato paste

scant ½ cup (105g) water

Preheat the oven to 350°F.

In a large bowl, whisk together the flour, cornmeal, dry milk, cumin, baking soda, salt, sugar, and chipotle powder. Cut in the shortening and tomato paste, then add enough water to make a workable dough. Gather the dough into a ball and divide it into two pieces.

Working with one piece at a time, roll the dough on a lightly floured surface to ⅛″ thickness. Cut it into 1½″ squares and bake the crackers for 20 minutes. Remove them from the oven and cool on the pan. Store in an airtight container.

NUTRITION INFORMATION PER SERVING: **3 crackers, 10g**

52 cal | 2g fat | 1g protein | 7g complex carbohydrates | 0g sugar | 0g dietary fiber | 0mg cholesterol | 96mg sodium

CRISP CRACKERS

Crackers may be made totally without leavening, in which case their texture comes solely from the inner steam created as they bake (as with a flaky pie crust). Unleavened crackers are generally tender and flaky (rather than crisp) if they're fairly thick, or quite hard (think hardtack) if they're rolled thin. Adding a leavening agent, either yeast or chemical (baking soda, baking powder, or cream of tartar), will produce a crisper, lighter cracker. These leaveners contribute to the mouth-feel we recognize as "crisp" by producing carbon dioxide gas, which is trapped within the cracker dough as it bakes. The mixture of air and baked dough is what transforms "tough" or "hard" into "crisp."

To produce crisp crackers, moisture that begins in the dough needs to leave the cracker as it bakes. This is why crackers are often "docked"—that is, pricked with a fork, in the case of the home baker. Not only do these holes allow steam to escape, they prevent the cracker from blowing up like a balloon. A typical cracker dough may contain 45% liquid; by the time the cracker is baked, that number should be down to 5% to 6%. Thus crackers need a thorough baking, either at a high temperature for a short amount of time, or at a lower temperature for a correspondingly longer length of time. Very thin cracker doughs (1⁄16″) seem to do better with a short, hot bake (although you need to watch them very carefully, as the thinner the cracker, the more quickly it goes from baked to burned). Thicker cracker doughs (up to ¼″) do better with a longer, slower bake, to completely dry out the interior of the cracker without burning the exterior.

ALMOND FLOUR CRACKERS

ABOUT 120 SQUARE CRACKERS

Delicious and versatile, these crackers (which happen to be gluten-free) can easily be customized from simple to savory to sweet. Try one of our four favorite flavor options, or experiment to create your own new favorite. Note that using finely ground, rather than coarsely ground, blanched almond flour will yield the crispiest crackers, although both types will work.

1 large egg

¼ teaspoon salt

½ teaspoon freshly ground black pepper

1¾ cups (168g) finely ground almond flour

Preheat the oven to 350°F.

Whisk together the egg, salt, and pepper.

Add the almond flour, stirring to make a cohesive dough.

Place the dough onto a sheet of parchment, or a piece of plastic wrap. Pat it out with your hands, and top with an additional piece of parchment or plastic wrap. Roll the dough out to about ⅛″ thickness; it should be about 10″ × 12″ or larger.

Remove the top paper, and use a pizza wheel or knife to cut 1″ squares. Move the cut crackers, along with their parchment, to the baking sheet. If you've used plastic wrap, spray the pan with nonstick baking spray, and transfer the crackers from the plastic to the pan.

Bake the crackers for 14 to 16 minutes, until they're light golden brown. The crackers around the perimeter will tend to brown more quickly, so transfer those to a cooling rack and return the pan to the oven to finish baking the remaining center crackers.

Cool the crackers completely before transferring them to an airtight bag for room-temperature storage.

VARIATIONS

CHEESE CRACKERS: Add ¼ teaspoon mustard powder, a dash of Tabasco or a pinch of cayenne pepper, and 1 cup (100g) finely grated cheese along with the egg, salt, and pepper.

SEEDY CRACKERS: Add 1 to 2 tablespoons (9g to 18g) sesame seeds, poppy seeds, or the seed blend of your choice along with the egg, salt, and pepper.

SPICY CRACKERS: Add 1½ teaspoons curry powder, plus ¼ teaspoon hot sauce (such as Sriracha or Tabasco) along with the egg, salt, and pepper for an extra kick.

CINNAMON SUGAR CRACKERS: Omit the black pepper, and sprinkle 2 table-spoons (25g) cinnamon sugar over the tops of the crackers before baking.

NUTRITION INFORMATION PER SERVING: **24 crackers, 30g**
140 cal | 13g fat | 6g protein | 3g complex carbohydrates | 1g sugar | 2g dietary fiber | 25mg cholesterol | 95mg sodium

THIN WHEAT CRACKERS

ABOUT 96 CRACKERS

These crisp, golden brown wheat crackers are much better than the ones you buy in the store. They owe their subtle nutty flavor to both whole wheat flour and sesame seeds.

1 cup (120g) unbleached pastry flour or unbleached all-purpose flour

1 cup (140g) whole wheat flour or white whole wheat flour

¼ cup (35g) sesame seeds

¼ cup (49g) sugar

½ teaspoon salt

4 tablespoons (½ stick, 56g) butter

scant ½ cup (105g) milk

coarse salt (optional)

Preheat the oven to 325°F.

In a large bowl, combine the flours, sesame seeds, sugar, and salt. Cut in the butter, then stir in the milk, adding just enough milk to form a workable dough.

Divide the dough into three pieces and roll it out ultra-thin, one piece at a time—1/16″, if you can manage it. Sprinkle with a bit of coarse salt, if desired, and use the rolling pin to press the salt into the dough.

Cut the dough into 1″ × 2″ rectangles. Transfer the crackers to baking sheets and bake for 20 to 25 minutes, until they begin to brown. Cool on a rack.

NUTRITION INFORMATION PER SERVING: **9 crackers, 50g**
148 cal | 5g fat | 3g protein | 21g complex carbohydrates | 5g sugar | 2g dietary fiber | 14mg cholesterol | 114mg sodium

WINE BISCUITS

ABOUT 32 BISCUITS

These sweet, peppery-hot biscuits are a variation on a traditional Italian favorite, *biscotti di vino*: hard, semisweet biscuits served with an after-dinner cheese, or as a pre-dinner aperitif. Enjoy them with a glass of sangria and you won't be sorry! The term "biscuit," as it's used here, refers to a hard, fairly dense cracker-type bread rather than the flaky, buttery bread variety.

2½ cups (300g) unbleached all-purpose flour

2 teaspoons coarsely ground black pepper

4 to 6 tablespoons (50g to 70g) sugar, to taste*

1 teaspoon salt

2 teaspoons baking powder

½ cup plus 2 tablespoons (140g) dry red wine

¼ cup (50g) vegetable oil

In a medium bowl, combine the flour, pepper, sugar, salt, and baking powder. In a separate bowl, whisk together the wine and vegetable oil. Add the liquid ingredients to the dry ingredients and beat vigorously until the mixture is smooth, about 1 minute. Cover the bowl and refrigerate the dough for at least 1 hour, or overnight.

Preheat the oven to 350°F.

These biscuits are traditionally shaped into a round, mini-bagel shape, but we found that they were more appealing when cut into shapes with a cutter out of rolled ½″ thick dough. If you want to make the more traditional shape, break off a piece of dough about the size of a walnut (about 20g) and roll it into a ball. Poke a hole in the middle of the ball to make a small bagel-shaped biscuit. Place it on a lightly greased or parchment-lined baking sheet. Repeat with the remaining dough.

Bake the biscuits for 35 to 40 minutes, or until they're golden brown (they'll actually look a bit purple from the red wine). Remove them from the oven and cool completely on a rack.

* The greater amount of sugar will make a biscuit that is just about as sweet as a cookie; the lesser amount will yield a more savory type of biscuit.

NUTRITION INFORMATION PER SERVING: 1 biscuit, 20g

72 cal | 3.3g fat | 1g protein | 7g complex carbohydrates | 2g sugar | 0g dietary fiber | 0mg cholesterol | 94mg sodium

CRISP SEEDED MEGA-CRACKERS

8 LARGE CRACKERS

We truly believe that if the four food groups consisted of chips, dips, crackers, and cheese, many people could die happy. From good old sour cream onion dip and rippled chips to a luscious St. André triple-crème cheese spread on a crostini, the combination of salty and savory and creamy and crisp is unbeatable. The following recipe makes snapping-crisp, saucer-size crackers that look lovely presented in a bread basket. (You can easily swap other small seeds for the sesame seeds.) We thank author Lora Brody, a fellow snack lover, for the inspiration behind these crackers.

3 cups (360g) unbleached all-purpose flour

1¼ teaspoons salt

½ teaspoon baking powder

⅔ cup (95g) toasted sesame seeds

1 teaspoon freshly ground black pepper

2 tablespoons (21g) olive oil

1 cup (224g) water, cool

In a medium bowl, whisk together the flour, salt, baking powder, seeds, and pepper. Stir in the olive oil, mixing thoroughly, then add the water, tossing with a fork until the dough becomes cohesive. Turn out the dough onto a lightly floured surface and knead and turn it over a few times to smooth it out. Divide the dough into eight pieces and allow them to rest, covered, for 15 minutes.

Preheat the oven to 450°F. If you have a baking stone, be sure to use it; it will make the crispest crackers.

Roll one or two pieces of dough (as many as will fit on your baking stone at once) as thin as possible; you'll make rounds 8˝ to 9˝ across. Using a peel or giant spatula, transfer the rounds to the stone and bake them for about 4 minutes, then flip them over and bake about 2 minutes on the second side, until they're golden brown on both sides.

If you don't have a baking stone, bake these on a lightly greased or parchment-lined baking sheet set on the middle rack of your oven; they'll take about 6 minutes on the first side, 4 minutes on the second. Remove the crackers from the oven as soon as they're brown and transfer them to a rack to cool. Repeat with the remaining dough rounds. Store crackers airtight.

NUTRITION INFORMATION PER SERVING: 1 cracker, 77g
254 cal | 9g fat | 7g protein | 36g complex carbohydrates | 0g sugar | 3g dietary fiber | 0mg cholesterol | 365mg sodium

Flatbreads

When you think flatbread, think big. Flatbreads take many forms, but they're often round—sometimes thin, sometimes soft and flexible (tortillas), sometimes crackly-crisp (crackerbread or crisp bread), sometimes sturdy enough to support a large helping of dip or cheese. Here we've included only those breads that are unleavened; leavened with a chemical leavener, like baking powder; or leavened just barely with yeast so that they remain flat.

Flatbreads, being much quicker and easier to make than yeast breads, are found all around the world in many different forms, from Ethiopia's *injera* (a soft, naturally leavened bread using teff flour) to Norway's *flatbrod* (a hard and crisp whole grain round) to China's *moo shu* pancakes. We'll just dip our toe into the waters here, examining some of the many delicious and beloved flatbreads that exist.

CARTA DI MUSICA

12 FLATBREADS

Also known as Sardinian parchment bread, this bread's colorful name comes from the dough, which is supposed to be rolled so thinly that you can read sheet music through it. It is best baked on a baking stone, where it crisps up beautifully. Carta di musica is the perfect vehicle for anything from roasted garlic to spoonfuls of caponata.

2 cups (240g) unbleached all-purpose flour	1¼ cups (284g) water
1 cup (161g) semolina	olive oil, for brushing
1½ teaspoons salt	2 teaspoons fresh rosemary (optional)

Preheat the oven for at least 40 minutes at 450°F; if you have a baking stone, put it in the oven before preheating. If working without a baking stone, preheat a baking sheet by putting it in the oven for 10 minutes so the breads are placed on a hot surface.

In a large bowl, whisk together the flours and the salt. Slowly add the water, stirring with a wooden spoon or dough whisk until the mixture forms a soft dough—all of the water may not be necessary. Knead the dough with your hands to form a ball. Place on a lightly floured work surface and knead until the dough is firm and smooth, but not sticky. Divide the dough evenly into twelve balls. Place the balls on a lightly floured surface. Flatten each ball into a 4″ round. Cover and let rest for 15 minutes. After dough has rested, generously flour the work surface and roll each portion of the dough as thin as possible into an 8″ or 9″ round.

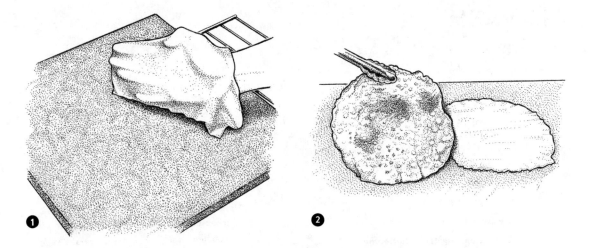

1. Carefully drape the rolled carta di musica over your hand, and place on the baking stone. **2.** The cooked, crisp carta di musica, left, and an unbaked piece on the right.

Place several rounds of dough on an ungreased baking sheet and place in the oven, or transfer to a baking stone using a baker's peel. Bake until the top of the bread is firm and lightly browned, 3 to 4 minutes. Turn the rounds over and bake until the other side is slightly browned. Transfer the bread to a rack to cool. Brush with olive oil and sprinkle with salt and rosemary, if using.

NUTRITION INFORMATION PER SERVING: **1 flatbread, 59g**
117 cal | 0g fat | 4g protein | 24g complex carbohydrates | 0g sugar | 1g dietary fiber | 0mg cholesterol | 267mg sodium

LAVASH

4 SHEETS

This easy-to-make unleavened bread is quite simple in both technique and ingredient list, which makes it an excellent go-to recipe for bakers of all levels. It is the ideal complement to any kind of spread, from soft butter to smoked salmon and cream cheese.

3½ cups (420g) unbleached all-purpose flour

1½ teaspoons salt

¾ teaspoon sugar

¼ cup (50g) vegetable shortening

1 large egg

1 cup (227g) milk

½ cup (70g) sesame seeds, toasted, or a combination of any small seeds you like

In a large bowl, whisk together the flour, salt, and sugar. Cut in shortening. Beat the egg and milk together and stir into the flour mixture, mixing well. The dough will be firm. Cover and let it rest for 30 minutes.

Preheat the oven to 375°F.

Divide dough into four pieces and roll each to ¹⁄₁₆″ thickness on the back of a lightly greased baking sheet or on a piece of parchment paper. Brush the lavash with water and sprinkle the tops with seeds. Go over the dough once more, lightly, to press the seeds into the surface. Bake for 12 to 15 minutes, until browned and crisp. Break into pieces and serve.

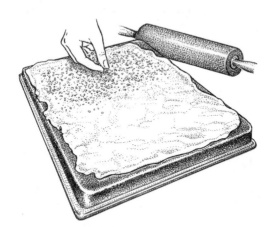

The dough can most easily be rolled thin on the back of a greased baking sheet. Brush with water, then sprinkle the top with seeds.

NUTRITION INFORMATION PER SERVING: ⅛ sheet, 19g

73 cal | 3g fat | 2g protein | 10g complex carbohydrates | 0g sugar | 1g dietary fiber | 7mg cholesterol | 116mg sodium

SEEDED CRACKERBREAD

3 PANS CRACKERBREAD

Crackerbread, an extra-thin focaccia type of loaf, is easy to make, bakes quickly, and can be broken up by hand into serving-size pieces at the table. Eat it with a meal or just grab pieces of it as a snack or with drinks; this is an all-purpose bread.

2½ teaspoons instant yeast

1½ cups (336g) water, lukewarm (110°F)

5 cups (600g) unbleached all-purpose flour

1 tablespoon (12g) sugar

1 tablespoon (18g) salt

1 tablespoon (13g) olive oil

¼ to ⅓ cup (35g to 46g) sesame or poppy seeds

coarsely ground pepper and salt, for sprinkling

Stir together yeast, water, flour, sugar, and salt. Knead them to form a smooth dough and place in a large greased bowl, turning to coat all over with oil. Cover it and let rise for 1 hour, or until nicely puffed.

Punch down the dough, shape into a ball, and let rest for 10 minutes. In the meantime, lightly oil the bottom of three half-sheet pans (13″ × 18″).

Divide dough into thirds. Take one third, place it on the bottom of a half-sheet pan, and roll it out as thin as you can; it should be ¹⁄₁₆″ or less. If dough resists rolling and keeps springing back, let it rest for 5 or 10 minutes, then start again. Dough should cover entire bottom of pan.

Preheat the oven to 450°F.

Lightly brush dough with oil and sprinkle with sesame or poppy seeds and coarsely ground pepper and salt, if desired. Bake for 7 to 10 minutes, until bread is very brown. Remove it from the oven and let cool; bread will become crisp as it cools, and is actually better 24 hours after you bake it.

NOTE: Any type of large flat pan will work here. You want a large enough pan—or enough smaller pans—to be able to roll the dough very thin. Since this bread bakes so quickly, you can do the whole thing using only one pan; it will simply take longer.

NUTRITION INFORMATION PER SERVING: ¹⁄₁₂ pan, 28g

66 cal | 1g fat | 2g protein | 12g complex carbohydrates | 0g sugar | 1g dietary fiber | 0mg cholesterol | 178mg sodium

SESAME CRISPS

8 CRISPS

Crisp and crunchy, nutty with the taste of sesame, these oversized ultra-thin crackers are one of our very favorite options for hors d'oeuvres. Using 00 or pastry flour creates a mellow, easy-to-roll dough.

1½ cups (168g) 00 flour or pastry flour	2 tablespoons (25g) olive oil
¾ teaspoon salt	½ cup (70g) toasted sesame seeds
⅓ cup (77g) water	sesame or garlic oil, for brushing

Combine all the ingredients to make a stiff dough. You can do this by hand, with the help of an electric mixer, or in a bread machine set on the manual cycle. Knead the dough for a minute or less; you don't need to develop the gluten—just make sure all the ingredients are thoroughly combined. Shape the dough into a flattened ball, cover it with plastic wrap, and set it aside to rest and relax at room temperature for 15 minutes.

Divide the dough into 8 equal pieces, each about the size of a golf ball (35g to 42g). Roll each piece into a ball, then flatten the balls. Cover them and let rest for 15 minutes.

Preheat the oven to 425°F. If you have a baking stone, place it on the floor of your gas oven, or on the lowest rack of your electric oven. If you don't have a baking stone, place a baking sheet on the lowest rack of the oven.

Transfer the dough to a lightly greased work surface. Working with one piece at a time, roll the dough into a thin 6″ circle. Set the circle aside and continue rolling the dough until you've got eight thin rounds.

Working quickly, pick up two pieces of dough and gently toss them onto the baking stone or baking sheet, making sure they lie flat. Close the oven door and bake for 3 minutes. Using a spatula or tongs, turn the rounds over and bake for 3 minutes on the other side, until the rounds are a light golden brown around the edges. (Check them after 2 to 2½ minutes to be sure they're not too brown; they can burn quickly.) Remove the crisps from the oven and quickly spray or brush them with sesame or garlic oil. Place on a rack to cool. Repeat with the remaining rounds. Eat immediately, or store in an airtight container.

NUTRITION INFORMATION PER SERVING: 1 crisp, 44g

145 cal | 6.6g fat | 3g protein | 18g complex carbohydrates | 0g sugar | 1g dietary fiber | 0mg cholesterol | 201mg sodium

Wraps and Tortillas

The wrap is nothing more than a variation on the traditional flour tortilla. Spinach powder, tomato powder, or a pinch of turmeric will add brilliant color and great flavor to wraps; you may also choose to turn a plain wrap or tortilla into one flavored with cheese, or herbs and spices, or garlic.

Wraps are an ideal vehicle for sandwich fillings. Just pile the filling onto the wrap, tuck in the ends, and roll it up. Flour tortillas can become burritos, and corn tortillas tacos, using the same technique.

PICNIC WRAPS

8 WRAPS

This thin, flexible bread is designed to be soft yet sturdy enough to stuff it full of hearty ingredients. By folding over the ends before rolling, the wrap is sealed to ensure safe transport to the sylvan picnic spot of your choice.

2 cups (240g) unbleached bread flour

3 tablespoons (28g) vegetable oil

½ to ¾ cup (112g to 168g) water

½ teaspoon salt

In a medium bowl, mix together the flour and oil. Gradually mix in the water and salt. Knead briefly, just until the dough is smooth.

1. A picnic wrap is pictured on the right; on the left is Soft Wrap Bread (page 132). **2.** Dry-frying the wrap will give it a freckled appearance. It should be ready to turn after 45 seconds of cooking on the first side.

Divide the dough into 8 equal pieces. Round them into balls, flatten slightly, and let them rest, covered, for at least 30 minutes.

Preheat an ungreased heavy frying pan over medium heat. Working with one piece of dough at a time, roll it out until it's about 8˝ in diameter. Fry the wrap for about 45 seconds on each side until it's a mottled brown. Cool and store in an airtight container.

NUTRITION INFORMATION PER SERVING: 1 wrap, 59g
170cal | 6g fat | 4g protein | 25g complex carbohydrates | 0g sugar | 1g dietary fiber | 0mg cholesterol | 134mg sodium

ROTI

8 ROTI

The world of Indian flatbreads is huge and varied, representing a host of cultures. Roti is just one of the many—the term *roti* is used to refer both generally to all of India's griddle-baked flatbreads collectively or specifically to either an unleavened, whole wheat bread within that category or a white flour, leavened, fat-enriched bread. We chose the latter to showcase here. Serve it as part of an Indian meal, of course, but also consider using it as a wrap, especially hot from the griddle.

3 cups (360g) unbleached all-purpose flour

1½ teaspoons baking powder

1 teaspoon salt

2 tablespoons (25g) vegetable oil

¾ to 1 cup (168g to 224g) water

In a large bowl, whisk together the flour, baking powder, and salt. Add the oil and enough water to form a dough that is soft but not sticky. Let rest for 30 minutes, then cut the dough into 8 equal pieces. Roll the dough into balls, then cover and let rest for 5 minutes. Roll out each piece on a floured board to make a 6˝ to 8˝ disk.

Heat a griddle over medium heat. Brush the griddle with oil, then brush the roti disks with oil on both sides. Place the roti on the griddle and cook until the top starts to blister. Flip roti and cook for 1 minute more. Serve warm, or cool completely and use as a wrap.

NUTRITION INFORMATION PER SERVING: 1 roti, 75g
180 cal | 4g fat | 4g protein | 32g complex carbohydrates | 0g sugar | 1g dietary fiber | 0mg cholesterol | 461mg sodium

SOFT CORNMEAL WRAPS

10 WRAPS

Just as tortillas often come in plain flour and cornmeal versions, so do our favorite wraps. Cornmeal adds a delicate golden color and a subtle hint of sweetness to these tender, pliable breads.

2 cups (240g) unbleached all-purpose flour

1 cup (137g) yellow cornmeal

1 teaspoon baking powder

1 teaspoon salt

¼ teaspoon instant yeast

2 tablespoons (18g) nonfat dry milk

2 tablespoons (21g) butter

1 cup (224g) water

In a medium bowl, mix together all the dry ingredients, then cut in the butter. Gradually mix in the water. Knead briefly, just until the dough is smooth.

Divide the dough into 10 pieces, weighing about 55g each. Round them into balls, flatten slightly, and let them rest, covered, for at least 30 minutes. This resting period improves the texture of the dough by giving the flour time to absorb the water, and it also gives the gluten time to relax, making the wraps easier to roll out.

Preheat an ungreased cast iron griddle or heavy frying pan over medium heat. Working with one piece of dough at a time (keep the remaining dough balls covered), roll out the balls until they're about 8″ in diameter. Fry the wraps in the ungreased pan for about 45 seconds on each side. (Or use a tortilla press.) Stack wraps on top of one another as you fry them to keep them soft and pliable. Serve warm or at room temperature. Store, tightly wrapped, in a plastic bag at room temperature. To store them longer than a few days, freeze them.

NUTRITION INFORMATION PER SERVING: 1 wrap, 55g

151 cal | 3g fat | 4g protein | 27g complex carbohydrates | 0g sugar | 2g dietary fiber | 0mg cholesterol | 275mg sodium

SOFT WRAP BREAD

8 BREADS

We use a rather unusual method to make this bread: boiling water is added to the flour, "cooking" the starch and making the resultant dough soft and easy to roll out. In addition, precooking the starch this way eliminates any possibility of a starchy taste in the final bread; all in all, we find these wrap-like rounds better tasting than conventional flour tortillas or other wraps. In texture, they're thicker and sturdier than a tortilla—and more like a pita bread. If you like the bread in your sandwich to be a substantial part of the whole, this is a good recipe for you.

3 to 3¼ cups (360g to 390g)
    unbleached all-purpose flour

1½ cups (336g) boiling water

¼ cup (42g) potato flour or ½ cup (43g)
    potato flakes

1¼ teaspoons salt

2 tablespoons (25g) vegetable oil

1 teaspoon instant yeast*

Place 2 cups (240g) of the flour in a bowl. Pour the boiling water over the flour and stir until smooth. Cover the bowl and set aside to cool the mixture for 30 minutes.

In a separate bowl, whisk together the potato flour and 1 cup (120g) of the remaining flour with the salt, oil, and yeast. Add this to the cooled flour/water mixture, stir, then knead for several minutes (by hand or mixer) to form a soft dough. The dough should form a ball, but will remain somewhat sticky. Add additional flour only if necessary; if kneading by hand, keep your hands and work surface lightly oiled. Place the dough in a greased bowl and let it rise, covered, for 1 hour.

Divide the dough into 8 pieces (about 84g each), cover, and let rest for 15 to 30 minutes. Roll each piece into a 7˝ to 8˝ circle and dry-fry them (fry without oil) over medium-high heat for 1 to 2 minutes per side, until they're puffed and flecked with brown spots. Adjust the heat if they seem to be cooking either too quickly or too slowly; cooking too quickly means they may be raw in the center, while too slowly will dry them out. Transfer the cooked breads to a rack, stacking them to keep them soft. Serve immediately, or cool slightly before storing in a plastic bag.

* This recipe works best with instant yeast because it dissolves during the kneading process, so you don't have to knead liquid into the dough. If you prefer to use active dry yeast, use only 1 cup boiling water for the initial dough, dissolve the yeast in ¼ cup warm water, and add this mixture to the dough along with the potato flour mixture. It'll be somewhat slippery at first, but will knead in and eventually become smooth.

NUTRITION INFORMATION PER SERVING: 1 bread, 98g

202 cal | 4g fat | 5g protein | 36g complex carbohydrates | 0g sugar | 2g dietary fiber | 0mg cholesterol | 336mg sodium

THIN CORNMEAL TORTILLAS

10 TORTILLAS

The following is a classic tortilla in texture: wafer-thin and pliable. However, it includes both flour and cornmeal, something a true tortilla would never do. We just happen to love the delicate sweetness that cornmeal adds.

1⅓ cups (160g) unbleached all-purpose flour

⅔ cup (91g) yellow cornmeal

¼ cup (50g) vegetable oil

½ cup plus 1 tablespoon (126g) water

½ teaspoon salt

In a medium bowl, mix together the flour, cornmeal, and oil. Gradually mix in the water and salt. Knead briefly, just until the dough is smooth.

Divide the dough into 10 pieces, weighing about 36g each. Round the pieces into balls, flatten them slightly, and let them rest, covered, for at least 30 minutes. This resting period improves the texture of the dough by giving the flour time to absorb the water, and it also gives the gluten time to relax, making the tortillas easier to roll out.

Preheat an ungreased cast iron griddle or heavy frying pan over medium heat. Working with one piece of dough at a time (keep the remaining dough balls covered), roll out each ball until about 8″ in diameter. Fry the tortillas in the ungreased pan for about 45 seconds on each side (or use a tortilla press). Stack tortillas on top of one another as you remove them from the pan, to keep them soft and pliable. Serve warm or at room temperature. Store, tightly wrapped, in a plastic bag at room temperature. To store tortillas longer than a few days, freeze them.

NUTRITION INFORMATION PER SERVING: 1 tortilla, 36g
130 cal | 6g fat | 2g protein | 17g complex carbohydrates | 0g sugar | 1g dietary fiber | 0mg cholesterol | 110mg sodium

CHAPTER FIVE

Yeast Breads

——

BREAD IS ONE OF THE FIRST FOODS of which we have a written record. It fills the stomach and tastes wonderful. Our earliest food memories probably include bread in some incarnation; it follows us through life like a constant friend, happy to stay in the background, but always present. Is there a better example of comfort food than warm bread and butter?

In years gone by, home bakers universally made bread at home. These days it's much more rare, as cookies, muffins, and other sweet treats have taken center stage in the kitchen of the modern baker.

But the plain truth is, here at King Arthur we find yeast bread easier to make than cake or biscuits or pie. Yes, it takes longer, but unlike other baked goods, its schedule is flexible. Start it in the morning, finish it at night; speed it up in a warm oven, slow it down in the refrigerator. It will happily bend itself to your agenda. And with the easy access most of us have to time-saving appliances— stand mixers, food processors, and so on—even the vigorous 10 minutes or so of required kneading can be taken out of your hands, quite literally. Good homemade bread is a goal any baker can easily achieve.

And what a broad landscape lies before us! Yeast bread is open to all kinds of variations. Even just among the categories of white, whole wheat, rye, and whole grain, there are myriad variations on each of those themes, ranging from white sandwich bread to crusty baguettes, light sandwich rye to raisin pumpernickel, and honey oatmeal bread to 10-grain loaf. And what's fascinating is, even when you've drilled right down to, say, rye bread, there's still not just one "right" recipe. You can use light, medium, or dark rye flour, or pumpernickel; add caraway, mustard, fennel or anise seeds; begin with a starter, or add pickle juice or sauerkraut; shape it into a sandwich loaf or a buxom round.

Join us as we explore the wonderful world of bread. You'll be helping to carry on a piece of the world's culture that's as ancient as the first tilled fields and as welcoming as a piece of warm buttered toast.

SEASONS OF CHANGE

Flour is porous, like a sponge. When the air around it is dry, flour will be dry. When the air is humid, flour will absorb the moisture in it. Just as a dry sponge can soak up more water than a wet sponge, so can dry flour. You'll find that during cold, dry months you'll often need more liquid when making a dough, and in hot, humid months, a bit less. Find a dough consistency that works well for you, then snap a mental picture of it; that's the consistency you're after all year long, no matter how the balance of ingredients may change.

You'll also find that, on rainy or stormy days (great days for baking anyway), when the barometric pressure is low, your bread will rise more quickly than it does ordinarily. This is because the dough doesn't have as much air to push against it; the air is not as dense or heavy as it is on clear days.

FITTING BREAD INTO YOUR SCHEDULE

The amount of yeast you use in your bread dough has a significant bearing on how quickly it will rise, and thus on your own schedule. By reducing the yeast, you ensure a long, slow rise rather than a series of quick rises and resultant falls.

You can reduce the yeast in most types of bread recipes (sweet breads being the exception) to produce a dough that will rise slowly over a long period of time, rather than one that rises for an hour in the bowl and half an hour in the pan before baking. This long rise is often much more convenient than the regular, short-rise method. In recipes calling for a packet of yeast (2¼ teaspoons), we recommend cutting the amount back to ½ to 1 teaspoon of instant yeast, depending on how long you want to let the dough ferment before the final shape-rise-bake process; ½ teaspoon would give you lots of flexibility, such as letting the dough rest for 16 to 20 hours; 1 teaspoon would be a good amount for an all-day or overnight rise (10 hours or so, at cool room temperature). If you're using active dry yeast, which isn't as vigorous as instant yeast, we'd up the range to ¾ to 1½ teaspoons.

The easiest, safest dough to subject to a long, slow rise is one containing only a small amount of sugar, if any, and no dairy products (eggs, milk, butter, etc.). Sweet doughs are notoriously slow risers, anyway; by cutting back on the yeast, you're just slowing them down even more. Sweet doughs are best slowed down by refrigeration, rather than reducing the amount of yeast. Also, doughs that contain dairy products (and shouldn't, for food safety reasons, be left at room temperature all day) should also be refrigerated if you want to slow them down.

Whole grain doughs are naturally slow-rising, due to the bran in the grain, which interferes with gluten development. If you'd like to slow down a familiar whole grain recipe, then do cut back on the yeast; if you're making a particular whole grain recipe for the first time, however, we recommend using the amount of yeast indicated and seeing just how long it takes the dough to rise fully. Often it takes longer than the directions say, and there's probably no need to slow things down even more.

Basic flour-water-yeast-salt doughs (which may also contain a bit of oil and/or sugar), such as those for baguettes, focaccia, and pizza, are the best candidates for an all-day countertop rise. Keep in mind, however, the vagaries of your own kitchen. If you bake bread all the time, your kitchen is full of wild yeast and any dough you make there will rise vigorously. If you seldom bake bread, or are just beginning, your kitchen will be quite "sterile"; your dough won't be aided by wild yeast and will rise more slowly than it would in a more "active" kitchen. We've found that here in our King Arthur kitchen, where we bake bread every day, we can cut the yeast back to ¹⁄₁₆ teaspoon in a 3-cup-of-flour recipe and get a good overnight rise. In a kitchen where bread is seldom baked, we needed ½ teaspoon of yeast to get the same effect. Use your judgment in rating your own kitchen as to "yeast friendliness."

Keep in mind, also, that this slow rise usually extends to the shaped loaf, as well as dough

(continued)

in the bowl. Once you've shaped your loaf, covered it, and set it aside to rise again, it may take 2 hours or more, rather than the usual 1 to 1½, to rise fully and be ready for the oven.

There's no hard-and-fast rule for the amount of yeast you should use in any particular recipe. It depends on how slow (or fast) you want the dough to rise; the composition of the dough itself (whole grain, sweet/dairy, or "straight"); and your kitchen. Be flexible and experiment; you'll soon discover the formula that will work just right for you, producing a ready-to-shape dough when you're ready to shape it.

————

HOW DOES YEAST WORK?

First, what is it? Yeast is a "thallophyte," a complete, smaller-than-we-can-see, one-celled fungus. Each cell is the same; that is, as they grow, they don't become differentiated to form more complex organisms like plants or animals. The name for all strains of bakers' yeast (with the exception of sourdough or wild yeast) is *Saccharomyces cerevisiae*.

The tiny pellets you see in a container of dried yeast are not single yeast cells, but agglomerations of many cells. It takes about 25 billion of them to make a gram (½₈ of an ounce). One yeast cell may be tiny, but in huge numbers they can certainly make their presence known— primarily by their waste products, which are very valuable to the baker. The most important waste products are carbon dioxide, which leavens bread; alcohol, which contributes to the bread's aroma; and organic acids, which give it flavor.

A mixture of flour and water creates one of the most favorable living conditions for yeast. It provides a good source of the carbohydrates and other minerals that yeast needs for nourishment. But beyond this, yeast also needs proper hydration, the right temperature, and an appropriate pH.

What are the optimum living conditions for yeast? The temperature should be in the range of 75°F to 90°F, although a dough can stray somewhat above or below these temperatures without undue effect.

If actively fermenting yeast is too cold for too long, the yeast cells slowly die. Thus, if you freeze a dough, it will remain viable only for a couple of months. On the other hand, yeast that is dormant, or not actively fermenting, can remain in the freezer (above 0°F, and not self-defrosting) for years at a time.

Yeast also needs access to the sugars and minerals in dough, and while it ultimately has the ability to break these down itself, bakers sometimes add a small amount of sugar to start the process. In addition, the pH of the liquid plays an important role. Soft (alkaline) water is relatively free of minerals. Because yeast has its own characteristic mineral content, it wants a growing medium that's similar. So it doesn't like soft water. Hard (acidic) water, on the other hand, contains lots of minerals and yeast will grow very quickly when it has access to such abundance. A small amount of ascorbic acid (vitamin C) can help correct water that is too soft. Slightly more yeast can help overcome water that is too hard.

Primer: How to Make a Loaf of Bread

In simplest terms, bread is a combination of flour, yeast, and water. Most bakers add salt, and from there the list of ingredients can grow in direct proportion to the baker's imagination. It's the basic ingredients you use, however, and how you treat them that makes or breaks your loaf of bread.

Start with the Flour

Flour is the dominant ingredient in bread, and thus carries much of the responsibility for its success or failure. While bread can be made from most any flour, the majority of yeast-leavened breads are most successfully made with a medium-to-high protein wheat-based flour. That means all-purpose or bread flour; the protein level on the side of the bag should read 3g to 4g per ¼-cup serving.

YEAST: ACTIVE DRY VS. INSTANT

You may substitute active dry yeast for the instant yeast called for in our recipes without making any changes in the amount; if the recipe calls for 2 teaspoons of instant yeast, use 2 teaspoons of active dry yeast.

While there's no need to dissolve active dry yeast before using it, you may still want to "proof" it to make sure it's healthy. Dissolve the yeast in a few tablespoons of the liquid in your recipe, along with a half teaspoon or so of sugar, or a tablespoon of flour. Wait 10 to 15 minutes; if you don't see any activity (small bubbles forming), try some newer yeast. If the yeast is active and producing bubbles, add the liquid mixture along with the other liquid ingredients.

Active dry yeast is a little bit slower off the mark than instant, as far as dough rising goes; but in a long (2- to 3-hour) rise, the active dry yeast catches up. If a recipe using instant yeast calls for the dough to "double in size, about 1 hour," you may want to mentally add 15 to 20 minutes to this time if you're using active dry yeast. When dough is rising, you need to judge it by how much it's risen, not how long it takes; cold weather, low barometric pressure, how often you bake, and a host of other factors affect dough rising times, so use them as a guide, not an unbreakable rule. Remember, bread-baking involves living things (yeast), your own personal touch in kneading technique, and the atmosphere of your kitchen. There are so many variables that it's impossible to say that "dough X will double in size in 60 minutes." Baking with yeast is a combination of art, science, and a bit of magic; stay flexible, and your bread will be just fine.

Flour can vary from region to region and season to season; just as a particular type of grape doesn't always produce the exact same kind of wine, the particular wheats used to make all-purpose and bread flour may produce a slightly different product from one growing season to the next. It's up to the flour manufacturer to ensure that the flour remains as consistent as possible; here at the King Arthur Baking Company, we have very high specification standards. It's up to you to discover which brand of flour works best for you.

Bread bakers rely on wheat flour because of its ability to form gluten. (For more information on wheat, flour, and gluten, see pages 452–461.) The protein in wheat flour, when combined with a liquid, forms long strands called gluten. These strands become elastic when you knead the dough; they're responsible for the final high-rising shape your bread assumes as it bakes. Other flours—rye, oat, corn—contain minimal amounts, if any, of this gluten; thus breads made with them alone won't be able to rise very high.

Combine It with Yeast, Any Other Dry Ingredients, and Liquid

Mix the yeast, salt, and sugar (if you're using it) into the flour. Once you combine the flour in your recipe with liquid, gluten starts to form. You'll notice that the dough starts to become cohesive very quickly; before you know it, it's following your spoon around the bowl (or the dough hook around the mixer). At this point—just as the dough has barely come together and is still extremely rough-looking—one option you have is to give the dough a 20-minute rest. This rest (called an autolyse by French bread bakers) allows the flour to absorb the liquid fully, making it easier to knead, and less likely that you'll make the mistake of adding too much flour as you go along. This step isn't crucial and can be skipped if you're in a hurry.

WHEN TO ADD THE SALT

There's much disagreement among professional bread bakers (and among ourselves—see page 228) about when to add salt to the dough, with the discussion centering on the preferred order of certain chemical reactions. Our preference is to combine all the basic dry ingredients with the flour—salt, sugar, instant yeast—and then to add the liquid. We don't feel it makes a discernible difference to hold the salt out until after the autolyse; and frankly, if we don't add it right at the beginning, we sometimes forget to add it at all—not a good thing!

A LITTLE SWEET, A LITTLE SALT

Can you make bread without sugar or salt? Sure. But keep the following points in mind.

- It won't taste very good. Both sugar and salt are flavor enhancers. Without salt in particular, your bread will taste flat. Cardboard is the best descriptor for saltless bread.
- It will rise very quickly. Both salt and sugar tend to temper the yeast's growth, allowing it to occur in a calm, regular manner. Without this tempering, the yeast grows very quickly and the dough rises too fast, without the chance to develop flavor.
- It may collapse. Both salt and organic acids, developed over a long, slow fermentation (rise), help strengthen the gluten in your loaf, allowing it to hold its shape until the hot oven does its job. Without them, your loaf is likely to rise and then collapse.

TOO MUCH SWEET, TOO MUCH SALT

If a little salt is good for your bread dough, is a lot even better? No. Too much salt attracts water in the dough, robbing the yeast of the liquid it needs to do its job. Sugar acts similarly; an "overdose" of sugar also coaxes your yeast to "overeat," resulting in yeast that acts like you do after Thanksgiving dinner: tired and lethargic.

We find that for a typical 3-cup-flour recipe, 1½ teaspoons salt and up to ¼ cup sugar won't result in any slowdown. More than that, you're tempting fate. To add more sugar for a sweeter bread, you may choose yeast that's designed specifically for sweet breads, or you may choose to increase the amount of yeast and give the dough a much longer window in which to rise.

Add the Remaining Ingredients

Now it's time to add any other ingredients you're using: butter or oil, eggs, whole grains, flavorings, or whatever your recipe calls for. The only ingredient you don't want to add at this point would be dried fruit or any other sweet add-in; sugar may leach from these ingredients into the surrounding dough, upsetting the sugar balance and slowing down the yeast. Combine thoroughly, using a mixer or your hands.

Time to Knead

Sprinkle your work surface with flour or spray with vegetable oil spray. Knead the dough until it's smooth and supple. It will become more and more elastic as you develop the gluten, until eventually it should feel like a baby's bottom—soft but springy. Take a break at about the 5-minute mark; giving the dough a 5-minute rest at this point allows the gluten to relax, making the remaining kneading a lot easier.

If you live in snow country, it's fairly certain your house will be a bit cool for optimum dough rising during the winter. There are a number of things you can do to help yeast remain warm and happily multiplying. First, seek out the naturally warm areas of your house, which may include the top of the water heater or the top of the refrigerator. Cover the top of your bowl of dough with lightly greased plastic wrap, wrap the bowl in a large dish towel or not-too-thick bath towel, and set it in this warm place. If you have a wood stove, any area near and above the stove (heat rises), such as a bookshelf, will be ideal. Ditto a radiator or hot air vent.

Second, for a more reliable, controllable source of heat, set a heating pad on low, swaddle it in a towel, and set your covered bowl on top. We've known a lot of bakers who've had great luck with this method. Or try this: Put your bowl of dough into the oven and turn on the oven light. Just the heat of the lightbulb(s) alone will warm the oven nicely. We've also heard of bakers setting their covered bowl of rising dough in a dishwasher that's just completed its cycle.

You can also make a temporary proofing box (a box for raising bread dough) out of a chest-type cooler. Put a cooling rack in the bottom of the cooler, then preheat the cooler by pouring a couple of cups of boiling water into it and shutting the lid. When your dough is ready, quickly open the top of the cooler, put in the bowl of dough, and shut the lid; the dough stays warm and moist and rises very nicely. If you're looking at a long rise, add another cup of boiling water every hour or so.

The First Rise

Put the kneaded dough into a lightly greased bowl or dough-rising bucket (see Tools, page 532) with a capacity two to three times the size of the dough. Cover the bowl with plastic wrap and let the dough rise, at warm room temperature (70°F to 80°F), until it's doubled in bulk or looks like the recipe tells you it should; not all doughs will double in bulk during this first rise.

Shaping

Pick the dough up out of the bowl and squeeze it gently to deflate it. Forget all that stuff you might have heard about punching down the dough or slamming it onto the counter. All this rough treatment does is (a) excite the gluten so that it becomes tough and resistant to shaping, and (b) drive the air out of the dough—those same gases you're counting on to make a tall, light loaf. So treat it gently.

Now it's up to you (and the recipe) to decide which shape your bread will take. A sandwich loaf? Baguette? Cloverleaf rolls? Pizza? Work on a lightly greased work surface to divide and/or shape the dough as the recipe directs.

The Second Rise

Most breads rise again once they're shaped. An exception would be ultra-flat breads, such as a thin-crust pizza or very thin flatbreads. Cover the shaped dough with thoroughly greased plastic wrap, a cake cover (for a round pan of rolls), or any other sturdy cover wide enough to cover the pan and tall enough for the dough to rise.

Again, your recipe will tell you how the dough should look at the end of its second rise. Sometimes dough needs to double; sometimes, for extra-light breads (such as ciabatta), it should at least triple. Sometimes it needs to rise just a bit before going into the oven to complete its rise. Follow your recipe.

THE PERFECT LOAF

You can tell if your bread is done if a digital thermometer pushed into the center of the loaf reads 190°F. Dense, whole grain hearth loaves should be baked to about 200°F to 210°F. We've come to rely entirely on our digital thermometer, and no longer use the traditional tapping method.

However, if you don't have a thermometer and want to check your bread the classic way—by sound—here's what to do: When you feel the bread is done, remove it from the oven, take it out of the pan and, holding it in one hand, give it a few quick, hard taps on the bottom with your index or middle finger. A loaf that's done will sound hollow, like a drum. Tapping that sounds muffled or dull means the loaf needs a bit more baking time. If that's the case, there's no need to put it back into the pan; simply place it right on the rack of the oven.

If you have tough hands (baker's hands!), you can do this quickly and quite easily without the aid of a potholder or mitt. If your hands are too sensitive to use this method, use a mitt or potholder to hold the loaf while you tap it with your bare finger.

STORING YEAST

A vacuum-sealed bag of yeast stored at room temperature will remain fresh up to its best-by date. Once the seal is broken, it should go into the freezer for optimum shelf life. A vacuum-sealed bag of yeast stored at high temperatures, however—for example, in a hot kitchen over the summer, or in a hot warehouse before delivery—will fairly quickly lose its effectiveness. After a while, if stored improperly, yeast cells will slowly become inactive (die). If you aren't using your yeast fairly quickly (or even if you are), it's a good idea to keep it in an airtight container in the freezer. It will keep for quite long periods of time that way (years in the freezer, if your freezer isn't self-defrosting). If you think you got old yeast, take it back to the store and ask for a new batch. Any business worth its salt will certainly replace it.

Baking

In general, crusty hearth breads bake for a short amount of time at a high temperature: 425°F to 450°F or hotter. Soft sandwich loaves or sweet breads bake at a lower temperature (350°F to 375°F) for a longer amount of time. A hot, fast bake produces a crisp crust; a slower, cooler bake yields a more tender crust. An exception to this is large breads without much fat or sugar, such as round country loaves. These breads need a lower temperature and longer time in the oven in order to bake all the way through; in the process, their crust tends to become thick and chewy rather than tender or crispy.

What should you do if your bread appears to be perfectly browned, but it's not ready to come out of the oven according to the times given in the recipe? This sometimes happens with breads that are high in sugar (especially honey) or fat. If your bread appears to be browning too quickly, carefully lay a sheet of aluminum foil over it; this should slow down the browning enough that the center has a chance to finish before the outside burns.

The bread is done when its interior temperature registers between 190°F (for most loaves) and 210°F (for heavier, denser country-style loaves). Remove it from the oven and transfer it from its pan to a cooling rack as soon as possible. Cooling bread left in a pan will steam, making the crust rubbery. For extra-crisp bread, turn off the oven, remove the bread from the pan, and set the bread back on the oven rack. Prop the door open a couple of inches and allow the bread to cool in the oven. This prevents steam from migrating from the bread's center and condensing on its crust, which would tend to soften the crust.

WHICH SIZE PAN?

The most common cause of poorly shaped pan loaves is using the wrong size pan. A good rule of thumb is as follows: A recipe using 2¾ to 3 cups flour and about 1 cup liquid will make a loaf of approximately 1 pound, which will rise to a nice shape in an 8½″ × 4½″ bread pan. Such a recipe will also work in a 9″ × 5″ pan, but will make a somewhat flatter loaf; the optimal amount of flour for a 9″ × 5″ pan is 3½ to 4 cups. To make a 1½-pound loaf, which will rise nicely in a 10″ × 5″ pan, use approximately 4½ cups flour and 1½ cups liquid.

If you're using the correct amount of flour and right size pan, and you think your bread is too flat, try letting it rise twice in the bowl before shaping and baking. This second rise not only gives the yeast more of a chance to do its work, but also improves your bread's texture and flavor. Flat-topped bread may also indicate your dough needs more flour, due to summer humidity; a slack dough tends to be flatter on top.

Cool It!

Warning! Tempting though it may be, it's better to wait 10 to 15 minutes before cutting into your bread. Until it has a chance to set as it cools a bit, it's very tender. Cutting into bread at this point tends to mar its shape, as well as allow too much moisture to escape, which can result in it becoming stale more quickly.

Sandwich and Pan Loaves

Pan bread—the soft, rectangular sandwich loaf we grew up with—has gotten a bad rap as the popularity of crusty artisan-style loaves has increased. Well, this is a big world; there's room for more than one type of bread. For toast and French toast, sandwiches and grilled cheese, stuffing or bread pudding or croutons, nothing beats a good loaf of close-grained, tender white bread. Or its siblings—oatmeal, whole wheat, and rye.

But this familiar bread doesn't stand alone. The same type of dough can be rolled into balls, built into a loaf, and called monkey bread; it can be spread with filling and rolled, to make a swirl loaf; it can even be enriched with eggs and butter to become an alluring brioche. The thread that joins all these loaves is texture; soft and light, they're ideal for little ones, as well as any of us looking for a comforting slice of toast or a perfect sandwich.

WHITE BREAD 101

The name of this bread refers to its basic nature—making it is child's play and the result is a delicious, fine-textured loaf, perfect for toast or sandwiches (especially peanut butter and jelly). The nonfat dry milk and potato flakes might not be common ingredients in your pantry, but they're responsible for the exceptionally tender and soft texture of this loaf, and worth seeking out if terrific sandwich bread is your goal.

3 cups (360g) unbleached all-purpose flour

2 teaspoons instant yeast

1¼ teaspoons salt

3 tablespoons (35g) sugar

4 tablespoons (½ stick, 56g) butter, at room temperature

¼ cup (35g) nonfat dry milk

¼ cup (42g) potato flour or ⅓ cup (21g) potato flakes

1⅛ cups (252g) water, lukewarm

Combine all the ingredients and mix and knead them together until you've made a soft, smooth dough. Adjust the dough's consistency with additional flour or water as needed—but remember, the more flour you add while you're kneading, the heavier and drier your final loaf will be. Cover and let the dough rise for 1 hour, until it's puffy (though not necessarily doubled in bulk).

Transfer the dough to a lightly greased work surface and shape it into an 8˝ log. Transfer the log to a lightly greased 8½˝ × 4½˝ loaf pan, cover the pan, and let the bread rise until the outer edge has risen about 1˝ over the rim of the pan, about 1 hour.

Preheat the oven to 350°F.

Uncover the pan and bake the bread for 35 to 40 minutes, tenting it lightly with aluminum foil for the final 10 to 15 minutes if it appears to be browning too quickly.

Remove the bread from the oven, take it out of the pan, and place it on a rack to cool completely. Once the bread is cool, brush it with melted butter, if desired; this will give it a soft crust.

NUTRITION INFORMATION PER SERVING: 1 slice, 55g

129 cal | 3g fat | 3g protein | 19g complex carbohydrates | 2g sugar | 1g dietary fiber | 9mg cholesterol | 179mg sodium

HELP! MY BREAD . . .

. . . IS COARSE, DRY, AND CRUMBLY

There are several causes for dry bread—bread that won't hold together in a sandwich—but the number one culprit is usually too much flour.

When you're kneading bread, and it's sticking to your hands, it's always a temptation to add more flour. But an overdose of flour will cause the resulting bread to be coarse-grained, crumbly, and dry. There are several solutions. First, use a dough scraper when you first start to knead, scooping underneath the dough and flopping it over on itself as you gradually sprinkle flour onto the dough. This is easier than constantly scraping the dough off your fingers. Second, once dough gets to the point where it's fairly kneadable by hand—though still sticky—try spraying your work surface and hands with nonstick vegetable oil spray. This will help you handle the dough without adding more flour. Third, let the dough remain a bit sticky. Yes, it's harder to work with, but the resultant loaf will have a much nicer texture.

A coarse grain in bread can also occur when bread is baked at too low a temperature. We like to bake loaf bread at 350°F or 375°F, while baguettes and other free-form loaves are usually baked at 425°F or 450°F. Another way to ensure your bread will have a fine grain is to let it rise twice in the bowl, rather than just once; this will also give better flavor, as the longer the dough rises, the more flavorful the bread will be.

Another cause of coarse-grained or dry bread is a lack of sufficient mixing or kneading. When making your dough, try adding only about ⅓ the flour to the liquid ingredients at first, then beat for about 2 minutes with a spoon or mixer; this ensures everything is well mixed. Mix in the remaining flour, then knead. Dough should be kneaded a good 8 to 10 minutes, at least. If you get tired, give the dough a rest after 5 minutes; this rest not only benefits you, it helps the dough as well, as the developing gluten has a chance to relax, making any further kneading that much easier and more effective.

Finally, crumbly bread may be caused by too much fat in the dough. The right amount of fat in a recipe will prevent moisture loss and staling. Too much fat, however, will prevent the gluten strands in the flour from bonding properly—thus the crumbling.

. . . HAS A WRINKLED TOP CRUST

Wrinkling occurs for several reasons. First, if bread rises too much it will develop a thin layer of air under the crust. If, at the same time, the crust dries out as it rises—if the dough is covered with a dry cloth or insufficiently covered—when you put the bread in the oven to bake, the crust doesn't allow steam from the interior of the bread to escape as readily as it would if it were more moist and porous. Instead, the crust absorbs the moisture. Additionally, once you take the bread out of the oven the interior continues to cook, sending off steam, while the

(continued)

outer crust rapidly cools and contracts. This causes moisture to condense on its surface, and you have the perfect recipe for wrinkling.

There are two things you can try to avoid this. First, let the bread rise only three-quarters of the way to full, then put it in a cold oven, set the temperature, and go from there. Your bread will require an additional 10 minutes or so of baking time, but its gradual rising as the oven heats will help prevent the top crust from separating from the interior.

Second, when your bread is done, turn off the oven, crack open the door, and leave the loaf in the oven for an additional 10 minutes. Steam from the interior will have an easier time evaporating through the crust into the hot oven air. Because the crust remains hot, the steam won't condense on it.

One more hint: If you want to brush your finished loaf with butter, wait until it's cool; fat forms a seal when applied to a hot loaf, preventing steam from escaping.

. . . GETS STALE TOO QUICKLY

Storing bread is a many-faceted challenge. If you can eat it quickly enough, wrap the bread in plastic and keep it on the kitchen counter or in a bread box. Bread will keep well for several days up to perhaps a week, depending on the weather. (In extremely hot, humid weather, bread will mold quickly at room temperature; you'll have to freeze it.)

Staling happens most quickly at refrigerator temperature—about five times faster than at room temperature. So don't store bread or other baked goods in the refrigerator; they're much better off at room temperature or in the freezer.

By the way, the best way to store crunchy-crusted, country-type loaves—typically sourdough-based—is neither in the freezer nor wrapped at room temperature. Instead, store the bread, cut side down, on the counter. This keeps the outer crust crunchy and the inner bread soft.

Interestingly, you can reverse the staling process by reheating, which sends all the molecules spinning back into their just-out-of-the-oven physical alignment. Reheating stale bread (stale bread, not rock-hard, days-old bread) to 140°F, the temperature at which starch gelatinizes, will make stale bread soft again for a short period of time.

ENGLISH MUFFIN TOASTING BREAD

ONE 8½" LOAF

This yeasty, coarse-textured bread makes the best toast ever, a perfect partner to jam or preserves. A purely mix-it-slap-in-the-pan-bake-and-eat-it loaf, it's earned a place of honor in our test kitchen's hall of fame.

3 cups (360g) unbleached all-
    purpose flour

1 tablespoon (14g) sugar

1½ teaspoons salt

¼ teaspoon baking soda

1 tablespoon (10g) instant yeast

1 cup (227g) milk

¼ cup (57g) water

2 tablespoons (25g) vegetable oil or
    olive oil

cornmeal, for sprinkling

Whisk together the flour, sugar, salt, baking soda, and instant yeast in a large bowl, or the bowl of a stand mixer. Combine the milk, water, and oil in a separate, microwave-safe bowl, and heat to between 120°F and 130°F. Be sure to stir the liquid well before measuring its temperature; you want an accurate reading. If you don't have a thermometer, the liquid will feel quite hot (hotter than lukewarm), but not so hot that it would be uncomfortable as bath water.

Pour the hot liquid over the dry ingredients in the mixing bowl. Using an electric beater, or stand mixer with beater attachment, beat at high speed for 1 minute; the dough will be smooth and very soft. If you don't have a stand or electric hand mixer, beat by hand for 2 to 3 minutes, or until the dough is smooth and starting to become elastic.

Lightly grease an 8½" × 4½" loaf pan, and sprinkle the bottom and sides with cornmeal. Scoop the soft dough into the pan, leveling it in the pan as much as possible.

Cover the pan, and let the dough rise until it's just barely crowned over the rim of the pan. When you look at the rim of the pan from eye level, you should see the dough, but it shouldn't be more than, say, ¼" over the rim. This will take about 45 minutes to 1 hour, if you heated the liquid to the correct temperature and your kitchen isn't very cold. While the dough is rising, preheat the oven to 400°F.

Remove the cover, and bake the bread for 22 to 27 minutes, until it's golden brown and its interior temperature is 190°F.

Remove the bread from the oven, and after 5 minutes, turn it out of the pan onto a rack to cool. Let the bread cool completely before slicing.

NUTRITION INFORMATION PER SERVING: **1 slice, 44g**
109 cal | 2g fat | 4g protein | 17g complex carbohydrates | 2g sugar | 1g dietary fiber | 1mg cholesterol | 245mg sodium

BACK-OF-THE-BAG OATMEAL BREAD

ONE 9″ LOAF

This tender, high-rising sandwich bread is soft enough for kids to enjoy, yet sturdy enough for all kinds of sandwich fillings. It also makes great toast, especially with jam or buttered alongside scrambled eggs. Bread flour ensures a high rise even in the presence of oats, which can inhibit gluten formation. In fact, the recipe was featured on our bread flour bag for quite some time and has become a perennial customer favorite for good reason: It's easy to make, uses simple ingredients, and we guarantee everyone in the family will love it!

DOUGH

3 cups (360g) unbleached bread flour

1 cup (99g) old-fashioned rolled oats

2 tablespoons (28g) butter, at room temperature

1½ teaspoons salt

3 tablespoons (40g) brown sugar or honey (63g)

2 teaspoons instant yeast

1¼ cups (283g) milk, lukewarm

TOPPING

1 large egg white

1 tablespoon (14g) water, cold

1 to 2 tablespoons (6g to 12g) old-fashioned rolled oats

In a large bowl, or in the bowl of a stand mixer, mix together all the dough ingredients to form a rough, shaggy dough.

Knead the dough, by hand or mixer, until it's springy though still somewhat soft, about 5 to 7 minutes. The dough may feel quite sticky at the beginning; don't be tempted to add more flour, as additional flour will make the loaf dry. If you're kneading by hand, try kneading on a lightly greased work surface rather than a floured surface.

Place the dough in a lightly greased bowl, cover, and allow it to rise at room temperature for 1 hour; it'll become quite puffy, though it may not double in bulk. If your kitchen is particularly cold (below 65°F), place the bowl of dough in your turned-off oven with the oven light on.

TO SHAPE THE DOUGH: Transfer the dough to a lightly oiled surface. Flatten the dough into a 6″ × 8″ rectangle. Fold the top down to the center (like you were folding a letter), pressing it firmly with the heel of your hand to seal. Pull the upper left and right corners into the center, pressing to seal. Repeat the first step (folding the top to the center and sealing) three or four more times, until you've created a 9″ to 10″ log. Tuck the ends under slightly, and turn the log over so its seam is on the bottom.

Place the log in a lightly greased 9″ × 5″ loaf pan, and tent the pan with lightly greased plastic wrap or the cover of your choice. Allow the dough to rise for 1 to 1½ hours, until it's crested about 1″ over the rim of the pan.

Toward the end of the rising time, preheat your oven to 350°F with a rack in the center.

TO ADD THE TOPPING: Uncover the risen loaf. Beat the egg white with the cold water. Brush the beaten white all over the top crust (you won't need it all), then sprinkle with the oats.

Bake the bread for 35 to 40 minutes, until it's golden brown. If the bread appears to be browning too quickly, cover it lightly with aluminum foil for the final 10 minutes of baking. When done, a digital thermometer inserted into the center of the loaf will register 190°F. If you don't have a thermometer, slide the bread out of its pan and tap its bottom with your fingers: You should hear a hollow thump.

Remove the bread from the oven and turn it out of the pan onto a rack to cool. Cool completely before slicing.

NUTRITION INFORMATION PER SERVING: 1 slice, 61g

160 cal | 2.5g fat | 5g protein | 24g complex carbohydrates | 8g sugar | 2g dietary fiber | 5mg cholesterol | 230mg sodium

GLUTEN-FREE SANDWICH BREAD

ONE 8½" OR 9" LOAF

This recipe yields a tender, tasty, high-rising loaf—perfect for a simple PB&J or BLT. Toast and spread it with butter and jam for breakfast, turn it into French toast, or make a gooey grilled cheese sandwich.

3 cups (468g) gluten-free all-purpose flour

3 tablespoons (35g) sugar

2 teaspoons instant yeast

1¼ teaspoons salt

1¼ teaspoons xanthan gum

1 cup (227g) milk, warmed

4 tablespoons (½ stick, 57g) butter, softened

3 large eggs

Place the flour, sugar, yeast, salt, and xanthan gum in a bowl, or the bowl of your stand mixer. Mix until combined.

Using a stand mixer, drizzle in the milk, beating all the time; the mixture will be crumbly at first, but once all the milk is added, it'll come together.

Add the butter and beat until thoroughly blended.

Beat in the eggs one at a time, beating each in thoroughly before adding the next. Scrape the bottom and sides of the bowl, then beat at high speed for 3 minutes, to make a very smooth, thick batter.

Cover the bowl, and let the batter rise for 1 hour.

Scrape down the bottom and sides of the bowl, gently deflating the batter in the process.

Grease an 8½″ by 4½″ loaf pan, or a 9″ × 4″ × 4″ pain de mie pan.

Scoop the dough into the pan. Press it level, using a spatula or your wet fingers.

Cover with greased plastic wrap, and set in a warm place to rise until the loaf barely crowns above the rim of the 8½″ × 4½″ pan, or until it comes to within about an inch of the rim of the 9″ pain de mie pan. This should take about 45 to 60 minutes. Toward the end of the rising time, preheat the oven to 350°F.

Bake the bread for 38 to 42 minutes, until golden brown. If you're using a pain de mie pan, leave the lid on the entire time. Remove the bread from the oven, turn it out of the pan, and cool on a rack.

Like a baguette, this bread has a short shelf life. For best texture, reheat or toast after the first day.

NUTRITION INFORMATION PER SERVING: 1 slice, 58g

154 cal | 4g fat | 3g protein | 23g complex carbohydrates | 3g sugar | 1g dietary fiber | 48mg cholesterol | 204mg sodium

HERBED MONKEY BREAD

ONE 8″ ROUND LOAF

This soft, pull-apart bread is a fun loaf for sharing. Use the smaller amount of oil if you simply want to drizzle the herb coating over the dough balls once they're in the pan. To thoroughly coat each dough ball before putting them in the pan, use the full 5 tablespoons of olive oil. This extra oil will give the bread a delicious crispy crust.

HERB COATING

3 to 5 tablespoons (35g to 67g) olive oil

1 tablespoon fresh thyme or
   1½ teaspoons dried thyme

2 tablespoons chopped fresh parsley or
   1 tablespoon (2g) dried parsley

1 teaspoon dried oregano

1 garlic clove, minced

DOUGH

1 recipe White Bread 101 (page 146)

Combine the oil, herbs, and garlic. Set the mixture aside.

Prepare White Bread 101 through its first rise. Grease the bottom and sides of a small (8″) tube or bundt-style pan, or a deep (2″ or deeper) 8″ cake pan or soufflé dish. Turn the risen dough onto a lightly floured work surface and divide it into 32 small pieces, each about the size of a chestnut and weighing approximately 21g. Place about a third of them in the bottom of the pan if you're using a small bundt-style pan. If you're using a cake pan, put about two-thirds of the pieces into it. Brush the dough in the pan with the herb coating. Continue to layer with the remaining balls, brushing the top layer with the remaining herb oil. (If you've used the greater amount of olive oil, dip each piece of dough into the oil to coat it completely before layering it into the pan.) Let the bread rise, covered, for 1 hour.

Preheat the oven to 375°F. Bake the bread for 30 to 35 minutes, until it's golden. Remove it from the oven and invert it onto a serving platter; the crispy bottom crust should be on top. Serve warm.

NUTRITION INFORMATION PER SERVING: **4 small pieces, 87g**

235 cal | 7g fat | 6g protein | 33g complex carbohydrates | 2g sugar | 1g fiber | 7mg cholesterol | 322mg sodium

DIVIDING DOUGH

When you're making monkey bread (or rolls or breadsticks), you need to divide the dough evenly into smaller pieces. The best way to do this is with a bench knife and a scale (see Tools, pages 531 and 541). Weigh the dough, then divide it in half, weighing each half to make sure they're the same size. Then, depending on how many pieces you want to end up with, keep dividing the halves in half, continuing to use the scale to make sure the pieces are all the same size.

An exception to this process is if you want to end up with a number of dough pieces that's not divisible by 4—say, 15 or 18 pieces of dough. In that case, you'll need to divide the dough into three pieces at some point, rather than two. It's up to you to figure out when that point is, depending on how many rolls or breadsticks you're making. (Now's the time to pull out those short division skills!)

UP-SIZING

Unlike many baking recipes, you can increase the size of most bread recipes simply by doubling or tripling all the ingredients. The exception is the yeast, when making a large batch of rolls or multiple loaves of bread; if you increase the amount of yeast at the same rate you increase everything else, you may find yourself with a lot of dough on your hands and not enough time to deal with it.

If you're doubling or tripling your recipe, simply double or triple all the ingredients, including yeast. But for larger batches, hold back on the yeast; 1 tablespoon of yeast is about right for 8 loaves or batches of rolls. The resulting dough will rise more slowly, which not only improves the bread's flavor, but gives you the time you need to work with the dough most effectively.

VERMONT WHOLE WHEAT HONEY OAT BREAD

TWO 8½" LOAVES

This lovely loaf is soft and mildly sweet, perfect for both sandwiches and toast. If you can find it, use Vietnamese cinnamon—a spicier, bolder variety that comes through beautifully in this bread.

2 cups (454g) boiling water

1 cup (99g) old-fashioned rolled oats

½ cup (78g) maple sugar or brown sugar (107g)

1 tablespoon (21g) honey

4 tablespoons (½ stick, 57g) butter

2½ teaspoons salt

1 teaspoon cinnamon

1 tablespoon (10g) instant yeast

1½ cups (170g) white whole wheat flour

4 cups (480g) unbleached all-purpose flour

In a large bowl, combine the water, oats, maple or brown sugar, honey, butter, salt, and cinnamon. Let cool to lukewarm (100°F to 110°F), which typically takes about 10 to 15 minutes; stir the mixture several times to help things along, if you like.

Add the yeast and flours, stirring to form a rough dough. Knead (about 10 minutes by hand, 5 to 7 minutes using a mixer) until the dough is smooth and satiny.

Transfer the dough to a lightly greased bowl, cover the bowl with lightly greased plastic wrap, and allow the dough to rise for 1 hour. Since the dough is warm to begin with (from the boiling water), it should become quite puffy.

Divide the dough in half, and shape each half into a loaf. Place the loaves in two greased 8½" × 4½" loaf pans.

Cover the pans with lightly greased plastic wrap and allow the loaves to rise until they've crowned about 1" over the rim of the pan, about 60 to 90 minutes.

Bake the loaves in a preheated 350°F oven for 35 to 40 minutes, tenting them lightly with aluminum foil after 25 minutes to prevent over-browning. Remove them from the oven when they're golden brown, and the interior registers 190°F on a digital thermometer.

Turn the loaves out onto a rack to cool.

NUTRITION INFORMATION PER SERVING: 1 slice, 89g

110 cal | 2g fat | 3g protein | 16g complex carbohydrates | 4g sugar | 1g dietary fiber | 5mg cholesterol | 180mg sodium

SANDWICH RYE BREAD

ONE 8½″ LOAF

To us, an excellent loaf of sandwich rye bread should be dark on the outside and light brown (almost a putty-beige color) on the inside. It should taste strongly of caraway and should have that distinctive rye bread flavor—a combination of caraway and the rye flour itself, with perhaps a hint of sour pickle. It should be shaped like sandwich bread and have a slightly chewy crust and a tender crumb. Finally, it should be moist enough to hold together when piled with pastrami or layered with ham and cheese and mustard.

This bread is all of that. Each of the four flours adds its own special characteristic: height and structure from the bread flour, flavor from the rye, texture from the pumpernickel, and added moistness from the potato flour. Pickle juice adds just the right amount of tang.

2 cups (240g) unbleached bread flour	1 tablespoon (12g) sugar
1 cup (112g) rye flour	2 teaspoons instant yeast
⅓ cup (39g) pumpernickel	¼ cup (50g) vegetable oil
¼ cup (42g) potato flour or ⅓ cup (21g) potato flakes	¼ cup (56g) dill pickle juice or sour pickle juice
1 tablespoon (7g) caraway seeds	1 cup (224g) water
1½ teaspoons salt	

Mix all the dry ingredients in a large bowl. Add the vegetable oil, pickle juice, and water and mix until a shaggy mass forms. Let the dough rest for 30 minutes; this resting period allows the flour to absorb the liquid fully, making it easier to knead.

Knead the dough for about 10 minutes; it should feel firm and smooth, though somewhat sticky. Put it into a greased bowl, cover the bowl, and let the dough rise until it's almost doubled in bulk.

Turn the dough onto a lightly oiled or lightly floured surface and shape it into an 8″ log. Place the log in a lightly greased 8½″ × 4½″ loaf pan, cover the pan with greased plastic wrap or a reusable cover, and let the loaf rise until it's just about crowned over the rim of the pan (about 60 to 90 minutes).

Preheat the oven to 350°F. Bake the bread for about 35 minutes, until it's a deep golden brown and its internal temperature registers 190°F on a digital thermometer. (If the bread appears to be browning too quickly, tent it with aluminum foil, shiny side up, for the final 10 minutes of baking.) Remove the bread from the oven, take it out of the pan, and cool it on a rack.

NUTRITION INFORMATION PER SERVING: 1 slice, 51g

126 cal | 3.5g fat | 3g protein | 20g complex carbohydrates | 1g sugar | 2g dietary fiber | 0mg cholesterol | 202mg sodium

VARIATION

SAUERKRAUT RYE LOAF: Use this bread to make a fantastic Reuben melt with corned beef and Swiss cheese layered on two slices of bread, cooked on the griddle like grilled cheese. You'll need coleslaw and Dr. Brown's Cel-Ray Tonic on the side, of course.

Prepare the sandwich rye dough, adding ¾ cup (112g to 140g) very well drained, chopped sauerkraut, and reducing the water to ¾ cup. Another nice addition is up to 4 teaspoons mustard seeds (yellow, brown, or a mix). Shape and bake the bread as directed above; it may take a bit longer to rise.

ONE POTATO . . .

Many traditional American bread recipes call for cooked potato or potato water as one of the ingredients. In the days before yeast was readily available, bakers had to rely on wild yeasts, present in the air, to leaven their breads. Yeast is attracted to starch, and the starch-filled water in which potatoes have been boiled is a good medium for capturing and propagating wild yeast.

It's this same starch that accounts for the crisp brown crust, moist airy interior, and wonderful keeping qualities of potato bread. The starch in potatoes (or in potato water) absorbs liquid as bread dough is kneaded, and holds onto that liquid as the bread bakes.

If you want or need potato water for your recipe, peel potatoes, leave them whole, and boil—using enough water to cover the potatoes fully—until tender, 25 to 30 minutes. The resulting water will be cloudy and full of starch, ideal for using in yeasted breads. (Yeast happily converts starch to sugar, so starch is an excellent food for yeast.)

Potato flour—dried, ground potatoes—and potato starch are both good stand-ins for potato water. Use 3 to 4 tablespoons (35g to 46g) potato flour or starch in a 3-cup-flour (1 pound) bread recipe.

CINNAMON SWIRL BREAD

ONE 8½" LOAF

This tender white bread, with its swirl of cinnamon in the center, cries out for toasting and buttering. The streusel topping adds just the right final touch.

The following recipe incorporates a few tips for success that we've discovered over the years. First, for a deep, dark, moist cinnamon swirl inside the bread, whirl sugar, cinnamon, and raisins or currants together in a blender or food processor until smooth. The fruit adds moistness as well as subtle flavor to the filling. And second, rather than brush the dough with butter before sprinkling on the filling, brush it with beaten egg. Butter acts as a barrier between the pieces of rolled-up dough, preventing them from cohering and giving you bread that "unravels" when you cut it. On the other hand, the protein in egg acts like glue, cementing the bread and filling together, and allowing much less (though still a bit) unraveling.

DOUGH

3 cups (360g) unbleached all-purpose flour

¼ cup (42g) potato flour or ⅓ cup (21g) potato flakes

¼ cup (35g) nonfat dry milk

1¼ teaspoons salt

½ teaspoon cinnamon

3 tablespoons (35g) sugar

2½ teaspoons instant yeast

4 tablespoons (½ stick, 56g) butter, at room temperature

1 cup (227g) water

FILLING

¼ cup (50g) sugar

1½ teaspoons cinnamon

¼ cup (42g) raisins or currants

2 teaspoons unbleached all-purpose flour

1 large egg beaten with 1 tablespoon (14g) water

TOPPING

2 tablespoons (28g) butter

2 tablespoons (25g) sugar

¼ teaspoon cinnamon

¼ cup (30g) unbleached all-purpose flour

TO MAKE THE DOUGH: In a large bowl, combine all the dough ingredients, mixing until the dough begins to come away from the sides of the bowl. Knead (about 10 minutes by hand, 5 to 7 minutes using a mixer) until the dough is smooth and satiny. Transfer the dough to a lightly oiled bowl, cover the bowl with plastic wrap, and set it aside to rise for 1 to 1½ hours; it will be puffy, if not doubled in bulk.

TO MAKE THE FILLING: Pulse filling ingredients except the egg wash in a food processor or blender.

TO ASSEMBLE: Transfer the dough to a lightly oiled work surface and shape it into a long, narrow rectangle, about 16″ × 8″. Brush the dough with some of the egg wash (set the remainder aside) and pat the filling gently onto the dough. Beginning with a short edge, roll the dough into a log. Pinch the side seam and ends closed (to keep the filling from bubbling out) and place the log in a lightly greased 8½″ × 4½″ loaf pan.

Cover the pan with lightly greased plastic wrap or a reusable cover and let the bread rise for about 1 hour at room temperature, or until it's crowned about 1″ over the rim of the pan.

TO MAKE THE TOPPING: In a small bowl or mini processor, mix together the butter, sugar, cinnamon, and flour until the mixture is crumbly. If you're using a mini processor, watch carefully; topping will go from crumbly to a cohesive mass in just a second or so. Brush the top of the loaf with some (or all) of the reserved egg wash and gently press on the topping.

Preheat the oven to 350°F. Bake the bread for about 45 minutes, tenting it lightly with aluminum foil for the final 15 minutes or so if it appears to be browning too quickly. Remove the loaf from the oven and after about 5 minutes, gently remove it from the pan. Some of the streusel will fall off, but you can alleviate this by first loosening all around the edges of the loaf with a knife, then turning the pan on its side and gently pulling it away from the loaf.

NUTRITION INFORMATION PER SERVING: 1 slice, 62g
171 cal | 5g fat | 4g protein | 22g complex carbohydrates | 6g sugar | 1g dietary fiber | 25mg cholesterol | 183mg sodium

CLASSIC 100% WHOLE WHEAT BREAD

ONE 8½″ LOAF

This is the bread that will convert anyone into a whole wheat bread lover. This 100% whole wheat recipe features the delightfully nutty taste of wheat in a fine-grained, moist, faintly sweet loaf. Use the lesser amount of water in summer or a humid climate and the greater amount in winter or dry weather.

1 to 1⅛ cups (227g to 255g) water, lukewarm

¼ cup (50g) vegetable oil

¼ cup (85g) honey, molasses, or maple syrup

3½ cups (397g) white whole wheat flour

2½ teaspoons instant yeast

¼ cup (35g) nonfat dry milk

1¼ teaspoons salt

In a large bowl, combine all the ingredients and stir until the dough starts to leave the sides of the bowl. For easiest, most effective kneading, let the dough rest for 20 to 30 minutes in the bowl; this gives the flour a chance to absorb some of the liquid, and the bran to soften. Transfer the dough to a lightly greased surface, oil your hands, and knead it for 6 to 8 minutes, or until it begins to become smooth and supple. (You may also knead this dough in a stand mixer or bread machine set to the dough cycle.) The dough should be soft, yet still firm enough to knead. Adjust its consistency with additional water or flour, if necessary.

Transfer the dough to a lightly greased bowl or large measuring cup, cover it, and allow the dough to rise until puffy though not necessarily doubled in bulk, about 1 to 2 hours, depending on the warmth of your kitchen.

Transfer the dough to a lightly oiled work surface, and shape it into an 8″ log. Place the log in a lightly greased 8½″ × 4½″ loaf pan, cover the pan loosely with lightly greased plastic wrap, and allow the bread to rise for about 1 to 2 hours, or until the center has crowned about 1″ above the rim of the pan. Toward the end of the rising time, preheat the oven to 350°F.

Bake the bread for 35 to 40 minutes, tenting it lightly with aluminum foil after 20 minutes to prevent over-browning.

Remove the bread from the oven, and turn it out of the pan onto a rack to cool. If desired, brush the top with melted butter; this will yield a soft, flavorful crust. Cool completely before slicing.

NUTRITION INFORMATION PER SERVING: 1 slice, 50g

150 cal | 3.5g fat | 5g protein | 19g complex carbohydrates | 5g sugar | 3g dietary fiber | 0mg cholesterol | 200mg sodium

CHEESE BREAD

ONE 8½″ LOAF

This golden loaf, soft and high-rising, has a nicely assertive sharp cheese flavor and aroma. Use it for the ultimate grilled cheese sandwich, or an excellent BLT. Cut any stale bread into cubes, drizzle with olive oil, and toast them in the oven for cheese croutons.

2¼ teaspoons instant yeast

¼ cup (56g) water

1 cup (227g) milk

1¼ teaspoons salt

1 tablespoon (12g) sugar

3½ cups (420g) unbleached all-purpose flour

1 cup (112g) finely grated cheddar cheese

½ cup (56g) finely grated Parmesan

2 tablespoons (28g) butter or vegetable oil (25g)

2 teaspoons tomato paste (optional, for color)

Combine all the ingredients and mix and knead them together until you've made a soft, smooth dough. Adjust the dough's consistency with additional flour or water as needed; this dough should be soft but not sticky. Cover and let the dough rise for 1 hour, or until it's puffy (though not necessarily doubled in bulk).

Transfer the dough to a lightly greased work surface and pat it into an 8″ log. Transfer the log to a lightly greased 8½″ × 4½″ loaf pan, cover the pan, and let the bread rise until the outer edge has just barely risen over the rim of the pan, about 45 minutes.

Preheat the oven to 350°F. Bake the bread for 35 to 40 minutes, tenting it lightly with aluminum foil for the final 10 to 15 minutes if it appears to be browning too quickly. Remove the bread from the oven, take it out of the pan, and place it on a rack to cool completely.

NUTRITION INFORMATION PER SERVING: 1 slice, 57g

150 cal | 5g fat | 6g protein | 19g complex carbohydrates | 1g sugar | 1g dietary fiber | 14mg cholesterol | 261mg sodium

BRIOCHE

ONE 9" ROUND LOAF

Brioche is a yeast bread that's so rich it can be eaten pleasurably with absolutely no adornment at all. Which isn't to say that orange marmalade or peach jam or butter wouldn't all be welcome additions.

Brioche can be shaped in the traditional *tête* shape—a fluted round with a jaunty top-knot—but it can also be made into sandwich loaves or shaped into balls and laid side by side to make a ring. You can even pile it into a loaf pan to make a kind of French monkey bread. However you shape it, brioche is a versatile loaf that can easily be sliced and served plain or toasted with jam or turned into French toast.

With all its butter, this is a difficult dough to develop by hand and we don't suggest trying it. A stand mixer or bread machine set to the dough cycle are ideal for the task; if you have access to either one, don't hesitate to tackle this recipe. It's only a tad more challenging than any other yeast bread recipe, and the results are out of this world.

DOUGH

2¾ cups (330g) unbleached all-purpose flour

1½ teaspoons instant yeast

¼ cup (57g) water, cool (about 70°F)

4 large eggs

2 tablespoons (25g) sugar

¾ teaspoon salt

16 tablespoons (2 sticks, 227g) unsalted butter, at cool room temperature, 65°F to 68°F

EGG WASH

1 large egg

1 tablespoon (14g) cold water

TO MAKE THE DOUGH: Place 1½ cups (180g) of the flour, the yeast, water, and eggs in the bowl of a stand mixer or the bucket of your bread machine set to dough mode. Beat at medium speed (or knead in the bread machine) until smooth. Cover the mixture and let it sit for 45 minutes. It will develop some bubbles, but not change very much due to the thinness of the batter. The yeast, however, is getting a jump-start.

Add the remaining 1¼ cup (150g) of flour, sugar, and salt. Beat for 8 to 10 minutes (switch to a dough hook if you're using a mixer), or knead in the bread machine, until the dough cleans the sides of the bowl and becomes shiny and elastic.

With the mixer or bread machine running, add the butter 2 tablespoons at a time, letting the butter become absorbed before adding the next chunk. Repeat until all of the butter is added.

Cover the dough and let it rise for 1 hour. It'll be very soft at this point and should have grown by about one-third. Turn the dough onto a lightly floured surface and fold it over several times. (Use a bench knife to scrape up any bits that stick to the table.) Place the dough in a greased bowl, cover the bowl, and refrigerate it for a minimum of 4 hours and up to about 16 hours. The dough will firm up considerably.

Remove the dough from the refrigerator and form it into a round loaf. Work quickly, because as the dough warms it becomes very sticky. Place it in a 9″ brioche pan. (We've chosen not to make the top-knotted brioche here; it's a fair trick to get the knob on top to stay centered throughout the rising and baking process, and as we don't like the look of tipsy brioches, we usually just form it into a plain round.) Allow the dough to rise for 1 to 1½ hours, until it's an inch above the edge of the pan and looks puffy. Preheat the oven to 375°F.

TO MAKE THE EGG WASH: Beat the egg and water and brush all exposed surfaces with the egg wash. Cut four slashes into the top of the loaf (see instructions, page 191). Bake the brioche for 40 to 50 minutes, until its internal temperature reads 190°F on a digital thermometer and it's golden brown. For brioche with lighter crust, tent it with aluminum foil after 20 minutes of baking.

Remove the brioche from the oven and cool it in the pan for 10 minutes. Turn it out of the pan and cool it completely on a rack. Serve the brioche when it's completely cool.

NUTRITION INFORMATION PER SERVING: 1 slice, 68g

268 cal | 18g fat | 5g protein | 19g complex carbohydrates | 2g sugar | 1g dietary fiber | 116mg cholesterol | 320mg sodium

JUICING UP YOUR BREAD

Adding a tablespoon of orange juice concentrate or vinegar or a pinch of ascorbic acid to bread dough will aid in its rising. Yeast loves to grow in an acidic environment. Basically, yeast requires only a bit of food and a bit of warmth to multiply. But like any living organism, it will grow slowly if given a minimal amount of food and comfort. Increase the food (sugar, diastatic malt powder), give it a comfortable (acidic) home, and watch the yeast and your bread dough take off.

A little extra acid works particularly well in rich sweet doughs, which often rise very, very slowly. In a side-by-side test we did with *kuchen*, a plain sweet dough, the kuchen with ascorbic acid rose 50% higher than the plain kuchen, in the same amount of time.

Sweet Breads

As soft as sandwich or pan breads, sweet breads add sugar (and often additional fat) to that formula to become even more tender and rich. Sweet bread dough is often braided, or braided and shaped into a wreath, fashioned into rolls and stuffed with filling, or spread with filling, rolled, and sliced. These breads may take a bit longer to make, due to their increased sugar content, so be sure to read the recipe all the way through before beginning, and allow yourself plenty of time from start to finish.

RASPBERRY CREAM CHEESE BRAID

2 BRAIDS

This sweet braided bread is impressive looking, but easy to make. The soft and pliable dough is a joy to work with—though the braiding *looks* challenging, it's anything but. This dough is also an ideal base for all manner of soft sweet breads: monkey bread, sweet glazed braids, hot cross buns, and the like. If you use all-purpose rather than pastry flour, expect a loaf that's a bit chewy (rather than totally tender). You'll need to increase the water by a couple of tablespoons, as well.

DOUGH

2 teaspoons instant yeast

¼ cup (57g) water, warm

¼ cup (50g) granulated sugar

3 cups (318g) unbleached pastry flour or all-purpose flour (360g)

6 tablespoons (84g) sour cream or yogurt

6 tablespoons (¾ stick, 84g) unsalted butter, softened

1¼ teaspoons salt

1 large egg

¼ teaspoon lemon oil or 1 teaspoon lemon zest

FILLING

1 package (227g) cream cheese, softened

2 tablespoons (28g) unsalted butter, softened

¼ cup (50g) granulated sugar

⅛ teaspoon salt

1 teaspoon vanilla extract

2 tablespoons (22g) Instant ClearJel or 3 tablespoons (23g) unbleached all-purpose flour

1 large egg

½ cup (168g) raspberry jam mixed with 2 tablespoons (22g) ClearJel or all-purpose flour (15g)

TOPPING (OPTIONAL)

1 large egg

1 tablespoon (14g) cold water

¼ cup (50g) coarse white sugar

TO MAKE THE DOUGH: In a large bowl, combine all the dough ingredients and knead the dough—by hand or mixer—until it's soft and pliable but not sticky.

Place the dough in a lightly greased bowl, cover with plastic wrap, and let sit in a warm place for about 45 minutes, or until doubled.

TO MAKE THE FILLING: In a medium bowl, beat together the cream cheese, butter, sugar, salt, and vanilla. Mix in the ClearJel or flour and the egg, scraping the bottom and sides of the bowl thoroughly.

Gently deflate the risen dough and divide it in half. Roll each half into a 15″ × 10″ rectangle and place each onto a lightly greased or parchment-lined baking sheet. Spread half of the jam in a 2½″-wide swath, lengthwise, down the center of each dough rectangle, leaving a 1″ border at the top and bottom.

Top the jam with half of the filling. Make 2½″ cuts every ¾″ down both long sides of the dough. Fold the two ends of the dough over the filling, then pull the cut strips up and over, alternating sides to look like a braid. Repeat with the remaining piece of dough.

Cover the braids and let them rise for 30 to 45 minutes, until they're puffy looking.

Preheat the oven to 350°F.

If desired, mix the egg and water and brush onto both braids (this will make a darker, shinier crust), or spritz the braids with water. Sprinkle with coarse sugar. Bake the braids for 32 to 36 minutes, until they're golden brown. Remove from the oven and let them cool for 15 minutes before slicing.

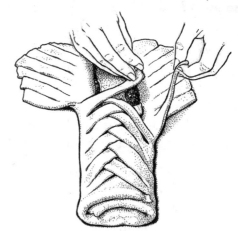

Make parallel cuts about 2½″ long at a 45° angle down each side of the braid, ¾″ apart. Take one strip at a time from alternate sides and bring them to the center. Let the ends overlap on top of the filling, continuing until the whole loaf is braided. Tuck in the ends. Brush with an egg wash and sprinkle with coarse sugar before baking, if desired.

NUTRITION INFORMATION PER SERVING: 1 slice, 33g

98 cal | 3g fat | 2g protein | 9g complex carbohydrates | 6g sugar | 1g dietary fiber | 21mg cholesterol | 110mg sodium

SOFT CINNAMON ROLLS

24 ROLLS

These are quintessential cinnamon rolls, stuffed with rich filling and slathered with thick white icing. The chief attribute setting these rolls apart from their peers is their texture. While all cinnamon rolls are delicious straight from the oven, they often harden up and become dry as they cool. These rolls will stay soft for several days thanks to *tangzhong*, the technique popularized by Asian bread making of cooking water with flour that produces a light, fluffy, moist yeast bread.

TANGZHONG (STARTER)

5 tablespoons (71g) water

5 tablespoons (71g) whole milk

3 tablespoons plus 1 teaspoon (28g) unbleached bread flour

DOUGH

4 cups plus 2 tablespoons (496g) unbleached bread flour

3 tablespoons (24g) nonfat dry milk

1¼ teaspoons salt

1 tablespoon (10g) instant yeast

¾ cup (170g) whole milk, lukewarm

2 large eggs

6 tablespoons (¾ stick, 85g) unsalted butter, melted

FILLING

¾ cup (142g) brown sugar, packed

4 teaspoons cinnamon

ICING

2 cups (227g) confectioners' sugar

pinch of salt

2 tablespoons (28g) unsalted butter, melted

½ teaspoon vanilla extract

2 to 3 tablespoons (28g to 43g) whole milk or cream, enough to make a thick but spreadable frosting

TO MAKE THE TANGZHONG: Combine all the starter ingredients in a small saucepan and whisk until no lumps remain.

Place the saucepan over medium heat, and cook the mixture, whisking constantly, until thick and the whisk leaves lines on the bottom of the pan. This will take only a minute or so. Remove from the heat and set it aside for several minutes.

TO MAKE THE DOUGH: Mix the tangzhong with the remaining dough ingredients until everything comes together. Let the dough rest, covered, for 20 minutes; this will give the flour a chance to absorb the liquid, making it easier to knead.

After 20 minutes, knead the dough—by hand or mixer—to make a smooth, elastic, somewhat sticky dough.

Shape the dough into a ball, and let it rest in a lightly greased covered bowl for 60 to 90 minutes, until puffy but not necessarily doubled in bulk.

TO MAKE THE FILLING: Combine the brown sugar and cinnamon, mixing until the cinnamon is thoroughly distributed.

Gently deflate the risen dough, divide it in half, and shape each piece into a rough rectangle.

Working with one piece at a time, roll the dough into an 18″ × 8″ rectangle.

Sprinkle half the filling onto the rolled-out dough.

Starting with a long edge, roll the dough into a log. With the seam underneath, cut the log into 12 slices, 1½″ each.

Repeat with the second piece of dough and the remaining filling.

Lightly grease a 9″ × 13″ pan. Space the rolls in the pan.

Cover the pan and let the rolls rise for 45 to 60 minutes, until they're crowding one another and are quite puffy.

While the rolls are rising, preheat the oven to 350°F with a rack in the bottom third.

Uncover the rolls, and bake them for 22 to 25 minutes, until they feel set. They might be just barely browned; that's fine. It's better to under-bake these rolls than bake them too long. Their interior temperature at the center should be about 188°F.

While the rolls are baking, stir together the icing ingredients, adding enough of the milk to make a thick, spreadable icing. The icing should be quite stiff, about the consistency of softened cream cheese.

Remove the rolls from the oven, and turn them out of the pan onto a rack. Spread them with the icing; it'll partially melt into the rolls.

Serve the rolls warm. Or cool to room temperature and reheat just before serving, if desired.

NUTRITION INFORMATION PER SERVING: 1 roll, 63g

190 cal | 5g fat | 4g protein | 18g complex carbohydrates | 16g sugar | 1g dietary fiber | 25mg cholesterol | 220mg sodium

FAVORITE STICKY BUNS

1 DOZEN BUNS

These gooey, dark gold buns feature thick cinnamon filling and a topping of rich brown sugar sauce sprinkled liberally with pecans. We guarantee these will rival (or surpass!) any bakery sticky buns you've ever enjoyed.

STARTER

2 cups (240g) unbleached all-purpose flour

1 cup plus 2 tablespoons (255g) water

1/16 teaspoon instant yeast

DOUGH

1½ cups (180g) unbleached all-purpose flour

¼ cup (32g) nonfat dry milk

2 tablespoons (21g) potato flour or ¼ cup (22g) dried potato flakes (optional, but makes a more tender bun)

¼ cup (21g) granulated sugar

2 teaspoons vanilla extract

1¼ teaspoons salt

2¼ teaspoons instant yeast

6 tablespoons (¾ stick, 84g) unsalted butter, at room temperature

FILLING

1 cup (196g) sugar

1½ tablespoons (11g) cinnamon

GLAZE

½ cup (154g) golden syrup or light corn syrup

1 tablespoon (14g) rum (optional)

3 tablespoons (42g) unsalted butter, melted

1 cup (213g) brown sugar

1 cup (105g) diced pecans

TO MAKE THE STARTER: Combine the flour, water, and yeast in a medium bowl, stirring until fairly smooth. Cover the bowl and let the mixture rest at room temperature (cooler than 75°F) overnight, or for 12 to 16 hours.

TO MAKE THE DOUGH: Combine the overnight starter with all the dough ingredients and mix and knead them together—by hand or mixer—to make a soft, smooth dough. Cover and let the dough rise for about 1 hour; it will become slightly puffy but won't double in bulk.

While the dough is rising, prepare the pans: two 9″ round cake pans or a 9″ × 13″ pan. Spray with nonstick pan spray or lightly grease with vegetable shortening or butter.

TO MAKE THE FILLING: Combine the sugar and cinnamon. Set aside.

TO MAKE THE GLAZE: In a small bowl, whisk together the syrup, rum (if using), and melted butter. Pour the glaze into the pan, or divide it evenly between the pans if you're using two pans. Sprinkle the brown sugar and pecans on top of the glaze.

TO ASSEMBLE: Transfer the dough to a lightly greased work surface and roll it into a rectangle approximately 14″ × 20″. Spread it with the prepared filling, leaving an uncovered strip about 1″ wide along one short end of the dough. Starting with the short end without the filling, roll the dough into a log and slice it into 12 slices, each about 1″ to 1¼″ wide. Place the buns in the prepared pan(s), leaving about ½″ between them. Cover the pan(s), and let the buns rise for 90 minutes; again, they won't rise much, they'll just seem to spread a bit.

Preheat the oven to 350°F. Bake the buns for 25 to 30 minutes, tenting them lightly with aluminum foil for the final 5 minutes if they appear to be browning too quickly. The finished buns will be golden brown. Loosen the edges of the buns with a knife, then carefully (the sugar is hot!) turn them out (upside down) onto a rack or parchment-covered baking sheet to cool, scraping any glaze that may have stuck to the pan onto the warm buns. Serve warm or at room temperature.

NUTRITION INFORMATION PER SERVING: 1 bun, 136g

473 cal | 15g fat | 6g protein | 31g complex carbohydrates | 48g sugar | 2g dietary fiber | 25mg cholesterol | 262mg sodium

PORTUGUESE SWEET ROLLS

16 ROLLS

Our take on traditional Portuguese sweet bread is simply a big round loaf broken down into smaller rolls, ideal for carrying in a brown bag lunch. Serve these soft, almost-sweet rolls with jam and double Devon cream just as you would a scone, for breakfast or tea.

1 tablespoon (10g) instant yeast

½ cup (113g) milk

6 tablespoons (¾ stick, 84g) unsalted butter

¼ cup (57g) water

1¼ teaspoons salt

3 cups (360g) unbleached all-purpose flour

¼ cup (46g) potato flour or ½ cup (46g) dried potato flakes

2 large eggs

⅓ cup (67g) sugar

2 teaspoons vanilla extract

¼ teaspoon lemon oil or 1½ teaspoons lemon zest

Mix and knead together all the ingredients—by hand or mixer—to form a soft, smooth dough. Transfer the dough to a lightly greased bowl, cover the bowl, and let the dough rise until puffy but not necessarily doubled in bulk, about 90 minutes, depending on the warmth of your kitchen.

Transfer the dough to a lightly greased work surface and divide it into 16 pieces. Round each piece into a smooth ball. Place the balls in a lightly greased 9″ × 13″ pan, two 9″ round cake pans, or a 14″ round pan. Cover the pan and let the rolls rise for about 1 hour; they should double in bulk.

Preheat the oven to 325°F. Bake the rolls for 30 minutes, tenting lightly with aluminum foil after the first 20 minutes. Remove them from the oven when they're golden brown and transfer them to a rack to cool.

NUTRITION INFORMATION PER SERVING: 1 roll, 62g
191 cal | 6g fat | 5g protein | 25g complex carbohydrates | 4g sugar | 1g dietary fiber | 40mg cholesterol | 193mg sodium

Small Breads and Rolls

Buns and bagels, rolls and pretzels—these small, single-serve breads are self-contained, each one an entity unto itself. All of them are easily obtainable at the grocery store or a nearby bakery, but if you love to bake, you'll want to try making them at home. Even the very freshest store-bought roll can't compare with a crusty homemade hard roll, or a soft, tender cloverleaf or crescent, hot from the oven.

SOFT ROLLS

16 DINNER ROLLS

Although we love crusty, crunchy artisan-style breads and rolls, it's comforting at times to drift back into childhood and the soft, squishy white rolls that graced so many of our tables, particularly at the holidays. Cloverleafs, crescents, fantans, knots—any baker worth their salt can put together a beautiful bread basket with just one simple dough and a few different shaping techniques.

The following rolls all begin with the dough for White Bread 101 (page 146).

Choose the shapes you want to create, and divide the dough into 16 pieces, or roll out as required. Shape according to the illustrations on page 170–171.

After shaping, let the rolls rise until puffy and almost double in size, about 1 hour. Preheat the oven to 350°F. Bake for 15 to 18 minutes, until golden brown with an internal temperature of 190°F.

Finished rolls can be brushed with butter for a delicious soft crust; a double coating of butter for a soft, satiny crust; or lightly dusted with flour, if you prefer.

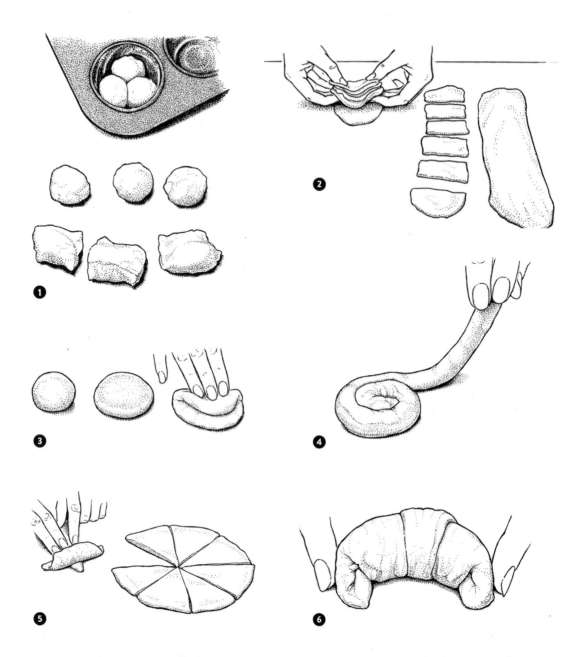

1. **Cloverleaf:** Divide each piece of dough into thirds. Roll each of the three pieces into a small ball. Place three balls into each well of a greased muffin pan. **2. Fantans:** Roll the dough into a 16˝ square. Cut the square in half, and cut each piece crosswise into 2˝ strips. Butter each strip, then cut into four 2˝ squares. Stack four squares on top of each other, and put them on edge in a greased muffin tin. **3. Parker House:** Roll each piece of dough into a ball, then flatten the ball with the heel of your hand or a rolling pin. Fold the circle just short of in half and press together. Place the roll, seam side up, on a greased baking sheet. **4. Snail:** Roll each piece of dough into a log, hold one end down, then wind the other around it to form a spiral or snail shape. Place into a greased muffin tin or on a baking sheet. **5 and 6. Crescent:** Divide the dough in half, and roll each half into a ¼˝ thick circle. Cut each circle into 8 wedges. Roll each wedge into a compact log, starting with the wider side and rolling toward the tip. Pinch the tip to seal the roll, then push the sides of the roll toward the center to form a crescent shape. Transfer the rolls to a lightly greased baking sheet, making sure to keep the tips on the bottom.

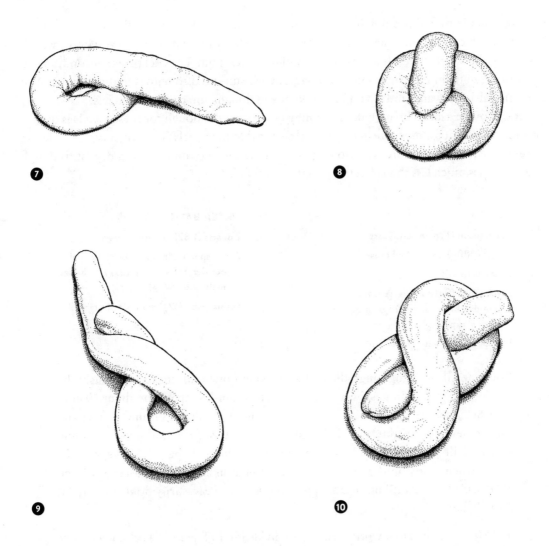

7 and 8. Single Knot: Roll each piece of dough into a log roughly 4″ long. Tie the dough in a simple knot, leaving one end in the center of the top and tucking the other underneath. Place on a lightly greased or parchment-lined baking sheet.
9 and 10. Double Knot: Roll each piece of dough into a rope 8″ long. Make a loop with the top half of the dough, giving the closed end a ½″ overlap of dough. Turn this loop over so the long piece is on top. Wind the long piece behind the overlap, and bring the end back up through the loop to make a figure 8.

BAGELS

8 BAGELS

It's fairly simple to find top-notch bagels in bakeries and bagel shops. With all kinds of good bagels available just about wherever you turn, why make your own? First, so you know what's in them—who wants things like azodicarbonmide in their pumpernickel bagel? Second, so you can customize them to taste, as in pesto bagels with sun-dried tomatoes and pine nuts. And third, it's fairly easy and fun! If you can make bread dough, you can make bagels.

If you're a seasoned bread baker, you may notice that the dough for these bagels is quite a bit stiffer than that for most breads. This is to ensure that the bagels attain their typically dense, close-grained, chewy texture; you don't want them rising very much, and a dry (stiff) dough naturally rises much less than a wetter dough.

DOUGH

1 tablespoon (10g) instant yeast

4 cups (480g) unbleached bread flour

2 teaspoons salt

1 tablespoon (9g) non-diastatic malt powder, brown sugar (13g), or barley malt syrup (22g)

1½ cups (340g) water, lukewarm

WATER BATH

2 quarts (1.82kg) water

2 tablespoons (18g) non-diastatic malt powder, brown sugar (27g), or barley malt syrup (43g)

1 tablespoon (12g) granulated sugar

Combine all the dough ingredients in a mixing bowl and knead vigorously, by hand for 10 to 15 minutes, or by machine on medium-low speed for about 10 minutes. Since you're using a high-protein bread flour, it takes a bit more effort and time to develop the gluten. The dough will be quite stiff; if you're using a stand mixer it will "thwap" the sides of the bowl and hold its shape (without spreading at all) when you stop the mixer. Place the dough in a lightly greased bowl and set it aside to rise until noticeably puffy though not necessarily doubled in bulk, 1 to 1½ hours.

Transfer the dough to a work surface and divide it into 8 pieces. Working with one piece at a time, roll it into a smooth, round ball. Cover the balls with plastic wrap and let them rest for 30 minutes. They'll puff up very slightly.

While the dough is resting, prepare the water bath by heating the water, malt powder, and sugar to a very gentle boil in a large, wide-diameter pan. Preheat the oven to 425°F.

Use your index finger to poke a hole through the center of each ball (see illustration on next page), then twirl the dough on your finger to stretch the hole until it's about 2″ in diameter (the entire bagel will be about 4″ across). Place the bagel on a lightly greased or parchment-lined baking sheet and repeat with the remaining pieces of dough.

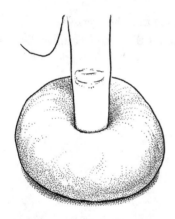

After forming the dough into a ball, poke a hole through the center with your finger. Stretch this opening (twirling the dough around your finger works well) until you have a hole 2″ across.

Transfer the bagels, four at a time if possible, to the simmering water. Increase the heat under the pan to bring the water back up to a gently simmering boil, if necessary. Cook the bagels for 2 minutes, gently flip them over, and cook 1 minute more. Using a skimmer or strainer, remove the bagels from the water and place them back on the baking sheet. Repeat with the remaining bagels.

Bake the bagels for 20 to 25 minutes, until they're as deep a brown as you like, turning them over after about 15 minutes, which will help them remain tall and round. Remove the bagels from the oven and cool completely on a rack.

NUTRITION INFORMATION PER SERVING: 1 plain bagel, 111g

211 cal | 1g fat | 7g protein | 43g complex carbohydrates | 2g sugar | 2g dietary fiber | 0mg cholesterol | 536mg sodium

VARIATIONS

SESAME SEED BAGELS: Brush each bagel, just before baking, with a glaze made of 1 egg white beaten until frothy with 1 tablespoon of water. Glaze each bagel and sprinkle heavily with seeds.

ONION BAGELS: Bake bagels for 20 to 22 minutes (or until they're almost as brown as you like) and remove the pan from the oven, keeping the oven turned on. Working with one bagel at a time, glaze as instructed above and sprinkle with minced, dried onion. Return the bagels to the oven for no more than 2 minutes (the onions will burn if the bagels are left in longer than that).

CINNAMON RAISIN BAGELS: Knead about ⅔ cup (100g) of raisins into the dough toward the end of the kneading process. Just before you're done kneading, sprinkle your work surface heavily with cinnamon sugar and give the dough a few more turns; it will pick up the cinnamon sugar in irregular swirls. Divide the dough into 8 pieces, form each piece into a ball, and roll each ball in additional cinnamon sugar. Let rest and shape as directed above.

CLASSIC PRETZELS: The traditional street vendor pretzel, with its characteristic dark brown, highly glazed appearance, is difficult to make at home, since professional bakers often use food-safe lye to give pretzels their characteristic sheen. You can use bagel dough to make a dense, chewy, Philadelphia-style pretzel; it will lack only in appearance.

Prepare bagel dough up through its first rise. Divide the dough into 12 pieces and roll each piece into a 25″ to 30″ rope. Shape ropes into pretzels (see illustrations) and simmer and bake as directed in the bagel recipe, understanding that the pretzels are larger and will be a bit more challenging to deal with as you move them from counter to water bath to baking sheet.

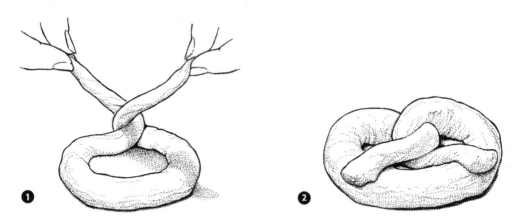

1 and 2. Form the rope of dough into a circle, leaving 4˝ free on each end of the rope. Twist these ends around each other, and fold the twist down the middle of the circle. Press the ends of the dough to the outside of the ring to make the pretzel shape.

ENGLISH MUFFINS

10 TO 12 MUFFINS

Sure, you can buy excellent English muffins, but for those of you who like the challenge of making your own, this is a great recipe.

We find these muffins are best made the day before you want to serve them. You may certainly sample them straight off the griddle, but they can be a bit gummy at that point; they definitely benefit by drying out for a day.

STARTER

1½ cups (180g) unbleached all-purpose flour

¾ cup (170g) water

⅛ teaspoon instant yeast

DOUGH

1¾ cups (210g) unbleached all-
purpose flour

2 tablespoons (14g) cornstarch

1 teaspoon instant yeast

1 teaspoon salt

2 tablespoons (25g) sugar or non-
diastatic malt powder

2 teaspoons baking powder

2 tablespoons (28g) butter, melted

¾ cup (170g) milk, warm

1 to 2 tablespoons (10g to 20g)
cornmeal, for sprinkling on the pan
(if you're baking the muffins)

TO MAKE THE STARTER: Mix the flour, water, and yeast in a medium bowl to form a smooth batter. Cover and leave at room temperature for at least 4 hours, or up to 16 hours. The starter should be puffy and full of holes when it's ready to use.

TO MAKE THE DOUGH: In a large bowl, beat together the starter and all the dough ingredients to form a smooth, very soft dough. The dough needs to be beaten for 5 to 8 minutes, so unless you feel like giving your biceps a good workout, we suggest using a stand mixer. Cover the bowl and place it in a warm spot until the dough has doubled in size, about 1 hour.

Now you can bake the English muffins in the oven or dry-fry them on the stovetop. Read both sets of directions first to decide which you want to do.

TO PREPARE MUFFINS FOR BAKING: Lightly grease 10 to 12 English muffin rings (nonstick spray works well) and place the rings on a lightly greased or parchment-lined baking sheet that's been sprinkled with a small amount of cornmeal. (The cornmeal isn't really necessary, but it makes the muffins look more authentic.) Stir the dough, then drop a scant ¼ cup into each ring. Sprinkle lightly with cornmeal. Smooth the dough with your fingers, dipped in water first. If you don't have English muffin rings, simply drop the soft dough onto the pan and shape it with your fingers. The muffins won't be as symmetrical, but their taste will be just fine.

Cover the pan and place in a warm place to rise for 1 hour, or until the muffins have grown by at least a third.

TO BAKE ENGLISH MUFFINS: Preheat the oven to 350°F. If you've used muffin rings, place a clean baking sheet atop the muffins, which keeps them flat on both sides (rather than crowned on the top) so they'll fit better in the toaster slot. (If you're not using muffin rings, don't put a pan on top of them—they'll squish.) Bake the muffins for 25 minutes, until they're lightly browned on both sides. (The bottoms will be more brown than the tops, just like the ones you buy at the store.) The muffins may be fork-split and eaten immediately (they'll be soft) or, for crunchier muffins, cool them completely, split them, and toast.

TO DRY-FRY ENGLISH MUFFINS: Let the dough rise for 1½ hours, until it's very puffy looking. Preheat a griddle to 325°F. Lightly grease English muffin rings. Place the rings on the griddle. Lightly stir the dough, then use a ¼-cup measure or muffin scoop to fill each ring about a third full. If you're not using muffin rings, simply drop the dough by ¼-cupfuls onto the griddle. Dry-fry the muffins (fry without grease) for 10 to 12 minutes on the first side before turning them over to cook on the other side. You'll know the muffins are ready to turn when the top side has formed a dry skin. Cook the muffins for about half the time you cooked them on the first side, remove them from the griddle, carefully remove the rings, and allow them to cool.

NUTRITION INFORMATION PER SERVING: 1 muffin, 82g

179 cal | 3g fat | 5g protein | 30g complex carbohydrates | 2g sugar | 1g dietary fiber | 8mg cholesterol | 108mg sodium

HOT BUTTERED PRETZELS

8 PRETZELS

Pretzels come in a few forms: crisp and hard in bags at your grocery store; bagel-like and chewy from a street vendor; or, if you're lucky and in the right place, soft, buttery, and tender, like those this wonderful recipe yields.

DOUGH

2½ cups (300g) unbleached all-purpose flour

½ teaspoon salt

1 teaspoon sugar

2¼ teaspoons instant yeast

⅞ to 1 cup (196g to 224g) water, warm*

TOPPING

½ cup (112g) water, warm

1 teaspoon sugar

coarse, kosher, or pretzel salt (optional)

3 tablespoons (42g) salted butter, melted

Place all the dough ingredients in a bowl and beat until well combined. Knead the dough, by hand or mixer, for about 5 minutes, until it's soft, smooth, and quite slack. Transfer the dough to a lightly greased bowl, cover, and let it rise for 30 minutes.

Preheat the oven to 475°F. Prepare two baking sheets by spraying them with vegetable oil spray or lining them with parchment paper.

Transfer the dough to a lightly greased work surface and divide it into 8 equal pieces (about 63g each). Let the pieces rest, uncovered, for 5 minutes.

Roll each piece of dough into a long thin rope (around 28″) and twist each rope into a pretzel (see illustration, page 174). Dip the pretzels in the warm water mixed with 1 teaspoon sugar, and place them on the baking sheets. Sprinkle them lightly with the salt, if using. Let them rest, uncovered, for 10 minutes.

Bake the pretzels for 8 to 9 minutes, until they're golden brown, reversing the baking sheets midway through.

Remove the pretzels from the oven and brush them thoroughly with the melted butter. Keep brushing the butter on until you've used it all; it may seem like a lot, but that's what gives these pretzels their ethereal taste. Eat the pretzels warm, or reheat them in an oven or microwave.

* Use the greater amount in the winter, the lesser amount in the summer, and somewhere in between in the spring and fall. Your goal is a soft dough.

NUTRITION INFORMATION PER SERVING: **1 pretzel, 85g**
171 cal | 5g fat | 4g protein | 27g complex carbohydrates | 1g sugar | 1g dietary fiber | 12mg cholesterol | 444mg sodium

VARIATION

SOFT BREADSTICKS: For soft, fat, chewy breadsticks, prepare the pretzel dough up through its first rest. Divide it into 24 pieces and shape each piece into an 8˝ to 10˝ breadstick. Transfer the breadsticks to a lightly greased or parchment-lined baking sheet, brush with warm water, and sprinkle with salt (for salt sticks) or seeds. Let rest and bake as directed in the preceding pretzel recipe.

FREEZE!

Most yeast doughs respond very well to being refrigerated or frozen for a while. The exceptions are doughs very high in milk, eggs, and/or sugar, which tend to start fermenting after several days in the refrigerator (they do better in the freezer); or doughs with a lot of added fresh ingredients, such as cheese, fruit, or vegetables. These doughs tend to become watery when frozen, then thawed.

We've discovered the best way to produce freezer dough is to prepare your dough, let it rise once, deflate it, and freeze it before it can rise again. With loaf bread dough, we shape the dough, place it in a greased loaf pan, place the pan inside a plastic bag, seal it, and freeze for 24 hours; then remove it from the pan, wrap it tightly in plastic, then in aluminum foil, and return to the freezer.

When you want to bake bread, unwrap the dough, place it in a greased loaf pan, cover it with lightly greased plastic wrap, and let it thaw and rise at room temperature. Typically, it will take about 4 hours for the dough to thaw and begin to rise, and another hour or so for it to rise fully; these times, of course, depend on the temperature of your kitchen. You also may thaw the dough by placing it in its greased pan in the refrigerator overnight, then removing it for its final rise the next morning.

For best results, yeast bread or rolls should only be stored in the freezer for 2 to 3 weeks before thawing and baking.

CRUSTY HARD ROLLS

12 ROLLS

These feathery light hard rolls have a delicious shiny, crunchy crust, partly the result of allowing them to proof overnight in the refrigerator, partly from an egg-white wash applied just prior to baking. This recipe starts with a poolish (pool-EESH), a premixed starter of flour, water, and a touch of yeast. Stirred together 12 to 16 hours before the remainder of the dough, the organic acids and alcohol produced by the growing yeast do wonders for both the bread's taste and its texture. Poolish is an idiomatic French word for Polish, as in Poland, which is where the French believe this type of starter originated.

POOLISH

1 cup (120g) unbleached all-
    purpose flour

½ cup (113g) water

⅛ teaspoon instant yeast

DOUGH

3½ cups (420g) unbleached all-
    purpose flour

1 cup (227g) water

1½ teaspoons salt

½ teaspoon instant yeast

WASH

1 large egg white

½ cup (113g) water

TO MAKE THE POOLISH: Mix together the ingredients until smooth, cover, and let rest at room temperature overnight.

TO MAKE THE DOUGH: Combine the poolish and all the dough ingredients and mix and knead them together—by hand or mixer—until you've made a soft, somewhat smooth dough. It should be cohesive but the surface should still be a bit rough; don't

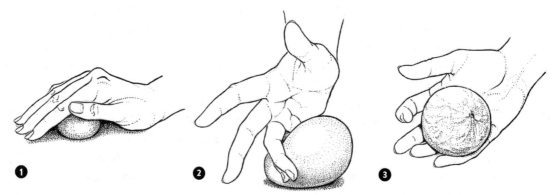

1. To roll a piece of dough into a round ball, place it on an unfloured, ungreased work surface. **2.** Cup your fingers lightly over the dough, and roll it quickly and gently in a circular motion, using the very top of your palm (at the base of your fingers) and applying the barest amount of downward pressure. **3.** Rolling the dough this way creates a tight, smooth top with a small "belly button" on the bottom.

knead it until completely smooth. Cover and let the dough rise for 3 hours, gently deflating it and turning it over after 1 hour, and again after 2 hours.

TO ASSEMBLE: Turn the dough onto a lightly greased or floured work surface. Divide it into 12 pieces, about 56g each. Shape the pieces into balls and firm them up by rolling them under your lightly cupped fingers on an unfloured work surface (see illustrations). Place the rolls on a parchment-lined baking sheet, cover them, and let them rise for 1½ to 2 hours, until they've doubled in size. Refrigerate them, covered, for several hours, or overnight.

Preheat the oven to 425°F.

Remove the rolls from the refrigerator. Whisk together the egg white and water and brush this wash on the rolls (you won't use it all). Slash a ¼″ deep cut across the top of each roll and bake for 30 to 35 minutes, until they're a deep golden brown. Remove them from the oven and cool on a rack. For an extra-crisp crust, let them cool in the turned-off oven with the door propped open.

The ball on the left still has a shaggy, rough surface. Continue rolling under your cupped hands to get a smooth, round ball (right).

NUTRITION INFORMATION PER SERVING: **1 roll, 82g**
152 cal | 0g fat | 5g protein | 32g complex carbohydrates | 0 g sugar | 1g dietary fiber | 0 mg cholesterol | 272mg sodium

ROLLING ROLLS

When the recipe directs you to shape pieces of dough into smooth balls, the process involves rounding the pieces on an unfloured, ungreased work surface. This is important; if you try to roll the balls of dough on a work surface covered with flour or coated with oil, you'll lack the dynamic tension between dough and rolling surface necessary for the rolls to become round. If the dough is very sticky, use a very light coating of oil on your work surface; never use flour.

BEAUTIFUL BURGER BUNS

8 LARGE BUNS

Soft, subtly sweet, and golden yellow from the butter and egg, these simple buns are perfect for burgers, but are also excellent for any kind of sandwich. You can even turn them into dinner rolls by shaping them into round balls and crowding them close together in a pan. This recipe came to us from a baker named Ellen Dill, and was quickly adopted as everyone's favorite soft bun.

DOUGH

1 cup (227g) water

2 tablespoons (28g) butter, at room temperature

1 large egg

3¼ cups (390g) unbleached all-purpose flour

¼ cup (50g) sugar

1 teaspoon salt

1 tablespoon (10g) instant yeast

1 teaspoon onion powder (optional)

½ teaspoon dried minced onion (optional)

TOPPING

3 tablespoons (43g) butter, melted

Combine all the ingredients and mix and knead them together to make a soft, smooth dough. Place the dough in a lightly greased bowl, cover it, and let it rise for 1 hour.

Divide the dough into 8 pieces and shape each piece into a flattened ball. Place the buns on greased baking sheets, cover, and let rise 30 to 40 minutes, until they're quite puffy. Brush the buns with about half of the melted butter.

Preheat the oven to 375°F. Bake the buns for 15 to 18 minutes, until they're golden brown. Remove them from the oven, brush with the remaining melted butter, and cool them on a rack. Split and use for burgers or sandwiches. For burgers, butter the split sides and fry them, buttered side down, until they're golden brown and warmed through.

NUTRITION INFORMATION PER SERVING: 1 bun, 90g
211 cal | 4g fat | 6g protein | 32g complex carbohydrates | 6g sugar | 1g dietary fiber | 35mg cholesterol | 276mg sodium

AMISH DINNER ROLLS

24 ROLLS

This exceptional recipe was inspired by one in a small handwritten Amish cookbook; thus its name. Dense yet still tender, moist but not at all heavy, these are the quintessential soft dinner rolls. Mashed potato gives them both their soft texture and staying power: They'll remain moist and fresh-tasting at room temperature for several days, so consider them a good candidate for making ahead.

2 large eggs

⅓ cup (67g) sugar

2 teaspoons salt

6 tablespoons (¾ stick, 85g) unsalted butter, softened

1 cup (213g) unseasoned mashed potatoes, lightly packed

2½ teaspoons instant yeast

¾ cup (170g) water, lukewarm (water in which the potatoes were boiled, if possible)

4¼ cups (510g) unbleached all-purpose flour

Mix and knead all the ingredients together to make a smooth, soft dough.

Place the dough in a lightly greased bowl, cover the bowl with plastic wrap, and let the dough rise until it's doubled in bulk, about 90 minutes.

Gently deflate the dough, and divide it into 24 balls. Round each ball into a smooth roll.

Place the rolls in a lightly greased 9″ × 13″ pan. Cover the pan with lightly greased plastic wrap and let them rise for 1½ to 2 hours, until they're quite puffy. Toward the end of the rising time, preheat the oven to 350°F.

Bake the rolls for 20 to 25 minutes, until they're golden brown and feel set. Remove them from the oven and turn them out of the pan onto a rack. Brush with melted butter, if desired.

Serve rolls warm, or at room temperature.

NUTRITION INFORMATION PER SERVING: 1 roll, 48g

127 cal | 5g fat | 3g protein | 17g complex carbohydrates | 3g sugar | 0g dietary fiber | 24mg cholesterol | 174mg sodium

JAPANESE MILK BREAD ROLLS

8 ROLLS

Also known as Hokkaido milk bread, these rolls are incredibly soft and airy thanks to a simple technique involving a roux "starter," known as *tangzhong*. The roux is mixed into the final dough, producing wonderfully tender bread each and every time.

TANGZHONG (STARTER)

3 tablespoons (43g) water

3 tablespoons (43g) whole milk

2 tablespoons (15g) unbleached bread flour

DOUGH

2½ cups (300g) unbleached bread flour

2 tablespoons (16g) nonfat dry milk

¼ cup (50g) sugar

1 teaspoon salt

1 tablespoon (10g) instant yeast

½ cup (113g) whole milk

1 large egg

4 tablespoons (½ stick, 57g) butter, melted

TO MAKE THE TANGZHONG: Combine all the ingredients in a small saucepan and whisk until no lumps remain.

Place the saucepan over low heat and cook the mixture, stirring constantly, until thick and the spoon or spatula leaves a line on the bottom of the pan, about 3 to 5 minutes. Transfer the tangzhong to a small mixing bowl and let it cool to room temperature.

TO MAKE THE DOUGH: Combine the tangzhong with the dough ingredients, then mix and knead to make a smooth, elastic dough.

Shape the dough into a ball and let it rest in a lightly greased, covered bowl for 60 to 90 minutes, until puffy but not necessarily doubled in bulk. Gently deflate the dough, divide it into 8 equal pieces, and shape each piece into a ball.

Place the rolls into a lightly greased 8˝ or 9˝ round cake pan. Cover the pan and let the rolls rest for 40 to 50 minutes, until puffy.

Preheat the oven to 350°F. Brush the rolls with milk and bake for 25 to 30 minutes, until golden brown on top; a digital thermometer inserted into the center of the middle roll should read at least 190°F.

Remove the rolls from the oven. Allow them to cool in the pan for 10 minutes, then transfer them to a rack to cool completely.

NUTRITION INFORMATION PER SERVING: 1 roll, 90g

250 cal | 8g fat | 8g protein | 28g complex carbohydrates | 9g sugar | 1g dietary fiber | 40mg cholesterol | 320mg sodium

GRUYÈRE-STUFFED CRUSTY LOAVES

4 MINI LOAVES OR 2 STANDARD-SIZE LOAVES

Who doesn't love warm bread and cheese? Fresh from the oven, a lava-flow of aromatic cheese melts down the sides of these crusty loaves, made light and chewy thanks to the use of bread flour. They're like a grilled cheese sandwich in roll form, and they make a very nice partner for soup or salad. When making the dough, consider the weather and use the greater amount of water in winter, when conditions are dry; and the lesser amount in summer, when the air is humid.

STARTER

1¼ cups (149g) unbleached bread flour

1 teaspoon salt

½ teaspoon instant yeast

½ cup (113g) water, cool

DOUGH

1 cup plus 2 tablespoons to 1¼ cups
    (255g to 284g) water, lukewarm

1 teaspoon salt

3½ cups (418g) unbleached bread flour

½ teaspoon instant yeast

FILLING

1 tablespoon (16g) garlic oil (optional)

2½ cups (283g) grated Gruyère cheese,
    or the cheese of your choice (sharp
    cheddar or a mixture of provolone
    and mozzarella are good)

TO MAKE THE STARTER: Mix the flour, salt, yeast, and water in a medium bowl until well combined; the starter will be stiff, not soft and liquid. Cover and let rest overnight at room temperature (65°F to 75°F is ideal); it'll become bubbly.

TO MAKE THE DOUGH: Combine the risen starter with the water, salt, flour, and yeast. Knead to make a smooth dough.

Place the dough in a lightly greased bowl, cover, and let it rise until it's nearly doubled in bulk, about 1½ to 2 hours.

Gently deflate the dough and turn it out onto a lightly floured surface, or a piece of parchment. Pat and stretch it into a ¾″ thick rectangle, about 9″ × 12″. Spritz with water (or brush with garlic oil, if using), and sprinkle with the grated cheese.

Starting with a long side, roll the dough into a log, pinching the seam and ends to seal. The cheese will try to fall out; that's fine, just try to enclose as much as possible, then pack any errant cheese into the ends before sealing.

Place the log, seam-side down, on a lightly floured or lightly oiled surface (or leave it on the parchment and place the parchment on a baking sheet, for easiest transport).

Gently cut the log into four crosswise slices, for mini loaves; or simply cut the dough in half, for two full-size loaves. A large sharp knife or serrated knife works well here. If for some reason you fail to cut all the way through the dough at the bottom, simply take a pair of scissors and snip through the dough.

Place the loaves on one (for two loaves) or two (for four mini loaves) lightly greased or parchment-lined baking sheets, cut side up.

Cover the loaves and let rise until they're puffy but not doubled in bulk, about 1 to 1½ hours. Toward the end of the rising time, preheat the oven to 425°F. If you're baking two loaves, position a rack in the center of the oven. If you're baking four loaves, place two racks toward the center of the oven with just enough room in between to accommodate the rising loaves.

Spread the loaves open a bit at the top, if necessary, to more fully expose the cheese. Spritz with warm water.

Bake for 25 to 35 minutes (for the mini loaves), or 35 to 40 minutes (for the full-size loaves), or until the cheese is melted and the loaves are a deep golden brown. If you're baking four loaves on two pans, rotate the pans halfway through the baking time: top to bottom, bottom to top. Remove the pans from the oven and cool the bread right on the pans. The bread is best served warm.

NUTRITION INFORMATION PER SERVING: 1 slice, 40g
100 cal | 3g fat | 5g protein | 13g complex carbohydrates | 0g sugar | 1g dietary fiber | 10mg cholesterol | 260mg sodium

STARTER, SPONGE, POOLISH, BIGA . . . I'M CONFUSED!

A wide array of methods to help jump-start your bread's rising (fermentation) process fall under the heading of preferments—as in PRE-ferments, something that happens before the first major fermenting (rising) of your bread dough. All the terms below refer to a type of starter, a combination of flour, water, and yeast prepared prior to the main body of the dough when making bread.

How do you know which, if any, of these preferments to use? When you're just getting started, rely on your recipe; if it calls for a particular preferment, use it. Once you've become acquainted with the various types, use the one that fits your schedule, and that you feel produces the best flavor and texture in your bread.

The term "starter," often used as a generic substitute for the word "preferments," can also refer specifically to sourdough starter, a mixture of flour, water, and wild yeast used to provide the leavening (and wonderful flavor) in bread.

A sponge is typically made by using all of the liquid, half of the flour, and half of the yeast in a bread recipe. These three elements are mixed together, placed in a cool spot, and left to bubble for 3 to 10 hours or so. The remaining dough ingredients are added, and the bread is kneaded, shaped, raised, and baked as directed.

Poolish and biga are overnight starters, both utilizing domestic yeast (as well as wild). Poolish is a wet starter (the consistency of thick pancake batter), made from flour, water, and a touch of yeast (about 1/16 teaspoon).

A biga—the Italian name for a starter—can be either wet (batter-like consistency) or dry (stiff dough consistency). Like the poolish, it begins with flour, water, and a tiny bit of yeast. It can develop overnight, or for up to 3 days. As it develops, it will become more acidic and complex in flavor. The longer you let the biga develop, the more sour it will become.

Why are some bigas wet and some dry? This has to do with how much time you want to spend developing them, and how sour you want your bread to be. A wet biga will produce acetic acid, the acid that makes bread taste sour, more quickly than a dry biga. Most often, use a wet biga if you want to make dough within 10 to 12 hours; a dry one if you'd like to wait longer.

Levain is the French incarnation of what we know as sourdough starter. But, rather than taking the form of a slurry, a fairly liquid combination of flour and water, a levain is in the form of a dough, and the bread it leavens is not particularly sour. Because of the diet it has during its initial days, it develops a high enough concentration of wild yeast that it can leaven bread without the addition of commercial yeast. The slight acidity imparted by the levain allows the flavor of breads made with it to improve over time.

A chef or *mère* (they're the same thing) is actually just part of a levain. In order to make bread, you break off part of the levain (it's stiff and doughlike); this piece is called a chef or *mère*. The chef or *mère* is fed with additional flour or water and allowed to ferment; this process can be followed up to three times, each time the chef's flavor becoming more complex, before finally it's used as the leavening agent in a bread recipe.

Hearth or Country Breads

When you hear the phrase "artisan bread," what comes to mind? A crusty, chewy loaf, perhaps loaded with pecans and dried cherries, or scented with fresh herbs. Or maybe a big round of sourdough with a shower of seeds on top. Or perhaps just the ultimate baguette.

What distinguishes artisan breads from others is the time that goes into them: most are made with an overnight (or longer) starter. As opposed to true sourdough, which is leavened by wild yeast, these loaves are often prepared using commercial yeast, but the flavor that develops from a series of long, slow rises is what sets them apart.

Most artisan-style hearth breads rely on just four ingredients: flour, water, yeast, and salt. Some include olive oil or other fat, but most are fairly simple breads. How, then, can there be such an incredible variety of breads made from these four basic ingredients? The methods used to make the dough, the time the dough is given to develop flavor, and the way the loaves are shaped and baked have an enormous effect on the final product. The following are some hints that we've come up with over the years that will help you successfully make artisan-style breads at home.

CHOOSING YOUR INGREDIENTS: Use unbleached, unbromated flour with a protein level between 10.5% and 12%. If your water has a strong chlorine taste/smell or other off-flavors, use bottled water. To eliminate chlorine from tap water, let the water sit in an open container for a few hours. There are many different yeasts on the market, each with its own following. We recommend instant yeast because it's so easy to use, easy to store, and can withstand some mishandling.

TIME: Flavor comes from long, slow fermentation (rising) at relatively low temperatures. An ambient rising temperature of 70°F to 80°F results in the best-flavored bread. Using a preferment (a sponge, poolish, biga, or levain) helps develop even more flavor.

USE LESS YEAST: If you plan to use a preferment and allow time for a long first rise, you can use less yeast. Using less yeast allows the dough to develop slowly, leaving time for all the enzymatic and chemical changes that lead to flavorful bread.

USE MORE WATER: Wetter is usually better. A slack dough allows for a more active fermentation and complete development of the gluten structure. A hydration of 65% or more based on total flour weight is a good place to start. (Consider the weight of the flour is 100%, then divide the weight of the water by the weight of the flour to find the hydration level. For example, if your flour weighs 336g, using 168g of water would give you 50% hydration.)

MIX (KNEAD) LESS: Mix and knead your dough less than to full development. The gluten continues to develop during fermentation, so if you knead the dough fully it will be hard to handle after fermentation; it will be too strong to shape properly and won't rise to its full volume in the oven. Full development is reached when your dough is very smooth, cleans the sides and bottom of the bowl, and will stretch—without tearing—to make a transparent "window," that is, you can see light through it. Dough at less than full development will be slightly sticky to the touch, won't be totally smooth, and will tear after stretching a small amount.

HANDLE WITH CARE: Handle dough gently during shaping. When you're deflating dough at any point during its fermentation process, simply fold it over gently onto itself. And when you're shaping, you don't want to expel all the air; just make the dough smooth, without huge air pockets.

BAKING WITH STEAM: Bake breads directly on a baking stone with steam in the oven for the first 10 minutes. It's nearly impossible to get the amount of steam in a home oven that a professional steam-injected oven has. That said, a good home approximation is putting a cast iron skillet into the bottom of the oven, preheating the oven for at least 30 minutes on the highest heat possible, and pouring boiling water (⅓ to ½ cup, 75g to 113g) into the hot pan just after the bread is put in. This method should allow you to keep the outside surface of the dough moist enough to let the loaf expand. Spritzing the loaves with water just before baking also helps.

THOROUGH BAKING: Bake the loaves until they've reached an internal temperature of 190° to 210°F and the crust is medium to dark brown. Much of the flavor of bread is concentrated in the crust, and the darker the crust (within reason, of course; don't let it blacken), the more flavorful the bread.

ADDING DRIED FRUIT

When making a yeast bread with fruit, be aware that the fruit will inevitably release some of its sugar into the dough, which will change the sugar ratio and may slow your bread's rise. To impact rising time as little as possible, do the following:

- If you're using raisins or other fruits that can remain whole (currants, dried cranberries, etc.), don't soak them first; it isn't necessary and it allows their sugar to begin leaching out.
- When adding fruits that need to be chopped (dried apricots, large pieces of dried pineapple, etc.), leave the fruit pieces as large as possible; the finer you chop the fruit, the more sugar it will release into the dough.
- Don't add fruit to your initial dough; let it go through its first rise, then briefly knead the fruit in before shaping. This gives the yeast a good strong start before you add the fruit.

RAISIN PECAN RYE BREAD

1 LOAF

There's something very right about the combination of rye flour, raisins, and pecans. The subtle earthy flavor of rye, the nuttiness of the pecans, and the sweetness of raisins combine to make a bread whose flavor seems to hit all the high notes at once. This dense, moist bread is delicious spread with butter (toasted or not); or serve it with Roquefort or another assertive cheese.

BIGA

⅛ teaspoon instant yeast

1 cup (120g) unbleached all-purpose flour

⅓ cup (76g) water

DOUGH

1½ teaspoons salt

3 tablespoons (40g) brown sugar

½ cup (56g) rye flour

½ cup (56g) pumpernickel flour

1 cup (120g) unbleached all-purpose flour

¾ cup (170g) water

2 teaspoons instant yeast

2 tablespoons (28g) butter

½ cup (53g) chopped pecans

1 cup (147g) currants or raisins

TO MAKE THE BIGA: Stir together the yeast, flour, and water. The dough will be quite stiff. Place it in a lightly greased bowl, cover it, and let it rest at room temperature overnight.

TO MAKE THE DOUGH: The next day, combine the biga with the remaining ingredients (except the pecans and fruit) in a large mixing bowl, or in the bowl of a stand mixer, mixing to form a shaggy dough. Knead the dough until smooth, then place it in a lightly greased bowl and let it rest for 1 hour; it will become quite puffy, but it may not double in bulk.

Transfer the dough to a lightly greased work surface, gently deflate it, and knead in the nuts and fruit. Shape the dough into a slightly flattened ball and place it on a lightly greased baking sheet. Cover the pan with a reusable cover or lightly greased plastic wrap. Let the loaf rise for 45 minutes to 1 hour, until it's puffy.

Preheat the oven to 350°F. Bake the bread for about 40 minutes (tenting it lightly with aluminum foil for the final 15 minutes) until its interior registers 190°F on a digital thermometer. Remove the bread from the oven and cool it on a rack.

NUTRITION INFORMATION PER SERVING: 1 slice, 79g

236 cal | 6g fat | 6g protein | 38g complex carbohydrates | 3g sugar | 2g dietary fiber | 9mg cholesterol | 214mg sodium

VARIATION

RAISIN RYE CRISPS: The preceding recipe makes a very nice sandwich or toasting bread. But, to make rye crisps—delightfully crunchy slices of oven-toasted bread— we use more rye and less wheat flour. This makes a denser bread, so it's easier to slice into crisps. In addition, we shape the breads differently: The bread for crisps is formed into two baguettes, to be sliced crosswise. These small, oval slices show less tendency to crumble, and also toast more evenly than would a large sandwich slice.

Prepare the biga as directed above. The next day, when making the dough, change the flour amounts to ⅔ cup (70g) each rye and pumpernickel flours, and ⅔ cup (81g) unbleached bread flour. Reduce the amount of yeast from 2 teaspoons to 1½ teaspoons. Prepare dough as directed up to the point when it's ready to shape.

Transfer the dough to a lightly oiled work surface and divide it in half. Shape each half into a thin baguette about 15″ long. Place the baguettes on a baking sheet and cover them with a dough cover or lightly greased plastic wrap. Let the baguettes rest for 1 hour. They won't appear to rise very much; that's OK.

Preheat the oven to 350°F. Bake the loaves for about 30 minutes, or until they're brown and their interior registers 190°F on a digital thermometer. Remove them from the oven and place on a rack to cool. When the bread is cool, wrap each loaf loosely in a clean dish towel and let them rest overnight.

The next day, cut the bread, making slightly diagonal cuts (as if you're making biscotti) into ¼″ slices. Place the slices in a single layer on ungreased baking sheets.

Preheat the oven to 275°F. Bake the slices for 25 to 30 minutes, until they're a light golden brown and very crisp. Remove from the oven and let them cool on the baking sheets. When the crisps are completely cool, store them in an airtight container.

CURRANTS VS. RAISINS

We like to use currants in place of raisins in bread that will be served in medium-to-thin slices; the smaller currants are more likely to remain embedded in the bread, rather than being ripped out by the knife as it cuts.

BAGUETTES

3 BAGUETTES

The first goal of every budding artisan bread baker is a crusty, flavorful baguette. Let this recipe be the starting point on a journey that may last for quite a long time—the "perfect" baguette is a serious challenge for any home baker.

This recipe makes use of a poolish (see description, page 185) to enhance the baguettes' flavor. Notice the symmetry of the ingredient amounts: nearly equal amounts of flour and water (by weight) in the poolish; in the dough, the same amount of water again and double the amount of flour. These are the classic French proportions for a baguette.

POOLISH

1¼ cups (150g) unbleached all-
   purpose flour

⅔ cup (152g) water, cool (approximately
   60°F)

⅛ teaspoon instant yeast

DOUGH

generous 2½ cups (300g) unbleached
   all-purpose flour

1½ teaspoons instant yeast

2 teaspoons salt

⅔ cup (152g) water, cool (approximately
   60°F)

TO MAKE THE POOLISH: Combine the flour, water, and yeast in a medium bowl and mix just until blended. Let the poolish rise for 12 hours or so (overnight is usually just fine). It should dome slightly on top and look aerated and spongy. Try to catch it before it starts to fall, as it will be at its optimum flavor and vigor when it's at its highest point. On the other hand, don't make yourself crazy about this; we've used plenty of starters that are either pre- or post-prime and they work fine.

TO MAKE THE DOUGH: Place the flour, yeast, and salt in a mixing bowl or the bowl of a stand mixer. Add the poolish and water and mix the dough until it just becomes cohesive, about 30 seconds. (It's OK if there's still flour in the bottom of the bowl.) Cover and let the dough rest for 20 minutes. This resting period allows the flour to absorb the liquid, which will make kneading much easier.

Knead the dough, using your hands or a stand mixer, for about 6 to 8 minutes by hand, or 4 to 5 minutes at medium-low speed in your mixer, until it's cohesive and elastic but not perfectly smooth; the surface should still exhibit some roughness. You'll want to knead this dough less than you think you should; while it will shape itself into a ball, it won't have the characteristic "baby's bottom" smoothness of fully kneaded dough. You aren't kneading this dough all the way because you'll give it a nice long rise, and during that rising time the gluten continues to develop. If you kneaded the dough fully before rising, the gluten would become unpleasantly stiff during the long rise.

Transfer the dough to a lightly oiled bowl (or oil your mixer bowl and leave it in there). Cover and let it rise for 2 hours, folding it over after the first hour (or more frequently if the dough is very slack or wet; folding helps strengthen the gluten). To fold the dough, lift it out of the bowl, gently deflate it, fold it in half, and place it back in the bowl; this expels excess carbon dioxide and redistributes the yeast's food.

Divide the dough into three pieces and gently form them into rough logs. Let them rest for 20 minutes, then shape into long (13″ to 14″), thin baguettes. Let the baguettes rise, covered, in the folds of a linen or cotton couche (see Tools, page 531) until they've become noticeably puffy, 30 to 40 minutes. If you don't have a couche, place them in a perforated triple baguette pan, or on a lightly greased or parchment-lined baking sheet, and cover them lightly with a reusable cover or greased plastic wrap.

Preheat the oven and baking stone to 500°F. (Baguettes baked on a stone will have a crispier crust, but those baked on a pan will be just as tasty, if not equally crunchy.) Just before putting the loaves into the oven, use a lame (see Tools, page 532) or sharp serrated knife to gently make four diagonal cuts in each loaf. These cuts should angle into the dough at about 45° (in other words, don't cut straight down) and should be a good ¼″ deep. Be gentle but quick; if you hesitate and drag your lame or knife through the dough, it will stick rather than cut.

Spray the loaves heavily with warm water; this will somewhat replicate a steam oven. (For other ways to create steam, see page 227.) Put the loaves in the oven. Reduce the oven heat to 475°F and bake the loaves for 20 minutes or so. Remove the loaves from the oven when they're a deep golden brown and transfer them to a rack to cool. Listen closely just as you take the loaves out of the oven; you'll hear them "sing," crackling as they hit the cool air of your kitchen. Let the loaves cool completely before slicing; if you can't wait, understand that the texture of the loaves where you cut them may be gummy as they still contain moisture, which will migrate out as they cool.

NUTRITION INFORMATION PER SERVING: **2 slices, 39g**
76 cal | 0g fat | 2g protein | 16g complex carbohydrates | 0g sugar | 16g dietary fiber | 0mg cholesterol | 214mg sodium

VOLLKORNBROT

ONE 13″ LOAF

This traditional whole grain loaf is deeply rye-flavored with a fine-grained, dense texture. It requires very little in the way of hands-on time or kneading. Enjoy thin slices with smoked salmon, fruit preserves, or a simple pat of butter. It will keep for weeks wrapped tightly in the refrigerator, or for months in the freezer.

STARTER

3¾ cups (398g) pumpernickel flour

1¼ cups (397g) water, lukewarm

2 tablespoons (21g) ripe (fed) sourdough starter or ¼ teaspoon instant yeast

SOAKER

2⅓ cups (283g) rye chops

1¼ cups (284g) water, lukewarm

DOUGH

2 cups (212g) pumpernickel flour

¼ cup (57g) water, lukewarm

1 tablespoon (16g) salt

½ cup (71g) sunflower seeds

2 teaspoons instant yeast

TO MAKE THE STARTER: Mix all the ingredients until smooth. Cover and let rest at room temperature overnight.

TO MAKE THE SOAKER: Combine the rye chops and water. Cover and let rest at room temperature overnight.

The next day, lightly grease the inside of a 13″ pain de mie (Pullman loaf) pan, then dust with pumpernickel flour.

TO MAKE THE DOUGH: In a large bowl, combine the starter, soaker, and dough ingredients. Mix the dough, by hand or using a stand mixer, until it becomes dense and sticky, but still loose; it won't require a lot of mixing.

Transfer the dough directly to a lightly greased work surface and form it into a 13″ log. Place the log in the prepared pan.

Sprinkle a thin layer of pumpernickel flour over the surface of the dough, cover with plastic wrap or a reusable cover, and allow the dough to sit for 60 minutes, until just slightly risen. You'll see cracks in the flour on top as the dough expands.

Toward the end of the rising time, preheat the oven to 450°F.

Uncover the bread and bake the loaf (without the lid on the pan) for 15 minutes, then reduce the oven temperature to 425°F and bake for 50 to 60 minutes longer, until the surface is cracked and dark brown.

Remove the bread from the oven, take the bread from the pan, and transfer it to a baking sheet. Bake for another 5 to 10 minutes, until the loaf's internal temperature reaches at least 205°F on a digital thermometer inserted into the center.

Remove the loaf from the oven and transfer it to a rack to cool completely. Wrap the cooled bread in a towel, or place it in a paper bag and let it rest for at least 24 to 48 hours before slicing.

NUTRITION INFORMATION PER SERVING: 1 slice, 53g
105 cal | 2g fat | 4g protein | 19g complex carbohydrates | 1g sugar | 4g dietary fiber | 0mg cholesterol | 226mg sodium

CRUSTY ITALIAN BREAD

1 BRAIDED LOAF

The term "Italian bread" is as uninformative a term as, say, "American soup." There are as many types of Italian bread as there are regions in Italy and bakers within those regions. The following recipe will make what many would consider a typical bakery-style Italian loaf: a golden brown, buxom braid, sprinkled with sesame seeds, with a crisp and crunchy crust.

BIGA

1 cup (227g) water, cool (about 65°F)

2 cups (240g) unbleached all-purpose flour

¼ teaspoon instant yeast

DOUGH

½ cup (114g) water, cool (about 65°F)

2 to 2½ cups (240g to 300g) unbleached all-purpose flour

2 teaspoons instant yeast

1½ teaspoons salt

TOPPING

1 egg white lightly beaten with 1 tablespoon (14g) water

sesame seeds

TO MAKE THE BIGA: Combine the biga ingredients in a large bowl, mixing just until a cohesive dough forms. Cover and let the starter rest for 12 to 16 hours at room temperature. When the biga is ready, it will be filled with craters and large bubbles.

TO MAKE THE DOUGH: Add the water to the biga and mix until smooth. Add the flour, yeast, and salt and knead the dough until it's fairly smooth but not necessarily elastic, about 3 minutes by stand mixer, or 5 minutes by hand. (The gluten will continue to develop as the dough rises, so you don't want to develop it fully during the kneading process.)

Place the dough in a lightly greased bowl, cover, and let the dough rise at room temperature for 1½ hours. To help develop the gluten and distribute the yeast's food, gently deflate the dough and turn it over every 30 minutes during the rising time (see illustration, page 195).

Preheat the oven to 425°F. Divide the dough in thirds and roll each third into a 20″ long rope. Braid the ropes. Set the braid on a lightly greased baking sheet, cover, and let rise for 1 to 1½ hours, until just puffy. Gently brush the braid with beaten egg white and sprinkle with sesame seeds. Put the bread in the oven and bake for 25 to 35 minutes, until golden brown and its internal temperature reaches 190°F. Take the bread out of the oven and cool it on a rack.

NUTRITION INFORMATION PER SERVING: 1 slice, 56g
102 cal | 0g fat | 4g protein | 23g complex carbohydrates | 0g sugar | 1g dietary fiber | 0mg cholesterol | 204mg sodium

CIABATTA

2 LOAVES

This airy white hearth bread from Italy's Lake Como region receives its name from its appearance: the finished loaf, a fat oval, looks like a homely, comfortably broken-in slipper. It takes a slack dough to make light bread: This dough is so slack (wet) that it must be kneaded by machine, not hand.

The texture of this bread is what sets it apart. The interior is soft and porous, with large irregular holes, while the crust is crunchy and crisp, rather than chewy. Serve ciabatta with pasta, where it's great for soaking up sauce. Or use it to make a delightfully overstuffed sandwich.

BIGA

¼ teaspoon instant yeast

½ cup (114g) water

1½ cups (180g) unbleached all-purpose flour

DOUGH

1 teaspoon instant yeast

2 teaspoons nonfat dry milk

1½ teaspoons salt

¾ cup plus 3 tablespoons (213g) water*

1 tablespoon (11g) olive oil

2 cups (240g) unbleached all-purpose flour

TO MAKE THE BIGA: Mix all the ingredients in a medium bowl, cover the bowl, and let rest for about 12 hours, or overnight.

TO MAKE THE DOUGH: Use your fingers to pull the biga into walnut-size pieces, and place the pieces in the bowl of a stand mixer. Add all the dough ingredients to

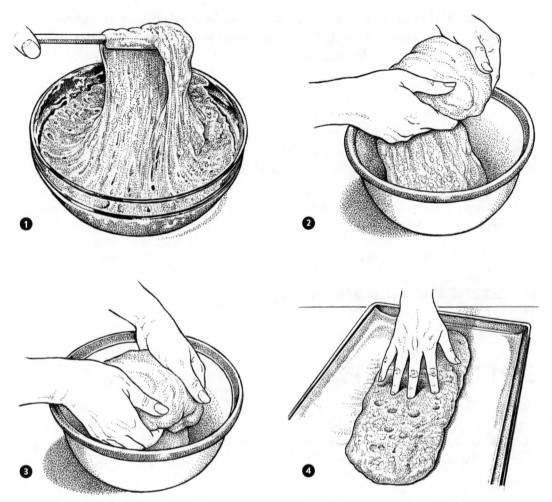

1. The dough will be wet and sticky. **2 and 3.** Gently deflating the dough and turning it over will help to develop its gluten. **4.** Pat the dough into a rough oval about 10″ long and 4″ wide. Press into the dough with your fingers to dimple it, as shown.

the biga and beat slowly with a flat beater paddle or beaters for about 3 minutes. Replace the beater paddle with the dough hook(s), increase the speed to medium, and knead for 10 minutes. The dough should be very sticky and slack. Transfer the dough to a lightly greased bowl or dough-rising bucket, cover the bowl or bucket, and let the dough rise for 2 to 3 hours, gently deflating it and turning it over every 45 minutes or so.

Transfer the dough to a lightly greased work surface and use a bench knife or dough scraper to divide it in half. Working with one half at a time, shape the dough into a rough log. Transfer the log to a parchment-lined baking sheet, or one sprinkled with cornmeal or semolina, and flatten it into an irregular 10″ × 4″ oval. Use your fingers—your entire finger, not just the tip—to indent the surface of the dough vigorously and thoroughly. Repeat with the remaining piece of dough. Cover the loaves with heavily greased plastic wrap or a reusable cover, and set them aside to rise until very puffy, 2 to 3 hours, depending on the warmth of your kitchen.

Half an hour before you want to bake the bread, preheat the oven to 425°F. Spritz water into the oven with a clean plant mister for about 5 seconds. Place the bread in the oven and spritz water into the oven three more times during the first 10 minutes of baking. Bake the loaves for a total of about 25 minutes, or until they're a deep golden brown and their interior temperature measures 210°F. Remove the loaves from the pan and return them to the oven. Turn off the oven, crack the door open a couple of inches, and let the loaves cool completely in the oven. Dust the loaves generously with flour.

* Use an additional 2 to 3 tablespoons of water in the winter, or in very dry weather conditions.

NUTRITION INFORMATION PER SERVING: 1 slice, 51g

103 cal | 1g fat | 3g protein | 20g complex carbohydrates | 0g sugar | 1g dietary fiber | 0mg cholesterol | 269 mg sodium

SWEDISH LIMPA

1 LOAF

This orange- and spice-scented Swedish rye is a Scandinavian favorite. It's especially good toasted and spread with sweet butter.

2 cups (240g) unbleached bread flour

½ cup (57g) whole wheat flour

½ cup (53g) pumpernickel flour

¼ cup (78g) dark corn syrup

2½ teaspoons instant yeast

1½ teaspoons each: caraway, fennel, and anise seed

1 tablespoon (3g) orange zest

1½ teaspoons salt

¼ cup (32g) nonfat dry milk

1 to 1¼ cups (227g to 284g) water

4 tablespoons (½ stick, 57g) butter or ¼ cup vegetable oil (50g)

In a large bowl, mix together all the ingredients until a rough dough forms, then knead (about 10 minutes by hand, 5 to 7 minutes by machine) until the dough is smooth and satiny. Transfer the dough to a lightly greased bowl, cover the bowl with lightly greased plastic wrap, and let the dough rise for 1 hour. It will become somewhat puffy, but probably won't double in bulk.

Shape the dough into a slightly flattened ball and place it on a lightly greased or parchment-lined baking sheet. Cover with a reusable cover or lightly greased plastic wrap and let it rise for 1¼ to 1½ hours, until it's puffed up noticeably.

Preheat the oven to 350°F. Place the bread in the oven and bake for 35 minutes, tenting it with aluminum foil for the final 10 minutes if it appears to be browning too quickly. When the internal temperature reaches 190°F, remove the bread from the oven and place it on a rack to cool.

NUTRITION INFORMATION PER SERVING: 1 slice, 54g
139 cal | 4g fat | 4g protein | 20g complex carbohydrates | 4g sugar | 2g dietary fiber | 9mg cholesterol | 220mg sodium

NO-KNEAD CRUSTY WHITE BREAD

3 OR 4 LOAVES

The most basic of all no-knead loaves, this is a wonderful way to get into baking yeast breads. The easy stir-together dough rests in your refrigerator, developing flavor all the time, until you're ready to bake. About 90 minutes before you want to serve bread, grab a handful of dough, shape it, let it rise, then bake for 30 minutes. The result? Incredible, crusty artisan-style bread. If you're a first-time bread baker, you'll never believe this bread came out of your own oven. And even if you're a seasoned bread baker, you'll love this recipe's simplicity.

The flour/liquid ratio is very important in this recipe, so measure carefully. Your best bet is to weigh the flour; or measure it by gently spooning it into a cup, then sweeping off any excess.

When we say "lukewarm" water, we mean about 105°F, but don't stress over getting the temperatures exact here. Comfortably warm is fine; "ouch, that's hot!" is not. Yeast is a living thing; treat it nicely.

7½ cups (900g) unbleached all-purpose flour

3 cups (681g) water, lukewarm

1 tablespoon (18g) salt

1½ tablespoons (14g) instant yeast

Mix and stir everything together to make a very sticky, rough dough. If you have a stand mixer, beat at medium speed with the beater blade for 30 to 60 seconds. If you don't have a mixer, just stir aggressively with a big spoon or dough whisk until everything is combined.

Next, you're going to let the dough rise. If you've made the dough in a plastic bucket, you're all set—just let it stay there, covering the bucket with a lid or plastic wrap; a shower cap actually works well here. If you've made the dough in a bowl that's not at least of 6-quart capacity, transfer it to a large bowl; it's going to rise a lot. There's no need to grease the bowl, though you can if you like; it makes it a bit easier to get the dough out when it's time to bake bread.

Cover the bowl or bucket, and let the dough rise at room temperature for 2 hours. Then refrigerate it for at least 2 hours, or for up to about 7 days. (If you're pressed for time, skip the room-temperature rise, and stick it right in the fridge.) The longer you keep it in the fridge, the tangier it'll get; if you chill it for 7 days, it will taste like sourdough. Over the course of the first day or so, it'll rise, then fall. That's fine; that's what it's supposed to do.

When you're ready to make bread, sprinkle the top of the dough with flour; this will make it easier to grab a hunk. Grease your hands and pull off about ¼ to ⅓ of the dough—a 392g to 532g piece, if you have a scale. It'll be about the size of a softball, or a large grapefruit.

Plop the sticky dough onto a floured work surface, and round it into a ball, or a longer log. Don't fuss around trying to make it perfect; just do the best you can.

Place the loaf on a piece of parchment if you're going to use a baking stone, or on a lightly greased or parchment-lined baking sheet. Sift a light coating of flour over the top; this will help keep the bread moist as it rests before baking. Drape the bread with greased plastic wrap, or cover it with a reusable cover.

Let the loaf warm to room temperature and rise; this should take about 60 minutes (or longer, up to a couple of hours, if your house is cool). It won't appear to rise upward that much; rather, it'll seem to settle and expand. Preheat your oven to 450°F while the loaf rests. If you're using a baking stone, position it on a middle rack while the oven preheats. Place a shallow metal or cast iron pan (not glass, Pyrex, or ceramic) on the lowest oven rack, and have 1 cup of hot water ready to go.

When you're ready to bake, take a sharp knife and slash the bread 2 or 3 times, making a cut about ½″ deep. The bread may deflate a bit; that's OK, it'll pick right up in the hot oven.

Place the bread in the oven—onto the baking stone, if you're using one, or simply onto a middle rack, if it's on a pan—and carefully pour the 1 cup hot water into the shallow pan on the rack beneath. It'll bubble and steam; close the oven door quickly.

Bake the bread for 25 to 35 minutes, until it's a deep, golden brown.

Remove the bread from the oven and cool it on a rack.

NUTRITION INFORMATION PER SERVING: 1 slice, 50g
100 cal | 0g fat | 4g protein | 20g complex carbohydrates | 0g sugar | 1g dietary fiber | 0mg cholesterol | 220mg sodium

NO-KNEAD HARVEST BREAD

1 LOAF

Plan ahead for this easy bread, which gets its incredible flavor from an overnight or all-day rise. Packed with whole grains, dried fruit, and nuts, it uses bread flour to guarantee a strong rise and satisfying chew. For the best crust, bake in a ceramic bread crock or a covered clay baker.

3¼ cups (390g) unbleached bread flour

1 cup (113g) whole wheat flour

2 teaspoons salt

½ teaspoon instant yeast

1¾ cups (397g) water, cool

¾ cup (86g) dried cranberries

½ cup (75g) golden raisins

1 cup (113g) coarsely chopped pecans or walnuts

Mix the flours, salt, yeast, and water in a large bowl. The dough will rise quite a bit, so be sure your bowl is large enough. Stir, then use your hands to bring the sticky dough together, making sure to incorporate all the flour.

Work in the fruits and nuts.

Cover the bowl with plastic wrap and let the dough rest at room temperature overnight, or for at least 8 hours.

Turn the dough out onto a lightly floured surface and form it into a log or round loaf to fit your 14″ to 15″ long lidded stoneware baker; 9″ × 12″ oval deep casserole dish with cover; or 9″ to 10″ round lidded baking crock.

Place the dough in the lightly greased pan, smooth side up.

Cover and let rise at room temperature for about 2 hours, until it's become puffy.

Using a sharp knife or lame, slash the bread in a crosshatch pattern. Place the lid on the pan, and put the bread in the cold oven. Set the oven temperature to 450°F, and put the bread into the oven.

Bake the bread for 45 to 50 minutes (start the timer when you place the bread into the cold oven). Remove the lid and continue to bake for another 5 to 15 minutes, until it's deep brown in color, and a digital thermometer inserted into the center registers about 205°F.

Remove the bread from the oven, turn it out onto a rack, and cool completely before slicing.

NUTRITION INFORMATION PER SERVING: 1 slice, 77g
196 cal | 5g fat | 5g protein | 26g complex carbohydrates | 7g sugar | 3g dietary fiber | 0mg cholesterol | 293mg sodium

PANE BIANCO

1 LOAF

Combining a stunningly impressive appearance with the comfortingly familiar flavor of pizza, this uniquely S-shaped loaf has wonderfully soft texture. The technique is actually quite simple, and although we fill it with fresh basil, tomatoes, garlic, and cheese, you can swap in other ingredients (such as mozzarella or fresh oregano). The recipe comes by way of Dianna Wara of Washington, Illinois, who took first place with it in the first-ever National Festival of Breads. We've since simplified it a bit, while retaining its award-winning characteristics.

DOUGH

3 cups (360g) unbleached bread flour

2 teaspoons instant yeast

1¼ teaspoons salt

1 large egg

½ cup (113g) milk, lukewarm

⅓ cup (75g) water, lukewarm

3 tablespoons (37g) olive oil

FILLING

¾ cup (85g) grated Italian-blend cheese

½ cup (113g) oil-packed sun-dried tomatoes or oven-roasted tomatoes

3 to 6 cloves garlic, peeled and minced

⅓ cup chopped fresh basil, green or purple

TO MAKE THE DOUGH: Combine all the dough ingredients in a bowl and mix and knead—by hand or using a mixer—to make a smooth, very soft dough. The dough should stick a bit to the bottom of the bowl if you're using a mixer.

Place the dough in a lightly greased bowl, cover, and let it rise until it's doubled in size, about 45 to 60 minutes.

Meanwhile, thoroughly drain the tomatoes, patting them dry. Use kitchen shears to cut them into smaller bits. Shears are also useful for slicing/chopping the basil.

Gently deflate the dough. Flatten and pat it into a 22″ × 8½″ rectangle. Spread with the cheese, tomatoes, garlic, and basil.

Starting with one long edge, roll the dough into a log the long way. Pinch the edges to seal. Place the log seam-side down on a lightly greased or parchment-lined baking sheet.

Using kitchen shears, start ½″ from one end and cut the log lengthwise down the center about 1″ deep, to within ½″ of the other end.

Keeping the cut side up, form an "S" shape. Tuck both ends under the center of the "S" to form a figure 8; pinch the ends together to seal.

Cover and let rise in a warm place until double in size, 45 to 60 minutes.

While the loaf is rising, preheat the oven to 350°F.

Uncover the bread, and bake it for 35 to 40 minutes, tenting it with foil after 20 to 25 minutes to prevent over-browning.

Remove the bread from the oven and transfer it to a rack to cool. Enjoy warm or at room temperature.

NUTRITION INFORMATION PER SERVING: **1 slice, 41g**
100 cal | 3g fat | 5g protein | 14g complex carbohydrates | 1g sugar | 1g dietary fiber | 10mg cholesterol | 190mg sodium

---

WATCH THE DOUGH, NOT THE CLOCK

When making anything with yeast, it's best to let the dough rise to the point the recipe says it should, e.g., "doubled in bulk," rather than watching the clock. Rising times are only a guide; there are so many variables in yeast baking that it's impossible to say that bread dough will *always* double in bulk in a specific amount of time.

Yeasted Flatbreads

Yeasted flatbreads are a familiar sight in cultures all over the world. From Middle Eastern pita to Italian focaccia to that universally beloved flatbread—pizza—these loaves are short in stature but broad in their appeal. Flatbreads come in two types: those that are given yeast and encouraged to rise, and those that aren't. These flatbreads have the unmistakable flavor and texture that comes from yeast, which is different from cracker-style flatbreads.

Flatbreads are often topped with seeds, herbs, and spices, or any of a wide array of vegetables, cheeses, and even fruit. Or, like pita, they're designed to be split and filled once they're out of the oven. One thing all these breads have in common is their suggestion of community; when you serve a big, table-dominating flatbread, it demands a crowd, pulling off pieces, reaching across one another, talking and laughing and enjoying the meal—and one another.

THE EASIEST PIZZA YOU'LL EVER MAKE

FOUR 12″ PIZZAS

This is, hands down, the simplest path to homemade pizza. It's perfect for a weeknight (in fact, we recommend prepping some ahead and keeping it on hand for a speedy dinner) and also makes a fun base for a "do-it-yourself-party"—just mix up the dough, set out plenty of toppings and cheese, and let everyone do the rest. The recipe makes three or four 12″ pizzas (depending on how thick you like the crust). For a larger party, you can double it.

1 tablespoon (12g) sugar

1 tablespoon (9g) instant yeast

1 tablespoon (18g) salt

2 tablespoons (25g) olive oil

2 cups (454g) water, lukewarm

5½ to 6 cups (660g to 720g) unbleached all-purpose flour

Dissolve the sugar, yeast, and salt in the lukewarm water (and olive oil, if you're using it).

Add the flour, starting with 5½ cups (660g) flour and adding more as necessary to make a soft, smooth dough.

Knead the dough (with your hands or a mixer) until it's smooth and elastic, about 7 to 10 minutes.

Place the dough in a lightly greased bowl or other container, cover it, and let it rise for 1 to 2 hours—whatever fits your schedule.

Gently deflate the dough, and divide it into 4 pieces, for medium-crust pizza; or 3 pieces, for thicker crusts. Use a rolling pin to roll each piece, on a lightly greased surface, into a circle to fit a 12″ pizza pan. Let the dough rest several times to relax it and make it more cooperative. If you prefer a more artisan look to your crust, with scattered random air pockets throughout, hand-stretch the dough to size. Again, letting it rest periodically makes the job easier.

Place the rounds on pizza pans; on baking sheets; or, if you have a pizza stone in your oven, on parchment.

Preheat the oven to 450°F. While it's heating, get out your toppings, which you've prepared ahead. Good options are sliced pepperoni; sautéed mushrooms, onions, or peppers; cooked meats; olives; anchovies; and grated or shredded cheese.

Brush each crust with a bit of olive oil; spread sauce lightly over the surface, and add your favorite toppings. Sprinkle the top with grated cheese.

Bake the pizzas for 15 to 20 minutes, until they're golden brown, the toppings are hot and bubbly, and the cheese is melted. Remove the pizzas from the oven.

Immediately transfer pizzas to a cooling rack, so their bottoms don't get soggy. After about 10 minutes (to allow the toppings to set), slice and serve; a pair of scissors is a great cutting tool.

NUTRITION INFORMATION PER SERVING: **1 slice without toppings, 40g**

90 cal | 1g fat | 3g protein | 16g complex carbohydrates | 1g sugar | 1g dietary fiber | 0mg cholesterol | 270mg sodium

CRISPY CHEESY PAN PIZZA

ONE 9" OR 10" PIZZA

With its crispy golden edges, gooey layer of cheese (right to the edge!), and thick yet delicate crust, this pan pizza has a texture and taste that makes you want more. Plus, the crust has just five simple ingredients, making it easy to pull off in a home kitchen. Our recipe incorporates four baking "tricks." An untraditional, nearly no-knead method of folding the dough creates airy pockets in the crust. An overnight refrigerated rest allows the dough time to develop maximum flavor. Baking in a cast iron pan makes an audibly crispy crust for your flavorful assortment of toppings. And finally, the unique layering of cheese beneath the sauce acts as a barrier to minimize sogginess.

Our base cheese of choice is a block of low-moisture mozzarella, coarsely grated. If you experiment with other cheese, choose ones that melt well: Fontina, cheddar, Jack, provolone, and Gouda are all good candidates. For an extra hit of flavor, sprinkle freshly grated hard cheese (such as Parmesan) and/or fresh herbs (oregano, basil, thyme) over the hot pizza just before serving. This recipe can easily be doubled to feed a larger crowd—simply divide the dough between two pans.

CRUST

2 cups (240g) unbleached all-
  purpose flour

¾ teaspoon salt

½ teaspoon instant yeast

¾ cup (170g) water, lukewarm

1 tablespoon (13g) plus 1½ tablespoons
  (18g) olive oil for the pan

TOPPING

6 ounces (170g) grated mozzarella
  (about 1¼ cups, loosely packed)

⅓ to ½ cup (74g to 113g) tomato sauce
  or pizza sauce

Place the flour, salt, yeast, water, and 1 tablespoon (13g) of the olive oil in the bowl of a stand mixer or other large mixing bowl.

Stir everything together to make a shaggy, sticky mass of dough with no dry patches of flour. This should take 30 to 45 seconds in a mixer using the beater paddle; or about 1 minute by hand, using a spoon or spatula. Scrape down the sides of the bowl to gather the dough into a rough ball; cover the bowl.

After 5 minutes, uncover the bowl and reach a bowl scraper or your wet hand down between the side of the bowl and the dough, as though you were going to lift the dough out. Instead of lifting, stretch the bottom of the dough up and over its top. Repeat three more times, turning the bowl 90° each time. This process of four stretches, which takes the place of kneading, is called a fold.

Re-cover the bowl, and after 5 minutes do another fold. Wait 5 minutes and repeat; then another 5 minutes and do a fourth and final fold. Cover the bowl and let the dough rest, undisturbed, for 40 minutes. Then refrigerate it for a minimum of 12 hours, or up to 72 hours. It'll rise slowly as it chills, developing flavor; this long rise will also add flexibility to your schedule.

About 3 hours before you want to serve your pizza, prepare your pan. Pour 1½ tablespoons (18g) olive oil into a well-seasoned cast iron skillet that's 10″ to 11″ diameter across the top, and about 9″ across the bottom. Heavy, dark cast iron will give you a superb crust; but if you don't have it, use another oven-safe heavy-bottomed skillet of similar size, or a 10″ round cake pan or 9″ square pan. Tilt the pan to spread the oil across the bottom and use your fingers or a paper towel to spread some oil up the edges, as well.

Transfer the dough to the pan and turn it once to coat both sides with the oil. After coating the dough in oil, press the dough to the edges of the pan, dimpling it using the tips of your fingers in the process. The dough may start to resist and shrink back; that's OK, just cover it and let it rest for about 15 minutes, then repeat the dimpling/pressing. At this point the dough should reach the edges of the pan; if it doesn't, give it one more 15-minute rest before dimpling/pressing a third and final time.

Cover the crust and let it rise for 2 hours at room temperature. The fully risen dough will look soft and will jiggle when you gently shake the pan: think soft marshmallow.

About 30 minutes before baking, place one rack at the bottom of the oven and one toward the top (about 4″ to 5″ from the top heating element). Preheat the oven to 450°F.

When you're ready to bake the pizza, sprinkle about three-quarters of the cheese (a scant 1 cup) evenly over the crust. Cover the entire crust, no bare dough showing; this will yield caramelized edges. Dollop small spoonfuls of the sauce over the cheese; laying the cheese down first like this will prevent the sauce from seeping into the crust and making it soggy. Sprinkle on the remaining cheese.

Bake the pizza on the bottom rack of the oven for 18 to 20 minutes, until the cheese is bubbling and the bottom and edges of the crust are a rich golden brown (use a spatula to check the bottom). If the bottom is brown but the top still seems pale, transfer the pizza to the top rack and bake for 2 to 4 minutes longer. On the other hand, if the top seems fine but the bottom's not browned to your liking, leave the pizza on the bottom rack for another 2 to 4 minutes. Home ovens can vary a lot, so use the visual cues and your own preferences to gauge when you've achieved the perfect bake.

Remove the pizza from the oven and place the pan on a heatproof surface. Carefully run a table knife or spatula between the edge of the pizza and side of the pan to prevent the cheese from sticking as it cools. Let the pizza cool very briefly; as soon as you feel comfortable doing so, carefully transfer it from the pan to a cooling rack or cutting surface. This will prevent the crust from becoming soggy.

Serve the pizza anywhere from medium-hot to warm. Kitchen shears or a large pair of household scissors are both good tools for cutting this thick pizza into wedges.

NUTRITION INFORMATION PER SERVING: 2 slices, 186g
380 cal | 11g fat | 20g protein | 49g complex carbohydrates | 1g sugar | 2g dietary fiber | 10mg cholesterol | 980mg sodium

DOUBLE-CRUST PIZZA

1 PIZZA

Pizza comes under the heading of Things We Never Get Tired Of, just like chocolate cake or warm biscuits or ice cream. But how can you most easily enjoy homemade pizza at a picnic or for lunch? By making it portable. This pizza has a top crust to keep the filling soft, delicious, and contained.

This double-crust pizza is spectacular right out of the oven, the bubbly filling nesting inside a crisp, chewy crust. Later, it becomes more like a sandwich—less crisp, but still chewy and delicious.

POOLISH

1 cup (120g) unbleached all-
purpose flour

½ cup (112g) water

⅛ teaspoon instant yeast

DOUGH

2¼ cups (270g) unbleached all-
purpose flour

¾ cup (170g) water

1 teaspoon instant yeast

1 teaspoon sugar

1¼ teaspoons salt

1 tablespoon (13g) olive oil

TO MAKE THE POOLISH: In a mixing bowl, stir together the flour, water, and yeast. Set aside, covered, to rest at room temperature for 6 to 12 hours (overnight is fine).

TO MAKE THE DOUGH: Add the flour and water to the poolish, mix well, and let it rest for 20 minutes. Add the remaining dough ingredients, mixing and kneading briefly to form a semi-smooth dough. The dough should be slightly sticky and soft—and may still have a rough surface. We recommend kneading about 5 minutes in a stand mixer, or 6 to 7 minutes by hand. Cover and let the dough rise for 45 minutes; gently fold the edges to the middle, turn it over, and let it rise an additional 45 minutes. Prepare your choice of fillings (see below) while the dough is rising for the second time.

TO ASSEMBLE THE PIZZA: Divide the dough in half. Roll one half into a 14″ circle. Place it in a lightly greased round pizza pan, or on a lightly greased or parchment-lined pan big enough to hold it. Top with the filling of your choice, leaving a ½″ margin around the edge of the dough. Roll the second piece of dough into a 14″ circle. Place it over the top of the filling, pressing down all over. Pull the edges of the bottom dough up and over the edges of the top dough and press together to seal. Cut several small holes in the top to allow steam to escape while baking. Let the pizza rest and rise for 20 minutes.

Preheat the oven to 500°F. Bake the pizza for 30 to 35 minutes, until it's golden brown all over. Let it cool for about 5 minutes before cutting so the filling has time to settle.

Spinach and Cheese Filling

about 8 cups (280g) fresh spinach,
cleaned and torn, or two 10-ounce
packages frozen chopped spinach,
thawed and thoroughly squeezed dry

3 tablespoons (37g) olive oil

2 garlic cloves, peeled and minced

4 cups (312g) cleaned, sliced
mushrooms

½ teaspoon salt

1 teaspoon coarsely ground black pepper

1 cup (114g) crumbled feta cheese

½ cup (71g) pitted and sliced kalamata
olives (optional)

Clean and remove the stems from the spinach. Heat a large skillet until hot, add the oil and garlic, then immediately add the mushrooms. Stir with a heatproof spatula; the mushrooms will begin to give off their juice. After about 2 minutes, add the spinach, salt, and pepper. Cook just enough to wilt the spinach. Add the feta and olives (if using). Remove the pan from the stove and set aside until you're ready to use it.

NUTRITION INFORMATION PER SERVING: 1 slice, 215g

356 cal | 15g fat | 12g protein | 44g complex carbohydrates | 1g sugar | 4g dietary fiber | 25mg cholesterol | 991mg sodium

Ricotta and Basil Filling

1½ cups (340g) ricotta cheese

1 lightly packed cup shredded fresh basil

1 large (about 224g) green or red
pepper, seeded and chopped

½ teaspoon salt

1 teaspoon freshly ground black pepper

2 garlic cloves, peeled and crushed

¾ cup (84g) grated Parmesan cheese

1 cup (112g) grated cheddar cheese

1 cup (77g) French-fried onions
(optional)

Mix the ricotta with the cleaned and shredded fresh basil. Add the diced peppers, salt, black pepper, garlic, cheeses, and onions (if using). Set aside until you're ready to use it.

NUTRITION INFORMATION PER SERVING: 1 slice, 187g

359 cal | 12g fat | 17g protein | 43g complex carbohydrates | 0g sugar | 2g dietary fiber | 35mg cholesterol | 743mg sodium

PITA BREAD

8 PITAS

Pita bread is one of those things (like English muffins and soft pretzels) that most people simply don't think of making. "It's too hard. It won't work. They won't puff up." Forget all that! This is just a simple white bread recipe cooked in an unusual way. They'll puff up, and fresh, golden pita bread, hot from the oven, is a revelation. It makes those packaged pitas pale (literally) by comparison.

3 cups (360g) unbleached all-purpose flour

2 teaspoons instant yeast

2 teaspoons sugar

1½ teaspoons salt

1 cup (224g) water, lukewarm

2 tablespoons (25g) vegetable oil

In a large bowl, or in the bowl of a stand mixer, combine all the ingredients, mixing to form a shaggy dough. Knead the dough by hand (10 minutes) or by machine (5 minutes) until it's smooth. Place the dough in a lightly greased bowl and let it rest for 1 hour. It will become quite puffy, though it may not double in bulk.

Turn the dough onto a lightly oiled work surface and divide it into 8 pieces. Roll 2 to 4 of the pieces into 6˝ circles (the number of pieces depends on how many rolled-out pieces at a time can fit on your baking sheet). Place the circles on a lightly greased baking sheet and let them rest, uncovered, for 15 minutes.

Preheat the oven to 500°F. (Keep the unrolled pieces of dough covered. Roll out the next batch while the first batch bakes.) Place the baking sheet on the lowest rack in the oven and bake the pitas for 5 minutes; they should puff up. (If they haven't puffed up, wait a minute or so longer. If they still haven't puffed, your oven isn't hot enough; raise the heat for the next batch.) Transfer the baking sheet to the oven's middle-to-top rack and bake for an additional 2 minutes, or until the pitas have browned. Remove the pitas from the oven, wrap them in a clean dish towel (this keeps them soft), and repeat with the remaining dough. Store cooled pitas in an airtight container.

NUTRITION INFORMATION PER SERVING: **1 pita bread, 83g**
187 cal | 4g fat | 5g protein | 33g complex carbohydrates | 1g sugar | 1g dietary fiber | 0mg cholesterol | 401mg sodium

GOLDEN FOCACCIA

1 LARGE FOCACCIA

With its roughly dimpled surface and craggy interior, focaccia has become mainstream American, even appearing in some fast-food restaurants. While Americans may be used to soft, thick focaccia, this version is closer to the classic Italian bread: a rustic, everyday loaf that's usually a bit thinner than American-style. It can be crusty and chewy, thin and crisp, or whatever style the family prefers. If you want, you can use 1 cup (227g) of ripe (fed) sourdough starter rather than making your own as part of the recipe.

STARTER

½ cup (113g) water, cool

¹⁄₁₆ teaspoon (a big pinch) instant yeast

1 cup (120g) unbleached all-purpose flour

DOUGH

2¼ teaspoons instant yeast

½ cup (113g) water, lukewarm

2 cups (240g) unbleached all-purpose flour

1¼ teaspoons salt

2 tablespoons (25g) olive oil

TOPPING

2 tablespoons (25g) olive oil

fresh or dried rosemary

coarsely ground black pepper

coarse sea salt or kosher salt

TO MAKE THE STARTER: Mix the water and yeast, then add the flour, stirring until the flour is incorporated. The starter will be paste-like; it won't form a ball.

Cover and let rest at room temperature for about 14 hours; the starter will be bubbly. If you make this in the late afternoon, it'll be ready to go by the next morning.

TO MAKE THE DOUGH: Combine the overnight starter with the remaining dough ingredients, and mix and knead to make a soft, smooth, elastic dough. If you're kneading in a stand mixer, it should take about 5 minutes at second speed.

Place the dough in a lightly greased bowl, cover, and let it rise for 1 hour, or until it's noticeably puffy.

Use nonstick vegetable oil spray to lightly grease a large baking sheet (e.g., 18″ × 13″). Drizzle about 2 tablespoons (25g) olive oil over the spray; the spray keeps the bread from sticking, while the olive oil gives the bottom crust great crunch and flavor.

Gently pull and shape the dough into a rough rectangle and pat it into the pan. For thinner focaccia (½″ to ¾″ thick), pat it all the way to the edges of the pan. For thicker focaccia (¾″ to 1″ thick), don't pat all the way to the edges of the pan; leave an inch or so free around the perimeter.

Cover the pan and allow the dough to rise for 30 minutes. Use your fingers to make irregularly spaced dimples, pressing down firmly; your fingers should reach the bottom of the pan without actually breaking through the dough.

Re-cover the dough, and let it rise until it's noticeably puffy, about 1 hour. The dough should have expanded, but shouldn't seem fragile, or look like it might collapse. Toward the end of the rising time, preheat the oven to 425°F. If you have a pizza stone or baking stone, set it on a middle or lower-middle rack.

Spritz the focaccia heavily with warm water, and drizzle with the olive oil (enough to collect a bit in the dimples). Sprinkle with rosemary (or the herb of your choice), black pepper, and coarse salt, to taste.

Place the pan of focaccia onto the baking stone, or onto a middle oven rack. Bake the focaccia until it's light golden brown, about 20 to 25 minutes. Remove the focaccia from the oven, and immediately turn it out of the pan onto a rack to cool.

Enjoy focaccia hot from the oven, or warm; focaccia is best the same day it's made. But leftovers can be successfully reheated in a 350°F oven just until warmed through.

NUTRITION INFORMATION PER SERVING: **1 piece, 58g**
150 cal | 5g fat | 4g protein | 22g complex carbohydrates | 1g sugar | 1g dietary fiber | 0mg cholesterol | 270mg sodium

DIMPLING DOUGH

What does it mean to dimple dough? It's simply using your fingertips to poke fairly deep indentations in the dough; it's a technique used on both ciabatta and focaccia, to give them their distinctive craggy appearance (see illustration, page 195).

The trick is to be firm, yet gentle. You'll be poking risen dough; you don't want to deflate it. Don't punch the dough with your fingers; rather, lay a fingertip against the dough and press down until it's about half to two-thirds of the way to the bottom of the dough. Repeat until the dough is marked all over with indentations (not holes) at about 1½˝ intervals. Don't worry if the dough loses a bit of its loft during this process; it's almost inevitable. What you don't want is total deflation.

Celebration Breads

In many of the world's cultures, the signature holiday baked good is a traditional yeast bread. In Sweden, for instance, "dipping bread" is a centerpiece of a Christmas smorgasbord. Italians and Greeks are famous for their Easter breads, and come Christmastime in Germany, you'll find fruit-studded butter- and sugar-gilded *stollen* in shops everywhere. The following recipes represent a small sampling of the many ways the world's cultures use bread to celebrate. And although many of these breads originated as holiday-centric traditions, they are all wonderful ways to make any celebration more special. Who wouldn't welcome a warm loaf of chocolate babka at a birthday or an intricate cinnamon star bread at a graduation brunch?

CLASSIC CHALLAH

1 LOAF

This deeply golden, light-textured bread is traditionally served on the Jewish Sabbath and other holidays. The dough for this loaf is wonderfully smooth and supple, making it an ideal candidate for braiding. The simplest way to go is a three-strand braid, but feel free to try the slightly more complex four-strand braid, or even a six-strand braid, which makes a striking presentation.

DOUGH

½ cup (113g) water, lukewarm

6 tablespoons (74g) vegetable oil

¼ cup (85g) honey

2 large eggs

4 cups (480g) unbleached all-purpose flour

1½ teaspoons salt

1 tablespoon (10g) instant yeast

EGG WASH

1 large egg beaten with 1 tablespoon (14g) cold water

Combine all the dough ingredients and mix and knead until you have a soft, smooth dough.

Place the dough in a bowl, cover it, and let it rise for about 2 hours, or until it's puffy; it won't necessarily double in bulk.

Gently deflate the dough and transfer it to a lightly greased work surface.

You may braid the challah the traditional way, into a three-strand braid. For a fancier presentation, make a four- or six-strand braid.

Once you've decided which braid you're doing, divide the dough into the appropriate number of pieces. Roll each piece into a rope about 20″ long. If the dough starts to shrink back as you roll, cover it and let it rest for about 10 minutes, then resume rolling. The short rest gives the gluten a chance to relax.

Braid the loaf.

Gently pick up the braided loaf and place it on a lightly greased or parchment-lined baking sheet.

Cover the loaf with lightly greased plastic wrap, and let it rise until it's very puffy, 90 minutes to 2 hours at cool room temperature. Toward the end of the rising time, preheat the oven to 375°F.

TO MAKE THE EGG WASH: Whisk together the egg and water. Brush over the risen loaf.

Place the baking sheet atop another baking sheet; this will insulate the bread's bottom crust, and keep it from browning too much. Put the challah in the lower third of the oven, and bake it for 20 minutes. If it's a deep golden brown, tent it loosely with aluminum foil. If it's not as brown as you like, check it again at 30 minutes.

Once you've tented the challah, bake it for an additional 10 to 15 minutes, until the loaf looks and feels set and its interior registers at least 190°F.

Remove the bread from the oven and place it on a rack to cool.

While challah does tend to dry out after a day or so, it's always good toasted, or made into grilled sandwiches or French toast.

NUTRITION INFORMATION PER SERVING: 1 slice, 58g
180 cal | 6g fat | 5g protein | 24g complex carbohydrates | 4g sugar | 1g dietary fiber | 35mg cholesterol | 230mg sodium

PANETTONE

1 PANETTONE

Ubiquitous at Christmas, this sweet bread from Milan is golden, high-rising, and traditionally studded with citron and citrus peel. Although using a starter to make a sweet bread is unusual, the use of a biga—a flour, water, and yeast starter the consistency of a firm bread dough—gives bread added flavor and keeping qualities. We often use a biga when making ciabatta or other Italian loaves to help bring out the wheat flavor in breads that might otherwise seem a bit plain. But in a sweet bread—loaded with sugar, butter, and fruit—who needs a biga?

Well, we both do. Panettone made with a biga has a moist, fine texture and rises better than anything with that amount of sugar and fat has a right to. Although the dough still needs a big kick of instant yeast, the biga gives it the strength to take off and rise, despite the sugar and fat doing their best to retard the whole process.

The use of a biga makes this panettone traditional. What separates it from the norm is the fruits we use to flavor the bread, and the pan we bake it in. For those of you who turn up your nose at candied peel—citron, lemon, orange—we offer this dried-fruit version using pineapple, apricots, and golden raisins. And for those who don't have a traditional panettone pan—a tall, round loaf pan—or who've encountered difficulties using such a pan (raw center, burned crust), we suggest the use of a tube or angel food pan.

BIGA

1½ cups (180g) unbleached all-
    purpose flour

½ cup (113g) water

½ teaspoon instant yeast*

DOUGH

3 large eggs

8 tablespoons (1 stick, 113g) unsalted
    butter, cut into about 10 chunks

2½ cups (300g) unbleached all-
    purpose flour

⅓ cup (66g) sugar

5 teaspoons (15g) instant yeast*

1¾ teaspoons salt

2 teaspoons vanilla extract

⅛ teaspoon lemon oil or 2 teaspoons
    lemon zest

1½ cups (about 252g) dried fruit**

TO MAKE THE BIGA: Combine the flour, water, and yeast, kneading briefly to make a stiff dough. Place the dough in a lightly greased bowl and let it rise overnight at room temperature, about 12 hours.

TO MAKE THE DOUGH: In the bowl of a stand mixer, combine the biga with all the ingredients except the dried fruit. (This dough is very difficult to make by hand; we suggest the use of a machine.) Knead the dough until it's smooth and supple; it will seem very sticky at first but will come together nicely at the end. Place the dough in a lightly greased bowl and let it rest for 1 hour.

Knead the fruit into the dough, by hand or machine; knead only until the dough accepts the fruit, as overhandling will cause the fruit to release too much sugar into the dough, slowing the rise. Let the dough rest for 10 minutes, then shape it into a log about 24″ long. Place this log in the bottom of a lightly greased 9″ to 10″ tube pan or angel food pan, cover the pan, and set the dough aside to rise for 2 hours or so. It probably won't double in size but will puff up a bit.

Preheat the oven to 350°F. Bake the panettone for 45 minutes, tenting it with aluminum foil for the final 15 minutes of baking if it appears to be browning too quickly. The internal temperature of the dough should register 190°F to 205°F when it's done. Remove the panettone from the oven, turn it out of the pan, and cool on a rack.

* Instant yeast formulated for sweet doughs (e.g, SAF Gold Label) is a good selection here. If you use regular instant yeast, you may need to increase the rising times a bit.

** We use a mixture of dried apricots, pineapple, and golden raisins; chopped dates, dark raisins, and toasted walnuts would also be appropriate, as would dried cranberries and cherries.

NUTRITION INFORMATION PER SERVING: 1 slice, 52g

151 cal | 5g fat | 3g protein | 21g complex carbohydrates | 3g sugar | 2g dietary fiber | 45mg cholesterol | 145mg sodium

POTICZA

2 LOAVES

This traditional Slovakian bread (pronounced po-TEET-sah) features many thin, alternating layers of bread and sugar-nut filling. Each crosswise slice is an intricate combination of light and dark. Poticza is served at holidays, particularly Christmas and Easter, and on special occasions; while it's a bit time-consuming to make, it keeps well and makes an impressive presentation.

Thankfully, this is a great, easy-to-roll-out dough that makes a wonderful base for any filling. And if you don't want to do the folding and rolling required for the traditional loaf, make a simple wreath; we've included instructions for both shapes.

DOUGH

4 tablespoons (½ stick, 57g) butter

¼ cup (50g) sugar

1 teaspoon salt

¾ cup (170g) milk

2 large eggs

2½ teaspoons instant yeast

2 teaspoons vanilla extract

3 cups (360g) unbleached all-purpose flour

¼ cup (46g) potato flour or ½ cup (43g) dried potato flakes

FILLING

4½ cups (510g) chopped walnuts or pecans

¾ cup (149g) sugar

1 tablespoon (11g) Instant ClearJel

¼ teaspoon salt

2 teaspoons cinnamon

3 large eggs

¼ cup (57g) milk

¼ cup (78g) maple syrup

1 teaspoon vanilla extract

2 teaspoons orange zest (optional)

TOPPING

1 large egg, beaten with 2 tablespoons (28g) water

¼ cup (28g) finely chopped walnuts or pecans

TO MAKE THE DOUGH: Place the butter, sugar, and salt in a large mixing bowl. Bring the milk to a simmer on the stove or in the microwave and pour over the ingredients. Stir briefly, then let the mixture cool to lukewarm.

When cooled, whisk in the eggs, yeast, and vanilla. Whisk 1 cup of the all-purpose flour with the potato flour or potato flakes and stir into the wet ingredients. Add the remaining flour, mixing to form a soft dough.

Knead the dough for 8 to 10 minutes, until shiny and smooth. Cover the dough and let it rise for 1 hour, then refrigerate it for at least 1 hour, and as long as overnight.

TO MAKE THE FILLING: Put the nuts, sugar, Instant ClearJel, salt, and cinnamon in the bowl of a food processor or blender. Process in short bursts to grind the nuts.

With the machine running, add the eggs, milk, maple syrup, and vanilla. Add the orange zest (if using) and pulse to incorporate.

TO ASSEMBLE: On a greased work surface, roll the dough into a 26″ × 18″ rectangle, with a long side facing you. Spread the filling evenly over the surface, leaving 1″ of one long edge uncovered.

Roll the dough toward the uncovered edge, pinching to seal the seam and ends to enclose the filling.

Grease two 8½″ × 4½″ loaf pans and line with parchment. Cut the rolled dough in half. Bring the ends of each half together to make a ring shape. Place each ring in a pan with the seam facing down. Press the dough down gently with your hand to fill in the corners.

Cover the loaves and let them rise until puffy, up to 1½ hours. Toward the end of the rising time, preheat the oven to 350°F.

When the loaves have risen, brush the tops with the beaten egg and water and sprinkle with the finely chopped nuts.

Bake the loaves for 50 to 55 minutes. Check the tops after 20 minutes, tenting with foil if necessary to keep them from over-browning. The breads are done when the centers read 190°F when measured with a digital thermometer.

Remove the loaves from the oven and let cool in the pans on a rack for 20 minutes before tipping out of the pans and returning to the rack to finish cooling completely.

NUTRITION INFORMATION PER SERVING: 1 slice, 44g

173 cal | 14g fat | 4g protein | 1g complex carbohydrates | 7g sugar | 0g dietary fiber | 33mg cholesterol | 108mg sodium

WREATH VARIATION

Roll the dough into a 16″ × 28″ rectangle and cut it into two 16″ × 14″ pieces. Follow the directions above for spreading the filling then, starting with a long edge, roll each piece into a log. Place the logs on parchment-lined or lightly greased baking sheets and shape each into a circle (wreath), pinching the ends together. Cover and let them rise for 1½ hours, or until they've grown by at least one-third.

Preheat the oven to 350°F. Just before placing the wreaths in the oven, use scissors or a sharp knife to cut V shapes into them at about 3″ intervals. (Hold the scissors vertically above the loaf with the blades open about ½″. Stab down into the loaf about 1″, then bring the scissor blades together.)

Bake the wreaths for 30 to 40 minutes, until they're golden brown and a digital thermometer inserted in the center reads 195°F. Remove them from the oven and drizzle with the sugar glaze or icing of your choice, or brush with melted butter and sprinkle with sugar.

CINNAMON STAR BREAD

1 LOAF

This pull-apart-style sweet bread is a show-stopping riff on a classic cinnamon bun. As it bakes, the cinnamon-sugar filling caramelizes and gives the bread a wonderfully sweet and crunchy coating, while the interior remains soft and tender. It's a holiday breakfast treat that will disappear in a flash.

DOUGH

2 cups (240g) unbleached all-purpose flour

¼ cup (46g) potato flour or ½ cup (43g) dried potato flakes

¼ cup (32g) nonfat dry milk

¾ cup plus 2 to 4 tablespoons (199g to 227g) water, lukewarm, enough to make a soft, smooth dough

4 tablespoons (½ stick, 57g) butter, at room temperature

1 teaspoon vanilla extract

2 teaspoons instant yeast

2 tablespoons (25g) sugar

1 teaspoon salt

FILLING

1 large egg, beaten

½ cup (99g) sugar

1 tablespoon (9g) cinnamon

Sift the flour, potato flour or potato flakes, and dry milk through a strainer; this is an important step to prevent lumps in the dough. (If you're using instant mashed potatoes rather than potato flour you can skip this sifting step.)

TO MAKE THE DOUGH: Combine all the dough ingredients and mix and knead to make a soft, smooth dough.

Place the dough in a lightly greased bowl, cover, and let it rise for 60 minutes, until it's nearly doubled in bulk.

Divide the dough into 4 equal pieces. Shape each piece into a ball, cover the balls, and allow them to rest for 15 minutes.

On a lightly greased or floured work surface, roll 1 piece of dough into a 10˝ circle. Place the circle on a piece of parchment, brush a thin coat of beaten egg on the surface, then evenly sprinkle with ⅓ of the cinnamon sugar, leaving ¼˝ of bare dough around the perimeter.

Roll out a second circle the same size as the first, and place it on top of the filling-covered circle. Repeat the layering process—egg, cinnamon sugar, dough circle—leaving the top circle bare.

Place a 2½″ to 3″ round cutter in the center of the dough circle as a guide. With a bench knife or sharp knife, cut the circle into 16 equal strips, from the cutter to the edge, through all the layers.

Using two hands, pick up two adjacent strips and twist them away from each other twice so that the top side is facing up again. Repeat with the remaining strips of dough so that you end up with 8 pairs of strips.

Pinch the pairs of strips together to create a star-like shape with 8 points. Remove the cutter.

Transfer the star on the parchment to a baking sheet. Cover the star and let it rise until it becomes noticeably puffy, about 45 minutes.

While the star is rising, preheat the oven to 400°F.

Brush the star with a thin coat of the beaten egg. Bake it for 12 to 15 minutes, until it's nicely golden with dark brown cinnamon streaks; the center should register 200°F on a digital thermometer.

Remove the bread from the oven and allow it to cool for about 10 minutes before serving. Dust with confectioners' sugar and serve warm or at room temperature.

NUTRITION INFORMATION PER SERVING: 1 slice, 92g

250 cal | 7g fat | 7g protein | 28g complex carbohydrates | 14g sugar | 2g dietary fiber | 40mg cholesterol | 330mg sodium

CHOCOLATE BABKA

2 LOAVES

This overstuffed yeast loaf, filled with two kinds of chocolate, nuts, and cinnamon, is based on a traditional eastern European bread. A classic sweet bread, it's usually shaped in a twist and topped with streusel. Babka is a perennial best seller at Jewish bakeries in many major North American cities. Our thanks to Maggie Glezer, and her book, *A Blessing of Bread*, for the inspiration for this recipe.

DOUGH

1 to 1¼ cups (227g to 283g) water, lukewarm

2 large eggs

6¼ cups (750g) unbleached all-purpose flour

⅓ cup (42g) nonfat dry milk

2 tablespoons (18g) instant yeast

½ teaspoon cinnamon

½ cup (99g) sugar

2½ teaspoons salt

10 tablespoons (142g) unsalted butter, at room temperature

1 tablespoon (14g) vanilla extract

FILLING

½ cup (99g) sugar

½ teaspoon cinnamon

⅓ cup (28g) unsweetened cocoa

½ teaspoon espresso powder

4 tablespoons (½ stick, 57g) unsalted butter, melted

1 cup (113g) diced pecans or walnuts, toasted if desired

1 cup (170g) finely chopped semisweet chocolate or semisweet chocolate chips, mini chips preferred

TOPPING

1 large egg beaten with a pinch of salt until well combined

4 tablespoons (½ stick, 57g) unsalted butter, melted

½ teaspoon cinnamon

⅔ cup (76g) confectioners' sugar

½ cup (60g) unbleached all-purpose flour

Combine all the dough ingredients (starting with the lesser amount of water), mixing until everything is moistened. Add additional water, if necessary, to bring the dough together. Cover the bowl and let the dough rest for 20 minutes. Then mix/knead it until it's soft and smooth.

Place the dough in a lightly greased bowl and cover the bowl. The dough is going to rise for about 1½ to 2 hours, until it's quite puffy.

Gently deflate the dough and divide it in half. Set the pieces aside, covered, while you make the filling.

TO MAKE THE FILLING: Combine the sugar, cinnamon, cocoa, and espresso powder. Stir in the melted butter. The mixture will look grainy and slick; that's OK.

Shape each half of the dough into a 9″ × 18″, ¼″-thick rectangle. If the dough "fights back," let it rest for 10 minutes to relax the gluten, then stretch it some more. Don't be fussy about this; 19″ or 20″ is as good as 18″.

Smear each piece of the dough with half the filling, coming to within an inch of the edges.

Scatter half the nuts and half the chopped chocolate or chips over each piece. If using standard-size chips, process them in a food processor first to create smaller bits of chocolate and a less chunky filling.

Starting with a short end, roll each piece gently into a log, sealing the seam and ends. Working with one log at a time, use a pair of scissors or a sharp knife to cut the log in half lengthwise (not crosswise) to make two pieces of dough about 10″ long each; cut carefully, to prevent too much filling from spilling out. With the exposed filling side up, twist the two pieces into a braid, tucking the ends underneath. Repeat with the other log. Place each log into a lightly greased 9″ × 5″ loaf pan.

TO MAKE THE TOPPING: Brush each loaf with the beaten egg. Mix together the topping ingredients until crumbly and sprinkle half the topping over each loaf.

Tent each pan with plastic wrap, and let the loaves rise until they're very puffy and have crowned a good inch over the rim of the pan, 1½ to 2½ hours. Toward the end of the rising time, preheat your oven to 300°F.

Bake the bread for 35 minutes. Tent lightly with foil and bake for an additional 15 to 25 minutes (for a total of 50 to 60 minutes); the loaves should be a deep-golden brown.

To ensure the loaves are baked through, insert a digital thermometer into the center of one loaf. It should register at least 190°F.

Remove the loaves from the oven, and immediately loosen the edges with a heatproof spatula or table knife. Let the loaves cool for 10 minutes, then turn them out of the pans onto a rack to cool completely.

Slice the babka and serve it at room temperature; or rewarm individual slices briefly in a toaster, if desired.

NUTRITION INFORMATION PER SERVING: 1 slice, 66g
250 cal | 11g fat | 5g protein | 21g complex carbohydrates | 12g sugar | 2g dietary fiber | 35mg cholesterol | 200mg sodium

CHAPTER SIX

Sourdough

——

FLOUR AND WATER, mixed together and left alone, become something truly amazing: a sourdough starter, which then becomes sourdough bread. The leavening agents in this mixture are the yeast in your flour and the air of your kitchen. Faster, more reliable, and easily purchased leaveners exist (the most common being commercial yeast), yet none of them has the allure of sourdough. Perhaps it's because sourdough starters were, for ages, the only means of leavening bread, and have been treasured and passed down among bakers for generations.

A treasure they are—and what wonderful breads they make! Breads leavened with sourdough and given the time they need to develop have fantastically complex flavors that cannot be attained by any other method. Time for the dough to rest and rise, and plenty of it, is perhaps the most critical ingredient for crafting delicious sourdough breads.

There are many distinct varieties of sourdough throughout the world; we've chosen to present a sourdough starter here that's more a thick batter than a stiff dough. It's made mostly with white rather than whole grain flour, because we find it easy to work with and it's familiar to many of us.

How does a simple slurry of flour and water become a powerful leavener, strong enough to raise a dough much larger than itself? Wild yeast and friendly bacteria, called lactobacilli, settle and grow in the warm mass, and the leavening capability of a sourdough starter is a result of the by-products of these tiny living creatures, which are collectively called the sourdough's microflora.

Wild yeast is a tiny fungi—it's the white, dusty film you see on grapes and grains, and it exists all around us in varying degrees, in the air and settled on surfaces. The friendly bacteria, lactobacilli, busy themselves breaking down flour's complex carbohydrates into simple sugars—exactly what wild yeast needs for food. Wild yeast, feeding on the simple sugars, produces carbon dioxide bubbles that raise the dough when trapped in the gluten webbing. As by-products, the lactobacilli produce flavorful organic acids: lactic acid, which adds a rich, mellow flavor to bread; and to a lesser degree, and over a longer time, acetic acid, which can give sourdough bread a mouth-puckering tang.

Why is time important? The amount of wild yeast in a sourdough starter isn't nearly the multitudes we employ when we use domestic yeast. The less yeast, the slower carbon dioxide bubbles accumulate in the dough. The wild yeast organisms in a sourdough starter are reproducing rapidly as they feed, but it still takes time for them to produce the amount of carbon dioxide necessary to achieve the rise.

Time is also necessary to develop flavor. The sour flavor in sourdough bread comes from the acids produced as the lactobacilli work. As the acid accumulates, the flavor increases. Since they accumulate slowly, the baker who wants those flavors must allow the fermentation to stretch out over time. By understanding the roles of wild yeast and lactobacilli, and learning what does and does not spur these creatures to action, an attentive baker is able to adjust timing and temperature for the desired flavor characteristics.

Creating Your Own Sourdough Starter

There's something very special about inheriting a sourdough starter with a history, but starting your own from scratch is deeply gratifying as well. Though you may have a nostalgic attachment to your starter, especially if it has a long history, a new one in the same environment will contain the same resident microflora. The confidence of knowing you can start again will bring a certain freedom to your endeavors.

While there are many methods for starting a new starter, we recommend the following simple, reliable process, using nothing more than flour and water. Here's how to proceed:

Day 1

In a nonreactive container, combine the following:

½ cup (113g) water, cool
1 cup (113g) whole rye (pumpernickel) or whole wheat flour

Mix the water and flour thoroughly, cover loosely, and allow the mixture to rest (ferment) for 24 hours at about 70°F. If your house is cool, set the starter atop your water heater, refrigerator, or another appliance that might generate ambient heat. Your turned-off oven—with the light turned on—is also a good choice.

Day 2

Discard half the starter (113g, about ½ cup), and to the remainder add:

½ cup (113g) water, cool
1 scant cup (113g) unbleached all-purpose flour

Mix thoroughly, cover loosely, and let the mixture rest for 24 hours at 70°F.

Day 3, Day 4, Day 5, and Day 6

By the third day, you'll likely see some activity—bubbling; a fresh, fruity aroma, and some evidence of expansion. It's now time to begin two feedings daily, as evenly spaced as your schedule allows. For each feeding, weigh out 113g starter; this will be a generous ½ cup, once it's thoroughly stirred down. Discard any remaining starter.

Add a scant 1 cup (113g) unbleached all-purpose flour and ½ cup (113g) water to the 113g starter. Mix the starter, flour, and water, cover loosely, and let the mixture rest at room temperature for approximately 12 hours before repeating.

By the end of day 5, the starter should have at least doubled in volume. You'll see lots of bubbles; there may be some little "rivulets" on the surface, full of finer bubbles. Also, the starter should have a tangy aroma—pleasingly acidic, but not overpowering. If your starter hasn't risen much and isn't showing lots of bubbles, repeat discarding and feeding every 12 hours, as long as it takes to create a vigorous starter (risen and bubbly) within 6 to 8 hours of feeding.

RIPE STARTER   Sourdough starter that's ripe and ready to use has bubbles that break the surface and are visible throughout the starter. The creases are a sign that the starter has recently fallen after achieving its greatest volume.

Day 7, or as soon as your starter is established

When your starter is well established and ready to use in baking, stir it down and place ½ cup (113g) in a 2- to 4-quart nonreactive, wide-mouthed container. Feed it with 113g each flour and water; this will be your ongoing starter, the one you keep and feed. Use the remaining starter (up to about 1 cup, 226g) in your recipe. If your recipe calls for more than 1 cup of starter, give it a couple of feedings without discarding, until you've made enough for your recipe plus 113g to keep and feed again.

BE PATIENT!

If your young starter still doesn't appear active after the first week, don't be discouraged. Simply continue the twice-daily feeding schedule. It's not uncommon for sourdough starter to require more than a week to become established. Cool winter temperatures and the absence of wild yeast in your kitchen are factors that extend the time needed for a starter to become mature and ripe. The value of a long, slow process is a central theme in the world of sourdough, and while this may be your first encounter with this theme, it will certainly not be your last. Again and again we are reminded that *time* is a critical ingredient, with no substitute.

Care and Feeding of an Established Starter: Two Methods

ON THE COUNTERTOP (MAINTAINING YOUR STARTER AT ROOM TEMPERATURE)

As far as the sourdough bacteria are concerned, room temperature is the preferable environment for your starter. You can always stash it in the refrigerator when you need to, but do try this room-temperature process for a while. You'll learn a lot about your starter by observing it under these optimum conditions.

Starter that's kept at room temperature is more active than refrigerated starter, and thus needs to be fed more often. Room-temperature starter should be fed every 12 hours (twice a day) using the standard maintenance feeding procedure: discard all but ½ cup (113g), and feed that 113g starter with 113g each water and flour.

If you plan to use the starter the next day, feed it twice, with a minimum of 6 hours between feedings. The last feeding should be 6 to 8 hours before you want to use it.

IN THE REFRIGERATOR

If daily sourdough feeding is too much trouble, you can store your starter in the refrigerator and feed it once a week instead. Take the starter out of the fridge, stir well, and pour off all but ½ cup (113g). Add 113g of water and 113g of flour, mix until smooth, and cover. Let the starter rest on the counter until it starts bubbling (1 to 2 hours) before returning it to the refrigerator.

To create baking-ready starter, remove it from the refrigerator and feed it until it doubles in size within 6 to 8 hours of being fed and appears bubbly and vigorous, with a sharp, clean aroma. This could take up to several days, so allow yourself enough time. Measure out the amount called for in your recipe, retaining 113g for the future (and discarding any additional). Feed that 113g of retained starter and give it a couple of hours to get going before placing back in the refrigerator.

Baking Sourdough Bread

As you bake with sourdough, pay close attention to your results. Get into the habit of really looking at the bread closely and inhaling the aroma deeply; this is how your skill increases.

The dough of naturally leavened breads should be quite wet. Resist the temptation to add flour as you work. Even though the moisture makes the dough a bit more difficult to handle, the high percentage of water helps create beautifully open interiors and nice volume, and increases the shelf life of the baked loaf substantially.

You'll make better bread if you closely monitor the temperature of the dough throughout the process. Optimum temperature for fermenting dough is 75°F to

80°F. Dough that's too cold won't ferment adequately and will be dense, unless it's given a very long fermentation time. Dough that's too warm will ferment very quickly, and the resulting loaf will rise excessively, tend to have thick, pale crust and an off flavor, and will go stale more quickly than it should.

ESSENTIAL TOOL: A DIGITAL THERMOMETER

If we could choose only one tool to recommend for bread bakers, we'd have to settle on our trusty digital thermometer. Crafting great bread depends largely on working with ingredients at the proper temperatures, and this simple, inexpensive tool will increase your precision, and therefore your success, enormously.

Slowing Down Your Dough

How can we increase dough's fermentation time and build flavor without over-fermenting? Slow down the fermentation by decreasing the temperature. Once your bread has been shaped, allow it to rise (this should take an hour or so). When you see it beginning to rise and get puffy, cover it with plastic wrap and place it in your refrigerator. The bread will be ready to bake 12 to 24 hours later.

Professional bakers use special coolers for this technique that maintain a temperature of about 50°F, but the refrigerator is a practical alternative for home bakers. Refrigerator temperatures are a bit low and can seriously slow down the action of the dough, so place your dough on the top shelf if possible (it's usually slightly warmer near the top of the refrigerator). The dough may need some time at room temperature for the last bit of rising, but if the bread looks ready to go the minute you pull it from the fridge, it's fine to put it directly into the oven. Cold dough going into the oven will, however, reduce initial baking temperature in the oven, so compensate by preheating the oven 50°F higher than the recipe calls for. Once the bread is in the oven, reduce the heat to the recommended temperature and bake as usual.

AN EXPERIMENT: CHANGING FLAVOR AND KEEPING QUALITY

Mix a batch of your favorite sourdough. Shape three loaves and allow them to rise for 1 hour. Cover two with plastic wrap and place them in the refrigerator overnight. Allow the third loaf to rise and bake without refrigeration. The next morning, pull one of the loaves out of the refrigerator and bake it. That evening, pull out the last loaf and bake it. Taste all three loaves to see how they differ, then notice how they age over the course of the next couple of days.

Creating a Steamy Hearth in the Home Oven

The best way to create a hearth oven at home is to use a baking stone or steel. When we bake at home, we place a baking stone in the oven and preheat both for 45 minutes to an hour before it's time to bake. This gives the baking stone time to absorb and store heat, which is then transferred to the loaf when it's placed directly on the stone. When you put a loaf of risen dough onto a hot oven stone or baking steel (see Tools, page 532), the heat from the stone immediately flows into the dough. This intense heat stimulates the yeast into a feeding frenzy. The carbon dioxide produced by the yeast builds up in the dough and the loaf rises dramatically, which bakers describe as "oven spring." This increase in volume is facilitated by a steamy environment, because steam slows the formation of a rigid crust, allowing the dough to keep expanding. In a dry oven, the crust forms and hardens much more quickly than in a steamy oven, resulting in a baked loaf with low volume and a dense interior. Steam also produces a nicely caramelized crust: glossy, deep brown, and delicious.

Here's the method we recommend: Place an empty cast iron pan in the bottom of a preheating oven, on the rack beneath the baking stone. Put a kettle of water on the stove and bring it to a boil just before it's time to put the bread in the oven. Before opening the oven door, take time to arrange everything you'll need—the risen loaf on the baker's peel (see Tools, page 532) and the kettle of boiling water. When you're all set, proceed swiftly: Open the oven door, slide the loaf onto the baking stone and pour about ½ cup boiling water into the cast iron pan below. Be careful: Once the water gets poured into the pan, steam rises immediately and a steam burn can happen quickly.

Once the oven door is closed, resist the temptation to check on the bread for the first 20 minutes. The temperature must remain high for the crust to caramelize. Open the oven door after 20 minutes to allow the steam to escape and carefully remove the pan of water, because hearth breads should finish baking in a dry oven. A very steamy environment for more than 25 minutes will result in a tough crust.

Another excellent technique for achieving a steamy oven at home is to bake your bread in a Dutch oven or covered bread crock.

REVIVING A DORMANT OR NEGLECTED STARTER

Sometimes you may find yourself with a starter that has gone far too long without a feeding. Covered in a clear, dark gray liquid (alcohol, a by-product of yeast that's been deprived of oxygen), the starter will smell very strong and will lack bubbles or other signs of activity. You may fear that it's dead, but rest assured the microflora in this dormant starter are patiently waiting and will spring into action again as soon as they get a few good meals. Stir the liquid on top back into the starter, pour off all but ½ cup (113g), and feed it ½ cup (113g) and a scant 1 cup (113g) of flour twice a day until it's healthy, bubbly, and active. At each feeding, pour off about ½ cup (113g) of starter before adding the additional flour and water.

Very rarely, a severely neglected starter will turn ominously pink or reddish, show visible signs of mold, or smell decidedly putrid. In this case, discard the starter and begin again because harmful microorganisms have muscled their way into this batch.

THE AUTOLYSE

Some of the recipes in this chapter include a step called an *autolyse* (pronounced ahh-toe-lease), in which the flour, starter, and water are combined and allowed to rest for 20 to 30 minutes before the remaining ingredients are added and the dough is mixed. This simple step prepares the dough for the mixing or kneading that follows. When flour and water are first brought together, the gluten is disorganized and tangled, and it must be mechanically pulled apart by kneading before it can reassemble into organized long strands. An autolyse gives naturally occurring enzymes the chance to untangle the gluten, so less mixing is necessary to develop the dough. Salt and additional yeast, if used, are not added until after the autolyse, because they tighten the gluten—just the opposite of what an autolyse accomplishes. An autolyse also increases the dough's extensibility, which is its ability to stretch without pulling back like a rubber band. This makes the dough easier to shape and increases its ability to rise in the oven.

Sourdough Breads

PAIN AU LEVAIN

ONE 3-POUND LOAF OR TWO 1½-POUND LOAVES

This is a traditional French-style sourdough with a mildly sour flavor. It's an everyday bread, delicious but uncomplicated, and we enjoy mixing it by hand. You can make a single large loaf with this recipe, or divide the dough and make two smaller ones. Large round loaves of pain au levain are reminiscent of the loaves peasants baked for centuries in the communal ovens of Europe. Large loaves have a longer shelf life than smaller ones.

5 cups (600g) unbleached all-purpose flour

¾ cup (85g) whole wheat flour

1¾ cups (397g) water, at room temperature

2 cups (454g) ripe sourdough starter (page 223) (best measured by weight; volume varies with ripeness)

2½ teaspoons salt

Combine the flours in a large bowl. Add the water to the starter and stir into the flours. Mix by hand for 2 minutes, until the flour is thoroughly incorporated but not yet smooth. Cover the bowl loosely with plastic wrap and let the dough rest for 20 to 30 minutes.

Add the salt and knead the dough until it becomes smooth, supple, and slightly tacky. Avoid adding flour; the dough should be soft. The dough temperature should be 78°F to 80°F. Return the dough to the bowl, cover, and let rise for 1 hour. Turn the dough onto a lightly floured surface and fold it. Folding is a gentler and preferred alternative to "punching down" bread dough. The object is to develop the gluten while not de-gassing the dough. To fold, lightly dust the dough (still in the bowl) and your work surface with flour. Turn the dough out of the bowl onto the work surface—a flexible bowl scraper works perfectly for this step. Gently pull and pat the dough flat, without deflating all the bubbles, then fold the bottom third up and the top third down, as you would a letter. Turn the dough 90 degrees on your work surface and repeat the folds (top down, bottom up), so that now all four sides have been folded into the center. Pick up this folded package and deposit it gently, folded side down, back into the bowl. The dough will be noticeably tighter after the fold. Let it rise, covered, for another hour.

Divide the dough into two pieces, or keep it as one if you wish to make a single large round loaf. Pre-shape each piece into a loose ball by drawing the edges together, so

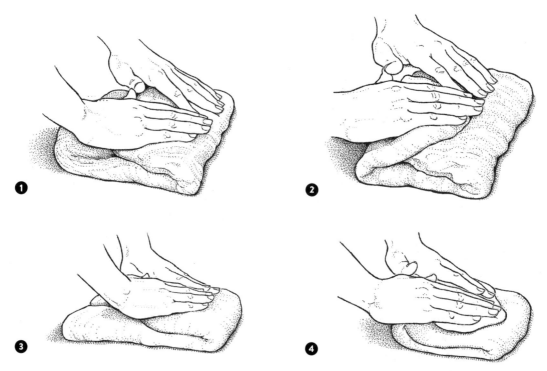

FOLDING SEQUENCE   **1.** Gently pat out the dough and fold the top edge two-thirds of the way toward the bottom edge. **2.** Bring the bottom edge halfway over the dough and pat lightly to seal. **3.** Turn the dough 90 degrees and fold the top edge two-thirds of the way toward the bottom edge. **4.** Bring the bottom edge halfway over the dough and pat lightly to seal. This four-step series is considered one fold, and the dough is now ready to be placed back in the bowl to rise again.

that one side becomes the outer surface, with all the corners coming together at the bottom of the ball. Place the dough smooth side up on a lightly floured surface. Cover and let it rest for about 20 minutes.

Shape the loaves into tight round *boules*—"boule" is French for "ball" and is often used to describe a round loaf of artisan bread—and place them, smooth side down and covered, in well-floured proofing baskets for 2 hours. An hour before baking, preheat the oven and baking stone to 450°F. When ready to bake, turn the loaves onto parchment paper set on a baker's peel, or a semolina-dusted peel, and score the loaves (most easily done with a sharp single-edged razor blade or a baker's lame). Slide the loaves onto the baking stone and fill the oven with steam as directed on page 227. Bake for 45 to 50 minutes for a large loaf (about 40 minutes for two loaves), until the crust is richly golden and the internal temperature of the loaf is about 200°F.

NUTRITION INFORMATION PER SERVING: 1 slice, 56g

105 cal | 0g fat | 3g protein | 22g complex carbohydrates | 0g sugar | 0mg cholesterol | 2g dietary fiber | 223mg sodium

Nuts (especially lightly toasted chopped pecans) or pitted dark olives are wonderful additions to this bread. Add about 1½ cups nuts or a generous cup of olives (168g) to the dough when the mixing is nearly finished. Nuts will tend to make the dough a bit drier, so you may need to add a touch more water. The opposite is true of olives. Also, if adding olives, reduce the salt in the recipe to 2 teaspoons. Try to enclose the nuts or olives in the dough as much as possible, as they're likely to burn if they're sticking out.

SHAPING BOULES

It takes practice to properly shape dough into perfectly round balls. You want to achieve a tight skin, with tension evenly distributed across the surface. For this step you don't want too much flour on your work surface. Cup both hands around the boule and drag it toward you, letting the skin of the boule get pulled tighter by the friction against the work surface. Rotate it in your hands as you drag it, so that the entire surface is tightened evenly and the resulting boule won't be lopsided. As the surface draws tighter, seal the edges together at the base with the side of your hand.

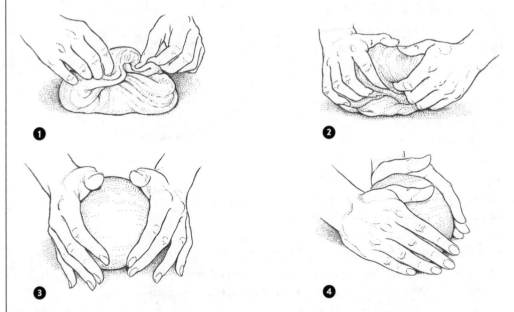

1. Gather the edges of the dough together. The point where all the edges come together will be the bottom seam of the shaped loaf. **2.** Turn the dough over and begin tightening the surface by pulling the loaf toward you repeatedly on an unfloured work surface. Continue to tuck the loose edges into the bottom of the ball. Roll the loaf sideways as you work to create an evenly round boule. The goal is equal tension over the loaf's surface. **3.** To further tighten and round the loaf, drag it across the unfloured work surface with cupped hands. Repeat this step several times, until you're satisfied that the boule is sufficiently tight. **4.** Once the boule is tight and round, seal the bottom seam. Turn the boule on its side, and press the seam together with the side of your hand as you roll the boule away from you.

PROOFING BASKETS

It's ideal to provide a cradle for your shaped loaf as it rises, especially for the wet doughs we recommend for artisan breads. A proofing basket serves as an effective cradle, preventing the loaf from spreading and flattening excessively as it rises, as it would if left to rise (or "proof") on a flat surface. There are several beautiful and effective proofing baskets on the market, from linen-lined French *bannetons* to German coiled wooden *brotformen*, and while they each lend a unique appearance to the finished loaf, they all serve as a supportive cradle in which to raise your dough. These are deluxe additions to your bread-baking tool kit—authentic proofing baskets can be pricey—but they will last and last. An economical option is to simply line a bowl, basket, or colander with a tea towel, or if you're handy with a needle and thread, sew a cotton or linen liner to fit a bowl or basket of your choosing.

Dust the proofing basket with enough flour to prevent the dough from sticking, but don't use too much. An excessive layer of flour stuck to the surface of the loaf will inhibit the development of good crust color, and lends a taste of dry flour to the finished bread. Place the shaped loaf into the floured basket smooth side down, let it rise, and then turn it out onto an oven peel directly from the basket. The floured coils of the *brotform* give the finished loaf a beautiful spiral pattern.

Examples of proofing baskets: a French linen-lined *banneton* (top), a German coiled *brotform* (left), and a homemade proofing basket, easily made by lining a bowl with a linen tea towel (right). The shaped loaf is placed bottom up in the basket for its final rise, then turned out of the basket onto a baking stone or pan to bake.

The rings of flour on this sourdough boule are characteristic markings of the coiled *brotform*. This loaf was scored in a circular pattern to enhance the appearance of the rings.

SCORING THE LOAF

Scoring, or "slashing," aids the loaf's expansion in the oven and prevents asymmetrical ruptures in the crust. To properly score a loaf, first mentally rehearse the cuts you will make, and then swiftly draw the blade through the dough, making cuts about ¼″ deep.

— QUICK BREADS —

Fresh Blueberry Scones

PAGE 74

— BREAKFASTS —
Zephyr Pancakes
PAGE 6

– SCALLION CHEDDAR SCONES PAGE 79

CRUNCHY CORNMEAL WAFFLE
PAGE 16

– POPOVERS PAGE 29

OUR FAVORITE SOUR CREAM COFFEECAKE PAGE 31

BANANA CHOCOLATE CHIP MUFFINS
PAGE 39

— BREAKFASTS —

Rich French Toast

PAGE 20

— PASTRY —

Traditional Danish Pastries

PAGE 439

QUICK BREADS

Simple Zucchini Bread

PAGE 60

—PASTRY—

Blitz Puff Pastry
PAGE 426

SOURDOUGH
Pain au Levain
PAGE 229

— YEAST BREADS —

Baguettes
PAGE 190

— YEAST BREADS —
Chocolate Babka
PAGE 218

PANE BIANCO PAGE 200

HOT BUTTERED PRETZELS
PAGE 176

CLASSIC CHALLAH PAGE 211

BAGELS PAGE 172

– FAVORITE STICKY BUNS
PAGE 167

YEAST BREADS
Gruyère-Stuffed Crusty Loaves
PAGE 183

— YEAST BREADS —
Beautiful Burger Buns
PAGE 180

— YEAST BREADS —
Ciabatta
PAGE 194

YEAST BREADS
Crispy Cheesy Pan Pizza
PAGE 203

— CAKES —

**Chocolate Mousse Cake
with Raspberries**
PAGE 334

— PASTRY —

Croissants de Boulanger

PAGE 437

CAKES
Chocolate Cake Pan Cake
PAGE 289

- PUMPKIN CHEESECAKE PIE
PAGE 396

- WHOOPIE PIES PAGE 257

BLACK AND WHITE COOKIES
PAGE 258

BUMBLEBERRY PIE
PAGE 383

FUDGE BROWNIES PAGE 274

— CAKES —
Classic Birthday Cake
PAGE 303

— CAKES —
Chiffon Cake
PAGE 322

— CAKES —
Lemon-Glazed Pound Cake
PAGE 310

Roasted Butternut Squash and Spinach Quiche

PAGE 418

EXTRA-TANGY SOURDOUGH BREAD

2 LOAVES

This bread, with its mellow tang, is perfect for those who like their sourdough bread noticeably sour, but not mouth-puckeringly so.

1 cup (227g) ripe sourdough starter (page 223)	5 cups (600g) unbleached all-purpose flour
1½ cups (340g) water, lukewarm	2½ teaspoons salt

Combine the starter, water, and 3 cups (360g) of the flour. Beat vigorously for 1 minute.

Cover and let rest at room temperature for 4 hours. Refrigerate overnight, for about 12 hours.

Add the remaining 2 cups (240g) flour and the salt. Knead to form a smooth dough.

Allow the dough to rise in a covered bowl until it's light and airy, with visible gas bubbles. Depending on the vigor of your starter, this may take up to 5 hours (or even longer). For best results, gently deflate the dough once an hour by turning it out onto a lightly floured work surface, stretching and folding the edges into the center, and turning it over before returning it to the bowl. Adding these folds will give you a better sense of how the dough is progressing, as well as strengthen it.

Gently divide the dough in half.

Gently shape the dough into two rounds or oval loaves, and place them on a lightly greased or parchment-lined baking sheet. Cover with lightly greased plastic wrap and let it rise until very puffy, about 2 to 4 hours (or longer; give them sufficient time to become noticeably puffy). Don't worry if the loaves spread more than they rise; they'll pick up once they hit the oven's heat. Toward the end of the rising time, preheat the oven to 425°F.

Spray the loaves with lukewarm water.

Slash the loaves. If you've made round loaves, try one slash across the center, and a curved slash on each side of it; or slash in the pattern of your choice. For oval loaves, two diagonal slashes are fine. Make the slashes fairly deep; a serrated bread knife, wielded firmly, works well here.

Bake the bread for 25 to 30 minutes, until it's a very deep golden brown. Remove it from the oven, and cool on a rack.

NUTRITION INFORMATION PER SERVING: 1 slice, 50g

110 cal | 0g fat | 3g protein | 21g complex carbohydrates | 1g sugar | 1g dietary fiber | 0mg cholesterol | 220mg sodium

WHOLE GRAIN FLOURS

The additional nutrients present in whole grain flours provide extra food for the sourdough microflora, and therefore increase fermentation and acid production. Whole rye flour in particular is recognized as adding more sour flavor to sourdough breads. But don't stop at wheat and rye: Flours made from other whole grains—such as barley, quinoa, or oats—are excellent candidates for sourdough baking.

———

WHEN YOU WANT A REALLY SOUR SOURDOUGH

Although you can't change the characteristics of your local wild yeast and lactobacilli, some conditions (a long slow rise after shaping) and ingredients (pickle juice) can be manipulated to increase the sour taste of your sourdough bread.

Be careful, though; it's possible to over-acidify dough, and the result is the infamous inedible "hockey puck." While acetic acid is great for achieving a sour flavor, too much acetic acid will break down the dough's gluten, resulting in a flat, dense loaf. If you prefer your bread very sour, you'll need to balance the factors of sour taste and good volume.

NO-KNEAD SOURDOUGH BREAD

1 LARGE LOAF

Characterized by its crusty, chewy texture, robust sourdough flavor, and rich golden color, this sourdough loaf has become a favorite in our test kitchen. It relies entirely on its starter for leavening, but with an active, bubbly starter, a little bit of patience, and minimal effort, you'll be amazed by the results. Note that the diastatic malt powder is optional, but will yield a deeper golden color and stronger rise.

1 cup (227g) ripe sourdough starter (page 223)

1¼ cups (397g) water, lukewarm

5 cups (600g) unbleached bread flour

1 tablespoon (18g) salt

2 teaspoons diastatic malt powder (optional, for deeper color and stronger rise)

Combine all the ingredients in a large bowl or a 6-quart food-safe plastic bucket.

Mix and stir everything together to make a sticky, rough dough. If you have a stand mixer, beat at medium speed with the paddle attachment for 30 to 60 seconds. If you don't have a mixer, just stir with a big spoon or dough whisk until everything is combined.

Cover the bowl with a piece of plastic wrap or the bucket with the bucket's lid, and let it rise for 1 hour.

Gently pick up the dough and fold it over on itself several times, cover it again, and let it rise for another hour.

Repeat the rising-folding process one more time (for a total of 3 hours), folding it again after the last hour. Then, place the bucket or bowl in the refrigerator, and let the dough rest for at least 8 hours (or up to 48 hours).

When you're ready to make bread, turn the dough out onto a well-floured work surface, and shape it into a rough ball. Leave the dough seam-side up, cover it, and let it rest on a floured surface for 15 minutes.

Next, shape the dough to fit the vessel in which you'll bake it: a 13″ log for a long covered baker, such as a glazed long covered baker; or a large boule (round) for a round baker, Dutch oven, or bread-baking crock. Place the shaped dough into the lightly greased or semolina-dusted base of the baker and cover it with the lid.

Let the loaf warm to room temperature and rise; this should take about 2½ to 3 hours. It won't appear to rise upward that much, but will relax and expand.

With a rack positioned in the middle, start preheating the oven to 500°F 1 hour before you're ready to bake.

Just before baking, dust the loaf with a fine coat of flour and use a lame or a sharp knife to make one or several ½″ deep slashes through its top surface. If you're baking a long loaf, one arched slash down the loaf lengthwise is nice, or if baking a round, a crosshatch or crisscross pattern works well.

Cover the baker with its lid and place it in the oven. Reduce the oven temperature to 450°F and bake the bread for 45 minutes.

Remove the cover of the baker and bake the bread for 10 to 15 minutes longer, until the bread is deep golden brown and crusty, and a digital thermometer inserted into the center of the loaf reads at least 210°F.

Remove the bread from the oven and transfer it to a rack to cool completely.

NUTRITION INFORMATION PER SERVING: 1 slice, 78g
160 cal | 1g fat | 6g protein | 33g complex carbohydrates | 0g sugar | 1g dietary fiber | 0mg cholesterol | 440mg sodium

Breads with *Levain de Pâte:* Sourdough Starter and Domestic Yeast

Breads that contain both wild (sourdough) and domestic yeast have the attributes of both: the complex flavor and extended keeping quality of sourdough and the greater volume, softer crumb, and speedier production of domestic yeast. A small amount of yeast is added to the dough at the final stage of mixing. This method, although not a "pure" sourdough, is widely used in the bakeries of Europe (in France it's known as the *levain de pâte* method).

SOURDOUGH BAGUETTES

6 BAGUETTES

Crisp and light, with a crackly brown crust, these baguettes are incredibly easy to make. Why the variation in the amount of yeast? The more yeast you use (and the more vigorous your starter), the faster your dough will rise. But speed can come at the expense of flavor; it's only over time that sourdough dough produces the lactic and acetic acids so critical to its taste. We suggest, if you feel your starter is nice and vigorous, to try making the bread with 1 teaspoon of yeast; and if you like those results and are willing to experiment, dropping the amount of yeast down until you reach your favorite combination of flavor and rising times.

1¼ cups (284g) water, lukewarm

2 cups (454g) ripe or discard sourdough starter (page 223)

4½ to 5 cups (540g to 600g) unbleached all-purpose flour

2½ teaspoons salt

2 teaspoons sugar

1 to 2 teaspoons instant yeast (depending on the vigor of your fed starter)

4 teaspoons (12g) vital wheat gluten

In a large bowl, combine the water, starter, and 3 cups (360g) of the flour, mixing until smooth.

Stir in the salt, sugar, yeast, and gluten, then an additional 1½ to 2 cups (180g to 240g) flour. Stir until the dough pulls away from the sides of the bowl, adding only enough additional flour as necessary; a slack (sticky) dough makes a light loaf.

Knead the dough on a lightly greased work surface for about 7 minutes in a stand mixer; or 8 to 10 minutes by hand. You may also knead this dough using the dough

EXTENDED CARE

If you decide that you want to take a vacation from sourdough baking, you can dry your starter to preserve it. Spread it out as thinly as possible between two pieces of parchment, let it dry at room temperature (this could take a day or up to five days). Break it into pieces and store it in an airtight container in a cool, dry place. To use it again, mix the pieces with water and stir to dissolve them, then feed it with flour, let it rest, and feed it again.

WHAT TO DO WITH YOUR EXCESS STARTER

One of the unsung pleasures of maintaining a sourdough starter is the gift of excess starter that you'll pour off at each feeding. Don't throw it away. It's a flavorful ingredient, ready to be used in a variety of delicious ways. Here we include several simple and delicious recipes for using your sourdough discard, and we encourage you to try them.

cycle on your bread machine; once it's finished kneading, transfer it to a bowl to rise, as directed below.

Turn the dough into an oiled bowl, cover the bowl, and let the dough rise until doubled in bulk, about 90 minutes. Gently deflate the dough and divide it into 6 pieces.

Shape each piece into a 16″ long loaf and place the loaves, at least 4″ apart, on parchment-lined baking sheets or in lightly greased baguette pans (French loaf pans). If you're using baguette pans, make the loaves 15″ long.

Cover the loaves with lightly greased plastic wrap and let them rise for 1½ to 2 hours, or until they're nice and puffy. Toward the end of the rising time, preheat your oven to 450°F.

For a classic look, make three diagonal slashes in each loaf, cutting about ¼″ deep. For taller, rounder baguettes, don't slash.

Bake the baguettes for about 25 minutes, or until they're a rich golden brown. If you baked in baguette pans, remove the loaves from the oven and unmold. Turn off the oven, return the loaves (without the pan) to the oven, and crack the oven door open a few inches. If you baked on parchment-lined baking sheets, simply turn off the oven and crack the oven door open a few inches. Letting the loaves cool right in the turned-off oven helps preserve their crunchy crust.

Remove the baguettes from the oven and cool them completely on a rack.

NUTRITION INFORMATION PER SERVING: 1 slice, 38g
85 cal | 0g fat | 3g protein | 17g complex carbohydrates | 0g sugar | 1g dietary fiber | 0mg cholesterol | 163mg sodium

SOURDOUGH WAFFLES

12 WAFFLES

This recipe uses the acidity of sourdough in reaction with baking soda for leavening. It makes the lightest, crispiest waffles in the world with a flavor that you won't find anywhere else. (You also can use this batter for pancakes.) When you use white whole wheat flour, the flavor remains light but you get the advantage of the vitamins in the wheat germ and the fiber in the bran.

For best flavor, make up the sponge the night before. Making waffles also creates an easy excuse to feed your starter without getting into anything very time-consuming. But knowing how waffles can be a spontaneous sort of thing (and having in desperation done it this way), you can also make these without waiting for the sponge to work.

SPONGE

1 cup (120g) unbleached all-purpose flour

1 cup (113g) white whole wheat flour

2 tablespoons (25g) sugar

2 cups (454g) buttermilk

1 cup (227g) ripe sourdough starter (page 223)

BATTER

2 large eggs, at room temperature

4 tablespoons (½ stick, 56g) butter, melted

¾ teaspoon salt

1 teaspoon baking soda

TO MAKE THE SPONGE: Mix together the flours and sugar in a medium nonreactive bowl. Stir in the buttermilk. (If you're doing this at the last minute, take the chill off it; a microwave does this nicely. Don't worry if it separates a bit.) Stir in your ripe sourdough starter and cover loosely with plastic wrap. Let sit at room temperature overnight, or for whatever shorter time span is practical.

TO MAKE THE BATTER: Beat together the eggs, butter, salt, and baking soda until light. Blend this mixture into the sponge, and see dramatic chemistry begin to happen.

Spray your waffle iron with a bit of vegetable oil pan spray. (This is probably necessary only for the first waffle.) Pour ½ to 1 cup batter onto the iron, depending on its size. Close the iron, and cook for approximately 2 minutes, or until the iron stops steaming. Remove gently with a fork.

Serve hot.

NUTRITION INFORMATION PER SERVING: 1 waffle, 92g

161 cal | 5g fat | 6g protein | 20g complex carbohydrates | 2g sugar | 2g dietary fiber | 47mg cholesterol | 292mg sodium

BUTTERY SOURDOUGH BISCUITS

6 TO 7 LARGE BISCUITS

These large biscuits are perfect for breakfast sandwiches. Their sourdough tang pairs nicely with savory fillings like eggs, cheese and bacon, but they're also fantastic as is. The sourdough flavor isn't overly pronounced, but adds a complexity that a regular biscuit lacks, much the way buttermilk can. As an added bonus, the aroma of these biscuits as they bake is one of the very best things around.

1 cup (120g) unbleached all-purpose flour

2 teaspoons baking powder

¾ teaspoon salt

8 tablespoons (1 stick, 113g) unsalted butter, cold

1 cup (227g) unfed or discard sourdough starter (page 223)

Preheat the oven to 425°F, with a rack in the upper third. Grease a baking sheet, or line it with parchment.

Combine the flour, baking powder, and salt. Work the butter into the flour until the mixture is unevenly crumbly.

Add the starter, mixing gently until the dough is cohesive.

Turn the dough out onto a lightly floured surface (a piece of parchment works well), and gently pat it into a 6″ round about 1″ thick.

Use a sharp 2⅜″ biscuit cutter to cut four rounds, cutting them as close to one another as possible. Gently push and pat the scraps into a 2½″ × 5″ rectangle. Cut two more biscuits. Push and pat the remaining scraps into a 1″-thick biscuit; it'll be slightly smaller than the others.

Place the biscuits onto the prepared baking sheet, leaving about 2″ between them; they'll spread as they bake.

Bake the biscuits in the upper third of your oven for 20 to 23 minutes, until they're golden brown.

Remove the biscuits from the oven, and serve warm.

NUTRITION INFORMATION PER SERVING: 1 biscuit, 80g

280 cal | 16g fat | 5g protein | 31g complex carbohydrates | 0g sugar | 1g dietary fiber | 40mg cholesterol | 420mg sodium

SOURDOUGH CRACKERS

ABOUT 100 CRACKERS

Here's the perfect solution to your discarded sourdough dilemma. The dried herbs, while optional, complement the tang of the sourdough perfectly—we like rosemary and thyme. These make a wonderful snack, and they're also sturdy enough to pair with dips like hummus.

1 cup (113g) white whole wheat flour

½ teaspoon salt

1 cup (227g) unfed or discard sourdough starter (page 223)

4 tablespoons (½ stick, 57g) butter, at room temperature

2 tablespoons (3g) dried herbs of your choice (optional)

oil, for brushing

coarse salt, for sprinkling

Mix together the flour, salt, sourdough starter, butter, and optional herbs to make a smooth (not sticky), cohesive dough.

Divide the dough in half and shape each half into a small rectangular slab. Cover with plastic wrap, and refrigerate for 30 minutes, or up to a couple of hours, until the dough is firm.

Preheat the oven to 350°F.

Very lightly flour a piece of parchment, your rolling pin, and the top of the dough.

Working with one piece at a time, place the dough on the parchment and roll it about 1/16″ thick. The dough will have ragged, uneven edges; that's OK. Just try to make it as even as possible.

Transfer the dough and parchment together onto a baking sheet. Lightly brush with oil and then sprinkle the salt on top.

Cut the dough into 1¼″ squares; a pizza wheel works well here.

Prick each square with the tines of a fork.

Bake the crackers for 20 to 25 minutes, until the squares are starting to brown around the edges. Midway through, reverse the baking sheets, top to bottom and front to back; this will help the crackers brown evenly.

When fully browned, remove the crackers from the oven and transfer them to a cooling rack.

NUTRITION INFORMATION PER SERVING: 5 crackers, 22g

57 cal | 2g fat | 2g protein | 7g complex carbohydrates | 0g sugar | 1g dietary fiber | 6mg cholesterol | 298mg sodium

INCREASING THE VOLUME OF YOUR STARTER

To increase the volume of your starter for a large recipe or use in more than one recipe at once, simply feed the starter as usual without discarding any. You may also increase volume by increasing the amount of flour and water you add at each feeding; just remember to follow the one-to-one ratio of equal parts (by weight) flour and water.

CHAPTER SEVEN

Cookies and Bars

———

THINK BACK—WAY, WAY BACK—to your earliest memories of food. We're guessing that somewhere in the mists of time lurks a childhood experience including cookies. Maybe it was a classic: the aroma of warm chocolate chip cookies filling the kitchen. Perhaps it was more contemporary: licking the filling out of Oreos or your first time baking a pan of brownies. But whatever time frame your personal era encompasses, cookies have managed to span it.

Cookies are one of the most popular categories of recipes; more bakers bake more cookies, more often, than they do anything else. And cookies—like bread, like pie, like any number of baked goods—are at their ravishing best when served fresh and warm from the oven.

Cookie recipes come in a variety of options, categorized both by technique (like drop and roll-out) and flavor (like chocolate, molasses, and sugar). The following collection of cookies represents just a sampling of the vast number of cookie recipes out there, but encompasses some of our very favorites.

TO SPREAD OR NOT TO SPREAD?

Why do some cookies flatten out as they bake, while others stand firm and leave the oven looking exactly as they did going in? In large part, it's the liquid in cookies that makes them flatten out. Liquids (or ingredients that act like liquid in the heat of the oven) will flow in all directions until the proteins in the flour and egg are cooked and set. Cookies made with a liquid sweetener, such as honey or molasses, tend to spread more than cookies made with a dry sweetener. These softer doughs benefit from chilling before being baked.

The rate at which cookies flatten depends on the rate at which their ingredients become liquid. A cookie made with shortening and granulated sugar will flatten more slowly than one made with butter. Butter contains water and melts at a lower temperature than shortening, giving the cookie more time to spread before setting. When cookies don't spread, it's because their ingredients "liquefy" so slowly that the dough structure actually sets up and hardens first.

Here are few tips for preventing cookies from flattening too much:

- Use vegetable shortening in recipes that call for it. Butter, margarine, and oil have lower melting points than shortening.
- If a recipe calls for butter and the spreading is excessive, add another ¼ cup of flour.
- Browning and cooling the butter before adding it won't change its melting point, but it does remove its water (while adding amazing flavor at the same time).

Other reasons cookies may spread:

- Check your oven temperature. Baking cookies in a too-cool oven allows the fat to melt before the rest of the cookie "sets up." Always turn the oven on to preheat before you begin to measure ingredients.
- Don't over-grease your baking sheet. Most cookies need only a touch of oil to keep them from sticking; don't overdo it.
- Watch the heat! If you place your dough on a hot baking sheet, the fat will melt before the cookies are even in the oven.
- Change the sugar content. Too much sugar can cause cookies to spread. Sugar is hygroscopic, which means it attracts water. Water molecules in your cookie dough, rather than being absorbed by the flour, are attracted by the sugar (which doesn't absorb the water, but simply attracts it). The dough remains soft and "liquid" and spreads as it bakes. By cutting back on the sugar, you're increasing the amount of water that will be absorbed by the flour, thus stiffening the dough and preventing spread. Try cutting back the sugar in your recipe by a quarter and see what happens.

However, if you want your cookies to spread and flatten more, try baking soda if there's an acidic ingredient in the recipe (brown sugar, maple syrup, or sour cream). Use ¼ teaspoon baking soda per cup of flour. Cookies that use baking powder may be slightly acidic, which means they'll bake faster and spread less. Baking soda reduces the acidity so the cookies will spread a bit more and brown faster. They'll also be more crisp.

Drop Cookies

These are by far the simplest cookies to make. Drop cookie dough is mixed up, then dropped—from a spoon or cookie scoop—onto a sheet to bake. Drop cookie dough is the "wettest" of all the cookie doughs; therefore, it's also the most likely to spread too much as it bakes. To prevent this, and to make the dough easier to handle, drop cookie dough is often refrigerated for up to 24 hours before being baked. This is a good cookie to bake with kids; the steps are few, but the rewards are many.

SIMPLE SUGAR COOKIES

ABOUT EIGHTEEN 3″ COOKIES

These cookies are simple, but still memorable. Although the template is basic, we fancied ours up just a bit with the addition of vanilla and nutmeg, a combination that simply sings "sugar cookie." While you could probably pat these out and cut them with a cutter, we find it so much easier to simply drop them onto a baking sheet with a cookie scoop, then flatten them with the bottom of a drinking glass dipped in sugar (or not, as you please). Using shortening as the fat, rather than butter, gives them a more tender texture.

½ cup (91g) vegetable shortening

⅔ cup (133g) sugar

¼ cup (56g) buttermilk

1 tablespoon (14g) vanilla extract

⅛ to ¼ teaspoon nutmeg, to taste

2 cups (240g) unbleached all-purpose flour

½ teaspoon baking soda

¼ teaspoon salt

Preheat the oven to 350°F.

In a large bowl, beat together the shortening and sugar until smooth. Add the buttermilk and vanilla, again beating until well combined. The mixture may look a bit curdled, which is OK.

Add the nutmeg, flour, baking soda, and salt to the wet ingredients and beat until the mixture forms a cohesive dough.

Drop the dough in round balls onto a parchment-lined baking sheet. They should be a bit bigger than a Ping-Pong ball, a bit smaller than a golf ball. Using a cookie scoop (or a small ice cream scoop that holds about 2 level tablespoons of liquid) makes this task extremely simple. Leave about 2″ between the dough balls, as they'll spread as they bake. If you want a crisp cookie, flatten the cookies as described above. If you like a chewier center, leave them as is.

Bake the cookies for 16 to 18 minutes, until they're just beginning to brown around the bottom edges. Remove them from the oven and cool on a rack. As they cool, they'll become crisp. If you want them to remain crisp, store them in an airtight container when they're totally cool. If you want them to get a bit chewy, store them in a bag with a slice of apple.

NOTE: To make 4″ cookies, make balls of dough about 2″ in diameter. Flatten them and bake as directed above. Yield: about ten 4″ cookies.

NUTRITION INFORMATION PER SERVING: **1 sugar cookie, 30g**
124 cal | 5g fat | 1g protein | 17g complex carbohydrates | 8g sugar | 0g dietary fiber | 0mg cholesterol | 68mg sodium

HOW TO CHANGE YOUR COOKIE'S PERSONALITY

- For light whole wheat flavor, and added fiber and nutrition, try whole wheat flour in combination with unbleached all-purpose flour. The percentage you use is up to you; many cookies can be made with 100% whole wheat flour, although their taste and character will change noticeably. Start by substituting whole wheat for a quarter of the all-purpose flour and go from there. In addition, white whole wheat flour has a much milder flavor than traditional whole wheat flour.
- If the recipe calls for vanilla extract, and most do, add another flavoring as well, such as almond, lemon, or peppermint.
- Cookies made completely with butter have the best flavor, but because butter contains some milk solids, it tends to produce cookies with a firmer "bite." Try browning and cooling the butter in your recipe before mixing it in for a flavorful swap.
- Add 1 teaspoon espresso powder to a typical-size (2 to 3 cups of flour) chocolate or chocolate chip cookie recipe; it will make the chocolate sing!

SNICKERDOODLES

ABOUT 40 MEDIUM COOKIES

Everyone has their own (strong!) opinions about what makes the ultimate snickerdoodle, be it chewy and soft or thinner and crispier. While each person may have their own ideal version, this is what we consider a perfect snickerdoodle, thanks to a slight tang from the cream of tartar, plenty of cinnamon sugar, and extra-tender texture from the shortening.

1 cup (184g) vegetable shortening

1½ cups (298g) sugar

2 large eggs

1 teaspoon vanilla extract

2 teaspoons cream of tartar

1 teaspoon baking soda

½ teaspoon salt

2¾ cups (330g) unbleached all-purpose flour

½ cup (98g) cinnamon sugar (1 teaspoon cinnamon mixed into 1 cup [98g] sugar)

Preheat the oven to 400°F. Lightly grease (or line with parchment) two baking sheets.

In a medium bowl, beat together the shortening and sugar until smooth, then beat in the eggs, again beating until smooth. The mixture will become lighter, and lighter colored, as you beat; this is the result of air being absorbed.

Beat in the vanilla, cream of tartar, baking soda, and salt, then add the flour, mixing slowly until combined.

Place the cinnamon sugar in an 8″ or 9″ round cake pan.

Drop the soft dough by tablespoonfuls into the pan with the sugar, about 6 to 8 balls at a time. Gently shake the pan to coat the dough balls with sugar.

Place the cookies on the prepared baking sheets, leaving about 1½″ between them. Using the bottom of a glass, flatten each cookie until it's about ½″ thick. Repeat until you've used up all the dough.

Bake the snickerdoodles for 11 to 12 minutes, reversing the position of the pans (top to bottom, and back to front) midway through.

Remove the cookies from the oven once they're set and just starting to turn golden. Transfer them to a rack to cool completely.

NUTRITION INFORMATION PER SERVING: 1 cookie, 24g

101 cal | 4g fat | 1g protein | 5g complex carbohydrates | 9g sugar | 0g dietary fiber | 9mg cholesterol | 55mg sodium

CHEWY CHOCOLATE CHIP COOKIES

THIRTY-SIX 2½" COOKIES

Purportedly invented at the Toll House Restaurant (thus the cookie's alternate name, Toll House), in Whitman, Massachusetts, back in the 1930s, the chocolate chip cookie has become an iconic recipe. Everyone has a favorite recipe, from back-of-the-Nestlé's-bag to their mom's classic.

The following recipe yields a soft and chewy cookie (thanks in part to the brown sugar and corn syrup used as sweetener)—perfect for pairing with a cold glass of milk.

12 tablespoons (1½ sticks, 168g) unsalted butter, at room temperature

1¼ cups (266g) light brown sugar, packed

¼ cup (70g) light corn syrup

2 teaspoons vanilla extract

¾ teaspoon baking powder

¾ teaspoon salt

¼ teaspoon baking soda

1 large egg

2¼ cups (270g) unbleached all-purpose flour

1 cup (112g) chopped nuts (optional)

2 cups (336g) semisweet or bittersweet chocolate chips

Preheat the oven to 375°F.

Beat the butter, brown sugar, and corn syrup together until fluffy. Beat in the vanilla, baking powder, salt, and baking soda, and then mix in the egg. Beat well. Beat in the flour, then stir in the nuts (if using) and chocolate chips. Drop cookie dough by the rounded tablespoonful onto lightly greased or parchment-lined baking sheets. Bake for 12 to 14 minutes, just until lightly browned at the edges. For the chewiest cookies, do not overbake. The cookies will look slightly underdone in the middle, but will set up as they cool. Cool on the baking sheets for 5 minutes, and then transfer to a rack to cool completely.

NOTE: To be sure you have the amount of spread you like in a cookie, we recommend baking one cookie to test it. Then if it doesn't spread enough, simply flatten the cookies before baking. If it spreads more than you'd like, mix an extra ¼ cup of flour into the dough.

NUTRITION INFORMATION PER SERVING: 1 cookie (without nuts), 32g

143 cal | 7g fat | 1g protein | 6g complex carbohydrates | 14g sugar | 0g dietary fiber | 10mg cholesterol | 69mg sodium

CRISP CHOCOLATE CHIP COOKIES

ABOUT FORTY-TWO 2½″ COOKIES

Crunchy and packed with chocolate and nuts, these cookies are the favorite of everyone who opts for a crisp (rather than chewy) chocolate chip cookie.

8 tablespoons (1 stick, 113g) unsalted butter, at room temperature

½ cup (91g) vegetable shortening

1 cup (213g) dark brown sugar, packed

½ cup (98g) granulated sugar

2 teaspoons vanilla extract

¼ teaspoon almond extract (optional)

1 large egg

¾ teaspoon salt

1 teaspoon baking soda

2 cups (240g) unbleached all-purpose flour

1 cup (112g) chopped toasted nuts (optional)

2 to 2½ cups (336g to 420g) semisweet chocolate chips

Preheat the oven to 375°F.

In a large mixing bowl, beat together the butter, shortening, sugars, vanilla and almond extracts (if using), egg, salt, and baking soda. Beat until the mixture is smooth and light in color. Add the flour, nuts (if using), and chocolate chips, mixing on slow speed until thoroughly combined.

Scoop by tablespoonfuls onto lightly greased or parchment-lined baking sheets, spacing them 1½ to 2″ apart. Bake the cookies for 12 to 14 minutes. To check, put a spatula under one side of the cookie, and lift it off the sheet at a 45-degree angle. If the bottom stays together, the cookies are ready to come out of the oven. Transfer the cookies to a rack to cool.

NUTRITION INFORMATION PER SERVING: 1 cookie (without nuts), 36g

156 cal | 3g fat | 2g protein | 5g complex carbohydrates | 18g sugar | 0g dietary fiber | 16mg cholesterol | 56mg sodium

LACE COOKIES

FIFTY-FOUR 3″ COOKIES

These gossamer cookies have just enough flour in them to keep them from flowing off the baking sheet. They spread enormously to become "cookies made of lace." Like snowflakes, they should be a winter phenomenon, as they will easily become soft and limp in humid or warm weather.

3 tablespoons (23g) unbleached all-purpose flour	1 teaspoon salt
2¼ cups (217g) old-fashioned rolled oats	16 tablespoons (2 sticks, 224g) unsalted butter
2¼ cups (479g) light brown sugar, packed	1 large egg
	1 teaspoon vanilla extract

Preheat the oven to 375°F. Line a baking sheet with parchment paper.

In a large bowl, mix together the flour, oats, sugar, and salt. In a small saucepan, warm the butter until it's just melted. Mix this into the dry ingredients. In a small bowl, beat the egg with the vanilla and blend it into the rest of the ingredients.

Drop the dough in small spoonfuls onto the prepared baking sheet, allowing plenty of room for cookies to spread. Bake for 5 to 7 minutes, depending on the size of your cookies.

Let the cookies cool just enough on the parchment so you can get a spatula under without tearing them. If you wait any longer, they will stick tenaciously. Cool them thoroughly on a rack and store in a cool, dry, airtight container.

NUTRITION INFORMATION PER SERVING: 1 cookie, 19g

82 cal | 4g fat | 1g protein | 3g complex carbohydrates | 9g sugar | 0g dietary fiber | 14mg cholesterol | 45mg sodium

VARIATION

MOLDED LACE COOKIES: If you leave out the oats from the above recipe and increase the flour to ¼ cup (30g), you can mold these cookies in a number of ways while they are still warm. They can be placed in the lightly greased wells of a muffin tin to make pretty, edible "bowls" for ice cream or mousse, or they can be rolled around the handle of a wooden spoon. Once shaped, these can be dipped in chocolate and filled with sweetened mascarpone or ricotta cheese, whipped cream, mousse, or fresh berries.

MERINGUES

ABOUT 36 MERINGUES

Making egg whites into meringue is something we've always loved to do. It's magical to watch plain egg whites transform into a snowy white, lighter-than-air puff, creating a delicate, melt-in-your-mouth sweet. Although it might seem like magic, it's the oxygen, which, when beaten into egg whites with a bit of acid to stabilize everything, creates both a light color and airy texture. Add sugar and you've got meringue. Meringues are innately versatile and can be flavored with your favorite extract or flavoring.

2 large egg whites

¼ teaspoon cream of tartar

dash of salt

½ cup (98g) sugar, plus more
for sprinkling

1 teaspoon vanilla extract

Preheat the oven to 200°F. Line a baking sheet with parchment paper or aluminum foil, shiny side up.

In a large bowl, combine the egg whites, cream of tartar, and salt. Beat until soft peaks form, then gradually add the sugar, continuing to beat until the mixture is stiff and glossy. Add the vanilla at the end.

Drop the meringue by large teaspoonfuls onto the prepared baking sheet and sprinkle each meringue with a bit of sugar. Bake for 1½ hours. Turn off the heat and leave the meringues in the oven until they're completely cool, 3 hours or more. These are good to make in the evening; they can be left in the oven, with the heat turned off, overnight. Store them in an airtight container to keep them crisp.

NUTRITION INFORMATION PER SERVING: 3 meringues, 5g

31 cal | 0g fat | 0g protein | 0g complex carbohydrates | 8g sugar | 0g dietary fiber | 0mg cholesterol | 31mg sodium

VARIATIONS

COCOA MERINGUES: Sift together ¼ cup (28g) confectioners' sugar and 2 tablespoons (11g) unsweetened cocoa. Use ¼ cup (50g) granulated sugar while beating the egg whites and fold in the cocoa mixture and vanilla extract before baking.

CHOCOLATE CHIP MERINGUES: Fold in ½ cup (84g) mini chocolate chips (or any other flavored chips you like) or shaved chocolate before baking.

VERMONT MAPLE MERINGUES: Substitute the following for the sugar:

½ cup plus 1 tablespoon (84g)
granulated maple sugar

½ to 1 teaspoon maple flavor (to taste)

additional maple sugar, for sprinkling

OUR BAKERY'S COCONUT MACAROONS

ABOUT 24 MACAROONS

Standing tall with their lightly toasted edges, these chewy and moist cookies are a beloved and ever-popular favorite in our Vermont bakery, thanks to their intense coconut flavor.

MACAROONS

one 14-ounce can sweetened
   condensed milk

2 large egg whites

1 tablespoon (14g) vanilla extract

½ teaspoon salt

2½ cups (283g) shredded unsweetened
   coconut

3¼ cups (276g) shredded sweetened
   coconut

COATING (OPTIONAL)

1⅓ cups (227g) chopped bittersweet or
   semisweet chocolate or chocolate
   chips

Preheat the oven to 350°F. Lightly grease two baking sheets, or line with parchment.

TO MAKE THE MACAROONS: In a medium bowl, mix together all the ingredients (not including the chocolate for the coating) until thoroughly incorporated.

Scoop the dough by ⅛-cupfuls (2 tablespoons) onto the prepared baking sheets, leaving an inch of space between them; a jumbo cookie scoop works well here. Leave the macaroons as rounds, or use your hands or the flat side of a bench knife or dough scraper to shape the balls into pyramids.

Bake the macaroons for 16 to 18 minutes, until they're a light golden brown on top.

Remove the macaroons from the oven and allow them to cool on the pan.

TO MAKE THE OPTIONAL COATING: Melt (or temper, if desired) the chocolate in a double boiler or the microwave in short, 10-second increments, stirring until smooth.

Dip the bottoms of the cooled macaroons into the chocolate, then transfer them to a cooling rack or back to the baking sheet. Let rest until the chocolate sets.

NUTRITION INFORMATION PER SERVING: 1 cookie, 39g
196 cal | 15g fat | 3g protein | 5g complex carbohydrates | 10g sugar | 1g dietary fiber | 8mg cholesterol | 51mg sodium

FLOURLESS FUDGE COOKIES

16 LARGE COOKIES OR 32 SMALLER COOKIES

Ultra-chewy, rich chocolate cookies with no flour? Impossible! But it's true—these cookies get their texture from egg whites, and their flavor from cocoa powder (which actually is the only fat in the recipe). They're easy to make, by simply stirring together a few simple ingredients, scooping onto a pan, and baking.

3 large (106g) egg whites

2 teaspoons vanilla extract

2¼ cups (255g) confectioners' sugar

¼ teaspoon salt

1 teaspoon espresso powder (optional but good)

1 cup (85g) unsweetened cocoa, natural or Dutch-process

2 cups (227g to 340g) chocolate chips, chopped nuts, and/or chopped dried fruit (optional)

Lightly grease two baking sheets, or line with parchment and grease the parchment. Yes, grease the parchment; these cookies are sticky, and need to be baked on a greased surface.

Whisk together the egg whites and vanilla. In a separate bowl, whisk together the dry ingredients, except for the chips/nuts/fruit. Stir the wet and dry ingredients together. Scrape the bottom and sides of the bowl, and stir again until smooth. The sticky batter will be the consistency of a thick syrup. Add the chips and/or nuts, if you're using them.

Drop the syrupy batter onto the prepared baking sheets in 3″ circles (for large cookies), or 1¾″ to 2″ circles (for smaller cookies); a tablespoon cookie scoop or teaspoon cookie scoop, respectively, work well here. Let the cookies rest on the baking sheets for 30 minutes, while you preheat the oven to 350°F.

Bake the cookies for 7 minutes (for smaller cookies) or 8 to 9 minutes for the larger cookies. They should spread slightly, become somewhat shiny, and develop faintly crackly tops. Large cookies with added chips/nuts will need to bake for 10 minutes.

Remove the cookies from the oven, and allow them to cool right on the pan. When they're nearly cool, carefully loosen them from the pan with a spatula.

NUTRITION INFORMATION PER SERVING: 1 cookie, 28g

88 cal | 1g fat | 2g protein | 3g complex carbohydrates | 16g sugar | 1g dietary fiber | 0mg cholesterol | 47mg sodium

STORING COOKIES

SOFT AND SWEET

To keep chewy cookies soft, cover the baking pan loosely with a clean dish towel as soon as you take them out of the oven. Once they've cooled to just warm, remove the towel and wrap them in plastic wrap. The breathable dish towel allows cookies to release some of their moisture without trapping it all, which would make them rubbery; wrapping them in plastic helps contain what moisture is left.

Another way to ensure cookies' continued softness is to store them airtight with a cookie softener, also known as a sugar softener. This small piece of porous ceramic is soaked in water, then gradually lets out its moisture over time, keeping the cookies soft.

KEEP THEM CRISP

For crisp cookies, try cooling them in the turned-off oven, with the oven door ajar. In cool, dry weather, crisp cookies will stay that way for several days in a cookie jar or crock. Humid weather will make crisp cookies wilt, so if you're not going to eat them immediately, put them in an airtight container after they've cooled. You can even store them in the freezer. Just make sure to remove them from the bag while they're thawing so moisture won't condense on them as they come back to room temperature.

FREEZING COOKIES

If you want to bake holiday cookies and freeze them until you're ready to make up your gift bags, put them in a heavy-duty plastic freezer bag. Close the bag partway, use a drinking straw to suck out any excess air, and finish sealing the bag. Wrap the entire bag in heavy-duty aluminum foil before putting in the freezer for up to 2 months.

SOFT AND CHEWY OATMEAL-RAISIN COOKIES

26 COOKIES

These humble cookies may seem old-fashioned, but their signature oatmeal flavor and soft, chewy texture will never go out of style.

8 tablespoons (1 stick, 113g) unsalted butter, at room temperature

¼ cup (50g) granulated sugar

⅓ to ½ cup (71g to 106g) brown sugar, to taste

1 teaspoon cinnamon

¼ teaspoon allspice

½ teaspoon ginger

heaping ½ teaspoon salt

½ teaspoon baking soda

1 teaspoon vanilla extract

1 large egg

3 tablespoons (64g) honey

¾ cup (90g) unbleached all-purpose flour

1½ cups (149g) quick-cooking oats

1½ cups (213g) raisins

Lightly grease (or line with parchment) two baking sheets.

Beat together the butter, sugars, spices, salt, baking soda, and vanilla, mixing until smooth.

Beat in the egg, then the honey.

Stir in the flour, then the oats, then the raisins.

Cover the dough, and refrigerate it for 1 to 2 hours, until it's thoroughly chilled.

Drop the chilled dough by generous tablespoonfuls onto the prepared baking sheet; a tablespoon cookie scoop works well here. The cookies will spread, so leave 2″ or so between them.

Just before baking, preheat the oven to 375°F.

Bake the cookies for 10 minutes, until they're barely beginning to brown. Reverse the pans (top to bottom, bottom to top) midway through baking.

Remove the cookies from the oven, and cool right on the pan; or transfer to a rack if you need the pan for the next batch.

NUTRITION INFORMATION PER SERVING: 1 cookie, 31g

116 cal | 4g fat | 2g protein | 19g complex carbohydrates | 12g sugar | 1g dietary fiber | 17mg cholesterol | 50mg sodium

PEANUT BUTTER CRISSCROSSES

FORTY-EIGHT 2½" COOKIES

An all-time favorite, these golden cookies are slightly soft and mildly chewy (rather than crunchy), with satisfying peanut butter taste. They sport a crosshatch design on top—easily made with a fork—to give them their iconic appearance.

1 cup (182g) vegetable shortening

1 cup (196g) granulated sugar

1 cup (213g) brown sugar, packed

2 large eggs

1 teaspoon vanilla extract

1 cup (266g) peanut butter (smooth supermarket-style, not natural)

3 cups (360g) unbleached all-purpose flour

2 teaspoons baking soda

½ teaspoon salt

Preheat the oven to 350°F. Lightly grease a baking sheet.

In a large bowl, beat together the shortening, sugars, eggs, vanilla, and peanut butter. Sift together the flour, baking soda, and salt and add to the peanut butter mixture, stirring to combine.

Drop cookies by spoonfuls onto the prepared baking sheet and press down with a fork, making a crisscross design. Bake cookies for 10 minutes, or until lightly browned. Remove from the oven and cool on a rack.

NUTRITION INFORMATION PER SERVING: 1 cookie, 28g

129 cal | 7g fat | 3g protein | 6g complex carbohydrates | 9g sugar | 1g dietary fiber | 11mg cholesterol | 86mg sodium

WHOOPIE PIES

9 LARGE WHOOPIE PIES

Two saucer-shaped rounds of chocolate cake sandwiched around a marshmallow-y cream filling—that's the classic whoopie pie. Originally popular in New England and around Amish country, the whoopie pie has gradually spread throughout America, and for good reason: It's a delicious throwback.

CAKES

½ cup (91g) vegetable shortening

1 cup (213g) brown sugar, packed

1 large egg

1 teaspoon baking powder

1 teaspoon baking soda

1 teaspoon salt

1 teaspoon vanilla extract

¼ cup plus 2 tablespoons (32g) natural cocoa

2 cups (240g) unbleached all-purpose flour

1 cup (227g) milk

FILLING

1 cup (182g) vegetable shortening

1 cup (112g) confectioners' sugar

1⅓ cups (112g) marshmallow creme

heaping ¼ teaspoon salt dissolved in 1 tablespoon (14g) water

1½ teaspoons vanilla extract

Preheat the oven to 350°F. Line with parchment paper or lightly grease three baking sheets.

TO MAKE THE CAKES: In a large mixing bowl, beat together the shortening, brown sugar, egg, baking powder, baking soda, salt, and vanilla. In a separate bowl, whisk together the cocoa and flour. Add the dry ingredients to the shortening mixture alternately with the milk, beating until smooth.

Drop the dough by the ¼-cupful onto the prepared baking sheets, leaving about 2″ between each cake. Bake the cakes for about 15 minutes, or until they're firm to the touch. Remove them from the oven and cool completely on a rack.

TO MAKE THE FILLING: Beat together the shortening, sugar, and marshmallow, then stir in the salt water and vanilla. Spread half of the cakes with the filling; top with the remaining cakes.

NUTRITION INFORMATION PER SERVING: 1 whoopie pie, 196g

768 cal | 53g fat | 7g protein | 23g complex carbohydrates | 45g sugar | 2g dietary fiber | 89mg cholesterol | 441mg sodium

BLACK AND WHITE COOKIES

TWENTY 5″ COOKIES

These jumbo-size cookies, a New York City–bakery staple, are soft and cakey and would be quite plain save for the hint of lemon in the cookie and the assertive vanilla and chocolate icing on top. Although we provide a recipe, feel free to use your own favorite chocolate and vanilla icings. The only trouble with this cookie is figuring out which side to eat first!

COOKIES

8 tablespoons (1 stick, 113g) unsalted butter, at room temperature

½ cup (91g) vegetable shortening

1 teaspoon lemon zest

1½ teaspoons salt

2 teaspoons vanilla extract

1½ cups (294g) granulated sugar

2 large eggs

4½ cups (540g) unbleached all-purpose flour

1 teaspoon baking soda

1 teaspoon baking powder

1 cup (8 ounces, 224g) sour cream

ICING

8 tablespoons (1 stick, 113g) unsalted butter

½ cup (112g) plain full-fat yogurt, at room temperature

4¼ cups (482g) confectioners' sugar, divided

⅓ cup (56g) finely chopped unsweetened chocolate

Preheat the oven to 400°F. Lightly grease your baking sheets, or line them with parchment; the cookies will fill four baking sheets, so you may need to bake in batches.

TO MAKE THE COOKIES: In a large bowl, beat together the butter, shortening, zest, salt, and vanilla. Beat in the sugar, then the eggs, one at a time, beating well after each addition.

Whisk together the flour, baking soda, and baking powder. Add the flour mixture to the wet ingredients alternately with the sour cream, beginning and ending with the flour and adding the sour cream in three additions.

Using a muffin scoop, a ¼-cup measure, or an ice cream scoop, drop the dough onto the prepared baking sheets in nice round balls. Flatten each ball to a circle ¼″ to ⅜″ thick, about 4½″ across. Leave 2″ to 2½″ between each cookie.

Bake for 10 to 11 minutes, until there's a hint of brown at the edges. Cool for 5 minutes on a rack. Cover the pans with a clean dish towel while the cookies finish cooling to keep them soft. When they're completely cool, seal the cookies in a plastic bag so they stay soft. Let them rest for at least an hour before icing them.

TO MAKE THE ICING: Melt the butter in a large saucepan over low heat. Remove from the heat, then stir in the yogurt, and 4 cups of the confectioners' sugar. The icing will be soft and runny. Immediately separate it into two halves, 1 cup each. Add the remaining ¼ cup confectioners' sugar to half of the white icing, and the chopped unsweetened chocolate to the other half. Stir to melt the chocolate. Set the chocolate icing in a pan of hot water, or in a saucepan over very low heat, to keep it spreadable.

Dip one side of the top of each cookie into the white frosting and put it on a rack to drip and dry. As soon as you can handle the cookies without leaving fingerprints in the frosting, dip the other side of each cookie in the chocolate frosting.

NUTRITION INFORMATION PER SERVING: 1 cookie, 100g
364 cal | 13g fat | 4g protein | 20g complex carbohydrates | 39g sugar | 1g dietary fiber | 52mg cholesterol | 266mg sodium

SOFT MOLASSES COOKIES

FORTY 3″ COOKIES

These generously spiced cookies will stay soft, chewy, and pliable for days if you store them in a bag or cookie jar with a couple of pieces of cut apple. They may not be a favorite of kids—too many strong-tasting spices—but adults love them, and older folks especially seem to be transported back to their childhood when they take that first bite.

8 tablespoons (1 stick, 113g) unsalted butter, at room temperature

½ cup (92g) vegetable shortening

1½ cups (298g) granulated sugar, plus more for coating

½ cup (170g) molasses

2 large eggs, lightly beaten

4 cups (480g) unbleached all-purpose flour

1 teaspoon salt

2¼ teaspoons baking soda

2¼ teaspoons ginger

1½ teaspoons cloves

1½ teaspoons cinnamon

Lightly grease two baking sheets, or line them with parchment.

In a large mixing bowl, beat together the butter, shortening, and sugar. Beat in the molasses and eggs.

In a separate bowl, whisk together the flour, salt, baking soda, and spices. Stir the dry ingredients into the wet ingredients and blend until smooth. Refrigerate for 1 hour, or until the dough has stiffened sufficiently to handle easily.

Preheat the oven to 350°F.

Roll the dough into balls about the size of a golf ball—about 2 tablespoons (28g) of dough. Roll each ball in a sugar-filled shallow bowl to coat it. Place the cookies 2″ apart on the prepared baking sheets.

Bake the cookies for 13 minutes. They will have flattened, but won't have browned significantly. If you let them get brown around the edges, they'll be less chewy and moist. When you take them out of the oven they should still feel soft on top and be just barely colored. Cool the cookies completely on a rack and store them in a plastic bag with a slice of apple to keep them soft.

NUTRITION INFORMATION PER SERVING: 1 cookie, 33g

130 cal | 5g fat | 2g protein | 9g complex carbohydrates | 10g sugar | 0g dietary fiber | 20mg cholesterol | 107mg sodium

GINGERSNAPS

SEVENTY-TWO 1½″ COOKIES

These crisp, spicy rounds with their crackled, sugary tops make an ideal holiday cookie. But we prefer to savor them on a golden afternoon in late September, sitting outside in the fresh air.

2⅓ cups (273g) unbleached all-purpose flour

1 teaspoon ginger

1 teaspoon cinnamon

½ teaspoon cloves

½ teaspoon salt

2 teaspoons baking soda

¾ cup (137g) vegetable shortening

1 cup (196g) sugar

1 large egg

⅓ cup (112g) molasses

½ cup (98g) cinnamon sugar
   (2 teaspoons cinnamon mixed into
   1 cup [198g] granulated sugar)

Preheat the oven to 375°F. Lightly grease two baking sheets, or line them with parchment.

Sift together the flour, spices, salt, and baking soda in a small bowl. In a large bowl, beat the shortening, sugar, and egg together until light and fluffy. Beat in the molasses. Stir in the dry ingredients to make a soft, smooth dough.

Measure out slightly rounded teaspoonfuls of dough, shape into balls, and roll each in cinnamon sugar. Place the cookies 2″ apart on the prepared baking sheets. Bake for 10 minutes until golden brown. Cool on racks.

NUTRITION INFORMATION PER SERVING: 1 cookie, 12g

50 cal | 2g fat | 0g protein | 3g complex carbohydrates | 5g sugar | 0g dietary fiber | 0mg cholesterol | 40mg sodium

FLOURLESS PEANUT BUTTER CHOCOLATE CHIP COOKIES

18 COOKIES

This may be the simplest cookie recipe you'll ever make. It's hard to imagine that so few ingredients can create such perfection, but after one bite, you'll be a believer. Naturally flourless, this recipe is an excellent option for gluten-free bakers.

1 cup (269g) smooth supermarket-style peanut butter

¾ cup (161g) brown sugar, packed

½ teaspoon baking soda

pinch of salt

1 large egg

1 teaspoon vanilla extract

½ cup (85g) chocolate chips or mini chips

Preheat the oven to 350°F. Line a baking sheet with parchment.

Beat the peanut butter, brown sugar, baking soda, and salt at medium speed of your mixer, until well blended.

Add the egg and vanilla, and beat on low-medium speed until incorporated.

Stir in the chocolate chips.

Scoop the dough by the tablespoonful onto the prepared baking sheet (a tablespoon cookie scoop is best for this job) and push the top of the dough to flatten just slightly.

Bake the cookies for 8 to 10 minutes. The tops should be slightly crinkled; you'll want to pull them before they begin to brown on the edges. Remove the cookies from the oven, and cool right on the pan.

NUTRITION INFORMATION PER SERVING: 1 cookie, 31g
150 cal | 9g fat | 4g protein | 3g complex carbohydrates | 12g sugar | 1g dietary fiber | 10mg cholesterol | 125mg sodium

Rolled Cookies

Generally drier than drop cookie dough, rolled cookie dough is almost identical to pie crust in texture and consistency. And you can roll it out the same way: gently, using a sufficient amount of flour and sliding a spatula underneath frequently to ensure the dough isn't sticking to your work surface. Once rolled cookie dough has reached a sufficient thinness (typically ranging from ⅛″ to ¼″), it's cut with a shaped cutter, baked, and often decorated. You can also press decorations, such as colored sugar, into the cookies before they're baked.

GINGERBREAD ROLLOUT COOKIES

FORTY-TWO 4½″ COOKIES

This is an excellent dough for cutout cookies because it holds a shape with very little distortion. The result: a very crisp, medium-spicy cookie with any design you like.

COOKIES

16 tablespoons (2 sticks, 226g) unsalted butter, at room temperature

1 cup (213g) brown sugar, packed

1½ teaspoons salt

1½ teaspoons allspice

2 teaspoons ginger

1 teaspoon cloves

2 teaspoons cinnamon

1 cup (336g) molasses

1 large egg

5½ cups (660g) unbleached all-purpose flour

1½ teaspoons baking soda dissolved in ¼ cup (57g) water

SHINY COOKIE GLAZE

3½ cups (392g) confectioners' sugar, sifted

6 tablespoons (84g) milk

3 tablespoons (45g) pasteurized egg whites or ¼ cup (43g) meringue powder*

1 teaspoon vanilla, almond, or other extract of your choice

Beat the butter, brown sugar, salt, and spices together. Add the molasses and egg and mix well. Stir in half (330g) of the flour and the soda dissolved in water, mixing until well combined. Add the remaining flour. Depending on the power of your mixer, you may need to add the last bit of flour by hand and knead it in. Divide the dough in half and wrap well. Refrigerate for several hours or overnight. The dough changes over the resting period, making it easier to work with and adding flavor to the cookies.

Preheat the oven to 350°F.

Work with half the dough at a time on a well-floured surface. Roll the dough ¼″ thick. Use cookie cutters to cut the cookies into shapes. Transfer the cookies to ungreased baking sheets, leaving about ½″ between them. Bake for 8 to 10 minutes, being careful not to overbake. The cookies will still be soft when done. Let them rest on the baking sheet to firm up before transferring to a rack to cool.

TO MAKE THE GLAZE: Place the sifted confectioners' sugar in a medium bowl. In a separate bowl, stir together the milk and egg white and add to the sugar. Mix by hand or at the mixer's lowest speed until the glaze is the consistency of molasses. Adjust the consistency with a tablespoon (14g) of water if necessary. Mix in the extract. Keep the glaze covered while working with it, to keep it from forming a skin.

Dip the cooled cookies in the glaze, then sweep a spatula over the top of each cookie to remove the excess. Place on a rack for several hours or overnight to let the glaze harden and dry.

* If using meringue powder, mix it in with the confectioners' sugar before adding the liquids, and mix for 4 to 5 minutes to allow the mixture to become smooth.

NUTRITION INFORMATION PER SERVING: 1 glazed cookie, 33g
120 cal | 3g fat | 1g protein | 7g complex carbohydrates | 14g sugar | 0g dietary fiber | 12mg cholesterol | 58mg sodium

ROLLING? NOT A NECESSITY

Sliced cookies: Roll the dough into a log about 1½″ to 2″ in diameter. Before chilling the log, roll it in chopped nuts, seeds, or shaved chocolate for some extra texture and flavor, if desired. If it doesn't roll easily into a log right after you've made the dough, chill it for a while until it becomes more cooperative. You can also press it into a clean, lightly greased juice can to give it the appropriate shape. Or slit the cardboard tube from a roll of paper towels lengthwise; wrap the cookie roll in plastic and press it into the tube. The tube will help it keep its shape as it chills. Let the dough chill until it's quite hard, or freeze it. To bake, slice it into ⅛″ to ¼″ thick rounds.

Hand-rolled cookies: An easy way to handle roll-out dough after it's been chilled is to roll balls of dough between your hands (a fun technique for kids). Then put the balls of dough on a lightly greased baking sheet and press them flat with a fork or the bottom of a glass that's been dipped in flour, sugar, or cocoa.

ALL-PURPOSE CUTOUT COOKIES

ABOUT 42 COOKIES

Cutout cookies should be thin, light, and crisp, sturdy enough to decorate, and tender rather than hard. This is one of our favorite cutout cookie recipes; it plays a starring role in our holiday preparations.

½ cup (91g) vegetable shortening

8 tablespoons (1 stick, 113g) unsalted butter, at room temperature

½ cup (107g) brown sugar, packed

½ cup (98g) granulated sugar

½ teaspoon salt

1 teaspoon baking powder

2 teaspoons vanilla extract

1 large egg

2½ cups (300g) unbleached all-purpose flour

½ cup (56g) white rice flour or cornstarch

In a large bowl, beat together the shortening, butter, sugars, salt, baking powder, and vanilla. When well blended, add the egg, beating until fluffy. Whisk the flours and/or cornstarch together and stir in. Divide the dough in half, form into disks, wrap well, and refrigerate for 30 minutes.

Preheat the oven to 350°F. Lightly grease two baking sheets, or line them with parchment.

Remove the chilled dough from the refrigerator and roll it ⅛″ thick on a lightly floured surface. Cut with cookie or biscuit cutters, place the cookies on the prepared baking sheets, and bake them for 8 to 10 minutes, until they're very lightly browned on the edges. Remove them from the oven and cool on racks.

NUTRITION INFORMATION PER SERVING: 1 cookie, unfrosted, 20g

93 cal | 5g fat | 1g protein | 6g complex carbohydrates | 5g sugar | 0g dietary fiber | 11mg cholesterol | 40mg sodium

LINZER COOKIES

42 TO 48 COOKIES

Linzer cookies are a traditional Christmas cookie from Austria and have been lovingly adopted elsewhere around the world. Traditionally made with nut flour, these cookies are sandwiched around jam or preserves—with one cookie featuring a decorative cutout, so the filling peeks through. You'll often see them made with a crisp sugar cookie dough.

COOKIES

½ cup (91g) vegetable shortening

4 tablespoons (56g) butter, at room temperature

¼ cup (56g) sour cream

½ cup (98g) granulated sugar

½ cup (107g) brown sugar, packed

½ teaspoon salt

1 teaspoon baking powder

1 teaspoon vanilla extract

1 large egg

2½ cups (300g) unbleached all-purpose flour

½ cup (56g) cornstarch

FROSTING

2 tablespoons (28g) butter, melted

2 cups (224g) confectioners' sugar

½ teaspoon almond extract

3 to 4 tablespoons (42g to 56g) milk or cream

FILLING

¾ cup (252g) seedless raspberry jam

TO MAKE THE COOKIES: In a large bowl, beat together the shortening, butter, sour cream, sugars, salt, baking powder, and vanilla. Add the egg, beating until fluffy. Whisk the flour and cornstarch together and stir in. Divide the dough in half, form into disks, wrap well, and refrigerate for 30 minutes.

Preheat the oven to 350°F. Lightly grease two baking sheets, or line them with parchment.

Remove the chilled dough from the refrigerator and roll it ⅛″ thick on a lightly floured surface. Cut into 2½″ to 3″ rounds. Cut a smaller shape (circle, diamond, heart, or other shape, depending on the cutters you have) in the center of half of the rounds to make the tops of the cookies. (You can buy special Linzer cookie cutters made just for cutting out these cookies.) Place the cookies on the prepared baking sheets and bake them for 8 to 10 minutes, until they're very lightly browned on the edges. Remove from the oven and cool on racks.

TO MAKE THE FROSTING: Combine the frosting ingredients and put a thin layer of frosting on the cookies with cutouts. Place them on a rack to drain and dry.

TO ASSEMBLE: Place ½ teaspoon of jam on the unfrosted cookie circles, then place the frosted cutouts on top.

NUTRITION INFORMATION PER SERVING: 1 cookie, 42g

123 cal | 4g fat | 1g protein | 8g complex carbohydrates | 13g sugar | 0g dietary fiber | 10mg cholesterol | 43mg sodium

VARIATION

For a more traditional Linzer dough, replace ½ cup (60g) of the flour with ½ cup (48g) almond flour.

Shaped, Stamped, and Filled Cookies

As cookie dough goes from drop (wet) to rolled (drier), it becomes easier to handle. Rather than rolling out cookies, the same type of dough can be shaped in a number of alternate ways. It can be rolled into individual balls by hand and stamped with a cookie stamp or flattened with the bottom of a drinking glass (to ensure it bakes to the desired thickness); rolled into a rectangle, spread with filling, and folded or rolled up so the filling is enclosed; pressed into a cookie mold and unmolded onto a pan to bake; baked in a decorative shortbread pan; or baked in a log, sliced, and baked again, in the style of biscotti and *mandelbrot*. British shortbread and German *springerle* are prime examples of this type of cookie.

SHORTBREAD

32 COOKIES

These cookies are a perfect example of how delicious simplicity can be. Butter, sugar, and flour are all it takes to make a complex, crispy cookie that takes on more personality if aged for some days in an airtight container.

16 tablespoons (2 sticks, 226g) unsalted
butter, at room temperature

1 teaspoon salt

¾ cup (147g) sugar

2 cups (240g) unbleached all-
purpose flour

In a medium bowl, beat the butter, salt, and sugar together. Add the flour and blend until the mixture is cohesive. To shape, roll the dough into 1½″ balls, press with a cookie stamp (or the bottom of a glass dipped in sugar, to prevent it from sticking), and chill in the freezer for 30 minutes before baking. Or form the dough into a long roll, 1½″ to 2″ in diameter, cover with parchment paper, and freeze until very firm.

When ready to bake, preheat the oven to 300°F. If you've made a roll of dough, slice the roll into cookies no thinner than ¼″ and prick each cookie twice with a fork (or stamp with a stamp). You can also press the dough into a shortbread mold; no need to freeze it. Bake on ungreased baking sheets for about 20 minutes. Watch the cookies carefully. When the bottoms are a light sand color, remove them from the oven and transfer to a rack to cool completely.

Store the cookies in tins lined with waxed or parchment paper. You'll find that shortbread improves with a little age.

NUTRITION INFORMATION PER SERVING: 1 cookie, 26g
123 cal | 8g fat | 1g protein | 7g complex carbohydrates | 6g sugar | 0g dietary fiber | 23mg cholesterol | 46mg sodium

DO YOU HAVE DESIGNS ON YOUR COOKIES?

If using cookie stamps or shortbread molds, it's important you use a dough recipe that's designed to be stamped (or molded); such a recipe won't include any leavening (as this would erase the design), and the type of fats used will be carefully paired to the liquid in the recipe to ensure the design stays its sharpest.

VARIATIONS

ALMOND OR PECAN SHORTBREAD: Add ¾ teaspoon almond extract to the dough and roll the balls of dough in finely chopped almonds or pecans before pressing flat to bake.

CINNAMON CAPPUCCINO SHORTBREAD: Replace ¼ cup (30g) of the flour with ¼ cup (21g) unsweetened cocoa and add 1 teaspoon of espresso powder and 1 large egg to the dough. Roll the balls of dough in cinnamon sugar before pressing flat to bake.

LEMON SHORTBREAD: Add 1 tablespoon of lemon zest (or ½ teaspoon lemon extract or ¼ teaspoon lemon oil) and 1 teaspoon of lemon juice to the dough; roll the balls in granulated sugar before pressing flat to bake.

MAPLE SHORTBREAD: In place of ¾ cup (149g) sugar, use ¼ cup (50g) granulated sugar, ¼ cup plus 1 tablespoon (49g) pure granulated maple sugar, and ½ to 1 teaspoon maple extract (optional, for increased maple flavor).

PEPPERMINT SANDWICH COOKIES

ABOUT 30 FILLED COOKIES

After baking these crispy cookies, fill them with wintry peppermint filling and roll the edges in pearl sugar or crushed candy canes for a treat that's sweet, bracing, and beautiful to look at.

DOUGH

16 tablespoons (2 sticks, 226g) unsalted butter, at room temperature

1 cup (198g) granulated sugar

1½ teaspoons baking powder

1 teaspoon salt

1 tablespoon (14g) vanilla extract

2 cups (241g) unbleached all-purpose flour

FILLING

8 tablespoons (1 stick, 113g) unsalted butter

6 tablespoons (71g) vegetable shortening

3¾ cups (425g) confectioners' sugar

¼ teaspoon salt

1 teaspoon vanilla extract

1 teaspoon peppermint extract or ¼ teaspoon peppermint oil

1 cup (191g) crushed candy canes or pearl sugar, for rolling

Preheat the oven to 350°F. Line two baking sheets with parchment.

TO MAKE THE DOUGH: In a large mixing bowl, beat together the butter, sugar, baking powder, and salt until fluffy.

Add the vanilla and flour and mix until combined. Scoop the dough into 1˝ balls.

Place the dough balls onto the prepared baking sheets, leaving 1½˝ between them. Use the bottom of a glass dipped in sugar to flatten the balls to about ¼˝ thick.

Bake the cookies until they're light brown around the edges, 9 to 11 minutes. Remove them from the oven and let them cool on the pan.

TO MAKE THE FILLING: In a small saucepan, melt the butter over low heat until it separates and starts to simmer. Cook until the liquid portion of the butter is clear, not cloudy. There will be foamy-looking solids floating in the butter; that's OK. If they start to brown, turn the heat down.

In a large bowl, combine the shortening, confectioners' sugar, salt, and melted butter. Mix until the filling comes together; add the vanilla and peppermint extracts.

TO ASSEMBLE: Turn half the cookies over. Take a tablespoon of filling, roll it into a ball, and flatten it into a 2″ disk. Place on the bottom of one cookie and top with a second, pressing down gently until the filling peeks out around the edges.

Roll the edges of the cookies in the crushed candy canes or pearl sugar.

NUTRITION INFORMATION PER SERVING: 1 filled cookie, 30g

158 cal | 11g fat | 1g protein | 6g complex carbohydrates | 8g sugar | 0g dietary fiber | 24mg cholesterol | 95mg sodium

ALMOND CLOUD COOKIES

21 COOKIES

The name says it all: These cookies have a thin, shell-like surface that reveals a moist and light almond-flavored center. A perennial favorite at our bakery, they're also gluten-free.

1¼ cups (454g) almond paste

1 cup (198g) granulated sugar

¼ teaspoon salt

2 large egg whites, lightly beaten

1 teaspoon almond extract

confectioners' sugar, for dusting

Lightly grease two baking sheets, or line them with parchment.

Mix together the almond paste, sugar, and salt until the mixture is uniformly crumbly. Add the egg whites one at a time, mixing to make a smooth paste. Stir in the almond extract.

Scoop the dough by heaping tablespoonfuls onto the prepared pans.

Dust the cookies generously with confectioners' sugar, then use three fingers to press an indentation into the center of each cookie. Refrigerate the shaped cookies, uncovered, for at least 2 hours or as long as overnight.

When you're ready to bake, preheat the oven to 325°F.

Bake the cookies for 20 to 25 minutes, just until they're brown around the edges. Remove them from the oven and let them cool right on the pan.

NUTRITION INFORMATION PER SERVING: 1 cookie, 36g

142 cal | 6g fat | 2g protein | 3g complex carbohydrates | 18g sugar | 1g dietary fiber | 0mg cholesterol | 35mg sodium

FAUX-REOS

ABOUT 50 SANDWICH COOKIES

Very thin and crunchy, with an intensely chocolate, not-too-sweet taste, these dark, almost black cookies look very professional when pressed with a cookie stamp. Though you'll never duplicate exactly the look of an Oreo, this homemade version comes close to matching the taste and texture of those store-bought favorites.

COOKIES

1 cup plus 2 tablespoons (221g) granulated sugar

12 tablespoons (1½ sticks, 168g) unsalted butter, at room temperature

½ teaspoon salt

1 large egg

1 tablespoon (14g) water

1 teaspoon vanilla extract

1½ cups (180g) unbleached all-purpose flour

¾ cup (63g) Dutch-process cocoa or black cocoa

FILLING

1 teaspoon plus a heaping ¼ teaspoon (½ envelope) unflavored gelatin

2 tablespoons (28g) water

½ cup (91g) vegetable shortening

1 teaspoon vanilla extract

2½ cups (280g) confectioners' sugar

TO MAKE THE COOKIES: In a medium bowl, beat together the sugar and butter. Add the salt, egg, water, and vanilla and beat until smooth. Beat in the flour and cocoa until thoroughly combined; the dough will be very stiff.

Roll the dough into balls about the size of a shelled chestnut (about 2 level measuring teaspoons of dough). Place the balls on parchment-lined or lightly greased baking sheets and flatten each ball until it's ⅛″ thick, using the bottom of a glass dipped in cocoa powder. You may also use a cookie stamp, for a more realistic "Faux-reo" effect. To get a nice crisp cookie, it's important to press them thin; use a ruler on the first one so you can see just how thin ⅛″ is. (If you press them thinner than ⅛″, you run the risk of having them burn.) Place the baking sheets in the refrigerator to chill the dough for 30 minutes.

Bake the cookies for 18 minutes in a preheated 325°F oven. It's important to bake them just the right amount of time: too little and they won't crisp properly; too much and they'll scorch. Watch them closely at the end of the baking time, and at the first sign of darkening edges or first whiff of scorching chocolate, remove them from the oven immediately. Remove the cookies from the baking pans and cool them completely on a rack.

TO MAKE THE FILLING: Soften the gelatin in a cup containing the 2 tablespoons (28g) of cold water, then place the cup in a larger dish of hot water and leave it there until the gelatin is completely dissolved and the liquid is transparent. Remove the cup of gelatin from the hot water and let it cool until it's room temperature but hasn't begun to set.

In a medium bowl, beat the shortening, then add the vanilla and confectioners' sugar a little at a time, beating until the mixture is light and creamy. Beat in the gelatin.

Sandwich the cookies, using about 1½ teaspoons filling for regular Faux-reos, more for double-stuffed. (You'll have some filling left over if you fill the cookies moderately.)

NUTRITION INFORMATION PER SERVING: **1 sandwich cookie, 23g**

102 cal | 5g fat | 1g protein | 3g complex carbohydrates | 10g sugar | 1g dietary fiber | 13mg cholesterol | 24mg sodium

FILLING VARIATIONS

CAPPUCCINO FILLING: Substitute 1 teaspoon espresso powder and ¼ cup (21g) sifted unsweetened cocoa for ¼ cup (28g) of the confectioners' sugar.

PEANUT BUTTER FILLING: Cut the shortening amount to ¼ cup (46g) and add ¾ cup (203g) smooth peanut butter to the remaining shortening when it's whipped.

A DECADENT DIP

What's the best way to gild a cookie with chocolate? Start by slowly melting the chocolate of your choice; the easiest way is in a microwave. Heat the chocolate, stirring occasionally, until it's very soft and partially melted but some chunks still remain. Remove the chocolate from the heat and stir until smooth; melting chocolate this way, so that it never gets overly warm, helps it stay smooth and shiny.

If the chocolate is the consistency you like, go ahead and start spreading. For a more liquid chocolate, for drizzling or smooth dipping, stir in vegetable shortening about a teaspoon at a time (up to a maximum of 1 tablespoon shortening per 1 cup melted chocolate), until the chocolate is the proper consistency. Why shortening instead of vegetable oil? Because once the chocolate cools the shortening will become solid again, helping the chocolate to set up.

TRADITIONAL ITALIAN BISCOTTI

ABOUT 60 BISCOTTI

The Italian biscotti has its etymological origin in the Middle French *bescuit*, which referred to a type of sailor's bread, and literally means "twice cooked." The German *zwieback* means the same thing. So, zwieback, the current French *biscotte*, biscotti, and rusk all refer to variations on a theme: a bread that is baked once, sliced, then baked again until it's very dry. From its original consumption as a bread suitable for long ocean voyages, it's evolved into a snack bread ideal for dipping into coffee or tea, as well as a type of teething biscuit beloved by gap-toothed 1-year-olds and their parents. This recipe uses the traditional flavors of anise and lemon to produce a taste that's evocatively Italian.

4 tablespoons (½ stick, 56g) butter, at room temperature

¼ cup (46g) vegetable shortening

¾ cup (147g) sugar

3 large eggs

1 teaspoon vanilla extract

1 teaspoon anise extract or 1 tablespoon aniseed

⅛ teaspoon lemon oil or 1 teaspoon lemon extract

1 teaspoon baking powder

¼ teaspoon salt

3 cups (360g) unbleached all-purpose flour

1½ cups (168g) whole blanched almonds or whole blanched hazelnuts, toasted

Preheat the oven to 375°F.

Lightly grease one or two baking sheets, or line them with parchment.

In a large bowl, beat together the butter, shortening, and sugar, then add the eggs one at a time, beating well after each addition and scraping down the bowl midway through. Beat in the vanilla, anise, lemon, baking powder, and salt. Mix in the flour 1 cup at a time to make a cohesive, well-mixed dough. Add the nuts, mixing until they're distributed throughout the dough.

Transfer the dough to a lightly floured or lightly greased work surface. Divide it into three fairly equal pieces and shape each piece into a rough 12″ log. Transfer each log to the prepared baking sheet, leaving about 3″ between them; you may need to use two baking sheets. Wet your fingers and pat the logs into smooth-topped rectangles 12″ long x 2½″ wide x ⅞″ thick.

Bake the logs for 20 to 25 minutes, until they're beginning to brown around the edges. Remove them from the oven and let rest for 20 minutes. Lower the oven temperature to 300°F.

Gently transfer the logs to a cutting surface and use a serrated knife to cut them on the diagonal into ½″ wide slices. Because of the nuts and the nature of the dough, the biscotti at this point are prone to crumbling; just be sure to use a slow, gentle sawing motion and accept the fact that some bits and pieces will break off. Carefully transfer the slices, cut sides up, to a parchment-lined or ungreased baking sheet. You can crowd them together, as they won't expand; about ¼″ breathing space is all that's required.

Return the biscotti to the oven and bake them for 20 minutes. Remove from the oven, quickly turn them over, and bake for an additional 20 minutes, or until they're very dry and beginning to brown. Remove them from the oven, cool completely, and store in an airtight container.

NUTRITION INFORMATION PER SERVING: **1 biscotti made with almonds, 16g**
63 cal | 3g fat | 1g protein | 5g complex carbohydrates | 2g sugar | 1g dietary fiber | 16mg cholesterol | 38mg sodium

VARIATIONS

ALMOND APRICOT: Use 1 teaspoon almond extract and omit the anise and lemon extracts. Substitute 1 cup (114g) lightly toasted, coarsely chopped almonds and ¾ cup (96g) chopped dried apricots for the nuts.

HAZELNUT WHITE CHOCOLATE: In place of the anise and lemon extracts, increase the vanilla extract to 2 teaspoons. Substitute 1 cup (142g) lightly toasted blanched whole hazelnuts and ¾ cup (128g) white chocolate chips or chunks for the nuts.

CRANBERRY ORANGE: In place of the anise and lemon extract, use 1 tablespoon orange zest and/or ¼ teaspoon orange oil. Substitute 1 cup (114g) dried cranberries for the nuts.

Bars and Squares

Brownies are the first recipe that comes to mind when we talk about bar cookies and squares, but that's just the beginning.

The term encompasses everything from blondies to hermit bars—in other words, all manner of sweets baked in a pan that can be easily cut and eaten out of hand. An easy substitute for the cookie-baking process, bars often involve the same dough you'd use for cookies, but spread in a pan instead of shaped into balls. Being sturdy and straight-edged, they're simple to transport and ideal for a crowd.

Bars and squares come in two basic types, which we'll categorize as one-step and two-step. The one-step bar, the most familiar of which is the brownie, involves mixing dough, spreading it into a pan, and baking. The two-step bar includes an initial bake of its crust, then the addition of filling and additional baking, if necessary. The lemon square is a good example of the two-step bar.

DOES THE PAN MAKE A DIFFERENCE?

Absolutely, for cookies and bars both—though for different reasons.

When a bar recipe calls for a certain size pan, it is because the recipe has been developed using that size pan with the indicated baking temperature and time. Use a pan that's larger and the dough will be thinner and bake more quickly; a smaller pan will make the bars thicker and require longer baking. You may certainly choose a different size pan than what the recipe recommends, but be aware of the ramifications such a switch will trigger. When going from a larger to a smaller pan, never fill the smaller pan more than two-thirds full—it might bubble over.

The size of pan you use for your cookies has more to do with the size of your oven than anything else. Cookies should be baked on a pan that has at least 2″ of clearance on all sides in the oven for best heat circulation. A pan that covers the entire oven rack may cause cookies to burn on the bottom.

In addition, bright, shiny baking sheets are more likely to produce a cookie that's golden brown on the bottom rather than burned. A darker, thinner baking sheet heats faster and hotter than a shiny sheet, meaning your cookie's bottoms will brown much faster than their tops. Put the baking sheets in the middle or lower third of the oven. If all you have are dark, thin pans, try nesting them one within the other—the thin layer of air between the pans will act as insulation, helping to prevent cookies from burning.

FUDGE BROWNIES

TWENTY-FOUR 2″ BROWNIES

Fudgy, cakey, fudgy, cakey . . . can't make up your mind? If you're looking for a brownie that's right in between those two styles, you've found it. These brownies combine a fudge brownie's ultra-moist texture with a subtle cake-like rise, for the best of both worlds.

4 large eggs

1¼ cups (106g) Dutch-process cocoa

1 teaspoon salt

1 teaspoon baking powder

1 teaspoon espresso powder (optional, for enhanced flavor)

1 tablespoon (14g) vanilla extract

16 tablespoons (2 sticks, 227g) unsalted butter

2¼ cups (447g) sugar

1½ cups (180g) unbleached all-purpose flour

2 cups (340g) chocolate chips

Preheat the oven to 350°F. Lightly grease a 9″ × 13″ pan.

In a medium bowl, beat the eggs with the cocoa, salt, baking powder, espresso powder (if using), and vanilla for about 1 minute at medium speed in a mixer or by hand until smooth. You can do this while you're melting your butter (next step).

In a medium microwave-safe bowl, or in a saucepan set over low heat, melt the butter, then add the sugar and stir to combine. Or simply combine the butter and sugar, and heat, stirring, until the butter is melted. Continue to heat (or microwave) briefly, just until the mixture is hot (about 110°F to 120°F), but not bubbling; it'll become shiny looking as you stir it. Heating the mixture to this point will dissolve more of the sugar, which will help produce a shiny top crust on your brownies.

Add the hot butter/sugar mixture to the egg/cocoa mixture, stirring until smooth.

Add the flour and chips, stirring until smooth. Again, adding the chips helps produce a shiny top crust.

Spoon the batter into the prepared pan.

Bake the brownies for 28 to 32 minutes, until a toothpick inserted into the center comes out clean, or with just a few moist crumbs clinging to it. The brownies should feel set on the edges, and the center should look very moist, but not uncooked. Remove them from the oven and cool on a rack before cutting and serving.

NUTRITION INFORMATION PER SERVING: 1 brownie, 63g
260 cal | 8g fat | 3g protein | 9g complex carbohydrates | 27g sugar | 2g dietary fiber | 55mg cholesterol | 130mg sodium

BLONDIES

TWENTY-FOUR 2″ SQUARES

Brown sugar gives a deeply caramelized flavor to these chewy, rich blondies: the unsung hero of the bar cookie world. They might seem less enticing than a dark chocolate brownie, but with the right recipe, they're just as memorable . . . and as difficult to stop eating!

8 tablespoons (1 stick, 113g) unsalted butter, at room temperature

2 cups (426g) brown sugar, packed

½ teaspoon salt

1 teaspoon baking powder

2 teaspoons vanilla extract

1½ cups (180g) unbleached all-purpose flour

3 large eggs

1½ cups (168g) chopped pecans or walnuts

Preheat the oven to 350°F. Lightly grease a 9″ × 13″ pan.

Melt the butter in the microwave or in a saucepan set over medium heat. In a medium bowl, mix the melted butter with the brown sugar, salt, baking powder, and vanilla. Stir in the flour, then the eggs, one at a time. Stir in 1 cup of the nuts. Scoop the batter into the prepared pan and sprinkle the remaining nuts on top.

Bake the blondies for 30 to 35 minutes, until the top is shiny but the middle is still gooey (though not liquid). Remove them from the oven and cool completely before slicing.

NUTRITION INFORMATION PER SERVING: 1 brownie, 76g

321 cal | 12g fat | 3g protein | 7g complex carbohydrates | 45g sugar | 1g dietary fiber | 37mg cholesterol | 91mg sodium

VARIATIONS

CHEWY CHOCOLATE CHIP COOKIE BARS: Add ½ teaspoon butterscotch flavoring and 1½ cups (255g) semisweet chocolate chips.

S'MORE GRANOLA BARS

SIXTEEN 2¼″ SQUARES

The words "s'mores" and "granola bars" conjure up memories of smoky campfires, the smell of toasting marshmallows and melting chocolate wafting in the air, a leafy canopy overhead, and the good feeling of a heavy pack resting on your hips, the cool mountain air. These simple-to-make bars channel the experience of all of it.

- 6 tablespoons (¾ stick, 84g) unsalted butter
- ¼ cup (53g) light brown sugar, packed
- 6 tablespoons (112g) golden syrup, maple syrup, or dark corn syrup
- 2¼ cups (217g) old-fashioned rolled oats
- ½ cup (60g) unbleached all-purpose flour
- ½ teaspoon salt
- 1 cup (98g) graham cracker crumbs
- 1 cup (168g) semisweet or bittersweet chocolate chips
- 1¼ cups (154g) mini marshmallows

In a medium saucepan set over medium heat, melt and stir together the butter, brown sugar, and syrup, cooking until the sugar has dissolved. Stir in the oats, flour, salt, and graham cracker crumbs.

Press slightly more than half of the mixture into a lightly greased 9″ square pan. Let cool completely. Preheat the oven to 350°F. Sprinkle the chocolate chips evenly over the top, then the marshmallows. Top with the remaining crust mixture. Bake the bars for 15 to 20 minutes. Remove them from the oven and let them rest for 20 minutes, then cut into squares while still slightly warm.

YULETIDE TOFFEE SQUARES

96 SMALL PIECES

These squares—a holiday favorite—are a marriage between cookie and candy. Each decadent piece has the combined flavors of toffee, a meltingly buttery yet crisp base, just-thick-enough slathering of chocolate, and a dusting of finely chopped nuts. We consider these faux candy bars a pressed-for-time baker's best friend.

4½ cups (434g) old-fashioned rolled oats

1 cup (213g) brown sugar, packed

12 tablespoons (1½ sticks, 168g) unsalted butter, melted

¾ cup (231g) light corn syrup

1 tablespoon (14g) vanilla extract

½ teaspoon salt

2 cups (336g) semisweet chocolate chips

2 tablespoons (23g) vegetable shortening

⅔ cup (about 84g) chopped nuts

Preheat the oven to 450°F. Lightly grease a 15″ × 10″ pan.

Combine the oats, sugar, butter, corn syrup, vanilla, and salt and mix well. Press the mixture into the pan, using lightly greased hands to help the process along.

Bake the crust for 12 to 15 minutes, or until it's a light golden brown. Remove the pan from the oven and cool completely on a rack.

In a medium saucepan set over very low heat, melt the chocolate and shortening together, stirring constantly until smooth. Spread the mixture evenly over the crust and sprinkle with the chopped nuts.

Cover very loosely and chill the bars in the pan until the chocolate is firm. Remove from the refrigerator and cut into squares. The easiest way to do this is to use a chef's knife to cut the bars into long strips while they're still in the pan, then transfer each long strip to a cutting board to cut into bite-size pieces.

CHOCOLATE MINT SQUARES

ABOUT 36 SMALL 1″ SQUARES

Peppermint seems to appear during the holidays and disappear just as quickly once the New Year has arrived, but we're in favor of embracing the flavor all year long. These dense, rich bars boast a layer of white icing offset by a drizzle of bitter chocolate.

DOUGH

2 ounces (56g) unsweetened chocolate

8 tablespoons (1 stick, 113g) unsalted butter

1 cup (196g) granulated sugar

¼ teaspoon salt

2 large eggs

½ cup (60g) unbleached all-purpose flour

½ cup (56g) chopped walnuts or pecans

½ teaspoon peppermint extract or peppermint oil*

FROSTING

1 cup (112g) confectioners' sugar

2 tablespoons (28g) butter, melted

¾ teaspoon peppermint extract or peppermint oil*

1 tablespoon (14g) milk

GLAZE

1 ounce (28g) bittersweet chocolate

1 tablespoon (14g) butter

Preheat the oven to 350°F. Lightly grease a 9″ square pan.

TO MAKE THE DOUGH: In a double boiler, or in a microwave, melt together the chocolate and butter. In a medium bowl, beat together the sugar, salt, and eggs. Add the chocolate mixture, stirring to combine, then the flour, nuts, and peppermint, mixing until well blended.

Pour the batter into the prepared pan. Bake the bars for 25 minutes. Remove them from the oven and cool to room temperature.

TO MAKE THE FROSTING: Whisk together the sugar, butter, peppermint, and milk in a small bowl. Spread the frosting over the cooled bars in a thin layer.

TO MAKE THE GLAZE: In a double boiler or in a microwave, melt together the chocolate and butter. Drizzle this over the frosted bars. Refrigerate the bars until they're well chilled. To serve, cut into 1½″ squares.

* Peppermint oils vary in strength; add them judiciously, tasting as you go.

NUTRITION INFORMATION PER SERVING: **1 square made with walnuts, 22g**
99 cal | 6g fat | 1g protein | 2g complex carbohydrates | 8g sugar | 0g dietary fiber | 25mg cholesterol | 20mg sodium

HERMIT BARS

ABOUT ONE HUNDRED 1″-SQUARE BARS

Everyone thinks there's ginger in these soft, chewy bars, but the key ingredient is actually allspice. Among the many virtues of this recipe is that it keeps for weeks in an airtight container. (It also ships very, very well.) As they bake, they'll puff up in the oven and the top will get shiny. As soon as you see this, pull the pan from the oven. The top will fall back down and the interior of the cookies will have an almost fudgy consistency. If you leave them in the oven longer, they'll be more cake-like and won't be as moist and irresistible.

BARS

1⅓ cups (280g) granulated sugar

½ cup plus 2 tablespoons (112g) vegetable shortening

4 tablespoons (½ stick, 56g) butter, at room temperature

¼ cup (84g) molasses

¾ teaspoon salt

¾ teaspoon allspice

¾ teaspoon cinnamon

1¾ teaspoons baking soda

2 large eggs

5 cups (600g) unbleached all-purpose flour

⅓ cup (74g) water

2 cups (336g) raisins

GLAZE

1 cup (112g) confectioners' sugar, sifted

3 tablespoons (42g) milk

Preheat the oven to 350°F. Lightly grease a 10″ × 15″ jelly roll pan, or a 9″ square pan and 8″ square pan (or 9″ round pan) to approximate the size of the jelly roll pan.

TO MAKE THE BARS: In the bowl of a stand mixer or by hand in a large bowl, beat together the sugar, shortening, and butter at medium speed until fluffy. Add the molasses, salt, spices, and baking soda. Mix for 1 minute, then stop the mixer and scrape down the sides of the bowl. Add the eggs one at a time, beating well after each addition. Add half the flour. Once it's mixed in, add the water, then the other half of the flour. When the batter is completely mixed, add the raisins and stir until combined.

Spread the batter in the prepared pan(s). Bake the hermits for 18 to 20 minutes, until their edges are light brown and the top is shiny. Remove from the oven and cool them in the pan completely before glazing.

TO MAKE THE GLAZE: Stir together the glaze ingredients until they're smooth—it will be quite thin. Use a pastry brush to brush it on top of the hermits.

NUTRITION INFORMATION PER SERVING: **1 square, 13g**

47 cal | 1g fat | 1g protein | 5g complex carbohydrates | 4g sugar | 0g dietary fiber | 5mg cholesterol | 37mg sodium

GINGER SQUARES

ABOUT 54 SQUARES

English bakers have long been famous for their gingerbread and the numerous forms it can take, from sticky toffee pudding to gingerbread men (supposedly "invented" by Queen Elizabeth I). Our recipe for thin, chewy gingerbread topped with streusel and crystallized ginger was inspired by a sample from Cornwall, England, where a locally famous bakery sells it, wrapped in foil.

BATTER

1¼ cups (150g) unbleached all-purpose flour

2 teaspoons ginger

1 teaspoon allspice

¾ teaspoon salt

¼ teaspoon baking soda

½ cup (77g) diced crystallized ginger

¼ cup (84g) molasses

2 large eggs

1⅓ cups (283g) dark brown sugar, packed

4 tablespoons (½ stick, 56g) unsalted butter, melted

STREUSEL TOPPING

1⅓ cups (160g) unbleached all-purpose flour

8 tablespoons (1 stick, 113g) unsalted butter, at room temperature

pinch of salt

¾ cup (160g) dark brown sugar, packed

½ cup (77g) diced crystallized ginger

Preheat the oven to 350°F. Lightly grease a 9″ × 13″ pan.

TO MAKE THE BATTER: In a medium bowl, whisk together the flour, ginger, allspice, salt, baking soda, and crystallized ginger.

In a separate bowl, stir together the molasses, eggs, brown sugar, and melted butter. Combine the wet and dry ingredients, beating until smooth. Spread the batter in the prepared pan and bake the bars for 20 minutes. While the batter bakes, prepare the topping.

TO MAKE THE TOPPING: Using a pastry blender, electric mixer, or your fingers, mix together the flour, butter, salt, and brown sugar until it's fairly well blended; some chunks of butter can remain. Mix in the crystallized ginger. Once the first bake is done, sprinkle on the streusel and bake for an additional 25 minutes, until the streusel is a deep golden brown. Remove the bars from the oven and run a knife around the edges of the pan to loosen them. Allow them to cool, then cut them into 1½″ squares.

NUTRITION INFORMATION PER SERVING: 1 square, 24g

90 cal | 3g fat | 1g protein | 5g complex carbohydrates | 10g sugar | 0g dietary fiber | 18mg cholesterol | 53mg sodium

LEMON SQUARES

THIRTY-FIVE 2″ SQUARES

We always feel that spring has truly arrived when we smell the lilacs and see rhubarb at the farmers' market, and this is just the dessert to welcome the season.

CRUST

8 tablespoons (1 stick, 113g) unsalted butter, at room temperature

¼ cup (50g) granulated sugar

½ teaspoon salt

2 teaspoons vanilla extract

2½ cups (300g) unbleached all-purpose flour or unbleached pastry flour

2 large eggs

FILLING

8 tablespoons (1 stick, 113g) unsalted butter, melted

1¼ cups (245g) granulated sugar

2 tablespoons (18g) cornmeal

2 tablespoons (14g) cornstarch

½ teaspoon salt

4 large eggs

½ cup (112g) fresh lemon juice (from 2 to 3 large lemons)

TOPPING

confectioners' sugar, for dusting

Preheat the oven to 350°F. Lightly grease a 10″ × 15″ jelly roll pan, or a 9″ square pan and 8″ square pan (or 9″ round pan) to approximate the size of the jelly roll pan.

TO MAKE THE CRUST: In a medium bowl, beat the butter until fluffy. Beat in the sugar, salt, and vanilla. Stir in the flour and eggs, mixing until well blended. If you're using a hand mixer, you'll need to finish kneading in the flour by hand, as this dough is quite stiff.

Press the dough into the pan, being sure to press it up to the top edge of the pan. Prick the dough all over with a fork. Bake the crust for 8 minutes; it won't brown much, just become set. Leave the oven on.

TO MAKE THE LEMON FILLING: In a medium bowl, whisk together the melted butter, sugar, cornmeal, cornstarch, salt, eggs, and lemon juice. Top the baked crust with the lemon filling. Return it to the oven and bake for an additional 25 to 28 minutes, until the top is lightly browned.

Cool the bars completely, then dust with confectioners' sugar before cutting into squares.

NUTRITION INFORMATION PER SERVING: 1 lemon square, 37g

116 cal | 5g fat | 2g protein | 8g complex carbohydrates | 8g sugar | 0g dietary fiber | 48mg cholesterol | 73mg sodium

NO-BAKE PEANUT BUTTER CHOCOLATE SQUARES

ABOUT 24 SQUARES

This is one of those recipes you can make at home that emulates a store-bought treat almost perfectly: in this case, peanut butter cups.

1½ cups (213g) graham cracker crumbs

16 tablespoons (2 sticks, 226g) unsalted butter, melted

2½ cups (283g) confectioners' sugar

1 cup (269g) supermarket-style peanut butter, crunchy or smooth

1 cup (170g) chocolate chips

In a large bowl, combine the graham cracker crumbs, butter, sugar, and peanut butter. Mix until well combined.

Spread the mixture in a lightly greased 9″ × 13″ pan. Chill in the refrigerator for approximately 10 minutes.

While the peanut butter layer is chilling, melt the chocolate chips, in a microwave or in a double boiler on top of the stove. Spread the chocolate over the peanut butter.

Cut into squares. Return them to the refrigerator to chill for at least 1 hour.

NUTRITION INFORMATION PER SERVING: 1 square, 48g

251 cal | 16g fat | 3g protein | 26g complex carbohydrates | 18g sugar | 1g dietary fiber | 20mg cholesterol | 115mg sodium

ALMOND TOFFEE BARS

ABOUT 48 SQUARES

This recipe makes rich, buttery squares gilded with a dark caramel topping.

COOKIE BASE

16 tablespoons (2 sticks, 226g) unsalted
  butter, at room temperature

1 teaspoon almond extract

½ cup (56g) confectioners' sugar

2 cups (240g) unbleached all-
  purpose flour

½ teaspoon baking powder

½ teaspoon salt

TOPPING

1 cup (213g) brown sugar, packed

5⅓ tablespoons (⅔ stick, 75g) unsalted
  butter, at room temperature

¼ cup (56g) milk

1 cup (84g) sliced almonds

Preheat the oven to 350°F. Lightly grease a 10″ × 15″ jelly roll pan, or a 9″ square pan and 8″ square pan (or 9″ round pan) to approximate the size of the jelly roll pan.

TO MAKE THE COOKIE BASE: In a medium bowl, beat the butter, then add the almond extract and the confectioners' sugar, beating continuously. Sift together the flour, baking powder, and salt and stir the dry ingredients into the wet ingredients. Press the dough into the prepared pan, coming up the sides just a little. Bake the crust 15 to 20 minutes, until it's golden brown. Set it aside.

TO MAKE THE TOPPING: Combine the brown sugar, butter, and milk in a saucepan, stirring over low heat just until the brown sugar is dissolved and the butter has melted. Spread this mixture over the cookie base. Sprinkle with the sliced almonds.

Put the pastry under the broiler until the top bubbles, 3 minutes at the most. After 2 minutes, open the oven door and watch the bubbling action. As soon as the nuts are golden brown, remove the bars from the oven. (It's easy to burn the topping if you're not careful.) When cool, cut into small (1½″) squares.

NUTRITION INFORMATION PER SERVING: 1 square, 21g

98 cal | 6g fat | 1g protein | 4g complex carbohydrates | 5g sugar | 0g dietary fiber | 15mg cholesterol | 86mg sodium

CAMELOT DREAM BARS

24 BARS

These sweet, sticky bars may not be much to look at, but just one taste and you'll be hooked. Filled with coconut, toasted pecans, and brown sugar, they're a nice change from a brownie.

CRUST

8 tablespoons (1 stick, 113g) salted butter, at room temperature

¾ cup (160g) brown sugar, packed

1 cup plus 2 tablespoons (135g) unbleached all-purpose flour

TOPPING

2 large eggs

2 teaspoons vanilla extract

¾ cup (160g) brown sugar, packed

¼ teaspoon salt

1 teaspoon baking powder

¼ cup (30g) unbleached all-purpose flour

1 cup (113g) pecan pieces, toasted

1½ cups (156g) flaked sweetened coconut

Preheat the oven to 350°F. Grease a 9″ × 13″ pan. For easiest removal, line the pan with parchment, and grease the parchment.

TO MAKE THE CRUST: In a medium bowl, beat the butter and brown sugar until light and fluffy. Add the flour, stirring until just combined.

Pat the mixture into the prepared pan. Lightly flour your fingers as you press the dough into the pan; it's sticky, and will cover the bottom of the pan with only a thin layer.

Bake the crust for 15 to 20 minutes, until bubbly and beginning to brown. Remove it from the oven, and let it cool while you prepare the topping.

TO MAKE THE TOPPING: Beat together the eggs, vanilla, brown sugar, salt, and baking powder. Gently beat in the flour, then mix in the toasted pecans and coconut.

Spread the topping mixture over the baked crust. Return the bars to the oven, and bake for 20 to 25 minutes, until they're starting to turn golden brown.

Remove the bars from the oven. After a few minutes, loosen the edges with a knife.

After 5 more minutes, carefully turn the warm bars out onto a piece of parchment or foil, topping side down. Quickly cut them into squares. When they've set and are no longer fragile, place the squares, topping side up, on a rack to cool.

NUTRITION INFORMATION PER SERVING: 1 bar, 40g

170 cal | 9g fat | 2g protein | 6g complex carbohydrates | 16g sugar | 1g dietary fiber | 25mg cholesterol | 90mg sodium

DATE SQUARES

THIRTY-SIX 1½″ SQUARES

If you've never had the pleasure of eating a date square, with its two layers of crumbly, crunchy, sweet oatmeal crust sandwiching a gooey layer of smooth date filling—you've missed out. It's best to eat them over a plate, as much of the crust inevitably crumbles away as you take a bite.

Most recipes for date bars yield a homogeneous, rather than layered, mixture of dates and oatmeal, not at all what we remember of the traditional version. In desperation, we finally went ahead and made up our own recipe and have been enjoying it ever since.

FILLING

3 cups (447g) chopped dates

1 cup (224g) water

heaping ¼ teaspoon salt

1 tablespoon plus 1 teaspoon (19g) lemon juice

2 teaspoons vanilla extract

CRUST

1½ cups (147g) old-fashioned rolled oats

1½ cups (180g) unbleached all-purpose flour

1 cup (213g) brown sugar, packed

¾ teaspoon baking soda

¾ teaspoon salt

12 tablespoons (1½ sticks, 168g) unsalted butter, melted

½ cup (56g) chopped walnuts or pecans

Preheat the oven to 350°F. Lightly grease a 9″ square pan.

TO MAKE THE FILLING: In a small saucepan, combine the dates, water, salt, and lemon juice. Bring the mixture to a boil, reduce the heat to low, and simmer for 3 to 4 minutes, until the water is absorbed and the mixture has thickened somewhat. Remove the pan from the heat, stir in the vanilla, and set aside to cool while you prepare the crust.

TO MAKE THE CRUST: In a medium bowl, whisk together the oats, flour, brown sugar, baking soda, and salt. Stir in the melted butter.

TO ASSEMBLE: Press 2½ cups of the crust mixture into the prepared pan, smoothing it out to completely cover the bottom of the pan with no gaps. Top the crust with the date filling. Add the walnuts to the remaining crust mixture and sprinkle it over the filling.

Bake the squares for 30 minutes, or until the crust is golden brown. Remove the squares from the oven and allow them to cool before cutting.

NUTRITION INFORMATION PER SERVING: **1 square, 41g**

134 cal | 5g fat | 2g protein | 14g complex carbohydrates | 6g sugar | 2g dietary fiber | 11mg cholesterol | 90mg sodium

CHAPTER EIGHT

Cakes

———

HAVE YOU EVER NOTICED that all of life's happy milestones—birthdays, graduations, weddings, anniversaries—are marked by cake? Every time the occasion turns festive, there's a cake, right at its center. It's a harbinger of celebration—who can think about anything but a party upon seeing a layer cake swathed in frosting and crowned with brightly lit candles?

But what makes cake different from other baked goods? Cake (particularly cupcakes) and muffins are actually quite similar, but on the whole, cake (especially in its layered form) is a much grander, more festive choice. And cake, although perceived by some as a more formal dessert, is also the essence of comfort food in its most basic form: sweet, soft, and straightforward in flavor (think chocolate and vanilla).

Cakes, like most baked goods, come in a wide variety of types. There's the dense flourless chocolate cake, a fudge-frosted yellow cupcake, delicate angel food, creamy New York cheesecake, an impossibly light jelly roll swirled around a filling of whipped cream and raspberry jam, or a three-tiered carrot cake swathed in cream cheese frosting. All are cake, but so different in flavor, texture, and form. You could bake a cake every day of the year and not come close to traversing their wide world. And, if you're a passionate baker, the wideness of that universe is somehow comforting; no matter what, you'll never run out of new cake recipes to try.

Easy or One-Bowl Cakes

When you think of comfort food in cake form, what comes to mind? A rustic raisin-studded apple cake, drizzled with caramel icing? Gingerbread with a dollop of whipped cream? How about everyone's favorite, carrot cake with cream cheese icing? These cakes, often containing a wide array of ingredients, and usually dense rather than light, are called one-bowl cakes because you need only one bowl to prepare them. The simplest of all the cakes, they're stirred together like muffins, although usually this stirring comes closer to beating. Because of the tenderizing properties of their high amounts of both sugar and fat, these cakes are able to withstand a fairly heavy workout without becoming tough.

The leavening in this type of cake comes almost entirely from chemicals, either baking powder, baking soda, or a combination. A small amount of air is created through beating, but nothing like what occurs in butter or foam cakes, which rely much more heavily on the physical technique used in their preparation, rather than on the baking powder or baking soda in the list of ingredients.

CHOCOLATE CAKE PAN CAKE

ONE 8″ SQUARE OR 9″ ROUND CAKE

This dark, moist, and delicious chocolate cake epitomizes how simple cake can be. Using vegetable oil instead of butter means you can just stir it all together quickly, and also makes it vegan. Over the years, this cake has been one of King Arthur's most requested recipes. It's truly a cake for all reasons and all seasons.

CAKE

1½ cups (180g) unbleached all-purpose flour

1 cup (198g) sugar

¼ cup (21g) unsweetened cocoa

½ teaspoon salt

½ teaspoon espresso power (optional)

1 teaspoon baking soda

1 teaspoon vanilla extract

1 tablespoon (14g) cider or white vinegar

⅓ cup (67g) vegetable oil

1 cup (227g) cold water

ICING (OPTIONAL)

1½ cups (255g) semisweet chocolate chips

½ cup (113g) half-and-half

Preheat the oven to 350°F. Lightly grease an 8″ square or 9″ round pan that's at least 2″ deep.

Whisk the dry ingredients together in a medium bowl. Whisk the vanilla, vinegar, vegetable oil, and water in a separate bowl. Pour the wet ingredients into the bowl of dry ingredients, stirring until thoroughly combined. Pour the batter into the prepared pan.

Bake the cake for 30 to 35 minutes, until a cake tester or toothpick inserted into the center comes out clean, or with a few moist crumbs clinging to it.

Serve the cake right from the pan, or let it cool, and frost it with a simple chocolate icing: Heat the chocolate chips with the half-and-half until the chips melt. Stir until smooth, and pour or spread over the cake. For a nondairy icing, substitute ⅓ cup cold brewed coffee (or water) for the half-and-half.

Store cake, well covered, at room temperature for several days; freeze for longer storage.

VARIATION
GLUTEN-FREE: Swap the 1½ cups (180g) unbleached all-purpose flour for an equal amount of Gluten-Free Measure for Measure Flour.

NUTRITION INFORMATION PER SERVING: **1 square, 70g**
220 cal | 10g fat | 3g protein | 12g complex carbohydrates | 21g sugar | 2g dietary fiber | 0mg cholesterol | 160mg sodium

APPLE CAKE

ONE 9″ × 13″ CAKE

Apples and ginger have a natural affinity for each other, as this moist, flavorful cake demonstrates.

1 cup (113g) whole wheat flour

1⅓ cups (160g) unbleached all-purpose flour

1 cup (198g) granulated sugar

1 cup (213g) brown sugar, firmly packed

2 teaspoons baking soda

¾ teaspoon salt

2 teaspoons apple pie spice or 1 teaspoon cinnamon plus ½ teaspoon each allspice and nutmeg

8 tablespoons (1 stick, 113g) unsalted butter, softened

3 tablespoons (42g) minced crystallized ginger (optional)

4 cups (452g) cored, chopped, unpeeled apples

½ cup (57g) diced pecans or walnuts

½ cup (85g) raisins, golden raisins, or currants

2 large eggs

Preheat the oven to 325°F. Grease and flour a 9″ × 13″ pan.

In a large mixing bowl, whisk together the flours, sugars, baking soda, salt, and spice(s). Cut the softened butter into chunks and add it along with the ginger, apples, nuts, raisins, and eggs. Beat at medium speed until well blended.

Turn the batter into the prepared pan and smooth the top. Bake the cake for 45 minutes, or until it springs back when lightly touched in the center. Remove it from the oven and cool completely on a rack. Leave the cake in the pan and frost with Brown Sugar Frosting (page 347), if desired.

NUTRITION INFORMATION PER SERVING: 1 square, unfrosted, 96g

279 cal | 4g fat | 9g protein | 22g complex carbohydrates | 27g sugar | 3g dietary fiber | 42mg cholesterol | 274mg sodium

CARROT CAKE

ONE 9″ × 13″ CAKE OR 3-LAYER 8″ CAKE

Carrot cake is a touchstone dessert. We know lots of people for whom nothing else will do on their birthdays. But if someone asks you for carrot cake, make sure to ask which kind they're thinking about, since there are really two distinct styles. One camp garnishes with raisins and nuts, while the other heads for crushed pineapple or coconut. This recipe will work perfectly well either way, but if you're the sort for whom too much is just enough, put all of them in. It's moist and flavorful enough to stand on its own with just a dusting of confectioners' sugar, but we know of no better way to enjoy cream cheese frosting than with carrot cake!

4 large eggs

1½ cups (298g) vegetable oil

2 teaspoons vanilla extract

1¾ cups (347g) sugar

2 cups (240g) unbleached all-purpose flour

1½ teaspoons baking powder

2 teaspoons baking soda

1 teaspoon salt

1 tablespoon cinnamon

½ teaspoon nutmeg

2½ cups (248g) finely grated carrots

1 cup (114g) chopped pecans or walnuts

1 cup (113g) shredded or flaked coconut*

1 can (170g) crushed pineapple, drained*

Preheat the oven to 350°F. Grease a 9″ × 13″ pan or three 8″ round pans.

In a large bowl, beat the eggs and add oil while mixer is running. Add vanilla, then gradually add the sugar. You'll have a thick, foamy, lemon-colored mixture. In a separate medium bowl, whisk together the flour, baking powder, baking soda, salt, and spices. Add these dry ingredients to the wet mixture, stirring to make a smooth batter. Add the carrots and nuts, then additional garnishes of your choice (coconut, pineapple, and/or raisins).

Pour the batter into the prepared pan(s) and bake for 45 to 50 minutes (for a 9″ × 13″) or 35 minutes (for rounds). Cake is done when a cake tester or toothpick inserted in the center comes out clean. Cool in the pan for 10 minutes, then turn out to cool completely. Dust with confectioners' sugar or frost with Cream Cheese Frosting (page 349), or the icing of your choice.

* Or substitute 2 cups (340g) raisins for the coconut and pineapple.

NUTRITION INFORMATION PER SERVING: 1 square, unfrosted, 77g

280 cal | 19g fat | 3g protein | 11g complex carbohydrates | 15g sugar | 1g dietary fiber | 36mg cholesterol | 257mg sodium

GINGERBREAD PLUS

ONE 9″ × 13″ CAKE

Moist, gingery, and dense (but not heavy), this single-layer cake evokes an old-fashioned child-hood, one where you may have sat at the kitchen table after school eating a square of warm gingerbread adorned with whipped cream. The original recipe that inspired this extra-gingery version comes from Karyl Bannister of Southport, Maine.

¾ cup (160g) light brown sugar, packed

¼ cup (84g) molasses

½ cup (140g) Ginger Syrup (see following recipe), golden syrup, or light corn syrup

8 tablespoons (1 stick, 113g) unsalted butter, melted

¼ cup (49g) vegetable oil

2 large eggs

2½ cups (300g) unbleached all-purpose flour

2 teaspoons baking soda

1 tablespoon ginger

1 teaspoon cinnamon

½ teaspoon nutmeg

½ teaspoon salt

⅔ cup (128g) minced crystallized ginger (optional)

1 cup (227g) boiling water

Preheat the oven to 350°F. Lightly grease a 9″ × 13″ pan.

In a medium bowl, mix together the brown sugar, molasses, syrup, melted butter, oil, and eggs, beating until smooth. Stir in the flour, baking soda, spices, salt, and crystallized ginger (if using). Then carefully stir in the water; go slowly, as it will want to splash up. Scrape the sides and bottom of the bowl and stir in any of the pasty patches that have gathered there.

Pour the batter into the prepared pan. Bake for 30 to 40 minutes, until a cake tester or toothpick inserted in the center comes out clean. While still warm, brush with additional Ginger Syrup, if desired.

NUTRITION INFORMATION PER SERVING: 1 piece, 70g

215 cal | 9g fat | 2g protein | 12g complex carbohydrates | 20g sugar | 1g dietary fiber | 38mg cholesterol | 228mg sodium

Ginger Syrup

2¾ CUPS

Bitingly hot and sweet, this ginger syrup is a snap to make. Drizzle it over gingerbread, biscuits or scones, pancakes, or oatmeal. It's a wonderful addition to tea, too.

4 cups (about 369g) fresh ginger, unpeeled, cut into ¼˝ thick slices

3½ cups (695g) sugar
3½ cups (795g) water

In a large heavy-bottomed saucepan, bring the ginger, sugar, and water to a boil. Simmer the mixture for 45 minutes to 1 hour, until it registers 216°F to 220°F on a digital thermometer. The lower temperature will give you a thinner syrup, one that's easy to stir into drinks; the higher temperature will yield a thicker syrup, more the consistency of corn syrup. (You can't tell how thick the syrup will be while it's still hot; you have to go by its temperature, as it'll thicken as it cools.)

Remove the pan from the burner and carefully strain the syrup into a nonreactive container. Store in the refrigerator.

NUTRITION INFORMATION PER SERVING: 1 tablespoon, 34g

9 cal | 0g fat | 0g protein | 2g complex carbohydrates | 2g sugar | 0g dietary fiber | 0mg cholesterol | 2mg sodium

A VERY LIGHT FRUITCAKE

THREE 8½" × 4½" FRUITCAKES

Fruitcake seems to elicit either groans of dismay or timid—very timid—admissions of pleasure. While for some people, fruitcake is simply fodder for culinary jokes, for others it's a time-honored Christmas tradition.

We like the following recipe because it omits the usual citron and peel, a plus if you're not a fan of those somewhat bitter fruits. With its light-colored, mild-flavored cake cradling a variety of dried fruits, this is a version even non-fruitcake-lovers will embrace. If candied fruit isn't to your liking, skip it and add more dried fruit.

FRUIT

2¼ pounds (6 cups, 1021g) your favorite dried fruits

1 cup (170g) candied red cherries

¼ cup (57g) brandy, rum, or whiskey (or substitute apple juice or water)

CAKE

16 tablespoons (2 sticks, 227g) unsalted butter

1 cup (198g) granulated sugar

½ cup (107g) brown sugar

2 teaspoons baking powder

½ teaspoon salt

½ teaspoon ginger

1 teaspoon cinnamon

½ teaspoon nutmeg

4 large eggs

¼ cup (85g) honey

3 cups (360g) unbleached all-purpose flour

¾ cup (170g) milk

2 cups (227g) diced pecans or walnuts (optional)

TO PREPARE THE FRUIT: Combine the dried fruit and the liquor (or water or juice) in a nonreactive bowl, cover, and allow to sit and macerate overnight.

Preheat the oven to 300°F. Lightly grease three 8½" × 4½" loaf pans or smaller pans of your choice.

TO MAKE THE CAKE: Beat together the butter, sugars, baking powder, salt, and spices until well blended. Beat in the eggs and honey, beating until fluffy. Add the flour and beat until smooth. Beat in the milk, scrape the sides and bottom of the bowl, then mix in the fruit (don't drain it) and the nuts. Spoon the batter into the prepared pans. Fill them about three-quarters full.

Bake the cakes for 40 to 70 minutes, depending on the size of the pans; the full-size cakes will take the longer amount of time. When the cake is done, it will be a light golden brown all over and a cake tester or toothpick inserted into the center will come out clean.

Remove the fruitcakes from the oven, allow them to cool for 10 minutes, then turn them out of the pans. Brush them with brandy or the liquor of your choice (or apple juice) while they're still warm. When they're completely cool, wrap them well and let rest at least 24 hours before serving.

This cake can be made several weeks ahead; just brush it with brandy, rum, whiskey, or simple syrup and wrap it tightly in plastic wrap. For long-term storage (up to two months), brush with the liquor of your choice once a week, keeping the cake tightly wrapped between times. If you don't choose to brush the cake with liquor, freeze it for up to two months before serving.

NUTRITION INFORMATION PER SERVING: 1 slice, 51g
162 cal | 5g fat | 2g protein | 20g complex carbohydrates | 9g sugar | 2g dietary fiber | 29mg cholesterol | 55mg sodium

Traditional Fruitcake

If your idea of fruitcake is dark and lustrous, try the following variations on the preceding recipe:

Use a total of 1½ cups (320g) brown sugar, omitting the granulated sugar.

Substitute the fruits of your choice, including mixed dried peel and citron.

Add 2 tablespoons unsweetened cocoa for color.

ONE-BOWL CHOCOLATE MINT CAKE

ONE 2-LAYER 9″ CAKE

Deep, dark chocolate cake, layered around a rich and creamy filling, then glazed with sumptuous fudge glaze—what's not to love? The hint of mint comes from a garnish of crushed peppermint candies or crumbled chocolate mint cookies (hello, Girl Scouts!), but you could also substitute a chocolate-covered espresso-bean garnish instead to make this a chocolate mocha cake. We recommend filling this cake with the Seven-Minute Frosting on page 345 and icing it with the Chocolate Glaze on page 348.

1¾ cups (343g) sugar

2¼ cups (270g) unbleached all-purpose flour

2 tablespoons (14g) cornstarch

¾ cup (64g) Dutch-process cocoa

¼ cup (35g) buttermilk powder*

1 teaspoon baking powder

1 teaspoon baking soda

1 teaspoon salt

2 large eggs

¾ cup (170g) water*

½ cup (99g) vegetable oil

2 teaspoons vanilla extract

1 cup (227g) hot water

crushed peppermint candies or crumbled chocolate mint cookies, to garnish

Preheat the oven to 350°F. Lightly grease and flour two 9″ round cake pans.

TO PREPARE THE CAKE: In a large bowl, stir together the sugar, flour, cornstarch, cocoa, buttermilk powder, baking powder, baking soda, and salt. Add the eggs, water, oil, and vanilla; beat on medium speed for 2 minutes. Stir in the hot water; the batter will be thin. Pour the batter into the prepared pans.

Bake the cakes for 30 to 35 minutes, or until a cake tester inserted into the center of one comes out clean. Cool for 10 minutes in the pans, then turn them out to cool completely on a rack.

TO ASSEMBLE THE CAKE: Place 1 layer of cake, top side down, on a serving platter. Spread with the filling. Top with the remaining cake layer, also putting it top side down. Pour the Chocolate Glaze very slowly over the top of the cake. If the mixture is too thin and runs off, let it cool longer. Sprinkle the top with the crushed peppermint candy or chocolate mint cookies.

* If desired, substitute ¾ cup (170g) fresh buttermilk for the buttermilk powder and water.

NUTRITION INFORMATION PER SERVING: **1 piece, 105g**

330 cal | 16g fat | 4g protein | 45 g carbohydrates | 27g sugar | 1g dietary fiber | 45 mg cholesterol | 310 mg sodium

A Butter Cake Primer

Butter cakes are a bit more involved than one-bowl cakes. Their preparation is lengthier, both before going into the oven and afterward; they're nearly always iced, and often stacked in layers and decorated as well. Devil's food cake, yellow layer cake, white wedding cake, pound cake: All of these are familiar examples of butter cake. Aside from pound cake, which in the old days was leavened by nonchemical means (and sometimes still is), all of these cakes get their light texture from both a chemical leavener and the air beaten into the batter before it's spooned into the pan.

Making a butter cake (or creamed cake; they're the same thing), the most common of all American cakes, takes a bit more skill and attention to detail than making a one-bowl cake. But it's easy to make if you follow the recipe instructions carefully. A butter cake's texture depends on the ingredients you use, how you mix them, and how you bake the cake. Here's the process, one step at a time.

Flour

The role of flour in a butter cake is to provide just enough framework to support the cake as it rises in the oven. Because the cake has other supports as well, such as protein from dairy products and eggs, the cake isn't relying solely on the protein in the flour to enclose air pockets and support the cake. In yeast bread, there's often no other framework to trap air bubbles, so a high-gluten flour is necessary. But if cake is made with high-gluten flour, and the batter is beaten (to trap air), the final product will be tough.

We've experimented with baking cakes with all-purpose flour (11.7% protein), pastry flour (9% protein), and bleached cake flour (8% protein). We found that while the cakes with the pastry flour had a more tender crumb, they were also more crumbly. Cakes made from bleached cake flour were also tender, fine-grained, and high-rising, but again, their texture was crumbly. Cakes made with all-purpose flour were a shade denser and held together well. You can also opt for unbleached cake flour, which dilutes the protein level of all-purpose flour with added starch. These have the structure of an all-purpose flour cake with a more tender, finer grain. If you don't have pastry or cake flour and want to lighten your all-purpose flour, substitute 1 tablespoon of cornstarch for 1 tablespoon of flour in each cup of flour in the recipe. The key is to handle the batter lightly when you're incorporating the flour so that you don't activate the gluten too much.

Butter

The most important thing to remember about butter is that it needs to be at cool room temperature. Creaming the butter with the leavener, sugar, and flavors is usually the first step. Creaming butter means to beat it to incorporate air, which expands with the heat of the oven and help of leaveners. If the butter is at cool room temperature (around 65°F), the fat is pliable enough to expand and encapsulate millions of minuscule air bubbles. A caveat: Creaming can be taken too far; beating for too long can cause the aerated butter/sugar mixture to become so fragile that it collapses, and sunken cake layers are the result.

The best way to bring butter to room temperature is to let it sit out on the counter. We're often in a rush and tempted to microwave butter to get it to room temperature. However, microwaved butter isn't uniformly softened; it comes out with a few melted spots, more or less soft with some still-cold zones. This isn't a positive scenario for cake; a liquid fat has nowhere near the capacity to contain air that a solid, room-temperature fat does. And neither does a cold one. Once butter has been melted, you need to use it for something other than a butter cake. And don't think that by refrigerating melted butter you can bring it back to its original state. The emulsion of water and fat has been broken in the heating process, and a once-melted fat cannot hold air the way a room-temperature fat can.

Because the butter is creamed until it has trapped a lot of air (i.e., it's become light and fluffy), it becomes one of the cake's chief leaveners. Fat also permeates the batter and serves to soften it, contributing to the tender texture of the cake. If you refrigerate a butter cake, the fat hardens and the cake will be quite stiff; this type of cake is best stored at room temperature or, if it absolutely needs to be refrigerated (e.g., it has a whipped cream or other perishable filling or frosting), it should be brought to room temperature before serving.

Sugar

Sugar serves five purposes in a cake. When it's creamed with butter, it helps increase butter's ability to hold air; as you add sugar to the creamed butter and continue to whip, you'll notice an increase in volume. The second purpose is flavoring. The third is to help absorb moisture, which prevents the cake from drying out. The fourth is to help in the browning of the cake. Both the starch content of the flour and the browning of sugar that occurs as it's exposed to heat contribute to a lightly browned cake. The final purpose is to enhance tenderness; sugar binds with the proteins in the flour, preventing them from forming the long, elastic (tough) protein chains known as gluten.

Eggs

The eggs used in cake, like the butter, need to be at room temperature. If you add cold eggs to room-temperature butter, the butter cells will turn solid and actually break, releasing all of the air that you've just beaten into them. If the recipe calls for separated eggs, separate the yolks and whites as soon as you take the eggs out of the refrigerator. If you try to separate a room-temperature egg, you're likely to end up with egg yolk in the whites.

If the recipe calls for beating the yolks and whites separately, the whites must be beaten in a bowl that has no trace of fat, or they won't expand to their full capacity. The addition of cream of tartar (an acid) stabilizes the alkaline egg whites and they'll hold their beaten volume while you incorporate them into the cake batter.

Eggs are able to expand to many times their original volume when they're whipped. The air that's beaten into them is also a primary leavener in cakes. In the oven, the proteins in the egg white set first and help maintain the structure of the cake. The egg yolks contain lecithin, a type of fat, which helps to soften the texture of the cake.

Baking Powder and Baking Soda

Double-acting baking powder is a combination of two acids, sodium acid pyrophosphate and tartaric acid; an alkaline, sodium bicarbonate, a.k.a. baking soda and cornstarch. Some baking powder contains aluminum; some does not. When baking powder is beaten with butter and sugar at the beginning of the cake preparation process, it begins to react with the moisture in the butter, giving off tiny bubbles of carbon dioxide that will eventually help to leaven the cake. In the oven, the heat causes a second round of leavening ("double-acting") to occur, hence cakes continue to rise in the oven. To make your own baking powder, mix ½ teaspoon cream of tartar with ¼ teaspoon baking soda. This mixture has the leavening power of 1 teaspoon of baking powder.

Baking soda is an alkali and needs an acid in the batter to react to it. Usually buttermilk, yogurt, natural unsweetened cocoa (not Dutch-process), or a citrus fruit juice will do the job.

Liquids

Liquids moisten the baking powder and/or baking soda (if they're used), which allows them to react and leaven the batter. They're also absorbed by the flour, activating its gluten, which helps to build the cake's structure. In addition, if the liquids are dairy-based (such as milk or buttermilk), their proteins contribute to the structure of the cake, and their fats add tenderness.

Cocoa Powder

Natural cocoa powder is an acidic ingredient. When added to a mixture that contains baking soda (an alkali), it reacts to produce carbon dioxide, which leavens baked goods.

Dutch-process cocoa powder has been treated to reduce its acidity and needs to be used in combination with baking powder. If it's used with baking soda alone, the pH is too alkaline and the resulting cake will be dense, heavy, and soapy tasting.

If your recipe calls for Dutch or natural cocoa, use the one that's specified. If you're not sure which to use, remember the following: If the recipe calls for baking soda alone, or for baking soda and baking powder and the amount of baking soda is more than the amount of the baking powder, use natural cocoa powder.

If the recipe calls for baking powder, or for both baking powder and baking soda but the amount of the baking soda is less than the baking powder, use Dutch-process cocoa powder.

If the recipe doesn't call for leavening, you may use either kind of cocoa. Dutch-process cocoa has a smoother, mellower flavor and a darker, redder color.

Making the Cake

The first step is to cream or whip the butter to incorporate air. The fat needs to be solid (you can't substitute oil), and it needs to be at cool room temperature. Beat until the butter lightens in color and is smooth, with no lumps.

Next, add the leavener, salt, flavors, and sugar to the beaten butter; as you beat, the mixture will again increase in volume. This second step of creaming separates the encapsulated air bubbles and evenly incorporates them into the mixture. You need to beat this mixture until it's very light and fluffy, which may take up to 2 minutes in a stand mixer; longer in a hand-held one.

Next come the eggs, which need to be at room temperature, and added one at a time. If they're cold, or are poured in all at once, they'll cause the butter and sugar mixture to deflate and curdle or separate. Any cold ingredients will cause the butter to harden, seize up, and collapse, thus releasing the air bubbles. After each egg is added and absorbed, stop the mixer and scrape the sides and bottom of the bowl. The mixture may begin to look curdled between the second and third egg. If this happens, add a tablespoon or two of the recipe's dry ingredients. The flour mixture will help to stabilize the emulsion. The mixture should be light in color and fluffy, but not collapse when lightly touched.

The next step is to add the flour and liquid(s) alternately to the creamed butter

WHAT'S THE TEMPERATURE OF A FULLY BAKED CAKE?

How do you know when a cake is done? Almost every recipe you read gives a similar set of descriptions for what the cake should look like before taking it out of the oven: springs back in the center when touched gently, beginning to pull from the side of the pan, even hearing the slightest crackling noise from bubbles in the batter popping. We decided to put more concrete standards to use and measure the internal temperatures of different types of cakes when they exhibited the characteristics described above. Here is what we found for the types of cakes in this chapter:

TYPE OF CAKE	SIZE OF PAN	INTERNAL TEMPERATURE
CHOCOLATE BUTTER CAKE	9″ round	209°F
JELLY ROLL SPONGE	10″ × 15″	191°F to 194°F
CHIFFON	9″ round	210°F
POUND	9″ × 5″	205°F

mixture. By adding these heavy ingredients gradually, they can be incorporated with the least deflation of the batter.

A light hand is also needed at this stage so that you don't release all of the air that's held in fragile suspension. First add a third of the flour, mixing just until it's absorbed. Then mix in half the liquid, and a third of the flour. Mix at medium-low speed until uniform. Stir in the rest of the liquid and end with flour, which binds everything together. Scrape the sides and bottom of the bowl, mix for another 20 seconds, and stop mixing; your batter is ready.

Lightly grease and flour your cake pan(s). A typical layer cake makes 6 cups of batter and can be baked in three 8″ round pans, two 9″ round pans, a 9″ × 13″ pan, or 24 cupcake molds. If you use a vegetable oil pan spray and your cakes always stick in the pans, try sprinkling 2 tablespoons of all-purpose flour into the greased pan(s) and shake and rotate it until every surface is covered with a light dusting. Shake the pan over the trash bin to get out any extra flour before spooning in the batter.

Alternatively, you can add a layer of parchment to the bottom of the pan. Grease the pan, add the parchment, and grease and flour the parchment. This provides extra insurance that your cake will come out of the pan easily.

Next pour or spoon the batter into the prepared cake pan. Smooth the top with a spatula, making the sides slightly higher than the center, which keeps the cake from "doming" too much. Fill the pan no more than three-quarters full. Place the pans in a preheated oven. If you're baking in a dark pan, be sure to reduce the oven heat by 25°F; you'll probably need to reduce the baking time by 10% as well.

You know the cake is done when a cake tester (a broom straw, in our grandmothers' day) inserted into the center of the cake comes out clean, or with just the hint of a moist crumb. In addition, a cake that's done will spring back when pressed lightly in the center, and should have begun to barely pull away from the sides of the pan. If the cake is chocolate, its aroma should have begun to fill the kitchen. A tried-and-true way to know is to insert a digital thermometer into the center of the cake (see page 301).

After baking, remove the cake from the oven and place it on a rack to cool for 10 to 15 minutes with the pan upright. Then loosen the sides with a thin-bladed spatula or table knife and carefully turn it out of the pan back onto the cooling rack. With this method, we make perfect cakes without torn or gouged crusts—most of the time!

DEVIL'S FOOD CAKE

ONE 2-LAYER 9" ROUND, ONE 3-LAYER 8" ROUND, OR ONE 9" × 13" CAKE

This cake is moist and tastes deeply of dark chocolate. It can easily pair with any number of frostings, and since chocolate is such a versatile partner, there's no end of possibilities for what you can create. Opt for Cherry Filling (page 351) for a Black Forest Cake, Peanut Butter Frosting (page 348) for a candy bar–style classic, or Seven-Minute Frosting (page 345) for a snack cake-esque treat . . . it's no wonder this cake is associated with being sinfully delicious! And speaking of sin, whence the name devil's food? The combination of natural cocoa powder and baking soda produces a cake with a very slight reddish (devilish) tint.

12 tablespoons (1½ sticks, 170g) unsalted butter, softened	2 cups (240) unbleached all-purpose flour
1¾ cups (347g) superfine or granulated sugar	¾ cup (64g) unsweetened cocoa, natural (not Dutch-process)
½ teaspoon salt	4 large eggs
1½ teaspoons baking soda	1½ cups (340g) milk or water
2 teaspoons vanilla extract	

Preheat the oven to 350°F. Grease and flour two 9" round cake pans, two or three 8" round pans, or a 9" × 13" cake pan.

In a large bowl, cream together the butter, sugar, salt, baking soda, and vanilla until fluffy and light, at least 3 minutes. In a separate bowl, whisk together the flour and cocoa. If lumps remain, sift the mixture.

Add the eggs to the butter mixture one at a time, beating well after each addition. Slowly blend one-third of the flour mixture into the creamed mixture, then half the milk, another third of the flour, the remaining milk, and the remaining flour. Be sure to scrape the sides and bottom of the bowl occasionally throughout this process.

Divide the batter evenly between the prepared pans. Bake the cakes for 30 to 35 minutes (a bit longer for the 9″ × 13″ cake, shorter if you've used three 8″ pans), until a cake tester or toothpick inserted into the center comes out clean, and the sides of the cake begin to pull away from the pan. Remove the cakes from the oven, cool them for 5 to 10 minutes, then remove them from the pan and place on a rack to cool completely.

NUTRITION INFORMATION PER SERVING: 1 slice of 2-layer cake, without frosting, 87g

252 cal | 11g fat | 5g protein | 13g complex carbohydrates | 21g sugar | 2g dietary fiber | 77mg cholesterol | 217mg sodium

CLASSIC BIRTHDAY CAKE

ONE 2-LAYER 8″ OR 9″ CAKE

No birthday cake is quite so iconic as the classic yellow layer cake with its sturdy yet tender crumb. We spent months testing and tweaking to create this version, which nails that elusive bakery flavor and structure and yet is approachable enough for even the most novice baker. Finish it with your favorite frosting—we like chocolate!

2 cups (240g) unbleached all-purpose flour

1¼ teaspoons salt

2 teaspoons baking powder

4 large eggs, at room temperature

2 cups (397g) sugar

1 tablespoon (14g) vanilla extract

⅛ teaspoon almond extract (optional)

1 cup (227g) milk (whole milk preferred)

4 tablespoons (½ stick, 57g) butter, cut into pats

⅓ cup (67g) vegetable oil

Preheat the oven to 325°F with a rack in the center. Lightly grease two 8″ × 2″ or 9″ × 2″ round cake pans; for extra protection against sticking, line the bottom of the pans with parchment rounds (you can cut these yourself or use precut 8″ or 9″ rounds), and grease the parchment. If your 8″ pans aren't at least 2″ deep, use 9″ pans.

In a small bowl, combine the flour, salt, and baking powder. Set aside.

In a large mixing bowl, either using an electric hand mixer or a stand mixer with whisk attachment, beat the eggs, sugar, vanilla, and almond extract, if using, until thickened and light gold in color, about 2 minutes at medium-high speed. If your stand mixer doesn't have a whisk attachment, beat for 5 minutes using the paddle attachment. The batter should fall in thick ribbons from the beaters, whisk, or paddle.

Add the dry ingredients to the mixture in the bowl and mix—by hand or on low speed of a mixer—just enough to combine. Scrape the bottom and sides of the bowl, then mix again briefly, to fully incorporate any residual flour or sticky bits.

In a saucepan set over medium heat or in the microwave, bring the milk just to a simmer. Remove the pan from the heat and add the butter and oil, stirring by hand until the butter has melted.

Slowly mix the hot milk/butter/oil mixture into the batter, stirring on low speed of a mixer until everything is well combined. Scrape the bowl and mix briefly, just until smooth.

Divide the batter evenly between the two pans. You'll use about 2¾ cups (about 580g) in each.

Bake the cakes until the edges are pulling away from the sides of the pan, a cake tester or toothpick inserted into the center comes out clean, and the top feels set. This should take 26 to 30 minutes for two 9″ pans, or 38 to 42 minutes for two 8″ pans; a digital thermometer inserted into the center of the cakes should read 205°F. Remove the cakes from the oven, carefully loosen the edges, and allow them to cool for 15 minutes in the pans. Then turn them out of the pans and transfer them to a rack, right-side up to cool to room temperature. Frost and assemble as desired.

NUTRITION INFORMATION PER SERVING: 1 slice, 131g

480 cal | 22g fat | 5g protein | 16g complex carbohydrates | 53g sugar | 2g dietary fiber | 85mg cholesterol | 300mg sodium

TENDER WHITE CAKE

ONE 2-LAYER 8″ OR 9″ CAKE, ONE 9″ × 13″ CAKE, OR 20 TO 24 CUPCAKES

An excellent go-to cake, perfect for birthdays and special occasions, yet simple enough for everyday cupcakes. Vanilla and almond flavors combine to give you smooth, mellow flavors reminiscent of your favorite bakery cakes. Using unbleached cake flour results in a high-rising cake with a moist, tender crumb. The cake also uses the paste method, so no need to cream the butter and sugar. We do recommend a stand mixer for this cake, or a sturdy hand mixer.

2¾ cups (326g) unbleached cake flour

1⅓ cups (333g) sugar (superfine is best)

1 tablespoon baking powder

¾ teaspoon salt

12 tablespoons (1½ sticks, 170g) unsalted butter, softened

4 large egg whites plus 1 whole large egg, at room temperature

1 cup (227g) full-fat yogurt or whole milk, at room temperature

2 teaspoons vanilla extract

1 teaspoon almond extract

Preheat the oven to 350°F. Prepare two 8″ × 2″ or 9″ × 2″ round pans; a 9″ × 13″ × 2″ pan; or 2 standard cupcake pans (20 to 24 cupcakes total) by greasing and flouring, or lining with parchment, then greasing the parchment. Make sure your 8″ round pans are at least 2″ deep; if they're not, use one of the other pan options.

Mix all the dry ingredients on slow speed to blend. Add the soft butter and mix until evenly crumbly, like fine damp sand. It may form a paste, depending on the temperature of the butter, how much it's mixed, and the granulation of the sugar used.

Add the egg whites one at a time, then the whole egg, beating well after each addition to begin building the structure of the cake. Scrape down the sides and bottom of the bowl after each addition.

In a small bowl, whisk the yogurt (or milk) with the vanilla and almond extracts. Add this mixture, one-third at a time, to the batter. Beat 1 to 2 minutes after each addition, until fluffy. Be sure to scrape down the sides and bottom of the bowl.

Pour the batter into the prepared pans. Bake for 25 to 30 minutes for 8″ or 9″ rounds; 23 to 26 minutes for a 9″ × 13″ cake; or 20 minutes for cupcakes. A cake tester or toothpick inserted into the center will come out clean when done. Remove from the oven, remove from the pan, if desired (not advisable for a 9″ × 13″ cake), cool on a rack, and frost as desired.

VARIATION

COCONUT CAKE: To make coconut cake, make the following adjustments: Substitute 2 to 3 drops coconut flavor or 1 teaspoon coconut extract for the almond extract and fold 1 cup (85g) toasted coconut into the batter. Finish with Quick Buttercream Frosting (page 341), substituting 2 to 3 drops coconut flavor (or 1 teaspoon coconut extract) for half of the vanilla. Decorate the frosted cake with sweetened shredded coconut.

NUTRITION INFORMATION PER SERVING: 1 piece, 57g

180 cal | 7g fat | 3g protein | 11g complex carbohydrates | 16g sugar | 0g dietary fiber | 25mg cholesterol | 160mg sodium

---

CAKES OR CUPCAKES?

Any cake batter can be baked as a cupcake. We recommend greasing the insides of cupcake papers with pan spray to keep tender cakes from tearing when the papers are removed.

Fill lined cupcake wells about two-thirds full; a muffin scoop is a good way to get a precise, uniform result. Bake at the recipe's recommended temperature for 22 to 27 minutes, checking at the lower end of the bake time. When a cake tester inserted in the center of a cupcake comes out clean, the cupcakes are done.

BOSTON CREAM PIE

ONE 2-LAYER 9″ CAKE

The original Boston Cream Pie, created at Boston's Parker House hotel in the nineteenth century, featured sponge cake layered with cream and iced with chocolate fondant. Our updated recipe reflects the more modern version (that you probably know and love): tender vanilla layers sandwiched around a rich pastry cream, then topped with a dark chocolate ganache. We think even those loyal to the traditional version will love this cake.

CAKE

2 cups (397g) sugar

4 large eggs

⅓ cup (67g) vegetable oil

2 cups (240g) unbleached all-purpose flour

1¼ teaspoons salt

2 teaspoons baking powder

4 tablespoons (½ stick, 57g) butter, at cool room temperature (65°F to 68°F)

1 cup (227g) whole milk

2 teaspoons vanilla extract

FILLING

2½ cups (567g) whole milk

½ cup (99g) sugar

¼ teaspoon salt

⅓ cup (39g) cornstarch

3 large egg yolks

1 large egg

2 teaspoons vanilla extract

GLAZE

⅓ cup (57g) chopped dark chocolate or chocolate chips

¼ cup (57g) heavy cream

½ teaspoon vanilla extract

TO MAKE THE CAKE: Preheat the oven to 325°F. Lightly grease two 9″ round pans.

Beat the sugar and eggs together until they're light and fluffy, about 2 minutes at medium-high speed using an electric or stand mixer. Slowly beat in the vegetable oil.

Add the flour, salt, and baking powder to the egg mixture in the bowl, beating just enough to combine. Scrape the bottom and sides of the bowl, then beat again, to fully incorporate any sticky bits.

In a saucepan set over medium heat, bring the butter and milk just to a boil. Add the vanilla. Remove the pan from the heat and stir the mixture until the butter is completely melted.

Slowly add the hot milk mixture to the cake batter, mixing until everything is well combined. Scrape the bowl and mix briefly, just until smooth. The batter will be very thin.

Divide the batter evenly among the prepared pans.

Bake the cakes for 30 to 35 minutes, until a cake tester or toothpick inserted into the center comes out clean, and the top feels set when lightly touched. Remove the cakes from the oven, cool them in the pans for 10 minutes, then turn them out onto a rack to cool completely.

TO MAKE THE FILLING: In a medium saucepan, stir together 2 cups (454g) of the milk, the sugar, and the salt. Bring to a simmer over medium heat, stirring to dissolve the sugar.

Meanwhile, whisk the cornstarch, egg yolks, and whole egg with the remaining ½ cup (113g) milk.

Whisk some of the hot milk mixture into the egg yolks/cornstarch mixture to temper the yolks. (This keeps them from turning to scrambled eggs when you add them to the simmering milk.)

Pour the egg/milk mixture back into the remaining simmering milk in the pan, pouring it through a strainer to capture any bits of egg.

Bring the mixture to a low boil over medium heat (this may happen very quickly), stirring constantly with a whisk, and cook for 2 minutes; the mixture will thicken significantly.

Remove the filling from the heat and stir in the vanilla.

Transfer the filling to a heatproof bowl, and top it with a piece of buttered plastic wrap (make sure it touches the top of the filling so it doesn't develop a skin). Refrigerate until cool.

When the cakes and pastry cream are completely cool, spread the filling in an even layer over one layer, then stack the second layer on top. Set aside.

TO MAKE THE GLAZE: Melt the chocolate and cream together, stirring until smooth and lump-free. Add the vanilla and stir well. Let the glaze sit for about 10 minutes to cool a bit and thicken just a touch. Pour the glaze over the filled cake. Serve immediately, or cool to room temperature, and refrigerate until ready to serve.

NUTRITION INFORMATION PER SERVING: 1 slice, 98g

313 cal | 11g fat | 6g protein | 53g complex carbohydrates | 33g sugar | 1g dietary fiber | 148mg cholesterol | 326mg sodium

Pound Cakes

A subset of butter cakes, pound cakes were originally made from a pound each of flour, sugar, butter, and eggs. Over the years the proportions have changed somewhat and flavors have been added, but the result is still a very fine-textured, moderately heavy, and moist cake, perfect for slicing and serving as a base for fruit or ice cream.

One of our very favorite ways to serve pound cake is to brush both sides of a slice with butter, then sauté it, as you would a grilled cheese sandwich. When it's golden brown, remove it from the heat and top with ice cream, choosing a flavor that's complementary to the cake. Add fudge sauce and whipped cream and you've reached cake nirvana.

ORIGINAL POUND CAKE

ONE 9″ × 5″ CAKE

Pound cake is the original "grandmother" of all butter cakes. This particular pound cake is incredibly rich. It's wonderful on its own, but is also a nice blank canvas to top with anything from fresh fruit to loosely whipped cream with a touch of citrus zest. While traditional pound cake won't include baking powder, we add just a bit to help leaven and lighten the cake.

16 tablespoons (2 sticks, 227g) salted butter, at room temperature (at least 65°F)

1 cup (198g) sugar

4 large eggs, at room temperature

2 cups (240g) unbleached all-purpose flour

1½ teaspoons baking powder

½ teaspoon salt

½ cup (113g) milk, at room temperature

1 tablespoon (14g) brandy, sherry, rum, or the liquor of your choice (optional)

1 teaspoon vanilla extract, almond extract, or a combination

Preheat the oven to 350°F. Lightly grease a 9″ × 5″ loaf pan.

In a large bowl, beat the butter until very light. Beat in the sugar gradually and then the eggs, one by one. Scrape the bottom and sides of the bowl, and beat until the mixture is very light and fluffy.

In a separate bowl, whisk together the flour, baking powder, and salt.

In another small bowl, whisk together the milk, alcohol of your choice (if using), and extract.

Alternately add the wet and dry ingredients to the butter / sugar / egg mixture, starting and ending with the flour. Stir to combine after each addition.

Pour the batter into the prepared pan, smoothing the top.

Bake the cake for 60 to 65 minutes, until the top springs back when lightly pressed, and a cake tester or toothpick inserted into the center comes out clean. If the cake appears to be browning too quickly, tent it with foil for the final 15 minutes of baking.

Remove the cake from the oven and loosen its edges. Wait 5 minutes, then carefully turn it out of the pan onto a rack to cool.

Store, wrapped in plastic, for a day or two before serving. Wrap well and freeze for longer storage.

NUTRITION INFORMATION PER SERVING: **1 slice, 57g**

210 cal | 12g fat | 3g protein | 11g complex carbohydrates | 11g sugar | 0g dietary fiber | 70mg cholesterol | 125mg sodium

LEMON-GLAZED POUND CAKE

ONE 8½″ × 4½″ LOAF OR 1 BUNDT CAKE

The sunny taste of citrus is showcased in this buttery pound cake. When pouring the glaze, do so slowly, which will allow the warm cake to better absorb all that tart, tangy, sweet liquid.

CAKE

14 tablespoons (198g) unsalted butter, softened

6 tablespoons (3 ounces, 85g) cream cheese, at room temperature

½ teaspoon salt

1½ cups (297g) sugar

1 teaspoon baking powder

2 teaspoons vanilla extract

½ teaspoon lemon oil or 1 tablespoon lemon zest

1¾ cups (210g) unbleached all-purpose flour

5 large eggs

GLAZE

¼ cup (57g) fresh lemon juice

½ cup (99g) sugar

Preheat the oven to 350°F and grease two 8½″ × 4½″ loaf pans or a 9- to 10-cup tube or Bundt pan.

TO MAKE THE CAKE: In a medium bowl, beat together the butter and cream cheese until soft and fluffy. Add the salt, sugar, baking powder, vanilla, lemon, and flour and beat for 5 minutes; the batter will be stiff.

Add 1 egg, beating until well combined. Continue to add the eggs, one at a time, beating well and scraping the sides and bottom of the bowl after each addition.

When done, the batter will be very fluffy. Spoon the batter into the prepared pan(s).

Bake the cake for 55 to 60 minutes (for the tube or Bundt pan) or 35 to 40 minutes (for the two loaf pans), or until a cake tester or toothpick inserted into the center comes out clean.

TO MAKE THE GLAZE: Just before the cake is done, combine the lemon juice and sugar and heat over low heat (or in the microwave) until the sugar has dissolved; don't let the mixture boil.

Remove the cake from the oven and let it cool for 10 minutes in the pan. Turn it out onto a rack or serving platter. Poke the top all over with a cake tester or toothpick and gradually drizzle the glaze over it, pausing occasionally to let it sink in. Let the cake cool for several hours before slicing.

NUTRITION INFORMATION PER SERVING: 1 slice, 74g

268 cal | 14g fat | 4g protein | 9g complex carbohydrates | 24g sugar | 0g dietary fiber | 101mg cholesterol | 134mg sodium

CREAM CHEESE POUND CAKE

ONE 9″ × 5″ LOAF OR 1 BUNDT CAKE

This pound cake—a rich dark brown outside with a fine golden crumb—gets its plush, velvety crumb and slight tang from the addition of cream cheese. It's a fun one to play around with by adding different flavorings (such as almond extract, lemon zest, or dried coconut).

8 tablespoons (1 stick, 113g) unsalted butter, at room temperature

¾ cup (6 ounces, 170g) full-fat cream cheese, at room temperature

½ teaspoon salt

1 cup (198g) sugar

2 teaspoons vanilla extract

½ teaspoon baking powder

1¾ cups (210g) unbleached all-purpose flour

4 large eggs, at room temperature

1 cup (60g) unsweetened coconut flakes (optional)

1 cup dried fruit or nuts (optional)

Preheat the oven to 350°F. Grease a 9″ × 5″ loaf pan or 9-cup tube or Bundt pan.

In a medium bowl, beat together the butter and cream cheese until soft and fluffy. Add the salt, sugar, vanilla, and baking powder and beat for 5 minutes. Add the flour, beating well and scraping the bottom and sides of the bowl occasionally. The batter will be stiff.

Add the eggs one at a time, beating well and scraping the sides and bottom of the bowl after each addition. When done, the batter will be very fluffy. Fold in up to 1 cup of dried flaked coconut or dried fruit or nuts.

Spoon the batter into the prepared pan. Bake the cake for 55 to 60 minutes for the 9″ × 5″ loaf pan, or 45 to 50 minutes for the tube or Bundt pan. A cake tester or toothpick inserted into the center of the loaf should come out clean.

Remove the cake from the oven and let it cool for 15 minutes in the pan. Turn the cake out onto a rack or serving platter. Let the cake cool for several hours for best slicing. The cake will be dark brown on the edges and golden on top. Serve the cake at room temperature; store it well wrapped at room temperature.

NUTRITION INFORMATION PER SERVING: 1 slice, 76g

268 cal | 15g fat | 5g protein | 30g complex carbohydrates | 16g sugar | 1g dietary fiber | 107mg cholesterol | 174mg sodium

CHOCOLATE POUND CAKE

ONE 10˝ CAKE

Moist, light, and with just the right degree of richness, this versatile cake is an excellent riff on a classic pound cake and ideal for a chocolate craving. Complement it with whipped cream, frozen yogurt, fresh fruit, or raspberry sauce. Glaze it, or simply dust it with confectioners' sugar. Swirling a cup of chocolate chips, chopped nuts, coconut, or dried fruit into the batter only widens the horizon.

16 tablespoons (2 sticks, 227g) unsalted butter, softened

2½ cups (495g) sugar

2 teaspoons vanilla extract

½ teaspoon baking powder

½ teaspoon baking soda

1 teaspoon salt

5 large eggs, at room temperature

3 tablespoons (21g) espresso powder

¼ cup (57g) water, warm

¾ cup (170g) buttermilk

1 cup (85g) unsweetened Dutch-process cocoa

2 cups (240g) unbleached all-purpose flour

Preheat the oven to 325°F. Lightly grease a 10˝ (12-cup) tube pan or 12-cup Bundt pan.

Cream the butter in a medium bowl until light and fluffy, and continue to beat while gradually adding the sugar, then the vanilla, baking powder, baking soda, and salt. Beat the mixture at high speed for 2 to 3 minutes. Add the eggs one at a time, beating well after each addition and scraping the sides of the bowl occasionally.

In a small bowl, dissolve the espresso powder in the warm water and combine this with the buttermilk. In a separate bowl, sift or whisk together the cocoa and flour. Beat the dry ingredients into the egg mixture alternately with the liquid. (This part can be pretty messy, so try adding the dry ingredients just by the spoonful at first.) Blend well and pour into the prepared pan.

Bake the cake for about 1 hour and 20 minutes, or until a cake tester or toothpick inserted into the center comes out clean. Remove the cake from the oven and place it (in its pan) on a rack to cool for at least 15 minutes. Turn out the cake onto the rack and let it cool completely.

NUTRITION INFORMATION PER SERVING: 1 slice, 99g

325 cal | 15g fat | 5g protein | 14g complex carbohydrates | 28g sugar | 3g dietary fiber | 119mg cholesterol | 198mg sodium

SCANDINAVIAN GOLD CAKE

ONE 10″ CAKE

The addition of almond flour in this vanilla- and almond-scented cake adds extra flavor and a lightly flecked appearance.

CAKE

16 tablespoons (2 sticks, 227g) unsalted butter, softened

1⅓ cups (263g) sugar

½ teaspoon salt

1½ teaspoons baking powder

½ teaspoon almond extract

1 teaspoon vanilla extract

1 cup (99g) toasted almond flour

1¾ cups (210g) unbleached all-purpose flour

6 large eggs, at room temperature

GLAZE

2 cups (227g) confectioners' sugar, sifted

¼ cup (57g) heavy cream or evaporated milk

1 teaspoon vanilla extract

¼ teaspoon almond extract

Preheat the oven to 325°F. Grease and flour a 10″ tube pan or a 12-cup Bundt pan.

In a large bowl, beat the butter until it's soft. Add the sugar, salt, baking powder, and flavorings. Beat them together until well blended and no lumps remain.

Add the flours and mix; it will be crumbly. Beat in the eggs one at a time, mixing until each is absorbed, and scraping the bottom and sides of the bowl after each addition. The batter will become fluffy after the third or fourth egg has been added.

Scrape the batter into the pan and level it with a spatula. Bake the cake for about 1 hour, until a cake tester or toothpick inserted in the center comes out clean and the edges pull away from the pan.

Remove the cake from the oven and place it on a rack to cool. Turn it out of the pan after about 10 minutes to cool completely.

Mix all the glaze ingredients together, adding a bit of water if needed to make it spreadable. Use a spatula to spread it over the top of the cake. Let the glaze set for a few minutes before serving.

NUTRITION INFORMATION PER SERVING: **1 slice, 100g**

392 cal | 21g fat | 6g protein | 11g complex carbohydrates | 37g sugar | 1g dietary fiber | 132mg cholesterol | 160mg sodium

Foam Cakes

The broad category of foam cakes encompasses everything from sponge cake and hot milk cake to genoise and angel food; the common denominator for these cakes is their very light and delicate texture, derived mainly from beating air into eggs. Most are significantly lower in fat than butter cakes; when they do contain fat, it's in the form of vegetable oil or the fat in egg yolks. For that reason, these cakes are often layered with a rich filling, fruit, or some other element to complement their simplicity.

Foam cakes are one of the very earliest genres of cake. Taking over from yeast-risen cakes in the mid-1700s, they quickly became a favorite of the wealthy, who had both the white flour and the access to sweeteners (to say nothing of the servants who beat the eggs) necessary for foam cakes. The cakes were baked in a variety of sizes and shapes, fancifully decorated, and otherwise honored as the centerpiece of the banquet table.

Nowadays, foam cakes are commonly found in all manner of forms. Two of Italy's most familiar cake-based creations, tiramisù and cassata, are based on foam cakes. Mexico's famous celebration cake, tres leches, starts with a foam cake. Many French desserts are based on a classic genoise. And in the realm of retro desserts, pineapple upside-down cake relies on a light-textured foam cake to hold its heavy crown of pineapples and sugar in place.

JELLY ROLL

ONE 9″ TO 9½″ CAKE

The basis for a jelly roll—sponge cake—is made with more eggs, less fat, and less flour than typical cakes. Leavened mainly by air that is beaten into and held by whole eggs, sponge cake may also be boosted with a chemical leavener, either baking soda or baking powder.

A light and airy cake, sponge cake is similar to angel food, but, because of the addition of egg yolks and a minimal amount of fat in the form of unsalted butter, it's more tender and less springy. Typical sponge cake applications include not only jelly rolls, but trifles, "maryann" cakes (the yellow, spongy cake that forms the base of some kinds of berry shortcakes), and petits fours. Despite the name, we recommend using jam or preserves, not jelly, in the filling. We find jelly too thin to hold up as the cake is rolled.

SPONGE CAKE

¾ cup (90g) unbleached all-
   purpose flour

¾ teaspoon baking powder

¼ teaspoon salt

4 large eggs, at room temperature

¾ cup (149g) sugar

1 teaspoon vanilla extract

FILLING

1 heaping cup (350g) jam, preserves, or
   any thick fruit purée

Preheat the oven to 400°F. Line the bottom of a 10″ × 15″ jelly roll pan with waxed paper or parchment.

In a small bowl, sift together the flour, baking powder, and salt. Set aside.

In a large bowl, beat the eggs until foamy. Sprinkle in the sugar gradually, beating all the while, and continue beating until the batter is very thick and light lemon in color, 3 to 8 minutes. The batter will have doubled in volume. When the batter is sufficiently aerated, it should fall from the beaters in a thick ribbon and mound on top of the remaining batter in the bowl temporarily, before being reabsorbed. Just before you stop beating the batter, add the vanilla.

Gently fold in the flour mixture, using a rubber spatula or whisk. Spread the batter evenly into the prepared pan.

Bake the cake for 12 to 14 minutes, until it's golden brown and springy to the touch. Remove the cake from the oven and invert it onto a clean dish towel that's been lightly sprinkled with confectioners' sugar. Peel off the paper and, using scissors, a sharp knife, or a rolling pizza wheel, trim the crusty edges of the cake, if necessary. Starting with a short end, roll the cake and towel together into a log, and cool completely on a rack.

Just before serving, unroll the cake, spread it with the jam, preserves, or fruit purée, and re-roll it. Place the jelly roll on a plate, seam side down, and dust it with confectioners' sugar.

NUTRITION INFORMATION PER SERVING: 1 slice, 86g

225 cal | 3g fat | 4g protein | 12g complex carbohydrates | 35g sugar | 1g dietary fiber | 122mg cholesterol | 125mg sodium

---

JELLY ROLL TIPS

For easiest handling, we strongly suggest using parchment paper if you're baking sponge cake in a jelly roll pan. Another hint: When a sponge type of cake is done, you should be able to hear a very faint crackling noise, as some of the air pockets rupture.

TRADITIONAL ANGEL FOOD CAKE

ONE 10″ CAKE

Angel food cake is one of the most versatile desserts we know. You can eat it plain, top it with fruit, serve it under a drizzle of warm chocolate sauce, or frost it (we like to use an equally ethereal option such as Seven-Minute Frosting [see page 345]). Aptly named, this cake is exceptionally light and airy in texture and pale white in color—befitting a host of angels.

1 cup (120g) unbleached cake flour or unbleached all-purpose flour

1½ cups (298g) sugar

12 large (425g) egg whites, at room temperature

½ teaspoon salt

1 teaspoon vanilla or almond extract, or a combination

1½ teaspoons cream of tartar

Preheat the oven to 325°F. Don't grease or flour your angel food cake pan. A 10″ round pan or an angel food loaf pan will fit this recipe well.

In a large bowl, whisk together the flour and ¾ cup (149g) of the sugar. Set aside.

In a large bowl, combine the egg whites, salt, and extract. Beat until the mixture is just frothy, then sprinkle the cream of tartar on top and continue beating until the mixture forms stiff, glossy peaks.

Add the remaining sugar, ¼ cup (50g) at a time, then gradually fold in the dry ingredients.

Spoon the batter into the pan, and bake the cake for 40 to 45 minutes, or until it's golden brown and the top springs back when lightly touched.

Remove the cake from the oven and set it upside down with a bottle through its center cone to keep its top from flattening on the counter. Let the cake cool for 1½ hours. This cooling period sets the structure and keeps the cake from collapsing.

Loosen the edges of the cake with a knife and remove it from the pan.

Store the cake, covered, on the counter for up to a week. Freeze, well wrapped, for up to 3 months.

NUTRITION INFORMATION PER SERVING: 1 slice, 53g
100 cal | 0g fat | 4g protein | 6g complex carbohydrates | 19g sugar | 0g dietary fiber | 0mg cholesterol | 115mg sodium

TIRAMISÙ

1 CAKE

This quintessential Italian dessert is rich and delicious, loaded as it is with mascarpone, coffee liqueur, and espresso. *Tiramisù* means "pick me up" in Italian. Not only will it pick you up, it will carry you away. Best of all, it's easy and can be made early in the day for a dinner ahead. While it will keep overnight, know that the layers will meld together as they soften, becoming less distinct.

MASCARPONE FILLING

1 pound (454g) mascarpone cheese or
   1 pound (454g) cream cheese plus
   2 tablespoons (28g) sour cream

2 cups (454g) heavy or whipping cream

1½ cups (170g) confectioners' sugar

2 teaspoons vanilla extract

1 recipe sponge cake baked in a jelly roll
   pan (page 315)

½ cup (113g) espresso or coffee-flavored
   liqueur (or a mixture of ¼ cup [56g]
   of each)

1 tablespoon (5g) unsweetened cocoa
   (preferably Dutch-process, for its
   darker color and flavor)

½ cup (85g) grated or curled semisweet
   or milk chocolate

TO PREPARE THE FILLING: In a food processor or medium bowl, beat the mascarpone or cream cheese/sour cream mixture until soft. Add the cream, sugar, and vanilla and beat until smooth. Refrigerate the filling until you're ready to assemble the cake.

TO ASSEMBLE THE DESSERT: Cut the cake into three 5″ × 10″ slices. Brush each slice with the espresso or coffee-flavored liqueur. Let the cake sit for a few minutes to absorb the liquid, then brush it again. Place one slice on a serving platter and top it with one-third of the filling, top it with a second layer and another third of the filling, then place the third layer of cake on top. Cover the top and sides with the remaining filling, dust with cocoa, and top with chocolate for garnish. Wrap the cake well and refrigerate it for several hours (or overnight) before serving.

NUTRITION INFORMATION PER SERVING: 1 slice, 102g

323 cal | 18g fat | 6g protein | 32g complex carbohydrates | 20g sugar | 0g dietary fiber | 133mg cholesterol | 204mg sodium

GENOISE

1 CAKE

Genoise is a type of sponge cake enriched with butter and egg yolk. With its mild flavor, it's used as a base for a wide range of European-style tortes and cream-filled cakes. To that end, it's nearly always brushed with a flavored syrup, which helps keep it moist and adds a complementary flavor to the finished cake.

While genoise isn't hard to make, it takes careful attention to detail as well as a light touch: Fold the flour into the batter gently or you'll end up with a dense cake.

6 large eggs, at room temperature

1 egg yolk, at room temperature

¾ cup (149g) sugar (superfine is best)

⅛ teaspoon salt

¾ cup (90g) unbleached all-
    purpose flour

1 tablespoon cornstarch

4 tablespoons (½ stick, 57g) butter,
    melted and slightly cooled

2 teaspoons vanilla or almond extract (or
    one of each)

Preheat the oven to 350°F. Grease and flour (or line with parchment) two 9″ round pans, three 8″ round pans, a 10″ × 15″ jelly roll pan, or a 9″ × 3″ springform pan.

Place the eggs and egg yolk, ½ cup (99g) of the sugar, and the salt in a heatproof bowl and immerse the bottom of the bowl in warm water. Whisk over the warm water until the sugar dissolves; you'll be able to feel if the sugar has dissolved by rubbing a small amount of the batter between your fingers—it shouldn't feel gritty. Check the temperature of the batter occasionally; don't let it go over 110°F, as the eggs may

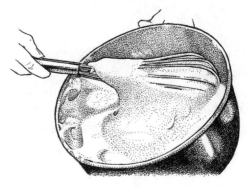

The eggs should be very light and fluffy when they are properly beaten. Use a hand whisk to gently fold the flour mixture into the beaten eggs without deflating them.

begin to cook. You're after batter that's just warm to the touch. Once the sugar has dissolved, remove the bowl from the hot water. Using an electric mixer, beat the egg mixture on high speed until it becomes very light and fluffy. This will take up to 10 minutes. It should double (or more) in volume and be very thick.

Whisk together the flour, cornstarch, and remaining ¼ cup (48g) sugar to eliminate any lumps and aerate the mixture. Using very low speed on an electric mixer, or a hand whisk, gently fold the flour mixture into the eggs, about a third at a time. In a small bowl, stir together the butter and extract. Mix about a third of the flour /egg mixture into the butter, then fold that back into the remaining batter. Spoon or pour the batter into the prepared pans, smoothing the surface.

Bake the 8″ or 9″ round layers for 20 to 25 minutes, the jelly roll for 14 to 18 minutes, or the springform for 30 to 35 minutes. All should be light golden in color and spring back when touched lightly in the center. Allow to cool in the pans for 15 minutes.

NUTRITION INFORMATION PER SERVING: 1 slice, 30g

80 cal | 5g fat | 3g protein | 5g complex carbohydrates | 5g sugar | 0g dietary fiber | 102mg cholesterol | 41mg sodium

VARIATION

CHOCOLATE GENOISE: To make a chocolate genoise, cut the amount of flour to ½ cup (60g) and whisk it together with ¼ cup (21g) Dutch-process unsweetened cocoa before folding it into the egg/sugar mixture.

GLUTEN-FREE ALMOND ROLL

1 ROLL CAKE

This naturally gluten-free cake relies on almond flour to create a tender and moist version of a classic yule log. Slice into it and you'll find a swirl of delicately almond-flavored cake around a filling of decadent chocolate whipped cream flavored with a touch of liqueur. If you prefer to make a nonalcoholic cake, combine ½ teaspoon almond, orange, or vanilla extract with 2 tablespoons (28g) heavy cream, milk, or water and use that in place of the liqueur.

CAKE

2¼ cups (216g) almond flour

1½ teaspoons baking powder

¼ teaspoon salt

9 large eggs, separated, at room temperature

1 cup (213g) brown sugar, packed

1 teaspoon almond extract

FROSTING

1¾ cups (397g) heavy cream

¼ cup (21g) unsweetened cocoa, Dutch-process preferred

⅓ cup (67g) superfine sugar or granulated sugar

3 tablespoons (43g) Amaretto, Grand Marnier, or the liqueur of your choice

confectioners' sugar, for dusting

Preheat the oven to 350°F. Lightly grease a half-sheet pan (13″ × 18″), line it with parchment, and lightly grease the parchment.

TO PREPARE THE CAKE: In a small bowl, mix together the almond flour, baking powder, and salt until evenly blended. Set aside.

In a large bowl, beat the egg yolks and brown sugar until the mixture is very light and falls in thick ribbons from the beater, about 3 minutes. Stir in the almond extract, then fold in the dry ingredients.

In another bowl with clean beaters, whip the egg whites until stiff peaks form. Fold a quarter of the whites into the yolk mixture to lighten it, then fold in the rest just until combined.

Pour the batter into the prepared pan, spreading it to the edges and into the corners with an offset spatula, quickly with as little back and forth as possible.

Bake the cake for 15 to 18 minutes, until the top is golden brown and a cake tester or toothpick inserted in the center comes out clean.

Remove from the oven and cool completely in the pan. Unlike a typical jelly roll, you don't roll this in a towel while still warm; it's too fragile.

TO PREPARE THE FROSTING: Whip the cream until soft peaks form. Sift the cocoa powder over the cream, then whip just until stiff peaks form. Fold in the sugar and liqueur.

TO ASSEMBLE: Run a thin spatula around the edges of the cake to loosen it. Dust the top of the cake with confectioners' sugar. Place a kitchen towel or piece of parchment over the cake. Place another sheet pan on top and flip the entire cake over. Remove the pan and parchment from the bottom of the cake.

Spread two-thirds of the frosting over the cake, leaving an inch of one long side bare. Starting with the uncovered long side, roll the cake into a log and place on a serving platter, seam side down. Cover the outside of the cake with the remaining frosting, and refrigerate until ready to serve.

The cake is better when served the next day, as it becomes more moist and tender. Store leftovers in the refrigerator for up to 3 days.

NUTRITION INFORMATION PER SERVING: 1 slice, 80g
258 cal | 17g fat | 6g protein | 2g complex carbohydrates | 18g sugar | 2g dietary fiber | 119mg cholesterol | 78mg sodium

CHIFFON CAKE

ONE 10″ CAKE

Chiffon cakes were a significant phenomenon of the fifties, touted in some cookbooks as the first new cake in one hundred years. Light as air but with the richness of a butter cake, chiffon cakes were "invented" by a Los Angeles insurance salesman, Harry Baker, who kept the formula secret for many years, baking and selling cakes to movie stars and some of the area's finest restaurants. In 1947, he sold his secret recipe to General Mills. And what is the secret? Vegetable oil.

Chiffon cakes may be baked either in tube (angel food) pans or round cake pans. Like angel food cakes, they must be cooled upside down to maintain their full height. They freeze well and make a good base for baked Alaska or other cold filled cakes, because unlike butter- or shortening-based cakes, they retain their soft texture in the refrigerator.

7 eggs, separated, at room temperature

½ teaspoon cream of tartar or 1 teaspoon lemon juice

1½ cups (297g) sugar

2 cups (240g) unbleached all-purpose flour

2½ teaspoons baking powder

¾ teaspoon salt

½ cup (99g) vegetable oil

¾ cup (170g) milk, at room temperature

2 teaspoons vanilla extract

1 teaspoon almond extract

Preheat the oven to 325°F.

In a large bowl, beat the egg whites with the cream of tartar or lemon juice until foamy. Gradually add ½ cup (99g) of the sugar and continue beating until stiff and glossy. Set aside.

Whisk together the remaining 1 cup (198g) sugar with the flour, baking powder, and salt. In a separate bowl, beat the oil, milk, egg yolks, and flavorings until pale yellow. Add the dry ingredients and beat until well blended, about 2 minutes at medium speed using a stand mixer, or longer with a hand mixer.

Gently fold in the whipped egg whites, using a wire whisk. Be sure to scrape the bottom of the bowl so the batter is well blended. Pour the batter into an ungreased 10″ tube pan or angel food pan, or two 9″ round ungreased cake pans. If it's in a tube or angel food pan, bake it for 1 hour. If you're using two 9″ cake pans, bake for about 50 minutes. Don't open the oven during the first 45 minutes of baking; the cake will rise high above the pan, then settle back almost evenly. It's done when a finger gently pressed in the center doesn't leave a print; you'll be able to hear a crackling sound if you listen carefully.

Remove the cake from the oven and cool it upside down for 30 minutes before removing it from the pan. If you've used a tube pan, set it atop a thin-necked bottle, threading the bottle neck through the hole in the tube. When the cake is completely cool, run a knife around the outside edge and around the tube. Turn the pan upside down and tap it to remove the cake. Frost the cake and cut it just before serving. Dip a serrated knife in hot water between each slice if you want smooth, even pieces.

NUTRITION INFORMATION PER SERVING: **1 slice (unfilled) cake**
165 cal | 7g fat | 4g protein | 10g complex carbohydrates | 10g sugar | 0g dietary fiber | 79mg cholesterol | 168mg sodium

VARIATIONS

LEMON OR ORANGE CHIFFON: Replace the cream of tartar with 1 tablespoon (14g) of lemon or orange juice; eliminate the almond extract and 1 teaspoon of the vanilla extract. Fold in 1 tablespoon lemon or orange zest or add ½ teaspoon lemon or orange oil at the same time you add the vanilla.

CHOCOLATE CHIFFON: Decrease the amount of flour to 1½ cups (180g), use buttermilk instead of regular milk, and sift ½ cup (42g) natural cocoa into the flour/baking powder mixture.

VANILLA CHIFFON: Increase vanilla extract to 1 tablespoon (14g) and omit the almond extract.

TRES LECHES CAKE

ONE 9″ × 13″ CAKE

This golden sponge cake from Latin America is liberally soaked with tres leches (three milks: condensed, evaporated, and heavy cream), and would seem, at first read-through of the recipe, to be unbearably sweet—to say nothing of sogginess. But the cake itself is only mildly sweet; and it's literally a sponge cake, soaking up and holding the liquid so that each mouthful is a just-sweet-enough, super-moist delight. It's particularly nice served with a dusting of cinnamon or diced mango, pineapple, or other tropical fruits.

CAKE

6 large eggs, separated, at room temperature

½ teaspoon cream of tartar or ¼ teaspoon lemon juice

1½ cups (298g) sugar

⅓ cup (75g) water, cold

2 teaspoons vanilla extract

1 teaspoon almond extract

2 teaspoons baking powder

½ teaspoon salt

1½ cups (180g) unbleached all-purpose flour

TOPPING

½ cup (113g) heavy cream

1 can (397g) sweetened condensed milk

1 can (340g) evaporated milk or 1½ cups (340g) half-and-half

2 teaspoons vanilla extract, or 1 tablespoon (14g) brandy or light rum

FROSTING

1½ cups (340g) heavy cream

¼ cup (50g) sugar

Preheat the oven to 350°F. Lightly grease a 9″ × 13″ pan; line it with parchment and grease the parchment, if you plan on turning the cake out onto a serving platter. Your pan must be at least 2″ deep; this is a high-rising cake.

TO PREPARE THE CAKE: In a large bowl, combine the egg whites and cream of tartar or lemon juice, and beat the whites until soft peaks form. Set aside.

In another large bowl, beat the egg yolks until well combined. Add the sugar, and beat until the mixture comes together and thickens. When you stop beating, the mixture should fall from the beater(s) in ribbons as you lift them out of the bowl.

Add the water and extracts to the egg yolk mixture, beating to combine.

Stir in the baking powder, salt, and flour, beating just to combine.

Gently and thoroughly fold in the beaten egg whites, stirring until no streaks of white show.

Scoop the batter into the prepared pan, gently smoothing the top.

Bake the cake for 28 to 30 minutes, until a toothpick or cake tester inserted into the center comes out clean. Remove it from the oven, and set it on a rack. Loosen the edges with a spatula or table knife.

After 20 minutes, gently turn the cake out onto a serving platter, turning it upright, if desired. You can also leave it face-down if you like; you'll be topping it with whipped cream, so any imperfections on the bottom crust will be hidden. You may also choose to serve the cake right from the pan; in which case, leave it where it is. Allow the cake to cool to room temperature.

TO PREPARE THE TOPPING: Combine the cream, condensed milk, evaporated milk or half-and-half, and vanilla or liquor, stirring thoroughly.

Poke the cake all over with a fork. Pour the milk mixture over the cake slowly, stopping occasionally to allow it to soak in. This seems like a lot of liquid for the cake to absorb; but don't worry, it will.

Cover the cake and refrigerate it for several hours before serving.

Just before serving, make the frosting: Whip the heavy cream with the sugar until the cream is stiff enough to spread. Spread the cream over the top of the cake, swirling it with your spatula.

NUTRITION INFORMATION PER SERVING: **1 piece, 70g**
190 cal | 7g fat | 4g protein | 6g complex carbohydrates | 23g sugar | 0g dietary fiber | 70mg cholesterol | 140mg sodium

PINEAPPLE UPSIDE-DOWN CAKE

ONE 9″ CAKE

This classic cake, with its moist, flavorful topping of pineapple rings and cherries (nuts optional), has been an American favorite for at least 90 years. It became popular after an early twentieth-century Dole engineer invented a machine that would slice that company's signature product—pineapple—into perfect rings. The first recipe appeared in print in 1923. The buttery, brown sugar base is just the right foil for the tropical fruit.

TOPPING

4 tablespoons (½ stick, 57g) butter

½ cup (107g) light brown sugar

¼ teaspoon cinnamon

¼ teaspoon ginger

one 20-ounce can pineapple rings in juice, drained

candied red cherries or maraschino cherries

pecans or walnuts, halved or diced (optional)

CAKE

3 tablespoons (43g) butter, at room temperature (at least 65°)

¾ cup (149g) granulated sugar

1 large egg, at room temperature

½ teaspoon salt

1¾ teaspoons baking powder

1 teaspoon vanilla extract

⅛ teaspoon coconut flavor (optional)

1⅓ cups (160g) unbleached all-purpose flour

½ cup (113g) milk, at room temperature

Preheat the oven to 375°F. Lightly grease a 9″ round cake pan.

TO PREPARE THE TOPPING: Melt the butter, and mix with the brown sugar, cinnamon, and ginger. Spoon the mixture into the prepared pan.

Space the pineapple rings atop the brown sugar mixture. Place a cherry in the center of each ring. If you're using nuts, scatter them in any empty spaces.

TO PREPARE THE CAKE: Beat the butter and sugar until fairly smooth.

Beat in the egg, then the salt, baking powder, vanilla, and coconut flavor.

Add the flour alternately with the milk, mixing at medium speed and beginning and ending with the flour. Once the last of the flour is added, mix briefly, just until smooth.

Spoon the thick batter into the prepared pan, spreading it to the edges of the pan. It may not cover the pineapple entirely; that's OK.

Bake the cake for 30 to 35 minutes, until a cake tester or toothpick inserted into the center comes out clean.

Remove the cake from the oven, wait 3 minutes, then turn the pan over onto a serving plate. Wait 30 seconds, then lift the pan off. If anything sticks in the pan, just lift it out and place it back on the cake. Serve warm or at room temperature.

Cheesecake

For something that's really so simple to make, and that produces such a rich, soul-satisfying dessert, it's amazing that we aren't all making cheesecake more frequently. (If you are, we applaud you!) This is another dessert with a long history, an antecedent of it being noted in print as early as the fifteenth century.

NEW YORK CHEESECAKE

ONE 10˝ CHEESECAKE

Known for being ultra-creamy and rich, New York cheesecake uses sour cream or cream cheese, which, along with a hint of lemon, gives the dense, luscious filling a touch of tang. Baked in a cookie crust, this cheesecake typically sports a thick topping of fruit compote.

CRUST

1½ cups (180g) unbleached all-purpose flour

⅓ cup (65g) sugar

¼ teaspoon salt

8 tablespoons (1 stick, 113g) unsalted butter, at room temperature

1 large egg, at room temperature

FILLING

4 cups (2 pounds, 907g) cream cheese, at room temperature

1¾ cups (347g) sugar

3 tablespoons (24g) unbleached all-purpose flour

zest of 1 lemon

¼ teaspoon salt

1 teaspoon vanilla extract

5 large eggs, at room temperature

½ cup (113g) sour cream, at room temperature

GLAZE

1 cup (227g) water

½ cup (99g) sugar

1½ to 2 tablespoons (11g to 14g) cornstarch

two (14.5-ounce) cans tart cherries in water, drained, or 4 cups (454g) fresh or frozen fruit

Preheat the oven to 400°F. Lightly grease a 10˝ springform pan.

TO PREPARE THE CRUST: In a mixing bowl with a paddle, combine the flour, sugar, salt, and butter. Mix until the mixture is crumbly, then add the egg and continue to mix until a soft dough forms.

Press the dough on the bottom and an inch up the sides of the prepared pan; prick it all over with a fork, and bake for 15 minutes, until light golden brown. Remove from the oven and cool to room temperature. Reduce the oven temperature to 325°F.

TO PREPARE THE FILLING: Place the cream cheese in a large mixing bowl with a paddle. Add the sugar and flour and mix at low speed until there are no lumps. Scrape the bottom and sides of the bowl at least twice during this process, to be sure no cheese is sticking.

Add the lemon zest, salt, and vanilla, and mix to combine. Add the eggs, one at a time, mixing until incorporated and scraping the mixing bowl between additions. Stir in the sour cream.

Pour the filling over the crust and bake for 45 to 50 minutes, until the edges of the cake are set an inch in from the edge. The middle should still jiggle when you nudge the pan; in fact, the cake will look underbaked. Measure the temperature of the cake an inch from the edge: When it reaches 175°F, turn off the oven.

Prop open the door, and let the cheesecake cool slowly in the oven for 1 hour. During this time the center will finish setting. Cooling the cake slowly will keep the top from cracking and ensure a smooth, even texture inside.

TO PREPARE THE GLAZE: Whisk together the water, sugar, and cornstarch in a medium saucepan until the cornstarch dissolves. Place over medium heat and cook, stirring constantly, until the mixture boils, becomes clear, and thickens.

Remove from the heat and add the drained cherries or fruit. Let the mixture cool to room temperature, then spoon it over the cooled cheesecake. Refrigerate the cake until you're ready to serve.

NUTRITION INFORMATION PER SERVING: 1 slice, 102g
347 cal | 23g fat | 7g protein | 9g complex carbohydrates | 21g sugar | 0g dietary fiber | 128mg cholesterol | 217mg sodium

PUMPKIN CHEESECAKE

ONE 9″ OR 10″ CHEESECAKE

The rich flavor of cheesecake melds beautifully with the color and sweet, hearty taste of pumpkin. To make this cake even more memorable, we've added a spicy gingersnap crust.

CRUST

4 tablespoons (½ stick, 57g) butter, melted

1¼ cups (191g) gingersnap crumbs

¼ to ½ teaspoon ginger (optional, for more ginger flavor)

2 tablespoons (27g) brown sugar

CHEESE FILLING

3 cups (24 ounces, 680g) cream cheese, at room temperature

1¼ cups (248g) granulated sugar

¼ teaspoon salt

2 tablespoons (14g) cornstarch

5 large eggs

1 tablespoon (14g) vanilla extract

1 cup (227g) heavy cream

½ cup (113g) pumpkin purée

½ teaspoon cinnamon

¼ teaspoon ginger

pinch of allspice

Preheat the oven to 350°F.

TO MAKE THE CRUST: Use a food processor or blender to blend together the butter, gingersnaps, ginger, and brown sugar until the mixture is evenly crumbly. Press the crumbs into the bottom and about ½″ up the side of a 9″ springform pan. Bake the crust for 12 to 14 minutes, just until it's set. Set aside to cool. Reduce the oven temperature to 325°F.

TO MAKE THE FILLING: Using an electric mixer set on low speed, beat the cream cheese until it's soft and no lumps remain. Add the sugar, salt, and cornstarch and mix until well blended. Beat in 4 of the eggs one at a time, being sure the mixture is smooth and scraping the bottom of the bowl after each addition. Add the vanilla and heavy cream, stirring just until the mixture is smooth.

Remove 1 cup of batter from the bowl and combine it with the pumpkin purée, 1 egg, and spices.

Pour the vanilla cheesecake batter into the cooled crust. Drop tablespoonfuls of the pumpkin batter over the vanilla batter. Use a knife to swirl the pumpkin through the batter (see illustration).

Bake the cake at 325°F for 40 to 55 minutes. The internal temperature, when measured an inch from the outside edge, should be 165°F or above, and the middle should jiggle. Turn off the oven, open the door slightly, and let the cheesecake cool slowly for 1 hour in the turned-off oven. Remove it from the oven, run a knife around the top edge of the pan to free the cake (so it can contract as it cools), then refrigerate overnight before serving.

NUTRITION INFORMATION PER SERVING: 1 slice, 138g

432 cal | 29g fat | 7g protein | 24g complex carbohydrates | 24g sugar | 1g dietary fiber | 147mg cholesterol | 307mg sodium

---

SMOOTH OPERATOR: KEEPING CHEESECAKE FROM CRACKING

Cracks occur in a cheesecake when they're overbaked; the proteins in the batter tighten and shrink as they cook, creating fissures in the surface. The trick is to stop baking before the cake is done. For a perfect cheesecake, turn off the oven and prop open the door when the cake's temperature measures 175°F on a digital thermometer an inch in from the edge (leave the cake inside). Carryover cooking will finish the cake's center and give you a perfectly smooth finish.

CHOCOLATE CHEESECAKE

ONE 9″ CAKE

This straightforward chocolate cheesecake is everything you want it to be: rich and dense with a bold chocolate flavor. Not only that, it's simple to put together, requiring neither special ingredients, nor a fussy water bath.

CRUST

24 (269g) vanilla-filled chocolate sandwich cookies

¼ cup (28g) confectioners' sugar

4 tablespoons (½ stick, 57g) butter, melted

FILLING

½ cup (113g) milk, at room temperature

2 cups (340g) semisweet or bittersweet chocolate chips

1 teaspoon espresso powder (optional)

3 cups (24 ounces, 680g) cream cheese, at room temperature

1 cup (198g) granulated sugar

4 large eggs, at room temperature

1 teaspoon vanilla extract

2 tablespoons (15g) unbleached all-purpose flour

Preheat the oven to 375°F. Lightly grease a 9˝ springform pan.

TO MAKE THE CRUST: Crush, grind, or otherwise pulverize the cookies together with the sugar; a food processor works well here.

Add the melted butter, processing briefly or stirring until the mixture is evenly crumbly. Press the moist crumbs into the bottom and partway up the sides of the prepared pan. Place the pan on a baking sheet, to catch any potential drips of butter.

Bake the crust for 15 minutes. Remove it from the oven, and set it aside as you make the filling.

Reduce the oven heat to 350°F.

TO MAKE THE FILLING: Combine the milk and chocolate chips in a small saucepan or microwave-safe bowl or large cup. Heat, stirring frequently, until the chips melt and the mixture is smooth. Remove from the heat, stir in the espresso powder, and set the mixture aside.

In a large bowl, beat together the cream cheese and sugar at low speed, until thoroughly combined. Scrape the bottom and sides of the bowl, and beat briefly, just until smooth.

Add the eggs one at a time, beating to combine after each one.

Stir in the vanilla, then the flour.

Add the chocolate/milk mixture, beating slowly until thoroughly combined. Scrape the bottom and sides of the bowl; beat briefly, just until smooth.

Pour the batter atop the crust in the pan. Place the pan on a baking sheet; this will make it easier to get the cake in and out of the oven safely.

Bake the cake at 350°F for 45 to 50 minutes, until a toothpick inserted into the cake 1˝ from the outside edge comes out clean. A digital thermometer, inserted at the same point, should read 175°F. The center may not look set; that's OK.

Turn off the oven, crack the door open several inches, and allow the cake to cool in the oven for 1 hour. Remove the cake from the oven and set it on a rack to finish cooling. When it's completely cool, cover the cake, and refrigerate it until ready to serve.

NUTRITION INFORMATION PER SERVING: 1 slice, 98g

350 cal | 24g fat | 5g protein | 8g complex carbohydrates | 27g sugar | 2g dietary fiber | 85mg cholesterol | 190mg sodium

Special Occasion Cakes

For those moments in life that are particularly memorable, you'll want a dessert to match. For very special occasions, we turn to a collection of show-stopping cakes that are reliably impressive but also ones we've made and loved over and over again. These include flourless cakes, whose structure is based entirely on eggs, and mousse cakes, where the cake plays almost a secondary role to the whipped cream and filling. These cakes are more pure confection than cake, delighting us with their rich ingredients and sometimes whimsical presentation.

FLOURLESS CHOCOLATE CAKE

ONE 8″ CAKE

This flourless cake, featuring both chocolate and cocoa, is extremely rich! A chocolate ganache glaze takes it even further over the top. And, since it contains neither flour nor leavening, it's perfect for Passover or for anyone looking for a gluten-free cake.

CAKE

1 cup (170g) semisweet or bittersweet
    chocolate chips

8 tablespoons (1 stick, 113g) unsalted
    butter

¾ cup (149g) sugar

¼ teaspoon salt

1 to 2 teaspoons espresso powder
    (optional)

1 teaspoon vanilla extract (optional)

3 large eggs

½ cup (43g) Dutch-process cocoa

GLAZE

1 cup (170g) semisweet or bittersweet
    chocolate chips

½ cup (113g) heavy cream

Preheat the oven to 375°F. Lightly grease a metal 8″ round cake pan; cut a piece of parchment to fit, grease it, and lay it in the bottom of the pan.

TO MAKE THE CAKE: Put the chocolate and butter in a microwave-safe bowl, and heat until the butter is melted and the chips are soft. Stir until the chips melt, reheating briefly if necessary. You can also do this over a burner set at very low heat. Transfer the melted chocolate mixture to a mixing bowl.

Stir in the sugar, salt, espresso powder, and vanilla (if using). Espresso enhances chocolate's flavor much as vanilla does; using 1 teaspoon will simply enhance the flavor, while 2 teaspoons will lend a hint of mocha to the cake.

Add the eggs, beating briefly until smooth. Add the cocoa powder and mix just to combine.

Spoon the batter into the prepared pan.

Bake the cake for 25 minutes; the top will have formed a thin crust, and it should register at least 200°F on a digital thermometer inserted into its center.

Remove it from the oven, and cool it in the pan for 5 minutes.

Loosen the edges of the pan with a table knife and turn it out onto a serving plate. The top will now be on the bottom; that's fine. Also, the edges will crumble a bit, which is also fine. Allow the cake to cool completely before glazing.

TO MAKE THE GLAZE: Place the chocolate in a heatproof bowl. Heat the cream until it's not quite at a simmer, but showing fine bubbles around the edge. Pour the cream over the chocolate, stir very briefly to combine, and let rest for 5 minutes. Stir again—at first slowly, then more vigorously—until the chocolate is completely melted and the glaze is smooth. If any bits of chocolate remain, reheat briefly in the microwave or over a burner, then stir until smooth.

Spoon the glaze over the cake, spreading it to drip over the sides a bit. Allow the glaze to set for several hours before serving the cake.

NUTRITION INFORMATION PER SERVING: **1 piece, 76g**
300 cal | 20g fat | 4g protein | 6g complex carbohydrates | 27g sugar | 4g dietary fiber | 80mg cholesterol | 75mg sodium

CHOCOLATE MOUSSE CAKE WITH RASPBERRIES

ONE 2-, 3-, OR 4-LAYER 8″ OR 9″ CAKE

This intensely fudgy cake is filled with chocolate mousse and fresh raspberries, then swathed in rich chocolate frosting. With its four towering layers and striking appearance, it's perfect for the most special of occasions. Our thanks to Sharon Kurtz of Emmaus, Pennsylvania, for the award-winning recipe. Using both shortening and butter helps to stabilize the frosting in warmer temperatures, but you can use all butter if you prefer.

CAKE

1¾ cups (210g) unbleached all-purpose flour

2 teaspoons baking soda

1 teaspoon baking powder

1 teaspoon salt

2 cups (397g) granulated sugar

1 cup (85g) unsweetened cocoa, natural or Dutch-process

½ cup (99g) vegetable oil

1 cup (227g) buttermilk or yogurt, at room temperature

1 cup (227g) boiling water or hot brewed coffee

2 teaspoons vanilla extract

3 large eggs, at room temperature

FILLING

2 tablespoons (28g) butter, softened

1 cup (8 ounces, 227g) cream cheese, at room temperature

1 cup (113g) confectioners' sugar, sifted

½ teaspoon vanilla extract

⅛ teaspoon salt

⅔ cup (113g) semisweet chocolate chips, melted

1 teaspoon Instant ClearJel (optional)

1 cup (227g) heavy cream, at room temperature

½ cup (85g) mini semisweet chocolate chips (optional)

1½ to 2 pints fresh raspberries, washed and dried

FROSTING

½ cup (92g) vegetable shortening

8 tablespoons (1 stick, 113g) unsalted butter, at room temperature

¼ teaspoon salt

4 cups (454g) confectioners' sugar, sifted

½ cup (43g) unsweetened cocoa, natural or Dutch-process

¼ cup (57g) milk

1 teaspoon vanilla extract

Preheat the oven to 325°F. Lightly grease two 8″ round pans at least 2″ deep (and preferably 3″ deep), three 9″ round pans, or four 8″ round pans at least 1½″ deep. If you have parchment rounds, line the pans with parchment and grease the parchment. If your pan assortment doesn't include any of these particular combinations, you can bake the cake batter in batches; the unbaked batter won't suffer while awaiting its turn in the oven.

TO MAKE THE CAKE LAYERS: In a large bowl, whisk together the flour and remaining dry ingredients, or combine thoroughly using a stand mixer equipped with the whisk or beater attachment. Check to make sure there aren't any hard lumps in the mixture; if there are, press them through a sieve.

In a medium bowl or large measuring cup, combine the oil, buttermilk or yogurt, boiling water or coffee, and vanilla. Add to the dry ingredients and beat at medium speed for 30 seconds to 1 minute, until the batter is smooth.

Scrape the sides and bottom of the mixing bowl, then beat in the eggs one at a time. Mix on medium speed for another minute, or until smooth.

Divide the batter among the prepared pans. Bake for 45 to 50 minutes for two 8″ pans, or 25 to 30 minutes for three 9″ or four 8″ pans, until the cake just begins to pull away from the edges of the pans, and a cake tester or toothpick inserted in each center comes out with just a few moist crumbs. Remove from the oven and place on a rack to cool for 15 minutes. Run a table knife around the edge of each pan to free the crust, and turn the cakes onto the rack to cool completely. While the cake layers are cooling, make the filling.

TO MAKE THE FILLING: In a large bowl, combine the butter, cream cheese, ¾ cup (85g) of the confectioners' sugar, vanilla, and salt, mixing at medium-low speed until smooth. Melt the chocolate; a minute or less in the microwave should be sufficient to soften the chips enough that you can stir them until completely melted and smooth. Add the melted chocolate to the bowl and mix on medium-high speed for 1 minute, or until a bit lightened and fluffy.

Whisk together the remaining ¼ cup (28g) confectioners' sugar with the Instant ClearJel, if using. Beat the heavy cream until soft peaks form, then add the confectioners' sugar mixture. Beat just until the cream is stiff; guard against over-beating, which will turn the cream grainy. Fold the whipped cream into the cream cheese mixture; scrape the bowl, and stir to combine any sticky residue. Finally, fold in the mini chocolate chips, if using.

Split the cake layers horizontally if you've baked two deep 8″ cakes; trim any domes off the tops if you've baked three or four individual layers. Place the first layer on a serving plate (line the edges with strips of waxed or parchment paper to keep the plate clean), and spread it with one-third of the filling (1 cup; 227g). Cut a half pint of raspberries in half lengthwise (rather than around the circumference), and place them over the filling, covering its entire surface. Repeat until all the layers are stacked; place the last layer bottom-side up for a flat surface on top.

Once the layers are assembled with filling and raspberries, place the cake in the refrigerator or freezer for at least 30 minutes to firm it up. This will make frosting the cake much easier since the layers are less likely to slide around and chilling helps prevent the cake from shedding crumbs as you frost. While the cake is chilling, make the frosting.

TO MAKE THE FROSTING: In a large bowl, beat together the shortening, butter, and salt.

Sift the confectioners' sugar and cocoa through a strainer to remove any lumps, and gently beat into the butter mixture alternately with the milk. Add the vanilla. Beat on medium-high speed for 2 minutes, or until fluffy.

TO FINISH THE CAKE: For the best-looking cake, do the frosting in two steps. First, spread a very thin layer of frosting around the sides and across the top; this is called a crumb coat. You should actually be able to see the cake through the frosting in spots, it's that thin. Refrigerate the cake for 20 minutes to let this layer set up.

Once the cake is chilled, use the remaining frosting to coat it thoroughly and evenly. The frosting will be thin, but the cake should be completely coated, with no bare patches. If you have any leftover frosting, use it to pipe decorations on the top and/or around the base.

Refrigerate the cake until ready to serve. Garnish with fresh raspberries just before serving.

NUTRITION INFORMATION PER SERVING: 1 slice, 143g

453 cal | 25g fat | 4g protein | 11g complex carbohydrates | 46g sugar | 3g dietary fiber | 64mg cholesterol | 300mg sodium

COCONUT CAKE

ONE 2-LAYER 8″ OR 9″ CAKE

A very good coconut cake is a dessert in a class of its own. Too often, recipes are cloyingly sweet or far too one-note in flavor, but this version is neither of those things. A simple cream cheese frosting adds a touch of tang to balance out the sweetness, and the coconut flavor shines through. If you can't find coconut milk powder, substitute nonfat dried milk.

CAKE

3 cups (360g) unbleached cake flour or unbleached all-purpose flour

⅔ cup (71g) coconut milk powder

½ teaspoon salt

4 teaspoons (16g) baking powder

10 tablespoons (142g) unsalted butter, softened

1½ cups (298g) granulated sugar

6 large (210g) egg whites, at room temperature

1½ cups (340g) whole milk, at room temperature

1½ teaspoons vanilla extract

4 drops coconut flavor

FROSTING

15 tablespoons (213g) unsalted butter, at room temperature

1¼ cups (10 ounces, 283g) cream cheese, at room temperature

¾ teaspoon vanilla extract

⅜ teaspoon salt

¼ teaspoon coconut flavor (optional)

¼ cup plus 1 tablespoon (35g) coconut milk powder

4¼ to 4½ cups (482g to 510g) confectioners' sugar, sifted

GARNISH

1½ cups (128g) shredded sweetened coconut

Preheat the oven to 350°F. Grease and flour (or line with parchment circles and spray with nonstick spray) two 8″ square cake pans (or two 9″ round cake pans) that are at least 2″ deep. If you want a taller cake, use two 8″ round cake pans that are at least 2″ deep.

TO MAKE THE CAKE: Whisk together the flour, coconut milk powder, salt, and baking powder; set aside.

In a large bowl, beat together the butter and sugar until the mixture is extremely light and fluffy; scrape down the sides and bottom of the mixing bowl after 2 minutes of beating, and beat for at least 3 minutes more. Add one-quarter of the dry ingredients; mix until combined and scrape the mixing bowl.

In a medium bowl, combine the egg whites, milk, vanilla, and coconut flavor. Add one-third of the mixture to the ingredients in the bowl and mix until combined. Continue adding dry and wet ingredients by turns, until all are incorporated. Scrape the sides and bottom of the bowl one last time, and mix for another minute.

Divide the batter between the two pans. Place the pans inside larger pans; add water to the larger pans until it's halfway up the sides of the cake pans (alternatively, you can soak two cake strips—if you have them—and wrap them around the outside of the pans). Bake for 30 to 35 minutes, until the cake springs back when lightly touched in the center and the edges just begin to pull away from the sides of the pan. A cake tester or toothpick inserted into the center will come out clean, or with a few moist crumbs clinging to it.

Remove the cakes from the oven and place on a rack; remove the cake strips (if using) or remove from the larger pans. Let the layers cool for 20 minutes, then turn out of the pan and return to the rack to finish cooling completely before filling and frosting.

TO MAKE THE FROSTING: In a large bowl, combine the butter, cream cheese, vanilla, salt, and coconut flavor, if using. Beat the ingredients together at medium speed until smooth, scraping down the sides of the bowl as needed.

In a separate large bowl, sift the coconut milk powder and confectioners' sugar together. Gradually add the sugar mixture to the butter/cream cheese mixture, mixing at low speed until fully incorporated, then beating at medium-high speed until the frosting is light and fluffy.

TO FINISH THE CAKE: Split the cooled cake layers horizontally. Place half of one layer on a serving plate; spread with a scant cup of frosting. Place the other cake half on top, spread with another scant cup of frosting. Repeat with the remaining layers until you've used them all. Frost the top and sides of the cake with the remaining frosting.

TO DECORATE THE CAKE: Press some coconut onto the sides of the cake and sprinkle the remaining over the top.

Refrigerate the cake until ready to serve, and let it stand at room temperature for an hour before slicing and enjoying.

NUTRITION INFORMATION PER SERVING: 1 slice, 175g

520 cal | 20g fat | 6g protein | 20g complex carbohydrates | 63g sugar | 2g dietary fiber | 35mg cholesterol | 310mg sodium

BERRY BLITZ TORTE

ONE 2-LAYER 8″ CAKE

This fancy looking but oh-so-easy-to-make confection is our take on *kvæfjordkake*, Norway's national cake. It features layers of dense yellow cake topped with meringue, cinnamon, and almonds; and a rich, creamy filling studded with fresh berries.

FILLING

2½ cups (567g) whole milk

½ cup (99g) sugar

¼ teaspoon salt

⅓ cup (39g) cornstarch

3 large egg yolks

1 large egg

2 teaspoons vanilla extract

½ cup (113g) heavy cream, whipped (optional)

1½ to 2 cups (about 191g to 255g) fresh raspberries, sliced strawberries, blueberries, or blackberries

CAKE

8 tablespoons (1 stick, 113g) unsalted butter, at room temperature (at least 65°F)

½ cup (99g) sugar

¼ teaspoon salt

4 large egg yolks (save the whites for the topping), at room temperature

1 teaspoon vanilla extract

3 tablespoons (43g) milk

1 teaspoon baking powder

1 cup (120g) unbleached all-purpose flour

TOPPING

4 large egg whites, from above

¾ cup (149g) sugar

½ cup (50g) sliced or slivered almonds

½ teaspoon cinnamon

1 tablespoon (14g) sugar

TO MAKE THE FILLING: In a medium saucepan, stir together 2 cups (454g) of the milk, the sugar, and salt. Bring to a simmer over medium heat, stirring to dissolve the sugar.

Meanwhile in a separate bowl, whisk the cornstarch, egg yolks, and whole egg with the remaining ½ cup (113g) milk.

Whisk some of the hot milk mixture into the egg yolk/cornstarch mixture to temper the yolks. This keeps them from turning to scrambled eggs when you add them to the simmering milk.

Pour the egg/milk mixture back into the remaining simmering milk, pouring it through a strainer to capture any bits of egg. Bring to a boil over medium heat (this may happen very quickly), stirring constantly with a whisk. Cook for 2 minutes, stirring constantly; the mixture will thicken significantly.

Remove from the heat and stir in the vanilla extract.

Transfer the filling to a heatproof storage container and top it with a piece of buttered plastic wrap (make sure it touches the top of the filling so it doesn't develop a skin). Refrigerate until cool, or for up to several days.

Preheat the oven to 350°F. Lightly grease two 8″ round cake pans. Or lightly grease the pans, line with parchment rounds, and lightly grease the parchment as well.

TO MAKE THE CAKE: In a medium bowl, beat together the butter, sugar, salt, and egg yolks until well combined. Scrape the bowl and beat briefly to incorporate any sticky residue.

Beat in the vanilla, milk, baking powder, and flour; the batter will be stiff.

Spread the batter in the prepared pans (it will barely cover the bottom of the pans; that's OK).

TO MAKE THE TOPPING: Using an electric mixer or stand mixer with a whisk attachment, beat the egg whites until foamy; gradually add the sugar and continue to beat until the meringue is smooth, glossy, and somewhat stiff (but not stiff enough to form rigid stand-up points).

Spread the meringue on the cake batter. Sprinkle the almonds over the meringue. Mix the cinnamon with the sugar, and dust on top.

Bake the cakes for 30 minutes, until the almonds are lightly browned. The cakes will puff up significantly; don't worry, they'll settle as they cool.

Remove the cakes from the oven and allow them to cool for 15 minutes. Carefully and thoroughly loosen the edge of each cake, and gently turn it out onto a rack to cool completely. The best way to do this is to place a flat object (a giant spatula, a small baking sheet) atop the pan, and to turn everything over. Lift the cake pan off the cake, then place a cooling rack against the bottom of the cake. Turn everything back over again, so the rack is on the bottom. Some of the almonds will fall off during this process; just sprinkle them back on top.

When you're ready to finish the cake, remove the pastry cream from the refrigerator. Stir it gently, just to loosen it up enough to spread; stirring too vigorously can break it down and turn it watery. It'll probably have a few lumps; that's OK. For a slightly richer filling with greater volume, gently fold the optional whipped cream into the pastry cream. Again, don't beat the pastry cream; it'll be a bit lumpy, but that won't affect the taste.

TO ASSEMBLE THE CAKE: Place one of the cake layers, meringue side up, on a serving plate. Spread with the filling. Add a layer of fresh berries. Top with the second cake layer, meringue-side up.

Serve immediately or refrigerate until serving time.

NUTRITION INFORMATION PER SERVING: 1 slice, 240g

560 cal | 27g fat | 11g protein | 19g complex carbohydrates | 51g sugar | 3g dietary fiber | 240mg cholesterol | 290mg sodium

Frostings, Glazes, and Fillings

Here's the icing on the cake—and the filling inside. Some of the cakes in this chapter call for specific icings or fillings, but the following recipes can be paired with any cake as you see fit. While the world of frostings (particularly buttercreams) encompasses many more than we've included here—from German buttercream to French buttercream—this collection runs the gamut of styles and offers a baker plenty of variety (and deliciousness).

QUICK BUTTERCREAM FROSTING

2½ CUPS, ENOUGH TO FROST AN 8″ OR 9″ LAYER CAKE, 9″ × 13″ CAKE, OR 24 CUPCAKES

You may use all butter in this quick buttercream, but using vegetable shortening will make a frosting that will be a little firmer in warmer temperatures. Also, using the optional meringue powder, while not necessary, will help your frosting hold its shape. If you're frosting a layer cake, double the recipe to have enough frosting to pipe decorations.

8 tablespoons (1 stick, 113g) unsalted butter, at room temperature, or ½ cup (92g) vegetable shortening, or a combination

pinch of salt

1 tablespoon (14g) meringue powder (optional, for "holding powder")

1 teaspoon vanilla extract

2½ to 3 cups (283g to 340g) confectioners' sugar, sifted, or glazing sugar

2 to 4 tablespoons (28g to 57g) milk

Beat the butter and/or shortening until fluffy.

Beat in the salt, meringue powder, and vanilla.

Add the confectioners' or glazing sugar and 2 tablespoons (28g) of the milk and beat until smooth. Scrape the sides and bottom of the bowl.

Adjust the consistency of the frosting as needed by adding more confectioners' sugar or milk.

If you're not going to use the frosting right away, keep it at room temperature, covered, to prevent it from developing a dry crust.

NUTRITION INFORMATION PER SERVING: 1 heaping tablespoon, 29g

130 cal | 6g fat | 0g protein | 1g complex carbohydrates | 19g sugar | 0g dietary fiber | 20mg cholesterol | 10mg sodium

EASY CHOCOLATE BUTTERCREAM

2 TO 3 CUPS, ENOUGH TO FROST AN 8″ OR 9″ LAYER CAKE, 9″ × 13″ CAKE, OR 24 CUPCAKES

This is a simple chocolate frosting that's deliciously smooth and creamy. You can customize it for your particular taste by using unsweetened, bittersweet, or semisweet chocolate.

½ cup (84g) chopped unsweetened, bittersweet, or semisweet chocolate

4 tablespoons (½ stick, 56g) butter, at room temperature

⅛ teaspoon salt

4 to 5 cups (1 to 1¼ pounds, 454 to 567g) confectioners' sugar, sifted

2 teaspoons vanilla extract

6 tablespoons (84g) milk or cream

Place the chocolate in a heatproof bowl or measuring cup. In the microwave, or over simmering water, melt the chocolate about three-quarters of the way. Remove from the heat or microwave and stir the chocolate until it's completely smooth. Set aside to cool at room temperature.

In a large bowl, beat together the butter and salt until fluffy. Add about half of the confectioners' sugar and beat slowly until well blended. Add the vanilla and half the milk and beat until fluffy. Add the melted chocolate and mix until thoroughly blended. Scrape down the sides of the bowl and add the remaining sugar and milk alternately until they've been completely incorporated. Beat until the frosting is light and fluffy, adjusting the consistency with more milk or confectioners' sugar as needed. If you want some frosting left over to use in decorating, change the ingredient amounts as follows: 8 tablespoons (1 stick, 113g) unsalted butter, ⅔ cup (113g) chocolate, approximately 6 cups (1½ pounds, 680g) confectioners' sugar, and up to ½ cup (113g) milk or cream.

NUTRITION INFORMATION PER SERVING: 3 tablespoons (made with bittersweet chocolate and milk), 43g
167 cal | 5g fat | 0g protein | 1g complex carbohydrates | 31g sugar | 0g dietary fiver | 8mg cholesterol | 21mg sodium

ITALIAN BUTTERCREAM

7 TO 7½ CUPS, ENOUGH TO FILL AND FROST A 2- OR 3-LAYER CAKE,
WITH EXTRA FOR DECORATING

This is the frosting that you'll find on many wedding cakes. Its silky texture is unparalleled. It pipes like a dream, and can be flavored and colored in as many ways as you can imagine. It takes a little time to make, but it freezes quite well so you can make it ahead. To thaw it, simply defrost it in the refrigerator overnight, then let it come to room temperature before using; if it weeps or separates, whip it briefly in a mixer to bring it back together. If you want to customize this frosting, try adding 1 teaspoon to 2 tablespoons of your flavoring of choice, adjusting the amount as you like; vanilla extract, melted chocolate, citrus zest, and espresso powder are all good options.

SUGAR SYRUP

1¼ cups (248g) sugar

½ cup (113g) water

MERINGUE

½ cup (85g) meringue powder or 8 large egg whites, at room temperature, combined with 1 teaspoon cream of tartar

1 cup (227g) water

¼ teaspoon salt

⅓ cup (64g) sugar

FROSTING

48 tablespoons (6 sticks, 680g) unsalted butter, at room temperature

½ to ¾ cup (92g to 138g) vegetable shortening (optional)

1 to 2 teaspoons vanilla extract or flavoring of your choice

TO MAKE THE SYRUP: Combine the sugar and water in a small, nonstick (preferable, if you have one) saucepan. Bring to a boil over medium heat, stirring occasionally until the sugar dissolves. Cook, without stirring, until the syrup reaches at least 240°F. It can go as high as 248°F to 250°F. Just be sure it's within those temperatures before you take it off the stove.

TO MAKE THE MERINGUE: While the syrup is cooking, combine the meringue powder or egg whites and cream of tartar, water, and salt in the bowl of your mixer. Beat at high speed with the whisk attachment until the mixture first looks foamy, then turns white, and you begin to see tracks in the bowl. At this point, slowly sprinkle in the sugar with the mixer running. Increase the speed to high and beat until the mixture is stiff.

When the syrup gets above 240°F (115°C) and before it gets above 250°F (120°C), remove it from the heat and, with the mixer running at low speed, pour it down the side of the mixing bowl (not on the whisk or beaters if you can avoid it; that will send the syrup flying and start spinning sugar threads instead of incorporating it). Once the syrup is all in, leave the mixer running until the mixture cools to 80°F. You can help this process along by wrapping an ice pack around the mixing bowl.

Once the meringue is cool, add the butter, a few pieces at a time, with the mixer running at medium to medium-high speed. The meringue will deflate a bit, and may begin to look curdled. Don't lose heart! This stage is normal. Just keep the mixer running and adding the butter.

Soon the frosting will begin to bring itself together around the whisk, then in the rest of the bowl. Once most of the butter is in, add the vanilla or your choice of flavorings. If you're using the frosting for decorations, add the shortening in chunks at this point.

Use the buttercream within 4 hours or refrigerate until needed; bring it to room temperature before using it to frost or decorate.

NUTRITION INFORMATION PER SERVING: ¼ cup, 44g
213 cal | 18g fat | 1g protein | 0g complex carbohydrates | 12g sugar | 0g dietary fiber | 49mg cholesterol | 36mg sodium

SWISS BUTTERCREAM

5 CUPS, ENOUGH TO FILL AND FROST A 2- OR 3-LAYER CAKE OR 24 CUPCAKES

Swiss meringue is named for the meringue-making technique of beating egg whites and sugar over simmering water. This smooth and creamy frosting has one distinct advantage over Italian buttercream—it pipes just as nicely but it's a bit simpler to make, as there's no pouring of a hot sugar syrup required.

3 large (½ cup, 113g) egg whites, at room temperature

1¼ cups (248g) sugar

⅛ teaspoon salt

32 tablespoons (4 sticks, 454g) unsalted butter, at room temperature (at least 65°F)

1 to 2 teaspoons vanilla extract or flavoring of your choice

In the bowl of a stand mixer, combine the egg whites, sugar, and salt.

Place over a saucepan of simmering water (you should just barely see some lazy bubbles coming up), and whisk constantly until the mixture measures 161°F on a digital thermometer.

Attach the bowl to your mixer and beat the meringue with the whisk attachment until it's stiff.

Add the butter a few tablespoons at a time, with the mixer running. Let each blob of butter get completely mixed in before adding the next.

Once half the butter is in the bowl, stop and scrape the sides and bottom to make sure all the meringue is getting incorporated. Then finish adding the rest of the butter.

Beat in the flavoring of your choice.

If the frosting seems soft, chill for 15 minutes before using.

Store for up to 6 months in the freezer, or up to 1 week in the refrigerator.

NUTRITION INFORMATION PER SERVING: ¼ cup, 41g

214 cal | 18g fat | 1g protein | 0g complex carbohydrates | 12g sugar | 0g dietary fiber | 49mg cholesterol | 27mg sodium

SEVEN-MINUTE FROSTING

ABOUT 5 CUPS, ENOUGH TO FROST A 10" TUBE OR 2- OR 3-LAYER CAKE

Piling pillowy drifts of this snowy white frosting atop a cake is one of the prettiest (and easiest) ways to decorate. To make the unique texture this frosting is known for, egg whites and sugar are combined and beaten over simmering water for exactly seven minutes to dissolve the sugar and achieve a very light, fluffy texture.

1½ cups (298g) sugar

⅓ cup (74g) water, cold

2 large egg whites

2 teaspoons light corn syrup or
    ¼ teaspoon cream of tartar

pinch of salt

1 teaspoon vanilla extract

In the top of a double boiler, combine the sugar, water, egg whites, corn syrup or cream of tartar, and salt.

Beat with an electric mixer at low speed for 30 seconds, then set the pan over (but not touching) simmering water. Continue beating at high speed for about 7 minutes, or until it's stiff and glossy.

Remove from the heat, add the vanilla, and beat for another 1 to 2 minutes.

Use right away, as the frosting will set quickly.

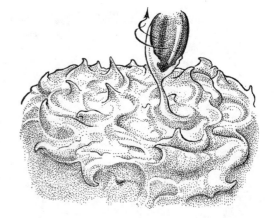

Use the back of a spoon or the tip of your icing spatula to make a swirl pattern in the frosting.

NUTRITION INFORMATION PER SERVING: 1 tablespoon, 19g

50 cal | 0g fat | 0g protein | 0g complex carbohydrates | 13g sugar | 0g dietary fiber | 13mg cholesterol | 20mg sodium

THICK FUDGE FROSTING

ABOUT 4 CUPS, ENOUGH TO FROST AN 8″ OR 9″ LAYER CAKE, 9″ × 13″ CAKE, OR 24 CUPCAKES

This thick chocolate frosting is poured, rather than spread, over the cake. As it cools it becomes glossy and smooth, very much like fudge.

8 tablespoons (1 stick, 113g) unsalted butter

¼ cup (21g) unsweetened cocoa

⅛ teaspoon salt

½ cup (113g) yogurt or sour cream

4 cups (1 pound, 454g) confectioners' sugar, sifted

1 teaspoon vanilla extract

In a medium saucepan, melt the butter over medium heat. When it has melted, stir in the cocoa, salt, and yogurt, then bring the mixture to a boil. Place the confectioners' sugar and vanilla in a mixing bowl, pour the hot cocoa mixture over it, and beat until smooth.

Pour the frosting slowly over the cake while warm; it will set as it cools. For a layer cake, pour ½ cup on the top of each layer and let the frosting set. If more is needed, reheat the frosting in the microwave for 20 seconds at half power and stir to dissolve any crystals; pour over the first layer of frosting.

For a 9″ × 13″ cake, leave it in its pan and pour the frosting evenly over the top. For cupcakes, dip the tops of the cupcakes into the warm frosting and let the excess drip back into the bowl. If the frosting thickens and begins to set before all the cupcakes are frosted, reheat as described above.

NUTRITION INFORMATION PER SERVING: 1½ tablespoons, 44g
178 cal | 6g fat | 1g protein | 31g complex carbohydrates | 29g sugar | 0g dietary fiber | 16mg cholesterol | 31mg sodium

BROWN SUGAR FROSTING

ABOUT 2½ CUPS, ENOUGH TO FROST A 9″ × 13″ CAKE

This frosting is akin in flavor to caramel or praline, or as we think of it, a spreadable version of brown sugar fudge. It's quite sweet, which makes it a natural pairing for fruit-forward cakes such as Apple Cake (page 290).

2¼ cups (255g) confectioners' sugar, sifted

7 tablespoons (99g) unsalted butter

⅔ cup (140g) brown sugar

¼ teaspoon salt

¼ cup (57g) milk

¾ teaspoon vanilla extract

Sift the confectioners' sugar into a bowl or onto a piece of parchment or waxed paper; set it aside.

Melt the butter in a medium saucepan over medium heat. Stir in the brown sugar and salt and cook, stirring, until the sugar starts to melt and the mixture becomes fairly smooth. While you may still notice a bit of grittiness from the sugar, you shouldn't see any melted butter pooled atop the sugar. Add the milk and bring to a boil.

Remove the syrup from the heat and pour it into a medium bowl (large enough to accommodate the confectioners' sugar). Let the syrup cool in the bowl for 10 minutes.

Pour the confectioners' sugar into the warm syrup in the bowl, then add the vanilla extract or other flavor. Whisk until everything is thoroughly combined. You need to work fast here; the frosting stiffens up quickly as it cools.

Pour the warm frosting onto your cake, spreading it over the entire surface.

NUTRITION INFORMATION PER SERVING: 2 tablespoons, 28g
114 cal | 4g fat | 0g protein | 20g complex carbohydrates | 19g sugar | 0g dietary fiber | 11mg cholesterol | 33mg sodium

CHOCOLATE GLAZE

1½ CUPS, ENOUGH TO GLAZE THE TOP OF AN 8″ OR 9″ CAKE

You can use this rich glaze alone to finish a cake, or you can pour it over a cake that's already sporting a layer of frosting, such as a peanut butter frosting or a chocolate buttercream for an extra-decadent dessert.

½ cup (113g) heavy cream

2 tablespoons (39g) corn syrup, light or dark

pinch of salt

1 heaping cup (175g) chopped semisweet or bittersweet chocolate or chocolate chips

Place all the ingredients in a small saucepan and warm over low heat, or put them in a microwave-safe bowl and microwave at low power. Heat, stirring often, until the chocolate has melted and the mixture is smooth. Cool, stirring occasionally, for 10 to 15 minutes, so that the glaze thickens slightly but is still pourable.

NUTRITION INFORMATION PER SERVING: 2 tablespoons, 33g

147 cal | 10g fat | 2g protein | 1g complex carbohydrates | 12g sugar | 0g dietary fiver | 21mg cholesterol | 47mg sodium

PEANUT BUTTER FROSTING

3 CUPS FROSTING, ENOUGH TO FROST AN 8″ OR 9″ LAYER CAKE, 9″ × 13″ CAKE, OR 24 CUPCAKES

This frosting is wonderful with chocolate cake, banana cake, a simple yellow cake, or even pound cake.

¾ cup (198g) creamy supermarket-style peanut butter

1½ teaspoons vanilla extract

4 cups (1 pound, 454g) confectioners' sugar, sifted

½ cup to 10 tablespoons (113g to 142g) milk

In a large bowl, combine the peanut butter and vanilla. Add the confectioners' sugar in three parts, alternating with the milk, stirring until you have a smooth, spreadable frosting.

NUTRITION INFORMATION PER SERVING: 3 tablespoons, 42g

160 cal | 6g fat | 3g protein | 1g complex carbohydrates | 23g sugar | 1g dietary fiber | 1mg cholesterol | 60mg sodium

CREAM CHEESE FROSTING

3 CUPS, ENOUGH TO FROST AN 8″ OR 9″ LAYER CAKE, 9″ × 13″ CAKE, OR 24 CUPCAKES

This frosting is rich but not overly sweet, and spreads beautifully. It's the perfect complement for Carrot Cake (page 291), of course, but also very nice on Apple Cake (page 290).

6 tablespoons (¾ stick, 85g) unsalted butter, at room temperature

1 cup (8 ounces, 227g) cream cheese, softened

1 teaspoon vanilla extract

4 cups (1 pound, 454g) confectioners' sugar, sifted

1 cup (113g) chopped nuts (optional)

½ cup (92g) minced crystallized ginger (optional)

2 to 4 tablespoons (28g to 57g) milk

In a medium bowl, combine the butter, cream cheese, and vanilla and beat them together until they're light and fluffy. Add the sugar gradually, beating well. Stir in the nuts and/or ginger, if using, then beat in the milk a little at a time, until the frosting is spreadable.

NUTRITION INFORMATION PER SERVING: 2 tablespoons, 40g

169 cal | 9g fat | 1g protein | 1g complex carbohydrates | 20g sugar | 0g dietary fiber | 18mg cholesterol | 32mg sodium

PASTRY CREAM

5 CUPS

This is the delicious custard filling you'll find in éclairs, napoleons, or Boston Cream Pie. The amount of sugar called for makes a pastry cream that is just barely sweet, perfect for profiteroles, as a base for the flavor combinations listed below, or for pastries that already include a sweet sauce. If you're planning to use the pastry cream for a pie or cake filling that you want a bit sweeter, increase the sugar to ¾ cup.

3 cups (681g) whole milk

½ cup (99g) sugar

¼ teaspoon salt

⅓ vanilla bean, split lengthwise, or
   2 teaspoons vanilla extract

¼ cup (28g) cornstarch

1 tablespoon (8g) unbleached all-
   purpose flour

4 large egg yolks

4 tablespoons (½ stick, 57g) butter

1 cup (227g) heavy cream, whipped to
   soft peaks

In a medium saucepan, stir together 2½ cups (568g) of the milk, the sugar, salt, and the vanilla bean. (If you're using vanilla extract, add it at the end.) Bring the mixture to a boil over medium heat.

Meanwhile, whisk the cornstarch, flour, and egg yolks with the remaining ½ cup (113g) milk.

Whisk some of the boiling milk mixture with the egg yolks. Pour the egg/milk mixture back into the remaining simmering milk. Doing this through a strainer will help prevent lumps later. Bring to a boil, stirring constantly with a whisk, until the mixture thickens; its temperature should reach 165°F. This is important: If the pastry cream doesn't reach 165°F on the stovetop, it won't set properly as it cools, and may be soft and runny. Remove from the heat and strain through a fine strainer into a bowl set in an ice bath. Stir in the butter and vanilla extract (if you're using it). If you're going to flavor the pastry cream, this is the time to do it (see options below). Rub a piece of butter over the surface of the cream, top with a piece of plastic wrap (make sure it touches the top of the pastry cream so it doesn't develop a skin), then refrigerate until cool.

To complete, fold the cooled cream into the whipped cream. Pastry cream will keep, covered in the refrigerator, for up to 5 days. After that it may start to weep.

NUTRITION INFORMATION PER SERVING: **about 6 tablespoons, 94g**
173 cal | 12g fat | 3g protein | 6g complex carbohydrates | 8g sugar | 0g dietary fiber | 106mg cholesterol | 81mg sodium

Flavoring Options

Pastry cream can be flavored in an infinite variety of ways. Here are some of our favorites:

CARAMEL: Add ¾ cup (213g) chopped caramel (21 to 23 individual unwrapped caramels) to the hot pastry cream, stirring until melted and the mixture is smooth.

CHOCOLATE: Add 1 cup (170g) chopped chocolate to the hot pastry cream, stirring until melted and the mixture is smooth.

HAZELNUT: Omit the butter and increase the sugar to ¾ cup (149g). Add ¾ cup (232g) praline paste to the hot pastry cream, stirring until well combined.

ORANGE: Increase the sugar to ¾ cup (149g). Add 1 teaspoon orange extract, ¼ teaspoon orange oil, or 3 tablespoons orange zest to the hot pastry cream.

PEANUT BUTTER: Add ¾ cup (206g) peanut butter to the hot pastry cream, stirring until melted and the mixture is smooth.

PISTACHIO: Omit the butter and increase the sugar to ¾ cup (149g). Add ¾ cup pistachio paste (232g) or blanched, puréed, shelled pistachios.

CHERRY FILLING

ABOUT 3 CUPS

This is the filling of choice for traditional Black Forest Cake, which features a combination of cherries and chocolate. Of course, no one would protest if you spooned it over pound cake either!

¼ cup (49g) sugar

2 tablespoons (14g) cornstarch

¼ cup (57g) water

¼ cup (57g) cherry brandy, white wine, or water

3 to 4 cups (439g to 452g) pitted fresh or frozen cherries (about 2 pounds unpitted)

1 cup (142g) dried sour cherries

Mix all the ingredients together in a medium saucepan, bring to a boil over medium-high heat, and cook until thickened, adding additional sugar to taste.

NUTRITION INFORMATION PER SERVING: about ¼ cup, 65g

97 cal | 0g fat | 1g protein | 18g complex carbohydrates | 4g sugar | 2g dietary fiber | 0mg cholesterol | 2mg sodium

LEMON CURD

1½ CUPS

This smooth, tangy curd is perfect when layered with fruit and cake in a trifle, or as a filling for a tart or cake. A smart way to get more juice from your lemons is to zest them first, then heat them in a microwave for 15 to 18 seconds.

4 large egg yolks

½ cup (113g) fresh lemon juice
(3 to 4 lemons)

zest of 3 lemons

⅛ teaspoon salt

1½ cups (298g) sugar

6 tablespoons (¾ stick, 85g) unsalted
butter

Stir all the ingredients together in the top of a double boiler set over medium heat. Whisk or stir constantly, being sure that nothing is sticking to the bottom. Continue to cook for 15 to 20 minutes, until the mixture starts to thicken; it should coat a spoon. The curd will thicken more as it cools. Remove it from the heat and spoon into a small bowl. Rub a piece of butter over the top, then place plastic wrap on the surface to prevent a skin from forming. Refrigerate until ready to use. The curd will keep, refrigerated, for 5 days.

NUTRITION INFORMATION PER SERVING: 2 tablespoons, 57g
203 cal | 5g fat | 1g protein | 1g complex carbohydrates | 29g sugar | 0g dietary fiber | 107mg cholesterol | 26mg sodium

VARIATIONS

LIME CURD: Substitute fresh lime juice for the lemon juice. Since limes are generally more tart than lemons, add an additional ¼ cup (50g) sugar and an additional 2 tablespoons (28g) butter to smooth the flavor.

RASPBERRY LEMON CURD: Reduce the sugar to 1 cup (199g) and substitute ½ cup (113g) raspberry-lemon juice for the lemon juice: mash 1 heaping cup (140g) raspberries with 2 tablespoons (28g) fresh lemon juice, then push through a fine sieve.

CHAPTER NINE

Pies and Tarts

———

AH, PIE! Flaky crust surrounding any manner of enticing fillings—from juicy berry to spiced apple to hearty vegetables and cheese—is one of the very nicest pleasures to be had. Add a scoop of vanilla ice cream to a fruit pie and we challenge you to come up with a more apt definition of bliss. This combination of a sweet or savory filling encased in a pastry crust has been a part of the world's culinary landscape for centuries. From the first written formula for a goat cheese and honey pie in a rye crust, published in Roman times, to the traditional meat-based pies in fourteenth-century Europe, pies have figured prominently in history. The pies baked by America's Pennsylvania Dutch heralded the shift toward sweet pies with their sweetened fruit fillings enclosed in a crisp crust. In the time since, pie has remained a steady companion of home bakers.

Though to some the phrase "easy as pie" might seem counterintuitive, it's not. Achieving a crisp and light pastry, with no soggy bottom, is an acquired skill, but a very doable task. And we believe it's one well worth learning. You can't just stir the ingredients together willy-nilly and expect to get great results. You'll need to consider the proportions of flour to fat to liquid, and practice and perfect your technique for rolling the dough. What's more, the baking time and temperature, as well as the pan you use, will help you achieve a crisp, golden crust.

A Pie Primer

Recipes for basic pie crust call for flour, fat, salt, and water; some add eggs, sugar, flavoring, vinegar, lemon juice, or buttermilk. The basic ratio (according to our grandmothers and the Culinary Institute of America) is 3:2:1—3 parts flour, 2 parts fat, and 1 part water. That ratio makes a very rich, tender crust.

Let's look at the ingredients, and how they interact in crust; this will help you decide which ingredients and method to use for the type of crust you prefer.

Flour

The best pie crust is made with a flour whose protein level is medium to low, 11% or lower. For pie-making purposes, the protein level indicates the amount of gluten, and in pie crust, the more developed the gluten, the tougher the pie crust. (You do need some gluten, in order for the crust to hold together.) Using equal parts unbleached all-purpose and pastry flours creates a crust that's easy to roll out, with enough structure to make it comfortable to move around. A crust made with only pastry flour will be very delicate and quite challenging to roll out, tending to crumble when you transfer it to the pie pan. An excellent crust can be made with only all-purpose flour, but good technique is critical so as not to over-develop the gluten. Crusts made with the all-purpose/pastry flour combination are tender but still easy to handle.

Salt

Salt plays two roles in pie crust. First, and most important, it adds flavor. Like bread made without salt, pie crust made without salt will be flat-tasting. Second, it firms up the gluten in the crust ever so slightly, making the dough easier to handle.

Because the salt-to-flour ratio in pie crust must be fairly exact for best flavor, we stick with table salt since its finer grains disperse more efficiently in the dough. Kosher or other large-flake granulations won't measure the same.

Sugar

Sugar may be added to pie crust dough for flavor and browning. The amount is usually about 1 tablespoon (12g) for 3 cups (360g) of flour. We've tested pie crusts side by side, using 1 tablespoon of sugar in one and none in the other. Truthfully, there was very little difference in browning, tenderness, crispness, or flavor. In our opinion, the amount of sugar used in most pie crust recipes is so small that it doesn't have a significant impact on texture, so use it if you like.

Buttermilk, Vinegar, or Lemon Juice

These liquids are often added to pie crusts because acids break down protein in the flour, so they'll help keep the crust tender, even if it's overworked a bit. Using a tablespoon of vinegar or lemon juice in the liquid for your dough will keep it from oxidizing and turning gray if you need to chill it in the refrigerator for up to 36 hours (any longer than that you should freeze the dough). In addition, adding dried buttermilk powder to a crust enhances its flavor.

Eggs or Egg Yolks

Whole eggs add protein, water, and fat to pie crust dough, along with color and flavor. Adding a lightly beaten egg as part of the crust's liquid will give you a sturdier crust without making it tough (this is desirable for a freestanding savory pie, for example). It will also enhance browning and texture. Adding just the yolk adds mostly fat, which will make a more golden, tender crust.

Fat

In our opinion, the fat you choose has the biggest influence on a pie crust. Fat plays two roles. The first is to coat the flour, thereby inhibiting the gluten development and creating tenderness. The water in a crust creates enough gluten to keep the crust together. The second role of fat is to create flakiness. By leaving some of the fat in larger pieces, it serves to separate the long strings of gluten. When flour and fat are formed in layers, the fat melts in the oven as the crust bakes, creating distinct layers in the cooked dough. When butter is part of the fat, the water in the solid butter turns to steam, creating even more flakiness.

Butter is a more brittle fat than lard or vegetable shortening. It's harder when cold and becomes softer and can separate when warmed to room temperature, so everything must be kept cool when working with butter. If the butter is overworked and warm, the water in it can leach out into the flour, making the crust tougher and leaving less in suspension to make steam (and flakiness) in the oven. Butter is also only about 81% fat, so you may need to use more butter and less water if substituting butter for lard or vegetable shortening in a recipe. Butter has the most pleasing flavor; the milk solids in it taste wonderful when fully baked and caramelized in pie crust.

Vegetable shortening has no water and keeps a consistent texture over a wide temperature range, making it easy to work with. It also makes a tender crust, as long as the dough isn't overworked. Using half shortening and half butter is a good place to start for beginning pie bakers; the shortening should be worked in first, to coat the flour, and the butter cut in after, left in larger, dime-size chunks.

CHILL THE DOUGH

Why do so many pie recipes tell you to chill the dough, find a cool surface on which to roll it, and use a rolling pin that's been placed in the freezer?

Because fat doesn't like heat; it melts and loses one of its main attributes, a just-right melting point in the oven. When you combine fat, flour, and a little water, the gluten in the flour is activated and strands start to form. If you don't handle the dough too much, the gluten will form shorter strands—enough to hold the crust together, but not so developed that the crust becomes hard when baked. Minute chunks of butter or fat separate these strands, preventing them from joining together. Once put into a hot oven, these strands quickly cook and retain their shape—with the fat holding them in place just until they're sturdy enough, at which time the fat melts, lending its flavor and tenderness to the dough. The result? Flaky pastry.

By the way, after you place your rolled-out crust into the pie pan, it never hurts to put it into the refrigerator or freezer while you're preparing the filling. Any fat that's beginning to get too warm and soft will firm right up again, and the gluten will have a chance to relax, which means the crust will shrink less as it cooks.

SALTED VS. UNSALTED BUTTER

All our pie recipes, as well as the other recipes in this book, assume the baker will use unsalted butter. Because salt can mask "off" flavors in butter, grocers like to fill their dairy case with salted butter, as it will seem fresh longer. If you buy unsalted butter, you'll have a better chance of getting a fresher product. In addition, we prefer to balance the salt-flour ratio in pie crust ourselves, rather than have to deal with the additional salt (¼ teaspoon salt per 113g butter) in salted butter.

We prefer, for reasons of taste and texture, to make pie crust with half butter and half vegetable shortening or lard. However, each to their own: A crust made with 100% shortening (or butter) is perfectly acceptable.

Lard was routinely used in decades past; it was an integral part of the farm economy, which used all parts of the pig. When rendered and cooled, it has large crystals that create tender, flaky crusts. Commercially available lard is usually hydrogenated, which increases shelf life but also adds trans fats. If you have access to locally produced fresh lard from a local butcher, it's wonderful to work with. We don't recommend using hydrogenated lard.

Water

Water binds the pie crust dough, activating its gluten so it holds together. In order to keep the fat as cold and solid as possible (for the best flaky crust), we recommend using ice water. Water is another element that needs to be precisely balanced in pie crust dough: too much, and you have a sticky, unrollable mess; too little, and the crust won't hold together or will crack around the edges as you roll it. Practice: Your hands are the great teachers here; the more frequently you make crust, the better you'll be at recognizing exactly what it should look and feel like before rolling.

There are a number of different types of crust within reach of the home baker. The three major types of basic pie crust—medium-flake, long-flake, and short-flake—all contain the same ingredients. The way the shortening and flour are combined gives each crust its name and characteristics. When you break a medium-flake pie crust with your fingers, it separates into flakes rather than breaking "clean." A long-flake crust breaks into larger flakes, almost shattering. A crust that breaks clean is called a short-flake crust or "short crust;" it's crisp and sandy-textured, rather than flaky. A French crust made this way is called *pâte brisée*; when it's sweetened, it becomes *pâte sablée*. We'll examine the most popular of all—medium-flake crust—and will then go on to show variations for short-flake and long-flake crusts.

BASIC PIE CRUST

ONE 9″ DOUBLE PIE CRUST

2½ cups (300g) unbleached all-
purpose flour, pastry flour, or a
combination of both

1¼ teaspoons salt

10 tablespoons (142g) unsalted butter
or vegetable shortening (113g), cold

6 to 10 tablespoons (85g to 142g) ice
water

Medium-Flake Method

MIX DRY INGREDIENTS. Whisk together the flour and salt in a bowl large enough that you'll be able to plunge both hands in to work with the dough.

CUT IN HALF OF THE FAT, COMBINING THOROUGHLY. The mixture should form very small, very even crumbs. If using a single type of fat, cut half of it into the flour. If using our recommended combination of shortening and butter, cut all the shortening into the flour and reserve the butter.

"Cutting the fat into the flour" simply means combining them. This first portion of the fat is worked into the flour to ensure tenderness. The pieces of cold butter or shortening should be combined until quite small: The mixture should be evenly crumbly, like coarse beach sand.

This can be done by plunging your hands into the bowl and working the pieces of fat with the flour, or you can use a pastry fork or pastry blender.

CUT IN REMAINING FAT. Cut or pinch the remaining fat into pats. Toss the chunks of fat into the flour mixture, mixing just enough to coat them with flour. Work in the fat by pinching it into flat shards with your fingers, or cut in lightly with a pastry cutter. Leave some larger chunks of fat intact along with the smaller ones. Combining flour with half the fat thoroughly, then combining with the remaining fat and leaving large chunks (pea-size, or even larger) will yield a medium-flake crust.

ADD WATER. Add the water, a tablespoon at a time, and toss with a fork to moisten the dough evenly. To test for the right amount of liquid, use your hands to squeeze a chunk of it together. If it sticks together easily, it's moist enough. If it falls apart, add a bit more water. When you're sprinkling water on the flour and fat mixture and tossing it around, keep grabbing small handfuls; the mixture should feel damp but not soggy. When the dough barely sticks together, add 1 more tablespoon (14g) of water. This should be just the right amount to yield a dough that's soft enough to roll nicely without cracking, but not so soft that it sticks to the counter and rolling pin.

TURN OUT DOUGH AND FOLD. Turn out the dough onto a piece of parchment. Use the paper to fold the dough in thirds like a business letter to bring it together. If necessary, use a spray bottle to spritz any dry crumbly spots with cold water and fold in thirds once again. Divide the dough in half, pat into flat disks about an inch thick, wrap both halves, and refrigerate for at least 30 minutes. This lets the flour hydrate while relaxing its gluten before rolling it out, which means easier rolling and no cracked edges.

ROLL OUT THE DOUGH. Flour your work surface—counter, tabletop, pastry board, or marble slab. Unwrap one piece of dough and put it on the floured surface. Whichever size pie you're making, you'll want to roll the crust to a diameter about 3″ to 4″ greater than the inside diameter of the pan. For example, for a 9″ pie pan, roll the crust to a 12″ to 13″ diameter. When rolling pie crust, be forceful but make it brief; the best pie crust is rolled from the center outward (to make an evenly round crust), with as few strokes as possible being used to stretch the crust to its desired size. Roll in only one direction, not back and forth. Pick up the crust with a giant or offset spatula and dust underneath it with flour from time to time, to keep it moving freely on the counter and under your rolling pin.

If the bottom crust cracks around the edges, it can be patched and will be hidden by the filling. If it's the top crust, just roll it large enough so the cracks extend to the edge, where they will disappear when you seal the top and bottom crusts.

Some recipes diverge from the typical 9″ pan to ones that are slightly larger or smaller. If you're making an 8″ pie, assume you'll have some dough left over; you can use it to decorate the top of the pie, or cut it in squares or other shapes, sprinkle it with cinnamon sugar, and bake it for 6 to 8 minutes along with the pie (watch carefully, as it'll only need a few minutes to brown). If you're making a 10″ pie, increase the flour to 3 cups (360g), salt to 1½ teaspoons fat to 14 tablespoons (198g), and water to 8 to 12 tablespoons (113g to 170g).

TRANSFER DOUGH TO PIE PAN. Next, transfer the rolled-out crust to a lightly greased pie pan. Greasing your pan will make removing the finished slices much easier, and it helps the bottom to brown and crisp. It's important to use a pie pan that conducts heat well. We prefer a dark metal pan, followed (in preference) by a ceramic or clear glass pan. We don't recommend light-colored metal pans as they don't produce as brown a crust as darker metal. The pan will also affect the baking time considerably. A dark metal pan will bake in the shortest time, followed by glass or ceramic. Shiny metal pans will take the longest (see Tools section, page 524). Hint: If using a thin, shiny, disposable pie pan, place the pie pan in a cast iron skillet (which retains heat) to be sure the pie is nicely browned on the bottom.

Using a spatula (or, if the crust isn't too thin and/or delicate, your fingers), fold the dough in half, then in half again the other way, so you've got a piece of dough that's just a quarter of what it was originally; it should be much easier to handle. Pick up the dough, place the corner in the center of the pie pan, and unfold it (see illustrations on next page). Or carefully and gently roll the crust onto your well-floured rolling pin and unroll it into your pie pan. Or use a giant spatula or small baker's peel to lift the entire crust and slide it into the pan.

COAT CRUST AND ADD FILLING. Brush the inside of the crust with lightly beaten egg white or milk. This very thin coating of protein will form a protective layer between crust and filling, helping to keep the crust from becoming soggy. Add the pie filling (or proceed to "Baking" on next page if baking an empty crust).

ROLL OUT AND ADD TOP CRUST (IF MAKING A TWO-CRUST PIE). Roll out the top crust, just as you did the bottom crust, making it about an inch less in diameter. (If you've added so much filling that it's heaped high in the pie shell, roll the top crust to the same size as the bottom crust.) Center the top crust over the filling.

Wet the edges to be sealed with a bit of milk or beaten egg white. The protein

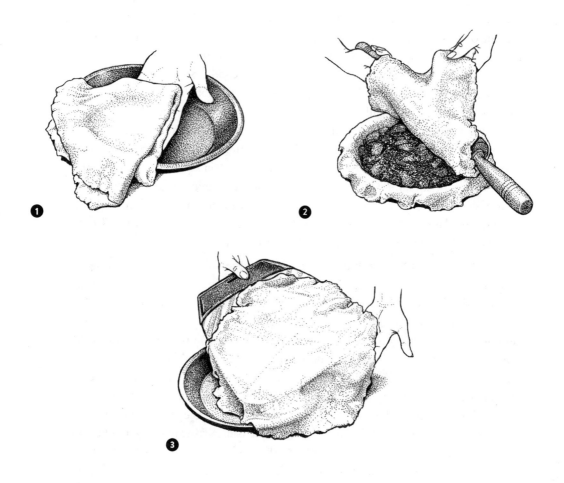

1 to 3. After rolling out, you can fold the bottom crust into quarters, roll the dough around a rolling pin, or use a giant spatula or small baker's peel to put it into your pie pan.

in either, when cooked, will bond with the starch in the flour and act as "glue" between the two crusts.

Making sure your crust is well sealed is key to avoiding the problem of having hot, bubbling fruit juice erupt from it. There are a number of decorative ways to seal a crust. If the filling is heaped high in the pan, a tall, finger-fluted seal is preferable to a thin, fork-tine seal; the taller edge gives the dough a better chance of containing the juices from the filling.

The steam that tries to force those juices out has to go somewhere, so it's important to make a few slits in the top crust of a pie. Once you've made sure there's a place for steam to escape, do your best to seal any other openings.

ADD GLAZE (OPTIONAL). You can bake a pie as is, but in most instances a wash or glaze makes it more attractive. Plain milk or cream will make a browner, slightly shiny crust. An egg beaten with a bit of water will intensify the color and create a glossy finish. Using only the white will give a clear finish; a whole egg or just the yolk will give a more golden result. In either case, a sprinkle of coarse sugar after brushing will add sparkle.

BAKING. Preheat the oven as the recipe directs. If you have one, a baking stone or steel is worth putting in the lower third of the oven before turning it on. Putting your pie pan on this heated surface transfers quick bottom heat, giving assurance against a soggy bottom crust. Some bakers swear by putting their pie plate into a cast iron pan before putting pan and plate into the oven together.

If the edges of the crust start to become too brown before the filling is done (for fruit pies, you should see bubbling all the way to the center of the pie), a pie crust shield (see below) is the easiest solution. Another option is to cover just the edges of the crust with a thin strip of aluminum foil before you put the pie in the oven. You can remove it for the last 10 minutes of baking to get more color on the edge, if needed.

When the pie is done, remove it from the oven and put it on a rack to cool.

BLIND BAKING. Some recipes call for you to blind bake a pie crust—that is, bake it without filling. Pies filled with fresh fruit, mousse, or cooked custard fillings are spooned into a fully cooked pastry shell. For some recipes (pumpkin pie) it's wise to blind bake the bottom crust partway before adding the filling and finishing it in the oven. This makes a pie with a much better chance of staying flaky and crisp.

To blind bake a pie crust, roll it out and place it in the pan. Next, "dock" it with a pastry docker or fork—prick it all over to avoid trapping steam underneath. At this point it's best to cover and refrigerate the rolled crust for 20 to 30 minutes; this will relax the gluten, firm the fat, and keep the crust from shrinking as it bakes.

To bake the chilled crust, line it with foil or parchment and weigh it down; otherwise steam released into the pan below the crust will cause it to dome like a blown-up balloon. In the past, bakers weighed down their pie crust with dry beans or uncooked rice. While these both work, they can be awkward to handle. You may also choose to use ceramic pie weights or a stainless steel pie chain; simply coil it onto the crust. The advantage of a pie chain is its ease of removal (use tongs to pick it up—it gets hot!). A creative solution instead of weights is to pour granulated sugar into the parchment-lined pie shell. It conforms faithfully to the pan's shape and does a great job of holding the crust's sides in place. The sugar will toast ever so slightly as the shell bakes in the oven, turning light golden brown and tasting wonderful. You can use the cooled sugar as you would in any other recipe after removing it from the pan.

For a fully blind-baked crust, bake it in a preheated 375°F oven for 20 to 25 minutes with the weights (use the longer time if using sugar); then remove the lining and weights and bake for an additional 15 minutes or until golden brown. For a partially baked crust—one that will finish baking with its filling—bake for 15 minutes with the weights, then remove the weights, fill, and bake as directed in the recipe.

Short-Flake Method

Whisk together the flour and salt. Using a pastry fork, pastry blender, or your fingers, cut or rub the fat you are using into the flour in one stage, until the mixture looks like bread crumbs. Add the water, a tablespoon at a time. Stir with a fork to moisten the dough evenly. To test for the right amount of moistness, use your hands to squeeze a chunk of it together. If it sticks together easily, it's moist enough. If it falls apart, add a bit more water. Turn it out onto a lightly floured surface. Divide the ball of dough in half, pat each half into a flat disk about an inch thick, wrap both halves, and refrigerate for at least 30 minutes before rolling out.

Long-Flake Method

For a tender, ultra-flaky crust, use the "long-flake" method. Whisk together all the dry ingredients, reserving a few tablespoons of the flour. Cut in half of the fat, working the mixture until it's crumbly.

Place the reserved flour on your work surface and coat the remaining fat (in a single piece) with the flour. Use a rolling pin or the heel of your hand to flatten the fat until it's about ½″ thick. Break this flour-coated fat into 1″ pieces and mix them into the dough just until they're evenly distributed; some of the pieces of flour-coated fat should break into smaller pieces.

Sprinkle the liquid over the dough while tossing with a fork. Stop mixing as soon as you can easily squeeze the dough into a ball. Visible pieces of fat should still appear in the dough. Flatten the dough into a disk and wrap it in plastic wrap or waxed paper. Refrigerate for at least 30 minutes. This resting period allows the flour to absorb the water, making the dough easier to roll out.

FREEZING FOR EXTENDED SHELF LIFE

Because freezing expands and contracts the water in a pie crust, which tends to break down its structure, crusts that freeze most successfully are made with a significant amount of fat, which remains more stable when frozen.

Pie shells can be frozen both unbaked and baked. If you freeze them unbaked, freeze them right in a pie plate. After they're solid, remove them, stack, and seal them in an airtight plastic bag.

Baked crusts can also be frozen the same way unbaked crusts are, in the pan and then removed to an airtight plastic bag. Frozen pie crusts are great to have on hand.

To freeze a whole fruit pie (don't try this with custard or cream pies—they'll become watery), prepare it up to the point of baking, but instead of putting it in the oven, wrap it well with plastic wrap. Then add a full wrapping of foil or a zippered plastic bag, just for insurance. Put the pie in the freezer, even if it's just overnight. When you're ready to bake it, don't defrost. Preheat the oven to 425°F, unwrap the pie, and pop it in the oven. Bake it at 425°F for 15 minutes, then lower the oven temperature to 350°F and bake for another 45 to 55 minutes, until the crust is brown and the filling is bubbly. Freezing the pie, even if only overnight (rather than refrigerating it) gives you much more latitude in your choice of when to bake and serve it.

Flour your work surface and roll the dough into a 12″ × 9″ (approximately) rectangle. If it isn't holding together well, use a spray bottle to lightly spritz or sprinkle any dry spots with cold water. Fold the dough into thirds (like a letter), then fold it into thirds the opposite way to form a rough square. Wrap it well and refrigerate again, for 30 minutes.

If the dough is made with all vegetable shortening, you'll be able to work with it directly from the refrigerator. A dough made with all butter will need to warm slightly (10 to 15 minutes) before rolling, as butter becomes brittle when it's refrigerated. Dough made with a combination of butter and shortening should rest for about 5 minutes at room temperature before rolling. Roll the dough to the size needed (about 13″ for a 9″ pie). Fill and bake as directed.

FOOD PROCESSOR PIE CRUST

ONE 9" DOUBLE CRUST

Pie crust is an ideal vehicle to take advantage of your food processor. Your machine, when using the pulse button, will very quickly cut in the fat or shortening with the flour. Because a food processor can heat up ingredients, it works best when you freeze the butter and/or shortening before putting them into the machine's bowl, and have an ice cube or two in the water that you'll be using. The consistency of your crust will depend on how thoroughly you mix the fat with the flour. The bigger the pieces of butter and shortening, the flakier your crust. Adding a little vinegar to the liquid in the recipe will help add to the crust's flakiness, too. It's OK if you see streaks of butter or shortening when you roll it out; they create flakiness when the crust is baking. If you process the mixture further until it looks like coarse cornmeal, you'll have a shorter flake and a smaller crumb when you cut into the crust.

8 tablespoons (1 stick, 113g) unsalted
    butter, cold

½ cup (92g) vegetable shortening

3 cups (360g) unbleached all-
    purpose flour or a combination of
    all-purpose and unbleached pastry
    flours

1 teaspoon salt

2 teaspoons vinegar

¼ to ½ cup (57g to 113g) ice water

Use a bench knife to cut a stick of butter into lengthwise strips. Flip the stick of butter on its side and repeat the process, then cut across the strips to get pea-size chunks.

Cut the stick of butter lengthwise into three slabs. Leave the slabs stacked, turn 90°, and make three lengthwise cuts to make 12 pencil-size strips.

With a bench scraper or knife, cut across the strips to make cubes of butter about ½" thick. Place the cubes in the freezer. Measure out the shortening and put it in the freezer, too. Leave the fats to firm up for at least 20 minutes while you gather the other things you need for your pie.

Place flour and salt in the bowl of your food processor fitted with the chopping blade. Turn on the machine for 5 seconds to mix the dry ingredients. Add the chilled fats and pulse for two seconds at a time, four times. Sprinkle the vinegar and ¼ cup (56g) of water over the dough. Pulse once more for only a second.

Take the mixture out of the machine and transfer to a mixing bowl or your work surface. The dough will still look crumbly and the butter should still be visible in rounded chunks. When you gather the dough in your hands, you will find that it is almost moist enough to hold together. Sprinkle it with 1 more tablespoon (14g) of water if necessary, mixing the dough with a fork, until the dough can be gathered together into a ball. Don't work or knead the dough any more than is necessary, or it will become tough. Divide the dough into two pieces and form each of them into a disk. Wrap each disk in plastic wrap and refrigerate for at least 30 minutes before rolling out.

NUTRITION INFORMATION PER SERVING: 1 unfilled double-crust slice, 83g

368 cal | 24g fat | 5g protein | 32g complex carbohydrates | 0g sugar | 1g dietary fiber | 83mg cholesterol | 268mg sodium

NO-ROLL PIE CRUST

ONE 9″ SINGLE CRUST

For simplicity, you can't beat this no-roll crust, which is made with vegetable oil. Crisp and tasty, it yields a nicely flaky crust with wonderful flavor. If you're intimidated by a rolling pin, this is the crust for you.

2 cups (240g) unbleached all-purpose flour

heaping ½ teaspoon salt

1 teaspoon sugar

⅜ teaspoon baking powder

7 tablespoons (87g) oil (canola, vegetable, olive, or peanut)

¼ cup (57g) water, cold

Whisk together the flour, salt, sugar, and baking powder. Whisk together the oil and water, then pour over the dry ingredients. Stir with a fork until the dough is evenly moistened.

Pat the dough across the bottom of the pie pan and up the sides. A flat-bottomed measuring cup or glass helps smooth the bottom. Crimp the edge or flatten with the tines of a fork.

NUTRITION INFORMATION PER SERVING: 1 unfilled slice, 34g

150 cal | 8g fat | 2g protein | 16g complex carbohydrates | 0g sugar | 1g dietary fiber | 0mg cholesterol | 100mg sodium

GLUTEN-FREE PIE CRUST

ONE 9″ SINGLE CRUST

We're particularly proud of the flaky texture of this crust, which can be difficult to achieve with gluten-free ingredients. Thorough baking and a golden brown color will give this crust a wonderful toasty flavor. The Instant ClearJel used here is optional; it's not packaged in a gluten-free facility, and thus isn't suitable for celiacs or for those with a strong allergy to gluten. Leave it out if you need.

1¼ cups (195g) gluten-free all-purpose flour

1 tablespoon (12g) sugar

2 teaspoons Instant ClearJel (optional)

½ teaspoon xanthan gum

½ teaspoon salt

6 tablespoons (¾ stick, 85g) unsalted butter, cold

1 large egg

2 teaspoons lemon juice or vinegar

Lightly grease a 9″ pie pan.

Whisk together the flour or flour blend, sugar, Instant ClearJel (if using), xanthan gum, and salt.

Cut the cold butter into pats, then work the pats into the flour mixture until it's crumbly, with some larger, pea-size chunks of butter remaining.

Whisk the egg and vinegar or lemon juice together until very foamy. Mix into the dry ingredients. Stir until the mixture holds together, adding 1 to 3 additional tablespoons (14g to 42g) cold water if necessary.

Shape into a ball and chill for an hour, or up to overnight.

Allow the dough to rest at room temperature for 10 to 15 minutes before rolling.

Roll out on a piece of plastic wrap, on a silicone rolling mat, or in a pie bag that's been heavily sprinkled with gluten-free flour or flour blend. Invert the crust into the prepared pie pan.

Fill and bake as your pie recipe directs.

NUTRITION INFORMATION PER SERVING: 1 unfilled slice, 43g
173 cal | 9g fat | 1g protein | 18g complex carbohydrates | 2g sugar | 0g dietary fiber | 49mg cholesterol | 156mg sodium

PÂTE SUCRÉE

Pâte sucrée (in French), *pasta frolla* (in Italian), and sweetened, enriched short-flake crust are all the same. Richer tasting, and sandy and crumbly rather than flaky, they're often used for fruit tarts but can be used for any sweet pastry. Egg, vanilla, butter (rather than shortening), and sugar distinguish this crust from its plainer medium- and short-flake cousins. This sweetened pastry falls midway between a classic pie crust and a cookie.

1¼ cups (133g) pastry or unbleached all-purpose flour

1 teaspoon nonfat dry milk (optional, but helpful for browning and tenderness)

¼ cup (50g) sugar

¼ teaspoon salt

8 tablespoons (1 stick, 113g) unsalted butter, cold

1 large egg yolk

1 teaspoon vanilla extract

1 tablespoon (14g) water

In a medium bowl, whisk together the dry ingredients, then cut in the cold butter. Whisk together the egg yolk, vanilla, and water and stir into the dry mixture; the dough should be crumbly but hold together when squeezed. Roll out the dough, or press it into the bottom and up the sides of a 9″ square or 10″ round tart pan (preferably with a removable bottom). Prick it all over with a fork and refrigerate for 30 minutes or longer.

Preheat the oven to 375°F.

To prepare a blind-baked, ready-to-fill crust, weigh down the crust with pie weights, a nesting pie pan, or line with parchment and fill with rice or dried beans. Bake for 10 to 12 minutes, until the crust is set. Remove weights, extra pan, or parchment and return to the oven to bake for another 6 to 8 minutes, until golden brown. Remove it from the oven and cool before filling.

NUTRITION INFORMATION PER SERVING: 1 unfilled slice, 44g

202 cal | 13g fat | 2g protein | 13g complex carbohydrates | 3g sugar | 1g dietary fiber | 60mg cholesterol | 69mg sodium

CITRUS-SCENTED TART DOUGH

THREE 8″ OR 9″ TARTS

This tart dough handles and rolls beautifully, and once it's baked, is strong enough to hold itself and whatever you fill it with without the aid of a pan. But the most amazing thing about this dough is the flavor: the citrus zest adds a brightness to any tart you make with it without overwhelming the filling. Since it makes a triple batch, we recommend freezing whatever you don't use right away; well-wrapped dough will keep for 3 to 4 months. The possibilities for fillings are endless; consider filling it, after blind baking, with a simple pastry cream or lemon curd topped with fresh berries. Another delicious idea is baking the tart shell, spreading a thin layer of chocolate ganache on the bottom, and then filling it with a raspberry mousse before chilling and serving.

1 cup (198g) sugar

zest of 1 lemon

zest of 1 orange

5 cups (530g) unbleached pastry flour
    or 4¾ cups (570g) unbleached all-
    purpose flour

1 teaspoon salt

24 tablespoons (3 sticks, 340g)
    unsalted butter, slightly softened

1 large egg

2 large egg yolks

1 to 2 tablespoons (14g to 28g) water

In a large bowl, combine the sugar and citrus zest, and stir to combine.

Add the flour and salt and whisk until well combined.

Cut the butter into small chunks and cut these into the dry ingredients; mix until the dough has a texture similar to rolled oats.

Add the egg and egg yolks, mix for another 2 minutes, then add the water, and mix 2 minutes more.

Take the dough out of the bowl and use the heel of your hand to smear the dough on the surface until it comes together in small pieces. Press the pieces together.

If necessary, sprinkle it with more water or flour to get a smooth consistency.

Divide the dough into three pieces, forming each into a 4″ disk. Wrap the disks and refrigerate them for at least an hour before rolling.

Take one piece of dough out of the fridge, allow it to soften for about 5 to 10 minutes, until it's pliable, and roll it out to fit a 9″ square (or 10″ round) tart tin, preferably one with a removable bottom. If you don't have a tart tin, use a 9″ pie pan.

Prick the dough all over with a fork; fill it with pie weights or a pie chain; or line it with waxed paper, and fill it about half full with dried rice or beans. Chill the dough again before baking, if possible.

Preheat the oven to 375°F.

Bake the tart shell until the edges are golden, about 14 minutes. Remove the weights and return to the oven.

Bake for 5 to 7 minutes, or until the bottom of the dough is set through and a light golden brown.

NUTRITION INFORMATION PER SERVING: 1 unfilled slice, 42g

186 cal | 11g fat | 3g protein | 19g complex carbohydrates | 2g sugar | 1g dietary fiber | 50mg cholesterol | 54mg sodium

Cookie Crumb Crusts

The easiest crusts of all to prepare are cookie crumb crusts, which are exactly what they sound like: crusts prepared from a mixture of crushed cookies, sugar, and butter. The crust is pressed into the pan rather than rolled out. Just about any crisp (as opposed to chewy or soft) cookie is a candidate for crushing and making into pie crust; we've given instructions for some of our favorites here.

GRAHAM CRACKER CRUST

ONE 9″ SINGLE CRUST

You can substitute chocolate cookies, vanilla wafers, or gingersnaps here, or peruse the cookie aisle and come up with your own crumb crust. Just make sure the cookies are crisp, not moist or chewy. Try a combination of gingersnaps and vanilla wafers, or gingersnaps and chocolate cookies. These crumb crusts are the perfect foundation for creamy fillings: Key lime pie, chocolate cream pie, and cheesecakes all combine happily with cookie crumb crusts.

1¾ cups (about 147g) graham cracker crumbs

¼ cup (28g) confectioners' sugar

6 tablespoons (¾ stick, 76g) unsalted butter, melted

Preheat the oven to 375°F.

In a medium bowl, combine the crumbs, sugar, and butter. Press the mixture into the bottom and partway up the sides of a 9″ springform pan, 9″ cheesecake pan, or 9″ deep-dish pie pan. If you're using a 9″ × 1½″ pan, you'll have ¼ to ½ cup extra crumbs. This can become a garnish for the pie, if you like.

Use a straight-sided measuring cup to press the crumbs into place and smooth out the bottom and sides of your crust.

To blind bake the crust (cookie crumb crusts are nearly always blind baked; no need to weigh it down), bake for 15 minutes, just until set and you smell the cookies toasting. Remove the crust from the oven, cool on a rack, and add the filling of your choice.

VARIATIONS

CHOCOLATE COOKIE CRUST: Replace the graham crackers with 2 cups of chocolate cookie crumbs; 40 chocolate wafer cookies (one 9-ounce package) will crush down to 2 cups of crumbs.

VANILLA WAFER CRUST: Replace the graham crackers with 2 cups of vanilla wafer cookie crumbs. About 71 small cookies (245g) will crush down to 2 cups of crumbs.

GINGERSNAP CRUST: Replace the graham crackers with 2 cups of crushed gingersnaps. About 43 gingersnaps (301g) will crush down to 2 cups of crumbs.

Fruit Pie Fillings

Certainly the largest, most varied, and one of the oldest pie categories is the fruit pie. There are many ways to prepare a fruit pie. The most common is to cut fruit into bite-size pieces (coring and/or peeling it first, if necessary); mix it with sugar and a thickener (to thicken the juices exuded as it bakes); spoon it into a prepared pie crust; top with another crust or with streusel and bake until the crust is golden and the fruit bubbly. Another way, and one we particularly like for berries, is to prebake the crust, sweeten and cook half the berries, then mix the cooked berries with uncooked fresh berries, and spoon the resultant filling into the crust. Top with whipped cream and you've got a summertime treat folks will swoon over. A third type of fruit pie, one made less frequently, involves sweetening the fruit, then cooking it on top of the stove—with or without any thickener—until it is about three-quarters of the way to the consistency you like. Spoon the cooked fruit into an unbaked crust, top with a second crust, and bake. Try this method if you consistently have problems with runny, watery fruit in your pies.

THICKENERS FOR PIES

There's a whole range of ingredients that will help you thicken the delicious fruit juices in your pie, so you can slice your creation. Each of them behaves a little differently and has a different degree of holding power, or gel strength. The simplest way to distribute the thickener for a fruit pie evenly throughout the filling is to combine it with the sugar and spices used to flavor the pie.

All-purpose flour has the lowest gel strength, and it will give an opaque, cloudy appearance to the fruit.

Cornstarch has the most holding power for its weight, but gives a cloudy, semitransparent look to the filling. Some people can detect its taste, as well.

Modified food starch (Instant ClearJel) has plenty of thickening power and will keep fillings thick through a greater range of temperatures. It will thicken a filling's liquid at room temperature, without cooking (this is why mixing it with sugar in advance is very important); it will also keep a filling thick through freezing temperatures and back. It gives an opaque, semitranslucent look to liquids.

Pie Filling Enhancer is a combination of modified food starch, superfine sugar, and ascorbic acid; it will thicken fruit pie fillings the same way Instant ClearJel does. Its advantage is the added ascorbic acid (a flavor enhancer) and superfine sugar, which prevents the food starch from clumping.

Arrowroot, tapioca flour, and potato starch will give you a clear, translucent filling. Potato starch has the most holding power, followed by arrowroot, with tapioca flour third.

Quick-cooking tapioca holds better than tapioca flour by volume, but works best if combined with the filling and given time to soften and absorb its juices (15 to 30 minutes) before baking. It will give a clear filling, but also a stippled and slightly sticky texture.

FRUIT	THICKENER	HOW MUCH TO USE PER CUP OF FRUIT
Apples Need the least amount of thickener, since they are less watery. They are also high in pectin, which helps them set up as filling.	All-purpose flour	1¾ teaspoons
	Instant ClearJel, arrowroot, or quick-cooking tapioca	½ teaspoon
	Cornstarch	½ teaspoon
Reduce sugar by ¾ teaspoon per cup	Pie Filling Enhancer	1½ teaspoons
	Tapioca flour	1 teaspoon
Blackberries and Raspberries Have a lot of liquid, and release even more if they've been frozen, so need more thickener.	All-purpose flour	1 tablespoon plus 1 teaspoon
	Instant ClearJel or arrowroot	2¾ teaspoons

(continued)

FRUIT	THICKENER	HOW MUCH TO USE PER CUP OF FRUIT
	Cornstarch or quick-cooking tapioca	1 tablespoon
Reduce sugar by 2½ teaspoons per cup	Pie Filling Enhancer	2 tablespoons
	Tapioca flour	1½ tablespoons
Blueberries Have a lot of pectin, so will need a little less thickener than other berries, especially when cooked with lemon juice and sugar.	All-purpose flour	1 tablespoon
	Instant ClearJel or arrowroot	2 teaspoons
	Cornstarch	2½ teaspoons
	Quick-cooking tapioca	1½ teaspoons
Reduce sugar by 2 teaspoons per cup	Pie Filling Enhancer	1 tablespoon plus 1 teaspoon
Cherries Fresh cherries will need slightly less thickener than canned or frozen.	All-purpose flour	1 tablespoon
	Instant ClearJel or arrowroot	2½ teaspoons
	Cornstarch	2 teaspoons
	Quick-cooking tapioca	1¼ teaspoons
Reduce sugar by 2 teaspoons per cup	Pie Filling Enhancer	1 tablespoon plus ½ teaspoon
	Tapioca flour	1½ tablespoons
Peaches, Stone Fruits Don't have quite as much pectin as apples; they're also juicier, so require more thickener.	All-purpose flour	2½ teaspoons
	Instant ClearJel or arrowroot	2½ teaspoons
	Cornstarch	2 teaspoons
	Quick-cooking tapioca	1½ teaspoons
Reduce sugar by 2½ teaspoons per cup	Pie Filling Enhancer	2½ teaspoons
	Tapioca flour	1½ tablespoons
Strawberry-Rhubarb The juiciest fruit combination with the least amount of pectin; requires the most thickener.	All-purpose flour	1 tablespoon plus 1½ teaspoons
	Instant ClearJel or arrowroot	1 tablespoon
	Cornstarch	1 tablespoon plus ¼ teaspoon
Reduce sugar by 1 tablespoon per cup	Pie Filling Enhancer	2 tablespoons
	Quick-cooking tapioca	2½ teaspoons
	Tapioca flour	1½ tablespoons

TOP CRUST TIPS

Just as your pie's bottom crust may be short- or long-flake, chocolate or ginger, sweet or savory, the top crust may also change its character to match the filling (or your own special taste). The simplest and most common top crust for a double-crust pie is simply a replication of the bottom crust; make double pie crust recipe and divide it in half—making one half (the bottom) just slightly larger than the other (the top). The top crust is rolled out, laid atop the filling, and sealed to the bottom crust.

Before you put the pie in the oven, cut several slits through it to allow steam to escape. This can be done as artfully as you want. Another way to be artful with your top crust is to use some of the pastry scraps to decorate it. Cut them into leaves, flowers, or something that's symbolic of what's in the pie, or the occasion the pie is for. Stick these on with a bit of water or egg beaten with a bit of water. If you paint them with a bit of the egg wash or a little milk or cream, they'll brown nicely and be more visible. Finally, the top crust of a fruit pie can be woven or cut into a lattice, an old-fashioned attractive treatment, particularly for pies with bright filling such as cherry or raspberry.

If you're making a single-crust pie, one that has only a bottom crust, make a tall fluted edge for cream or custard pies where the liquid comes right up to the rim of the pan. Clearly, it's easier to move this type of pie from counter to oven rack if there's a nice, tall dam containing the filling. By the way, if you really have trouble moving custard pies (pumpkin, etc.) into the oven, try this: Place the pie pan and empty crust on the pulled-out rack of the preheated oven, fill it, gently slide the oven rack into the oven, and shut the door.

A single-crust fruit pie is often topped with streusel (which can add "crumb," "streusel," or "Dutch" to the pie's name). The same streusel that tops fruit crisps or crumbles—with oats or without—is appropriate for fruit pies.

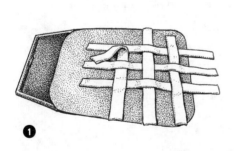 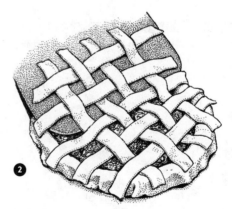

1 to 2. Cut strips of dough and weave together on a giant spatula or piece of parchment. Use the spatula or parchment to transfer the lattice to the top of the pie.

THE VERY FRESHEST FRUIT PIE

ONE 9″ PIE

Here's a very simple formula for fresh fruit pie that you'll find yourself making again and again. We first learned this method in East Machias, Maine, where this type of fresh blueberry pie appears each August. The genius of this pie lies in the method of keeping half of the fruit uncooked, which preserves the fresh fruit flavor, letting its ripeness shine unlike most styles of fruit pie.

4 cups (or a bit more; 680g) fresh whole berries, or other fruit, cut into pieces

⅔ to 1½ cups (131g to 299g) sugar, to taste

¼ cup (28g) cornstarch

1 cup (227g) water

1 tablespoon (14g) lemon juice

2 tablespoons (28g) butter

one 9″ single pie crust (see pages 358–369), blind baked

In a food processor or by hand, coarsely chop 1½ cups (168g) of the fruit. Put the sugar (starting with the lesser amount), cornstarch, and water in a saucepan and mix until smooth. Add the 1½ cups (168g) coarsely chopped fruit and cook over medium heat, stirring occasionally, until mixture is thick and semitransparent, 7 to 10 minutes. Stir in the lemon juice.

Add the butter and remaining 2½ cups (280g) fruit. Stir well and taste; add more sugar, if necessary, until it tastes good to you. Pour into the baked pie shell and chill until firm. Serve with whipped cream (we like it lightly sweetened and flavored with vanilla), if desired.

NUTRITION INFORMATION PER SERVING: 1 slice with blueberries, 167g
290 cal | 7g fat | 2g protein | 32g complex carbohydrates | 24g sugar | 5g dietary fiber | cholesterol varies | 217mg sodium

APPLE PIE

ONE 9˝ PIE

A slice of warm apple pie is the perfect end to any meal, from lunch to dinner (and we wouldn't say no to a cold slice for breakfast either). We've made many apple pies over the years, and this is our favorite classic version, with a comforting and familiar combination of spices, a flaky crust, and just the right amount of sweetness. One thing we do consistently endorse is using more than one kind of apple in the filling. This gives the filling a nice balance of texture and tartness.

8 cups (904g) peeled, sliced apple (from about 3¼ pounds whole apples)

2 tablespoons (28g) lemon juice

¾ cup (149g) sugar

2 tablespoons (15g) unbleached all-purpose flour

2 tablespoons (14g) cornstarch or Instant ClearJel

¼ teaspoon salt

1 teaspoon cinnamon

¼ teaspoon nutmeg

¼ teaspoon allspice

¼ cup (85g) boiled cider or undiluted apple juice concentrate

2 teaspoons vanilla extract (optional)

one 9˝ double pie crust (see pages 358–369)

2 tablespoons (28g) butter, diced in small pieces

Preheat the oven to 425°F. Lightly grease a 9˝ pie pan that's at least 2˝ deep. This will make serving the pie easier after it's baked.

TO MAKE THE FILLING: Combine the sliced apples and lemon juice in a large mixing bowl.

In a small bowl, whisk together the sugar, flour, cornstarch, salt, and spices. Sprinkle the mixture over the apples and stir to coat them. Stir in the boiled cider or apple juice concentrate and the vanilla (if using).

TO ASSEMBLE THE PIE: Take your pie crust dough out of the refrigerator and divide it into two pieces—one slightly larger than the other—if you haven't already. Roll the larger piece of pastry into a 13˝ circle. Transfer it to the prepared pan and trim the edges so they overlap the rim of the pan by an inch all the way around.

Spoon the apple filling into the pan. Dot the top with the diced butter.

Roll out the remaining pastry to an 11˝ circle. Carefully place the pastry over the apples. Bring the overhanging bottom crust up and over the top crust, pinching to seal the two and making a decorative crimp. Prick the crust all over with a fork to allow steam to escape. Or cut decorative vent holes, if desired. Alternatively, you can weave a lattice.

For extra crunch and shine, brush the top crust with milk (or an egg white beaten with 1 tablespoon [14g] of water), and sprinkle with coarse sugar. Place the pie in the refrigerator for 10 minutes to firm up the crust while the oven finishes heating.

Place the pie on a parchment-lined baking sheet. Bake the pie for 20 minutes, then reduce the oven temperature to 375°F and bake for 40 minutes more, until you see the filling bubbling inside the pie (and perhaps dripping onto the parchment). Check the pie after 30 minutes of baking time and cover the edges with foil or a pie shield to keep them from browning too quickly, if necessary.

When the pie is done—you should see the filling bubbling vigorously, either around the edges, or via any decorative vents—remove it from the oven.

Cool the pie completely before slicing—really. Cutting any fruit pie that's still warm is a messy business. The filling continues to thicken as the pie cools, and if you cut it too soon it will run out all over the place. It's better to bake the pie in advance, cool it completely, then warm each slice as needed after it's been cut.

VARIATION

CHEDDAR APPLE PIE: Swap ½ cup of the fat in your crust dough for ½ cup (57g) grated cheddar cheese.

NUTRITION INFORMATION PER SERVING: 1 slice, 205g

420 cal | 18g fat | 4g protein | 32g complex carbohydrates | 31g sugar | 4g dietary fiber | 25mg cholesterol | 270mg sodium

OLD-FASHIONED APPLE SLAB PIE

1 PIE

A flaky, tender crust encases a cinnamon-scented apple filling . . . that's a pie, right? In a manner of speaking! Here, we use all the components of a traditional round pie but we bake them in a rectangular pan. The result is a shallow pie, easy to slice into squares and simple to transport, too. We love it for bigger gatherings or parties, as it can yield a lot of small servings.

CRUST

2½ cups (300g) unbleached all-purpose flour

1 teaspoon salt

1 teaspoon baking powder

2 tablespoons (14g) confectioners' sugar

2 tablespoons (25g) buttermilk powder

¼ cup (25g) vegetable shortening

10 tablespoons (142g) unsalted butter, cold

1 teaspoon cider or white vinegar

6 to 10 tablespoons (85g to 142g) ice water

FILLING

1 cup (200g) panko bread crumbs or other coarse dry bread crumbs or 1 cup (25g) coarsely crushed cornflakes

8 cups (904g) peeled, cored, and sliced Granny Smith or other tart, firm apples—about 3¼ pounds (8 to 10 medium) whole apples

⅔ cup (131g) cinnamon sugar

TOPPING (OPTIONAL)

milk or cream

coarse white sugar

GLAZE (OPTIONAL)

1½ cups (170g) confectioners' sugar

⅓ cup (113g) boiled cider

small pinch of salt

½ teaspoon cinnamon

1 teaspoon milk or cream, if necessary to thin the glaze

Whisk together the flour, salt, baking powder, confectioners' sugar, and buttermilk powder.

Add the shortening, working it in until the mixture is evenly crumbly.

Cut the butter into small (about ½") cubes. Add the butter to the flour mixture, and work it in roughly with your fingers, a pastry cutter, or a mixer. Don't be too thorough; the mixture should be very uneven, with big chunks of butter in among the smaller ones.

Add the vinegar and 4 tablespoons (57g) water and toss to combine. Toss with enough additional water to make a chunky, fairly cohesive mixture. It should hold together when you gather it up and squeeze it in your hand.

Divide the dough into two pieces; one should represent about 40% of the dough, the other, about 60%. If you have a scale, this is easy; the smaller piece of dough should weigh about 245g, the larger piece, about 371g (if you've used about 7 to 8 tablespoons [99g to 113g] of water in the dough). If you don't have a scale and/or aren't good at math, eyeball it: The bottom crust needs to be larger than the top crust.

Shape each piece of crust into a rectangle; you're going to be rolling them into rectangles, so you might as well give yourself a head start. Cover with plastic wrap, and refrigerate for 30 to 60 minutes, until thoroughly chilled.

Take the larger piece of pastry out of the fridge and put it on a floured work surface. Roll it into an 11″ × 15″ rectangle. Don't worry about the ragged edges; they'll disappear under the top crust.

Place the crust in an ungreased 9″ × 13″ cake pan. Patch up any holes by pushing the pastry together with your fingers, or adding a pinch from the excess on the sides. Push the pastry up the sides of the pan a bit to make a shallow pastry container for the apples.

Put the crust in the fridge while you get the apples ready. Start preheating your oven to 350°F.

Take both crusts out of the fridge and spread the bread crumbs or crushed cornflakes evenly over the prepared bottom crust.

Spread the sliced apples atop the crumbs.

Sprinkle the cinnamon sugar over the apples.

Roll the remaining piece of pastry into a 9″ × 13″ rectangle. Again, don't worry too much about ragged edges.

Lay the top crust over the apples. Yes, apples will poke through. Seal the edges of the two crusts as well as you can. There'll be places where they don't quite meet. That's OK. If the whole thing has become warm and sticky and hard to work with, pop it in the fridge for 15 minutes to firm it up.

Just before baking, slash the crust 6 to 8 times to allow steam to escape. If desired, brush the crust with milk or cream, and sprinkle with coarse sugar.

Bake the slab for an hour; it'll be golden brown, and the filling should be bubbling. Remove it from the oven, and allow it to cool a bit before serving. If you choose to add the glaze, let it cool completely.

TO MAKE THE GLAZE (IF USING): Combine the confectioners' sugar, boiled cider, cinnamon, salt, and enough milk or cream (if necessary) to make the mixture thin enough to drizzle. Don't have boiled cider? Use plain milk or cream, maple syrup, honey, or thawed apple juice concentrate. Start with ¼ cup of any of these; if you've made this kind of icing before, you know it's easier to add more liquid than to try to take it away. Add enough liquid to make the glaze pourable.

Drizzle the glaze atop the slab.

NUTRITION INFORMATION PER SERVING: 1 square, 147g
320 cal | 14g fat | 4g protein | 26g complex carbohydrates | 20g sugar | 3g dietary fiber | 25mg cholesterol | 260mg sodium

MR. WASHINGTON'S CHERRY PIE

ONE 9″ PIE

In honor of George, of course. The sour cherries are important—not just any canned cherry will do. When you see them at the grocery store, stock up. If you can't find them, frozen tart cherries (thawed and drained) are a good alternative.

one 9″ double pie crust (see pages 358–369)

5 to 6 cups (three 14½ -ounce cans) sour cherries, packed in water

¾ cup (147g) sugar

¾ teaspoon cinnamon

¼ cup (42g) quick-cooking tapioca

1 teaspoon almond extract

½ teaspoon salt

2 tablespoons (28g) butter (optional)

Line a 9″ pie pan with one half of the rolled-out pie dough. Drain the cherries, reserving ⅔ cup (151g) of the water from one of the cans. Place the cherries and reserved liquid in a large mixing bowl. Combine the sugar, cinnamon, and tapioca. Stir into the cherries until evenly combined. Stir in the almond extract and salt. Let the filling sit for 20 minutes before filling the pie shell.

Preheat the oven to 425°F.

Spoon the filling into the pastry-lined pan and dot with butter, if using. Roll out the second crust and place on top of the filling. Cut a design (two cherries! a hatchet!) into the top to vent steam, and seal the top and bottom crust together, fluting with your fingers or a fork.

Place the pie on a foil-lined baking sheet and bake for 15 minutes. Reduce the heat to 350°F and bake for an additional 35 to 50 minutes, until the crust is golden brown and the fruit is bubbling. Take out of the oven and cool on a rack before slicing, so the filling can set up.

NUTRITION INFORMATION PER SERVING: 1 slice, 236g

438 cal | 9g fat | 5g protein | 40g complex carbohydrates | 16g sugar | 2g dietary fiber | 29mg cholesterol | 367 mg sodium

STRAWBERRY RHUBARB PIE

ONE 9″ PIE

Strawberries and rhubarb are a match made in heaven! This pie has wonderful flavor with the assertive tang from the rhubarb perfectly balanced by sweet, ripe strawberries. Bright and colorful, this pie is the essence of summer.

one 9″ double pie crust (see pages 358–369)

1¼ cups (248g) granulated sugar

5 tablespoons (53g) Instant ClearJel or 7½ tablespoons (57g) unbleached all-purpose flour

¼ teaspoon salt

3½ to 4 cups (420g to 480g) lightly packed diced rhubarb, fresh or frozen

3 cups (501g) hulled, quartered strawberries, fresh or frozen

1 tablespoon (14g) butter

coarse white sugar, for sprinkling

Line a 9″ pie pan (or two 6″ pie pans) with half the crust. Refrigerate while you make the filling, for at least 30 minutes.

Whisk together the sugar, Instant ClearJel or flour, and salt.

Toss the rhubarb and strawberries with the sugar mixture. Spoon the fruit into the pan(s), filling them about three-quarters full and mounding the filling a bit in the center.

Place dabs of the butter atop the filling. Return the pie to the refrigerator.

Preheat the oven to 425°F.

Roll out the remaining crust and cut it into star shapes, or any other shape you like.

Place the pastry shapes atop the filling. Brush with water and sprinkle with coarse sugar.

Bake the pie(s) for 30 minutes (for the 9″ pie), or 20 minutes (for the 6″ pies), then reduce the oven heat to 375°F and bake for an additional 30 to 40 minutes (9″ pie), or 20 to 25 minutes (6″ pies), until the filling is bubbling and the crust nicely browned.

Remove the pie(s) from the oven and let cool for an hour or so before serving.

The pie may be served warm, but it'll be a bit messy; it sets as it cools.

NUTRITION INFORMATION PER SERVING: 1 slice, 241g

567 cal | 26g fat | 7g protein | 79g complex carbohydrates | 35g sugar | 4g dietary fiber | 34mg cholesterol | 377mg sodium

GINGERED PLUM STREUSEL PIE

ONE 9″ PIE

While this is a fruit pie, the addition of ginger elevates it beyond an ordinary plum pie, giving it a kick of spice that will have people asking for the recipe over and over again.

FILLING

4 cups (680g) chopped plums

½ cup (107g) brown sugar, packed

1 tablespoon (11g) diced crystallized ginger

2 tablespoons (21g) quick-cooking tapioca

½ teaspoon cinnamon

½ teaspoon ginger

½ teaspoon lemon extract

TOPPING

¾ cup (90g) unbleached all-purpose flour

¾ cup (149g) granulated sugar

¼ teaspoon ginger

6 tablespoons (¾ stick, 85g) unsalted butter

one 9″ single pie crust (see pages 358–369)

1 large egg white, beaten

Preheat the oven to 375°F.

TO MAKE THE FILLING: Combine the plums, brown sugar, crystallized ginger, tapioca, cinnamon, ginger, and lemon extract.

Let the mixture sit for 15 minutes at room temperature.

TO MAKE THE TOPPING: Combine the flour, sugar, and ginger. Cut in the butter until the mixture resembles coarse crumbs. Set aside.

TO ASSEMBLE AND BAKE THE PIE: Roll out the pie dough and press it gently into a 9″ pie plate, crimping and trimming the edges as needed. Brush the inside of the unbaked pie crust lightly with the beaten egg white.

Spoon the filling into the crust.

Top the pie with the streusel topping.

Bake the pie for 50 minutes, or until the fruit is bubbling and the topping is golden brown.

Serve the pie warm or at room temperature, topped with whipped cream or ice cream (ginger is superb), if desired.

NUTRITION INFORMATION PER SERVING: 1 slice, 171g

421 cal | 17g fat | 5g protein | 67g complex carbohydrates | 36g sugar | 2g dietary fiber | 27mg cholesterol | 188mg sodium

BLUSHING PEACH PIE

ONE 9″ PIE

Ever since Auguste Escoffier paired peaches and raspberries in honor of Nellie Melba, this flavor combination has been bringing down the house. You can use prepared raspberry syrup, or make your own by simmering 1 cup (120g) raspberries, fresh or frozen, with ¾ cup (149g) of sugar until the sugar is dissolved, then straining out the fruit.

6 cups peeled, sliced peaches (12 to 14 peaches, 4 to 5 pounds, 1.8 to 2.3kg), or 2 one-pound (907g) bags of individually quick frozen peach slices, thawed

½ cup (113g) raspberry syrup

¼ cup (28g) tapioca flour or cornstarch (28g)

1 teaspoon lemon juice

¾ to 1 cup (149g to 198g) granulated sugar, to taste

¼ teaspoon salt

¼ teaspoon nutmeg

one 9″ double pie crust (see pages 358–369)

2 tablespoons (25g) coarse white sugar

Preheat the oven to 425°F.

In a large bowl, combine the peaches, raspberry syrup, tapioca flour, lemon juice, sugar, salt, and nutmeg.

Roll out half the pastry to a 13″ circle and fit it into a 9″ pie pan. Spoon the filling into the shell. Top with the other piece of rolled-out crust (make a lattice top, page 373, if desired) and sprinkle with coarse sugar. If not using a lattice top, cut several vents in the top crust.

Bake the pie for 15 minutes. Reduce the oven heat to 350°F and bake for an additional 35 to 50 minutes, until the crust is golden and the juices are bubbling. Remove the pie from the oven and cool it on a rack.

NUTRITION INFORMATION PER SERVING: 1 slice, 204g

368 cal | 13g fat | 4g protein | 38g complex carbohydrates | 23g sugar | 4g dietary fiber | 16mg cholesterol | 268mg sodium

BUMBLEBERRY PIE

ONE 9″ PIE

There you are, in high summer, the raspberries are at the end of their season and the blackberries are charging in. Blueberries are around also, and you have some of each but not enough of any to make a pie. That is the time for bumbleberry pie. These fruits are so used to starring roles on their own, we don't realize how delicious they can be in combination.

In the New England tradition of "use what you have," you can take this recipe and substitute cranberries for one of the berries. If it's midwinter and you need a taste of warmer times, most stores now carry quick-frozen berries. These work just fine and are easy to measure out when frozen. We recommend you thaw them (and drain, if necessary) before proceeding with the recipe.

2 tablespoons (28g) orange juice

1 teaspoon orange zest

2 cups (340g) blueberries

2 cups (240g) raspberries

2 cups (340g) blackberries

1 cup (198g) granulated sugar

¼ cup (28g) cornstarch or quick-cooking tapioca

one 9″ double pie crust (see pages 358–369)

2 tablespoons (25g) coarse white sugar

Place all the ingredients except the dough in a 2½-quart saucepan and simmer until filling is thickened. Cool to lukewarm.

Preheat the oven to 425°F.

Roll out half the pastry to a 13″ circle and fit it into a 9″ pie pan. Spoon the filling into the shell. Top with the other piece of rolled-out crust, and sprinkle with coarse sugar. Cut several vents in the top. Bake for 15 minutes, then lower the heat to 350°F and bake for another 35 to 50 minutes, until the top is evenly golden brown.

NUTRITION INFORMATION PER SERVING: 1 slice, 243g

447 cal | 13g fat | 5g protein | 53g complex carbohydrates | 24g sugar | 7g dietary fiber | 1mg cholesterol | 433mg sodium

VARIATION

BLUEBERRY PIE: Use all blueberries (6 cups) in the above recipe. Substitute lemon zest for the orange zest and add 2 tablespoons (29g) lemon juice and ½ teaspoon allspice or cinnamon to the filling.

BLUEBERRY HAND PIES

8 HAND PIES

These sweet and fruit-forward pastries can be served anytime and anywhere, thanks to their convenient portability. We use a sour cream dough here, which creates a sturdier crust—ideal for something hand-held. If you're using frozen berries, adjust the filling quantities of thickener to 2½ tablespoons (18g) cornstarch or 1½ tablespoons (17g) Instant ClearJel.

PASTRY

2 cups (240g) unbleached all-purpose flour

¾ teaspoon salt

½ teaspoon baking powder

16 tablespoons (2 sticks, 227g) unsalted butter, cold

½ cup (113g) sour cream, cold

FILLING

2 cups blueberries, fresh or frozen

2 tablespoons (14g) cornstarch or 1 tablespoon (11g) Instant ClearJel

⅓ cup (67g) granulated sugar

⅛ teaspoon salt (a large pinch)

1 tablespoon (14g) lemon juice

TOPPING

1 large egg, beaten

2 tablespoons (25g) coarse white sugar

TO MAKE THE PASTRY: Whisk together the flour, salt, and baking powder. Add the butter, working it in to make a coarse and crumbly mixture. Leave most of the butter in large, pea-size pieces.

Add the sour cream and stir until the mixture starts to come together in chunks. Turn it out onto a floured work surface and bring it together with a few quick kneads.

Pat the dough into a rough log and roll it into an 8″ × 10″ rectangle. Dust both sides of the dough with flour, and starting with a shorter end, fold it in three like a business letter.

Flip the dough over, give it a 90° turn on your work surface, and roll it again into an 8″ × 10″ rectangle. Fold it in three again.

Wrap the dough, and chill for at least 30 minutes before using.

TO MAKE THE FILLING: If you're using fresh berries, rinse and drain well. Place fresh or frozen berries in a saucepan. Whisk the cornstarch or Instant ClearJel with the sugar, and pour over the berries. Add the salt and lemon juice, stirring to combine.

Place the saucepan on a burner set to medium-high heat and cook, stirring, until the small amount of liquid in the bottom of the pan comes to a simmer. Reduce the heat to medium and continue to cook, stirring frequently, until the mixture starts to thicken, about 5 minutes. Transfer the cooked berries to a bowl and let cool to room temperature. It's fine to make the filling ahead of time and refrigerate until you're ready to use it.

Preheat the oven to 425°F; place a rack on the middle shelf. Line a baking sheet with parchment paper.

TO ASSEMBLE THE PIES: Roll the dough into a 14″ × 14″ square. With a straight edge and pastry wheel, or a 3½″ square cutter, cut out sixteen 3½″ squares.

Divide the filling among eight of the squares, using about a heaping tablespoon for each (a tablespoon cookie scoop works well here). Brush some of the beaten egg along the edges of each filled square.

Use a knife to cut a vent into each of the remaining eight squares; or use a decorative cutter of your choice.

Top each filled square with a vented square and press along the edges with the tines of a fork to seal.

Brush the top of each pie with the remaining beaten egg, and sprinkle with coarse sugar. Transfer the pies to the prepared baking sheet. If at any time during this process, the pies become sticky and hard to work with, simply refrigerate them for about 20 minutes, until firm.

Bake the pies for 18 to 20 minutes, until they're a light golden brown. Remove them from the oven and let cool for 20 minutes before serving.

NUTRITION INFORMATION PER SERVING: **1 hand pie, 120g**
400 cal | 27g fat | 5g protein | 26g complex carbohydrates | 12g sugar | 2g dietary fiber | 90mg cholesterol | 210mg sodium

Cream or Custard Pies

Cream and custard pies encompass everything from butterscotch to pumpkin. Custard pies are prepared by pouring an uncooked milk, egg, and sugar filling into an unbaked crust, then baking. Cream pies are usually made by spooning a flavored, fully prepared pastry cream into a fully baked crust (though they're sometimes baked, as with custard pies). Both are commonly topped with whipped cream or a baked meringue topping.

CUSTARD PIE

ONE 9″ PIE

Sweet, smooth, and oh-so-creamy, custard pie may seem humble but it shouldn't be overlooked. To make a custard pie that doesn't have a soggy bottom crust, we like to blind bake the crust for about 15 minutes in a 425°F oven (be sure to weigh it down to keep it from puffing), remove it from the oven, and brush it with beaten egg yolk. Return it to the oven and bake for 5 more minutes, to set the egg yolk. While the crust is baking, make the custard. Pour the hot custard into the hot pie shell and bake following the directions below. For best results, allow custard pie to cool and set for several hours before serving.

one 9″ single pie crust (see pages 358–369), blind baked as directed above

1 egg yolk, beaten (to brush on crust, as directed above)

1½ cups (340g) milk

1 cup (227g) heavy cream or half-and-half

⅓ vanilla bean,* split, or 2 teaspoons vanilla extract

¼ teaspoon salt

4 large eggs

⅔ cup (133g) sugar

¼ teaspoon nutmeg (freshly grated is best)

Preheat the oven to 425°F.

Scald the milk and cream with the piece of vanilla bean and the salt. (If using vanilla extract, just scald the milk and cream with the salt.) Remove the vanilla bean. In a medium bowl, whisk together the eggs and sugar (and vanilla extract, if using), then pour a quarter of the hot milk over the egg mixture and stir well. Pour the egg mixture into the remaining hot milk and stir well. Pour the custard into the hot, partially baked crust, and sprinkle it with the nutmeg. Use a crust shield or strips of aluminum foil to protect the edges of the crust from overbrowning.

Bake the pie for 10 minutes. Turn off the oven and, without opening the door, bake it for another 5 minutes. The mixture should look set around the edges but will still be wobbly in the middle. If it's not set at the edges, bake it for 5 minutes more. If you have a digital thermometer, remove the pie from the oven when it reaches 165°F in the center. If the mixture goes above 180°F, the custard will become watery. Cool the pie for several hours before serving.

* We like the sprinkle of brown flecks you get from using a vanilla bean. However, 2 teaspoons vanilla extract may be substituted for the bean. If using a bean, after scalding it, rinse it in cool water, dry it overnight, and cover it with sugar to make a lightly scented vanilla sugar.

NUTRITION INFORMATION PER SERVING: 1 slice, 116g

274 cal | 11g fat | 7g protein | 13g complex carbohydrates | 16g sugar | 0g dietary fiber | 187mg cholesterol | 226mg sodium

VARIATION

COCONUT CUSTARD PIE: Follow the directions for custard pie, adding 1 cup (85g) sweetened shredded coconut to the custard before pouring it into the pie shell.

CHOCOLATE CREAM PIE

ONE 9″ PIE

A true diner classic, this decadent dessert is beloved by fans of both chocolate and pie. The crust is blind baked, then filled with a cooked, cooled chocolate filling. Topped with lightly sweetened whipped cream, it's the perfect combination of crispy crust, dense chocolate filling, and airy cream topping. This is a tall pie with a generous amount of filling, which you can customize to your taste by using bittersweet, semisweet, milk chocolate, or any combination of these that you like.

Note here that your pie pan should be at least 2″ deep in order to hold all the filling. If, after forming the crust and pouring in the filling, you find yourself with leftover filling, simply pour it into a custard dish and refrigerate it until firm. It makes a delicious pudding.

one 9″ single pie crust (see pages 358–369), blind baked

2 tablespoons (28g) butter

1⅓ cups (227g) chopped semisweet chocolate

1 teaspoon vanilla extract

⅔ cup (131g) granulated sugar

3 tablespoons (21g) cornstarch

2 tablespoons (11g) unsweetened cocoa

1 teaspoon espresso powder (optional)

⅛ teaspoon salt

1 cup (227g) heavy cream

3 large egg yolks

2 cups (454g) milk

TOPPING

1 cup (227g) heavy cream

¼ cup (28g) confectioners' sugar

½ teaspoon vanilla extract

TO MAKE THE FILLING: Place the butter, chopped chocolate, and vanilla extract in a 2-quart mixing bowl; set aside.

In a medium saucepan off the heat, whisk together the sugar, cornstarch, cocoa, espresso powder, and salt. Add ½ cup (113g) of the heavy cream, whisking until the mixture is smooth and lump-free. Whisk in the egg yolks.

Place the saucepan over medium heat, and gradually whisk in the remaining ½ cup (113g) cream and milk. Bring to a boil, whisking constantly as the mixture thickens; boil for 1 minute. The temperature of the mixture will be around 200°F after 1 minute.

Remove the pan from the heat and pour the mixture over the reserved chocolate and butter. Whisk until the chocolate is melted and the mixture is smooth.

Pass the filling through a strainer into a bowl to remove any lumps. You can use the back of a ladle, a flexible spatula, or a wooden spoon to stir it through the strainer. Scrape the underside of the strainer once in a while with a clean spatula to help the process along.

Place plastic wrap or buttered parchment paper on the surface to prevent a skin from forming, and chill thoroughly. A shallow metal bowl with more surface area will chill the filling most quickly.

TO MAKE THE TOPPING: Place the heavy cream in a chilled mixing bowl. Whip until the whisk or beaters begin to leave tracks in the bowl.

Add the sugar and vanilla and whip until the cream holds a medium peak.

TO ASSEMBLE: Spoon the cooled filling into the cooled, baked pie crust. Level the top with the back of a spoon or an offset spatula. Spoon or pipe the whipped cream on top. If you're not planning on serving the entire pie at once, top individual slices with a dollop of whipped cream just before serving.

Chill the pie until ready to serve. For best slicing, refrigerate the pie overnight before serving.

NUTRITION INFORMATION PER SERVING: 1 slice, 146g
470 cal | 31g fat | 6g protein | 15g complex carbohydrates | 27g sugar | 1g dietary fiber | 120mg cholesterol | 160mg sodium

BANANA CREAM PIE

ONE 9″ PIE

Banana cream pie is an absolute standard in the world of pies. Many shortcut versions rely on a graham cracker crust and vanilla pudding, but this—our favorite version—pairs a real pastry crust with homemade cream filling, for what we believe will be your best banana cream pie experience yet! While it's optional, of course, freshly whipped cream is a wonderful complement to this pie.

one 9″ single pie crust (see pages 358–369), blind baked

½ cup (99g) sugar

2 tablespoons (15g) unbleached all-purpose flour

2 tablespoons (14g) cornstarch

½ teaspoon salt

2 large eggs

2 cups (454g) milk

6 tablespoons (¾ stick, 85g) unsalted butter, softened

½ teaspoon vanilla or almond extract

2 medium bananas, sliced ½″ thick

TO MAKE THE FILLING: In a medium heatproof bowl, whisk the sugar, flour, cornstarch, salt, and eggs together. In a medium saucepan, bring the milk just to a boil. Add the hot milk to the egg mixture gradually, whisking continually to make everything smooth. Return the egg/milk mixture to the saucepan, and cook over medium heat, stirring constantly, until the mixture thickens and starts to boil; this will happen quite quickly, so don't leave the stove. As soon as you see the pastry cream boil in the center, remove it from the heat and stir in the butter and vanilla or almond extract.

TO ASSEMBLE: Place the sliced bananas into the prebaked crust. Spoon the hot pastry cream over the bananas, smooth out the surface, and cover it with plastic wrap or a piece of parchment. Chill in the refrigerator until completely cold. Give it at least 6 hours; overnight is preferable. As the pie chills, the filling will thicken and set.

NUTRITION INFORMATION PER SERVING: 1 slice, 179g
375 cal | 22g fat | 8g protein | 37g complex carbohydrates | 19g sugar | 1g dietary fiber | 145mg cholesterol | 327mg sodium

LEMON MERINGUE PIE

ONE 9″ PIE

No pie lineup would be complete without lemon meringue, with its perfect combination of opposites—tart lemon with sweet meringue, flaky crust meeting smooth filling.

one 9″ single pie crust (see pages 358–369), blind baked

LEMON FILLING

6 tablespoons (42g) cornstarch

1⅓ cups (302g) water

1½ cups (298g) sugar

3 large egg yolks, slightly beaten

3 tablespoons (42g) butter

1 tablespoon lemon zest

½ cup (112g) fresh lemon juice (from 2 large lemons)

MERINGUE

3 egg whites, at room temperature

¼ teaspoon cream of tartar

6 tablespoons (77g) sugar

TO MAKE THE FILLING: In a medium saucepan, dissolve the cornstarch in the water. Add the sugar. Cook over medium heat, stirring, until the mixture thickens and comes to a boil. Boil, stirring, for 1 minute. Remove the pan from the heat and gradually add half of the hot mixture to the slightly beaten egg yolks. Blend the hot egg yolk mixture into the remaining filling in the pan and return the pan to the stove. Simmer the mixture, stirring, for 1 minute. Remove the pan from the heat. Stir in the butter, lemon zest, and lemon juice. Spoon the filling into the baked shell.

Preheat the oven to 400°F.

TO MAKE THE MERINGUE: In a large bowl, beat together the egg whites and cream of tartar until foamy. Gradually beat in the sugar, continuing to beat until the meringue is fairly stiff and glossy.

Spread the meringue atop the hot pie filling, using a knife to spread it completely over the surface of the pie. Make sure it's touching the crust all around; this will help to keep it from shrinking. (As for weeping, that's up to the weather; meringue pies almost always weep in hot, humid weather. As do we all. Adding cornstarch can help, see Mastering Meringue on the next page.

Bake the pie for 8 to 10 minutes, or until the meringue is golden brown. Remove it from the oven, and cool completely before serving.

NUTRITION INFORMATION PER SERVING: 1 slice, 109g

264 cal | 10g fat | 3g protein | 12g complex carbohydrates | 29g sugar | 0g dietary fiber | 84mg cholesterol | 69mg sodium

MASTERING MERINGUE

An ideal meringue is light, sweet, and holds up well, with no shrinking and little weeping.

Meringues consist of whipped egg whites and sugar. To make a meringue, you need a clean, non-plastic mixing bowl with no traces of fat in it. Any speck of fat in the bowl will coat the ends of the egg white's protein and that will cut the ability of the whites to hold air by more than half, so be sure yours is very clean. It's helpful to have your egg whites at room temperature (this gives them lower surface tension, and makes it easier to incorporate air). Many recipes call for salt and/or cream of tartar; these help to increase the holding power of the egg whites.

You can either use a whisk (and some elbow grease), or your electric mixer. The advantage to making meringue by hand (at least once) is that you become familiar with the stages that the whites go through. At first you have a puddle of clear liquid with some large bubbles. As you continue beating, the liquid becomes white with many smaller bubbles. Then the whisk begins to leave tracks in the whites. To test their progress, pull your whisk or beaters straight up out of the foam. If a point forms and then falls over immediately, you've got a soft peak. From here, 15 to 20 more strokes will bring you to a medium peak, and another 15 to 20 to stiff peaks.

It's extremely easy to overbeat meringue. When you start to see what look like grainy white clumps, you're beyond stiff peaks, and every stroke of the whisk or beater is tearing apart the network of air, water, and protein you've worked so hard to create. You'll also see a pool of clear liquid under the foam. You can still use that foam on top, but you can't really fix it completely other than to start over with new egg whites.

What about sugar? Sugar has two properties that affect egg whites. It, too, will coat the ends of the proteins in the whites, but if it's added too soon, it will take much longer to make a meringue stiff enough to be piped. If you're beating by hand, *don't* add the sugar until you've reached the medium-peak stage. If you're using a machine, start sprinkling sugar into the meringue after it gets to soft peaks. With a machine, the sugar will help give you a little extra leeway; you can go longer without overbeating the whites. For each egg white, use 2 tablespoons (25g) of sugar to make a soft meringue. Regular granulated sugar will work, but we advise the use of superfine that dissolves more quickly, making the meringue less grainy. For a stiffer meringue, use more sugar; up to 4 tablespoons (50g) per white.

Add ¾ teaspoon cornstarch per white with the sugar to keep it from "weeping" (exuding liquid) after baking, although if you're in very hot, humid conditions, weeping is inevitable. Be sure to fully cover your pie surface: 3 egg whites will give you plenty of meringue to cover a 9″ pie. If you're after a mile-high version, use 4 whites.

For finishing a pie, if your topping is between 1½″ and 2″ high, bake in a preheated oven at 350°F for 20 to 25 minutes, until the meringue is golden brown. If you're going for height, preheat to 300°F and bake for 35 to 45 minutes, to allow the meringue to cook through in the center.

CLASSIC KEY LIME PIE

ONE 9″ PIE

Creamy, tart, and sweet! Our ultimate version of the classic pie balances a lusciously smooth citrus filling with a nutty graham cracker crust. Emphasize the tropical vibe by adding ⅓ to ½ cup (35g to 53g) of toasted coconut to the crust if you like.

CRUST

1½ cups (128g) graham cracker crumbs

¼ cup (28g) confectioners' sugar

⅛ teaspoon salt

5 tablespoons (74g) unsalted butter, melted

FILLING

zest of 1 medium lime

3 large egg yolks

1¼ cups (14 ounces, 397g) sweetened condensed milk

⅔ cup (152g) bottled Key lime juice or freshly squeezed lime juice

⅛ to ¼ teaspoon lime oil (optional)

Select a pie pan whose inside top dimension is at least 9″ and whose height is at least 1¼″. Preheat the oven to 325°F.

Stir together all the crust ingredients, mixing until thoroughly combined. Press the crumbs into the bottom and up the sides of the pie pan.

Bake the pie crust for 15 minutes; it'll start to darken in color a bit. Remove it from the oven and place it on a rack to cool while you make the filling.

Whisk the grated lime zest and egg yolks at high speed of an electric mixer for about 4 minutes. The mixture will lighten in color and thicken somewhat, looking kind of like hollandaise sauce.

Stir in the sweetened condensed milk, mixing until smooth. Beat at high speed for 3 minutes; the filling will become slightly thicker and gain a bit of volume.

Add the lime juice, stirring just to combine. The mixture will thicken. Add lime oil to taste, if using.

Pour the mixture into the crust and return the pie to the oven. Bake for about 25 minutes, until it appears set around the edges, but still a bit wobbly in the center. The center should read about 145°F.

Remove the pie from the oven, and cool to room temperature. Refrigerate for several hours before serving.

NUTRITION INFORMATION PER SERVING: 1 slice, 103g

332 cal | 15g fat | 6g protein | 44g complex carbohydrates | 35g sugar | 1g dietary fiber | 102mg cholesterol | 166mg sodium

LEMON CHESS PIE

ONE 9″ PIE

Chess pie? No one seems certain where the name for this type of pie comes from. A simple combination of eggs, sugar, and butter, with the tiniest bit of flour or cornmeal for thickening, chess pies appeared in print as early as the late nineteenth century. Whatever its provenance, this lemon version of a simple chess pie is perfect for lemon lovers. This humble pie has no meringue to hide beneath; it's just citrus at its simple best.

CRUST

1½ cups (180g) unbleached all-purpose flour

1 tablespoon (13g) buttermilk powder (optional)

¼ teaspoon salt

¼ teaspoon baking powder

¼ cup (43g) vegetable shortening

4 tablespoons (½ stick, 57g) butter

3 to 5 tablespoons (43g to 71g) ice water

FILLING

1 tablespoon (10g) cornmeal

1½ tablespoons (11g) cornstarch

1⅔ cups (330g) sugar

½ teaspoon salt

6 tablespoons (¾ stick, 85g) unsalted butter, melted

¾ cup (170g) fresh lemon juice (from about 3 lemons)

5 large eggs

TO MAKE THE CRUST: Whisk together all the dry ingredients. Work in the shortening until it's well combined. Slice the butter into pats and add it to the flour mixture, working it in until it's unevenly crumbly, with some larger pieces of butter remaining.

Sprinkle 3 tablespoons (43g) of the water over the dough while tossing with a fork. Just as soon as the dough becomes cohesive (i.e., you can squeeze it into a ball easily), stop mixing; there should still be visible pieces of fat in the dough. Add up to 2 additional tablespoons (28g) water, if necessary, to make the dough come together.

Flatten the dough into a disk and wrap it in plastic wrap. Refrigerate for 30 minutes or longer; this resting period allows the flour to absorb the water and the gluten to relax, making the dough easier to roll out.

Flour your work surface and roll the dough into a 12″ × 9″ (approximately) rectangle. If it isn't holding together well, sprinkle it lightly with a couple of teaspoons of water. Fold the dough into thirds (like a letter), then fold it into thirds the opposite way, to form a rough square. Wrap it well and refrigerate again.

When you're "ready to roll," remove the dough from the fridge. Dough made with a combination of butter and shortening should rest for about 5 minutes at room temperature before rolling; dough made with all butter will need a 15-minute rest.

Roll the dough to a 12″ to 13″ circle and settle it gently into a 9″ pie pan; the pan shouldn't be over 1½″ deep. Flute or crimp the edge of the crust as desired. Place the crust in the refrigerator (no need to cover it) while you make the filling.

TO MAKE THE FILLING: Whisk together the cornmeal, cornstarch, sugar, and salt. Stir in the melted butter, then the lemon juice.

Whisk together the eggs briefly, then add them to the filling, stirring until everything is well combined.

Pour the filling into the chilled pie shell.

Bake the pie on the bottom shelf of a preheated 375°F oven for 45 to 50 minutes, or until the center is set. The top should be golden brown.

Remove the pie from the oven and allow it to cool before cutting and serving.

NUTRITION INFORMATION PER SERVING: 1 slice, 146g

425 cal | 19g fat | 7g protein | 64g complex carbohydrates | 42g sugar | 1g dietary fiber | 143mg cholesterol | 265mg sodium

PUMPKIN PIE

ONE 9″ PIE

Everyone has a favorite version of this Thanksgiving classic. This is ours—it's the one people request again and again. Mixing the filling a day in advance vastly improves this pie's flavor.

½ cup (99g) granulated sugar

½ cup (107g) brown sugar

1 tablespoon (8g) unbleached all-purpose flour

½ teaspoon salt

1 teaspoon cinnamon

1 teaspoon ginger

⅛ teaspoon cloves

⅛ teaspoon freshly ground black pepper (optional)

3 large eggs

2 cups (one 15-ounce can, 425g) pumpkin purée

1¼ cups (284g) light cream or evaporated milk

one 9″ single pie crust (see pages 358–369)

In a large bowl, whisk together the sugars, flour, salt, and spices.

In a large measuring cup, beat together the eggs, pumpkin, and cream or evaporated milk. Whisk into the dry ingredients. For best flavor, cover and refrigerate the filling overnight before baking.

Lightly grease a 9˝ pie pan that's at least 1½˝ deep. Roll the pie dough out to a 13˝ circle, and transfer to the pan. Crimp the edges above the rim; this will give you a little extra headroom to hold the filling when it expands in the oven. Refrigerate the crust while the oven preheats to 400°F.

When the oven is hot, place the pie pan on a baking sheet to catch any drips. Pour the filling into the unbaked pie shell.

Bake for 45 to 50 minutes, until the filling is set 2˝ in from the edge. The center should still be wobbly. Remove the pie from the oven and cool on a rack; the center will finish cooking through as the pie sits.

VARIATION

MASALA PUMPKIN PIE: Decrease cinnamon to ½ teaspoon, increase cloves to ¼ teaspoon and black pepper to ½ teaspoon. Add ½ teaspoon each ground coriander and turmeric, and ¼ teaspoon each cardamom and cumin to the filling.

NUTRITION INFORMATION PER SERVING: 1 slice, 172g

327 cal | 12g fat | 8g protein | 17g complex carbohydrates | 31g sugar | 2g dietary fiber | 96mg cholesterol | 329mg sodium

CHOCOLATE ICEBOX PIE

ONE 9˝ PIE

With a graham cracker crust and simple no-bake chocolate cream filling, this pie is a snap to put together in the high heat of summer.

CRUST

1¼ cups (177g) graham cracker crumbs

¼ cup (50g) granulated sugar

½ teaspoon cinnamon (optional)

5 tablespoons (71g) unsalted butter, melted

FILLING

⅓ cup (74g) water, hot

2 tablespoons (11g) Dutch-process cocoa

1 tablespoon (14g) vanilla extract

1⅓ cups (227g) bittersweet chocolate chips or chunks

1½ cups (340g) heavy cream

1 tablespoon (14g) granulated sugar

⅛ teaspoon salt

TOPPING

1 cup (227g) heavy cream

2 tablespoons (14g) confectioners' sugar

Preheat the oven to 375°F. Lightly grease a 9˝ pie pan.

TO MAKE THE CRUST: Combine the ingredients and press the mixture into the bottom and up the sides of the pan. Freeze the crust for 15 minutes (this will prevent overbrowning), then bake for 8 to 10 minutes, until it's lightly browned around the edges. Remove from the oven and cool completely.

TO MAKE THE FILLING: Combine the hot water, cocoa, and vanilla in a small measuring cup and set aside.

Heat the chocolate in a saucepan set over low heat on the stove, or in the microwave in 20-second bursts. Stir the chocolate until completely melted, and let cool for several minutes.

Whip the cream, sugar, and salt with a hand or stand mixer until soft peaks form.

Stir the cocoa mixture into the melted chocolate.

Using a whisk, fold the chocolate mixture into the whipped cream until no white streaks remain.

Spread the filling evenly into the cooled crust.

Refrigerate the pie for at least 1 hour before serving, or until the filling is firm.

TO MAKE THE TOPPING: Whip the cream and sugar together until the mixture is as firm (or soft) as you like. Slice the pie and serve with a dollop of the whipped cream.

NUTRITION INFORMATION PER SERVING: 1 slice, 153g

590 cal | 46g fat | 6g protein | 13g complex carbohydrates | 29g sugar | 3g dietary fiber | 100mg cholesterol | 170mg sodium

PUMPKIN CHEESECAKE PIE

ONE 9″ PIE

With its layers of sweetly spicy pumpkin and smooth, rich cheesecake nestled in a buttery crust, this pie has won over many a traditional pumpkin pie enthusiast. We suggest you make room for it on your Thanksgiving table.

one 9″ single pie crust (see pages 358–369) or gingersnap crust (page 370), blind baked

CHEESECAKE FILLING

1 cup (8 ounces, 227g) cream cheese, softened

⅓ cup (65g) sugar

1 large egg, lightly beaten

1 teaspoon vanilla extract

¼ cup (46g) diced crystallized ginger (optional, but good)

PUMPKIN FILLING

½ cup (99g) sugar

¼ teaspoon salt

¾ teaspoon ginger

¾ teaspoon cinnamon

¼ teaspoon nutmeg

¼ teaspoon allspice

1 cup (266g) pumpkin purée

⅔ cup (151g) light cream or
    evaporated milk

2 large eggs, lightly beaten

TO MAKE THE CHEESECAKE FILLING: In a medium bowl, place the cream cheese and let it warm to room temperature (this will make it easier to beat). When it has warmed, add the sugar and beat until fairly smooth. It may appear grainy, or a few lumps may remain; that's OK. Stir in the egg, vanilla, and ginger (if using) and spoon the filling into the pie crust.

TO MAKE THE PUMPKIN FILLING: In a medium bowl, whisk together the sugar, salt, and spices. Add the pumpkin, cream, and eggs and whisk gently until smooth. (You don't want to beat a lot of air into this mixture; just be sure it's thoroughly combined.) Gently spoon the pumpkin filling atop the cheesecake layer, filling to within ¼″ of the top of the crust. Do this carefully at first, so you don't disturb the cheesecake layer; once you've covered the cheesecake, you can be less careful. Depending on the depth of your pie pan, you may have leftover filling. Simply pour it into a custard cup or other small baking dish and bake it along with the pie, removing it from the oven when it appears set and a cake tester or toothpick inserted into the center comes out clean.

If you're using a pastry pie crust, place the pie in a preheated 425°F oven and bake it for 15 minutes. Reduce the oven temperature to 350°F and continue to bake for 40 to 45 minutes, covering the edges of the pie with a crust shield or aluminum foil if it seems to be browning too quickly. If you've prepared the pie with a gingersnap crust, bake it in a preheated 350°F oven for 50 to 60 minutes. The pie is done when it looks set but still wobbles a bit in the center when you jiggle it. (If you have a digital thermometer, the pie will register 165°F at its center when it's done.) Remove the pie from the oven, allow it to cool to room temperature, then refrigerate it until serving time. Serve with lightly sweetened whipped cream flavored with a pinch of ginger and a teaspoon of vanilla extract.

NUTRITION INFORMATION PER SERVING: 1 slice, 118g

274 cal | 15g fat | 6g protein | 13g complex carbohydrates | 16g sugar | 1g dietary fiber | 97mg cholesterol | 240mg sodium

OLD-FASHIONED PECAN PIE

ONE 9″ PIE

Sticky, gooey, toasty, nutty, sweet and salty, flaky and smooth—what other pie combines all the "opposites attract" attributes of a pecan pie? The flaky tender crust cradles a smooth, deep golden brown, ultra-sweet filling tempered by the addition of toasted pecans. We love this version as it has all the traditional flavors without the addition of corn syrup.

one 9″ single pie crust (see pages 358–369)

8 tablespoons (1 stick, 113g) unsalted butter

¼ cup (30g) unbleached all-purpose flour

2⅛ cups (456g) light brown sugar

½ teaspoon salt

6 tablespoons (85g) milk

3 large eggs, whisked briefly to combine

2 teaspoons vinegar

2 teaspoons vanilla extract

½ cup (57g) diced pecans

1 cup (113g) pecan halves

Preheat the oven to 375°F.

Roll out the pastry and place it in a greased 9″ pie plate. Flute the edges decoratively.

Melt the butter and set it aside to cool.

In a large bowl, mix together the flour, brown sugar, and salt. Add the milk and eggs and beat well.

Stir in the vinegar and vanilla, then the butter and diced pecans.

Pour the mixture into the crust and scatter the pecan halves on top.

Bake the pie for 47 to 50 minutes. When done, the top will be puffed up and set, and the center should just barely wobble when you jiggle the pan.

Remove the pie from the oven (the pie will finish setting up as it sits) and cool completely before slicing.

NUTRITION INFORMATION PER SERVING: 1 slice, 140g

415 cal | 25g fat | 9g protein | 1g complex carbohydrates | 38g sugar | 3g dietary fiber | 67mg cholesterol | 203mg sodium

CHOCOLATE PECAN PIE

ONE 9″ PIE

This gooey chocolate pie is traditionally served on Derby Day. The Kentucky Derby—the "run for the roses"—is an early May tradition in Kentucky, and a harbinger of spring for sports lovers all over the country. The crunch of pecans marries beautifully with the sticky, soft, and sweet chocolate filling. Serving each slice with a dollop of unsweetened whipped cream is a very good idea.

one 9″ single pie crust (see pages 358–369)

2 large eggs, at room temperature

1 cup (198g) sugar

½ teaspoon salt

½ cup (60g) unbleached all-purpose flour

8 tablespoons (1 stick, 113g) unsalted butter, melted and cooled

1 cup (168g) semisweet chocolate chips

1 cup (113g) chopped pecans, lightly toasted

1 tablespoon (14g) bourbon (optional)

1 teaspoon vanilla extract

Preheat the oven to 375°F.

Roll out the pastry and place it in a greased 9″ pie plate. Flute the edges decoratively.

Beat eggs on high speed with an electric mixer until light and pale yellow in color. Gradually beat in the sugar. Reduce speed to low and add the salt, flour, and butter, beating until thoroughly combined. Stir in the chocolate chips and nuts, then bourbon (if using) and vanilla.

Spoon the mixture into the crust. Bake until crust and top are golden brown, about 45 minutes. Serve warm.

NUTRITION INFORMATION PER SERVING: 1 slice, 99g

446 cal | 28g fat | 5g protein | 16g complex carbohydrates | 29g sugar | 2g dietary fiber | 75mg cholesterol | 201mg sodium

Tarts and Turnovers

Tarts and turnovers are offshoots of the classic fruit pie. A tart, which can range from full-size to bite-size, is a shallow, straight-sided pastry crust filled with cream and fruit, or fruit alone. A turnover is a half-moon or triangle of crust enclosing fruit filling. Tarts are often baked in removable-bottom pans, for ease of serving as well as a pretty presentation. Unlike pies, which often look rustic in a comforting, overstuffed way, tarts are almost military-looking in their neatness: a straight, even crust, berries lined up in rows like soldiers. Tarts are best served in more formal circumstances (i.e., on a plate, with a fork), as opposed to turnovers, which are the perfect "grab and go" picnic or lunchtime treat.

BERRY CREAM TART

ONE 9″ OR 10″ TART

You'll want to reach around and pat yourself on the back once you've made this tart. It looks like the centerpiece of a fancy bakery window. The trick to giving it (and any similar fruit dessert) such a polished look is simply brushing warm jam over the top of the berries.

one 9″ or 10″ pâte sucrée (page 367), blind baked

PASTRY CREAM FILLING

¼ cup (50g) sugar

1 tablespoon (8g) unbleached all-purpose flour

2 teaspoons cornstarch

¼ teaspoon salt

1 large egg

1 cup (227g) milk

3 tablespoons (42g) butter, softened

¼ teaspoon vanilla or almond extract

TOPPING

1 pint (284g) strawberries, sliced

1 pint (284g) blueberries

GLAZE

½ cup (170g) apricot jam

TO MAKE THE PASTRY CREAM: In a medium heatproof bowl, whisk together the sugar, flour, cornstarch, salt, and egg. In a small (1½-quart) saucepan, bring the milk to a boil. Add the hot milk to the egg mixture gradually, whisking continually to make everything smooth. Pour the liquid back into the saucepan and return to the heat to bring back to a boil. Stir continually with your whisk. (The mixture will thicken quickly and whisking will keep it from getting lumpy.) As soon as you see the pastry cream boil in the center, remove it from the heat and stir in the butter and vanilla or almond extract. Pour the pastry cream into the baked tart shell, place plastic wrap on the surface, and refrigerate. When you're ready to serve the tart, remove the wrap from the filling and top it with sliced strawberries and blueberries in alternating rows. If you're not going to serve the tart immediately, add the glaze to keep the berries looking their best.

TO MAKE THE GLAZE: Melt the apricot jam, then thin it with a little water if necessary. Strain or scoop out any solids, then brush the glaze over the berries to seal the top of the tart.

NUTRITION INFORMATION PER SERVING: 1 slice, 163g

352 cal | 18g fat | 6g protein | 44g complex carbohydrates | 18g sugar | 2g dietary fiber | 79mg cholesterol | 154mg sodium

SALTED CARAMEL AND CHOCOLATE TART

ONE 9″ TART

Simple and sophisticated, this tart tastes just as elegant as it looks with many flavors and textures encased inside the tender crust: toasted pecans, smooth caramel, and rich ganache. Can't find a caramel block? You can substitute individually wrapped caramel candies. You'll need about 60 of them, and they'll likely be firmer than the caramel block. To adjust for texture, melt them with ¼ cup (57g) of heavy cream instead of the 2 tablespoons called for below.

CRUST

6 tablespoons (¾ stick, 85g) unsalted butter, softened

¼ cup (50g) sugar

¼ teaspoon salt

½ teaspoon espresso powder (optional)

3 tablespoons (17g) Dutch-process cocoa

¾ cup (90g) unbleached all-purpose flour

½ cup (40g) pecan meal or ½ cup (48g) almond flour

CARAMEL FILLING

about 1¾ cups (496g) caramel from a block, cut into ½″ pieces

2 tablespoons (28g) heavy cream

¼ teaspoon salt

⅓ cup (47g) toasted, chopped pecans

CHOCOLATE FILLING

½ cup (113g) heavy cream

1 cup (170g) chopped dark chocolate or dark chocolate chips

TOPPING

⅓ cup (47g) toasted, chopped pecans

flaky sea salt, to finish

TO MAKE THE CRUST: Lightly grease a 9″ tart pan.

In a medium bowl, beat the butter, sugar, salt, and espresso powder together until smooth. Add the cocoa, flour, and pecan meal or almond flour and mix until the dough comes together.

Press the crust into the bottom and up the sides of the prepared pan. Prick the crust all over with a fork, then chill it in the freezer, uncovered, for 15 to 20 minutes or so, while you preheat the oven to 400°F.

Place the tart pan on a baking sheet and bake for 15 to 18 minutes, until you smell chocolate and the crust is set. Remove the crust from the oven and set it aside to cool.

TO MAKE THE CARAMEL FILLING: In a medium saucepan, heat the caramel, cream, and salt over medium-low heat, stirring regularly until melted and smooth. Remove from the heat.

Scatter the pecans over the bottom of the cooled crust then pour the caramel over the nuts. Place the caramel-filled tart in the freezer to firm up for 30 minutes.

TO MAKE THE CHOCOLATE FILLING: Heat the cream in a saucepan or a microwave until it begins to steam. Pour the hot cream over the chocolate in a bowl, let it sit for 5 minutes, then stir until melted and smooth. If necessary, reheat very briefly to soften any remaining hard bits of chocolate.

Pour the chocolate over the firm caramel, and sprinkle with the remaining pecans and flaky sea salt.

Refrigerate the pie for 1 hour or more before serving. It's best served chilled but not cold; remove the pie from the refrigerator about 15 to 20 minutes before serving.

NUTRITION INFORMATION PER SERVING: 1 slice, 95g

412 cal | 27g fat | 4g protein | 42g complex carbohydrates | 36g sugar | 2g dietary fiber | 33mg cholesterol | 182mg sodium

CHOCOLATE MOUSSE TART

ONE 9″ ROUND OR 4½″ × 13¾″ TART

This beautiful tart boasts both elegant appearance and incredible flavor. Pistachios, almonds, and coconut form the simple (and naturally gluten-free!) crust, which gets filled with a luscious chocolate mousse.

CRUST

¾ cup (92g) shelled salted pistachios

¾ cup (71g) almond flour

½ cup (57g) unsweetened shredded coconut

3 tablespoons (43g) butter or vegetable oil (37g)

3 tablespoons (59g) maple syrup

FILLING

1 cup (113g) confectioners' sugar

1 teaspoon Instant ClearJel (optional)

1 cup (227g) heavy cream

1 cup (8 ounces, 227g) cream cheese, softened

2 tablespoons (28g) butter, softened

½ teaspoon almond extract

⅔ cup (113g) chopped bittersweet chocolate

chopped pistachios or almonds, for garnish

Preheat the oven to 350°F. Have on hand a 9″ round or 4½″ × 13¾″ rectangular tart pan.

TO MAKE THE CRUST: Pulse the pistachios in a food processor. Be careful not to over-process into a paste.

In a medium bowl, combine the ground pistachios with the remaining crust ingredients. Stir until combined and crumbly-looking; it should hold together when you squeeze it. Press the mixture into the pan to cover the bottom and up the sides; the sides should be about ¼″ thick.

Place the pan on a baking sheet and bake for 15 to 20 minutes, or until the edges are golden brown. Remove from the oven, and let the crust cool completely.

TO MAKE THE FILLING: Whisk ¼ cup (28g) of the confectioners' sugar with the Instant ClearJel (if using). Whip the heavy cream to medium peaks, then add the sugar mixture. Continue whipping the cream until stiff peaks form.

In a medium bowl, combine the remaining confectioners' sugar with the cream cheese, butter, and almond extract, mixing until smooth. Set aside.

Melt the chocolate in a microwave or over simmering water.

Add the melted chocolate to the cream cheese mixture and beat to combine. Scrape the bowl, then fold the whipped cream mixture into the chocolate/cream cheese until evenly blended.

Pipe the filling into the cooled tart shell. Sprinkle with chopped nuts. Refrigerate until ready to serve.

NUTRITION INFORMATION PER SERVING: 1 piece, 105g

454 cal | 36g fat | 6g protein | 4g complex carbohydrates | 24g sugar | 3g dietary fiber | 65mg cholesterol | 145mg sodium

APPLE TURNOVERS

12 TURNOVERS

These lightly spiced pastry treats are reminiscent of apple pie but in a flakier, portable form! Be sure to cut the apples small to make the turnovers easier to fill.

DOUGH

2 cups (240g) unbleached all-purpose flour, plus ½ cup (60g) for dusting the butter

½ cup (40g) pecan meal

1 teaspoon salt

½ teaspoon baking powder

16 tablespoons (2 sticks, 227g) unsalted butter, frozen

½ cup (112g) sour cream

6 to 8 tablespoons (84g to 113g) water, cold

FILLING

2 pounds (4 cups, 907g) cored, peeled apples, cut into ½″ dice

⅓ cup (67g) sugar

½ teaspoon apple pie spice

1 tablespoon (7g) cornstarch

pinch of salt

1 tablespoon (21g) boiled cider or regular cider

1 tablespoon (14g) lemon juice

1 egg white beaten with 1 tablespoon (14g) water, for glaze

coarse white sugar, for topping

TO MAKE THE DOUGH: In a medium bowl, whisk together the dry ingredients and place them in the freezer. Unwrap the frozen sticks of butter and press the end of each stick into some of the "dusting" flour. This will help give you a grip on the butter while you're grating it. If you have a food processor with a medium-to-large shredding disk, use it; if not, use the coarse holes of a box grater to grate the butter by hand into large flakes.

Remove the dry ingredients from the freezer and use your fingers to toss the cold flour/butter together until they're evenly mixed. Stir the sour cream and cold water together. Add this mixture to the flour and butter. Use a dough scraper or spatula to fold and pat the mixture until it starts to hold together. You'll be able to see individual chunks of butter, which is OK; they shouldn't mix in. Pat the dough into a rough rectangle and fold it in thirds, like a letter. Pat it down again until it's about ½″ thick and fold in thirds a second time. Divide the dough in half. Place each half in the center of a piece of plastic wrap and form each piece into a 6″ square. Wrap the squares well and refrigerate for 30 minutes.

Remove one square of dough from the refrigerator and use the dusting flour to heavily flour both sides. Quickly roll the dough into a large (10″ × 12″) rectangle. Working with opposite shorter sides, fold the dough into thirds.

Use a rolling pin to flatten and widen the dough until it's about 5″ × 12″. Again, working with opposite shorter sides (the 5″ sides), fold the dough into thirds to form a rectangle of about 4″ × 5″. Return the dough to the refrigerator for 30 minutes, or until it's firm. Repeat with the remaining piece of dough. The dough may be prepared to this point up to 2 days before using, or up to 1 month before, if kept frozen.

TO FILL AND ASSEMBLE: Gently mix together the apples, sugar, spice, cornstarch, salt, cider, and lemon juice until well combined.

Preheat the oven to 400°F.

Divide the dough into two pieces; work with one piece at a time, keeping the other refrigerated. Remove one piece of dough from the refrigerator. (If it's been in the freezer, let it thaw, wrapped, until it's pliable.) Heavily flour both sides and roll it into a 10″ × 15″ rectangle.

Cut the dough into six 5″ squares. Spoon a scant ¼ cup of filling into the center of each square, moisten the edge of the dough, and fold the other half over to make a triangle. Pinch the edges of the triangle together or crimp with a fork and place it on an ungreased baking sheet. Repeat with the remaining pieces of dough. Brush each turnover with the egg white glaze, sprinkle with coarse sugar, prick them to make steam vents, and bake for 20 to 30 minutes, until golden brown. Remove the turnovers from the oven and cool them on a rack.

NUTRITION INFORMATION PER SERVING: 1 turnover, 90g

273 cal | 18g fat | 3g protein | 20g complex carbohydrates | 6g sugar | 1g dietary fiber | 47mg cholesterol | 209mg sodium

VARIATION

CHERRY OR BLUEBERRY TURNOVERS: Substitute pitted cherries or blueberries for the apples, omit the cider, and increase the cornstarch to 2 tablespoons (14g). Cook the filling in a saucepan until it thickens, then cool and use to fill the turnovers.

OPEN-FACED RUSTIC BERRY PIE

ONE 9″ PIE

Similar to a galette, this simple pie uses a "rustic" method of shaping the crust. All you have to do is roll out a big circle, pile the sugared berries in the middle, and gently fold the edges of the crust in toward the center, leaving about a 4″ wide circle of berries showing (that's the open-faced part). The goal is to bring the crust over the berries without tearing it; a crust with holes will allow leakage of the bubbling berry syrup. You can make evenly cut, artful, overlapping folds, or if you don't have the decorating gene, just flop the dough over the berries as best you can. Either way, it'll look enticing and delicious.

one 9″ single pie crust (see pages 358–369)	3 tablespoons (21g) quick-cooking tapioca or cornstarch
⅔ cup (133g) sugar	3 cups (510g) berries, fresh or frozen and thawed

Preheat the oven to 425°F.

Roll the crust into a 12″ to 13″ round and transfer the round to a pizza pan or baking sheet; if you use a baking sheet, the crust may (temporarily) hang off the edges, which is OK.

In a medium bowl, blend together the sugar and thickener. Add the berries, tossing to coat.

Mound the sugared berries in the center of the crust, leaving about a 3½″ margin of bare crust all the way around; the mound of fruit will be quite high. Using a pancake turner or a giant spatula, fold the edges of the crust up over the fruit, leaving 4″ to 5″ of fruit exposed in the center.

Bake the pie for about 35 minutes, or until the filling is beginning to bubble and the edges of the crust are brown. Remove it from the oven and let it cool for 15 to 30 minutes before cutting wedges.

NUTRITION INFORMATION PER SERVING: 1 slice, made with raspberries, 116g

253 cal | 9g fat | 3g protein | 24g complex carbohydrates | 16g sugar | 4g dietary fiber | 41mg cholesterol | 65mg sodium

TOASTER PASTRIES

16 TARTS

Toaster pastries have come a long way since their invention in 1964, from the original cinnamon brown sugar filling in a pastry crust, to the sugary confections in a wide variety of over-the-top flavors crowding the supermarket's cereal aisle today.

If you want to get back to basics, make your own. You can use several different fillings (we offer two classic versions here) for the amount of crust you'll have, so feel free to mix and match, and frost or not. The tarts are best eaten within a day or two.

PASTRY

8 tablespoons (1 stick, 113g) unsalted butter, at room temperature

1 cup (198g) granulated sugar

1 large egg

1 teaspoon vanilla extract

4 cups (480g) unbleached all-purpose flour

2 teaspoons cream of tartar

½ teaspoon baking soda

½ teaspoon salt

½ cup (113g) milk

FRUIT FILLING

1¼ cups (406g) thick jam (we like raspberry or strawberry)

¼ cup (30g) unbleached all-purpose flour

BROWN SUGAR FILLING

6 tablespoons (¾ stick, 84g) unsalted butter, softened

3 tablespoons (21g) unbleached all-purpose flour

¾ cup (160g) light brown sugar

1½ teaspoons cinnamon

¼ teaspoon salt

FROSTING

2½ tablespoons (35g) water or milk

1¼ cups (142g) confectioners' sugar

TO MAKE THE PASTRY: Cream the butter and sugar together in a large bowl. Add the egg and vanilla and beat well.

In a small bowl, blend the flour, cream of tartar, baking soda, and salt together. Alternately add the flour mixture and the milk to the butter mixture, beating the dough until it's well blended. Cover with plastic wrap and chill in the refrigerator for several hours, or overnight.

Just before you're ready to remove the dough from the refrigerator, prepare the filling(s).

TO MAKE THE FILLING: Mix the jam and flour together, or combine all the brown sugar–filling ingredients, stirring until smooth. Each filling recipe will make enough to fill all the tarts, so make double the amount of dough if you're making both batches of filling, or cut the filling ingredients in half.

Preheat the oven to 350°F.

TO ASSEMBLE: When the dough is well chilled, divide it into quarters and roll out each piece separately on a lightly floured work surface into a 12″ × 8″ rectangle about ⅟₁₆″ thick. Keep the other dough pieces chilled until you roll them out. Cut each rolled-out piece of dough into eight 3″ × 4″ pieces, trimming and discarding any uneven edges as you go.

Place the 3″ × 4″ rectangles from the first two dough quarters onto lightly greased or parchment-lined baking sheets. With a pastry brush or your finger, lightly moisten the outside edge of each rectangle. Spread slightly more than 1 tablespoon of filling onto each rectangle, leaving about a ⅛″ border all the way around.

When you've rolled and cut the remaining rectangles, place them on top of the bottom halves. Seal each tart all the way around with the flat side of a fork dipped into flour. Prick the top of each filled tart 10 to 12 times, to allow steam to escape. Bake the tarts for 18 to 20 minutes, until lightly golden brown. Remove them from the oven and transfer them to a rack to cool.

TO MAKE THE FROSTING: Simply stir the water or milk, ½ tablespoon at a time, into the confectioners' sugar until the mixture is of a spreadable consistency. Spread the frosting evenly onto the tarts; if you like, sprinkle each tart with some colored sugar for a finishing touch.

NUTRITION INFORMATION PER SERVING: 1 frosted tart made with raspberry jam, 99g
308 cal | 6.1g fat | 4g protein | 25g complex carbohydrates | 34g sugar | 1g dietary fiber | 33mg cholesterol | 64mg sodium

Savory Pies and Quiche

Savory pies might be eclipsed by their sweet brethren most of the time, but they have their distinct charms. The faint chill of a fall day or the definite cold of a winter night demands something comforting and filling. A slice of savory pie, paired with a crisp salad, fills this particular bill just fine.

A different sort of savory pie is the quiche, which can be thought of as a savory custard tart. Originating in France's Alsace-Lorraine, quiche is nearly as boundless in its variety as fruit pie, containing everything from cheese to meat to vegetables in almost infinite combinations. We like to team a mild cheese, such as Swiss, with more assertive vegetables, such as onions. On the other hand, a vegetable like zucchini teams well with a stronger-tasting cheese, such as sharp cheddar.

TOURTIÈRE (FRENCH-CANADIAN MEAT PIE)

ONE 9″ PIE

This traditional wintertime staple, often eaten with tomato chutney and a green salad, always elicits rave reviews. Feel free to use your favorite double-crust pie recipe, or try the one that follows. It's not a flaky crust, but it's very tender and easy to work with.

CRUST

¾ cup (168g) lard or ¾ cup (137g) vegetable shortening

⅓ cup (76g) boiling water

2¼ cups (270g) unbleached all-purpose flour

1½ teaspoons baking powder

½ teaspoon salt

FILLING

1 to 1½ teaspoons salt

2 cups (454g) water

2½ cups (336g to 392g, 1 large potato) peeled potatoes, cut into ½″ dice

½ pound (227g) ground beef

½ pound (227g) ground pork

1 cup (112g to 140g, 1 large onion) chopped onion

1 cup (84g to 112g, 1 to 2 celery ribs) chopped celery

2 garlic cloves, peeled and minced

¼ teaspoon cloves

1 teaspoon thyme

½ teaspoon sage

1 teaspoon freshly ground black pepper

TO MAKE THE CRUST: Place the lard or shortening in a bowl. Add the boiling water, then stir well to melt the fat. Add the flour, baking powder, and salt and mix with a spoon or electric mixer to make a smooth dough. Scrape half the dough out of the bowl onto a piece of plastic wrap, form it into a disk, and wrap well. Repeat with the remaining dough and refrigerate both dough disks while preparing the filling.

TO MAKE THE FILLING: Put the salt, water, and potatoes in a medium saucepan and bring the mixture to a boil over medium heat. Boil until the potatoes are fork-tender, then drain them, saving the water.

In a large frying pan, brown the meat, draining off any excess fat when finished. Add the onion, celery, garlic, spices, and potato water to the meat. Bring to a boil, then lower the heat to a simmer. Stirring occasionally, continue simmering the mixture for 30 minutes or longer, until the liquid has evaporated and the vegetables are tender.

Mash about half of the potato chunks and add them to the meat. Gently stir in the remaining chunks of potato. Remove the mixture from the heat and let it cool to room temperature.

TO ASSEMBLE: Preheat the oven to 450°F. Take one piece of dough out of the refrigerator, unwrap it, and dust both sides with flour. Roll it out to about ¼″ thick (or less if you prefer a thinner crust). Line a 9″ pie pan with the dough and fill it with the cooled meat mixture. Roll out the remaining dough disk and place it over the filling. Trim the excess from the dough and crimp the edges together with a fork or your fingers.

Bake the pie for 15 minutes. Reduce the oven heat to 350°F and bake for an additional 30 minutes, until the pie is golden brown. Let the pie cool for at least 15 minutes before slicing.

NUTRITION INFORMATION PER SERVING: **1 slice, 212g**
415 cal | 26g fat | 13g protein | 30g complex carbohydrates | 1g sugar | 2g dietary fiber | 55mg cholesterol | 440mg sodium

CLASSIC CHICKEN POT PIE

ONE 9″ × 13″ POT PIE

A very good chicken pot pie is one of the most comforting foods we know. The creamy filling plays a nice textural contrast against the flaky pastry crust. If you like, you can swap turkey for the chicken. If you'd like to use fresh uncooked vegetables rather than frozen, increase the amount of stock to 3 to 3½ cups (720g to 840g).

CRUST

1½ cups (180g) all-purpose flour

1 tablespoon (13g) buttermilk powder (optional)

¼ teaspoon salt

¼ teaspoon baking powder

4 tablespoons (½ stick, 57g) unsalted butter

¼ cup (43g) vegetable shortening

1 teaspoon white or cider vinegar

4 to 5 tablespoons (57g to 71g) ice water

FILLING

6 tablespoons (¾ stick, 85g) unsalted butter

6 tablespoons (43g) unbleached all-purpose flour

2½ cups (567g) chicken stock

6 to 7 cups (794g to 907g) boneless, skinless cooked chicken, cut into 1″ pieces

¼ teaspoon salt

freshly ground black pepper to taste

16 ounces (448g) frozen peas and carrots

8 ounces (224g) frozen pearl onions (use double the amount if you prefer)

TO MAKE THE CRUST: Combine the flour, buttermilk powder (if using), salt, and baking powder, then mix in the butter and shortening until crumbly, leaving some pea-size lumps.

Mix the vinegar with 4 tablespoons (57g) of the water. Sprinkle onto the dry ingredients, stir, and squeeze the dough together; if it's not totally cohesive, add an additional tablespoon (14g) of water (enough to make the dough stick together nicely, without crumbling).

Shape the dough into a flattened rectangle, wrap it in plastic wrap, and refrigerate for 30 minutes.

TO MAKE THE FILLING: Preheat the oven to 375°F. Heat the butter until melted, then stir in the flour. Gradually pour in the stock, whisking constantly. Cook and stir the sauce over medium heat until it comes to a boil, then reduce the heat and simmer for 5 minutes.

Stir in the chicken and salt. Add pepper and additional salt to taste, and the vegetables. Spoon the filling into a 9″ × 13″ (2- to 3-quart, or similar size) deep casserole dish.

Roll the crust out slightly larger than the dish. Place it on top of the filling; cut several vent holes, and use any scraps of dough to decorate.

Bake the pie for 50 to 60 minutes, until the crust is golden brown and the filling is bubbly.

NUTRITION INFORMATION PER SERVING: 1¼ cups, 309g

435 cal | 23g fat | 28g protein | 27g complex carbohydrates | 4g sugar | 4g dietary fiber | 90mg cholesterol | 1157mg sodium

FRESH TOMATO TARTS

2 LARGE TARTS

These light tarts are perfect for showcasing ripe summer tomatoes. Consider this recipe to be a light quiche, ideal for an appetizer, brunch, or lunch.

CRUST

2 cups (240g) unbleached all-purpose flour

½ cup (4 ounces, 113g) cream cheese

½ to ¾ teaspoon salt

2 tablespoons (25g) buttermilk powder (optional)

10 tablespoons (142g) unsalted butter, cold

3 to 4 tablespoons (43g to 57g) ice water

FILLING

6 large eggs, beaten

1½ cups (340g) milk

1 cup (113g) grated cheddar cheese

¼ teaspoon dried oregano

¼ teaspoon dried thyme

½ teaspoon salt

2 medium (340 to 397g) tomatoes, cut in ¼″ thick slices

TO MAKE THE CRUST: Put the flour in a mixing bowl, or in the bowl of a food processor. Add the cream cheese, salt, and buttermilk powder (if using). Mix together until everything is evenly crumbly. If you're using a food processor, just a few quick pulses are all you'll need.

Cut the cold butter into pieces and work it into the flour, leaving some visible pieces.

Sprinkle the dough with the cold water and toss. Squeeze the dough to determine if it holds together. If it's too dry, add water 1 tablespoon (14g) at a time, using just enough so the dough will hold together.

Divide the dough in half, to make two 9″ tarts. Flatten each piece of dough into a disk, wrap well, and refrigerate for 30 minutes or longer.

Once chilled, roll each piece of dough to a 12″ diameter.

Gently place the rolled-out pastry in the tart pan, smoothing it over the bottom and tucking it into the sides. Roll your rolling pin across the top of the pan to cut off the excess pastry. Peel the pastry away from the edge of the pan. You can bake these trimmings along with the tarts for a crunchy snack (baker's treat!).

Refrigerate the crusts while you prepare the filling.

TO MAKE THE FILLING: Preheat the oven to 425°F. Whisk together the eggs, milk, cheese, herbs, and salt. Divide the mixture between the two chilled shells. Lay the sliced tomatoes on top.

Bake in the preheated 425°F oven for 15 minutes, then reduce the oven temperature to 350°F and bake for another 10 to 15 minutes, until the crust is brown and the custard is set. Remove from the oven, and serve warm.

NUTRITION INFORMATION PER SERVING: 1 slice, 107g
214 cal | 14g fat | 7g protein | 15g complex carbohydrates | 2g sugar | 1g dietary fiber | 104mg cholesterol | 289mg sodium

SAVORY ZUCCHINI GALETTE

ONE 8″ TO 10″ GALETTE

With its tender crust and savory cheese and herb filling, this summery galette can be served in fat wedges as the main course for a warm-weather picnic; in smaller slices as a starter to a summer dinner, or in thin slivers as hors d'oeuvres for a cocktail party. The cheese powder in the crust is optional, but adds a wonderful depth of flavor to complement the cheese in the filling.

CRUST

1½ cups (159g) unbleached pastry flour or 1½ cups (180g) unbleached all-purpose flour

¼ cup (28g) Vermont cheddar cheese powder (optional)

½ teaspoon salt

8 tablespoons (1 stick, 113g) unsalted butter, cold

5 to 6 tablespoons (71g to 85g) water, cold

FILLING

1 large (340 to 397g) zucchini, sliced into ¼″-thick disks

2 teaspoons pizza seasoning or other dried herb and spice blend

½ pint cherry or grape tomatoes, halved

¾ cup (170g) ricotta cheese

¼ teaspoon salt

freshly ground black pepper, to taste

1 teaspoon fresh lemon zest (optional)

1 large egg

½ cup (57g) grated Parmesan cheese

EGG WASH

1 large egg, beaten with 1 tablespoon water

TO MAKE THE CRUST: Whisk together the dry ingredients. Work in the butter until the mixture is crumbly. Drizzle in 5 tablespoons (71g) of water, stirring gently until everything is evenly moistened. Add the final tablespoon (14g) of water if necessary to make a cohesive dough.

Pat the dough into a disk, wrap, and refrigerate for 30 minutes.

TO MAKE THE FILLING: Preheat the oven to 425°F. Lightly grease (or line with parchment) two baking sheets.

Place the zucchini slices on one pan and sprinkle with 1½ teaspoons pizza seasoning.

Place the tomato halves on the second pan and sprinkle with the remaining pizza seasoning.

Roast the zucchini and tomatoes until tender, about 15 to 20 minutes for the zucchini and 10 to 15 minutes for the tomatoes.

Remove the zucchini and tomatoes from the oven and allow to cool for 10 minutes.

Combine the ricotta, salt, pepper, lemon zest, and egg until evenly blended. Set aside.

TO ASSEMBLE THE GALETTE: On a lightly floured work surface, roll the dough into a 12˝ circle. Transfer the dough to a parchment-lined baking sheet.

Spread the ricotta mixture over the dough, leaving a 2˝-wide bare strip along the perimeter.

Sprinkle half the Parmesan over the ricotta, then shingle the zucchini slices over the cheese and scatter the tomato halves on top.

Fold the bare edges of the dough into the center.

Brush the exposed edges of the crust with egg wash and sprinkle the remaining Parmesan over the whole galette.

Bake the galette for 25 to 30 minutes, until the crust is golden brown and the filling is bubbling.

Remove the galette from the oven and allow it to cool for 5 to 10 minutes before serving.

NUTRITION INFORMATION PER SERVING: 1 slice, 153g

258 cal | 16g fat | 8g protein | 21g complex carbohydrates | 2g sugar | 1g dietary fiber | 68mg cholesterol | 355mg sodium

BASIC VEGETABLE QUICHE

ONE 9″ QUICHE

This is a wonderful master recipe to make use of any manner of vegetables you have on hand. We find that cooking vegetables before using them in quiche results in better flavor; this is true of all vegetables except tomatoes, which can be used raw but do need to be seeded and squeezed fairly dry. Slice or dice vegetables, then sauté in a bit of olive oil until lightly browned, seasoning sparingly with salt and less sparingly with pepper. Drain, cool, and add to quiche custard.

Alternatively, you can roast your vegetables in a 400°F oven for about 1 hour, or in a cooler oven for a longer amount of time, until golden. This is an ideal method for cooking lots of vegetables at once; use what you want in quiche, then save the rest for pasta sauce or as a delicious dish in themselves.

one 9″ single pie crust (see pages 358–369)

1 cup (113g) grated cheese, plus more for topping

1½ cups (340g) buttermilk or whole milk

3 large eggs

3 tablespoons (23g) unbleached all-purpose flour

½ teaspoon salt

½ to 1 teaspoon dried herbs (such as basil, thyme, oregano, marjoram)

1 teaspoon minced garlic (optional)

2 cups sautéed or roasted vegetables

Preheat the oven to 425°F.

Roll out pie crust and fit it into a 9″ pie or 10″ tart pan. Trim edges and crimp decoratively. Sprinkle with a thin layer of the cheese; this seals the crust, preventing it from becoming soggy. Set aside.

In a mixing bowl, combine buttermilk, eggs, flour, and salt. Beat until well mixed. Stir in herbs, garlic, vegetables, and cheese.

Pour vegetable mixture into prepared crust. Sprinkle with additional cheese, if desired. Bake on the bottom rack for 15 minutes, then reduce heat to 350°F and bake an additional 35 to 40 minutes, or until the crust is golden brown. Remove from the oven and cool completely on a rack before slicing.

NUTRITION INFORMATION PER SERVING: 1 slice, without extra cheese, 162g
229 cal | 12g fat | 10g protein | 19g complex carbohydrates | 3g sugar | 1g dietary fiber | 103mg cholesterol | 349mg sodium

QUICHE LORRAINE

ONE 9″ OR 10″ QUICHE

Quiche Lorraine, a rich, eggy cheese custard cradling bacon, eggs, ham, and chives in a golden crust, made an elegant splash in the fifties. Like pizza, its popularity in this country sprang from returning World War II veterans, who'd enjoyed it in France—particularly Paris, once that city was liberated. The notion of quiche was a simple leap from pie (which was common among home bakers at the time); it was no big deal to change the filling from sweet to savory.

Cold quiche makes a wonderfully elegant lunch alongside a simple salad. You can prepare it whole, or make individual quiches in the cups of a muffin pan.

one 9″ single pie crust (see pages 358–369)

¼ pound bacon (about 5 slices, 113g), diced

½ large (84g to 112g, a generous ¾ cup) onion, diced

¼ pound ham (a generous 3 cups, 113g), diced

1 cup (227g) milk

1 cup (227g) heavy cream

½ teaspoon salt

¼ teaspoon freshly ground black pepper

3 large eggs

2 tablespoons fresh chives

1 cup (113g) grated Swiss, Gruyère, or sharp cheddar cheese

Roll out the pastry dough to a circle 2″ to 3″ larger than the pan you're using. Place the crust into a lightly greased 9″ pie pan or 10″ tart or quiche pan. Build up the edges of the crust by folding excess dough under and then crimping it. Prick the bottom with a fork every 2″. Brush with lightly beaten egg white; this will help the crust remain crisp. Grease a sheet of foil and place it, greased side down, on top of the crust. Using another pie pan or pie weights, partially blind bake the crust in a preheated 425°F oven for 15 minutes. Set the crust aside. Turn the oven down to 350°F.

TO MAKE THE FILLING: Sauté the bacon until crisp. Pour off as much fat as possible, then add the onion and cook until soft. Add the ham and brown slightly. Remove from the heat and set aside.

In a medium saucepan, heat the milk and cream with the salt and pepper until the mixture is just below a simmer. Remove from the heat. Add some of the hot cream to the eggs, beat well, then stir the hot cream/egg mixture into the hot cream.

Layer the bacon mixture into the baked pie shell. Pour the egg/cream mixture into the shell, then sprinkle with chives and cheese.

Bake the quiche for 35 to 40 minutes. Be careful not to overbake it or it will be watery; the quiche is done when a knife inserted 2″ from the edge comes out clean, but the center is still wobbly. The temperature should register 160°F to 165°F on a digital thermometer. Don't be tempted to turn up the oven if the quiche seems to be taking a long time; the time from not sufficiently cooked to overbaked is short. Allow the quiche to cool for 15 minutes before serving.

NUTRITION INFORMATION PER SERVING: 1 slice, 201g
550 cal | 40g fat | 21g protein | 22g complex carbohydrates | 2g sugar | 1g dietary fiber | 283mg cholesterol | 904mg sodium

ROASTED BUTTERNUT SQUASH AND SPINACH QUICHE

ONE 9″ QUICHE

We've taken our favorite fall flavors and folded them into a quiche filling. Roasting the butternut squash ahead of time elevates its earthy flavor, and balsamic vinegar adds a tangy-sweet touch.

one 9″ single pie crust (see pages 358–369)

1 medium-large (227g) yellow onion, peeled

2 tablespoons (25g) olive oil

1 tablespoon (14g) balsamic vinegar

1½ cups (213g) cubed butternut squash

1 cup (227g) whole milk

5 large eggs

1 tablespoon fresh rosemary, chopped, or 1 teaspoon dried rosemary

½ teaspoon fresh thyme or ¼ teaspoon dried thyme

½ teaspoon salt

½ teaspoon freshly ground black pepper

1 cup (113g) grated cheddar cheese

1 cup (28g) chopped fresh baby spinach

Preheat the oven to 375°F.

Roll the prepared crust into a 12″ circle and press it gently into a 9″ pie pan. Prick it all over with a fork. Bake the crust for 10 minutes, then remove it from the oven and set it aside to cool.

TO MAKE THE FILLING: Quarter the onion and slice thinly. In a medium saucepan over medium-low heat, heat 1 tablespoon (12g) of the olive oil. Add the onion and cook, stirring occasionally, until caramelized and deep golden brown. This will take about 20 minutes. Right before the onion finishes cooking, add the balsamic vinegar to the pan and cook for a few more minutes.

While the onion is caramelizing, spread the cubed butternut squash on a parchment-lined baking sheet and toss it with the remaining olive oil, along with a couple of good dashes of salt and pepper. Roast the squash until it starts to brown and soften; this should take about the same amount of time as the onions (about 20 minutes).

In a large bowl, whisk together the milk and eggs. Add the rosemary, thyme, salt, and pepper. Add the caramelized onions, roasted squash, grated cheese, and baby spinach. Pour the mixture into the pie crust. Don't overfill! If you find you have too much filling, just leave a little out (you can always bake the extra alongside the quiche in a custard cup or oven-safe ramekin).

Bake the quiche for about 40 to 45 minutes. The edges should be golden brown and the center should feel just set.

Remove the quiche from the oven and let it cool on a rack. Serve warm or at room temperature.

NUTRITION INFORMATION PER SERVING: 1 slice, 162g
340 cal | 24g fat | 10g protein | 21g complex carbohydrates | 3g sugar | 2g dietary fiber | 125mg cholesterol | 390mg sodium

— CHAPTER TEN —

Pastry

———

WHILE MANY HOME BAKERS HAVE happily spent hours reading about and trying to reproduce the perfect baguette, there are fewer of us who've spent time trying to perfect a variety of classic French pastry, including classic puff pastry (*pâte feuilletée*), yeasted puff pastry (*viennoiserie*), and cream puff pastry (*pâte à choux*). Perhaps you're one of the determined who've made croissants by hand, or maybe you've read about the process, felt absolutely daunted, and went out to buy croissants at the bakery. But let us encourage you to give pastry a try at home! There is nothing (we repeat, *nothing*) that you can't master at home with the right guidance. The following recipes aren't exactly dauntless, but neither are they too daunting: If you're a dedicated bread baker, you'll thoroughly enjoy the long (although not particularly difficult) process involved in producing puff pastry, puff dough, and the incredibly flaky, delicate treats made from them. And there's a wide world of pastry-related recipes to try, from a stunning Paris-Brest round to savory cheese straws to a simple jam-topped almond puff loaf.

Pâte Feuilletée: Classic Puff Pastry

Classic puff pastry uses essentially the same ingredients (although a bit more butter) as pie crust; it's the way these ingredients are combined that makes this dough unique.

The French call it *pâte feuilletée* (pronounced paht foy yuh TAY), which means "pastry made leaflike." In fact, it has so many "leaves" that it's also called *mille-feuille* (meel FWEE), meaning "a thousand leaves." Each of these leaves consists of a layer of flour separated by a layer of butter. The expansion (puff) occurs because the butter layers create steam when exposed to the heat of an oven, expanding the space between the flour layers. Ultimately, in classic puff pastry, you want to create 729 layers of folded dough—not quite one thousand but, like the millipede (which really doesn't have a thousand legs), the effect is there.

How do you go about creating 729 layers of folded dough? One step at a time. First, dough made with flour, water, salt, and a tiny bit of butter is rolled into a square. Next, a layer of butter is put on top of the dough, enclosed by the dough, and rolled into a long rectangle. When this rectangle is folded in thirds, the layers of dough and butter begin. After rolling and folding a second time, you've completed two "turns." Classic puff pastry is made with six turns, usually with stints in the refrigerator to firm up the butter and relax the flour's gluten. So you see, it's not a difficult process; it just takes some time.

CLASSIC PUFF PASTRY: A PRIMER

Anyone who can fold a letter in thirds and hold a rolling pin can make puff pastry. You'll be surprised at how satisfying it is to create more layers and a more ethereal product with every fold. The first surprise is how malleable butter can be. After that, remember to pay attention to the temperature of both your work area and the butter; give the dough regular time-outs in the refrigerator and line up your edges as neatly as you can.

Step 1: Making the Dough

3½ cups (420g) unbleached all-
    purpose flour*

4 tablespoons (½ stick, 57g) butter,
    chilled

1½ teaspoons salt

1¼ cups (283g) water, cold

Place the flour in a mixing bowl and combine it with the chilled butter until the mixture resembles cornmeal. Add the salt to the water, stir well, then add to the flour. Mix gently with a fork or a dough whisk (see Tools, page 535) until you have a rough dough that pulls away from the sides of the bowl. If you need to add more water, do so a tablespoon at a time until the dough holds together. Turn out the dough onto a lightly floured surface and knead until it's smooth and a bit springy, 2 to 3 minutes. Pat it into a square, wrap it in plastic wrap, or place it in a large plastic bag and refrigerate for at least 30 minutes.

* You may substitute 1 cup (113g) unbleached pastry flour for 1 cup of the all-purpose flour or ½ cup (57g) cornstarch for an equal amount of all-purpose flour for a more tender final product.

Step 2: Preparing the Butter

½ cup (60g) unbleached all-
    purpose flour

28 tablespoons (3½ sticks, 397g)
    unsalted butter, softened but still
    cool to the touch

Using a mixer, a food processor, or a spoon, combine the flour and butter just until they are smooth and well blended. Lightly flour a piece of plastic wrap or waxed paper, and on it shape the butter/flour mixture into an 8″ square. Cover the butter and place it on a flat surface in the refrigerator for at least 30 minutes. Adding flour to the butter helps to stabilize it, so it won't "flow" out the seams when rolled.

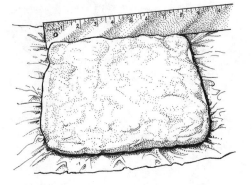

Combine the chilled butter and flour until smooth, then form it into an 8″ square on a piece of lightly floured plastic wrap. It will be about ¾″ thick.

Step 3: Rolling and Folding

TOOLS

flour, for dusting

rolling pin

yardstick or tape measure

pastry brush

Place the butter on the dough so it's rotated 45°. It will look like a diamond in the square.

Remove the dough from the refrigerator and put it on a lightly floured surface. Gently roll it into a square about 12″ across. Put the butter square in the center of the dough, at a 45° angle, so it looks like a diamond in the square.

Fold the flaps of the dough over the edges of the butter until they meet in the middle. Pinch and seal the edges of the dough together; moisten your fingers with a little water, if necessary. Dust the top with flour, then turn the dough over and tap it gently with the rolling pin into a rectangular shape. Make sure the dough isn't sticking underneath, and roll it from the center out into a larger rectangle, 20″ × 10″. (The barrel of most standard size rolling pins is 10″ long, so when the width of the rectangle matches the pin, you're in good shape. You'll need a tape measure to check the rectangle's length.)

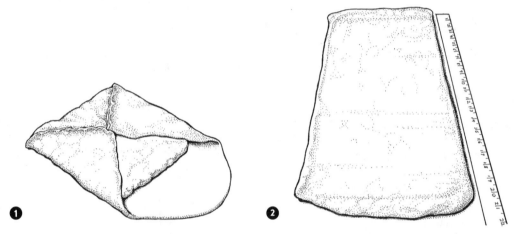

1. Bring the flaps of dough up and over the butter, and pinch the seams to seal them together. Use a little water on your fingers to ensure a tight seal if necessary, and try not to capture any air bubbles inside. **2.** Roll the dough-butter package from the center out into a 20″ × 10″ rectangle.

When the dough is the right size, lightly sweep off any excess flour from the top with your pastry brush. Fold the bottom third up to the center, and the top third over (like a business letter). Line the edges up on top of each other and even up the corners so they're directly atop one another. Tack the corners in place with a little water, then turn the dough package 90° to the right so it looks like a book ready to be opened. If the dough is still cool to the touch and relaxed, do another rolling and folding the same way.

If you've successfully rolled out the dough and folded it twice, you've completed two turns. Make a note of how many folds you've completed and the time, and then put the dough back in the refrigerator. Classic puff pastry gets six turns before being formed into finished shapes and should rest, chilled, for at least 30 to 50 minutes between every two turns.

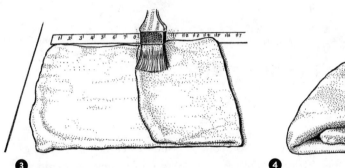
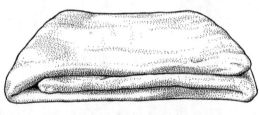

3. Use a pastry brush to sweep off any excess flour, then fold the dough in thirds, like a business letter. Take care to line the outside edges up directly over each other. **4.** Turn the folded dough 90° to the right, so it looks like a book ready to be opened. Be sure the corners are directly lined up over each other. Use a little water to stick them together to keep them from shifting if necessary.

Repeat the above folding and turning process two more times. When all six turns have been completed, wrap the dough well and refrigerate it for at least an hour (preferably overnight) before using. This recipe makes enough for twenty-four 4″ × 6″ pieces of dough, so you may want to take a portion of the finished pastry dough and freeze it for later. It will keep for 3 to 6 months, as long as it's tightly wrapped and no air gets to its surface in the freezer.

DUSTING, DUSTING . . .

As you work, keep the dough, work surface, and rolling pin well dusted with flour. Turn over the dough from time to time. As you roll, the top layers expand more than the bottom. By flipping it over, you'll even it out. Before folding the dough over on itself, use your pastry brush to sweep off any excess flour. This will help the dough stick to itself when you roll it again, so the layers don't slide around.

BUBBLES AND LEAKS

It's not unusual to have air trapped inside your laminated dough (dough layered with butter), making an awkward bubble. If this happens, simply pop the bubble with a toothpick and press down the dough with your fingers so it lies flat again. If you find yourself with a bare spot where butter is coming through, dust the leak with flour, pressing down lightly so the flour sticks, and continue on with the fold. Refrigerate the dough as soon as the fold is complete, to firm up the dough and the butter.

Pâte Feuilletée Rapide (Blitz Puff Pastry) and Fast and Easy Puff Pastry

As with any process that's time-consuming, someone is bound to come up with a way to save some of that time. *Pâte feuilletée rapide*—blitz puff pastry—is made with puff pastry ingredients, but the butter is cut into small pieces and added to the dough at the outset. Up to this point, it's much like a buttery pie crust; it strays off the pie crust path when the baker gives it a couple of folds, refrigerates it for 30 minutes or so, then gives it two more folds. The pastry is ready to use after another hour in the fridge. The "blitz" comes from adding the butter right to the dough and leaving out two of classic puff pastry's six turns.

If you don't want to bother with any turns at all, fast and easy puff pastry is the way to go. Flour and chunks of butter are mixed roughly, then held together by sour cream (which also serves to tenderize the flour's gluten). Baking powder gives this dough some added oomph in the oven. While it's nontraditional, and will yield pastry that's not quite as flaky or tender, it's a wonderful boon for the busy baker.

BLITZ PUFF PASTRY

As the name implies, this is a quicker way to make very flaky pastry dough. It's a perfectly good dough to use if you want to make napoleons or turnovers, without going through quite as much preparation time as with a classic puff pastry.

3 cups (360g) unbleached bread flour

24 tablespoons (3 sticks, 340g) unsalted butter, chilled, cut into ½" pieces

1 cup (227g) water, cold

2 teaspoons salt

Using a stand mixer with the paddle attachment, mix the flour and cold butter on low speed until the mixture forms large chunks.

Combine the water and salt in a small bowl and add to the flour/butter mixture. Mix on low speed, just until the dough begins to come together into a shaggy mass.

Turn out the dough onto a floured surface and fold it over on itself until it comes together (a bench knife can be helpful with gathering the dough at this point).

Form the dough into a block. Wrap in plastic wrap and refrigerate for 30 minutes. After this rest, remove from the refrigerator and give four letter folds, with rolling, as described on page 425. After the last fold, chill the dough for 30 minutes before using.

FAST AND EASY PUFF PASTRY

This pastry is very quick to put together and mimics the flakiness of classic puff pastry. The sour cream gives this dough a markedly tender texture. Be sure to have the butter well chilled before starting.

2 cups (240g) unbleached all-
   purpose flour

½ teaspoon salt

½ teaspoon baking powder

16 tablespoons (2 sticks, 227g) unsalted
   butter, cold

½ cup (113g) sour cream, cold

In a large bowl, whisk together the flour, salt, and baking powder.

Add the butter, working it in to make a coarse and crumbly mixture. Leave most of the butter in large, pea-size pieces.

Stir in the sour cream; the dough won't be cohesive. Turn it out onto a floured work surface, and bring it together with a few quick kneads.

Pat the dough into a rough log and roll it into an 8″ × 10″ rectangle.

Dust both sides of the dough with flour and, starting with a shorter end, fold it in three like a business letter.

Flip the dough over, give it a 90° turn on your work surface, and roll it into an 8″ × 10″ rectangle. Fold it in three again.

Chill the dough for at least 30 minutes before using. To make pastry, roll into desired size.

Freeze dough for prolonged storage, up to 2 months. To use, thaw in the refrigerator overnight.

CROISSANTS DE PÂTISSIER

12 CROISSANTS

Puff pastry croissants are called *croissants de pâtissier* because they're made by a pastry chef rather than a baker, who would make yeast-based *croissants de boulanger* (see page 437). Any puff pastry needs to be baked at a high temperature to create the steam that separates the layers of dough. All that moisture takes some time to cook out, so make sure you don't take your croissants out of the oven until they're a deep golden brown. If they come out of the oven too soon, the centers will still be damp and underdone.

½ recipe Classic Puff Pastry (page 422)
1 egg beaten with 1 tablespoon (14g) water, to glaze

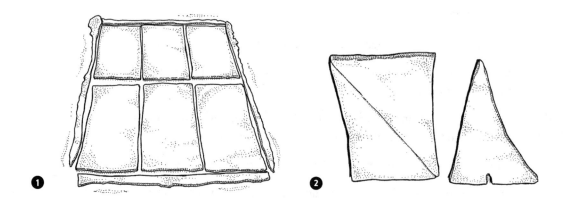

1. Roll the dough into a 12″ × 18″ rectangle; trim the edges with a sharp knife or pizza cutter. Cut the dough in thirds lengthwise, and in half across the middle. **2.** After cutting each piece of dough into two triangles, cut a ½″ notch in the center of the short side, closest to you.

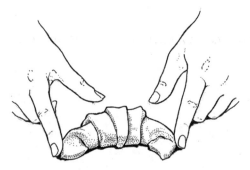

After rolling the croissant, bend the two ends toward the spot where the tip of the dough is tucked under.

TO SHAPE THE CROISSANTS: On a lightly floured surface, roll the dough into a 12″ × 18″ rectangle. Trim the edges of the dough all the way around by using a ruler and cutting straight down with a very sharp knife or a pizza wheel. This cuts off the folded edges that would inhibit the "puff."

Cut the dough in thirds lengthwise and in half through the middle. This will give you six 4″ × 9″ pieces. Cut these pieces in half diagonally and arrange them so the points of the triangles are facing away from you. It's OK to stretch them out slightly to elongate them when you do this. Cut a ½″ notch in the short edge of the triangle.

If you wish, put a dollop (no more than a heaping teaspoon) of filling (see variations on Croissants de Boulanger, pages 437–438, for options) in the center. Then roll up each triangle starting with the notched edge, working toward the tip. Make sure the point is tucked under the bottom of the croissant—if you have to stretch the dough a little to do so, that's OK. Form the crescent by bending the two ends toward the place where the dough's tip is tucked under the roll.

Place the croissants on a lightly greased or parchment-lined baking sheet. Cover and chill for at least 30 minutes. During that time, preheat the oven to 425°F.

TO BAKE THE CROISSANTS: Take the croissants out of the refrigerator, uncover them, and brush the tops with the beaten egg. Bake for 15 minutes; reduce the heat to 350°F and bake for another 10 to 15 minutes. The croissants should be a deep golden brown, even where the dough overlaps itself. Remove from the oven and cool completely on a rack.

NUTRITION INFORMATION PER SERVING: 1 unfilled croissant, 52g
205 cal | 15g fat | 2g protein | 15g complex carbohydrates | 0g sugar | 1g dietary fiber | 41mg cholesterol | 136mg sodium

---

FINISHING

When making croissants, it's traditional to finish them in a way that signals what's inside. Plain croissants need no more than the shine they acquire in the oven from the egg wash. Fruit-filled croissants are often glazed with sugar or honey, or drizzled with a simple icing or glaze. Almond-filled pastries should be glazed and sprinkled with toasted almond, sliced or chopped. Chocolate croissants get a thin stripe of melted chocolate. Savory filled croissants are usually made in a rectangular shape, with just enough filling showing at the ends to hint at what waits inside.

NAPOLEONS

16 PASTRIES

Most people assume this delightful combination of crisp pastry layers and creamy filling is in some way connected with Monsieur Bonaparte. Au contraire! The name is a French derivation of the word "Neapolitan": this style of pastry was originally made in Naples. It can be made with Classic Puff Pastry or a blitz dough. For filling, you can use a basic pastry cream or a flavored one, depending on your tastes.

½ recipe Classic Puff Pastry (page 422) or 1 recipe Blitz Puff Pastry (page 426)

GLAZE
2 cups (227g) confectioners' sugar, sifted

¼ cup (57g) heavy cream or milk, at room temperature

1 teaspoon corn syrup

½ ounce (14g) melted unsweetened chocolate

1 recipe Pastry Cream (page 350), chilled

fresh berries (optional)

On a lightly floured surface, roll out one half of the dough to a 14″ square, ⅛″ thick. Halfway through this process, transfer the dough to a piece of parchment paper, since it's difficult to move once it's been rolled very thin. Transfer the parchment and dough to a flat baking sheet. Prick the dough all over with a fork or a dough docker (see Tools, page 546), cover with a second sheet of parchment, and let it rest in the refrigerator for at least 30 minutes. Repeat this process with the other half of the dough.

Preheat the oven to 375°F.

After its rest, remove the dough from the refrigerator and place another flat-bottomed baking sheet on top of the parchment. Bake the dough sandwiched between the two pans for 20 minutes. Remove the top baking sheet and the paper underneath it, then return the uncovered pastry to the oven to continue baking for another 10 minutes, until the dough is a deep golden brown and baked all the way through. Remove from the oven and cool the pastry on a rack.

TO MAKE THE GLAZE: Place the confectioners' sugar in a bowl and stir in the cream and corn syrup. Remove ¼ cup of the mixture and, in a separate bowl, stir it into the melted chocolate.

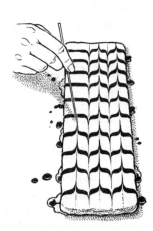

Cover the baked pastry sheets with an even layer of confectioners' sugar glaze. Pipe chocolate glaze in horizontal stripes, ¾″ apart. With a toothpick or the point of a paring knife, draw lines in alternating directions through the icing to pull the lines into points, as shown.

TO ASSEMBLE: Trim the edges of the cooked dough pieces with a serrated knife using gentle sawing motions, to make two 12″ squares. Cut each square into thirds, to make a total of six 4″ wide strips. Select the two best-looking strips of pastry and place them snugged up against each other on a piece of parchment or waxed paper. Pour the white glaze over the top to cover them completely. Smooth the glaze with an offset spatula. Pipe the chocolate glaze in narrow parallel lines across the top. With a toothpick or the tip of a paring knife, draw alternating lines perpendicularly through the chocolate stripes to pull them into a pattern. Carefully place tops on a rack to dry.

Take half of the chilled pastry cream and spread on two of the remaining strips of pastry; it should be about ¾″ thick. If you're using berries, push them down into this layer, then top with another strip of pastry. Repeat the process for the second layer, then put the iced strips on the top. Put the pastries in the refrigerator for half an hour to set up.

NUTRITION INFORMATION PER SERVING: **1 napoleon, 96g**
225 cal | 13g fat | 3g protein | 4g complex carbohydrates | 21g sugar | 0g dietary fiber | 93mg cholesterol | 69mg sodium

WHY TAKE THE PUFF OUT OF THE PASTRY?

Why go to all the effort of making puff pastry, only to bake it under the weight of another baking sheet? By limiting the vertical expansion of the layers while baking, they form themselves into an incredibly crisp pastry sheet that can carry the weight of the rich pastry cream on top. Covered baking also allows for slow caramelizing of the dough, yielding a deep, rich flavor. Napoleons are an excellent way to use scraps and trimmings from puff pastry dough, since there's no concern about the dough rising evenly.

CHEESE TWISTS

ABOUT THIRTY-SIX 12″ TO 14″ TWISTS

Don't you just love it when you discover a recipe that's easy to make, yet yields something that's not only delicious, but gives the appearance of having been difficult to execute? These tender, assertively cheesy pastries are absolutely addictive.

FILLING

1½ cups (150g) grated Parmesan cheese

2 teaspoons paprika

¼ teaspoon cayenne, or to taste*

EGG WASH

2 large eggs

2 tablespoons (28g) water

PASTRY

2 recipes Fast and Easy Puff Pastry
(page 427) or 1 recipe Blitz Puff
Pastry (page 426)

TO MAKE THE FILLING: Combine the Parmesan, paprika, and cayenne and set aside.

TO MAKE THE EGG WASH: Beat the eggs with the water in a small bowl, and set aside.

Preheat the oven to 400°F.

TO ASSEMBLE: Divide the dough into two pieces. Working with one piece at a time, roll it out into a 12″ × 24″ rectangle ⅛″ thick. Brush the entire surface with egg wash. Sprinkle half of the filling evenly over half of the dough. Fold the dough side without filling on it over to make a 12″ square, and roll it lengthwise, until the two halves stick together. You should have a rectangle of dough about 12″ × 13″. Repeat this process with the second piece of dough.

Using a rolling pizza cutter or a sharp knife, cut the dough crosswise into ¾″ wide strips, so that you have about 17 strips. Pick up a dough strip and twist the ends in opposite directions until the dough is a spiraled cylinder. Place the twists on a lightly greased or parchment-lined baking sheet and repeat with the remaining dough. Brush the tops lightly with egg wash, then sprinkle with salt. Bake the twists for 15 to 18 minutes, until they're golden brown. Remove from the oven and cool them on a rack before serving.

* This amount yields a twist that is noticeably but not assertively hot. Reduce or increase the amount of cayenne as you see fit.

NUTRITION INFORMATION PER SERVING: 1 twist, 34g

153 cal | 13g fat | 2g protein | 8g complex carbohydrates | 0g sugar | 0g dietary fiber | 46mg cholesterol | 40mg sodium

MINI ELEPHANT EARS

48 SMALL PASTRIES

These flat, crunchy, sweet pastry spirals are a delicious accompaniment to fresh berries.

2¼ cups (270g) unbleached all-purpose flour

¼ teaspoon salt

½ teaspoon baking powder

12 tablespoons (1½ sticks, 170g) unsalted butter, cut into ¼˝ pieces and frozen for 30 minutes

¾ cup (170g) sour cream, cold

½ to ¾ cup (98g to 147g) sugar

In a medium bowl, combine the flour, salt, and baking powder, then cut in the frozen butter, mixing until even crumbs form. Stir in the sour cream and gather the dough into a ball. Divide it in half, then cover and refrigerate for at least 1 hour, or overnight.

Remove one piece of the dough from the refrigerator, sprinkle your work surface heavily with sugar, and roll the dough into a 12˝ × 10˝ rectangle. Sprinkle more sugar over the dough and gently press it in with a rolling pin. Starting with the long sides, roll the edges of the pastry toward each other until they meet in the center, like a scroll. Repeat with remaining dough, wrap the scrolls, and refrigerate for at least 1 hour.

Preheat the oven to 425°F.

Using a serrated knife, gently cut each scroll into ⅓˝ thick slices and lay the slices on parchment-lined or lightly greased baking sheets.

Bake the pastries for 9 to 10 minutes, until the sugar on the bottom has begun to brown. Turn them over and bake for an additional 3 to 5 minutes, until the sugar is lightly browned on the other side. Watch closely—these go from golden brown to scorched very quickly. Remove the pastries from the oven and cool completely on a rack.

NUTRITION INFORMATION PER SERVING: **2 mini ears, 30g**
124 cal | 7g fat | 1g protein | 8g complex carbohydrates | 5g sugar | 0g dietary fiber | 19mg cholesterol | 38mg sodium

KRINGLE

THREE 10˝ ROUND KRINGLES

In the Midwest, and particularly in Wisconsin, kringle is a staple item in many bakeries. This festive confection—originally from Denmark—was traditionally formed into a pretzel shape, which has since evolved to a simpler wreath shape. Kringle is always made of some form of flaky sweet dough enclosing a sweet filling but the exact recipe varies—you'll find some with yeast doughs, some with a quick-bread base, and others with a tender sour cream– and butter-based pastry, which is the version we use.

We love this nut filling, but you can experiment with others (raspberry jam and caramel are common). Our recipe makes enough to fill one of the three kringles that the recipe yields, so either triple the filling or fill the other two with preserves, caramel, chocolate, or any other filling you like. Although the dough is very simple to put together, it requires gentle handling and thorough chilling, as it's quite soft.

DOUGH

2 cups (240g) unbleached all-purpose flour

½ teaspoon salt

16 tablespoons (2 sticks, 227g) unsalted butter, cold

1 cup (227g) sour cream

NUT FILLING (ENOUGH FOR ONE KRINGLE)

4 tablespoons (½ stick, 57g) butter, at room temperature

½ cup (113g) light brown sugar

¼ cup (30g) unbleached all-purpose flour

½ cup (57g) walnuts or pecans

½ cup (85g) raisins (optional)

TOPPING (ENOUGH FOR ALL THREE KRINGLES)

1 egg white

½ cup (110g) demerara or coarse white sugar

½ cup (57g) finely chopped nuts

TO MAKE THE DOUGH: In a medium bowl, whisk together the flour and salt. Cut in the butter until the mixture resembles coarse crumbs. Stir in the sour cream to create a soft dough. Wrap well and refrigerate overnight.

TO MAKE THE FILLING: Mix all the filling ingredients. Cover and refrigerate until you're ready to assemble the kringles. Bring the filling back to room temperature before using it, or it will tear the dough when you try to shape it.

Preheat the oven to 375°F.

TO ASSEMBLE: Take the kringle dough out of the refrigerator and divide it in thirds (each piece should weigh about 266g). Put two pieces back in the refrigerator. Take a 24˝ long piece of parchment and lightly flour the surface. Put the dough on the paper and lightly sprinkle it and your hands with flour. Roll the dough into a long,

5″ × 26″ strip. (It helps to go diagonally on your sheet of parchment; the strip will hang over the ends by an inch or so, but that's OK). Be sure to pick up the dough from time to time and sprinkle more flour underneath as necessary to keep it from sticking. With a dry pastry brush, carefully sweep any excess flour off the surface of the dough. Place the filling down the center of the dough, in a strip about 1″ wide. Gently take the edge closest to you (a bowl scraper or bench knife can help you here) and fold it up and over the filling. Brush the edge of the dough farthest away from you with egg white. Next, fold that edge to overlap the first, making a slightly flat, filled tube of dough. Brush off any excess flour, then carefully shape the dough into a circle. Seal the open ends together and brush the kringle with lightly beaten egg white. Sprinkle the top with the mixture of sugar and chopped nuts. Trim off excess parchment, and slide the kringle, riding on the parchment, onto a baking sheet. Repeat the process with the other two pieces of dough, varying the fillings as you like.

Bake for 25 minutes, or until evenly golden brown. Remove from the oven and cool on a rack. If desired, dust with confectioners' sugar before serving.

NUTRITION INFORMATION PER SERVING: 1 slice with nut filling, 29g
137 cal | 10g fat | 1g protein | 5g complex carbohydrates | 7g sugar | 1g dietary fiber | 19mg cholesterol | 26mg sodium

YEASTED PUFF PASTRY

This is the version of puff pastry found in France at the *boulangerie*, or bakery, as opposed to the classic puff pastry made at the patisserie. Sometimes it's sweet; sometimes it's not. But it, too, has many layers of butter rolled into it—not quite as many as puff pastry, but enough so that it's yeast dough at its most elegant. Yeasted puff dough is incredibly light but has more body than classic puff pastry. It can be made into Danish pastries, croissants, coffeecakes, or any number of pastries. The great advantage of this kind of dough is that once it's made, you can keep it for several days in the refrigerator, or you can even freeze it until the right occasion inspires you. It's easy to roll out, fill, and bake into a superlative breakfast.

DOUGH

2 large eggs plus enough warm water to make 2 cups liquid (454g)

¼ cup (49g) sugar

5½ to 6 cups (660g to 720g) unbleached all-purpose flour

2¼ teaspoons instant yeast

½ cup (42g) nonfat dry milk (optional, but will make a mellower, richer dough)

1 scant tablespoon (17g) salt

1 teaspoon vanilla extract (if making sweet pastry)

2 tablespoons (28g) butter, melted

BUTTER

**28 tablespoons (3½ sticks, 392g)
unsalted butter, cold**

½ cup (60g) unbleached all-
purpose flour, plus more for
sprinkling

TO MAKE THE DOUGH: Make a sponge by cracking the eggs into a 2-cup liquid mea-sure and adding enough warm water to equal 2 cups. Beat until blended and pour into a large mixing bowl or the bowl of your electric mixer. Add 1 tablespoon (12g) of the sugar, 3 cups (360g) of the flour, and the yeast. Mix until well blended. Cover and set aside at room temperature.

In a separate mixing bowl, blend together 2½ cups (300g) of the remaining flour, the rest of the sugar, the dry milk, and the salt. Set it aside.

TO MAKE THE BUTTER: Mix the butter and flour until they're smooth and well blended. You can do this with a mixer, a food processor, or with a spoon, by hand. Lightly flour a piece of plastic wrap or parchment, place the butter/flour mixture on it, and pat it into an 8˝ square (see illustration, page 423). Cover the butter and place it in the refrigerator on a flat surface for at least 30 minutes. Adding flour to the butter helps to stabilize it so it won't "flow" out of the seams when it's being rolled.

Turn your attention back to the dough. The yeast should have gotten to work and made the sponge bubbly and expanded by now. Give it a stir and blend in the vanilla and the melted butter. Stir in the flour/milk/salt mixture, mixing until you have a soft but kneadable dough.

Sprinkle flour on your kneading surface, turn out the dough, and knead for 8 to 10 min-utes, until it's bouncy and elastic. Wrap loosely and refrigerate for 30 minutes. You can also knead this dough in an electric mixer or in a bread machine.

MAKING THE TURNS: Follow the procedure for Classic Puff Pastry (page 422), giving a total of four turns to the dough. Wrap the dough loosely after its last turn, since the yeast will cause it to expand. Refrigerate for at least 2 hours, but prefer-ably overnight.

Use to make croissants (see Croissants de Boulanger, page 437) or a filled coffeecake.

CROISSANTS DE BOULANGER

24 CURVED OR 18 RECTANGULAR CROISSANTS

The croissants you'll find in French bread bakeries are often made with laminated yeast dough. Their texture is a bit sturdier and more flexible than those made from puff pastry, which is so flaky it practically shatters when pulled apart. The bread baker's croissant can be shaped into the familiar crescent, or it can be filled and folded into a rectangle before baking.

1 recipe Yeasted Puff Pastry (page 435)

EGG WASH
2 large eggs
2 tablespoons (28g) water

Preheat the oven to 400°F.

On a lightly floured surface, roll half of the dough into a 12″ x18″ rectangle. Trim the edges all the way around using a yardstick, cutting straight down with a very sharp knife or a pizza wheel. This cuts off the folded edges, which would inhibit the "puff." Repeat with the other half of the dough.

Cut the dough in thirds lengthwise and in half across the middle (see illustration, page 428). This should give you six 4″ × 9″ squares. Cut these squares in half diagonally and arrange them so the points of the triangles are facing away from you. It's OK to stretch them out slightly to elongate them when you do this. Cut a ½″ notch in the short edge of the triangle (see illustration, page 428). Roll the dough from this end toward the tip, making sure that the point of the dough is tucked under the bottom of the croissant. Push the outside edges toward the center to form the crescent shape.

PROOFING AND BAKING: Place the croissants on a parchment-lined baking sheet, use a reusable cover or greased plastic wrap to cover them, and let rise until almost doubled in size.

When fully proofed (20 to 30 minutes), beat the eggs and water together and brush the croissants with the egg wash. Bake for 18 to 22 minutes, until they're a deep golden brown, about 190°F with a digital thermometer.

NUTRITION INFORMATION PER SERVING: 1 plain croissant, 61g
223 cal | 16g fat | 3g protein | 15g complex carbohydrates | 2g sugar | 1g dietary fiber | 68mg cholesterol | 277mg sodium

VARIATIONS

ALMOND CROISSANTS: Roll Almond Filling (page 439) into a log about ¾″ in diameter and 3″ long. Place across the wide part of the triangle and with gentle

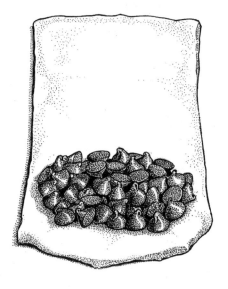

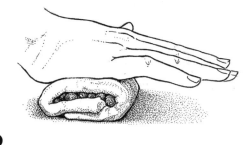

1. Place 2 tablespoons of filling or chocolate on the lower third of the rectangle. **2.** Press the folded croissant to flatten it slightly and keep it from unwinding during baking.

pressure roll it up. Make sure the point of the pastry ends up on the bottom. Gently curve the ends toward the point of the croissant and transfer it to the baking sheet.

CHOCOLATE CROISSANTS: Place 1 ounce (28g) of chocolate chips or chopped chocolate on the bottom third of the dough before rolling.

HAM AND CHEESE CROISSANTS: Trim a slice of ham to fit just inside the shape of the rectangle. Cut a slice of cheese to stack two pieces on the lower third of the rectangle. Shape as directed above.

NUTRITION INFORMATION PER SERVING: **1 chocolate croissant, 89g**
369 cal | 24g fat | 4g protein | 17g complex carbohydrates | 17g sugar | 1g dietary fiber | 68mg cholesterol | 277mg sodium

ALMOND PASTE, À LA MINUTE

To make your own almond paste, combine 1½ cups (144g) almond flour (make sure it's ground from blanched almonds), 1½ cups (170g) confectioners' sugar, 1 to 2 teaspoons almond extract (depending on how strong you want the flavor to be), and 2 tablespoons (40g) pasteurized egg whites in a food processor. Pulse, then process until the mixture is homogeneous and evenly moistened. Turn the mixture out on a work surface and knead it until it holds together. Divide into ½-cup pieces, wrap, and store airtight for up to 1 month, or freeze for longer storage.

Almond Filling

2 CUPS

This traditional croissant filling is pliable enough to be spread inside a coffeecake, and thick enough to be rolled into shapes.

¼ cup (63g) almond paste

¼ cup (49g) sugar

1 large egg

2 teaspoons brandy, rum, or almond syrup

½ teaspoon salt

¾ cup (64g) sliced almonds

1 cup (142g) cake crumbs*

Place the almond paste, sugar, egg, brandy, and salt in a food processor and purée until smooth. Pour the mixture into a mixing bowl and stir in the almonds and the cake crumbs. Refrigerate mixture until ready to use.

* To make cake crumbs, place six ½˝ slices of pound cake on an ungreased baking sheet and bake for 10 minutes at 300°F. Turn over, bake 10 minutes more, then cool. Process the slices in a food processor to make crumbs.

NUTRITION INFORMATION PER SERVING: 2 tablespoons, 26g
108 cal | 6g fat | 3g protein | 4g complex carbohydrates | 6g sugar | 1g dietary fiber | 23mg cholesterol | 96mg sodium

TRADITIONAL DANISH PASTRIES

24 DANISH PASTRIES

If there's one pastry that's familiar to just about any coffee drinker, it's the Danish. The version you'll make here is richer, fresher-tasting, and flakier than most you could buy. Danish pastry fillings are a matter of personal preference. Two of the most popular are raspberry and cheese, but feel free to experiment with other flavors, such as chocolate.

Make the recipe for Yeasted Puff Pastry (page 435), and include the following spices with the second addition of flour.

½ teaspoon cardamom

¼ teaspoon nutmeg

⅛ teaspoon cloves

Roll in the butter and give the dough four folds, as demonstrated on pages 424–425. Let the dough rest overnight.

Roll one-third of the dough into an 8″ × 16″ rectangle. With a pizza wheel or sharp knife, cut it in half lengthwise and then in quarters widthwise, so you have eight 4″ squares. For bite-size pastries, cut each square into four miniature squares.

TO MAKE POCKETS OR ENVELOPES: Take the 4″ squares, egg wash the edges, and place 2 teaspoons of filling in the center. (Be conservative with the amount of filling you place on these small pieces of dough, since it tends to occupy more space than you would think.) For pockets, take the opposite corners and bring them into the center and press them together. Take a scrap piece of dough and wrap around the overlap like a belt to keep it together while it bakes (see illustration). For an envelope, bring all four corners of the square to the center and press down to seal. You can put a little more filling on top of the center once the pastry is formed.

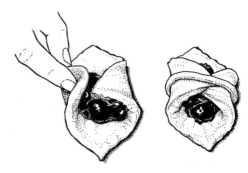

POCKETS   Place a spoonful of filling in the center of the dough square. Bring opposite points of the square together to form a pocket shape. Use a strip of scrap dough to "tie" the pocket together.

TO MAKE BEAR CLAWS OR COCKSCOMBS: (See illustration below). Instead of cutting squares, keep the dough in 4″ strips. Roll a ½″ diameter log of Almond Filling (page 439), and place it on the farthest edge of the strip. Egg wash the edge closest to you, roll the dough over the filling toward you, and press the edge together tightly. Roll the tube toward you a quarter turn, to make sure the seam is centered on the bottom, and press the tube flat with your fingers. With a sharp knife or a pair of kitchen scissors, make cuts through the dough every ½″ or so, stopping where the dough begins to bulge out around the filling. Cut the strip into 4″ pieces. Place on a baking sheet and bend slightly into a crescent to open the cuts.

TO MAKE FILLED ROUNDS: Roll the dough into an 8″ × 16″ rectangle, with the short side facing you. Brush the entire surface of the dough with egg wash and sprinkle the half closest to you with a layer of cinnamon sugar thick enough to cover the dough,

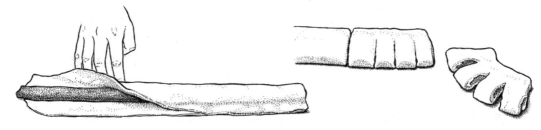

BEAR CLAWS   Cut the filled strip of dough with scissors, leaving a ½″ strip intact along the edge.

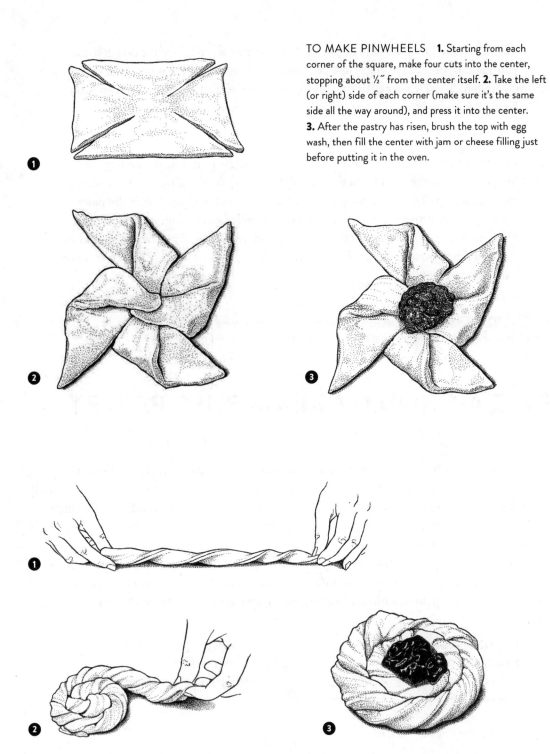

TO MAKE PINWHEELS **1.** Starting from each corner of the square, make four cuts into the center, stopping about ½″ from the center itself. **2.** Take the left (or right) side of each corner (make sure it's the same side all the way around), and press it into the center. **3.** After the pastry has risen, brush the top with egg wash, then fill the center with jam or cheese filling just before putting it in the oven.

FILLED ROUNDS **1.** Twist the ends of each strip of dough in opposite directions to form a spiral. **2.** Wind the twisted dough around itself like a snail, to form a round Danish. **3.** Place a tablespoon (21g) of jam or filling in the center after the dough has risen, just before baking.

leaving ½″ around the outside edge bare. Fold the uncovered half of the dough toward you, making sure all the edges line up. Lightly roll with a rolling pin to seal. Cut the dough into 1″ wide strips. Twist the strips to make spirals, then wind the spirals to form pinwheels. Place on a greased or parchment-lined baking sheet.

Preheat the oven to 400°F.

TO BAKE: Let the formed Danish rise for at least 20 minutes; depending on the temperature of the room, they may need as long as 90 minutes. They should look full and puffy; the longer they rise, the airier they will be. When the pastries are fully risen, brush them with egg wash and place any fillings on top. Bake for 18 to 22 minutes, depending on the shapes you've chosen. The Danish should be a deep golden brown all over. Remove from the oven, cool on a rack, and glaze or frost as you like.

NUTRITION INFORMATION PER SERVING: 1 Danish, filled with raspberry jam, 81g
277 cal | 16g fat | 3g protein | 16g complex carbohydrates | 12g sugar | 1g dietary fiber | 68mg cholesterol | 277mg sodium

PÂTE À CHOUX: CREAM PUFF PASTRY

3 CUPS, ENOUGH FOR 12 ÉCLAIRS OR 16 CREAM PUFFS

Pâte à choux (paht-ah-SHOO), which means literally cabbage paste (and refers to the similarity in shape between cream puffs and small cabbages), is also called choux paste, and commonly referred to as cream puff pastry. It's a cousin to popover batter, in that both baked products are leavened by steam, which expands them quickly and leaves large holes in their middles, ready to hold your choice of sweet fillings.

Pâte à choux is the basis for cream puffs (filled with whipped cream), éclairs (filled with pastry cream), and profiteroles (filled with ice cream). And of all the pastry recipes explored here, it ranks right up there with our fast and easy puff pastry as the easiest to make.

1 cup (227g) water

8 tablespoons (1 stick, 113g) unsalted butter

⅜ teaspoon salt

1¼ cups (150g) unbleached all-purpose flour

4 large eggs, at room temperature

Preheat the oven to 425°F.

Put the water, butter, and salt in a saucepan and bring the mixture to a rolling boil. Remove it from the heat and add the flour all at once. Stir vigorously. Return the pan to the burner and cook over medium heat, stirring all the while, until the mixture forms a ball; this should take only about a minute. Remove the pan from the heat and let the mixture cool for 5 to 10 minutes, to 140°F. It will still feel hot, but you should be able to hold a finger in it for a few seconds. Transfer the dough to a mixer and beat in the eggs one at a time; the mixture will become fluffy. Beat for at least 2 minutes after adding the last egg.

Form the choux paste into whatever shape you desire, using a spoon, or by putting the dough in a pastry bag and piping it.

Bake for 15 minutes, then reduce the oven temperature to 375°F and bake for an additional 15 minutes. Turn off the oven, open the door a crack, and leave the pastry inside to cool for 30 minutes. Remove from the oven to cool completely. Carefully split the pastry, fill, and frost as desired.

NUTRITION INFORMATION PER SERVING: **1 unfilled éclair, 40g**
105 cal | 8g fat | 1g protein | 7g complex carbohydrates | 0g sugar | 0g dietary fiber | 22mg cholesterol | 46mg sodium

IF THE CHOUX FITS

The principle behind choux paste is very simple: A hot oven creates steam, which lifts the dough high before it sets. What you might not know is that the ratio of liquid to flour to eggs is very flexible and can be adjusted depending on the texture you want. You can use amounts ranging from 1 part liquid to 2 parts flour to equal amounts of flour and liquid (all by volume). Using a higher percentage of flour will make a sturdier, crisper puff, more suitable for a heavy or wet filling. You can also increase crispness by using two egg whites in place of one of the whole eggs.

If you're seeking a tender, ethereal pastry that will be eaten soon after it's filled, use the higher amount of liquid. Our basic choux paste recipe is on this end of the spectrum.

CREAM PUFFS AND ÉCLAIRS

16 CREAM PUFFS AND 12 ÉCLAIRS

What is more delightful than these confections composed of crisp pâte à choux shells and cool, smooth custardy fillings? They're not nearly so difficult to prepare as their appearance might suggest. For best results, assemble these as close in time as you can to serving them, and store them and any leftovers in the refrigerator.

1 recipe prepared Pâte à Choux (page 442)

CREAM PUFF FILLING

2 cups (454g) heavy cream

¼ cup (50g) sugar, or to taste

1 teaspoon vanilla extract

CHOCOLATE ÉCLAIR FILLING AND GLAZE

½ recipe Pastry Cream (page 350)

1 cup (170g) chocolate chips or chopped semisweet chocolate

½ cup (113g) heavy cream

Preheat the oven to 425°F.

For cream puffs, using a generously filled tablespoon cookie scoop, or a level muffin scoop, drop the thick choux batter onto the prepared baking sheets in 3- to 4-tablespoon mounds. Space the mounds about 3″ apart, to allow for expansion. For éclairs, pipe the batter into 5″ logs about ½″ to ¾″ in diameter.

Bake the pastries for 15 minutes, then lower the heat to 350°F and bake until the sides are set, about 25 minutes more. Don't open the oven door while the pastries are baking.

Remove the pastries from the oven. Make a small slit in the top of each, and return them to the oven for 5 minutes, to allow the steam to escape. Place them on a rack to cool. When they're cool enough to handle, split each in half to make top and bottom pieces; splitting and exposing the centers to air will help keep them from becoming soggy.

TO MAKE THE CREAM PUFF FILLING: Pour the cream into a mixing bowl, and begin to whip it on high speed (using your mixer's whisk attachment, if you have one). Sprinkle in the sugar gradually as the cream whips. Whip until stiff, but be careful not to over-whip; cream should still look smooth.

Fill the bottom halves of the puffs with whipped cream, then replace their tops and serve.

TO MAKE THE ÉCLAIR FILLING: Prepare the pastry cream filling; you'll need about 3 cups of filling.

Spoon the filling into the éclair shells.

TO MAKE THE ÉCLAIR GLAZE: Place the chocolate chips or chunks and cream in a microwave-safe bowl or measuring cup.

Heat over low heat (or in the microwave) until the cream is very hot.

Remove from the heat, and stir until the chocolate melts and the icing is smooth. Spoon over the éclairs, spreading to the edges. Serve immediately.

NUTRITION INFORMATION PER SERVING: 1 filled pastry, 108g
310 cal | 27g fat | 5g protein | 10g complex carbohydrates | 5g sugar | 1g dietary fiber | 130mg cholesterol | 110mg sodium

SPICY CHEESE PUFFS

60 SMALL PUFFS

These tiny puffs are based on *gougère*, a French choux-type pastry that's typically flavored with Gruyère cheese, baked in a large ring, and served in slices as an appetizer. Our version makes individual light-as-air puffs. Serve them plain or gild the lily by filling them with tiny bits of cream cheese or chicken salad or savory dips. We include instructions for how to shape them as sticks instead of rounds, which makes for a delightful appetizer.

1 recipe Pâte à Choux (page 442)

1 teaspoon dry mustard

¼ teaspoon cayenne

1 teaspoon freshly ground black pepper

1 teaspoon paprika

1½ cups (170g) grated sharp cheddar cheese

¼ cup (25g) grated Parmesan cheese

Preheat the oven to 425°F.

Prepare choux paste as directed in the recipe, increasing the salt to 1 teaspoon and combining the spices above with the flour. Once the eggs are beaten in, beat in the cheeses. Use a small (teaspoon-size) cookie scoop or a pastry bag to drop or pipe cherry-size mounds of dough onto a lightly greased or parchment-lined baking sheet. For cheese sticks, fit a pastry bag with an open star tip with a ⅛″ to ¼″ opening. Pipe sticks the length of your choice; long sticks across a bowl of soup (about 8″ long) are impressive.

Bake the puffs for 15 minutes, reduce the oven temperature to 350°F, and continue to bake for an additional 10 to 15 minutes, until the puffs are golden brown. Turn off the oven, crack open the door, and let the puffs cool in the oven slowly; they'll dry out as they cool, which is the desired outcome.

If you're making sticks, bake them for a total of 14 minutes at the higher oven temperature, then turn off the oven, crack the door open, and let them cool in the oven for 5 minutes before taking them out and allowing them to cool completely on a rack. Store the puffs or sticks in an airtight container. If they become soft or soggy, reheat them in a preheated 400°F oven for 5 minutes.

ALMOND PUFF LOAF

TWO LOAVES

This recipe seems as if it can't be right—there's no sugar in the dough! But just follow the recipe and you'll be rewarded with a pastry that is remarkably elegant. The buttery crust supports a tender, almond-scented layer of airy pastry, which in turn is dressed up with a luxuriant layer of preserves. The glaze is the crowning touch, and when eaten all together, the results are simply captivating.

PASTRY

16 tablespoons (2 sticks, 227g) salted
    butter, cold and divided

2 cups (240g) unbleached all-
    purpose flour

1¼ cups (283g) water, cold

3 large eggs, at room temperature

1 teaspoon almond extract

TOPPING

¾ cup (255g) jam

½ cup (57g) chopped walnuts or
    almonds

ICING

1 cup (113g) confectioners' sugar

2 to 3 tablespoons (28g to 42g) milk

½ teaspoon vanilla extract

Preheat the oven to 350°F.

TO MAKE THE BASE: Cut 1 stick of butter into 1 cup of flour until the mixture forms coarse crumbs. Blend in ¼ cup cold water. Form the dough into a ball and divide it in half. On a greased baking sheet, pat each half into a 3″ × 11″ rectangle, spacing the rectangles 4″ apart. Slide a spatula dipped in cold water alongside and over the top of the rectangles to smooth out their surfaces.

TO MAKE THE PUFF PASTRY: Put remaining 1 cup of water in a saucepan and add the remaining stick of butter. Bring the mixture to a rapid boil, stirring until the butter melts completely. Add the remaining 1 cup of flour all at once, and stir until the mixture becomes smooth and pulls away from the side of the pan. Transfer the dough to a mixing bowl, and add the eggs one at a time, beating well after each. Beat in the almond extract. Divide this batter in half. Drop by spoonfuls on top of each pastry base, covering completely, top and sides. Bake for 1 hour, or until golden brown. Remove the pastries from the oven and immediately top with an even layer of jam (raspberry or apricot are particularly good) and chopped nuts. While the puffs are cooling, stir together the confectioners' sugar, milk, and vanilla to make a thin icing. When completely cool, drizzle the puffs with the icing.

NUTRITION INFORMATION PER SERVING: 1 slice, 55g

211 cal | 12g fat | 3g protein | 11g complex carbohydrates | 11g sugar | 1g dietary fiber | 57mg cholesterol | 12mg sodium

PARIS-BREST FRAMBOISE

ONE 8″ PARIS-BREST

This variation on a classic French pastry, one of France's most common uses for choux paste, is shaped in a wheel to commemorate an 1891 bicycle race from Paris to Brest. This ring of choux pastry is traditionally filled with a hazelnut and almond cream, but we've given a nod to springtime with raspberry mousse and fluffy whipped cream.

1 recipe Pâte à Choux (page 442)

RASPBERRY MOUSSE FILLING

3 cups (120g) frozen raspberries

1 cup (198g) granulated sugar

1 tablespoon (14g) lemon juice

1½ teaspoons unflavored powdered gelatin

¼ cup (57g) water, cold

1 cup (227g) heavy cream

GARNISH

½ pint (113g) fresh raspberries

1 cup (227g) heavy cream

¼ cup (28g) confectioners' sugar

½ teaspoon vanilla extract

Preheat the oven to 450°F.

To get a perfect pastry ring, trace around a dinner plate (an 8″ circle is the right size) on parchment, then turn over the paper (you don't want to bake on top of your ink or pencil) and place it on a baking sheet. You can pipe the choux around the inside edge of the circle, or use a scoop and drop mounds, just barely touching one another, around the circle. Bake for 15 minutes. Turn down the oven to 350°F and bake for another 5 to 10 minutes. Turn off the oven and let the pastry cool for 10 minutes, with the oven door propped open. Remove and let cool completely. Slice in half horizontally.

TO MAKE THE FILLING: In a medium saucepan set over medium heat, bring the frozen raspberries, sugar, and lemon juice to a simmer. Remove from the heat and press the fruit through a fine strainer; discard the seeds and any solids, reserving the purée. Set it aside to cool to room temperature. You should have at least 1½ cups.

In a small heatproof bowl or measuring cup, combine the gelatin and cold water. Let the mixture sit until all the water has been absorbed (this only takes a minute or so). Whip the cream until soft peaks form; set it aside. Heat the gelatin/water mixture over low heat until it becomes a clear liquid. Stir this into the raspberry purée, then fold in the whipped cream. Refrigerate the mousse for about 90 minutes, to let it begin to set up.

Fill the bottom half of the pastry ring with the raspberry mousse filling. Top the filling with half of the raspberries, then place the top half of the ring over them.

Whip the cream until it holds a medium peak, then add the confectioners' sugar and vanilla. Place the whipped cream in a pastry bag with a star tip and pipe cream rosettes on top. Decorate with fresh raspberries. Chill for 30 minutes or up to several hours (or longer) before serving. (The raspberry cream will hold its shape for several days if kept refrigerated, but the choux will lose its crispness over time.)

NUTRITION INFORMATION PER SERVING: 1 slice, 54g

142 cal | 12g fat | 1g protein | 7g complex carbohydrates | 2g sugar | 1g dietary fiber | 37mg cholesterol | 40mg sodium

ALMOND GALETTE

ONE 10″ GALETTE

In France, almond galette (known as Galette des Rois) is typically served on January 6: Epiphany, the Feast of the Kings. An ultra-buttery, exceptionally flaky pastry crust stuffed with almond filling, this is quite possibly the easiest "fancy" dessert you'll ever make.

CRUST

1½ cups (180g) unbleached all-purpose flour

¼ teaspoon salt

½ teaspoon baking powder

16 tablespoons (2 sticks, 227g) unsalted butter, cold

½ cup (113g) sour cream

FILLING

⅔ cup (170g) almond paste

6 tablespoons (¾ stick, 85g) unsalted
 butter, at room temperature

½ cup (99g) sugar

½ teaspoon salt

2 large egg yolks

1 teaspoon vanilla extract

⅓ cup (40g) unbleached all-
 purpose flour

½ cup (48g) almond flour or very finely
 ground whole almonds

GLAZE

1 large egg yolk

1 teaspoon water, cold

TO MAKE THE CRUST: Whisk together the flour, salt, and baking powder. Cut the cold butter into pats, and work it into the flour mixture until it's unevenly crumbly, with larger bits of butter remaining intact.

Stir in the sour cream. The dough will be craggy but cohesive. Turn the dough out onto a well-floured surface and bring it together, if necessary, with a few quick kneads.

Pat the dough into a rough square. Roll it into a rough 8″ × 10″ rectangle. Make sure the underside is sufficiently dusted with flour that you can move it around easily.

Starting with one of the shorter (8″) ends, fold the dough in thirds like a business letter. Flip it over (so the open flap is on the bottom) and turn it 90°. Roll the dough into an 8″ × 10″ rectangle again. Fold it in thirds again.

Wrap the dough in plastic wrap and place it in the refrigerator to chill for at least 30 minutes (or overnight).

When you're ready to proceed, preheat the oven to 400°F. Lightly grease a baking sheet, or line it with parchment.

Divide the pastry in half. Roll one half into a 10″ square.

Using a 10″ round template (e.g., a dinner plate), cut a 10″ circle. Set the circle onto the prepared baking sheet.

TO MAKE THE FILLING: Beat the almond paste, butter, sugar, and salt until thoroughly combined.

Add the egg yolks and vanilla, and beat until well incorporated.

Mix in the flours.

Roll the other piece of pastry into an 11″ square. Cut an 11″ circle.

TO ASSEMBLE THE GALETTE: Spread the filling over the smaller circle, leaving a 1″ rim around the edge of the pastry.

TO MAKE THE GLAZE: Mix the egg yolk and water together. Brush some glaze over the uncovered edge of the pastry.

Center the larger round of dough over the filled bottom crust, and smooth it over the filling. Using a fork, press and crimp the edge of the galette to seal.

Decorate the galette by using the back of a knife to trace a pattern on the surface; you'll just barely cut into the surface without cutting all the way through. Poke a vent hole in the center, and four additional small slits at other random spots, hiding the slits in the pattern you've drawn.

Brush an even coat of the glaze over the surface of the galette, then bake it for 30 to 35 minutes, or until it's golden. Don't be afraid to let it become deeply browned; this slight caramelization gives the butter in the crust wonderful flavor. Remove the galette from the oven, and cool it slightly right on the baking sheet.

NUTRITION INFORMATION PER SERVING: 1 slice, 86g

410 cal | 30g fat | 6g protein | 16g complex carbohydrates | 14g sugar | 2g dietary fiber | 105mg cholesterol | 180mg sodium

CHAPTER ELEVEN

Ingredients

THE KEY TO A BAKING MASTERPIECE is in its inception: choosing the ingredients. A fine hand and a quick mind are key attributes of the home baker, but knowledge and creativity won't make up for the wrong ingredients.

While baking success is a composed of several factors (a tested recipe, accurate measuring, good technique), it's also true that the single ingredient most responsible for a recipe's performance is the one most often taken for granted. Flour is the backbone of practically every baking recipe, and they can vary wildly from brand to brand, which is why using the best-quality flour you can is so important.

This chapter is devoted to giving you an objective review of most of the ingredients you'll encounter as a baker. Knowing which types of flour, fat, sweetener, liquid, salt, leavener, and other ingredients work best in the recipe you've chosen is not just important, it's imperative. Not all chocolate is created equal. Granulated sugar and powdered sugar are vastly different. Want to know more? Read on.

Flour

Wheat

The most fundamental ingredient for the baker is flour, since it's the foundation for the vast majority of baking recipes. The single most important thing for the baker to understand about flour is that all flour is *not* created equal. Knowing how different flours behave in the kitchen will allow you to be both creative and successful with your baking, because you'll be using the right tool for the right job.

In order to better understand flour, we need to gain insight into some basics and some history. When we think of flour we generally think of flour made from wheat. There's a reason for that. While flour can be ground from a number of different grains, it is only the flour milled from wheat that has the unique characteristics and abilities we associate with the word *flour*.

Wheat flour contains two proteins called glutenin and gliadin. When a flour that contains these proteins is mixed with a liquid, a stretchy substance called gluten is produced. Like any protein, it's pliable until cooked. After baking, it becomes firm and holds its shape. This combination of cohesion and elasticity allows a bread dough to capture and contain the carbon dioxide bubbles produced by yeast. As their numbers grow, the dough gets bigger. In short, gluten is the magic substance that allows a dough to rise, and it is found in the greatest abundance in wheat flour.

Other flours produce different amounts of gluten, giving them different baking behaviors. The amount of gluten is determined by the protein level of the flour. Protein levels for wheat from which flour is milled can vary from crop to crop, season to season. But there are even more significant variations in different types of wheat.

The Major Classifications of Modern Wheat

After eons of isolating and breeding more "user-friendly" characteristics, there are more than thirty thousand varieties of wheat today, each with its own merits. To bring some order to this, in the United States, wheat is grouped into six classes: hard red winter, hard red spring, hard white, soft red winter, soft white, and durum. These all have origins in seeds that were carried to the United States by people emigrating from Europe. As more wheat varieties are emerging from breeding facilities, those classifications will probably have some additions. It's worth noting that breeding plants is an ancient technique, wholly distinct from the creation of genetically modified plants. There is no commercially available genetically modified wheat in the United States at present. To make wheat types easier to understand, we'll look at current wheat varieties as some combination of the following: hard or soft, red or white, winter or spring.

Hard Wheats

Hard wheats are the high-protein wheats that contain more gluten-producing proteins than soft wheats and thus produce doughs with more structure and baked goods with a strong rise. Hard wheats, because they can produce more gluten, are therefore best for yeast-leavened goods. Physically, a hard wheat berry tends to be longer and more bullet-shaped than soft wheat berries, which are plumper. There are many more acres planted of hard wheats than soft wheats in this hemisphere.

Hard wheat berries can be either red or white, the color of the pigment in the bran. Most of the hard wheat in this country is red, but there is a growing percentage of white wheat being grown every year. Hard wheats, both red and white, can be either winter or spring varieties.

Winter wheat is grown from Texas north through Kansas, which is the largest wheat state, into mid-Nebraska. It is planted in the fall, grows until it's about 5˝ tall, and then with the onset of winter and cold weather, it becomes dormant under a good snow cover (vernalization). It resumes growing the following spring and is harvested in late spring and early summer. Hard winter wheat ranges between 10% and 12% protein, the right amount for artisan and home bread baking, where dough is often made by hand.

Spring wheat is grown primarily in the Dakotas, Minnesota, and Montana into Canada, where the climate is more severe. It is planted in the spring and harvested in late summer and early fall. Spring wheat flours range between 12% and 14% protein, high enough levels that doughs made from them are better developed by machine. Spring wheats are also a good choice when you're adding non-wheat (i.e., non-gluten-producing) ingredients to your dough.

Durum wheat is the hardest of the hard wheats, but it is in a category by itself. It is a more primitive wheat and, as such, its protein has very different characteristics. It doesn't create the elastic gluten that is characteristic of more modern hard wheats. It is usually milled into semolina (a golden-colored granulated flour with the consistency of Cream of Wheat), which is used primarily for pasta. It can also be milled into a finer golden flour that can be used for the same purpose, or in conjunction with other types of wheat in breads, cakes, and so on.

Soft Wheats

Soft wheats are the plump ones; they have a larger percentage of carbohydrates, meaning less protein, and thus less gluten-forming ability. These are used for baked goods that don't need a highly developed matrix of gluten strands, such as cakes,

TYPES OF WHEAT FLOUR

TYPE	PROTEIN LEVEL*	USES	WHEAT SOURCE	BAKING CHARACTERISTICS
King Arthur Unbleached Cake Flour	10%	Cakes, some muffins	Soft red	This flour/wheat starch blend creates moist and tender cakes or muffins.
King Arthur Pastry Flour	8%	Cakes, pastry	Soft red or white	Lower protein yields a more tender product without artificial chemicals
King Arthur Unbleached All-Purpose Flour	11.7%	Cakes, breads, pies, cookies, quick breads, and muffins	Hard red	Best all-around flour: Enough protein for good structure, but not so much that baked goods are tough or chewy.
King Arthur Unbleached Bread Flour	12.7%	Breads, pretzels, combined with whole grain or non-gluten flours	Hard red spring	Higher protein level gives more support to non-gluten flours such as rye; it also helps structure of whole grain breads. It makes excellent pizza crust and artisan loaves, which have a high water content.
King Arthur High-Gluten Flour	14.2%	Yeast products where a chewier texture is desired, such as bagels or pizza	Hard red spring	This flour has the highest protein level available; it's mostly used commercially, for bagels and pizza doughs.
King Arthur Self-Rising Flour	8.5%	Biscuits, dumplings, quick breads, pancakes, cakes	Soft red	A low-protein flour that has baking powder and salt added to it already; it saves time and makes wonderfully light baked goods.
King Arthur Premium 100% Whole Wheat Flour	14% (not all is gluten-forming; see page 460)	Recipes designed for whole grains; traditional artisan breads, sourdough, as an alternative to white flour with some recipe adjustments	Hard red spring	Ground from the entire wheat berry, whole wheat flour contains bran, germ, and endosperm. The oils in the germ can go rancid, so whole wheat flour should be stored airtight, in the freezer.
King Arthur White Whole Wheat Flour	12.5 % to 13% (not all is gluten-forming; see page 460)	Whole grain recipes where you want a lighter color and flavor; can be used to substitute for white flour, with some recipe adjustments	Hard white	Nutritionally identical to traditional whole wheat, the bran is lighter in color and has a milder, sweeter flavor.

*Percentages are based on King Arthur Baking Company product specifications.

biscuits, and pastry. These are almost all winter wheats. They're planted in the fall and winter in a state of dormancy to begin growing the following spring. Soft winter wheats are grown primarily east of the Mississippi, from Missouri and Illinois east to Virginia and the Carolinas in the South, and New York State in the North. There are also important crops of soft white wheat in the northern Pacific states.

Soft white flour has a greater absorption rate than soft red flour; that is, it has slightly more protein. Its protein is also more tolerant, meaning it retains its elastic characteristics during manipulation for a significantly longer period than does soft red. Soft whites are usually used for pastry flours. Soft reds are used for cake flour, which is sometimes bleached, chemically creating a "tougher" flour that can contain large amounts of fat and sugar but still produce a light cake.

From Wheat to Flour

Look at a wheat berry itself. In simplest terms, it is composed of the following:

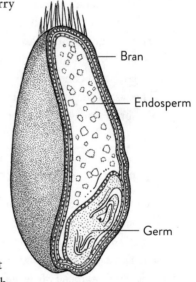

- **BRAN**, the outside coating that holds the wheat berry together and protects it.
- **GERM**, the embryo of a new wheat seedling were it to germinate.
- **ENDOSPERM** ("that which is within the seed"), the remaining part of the wheat berry that is the food or nutritive source for the growing wheat seedling.

While many espouse the use of whole grains for their nutritional value, there are some benefits to flours that don't contain the germ or bran. The most obvious is that the gluten-producing proteins are in the endosperm, not the germ or the bran. A bread dough made from flour ground from just the endosperm—white flour—will enjoy the greatest expansion and create the lightest loaf since there is nothing to interfere with the development of the gluten. The bran, no matter how finely ground, has sharp edges that tend to shred the strands of gluten that have been developed in a dough. When the gluten matrix is torn, some of the carbon dioxide bubbles created by the yeast escape, resulting in a denser loaf.

Second, the oil-rich germ, like any other vegetable oil, will eventually become rancid. Before the development of the refrigerator or freezer, storage of whole grains for any period of time was a real problem. Flour that doesn't contain the germ, if kept cool and dry and free of infestation, will keep almost indefinitely, with no loss in performance or nutritional value. All of these considerations made white flour very desirable.

Milling

Once the wheat berries are cleaned and tempered (soaked to bring them to a uniform moisture level), they're passed through the first set of steel rollers: the "first break." These rollers are corrugated and designed to break the berry into its constituent parts so the chunks of endosperm can begin to be separated from the bran and germ. With each successive pass through increasingly smooth rollers, the small chunks of endosperm are ground into flour and passed through a series of sieves with different mesh sizes, resulting in several "streams" of flour. The first stream produces what's known as "patent" flour, which contains the least amount of insoluble material. This can be equated with the earliest runs of maple sap that produce the fanciest syrup, the first cold-pressing of olives that produce extra virgin olive oil, or the first pressing of wine grapes that produces the highest quality wines.

With each successive rolling and sifting, streams of increasing mineral content are removed. The next major stream to come off is known as "First Clear Flour." This is significantly darker relative to patent flour. It is used often in making rye breads to add gluten-producing characteristics. "Second Clear Flour" follows "First," and contains an even greater level of non-endosperm (i.e., bran) material. The last is the lowest flour grade of all, often referred to as Red Dog. Along with the bran and germ that has been removed from the other flour streams, it is

---

STORING FLOURS AND GRAINS

Flours that don't contain the germ such as all-purpose bleached or unbleached, bread, white rye, and so forth, can be stored where it's cool and dry for an indefinite period of time. Whole grains are a different story. Once you rupture the oily germ of the berry by grinding it into flour, it's exposed to air and thus subject to oxidation. This simply means it will slowly become rancid. Freshly ground whole grains stored in cool and dry conditions will keep for about three months. If they're stored in an airtight container in the refrigerator, this time period can be extended for another three months. Freezing is by far the best way to store whole grain flours, but it won't stop oxidation entirely. When you're dealing with whole grains, the best bet is to buy small amounts and bake with them right away for the most delicious results.

All grains are subject to insect infestation. If you're going to have flour around at room temperature for any length of time, tuck in a bay leaf to discourage any "visitors." If you're going to be gone for any length of time, particularly over the summer, use all your flour or freeze it. Storage in an airtight container is advisable.

---

sometimes used as animal feed. With the growing awareness of the benefits of whole grains, all of these streams are frequently reunited in their proper proportions to make whole grain flours. When all the streams of endosperm are blended together, except for the "Clears" and "Red Dog," you have what is known as "straight" flour.

Additives

Once a flour has emerged from the milling process, a number of things can be added to it. During the 1940s, there was a temporary US Government mandate that white bread be "enriched," as it was a primary source of vitamins and minerals in people's diets, and the extraction of the wheat's bran and germ had removed many of them. As a result, small amounts of iron, niacin, thiamin, and riboflavin were added to white flour. The dietary landscape has changed considerably since then, and King Arthur Baking Company no longer adds enrichments to its flours, in keeping with its philosophy of simple, pure ingredients whenever possible. White flour is no longer required to be enriched.

That said, all-purpose flour usually has malted flour added to enhance its performance for yeast baking (the enzymes in the malt help convert the starch in the flour to sugars the yeast likes to eat). In some instances, flour is treated with other additives to produce certain characteristics. History and tradition have created a desire for white flour. Because it was difficult for medieval millers to separate the germ and the bran from the flour they milled, the small amounts of white flour produced were saved for the lord of the manor. Thus began the association of white flour with the upper classes. Before food safety laws were instituted in the early twentieth century, unethical millers accomplished this "whitening" by adding a variety of things to their flour: ground lime, chalk, alum, bone. In 1757, the English Parliament passed a law banning the addition of alum or anything else to flour, although it was generally ignored.

Contemporary millers are still in the business of making white flour. The first step in accomplishing this is to separate the bran and germ through the milling process itself. The next step is to "whiten" the remaining flour. Given time and exposure to air, flour will slowly oxidize and whiten on its own. This rest period, which should be around two weeks in the summer and up to a month in the winter, also changes flour's chemistry so that it will create a dough that is more responsive and elastic. However, rather than using time as an agent as King Arthur Baking Company does, many millers use chemicals to make this happen almost instantly. As the flour comes off the line at the mill, bleaching and oxidizing chemicals are added in order to quicken or actually replace this aging time.

Chlorine dioxide, benzoyl peroxide, and chlorine gas, all of which whiten and/or oxidize flour, are currently permissible additives. Benzoyl peroxide leaves benzoic acid, which, although it has an FDA GRAS (Generally Recognized As Safe) status, can be mildly toxic to the skin, eyes, and mucous membranes. This can be detected as a bitter aftertaste by people with an acute sense of taste. Benzoyl peroxide whitens flour but does not appreciably change its baking qualities. Chlorine gas reacts with the flour to change its absorbency, flavor, pH, and, in the case of some cake flours, its performance. After this reaction, the gas breaks down to leave hydrochloric acid, chloride (an electrolyte), and chlorite (which occurs naturally in unbleached flour). In baked goods where other ingredients do not mask it, it imparts a detectable flavor to people with sensitive palates.

The most controversial additive at present is potassium bromate, which is still in use both as an oxidizer and a conditioner in many commercially available flours. It has come under scrutiny, however, as tests with it have indicated that it is carcinogenic in animals and probably in humans. Since 1991, flour sold in California containing potassium bromate has had to carry a warning label. It is banned in Canada, Europe, and Japan. Although there are scientists who claim that there is no harmful residue left in bromated flour after baking, we are guessing that potassium bromate will ultimately also be retired as an additive.

King Arthur Baking Company Flours

In the late nineteenth century, when the effects of the roller milling process were really beginning to be felt, a lot of people wanted to get into the flour business. It looked like a burgeoning industry and a promising way to make money. Unfortunately, there were no federal standards or guidelines for milling flour. As a result, a lot of inconsistently milled and low-grade flour was produced, which was then "improved" with chemicals.

Messrs. Sands, Taylor, and Wood, the three who introduced the King Arthur brand of flour back in the 1890s (prior to that, the company had distributed but not milled its own flour), decided to take another approach. They developed a formula for a flour of the highest quality, something very specific and measurable. Since the protein level and its quality determine how a flour will behave in a recipe, a higher quality flour is one that is utterly consistent in its protein level; it will always perform in the same way. No other flour purveyor has more rigorous standards for the wheat from which its flour is milled, or a more consistently performing flour, than King Arthur.

This decision, to be purveyors of the finest flour possible, has stood us in good stead. King Arthur Baking Company has stood the test of time, the vagaries of the market, the decline in home baking, and the recent resurgence; it remains the finest flour available. Flour has been central to our business for more than two hundred years; it is the one ingredient on which we stake our reputation and around which the rest of our business is built. There's a very good reason that recipe testers, culinary schools, baking authors, and anyone who cares about quality chooses King Arthur Flours above all others.

In order to take full advantage of the predictable performance of our fine flours, you will need to have an understanding of each of them.

KING ARTHUR UNBLEACHED ALL-PURPOSE FLOUR is a patent flour with a protein level of about 11.7 %, milled from hard red wheat. The protein level of our flour is clearly higher than that of other all-purpose flour, which can range from as low as 10.5% to anywhere above 11%.

This distinction has its roots in our heritage. King Arthur Flour was formulated in 1896 with New England bread bakers in mind. The protein level of 11.7% is as high as can be adequately kneaded by hand. Because it is an unbleached flour, its protein hasn't been chemically toughened. It remains mellow enough that, when handled correctly, it will make wonderful quick breads, biscuits, cookies, and pastry. The protein in our King Arthur Unbleached All-Purpose Flour also has great "tolerance," meaning the gluten can be manipulated for a long time before it begins to break down. As far as the bread baker is concerned, it's a very forgiving flour. You can make a dough, deflate it several times or just ignore it all day, and it will still have enough strength to produce a wonderful loaf of bread. In fact, the bread will be better because the long fermentation will give it more complex and satisfying flavor. Our all-purpose flour is also an excellent flour for the bread machine.

SIR GALAHAD is the commercial bakery equivalent of our signature flour, King Arthur Unbleached All-Purpose Flour. It is used by commercial bakers who make artisan breads.

KING ARTHUR PASTRY FLOUR is an unbleached patent grade of soft white New York State wheat flour with a protein level of about 8%. It can be used as is to make tender cakes and pastry. It can be used in conjunction with our unbleached all-purpose flour to make French-type breads that have the characteristics of both flours. By combining the two in various proportions, you can create a protein that will produce the kind of texture you want in whatever you are baking. Our pastry flour is available through *The Baker's Catalogue* (see Where to Find It, page 550).

KING ARTHUR UNBLEACHED CAKE FLOUR, a blend of unbleached flour and wheat starch, was developed to give bakers a cake flour with trustworthy performance and ingredients, in keeping with the King Arthur Baking Company's quest for purity and lack of additives. With a protein level of 10%, our cake flour blend works well in cake recipes where the weight of the sugar in the recipe is less than the weight of the flour, and the eggs are less than that of the fat. White cakes made with our flour blend won't be as starkly white as those made with bleached flour, having a creamy ivory color instead. The texture of cakes made with this flour is moist and a little more close-grained than bleached flour recipes.

KING ARTHUR UNBLEACHED BREAD FLOUR is milled from hard red spring wheat and has a higher protein level than our all-purpose, about 12.7%. It is designed for yeast baking and its high protein is most adequately developed by mixer or machine; it's also well suited for high hydration breads with long fermentation times, such as the popular no-knead style of breads. It works well in recipes that call for non-gluten-producing flours such as rye, barley, corn, oat, teff, and the like. It is available both institutionally and at retail.

SIR LANCELOT HIGH-GLUTEN FLOUR is our highest protein flour, 14.2%. It is used primarily to make ultra-chewy bagels, or to lighten rye breads and for some pizza doughs. It is most effectively developed by machine. It is available institutionally and through *The Baker's Catalogue*.

KING ARTHUR PREMIUM 100% WHOLE WHEAT FLOUR is ground from the whole grain of hard red spring wheat with a protein level of about 14%. The protein level here is misleading, as a percentage of it is located in the germ and the bran and doesn't produce gluten. For practical baking purposes, calculate the amount of gluten-producing protein in whole grain flours, by using 75% of the amount given. This brings the level of gluten-producing protein to about 11.25%, an appropriate amount for yeast baking and kneading by hand. It should also be noted that the ground bran in the flour has sharp edges that can shear the gluten strands in the dough, inhibiting its rise. More liquid and longer fermentation times can ameliorate this and give better rising whole grain breads.

KING ARTHUR WHITE WHOLE WHEAT FLOUR was created in the early 1990s, when we were sent a sample of a new strain of whole wheat flour from a consortium of farmers in Kansas (now known as Farmer Direct Foods, Inc.) who had been working for some time with Kansas State University's wheat-breeding program. After we had baked with it we knew that we had something really exciting.

Some people find that traditional whole wheat flour has a flavor that's too strong for them. This new whole wheat flour seemed to be the answer to this. In baking with it, we found we could substitute it 100% for white flour in many breads with not a whisper of resistance from our loving children and spouses. What was the magic in it that made it taste so good? As we mentioned earlier, hard wheats in this country are almost always high-protein red wheats. This variety of wheat is also a hard, high-protein wheat; it's only difference is the color of the bran, which is much lighter than that of red wheat. The lack of a pigment called phenolic acid is the reason. Phenolic acid has a tannic flavor, similar to that in tea, and is perceived as bitter by some people. Its absence means that white whole wheat flour is a little sweeter and milder in flavor than traditional whole wheat flour.

White wheat flour is still whole wheat flour. It contains the bran, the germ, and all the nutritional benefits of whole wheat flour, and needs to be stored the same way. We recommend substituting it for 25% of the white flour in your recipe, to get a feel for how it performs. If you like what you get, you can increase the percentage until you find what works best for you. Some recipes, such as brownies, gingerbread, and banana bread, are perfectly wonderful using 100% white whole wheat.

Other Wheat Products

We've focused primarily on wheat as a flour. Here are some other options.

WHEAT BERRIES, any kind, can be used intact if they are soaked long enough (start with boiling water) to render them chewable. It is also possible to sprout them and add them to a bread dough, or you can even sprout them, dry them slowly, and grind them into flour to make your own diastatic malt (see page 467).

CRACKED WHEAT is the whole wheat berry cracked into pieces. It can be soaked just like wheat berries to add texture to bread. It can also be cooked into a delicious cereal to be eaten as such or added to bread. Cracked wheat won't sprout.

BULGUR WHEAT is cracked wheat that's been steamed (partially cooked) and dried before it's cracked. It can be added to bread doughs after a shorter soaking period. It also makes a very tasty substitute for rice.

WHEAT FLAKES are the wheat equivalent of oatmeal or oat flakes. They can be added straight to a bread dough for texture, or try substituting them for oats in a granola recipe.

WHEAT BRAN AND WHEAT GERM, available separately, can be added to whatever you're baking to increase the attributes of each or both in a final baked product.

VITAL WHEAT GLUTEN (or gluten flour) is flour that has been wet to activate the gluten-producing proteins, washed to remove the starchy part of the flour, and then dried and milled back to a flour-like consistency. This is not the same as high-gluten flour (see Sir Lancelot, page 460). It can be added, about 1 tablespoon (9g) per loaf, to bread doughs that contain low-protein flours or meals (such as ryes, oats, or corn) or a lot of extras (such as cheese, onions, dried fruit, or nuts) to produce lighter loaves.

Rye

Rye flours are associated with northern Europe and Scandinavia, primarily because rye is the grain that grows most successfully in those climates. In fact it was the backbone of most bread made during the Middle Ages. Today, rye is produced around the world, but most of the world's supplies are produced in northeastern Europe: Russia, Germany, Poland, Ukraine, and Belarus. Much of the rye we use in the United States comes from Canada.

Like wheat berries, rye berries contain an endosperm (the food source for a sprouting rye seedling), the bran (the outer coat of the berry), and the germ (the embryo that would produce a rye seedling if the berry were planted). Rye contains more minerals than wheat (iron, phosphorus, and potassium), but almost no gluten-producing protein. To make a loaf of rye bread that isn't as solid as a brick, you need to incorporate some wheat in your dough or understand a little of the chemistry of a rye dough.

Although rye contains about the same amount of protein as wheat does, it doesn't behave the same way in a dough. For a loaf of bread made completely with rye flour, to attain some volume, you have to look elsewhere for help. A component in rye flour is the pentosan, a kind of sugar. The molecules of pentosan contain 5 carbon atoms (as opposed to the 6-carbon-atom sugars we are familiar with as sweeteners). These pentosans, located in the cell walls of the endosperm, can absorb a great deal of water and become glutinous or gummy, which helps create the structure in an all-rye bread.

But along with pentosans, rye flour contains an enzyme, amylase, that very happily turns endosperm (starch) molecules into sugars. In a dough made with wheat, these enzymes are rendered inactive before the dough, or protein structure, "sets." In rye, however, the structure created by the pentosans continues to be attacked by those enzymes even after it has "set," which can create an unfortunate end product. The water contained by the pentosans is released, the structure begins to fail, and you wind up with something pretty heavy and soggy.

But if you change the pH of the dough, lower it, and make it "sour," you can slow down those enzymes and make them stop their destructive work. That way you wind up with the familiar flavor of the quintessential rye bread, slightly acidic, full of flavor (as well as being more digestible), and as full of volume as a rye bread can be. It also keeps exceptionally well.

Rye comes as "flour," "meal," or "chops." Rye flour is ground just from the endosperm of the rye berry and, like white wheat flour, does not contain the bran or the germ. Rye flour comes in a wide array of colors.

RYE FLOUR ground from the center of the endosperm is "white rye." Rye flour ground from a larger percentage of the endosperm, moving nearer the seed coat, is called "cream rye." Rye flour ground from the outside of the endosperm, after the white and cream ryes have been removed, is "dark rye." It is dark because it contains the greatest amount of ash, not because it is a whole grain flour. "Medium rye" is ground from the entire endosperm.

RYE MEAL is a coarser flour ground from the entire rye berry and is equivalent to whole wheat flour. Rye meal is available in three grinds: fine, medium, or coarse. Coarse rye meal is commonly called "pumpernickel flour." **Pumpernickel** is an affectionate German name given in fun, both to the meal and the hearty breads made with it, to describe their effect on the digestive system. (*Pumpern* is the German word for "intestinal wind" and *nickel* is a word for "demon" or "sprite.")

RYE CHOPS are the equivalent of cracked wheat and can add the same crunch to bread.

RYE FLAKES, berries that are steamed, then rolled, are like rolled oats; they add a slightly less intrusive texture. And the berries can be used whole in bread handled like wheat berries.

Corn

Most of the major classes of corn that we use today had been developed by Native Americans before the colonists arrived, with the exception of a hybrid that produced the dent corns that are the predominant and most productive corns we grow today. These we know more commonly as "field corn." With this hybrid, the American Corn Belt (Illinois, Iowa, and Nebraska) has become one of the most productive in the world, akin to the granary of the Kansas wheat fields.

Dent or field corn gets its name because of the dent that forms in the kernel as moisture evaporates from the endosperm. This is the type of corn developed by colonists that has become the powerhouse of the Corn Belt. Sixty percent is used for feed, but you'll also find it in cornmeals, sugars, syrups, cornstarch, vegetable substitutes for lard and butter, whiskey, and myriad nonfeed items; dyes, paints, oilcloth, oil for soaps, cellulose in press boards, insulating materials, ethanol fuel, and sundry chemicals.

CORNMEAL is the most common form of this grain that we use in baking. Most of the cornmeal you find on the grocer's shelf is made in large mills and is degermed and hulled, which means it will keep pretty indefinitely. There are a number of gristmills around the United States that still mill the whole kernel, including the germ. As with whole wheat flour, the oils in the germ are subject to rancidity so need to be stored in an airtight container in the freezer. Needless to say, these whole kernel meals are much more interesting and have much more flavor and texture than the large production ones.

Cornmeal comes in fine, medium, and coarse grinds, as well as in several colors, yellow being the most common. White is grown in the South and blue in the Southwest. Nutritionally, the yellow comes out on top as it contains beta-carotene, which translates to an additional 630 IU of vitamin A per cup (156g).

Like any non-wheat grain, it contains no gluten so needs some wheat to hold it together in a bread or muffin or cake. The early New England colonists used cornmeal in making Indian pudding, cornmeal mush, Johnny cake, and anadama bread.

CORN FLOUR is a more finely ground version of cornmeal.

CORNSTARCH is a more refined part of the starchy endosperm of the corn kernel, milled until it's essentially a powder. It is used primarily as a thickening agent, although a small amount can be added to wheat flour to temper its gluten-producing ability (essentially lowering its protein).

GRITS OR POLENTA are both made from ground dried corn; grits are usually finer in texture and frequently ground from white corn. They're cooked into a smooth porridge that's a staple in the South. Polenta is coarser in texture, usually ground from yellow corn, and has a sturdier, thicker texture when cooked. It can be served as a side dish or topped with anything you'd put on pasta. It gives a golden, hearty texture to breads it appears in.

HOMINY tastes distinctly different from corn. In order to eat dent corn, you need to either mill it (cornmeal) or remove the outer covering of the kernel. You just can't cook it until it's soft. To remove the kernels' armor, you need to soak them in an alkaline solution. This makes the endosperm swell, which cracks the case and releases the inside. This is then consumed as hominy or hominy grits.

Corn contains a lot of niacin, but it isn't nutritionally available in its untreated form. Soaking the kernels in water that's soaked in wood ashes (which is how Native Americans did it) not only frees the kernel, but also frees the niacin so it can be absorbed.

MASA HARINA is hominy that has been dried and ground, then used to make tortillas and tamales. It's already nutritionally superior to regular cornmeal, but traditionally these flatbreads were eaten with some kind of beans, the beans containing amino acids that complete those in the cornmeal and thus create a whole protein.

Oats

Unlike wheat berries, oats are harvested with hulls or husks that constitute about 25% of their weight. Before milling, these hulls need to be removed, which is not an easy task. Once the hulls are off, the remaining berries are called groats and look very similar to wheat berries. Nutritionally, oats contain a higher percentage of fat than wheat, about 7% versus 2%. (This means that about 17% of calories from whole oats come from fat.) Oats contain more protein as well, although it is not gluten producing. Oat bran is rich in water-soluble fiber, which helps reduce LDL blood cholesterol. Oats also contain more iron, B-vitamins, calcium, and calories than wheat.

To make old-fashioned rolled oats—their most familiar form—the oat groats, with the hulls removed, are first steamed to make them pliable, and then passed through rollers that flatten them. To make quick-cooking oats, the groats are first cut, then steamed and rolled to produce flakes that are thinner and consequently more quickly cooked. There are also "instant" flakes that are even thinner than the quick-cooking variety. These are so thin, however, that they tend to lose their identity when they're cooked and wind up pretty much as mush.

To make steel-cut or Irish oats (what the Scots call pinhead oats), whole oat groats are passed over steel drums perforated with holes large enough for the groats to fall into, but small enough so that they're held there about half-exposed. As the drum turns, a stationary blade cuts the groats in half as they pass by. Steel-cut oats are available in most grocery stores. They make a wonderful, nutty cooked cereal as well as a great addition, both for flavor and texture, to breads.

Oat flour is produced as a by-product of the cutting and flaking operations and is being used more and more in cereals, as an addition to breads and other baked goods, and in baby foods, as it's easy to digest. Except in breads, try substituting about 25% oat flour (either manufactured, or ground in your food processor from rolled oats) for the same amount of wheat flour, to create the typical nutty oat flavor. Because oats in any form are not gluten-producing, you'll have to use them in conjunction with wheat in bread making, probably not more than 15% of the flour used. In other baking, the percentage can be higher.

Gluten-Free Baking and Flours

Gluten is a combination of proteins in flour that form the elastic network responsible for baked goods' structure. The most common grains and flours that contain gluten include wheat, barley, and rye, as well as spelt, kamut, and other wheat relatives.

To replace gluten, a combination of gluten-free flours and a gelling agent, such as xanthan gum, are necessary to provide that structure in baked goods. These ingredients change the game considerably. Gluten-free baked goods can be wonderful, but they're never going to be exactly like the wheat flour–based products they're replacing.

The landscape for gluten-free baking has improved by leaps and bounds in the last decade, with excellent new gluten-free flour blends. King Arthur Baking Company spent years perfecting a range of products for gluten-free baking.

MEASURE FOR MEASURE: For cookies, quick breads, pancakes, cakes, and non-yeasted recipes, Measure for Measure seamlessly replaces the flour in your favorite recipes. A blend of rice flours, sorghum flour, tapioca and potato starches, and xanthan gum, it substantially eases the transition to gluten-free baking.

GLUTEN-FREE ALL-PURPOSE FLOUR: A blend of brown and white rice flours and potato starch, this blend is formulated for yeast baking. Best used in a recipe designed for gluten-free baking, which will likely also call for xanthan gum.

XANTHAN GUM: Because gluten-free baked goods lack the proteins necessary for structure-building, they can sometimes become crumbly, or not rise very well. Xanthan gum, a thickener, emulsifier, and stabilizer, improves the texture, "body," and rise of gluten-free baked goods.

Amaranth

Amaranth, also known as Inca wheat, is probably one of America's oldest crops. It was used as a food crop by both the Incas and Aztecs and was as prevalent as corn before the arrival of the Spanish. Amaranth disappeared because of its use in sacrificial ceremonies and the belief by the Spanish Church that, by eliminating it, the ceremonies would disappear as well. But it managed to survive wild in the mountainous regions of western South America and is now experiencing somewhat of a comeback because of its versatility and nutrition.

Amaranth is not a true grain. It is related to pigweed, also known as lamb's-quarters, which you often find as a volunteer in your garden. As a crop, it grows very quickly, is extremely hardy, and can survive where a lot of other "grass-crops' grains" crops will not. It is also useful in that the whole plant can be consumed. The "grain" itself is actually not much bigger than a poppy seed, but it occurs in huge numbers. These seeds also contain more of the amino acid lysine, which boosts its usable protein significantly more than grass-crops grains. Like oats, it also contains much soluble fiber.

Amaranth can be cooked and eaten as a cereal; it can be popped like popcorn; it can be ground into flour. Because it contains no gluten, it needs to be mixed with wheat flours for yeast-bread baking in similar amounts (about 15%) as soy flour. You can use it in much greater amounts in making pancakes or flatbreads. Amaranth can be found in health food stores.

Barley

Barley, another wild grass, with a nutrition profile similar to other grasses, has a history that is as old as wheat. Remnants have been found in a swath between North Africa all the way to Afghanistan. In ancient times, and even in modern historic times in Europe, barley played a much greater role than it does today, even greater than that of wheat. It was easier to grow in many places and, as a choice of grain for malting (beer and ale were consumed much the way we consume water today), it was felt to be the best choice. But as people discovered the gluten-producing properties of wheat protein, and what it meant for bread made with it, barley began to lose favor. It did persist as the grain used most by the lower classes and as a feed for animals. And it has persisted as the best grain for malting. In fact, the word for "barley" is a derivative of an old English word for beer.

In its heyday, the length of a barley grain became the foundation of our linear measurement system. Three of them laid end to end equaled an Anglo-Saxon *ynce* (later inch). The weight of a barley "grain" eventually became the "gram," the foundation of the metric system.

Although barley is available in several forms (pearled barley, scotch barley, barley grits), what the baker will most likely use is barley flour. This is roasted barley that has been ground into a nutty-flavored flour. Like wheat flour, it can be used for thickening. You can include it in any baked product by substituting it for wheat flour. Because it is not gluten producing, you probably don't want to use more than a couple of tablespoons per cup of wheat flour. Barley flour adds its own flavor to whatever you bake.

MALT is used primarily to make beers and ales. In Scotland, malt is strongly identified with whisky (in Ireland, whiskey). Although other grains can be malted, long periods of experience and experimenting have led people to believe that barley produces the best result.

Malt making used to be a much more visible process. In the Middle Ages, women were responsible for this task. Later, you would find a malt house in almost every village. Now malting is done at an industrial level so most of us don't even know what the process is or why it's done. To understand why one would make malt, first we should understand what it is and what it does.

DIASTATIC MALT is grain that has been sprouted, slowly dried at relatively low temperatures, and then ground into a powder. When grain begins to sprout, there is a rise in the level of enzyme activity that begins to break down the starch in the endosperm into simple sugars that the new seedling can feed on. This is primarily maltose, thus the name "malt." By allowing the grain to begin to sprout, then drying it at low temperatures, and finally grinding it, the enzymes are not destroyed. Once the enzymes are in some kind of wet medium, they become active again and continue to turn available starch to sugar. This sugar, intended for a new grain seedling, can also create a fine food for yeast, which in turn can be used for making either beer or bread. If you look on a bag of all-purpose flour, you'll see that there is a tiny amount of malt added. Wheat flour has its own enzymes, but often not enough to create a flour that will make good bread. So the level of enzyme activity is corrected by adding a bit of diastatic barley malt.

Malt for baking is dried slowly and at a very low heat. Malt for beer is also dried slowly, but after the berries have reached about 10% moisture and the enzymes are stabilized, the heat is increased, and the berries are then allowed to develop some color. The lighter colors are for pale ales, the darker colors for stronger flavored porters or stouts. As the color gets darker (and the flavors more pronounced), the enzyme activity becomes more and more compromised.

NON-DIASTATIC MALT is a malt powder that has been dried at temperatures high enough so the enzymes are destroyed and no longer active. This powder can be used simply as a sweetener with its associated malt flavor; it can be added to the water used to boil bagels to enhance their color.

MALT SYRUP is made from barley berries that have sprouted and are thus full of maltose, the sugar that gives malt its name. It can be either diastatic or non-diastatic. To make malt syrup, sprouted barley berries are soaked in water to allow the now-available sugars to dissolve. The water is strained off from the spent grain and then cooked down until it is a sweet syrup. Malt syrup is not quite as sweet as honey and not as strongly flavored as molasses. It has a characteristic malt flavor and can be used in baking like honey or molasses. If you want to replace sugar with it, you have to reduce the amount of liquid in your recipe by ¼ cup for every cup of malt syrup used.

Buckwheat

Buckwheat is not a grass like most of the other grains with which we bake (wheat, corn, rice, rye, oats). It's actually related to rhubarb and burdock and grows as vigorously as the latter. It probably originated in China (although some claim Russia) and is a minor crop in the United States. Because it blooms continuously throughout the summer, it is a good bee crop and makes a unique honey. Its hulls make great mulch as well as pillow filling. Buckwheat flour is non-gluten-producing and has an assertive flavor all its own that is somewhat of an acquired taste. It is used most familiarly in Russian pancakes (blini), particularly right before Lent, when they are served with almost anything, caviar being traditional, but also salmon, sour cream, jam—whatever tempts the baker.

Chickpea Flour

Chickpeas, also known as garbanzos, are a legume like soybeans, that nitrogen-fixing group of plants that can enrich the soil. They grow well in warm climates and historically were found in Egypt and the Levant, those countries that border the eastern coast of the Mediterranean. From there they found their way around the Mediterranean to Spain and east to India, where they found a receptive home. Chickpeas have always been a poor man's food. But just as we are discovering the nutritional value of a lot of "lesser" grains, so we have with chickpeas. Nutritionally, chickpeas have a higher fat content than other legumes, but they are rich in calcium and iron and are a good source of fiber.

In India, chickpeas are ground into a flour called *besan*, which is used for fillings for chapatis, dumplings, and noodles; as a thickener; and in batter for deep-fried foods. In southwestern France and in northwestern Italy, you'll find a street food that is a very thin pizza, a chickpea pancake fried in olive oil on a griddle. In Nice, it's called *socca*. Across the border, it's called *farinata*.

Millet

A native of Africa and Asia, millet has the ability to deal with arid climates and nutritionally deficient soils, which is why it has long been seen as a poor man's crop. But in addition to its ability to grow in harsh conditions, millet has other benefits. It's nutritionally similar to wheat but has a greater number of amino acids (the components in protein) than wheat and most of the other grains found in this country. Most millet grown today in the United States is used for animal and bird feed, but we can benefit from millet, too. Think of it like rice or bulgur. Try adding some to your next loaf of bread; it will give it lovely gold flecks and some delightful crunch. Just as we've learned to share oats with horses, we need to learn to share millet with the birds.

Quinoa

Quinoa ("keen-wah") is native to this hemisphere and was a staple of (and considered sacred by) the Incas. It self-seeds, and it too grows in extremes of temperature and altitude. Though technically not a grain, quinoa has more complete protein, iron, and vitamins B_1 and B_2 than the traditional grains that we consume, and can be a valuable addition to our culinary repertoires. When it's cooked a small "tail" is visible as the grain expands and takes on water. It, too, can be used like millet, bulgur, rice, and so on. Whole quinoa as well as quinoa flour, available at health food stores, can be added like soy flour, at about 15%, to any baked goods to enhance their nutritional value.

Rice

Rice is another grass that has adapted itself to almost every geographical area and climate. But unlike wheat, which began its geographical journey from the Middle East, and corn, which did the same in the Western Hemisphere, rice is an Eastern grass. It is said that it reached Europe with Alexander the Great about 300 BCE so it has a much shorter history in the Western world. But like wheat and corn, it feeds an enormous percentage of the world's population—more than half of it in fact—although it is still culturally Eastern.

Rice flour is not a large part of our baking heritage although it is often added to shortbread and other cookie recipes to make a sandier texture. It is a boon for people who have wheat (gluten) allergies as it can be combined with other ingredients for baking all manner of recipes.

Soy

Soybeans are unusual in that they're a plant that contains complete proteins, as well as an impressive array of vitamins and minerals.

Because it adds moisture to baked products, soy flour can also be used as a cholesterol-free egg substitute. In some recipes, where egg isn't used as a leavening agent, you can replace an egg with 1 tablespoon (9g) of soy flour and 1 tablespoon (14g) of water. Again, remember that you're also substituting the flavor of soy for the flavor of egg.

Soy flour is ground from roasted soybeans and is available either as full-fat soy flour, which contains the natural oils that are found in the soybean, or defatted soy flour, which has the oils removed during processing. Soy flour increases moistness in baked products and gives them a longer shelf life. Full-fat soy flour, like any whole grain, will become rancid, so if this is the flour you wish to use, we suggest buying it in small quantities and either using it quickly or storing it in the freezer.

Soy flour works particularly well in quick breads, muffins, pancakes, waffles, brownies, and other bars. In yeast breads, you can replace up to 15% of the recipe's wheat flour with soy flour.

BAKING WITH SOY

Like baked products that contain honey, baked products containing soy flour tend to brown more quickly, so lower your oven temperature by 25°F or shorten the baking time. In fried foods, such as doughnuts, soy flour reduces the amount of fat that is absorbed by the dough.

Teff

Teff, a tiny milletlike grain, is grown in Ethiopia and Eritrea and has been that region's primary cereal grain for thousands of years. Its name is an ancient Ethiopian, or Amharic, word meaning "lost" because it is, in fact, so easily lost in harvesting. Like amaranth, it has elevated levels of lysine making its protein more complete and more valuable for human consumption than that of other grass grains. It is also an excellent source of fiber and iron and has many times the amount of calcium and potassium found in other grains.

Teff is used to make injera, a fermented, foot-and-a-half-wide, sour-tasting pancake that is a mainstay in Ethiopia, both as a food and as an implement for eating. The fermenting process, which takes two or three days, gives the resulting pancake, which is cooked just on one side, a spongy surface with a lot of "eyes." (You'll recognize those from cooking wheat-based pancakes.) The pancake itself is used as a scoop and/or a container for their spicy stews and finally eaten itself soaked with the remaining juices.

Triticale

Triticale is a hybrid of wheat and rye, the first successful new grain crop created by combining species from two distinct genera. It was originally developed in Sweden in the late nineteenth century but didn't appear as "triticale" in the United States until just before World War II. In the Americas, it is grown primarily in northern United States and in Canada.

Milk, Cream, Cheese, and Eggs

Milk is a given in much of baking, along with flour, sugar, butter, and eggs. Somehow we feel reasonably comfortable substituting one form of milk for another in what we bake, just as we do on our cereal. It seems a matter of taste, preference, and/or dietary concern. Once we're beyond different types of fresh milk and into more esoteric forms, such as dry milk, evaporated milk, condensed milk, buttermilk, and sour milk, then questions begin to arise. There is also an interesting continuum between fresh and fermented dairy products. While we have found ways to extend the shelf life of milk by heating it enough to kill the organisms responsible for spoilage, other cultures have used those very organisms to create signature dairy products that would also be much less perishable than the original: the "cultures" of other cultures. These have identities quite beyond their original forms, and have taken on lives and culinary momentum of their own, independent of their food of origin. We know several of them as sour milk, sour cream, buttermilk, yogurt, crème fraîche, clotted cream, and most cheeses. Even European butter has been made from cream that has been allowed to develop character through the activity of its inherent bacteria.

Milk

Nutritionally, milk is an excellent source of complete protein, along with calcium, magnesium, and phosphorus, and a good dose of vitamins A, B_1, B_2, and riboflavin. In addition, it's usually fortified with vitamin D. Fresh milk is available in a fairly wide range of options, from whole milk, containing 8 grams of fat per cup (227g), to skim milk, with almost none, to options with various levels of fat in between. When it's combined with grains, you wind up with all the amino acids that create complete proteins. Just from a nutritional point of view, milk is a good alternative to water as the liquid to choose for baking.

But what, beyond nutrition, does milk contribute to baked goods?

Bread made with milk that contains at least some fat will have a lighter, softer texture than the same made with water. Milk also acts as a "conditioner," making a dough easier to handle and shape. The fat in the milk slows down fermentation somewhat so it makes the proofing process more flexible; that is, it allows a bread dough to retain gas better and therefore elongates the period of peak proof. Better gas retention also means that the resulting loaf will have greater volume than one made with water. The presence of milk sugar (lactose) and albumin (a protein found in milk) changes the crust of the bread as it goes through the Maillard Reaction (see sidebar). From a sensory point of view, this means a more richly browned crust as well as flavors and aromas that are unique to milk breads.

As for the bread itself, milk deepens flavor and creates a more tender crumb and a finer grain, which makes it easier to slice. And, as long as the milk you're using contains some fat, your bread will also stay fresher longer.

In quick breads, muffins, and cakes, milk can increase body and enhance the impact of other flavors.

In a pie crust, as in a bread crust, the Maillard Reaction (see sidebar) also plays a part in browning both the top and bottom crusts. Milk also makes the crust more tender and less apt to get soggy.

SCALDING: Milk was originally scalded to eliminate harmful bacteria, which is now done through pasteurization. There are certain enzymes in unpasteurized milk that can interfere with the growth of yeast. Many older recipes call for scalding milk before starting a yeast dough, but, unless you're using unpasteurized milk fresh from the cow, it's not necessary.

To scald milk, bring it to just short of a boil in a heavy saucepan. Look for bubbles just beginning to appear around the edge of the milk with a skim of coagulated protein covering the surface. Don't bring it to a full boil. Remove from the heat and cool.

PASTEURIZATION: This is a process that heats milk to 145°F to 150°F for about half an hour, or to 161°F for 15 seconds. Depending on the length and temperature of the process, this changes the flavor of the original milk; the longer and hotter you cook it, the more the milk's flavor changes. It does, however, disable certain bacteria and enzymes that can cause it to spoil.

ULTRAPASTEURIZATION: This is an even more intense heat treatment for a much shorter time (280°F for 2 seconds) that kills virtually all natural bacteria and renders the milk refrigerator-safe for one to three months. The flavor changes in this milk are more pronounced than that of pasteurized milk. Although this process is more common with cream, ultrapasteurized milk is beginning to show up more frequently. Once milk is opened, pasteurized or ultrapasteurized, it's best consumed within a week.

A GOLDEN BROWN CRUST

The Maillard Reaction is the caramelization that produces the lovely golden brown color of a bread's crust as it bakes. The long fermentation of the yeast in bread breaks down complex carbohydrates from the starches in flour to simple sugars. These simple sugars will caramelize at lower temperatures than sugar alone.

Lactose, unlike sucrose (table sugar), does not ferment; that is, yeast will not feed on it so it remains intact throughout mixing and baking. It is not a substitute for a sugar, which can be used to stimulate the growth of yeast, but it will contribute to the Maillard Reaction.

UHT MILK: This is a process used most frequently in Europe, but is increasingly being done on this side of the pond. UHT milk is heated to 282°F, held for several seconds, then cooled to 70 degrees in a pressurized system. Then it's packaged aseptically; that is, sealed from any outside contamination in a container that doesn't allow light through it. The benefit of treating milk this way is that it has a room-temperature shelf life of about nine months, which means it can be transported long distances without refrigeration. Once it has been opened it will spoil like any milk and must be refrigerated, which will give it one to two weeks.

DRY MILK is available in two versions, one that dissolves easily in water and a second that needs to be added to the dry ingredients in a recipe. The latter is processed with higher heat, which disables the protease enzymes that can interfere with the growth of yeast. The water-soluble type is most often available at grocery stores. The other is available in *The Baker's Catalogue* (see Where to Find It, page 550).

EVAPORATED MILK, either whole or skim, is milk that has had about half the water removed from it. It was developed during the nineteenth century, before refrigerators, as a way to deal with milk's propensity to "go off." Before refrigeration or pasteurization, milk had to be consumed very quickly because, in its raw state, it is quickly perishable. The high-heat process used in evaporating milk gives it a different flavor than fresh milk, although not necessarily unpleasing. It also is slightly darker in color. Because it's concentrated, the nutrients and the calories are concentrated as well. As a result, it adds richness to baked goods and can, in some instances, be substituted for cream. Evaporated whole milk has 340 calories and 20 grams of fat per cup (227g), while evaporated skim milk has just 200 calories and less than 1 gram of fat per cup. Which to use is up to you. It depends on what you're trying to accomplish. Both contain significantly less fat than cream.

SWEETENED CONDENSED MILK is simply evaporated milk that has sugar added to it, about 50% of the total volume. This was done as a preservative since such a sugar-saturated environment is lethal to most bacteria. Like evaporated milk, its nutrients and calories are also concentrated. The addition of sugar makes it even richer.

When mixed with an acidic ingredient, sweetened condensed milk does something almost magical. Its consistency changes from something that can only be described as gloppy to a substance that has some structural integrity, a loose solid that doesn't flow. This property, combined with the flavor juxtaposition of the sweet with the acidic, is found most famously in Key Lime Pie. You can also drizzle condensed milk over fruit as a topping. Unopened cans of condensed milk can be stored at room temperature for many months. You'll find that milk in an older can may be darker in color, but will be still be fine to use.

Cream

Creams, like milk, are pasteurized, and it's getting harder to find them not ultra-pasteurized. The least processed cream, however, will taste better and will whip more easily.

AMERICAN CREAMS go from "light" (20.6% fat), to "whipping" (31.3% fat), to "heavy" (about 37.6% fat). Then there is half-and-half (12% fat), and both dry and liquid nondairy creamers. Cream is usually used as a garnish, but there are some recipes for baked products that call for cream as the liquid with no added— or substantially reduced—butter or other fat. Because cream is halfway between milk and butter, it endows baked goods with the attributes of both: richness, tenderness, and wonderful flavor.

FRENCH CRÈME CHANTILLY (or, in English, chantilly cream) is essentially lightly whipped cream enhanced with some kind of flavor: vanilla or other extract, brandy, citrus zest, and so forth. This is used primarily as a garnish.

The British embrace cream more warmly than do we. A single cream (minimum 18% fat) is essentially like our light cream; from there, they move up to whipping cream (minimum 35% fat), which is closer to our heavy cream and where we stop in the cream department. They then go on to double cream (minimum 48% fat), and finally soar to clotted cream, which can come in between 55% and 60% fat. (Butter in either country is about 81% fat.) In both countries, there is ultrapasteurized cream that is extra-high-heat treated so its shelf life is longer. Because heat destroys the native bacteria and enzymes in the cream that will

---

HINT FOR WHIPPING CREAM

Whipped cream is simply cream with lots of air incorporated into it. At warm temperatures, the fat in the cream will more easily coalesce and turn to butter. To prevent this, keep the cream chilled, and if you think of it, chill the bowl and beaters as well. In hot weather, whip it over a bowl of ice. To avoid turning cream to butter, beat at high speed with an electric mixer until the cream begins to thicken, then lower the speed to medium and watch it carefully. Err on the side of leaving it too slack rather than almost butter. If you think you've gone a bit too far, beat in 2 or more tablespoons of milk or cream, which should rescue it. Finally, by using confectioners' sugar as a sweetener, the cornstarch that it contains will act as a stabilizer and help the whipped cream hold its shape. Whipped cream that is to be used as a filling needs to be beaten more stiffly than that which is to be used as a garnish.

For a lower-calorie garnish, try this: Whip ⅓ cup (75g) heavy cream until stiff. Stir in ⅔ cup (150g) nonfat plain or vanilla yogurt. If you find this too tart, try it at ½ cup (113g) cream and ½ cup (113g) yogurt.

---

naturally ferment them, they can never develop the flavors that untreated creams can. This makes them safe but not nearly as interesting.

Fermented Milk Products

Fresh cow's milk, which we Americans take so much for granted, does not exist in many cultures, and if it does, only ephemerally. Our commitment to fresh milk has caused us to take a different tack to preserve it as we described earlier; that of eliminating the naturally occurring bacteria found in raw milk by heating it in order to preserve its "freshness."

Another probable reason for the significant presence of fresh milk in our groceries is the fact that a large part of our population can still digest it. Strangely enough, this ability, which is characteristic of almost all western Europeans, is absent in three-fourths of the people from Eastern Europe, the Middle East, and the Far East. For reasons about which scientists are still speculating, these people stop producing lactase, the enzyme that allows them to digest lactose (milk sugar) before adulthood.

Many of these cultures, probably without really understanding the biological process they were implementing, allowed naturally occurring bacteria to ferment their native milks until they had undergone some inherent changes. This process of fermentation gave milk a texture and taste (as well as a natural shelf life) of its own. This is due to fermentation's byproduct, lactic acid, a substance that precludes or greatly retards the growth of many pathogens that are potentially harmful to humans (e.g., typhoid and typhus, tuberculosis, etc.). The bacteria involved in fermentation also "predigest" the lactose, which make the resulting products easier to digest for people with lactose intolerance. Nutritionally, fermented milk does have benefits beyond those of the milk that it was made from. Modern science is slowly confirming many of these claims.

Because each geographic area has its own native bacteria that are adapted to its particular climate, fermented milk products, as with sourdough breads, have their own regionally influenced characteristics. Warmer climates—and the bacteria congenial to them—produce a firmer, more acidic ferment; cooler climates produce a milder, looser product. Another important factor playing a part in the final product is the type of milk being fermented. Where the cow isn't part of a local agriculture, you'll find people using milk from sheep, goats, horses, water buffalo, and so on. Each has its own identity.

The resulting fermented milks and milk products are used in multiple ways; they can be liquid, solid, savory, or sweet. In whatever form, these foods have centuries of tradition behind them, and they've become an integral part of their native cuisines. All of these have quite a long life in the refrigerator, significantly longer than fresh milk.

Following are the soured milk products and soft, fresh cheeses that are meant to be eaten quickly. Most cultures have a cottage cheese, or a local variety of the same. In the United States, we have cream cheese as well; in Italy, ricotta, mozzarella, and mascarpone; in France, *fromage blanc*; in Germany, *quark*. These are the cheeses that are primarily used in baking, although you will find some recipes that contain grated hard cheeses.

Sour milk used to happen naturally as a result of the indigenous bacteria present in the milk. Now you can sour milk easily by adding 1 tablespoon (14g) of lemon juice or vinegar to 1 cup (227g) of fresh milk and letting it sit for 5 minutes.

FOR TENDER TEXTURE, INCREASE ACIDITY

Yogurt, buttermilk, sour milk, and sour cream can be used interchangeably pretty successfully in baking. All four products will produce rich and tender baked goods because of their acidity. Just be aware that each will produce a slightly different flavor and texture.

BUTTERMILK, which used to be the byproduct of butter making, is made nowadays by treating low-fat or nonfat milk with special bacteria. It's thinner than sour cream but thicker than sour milk. It's usually quite low in fat, but its thickness and slight acidity make it taste much richer than it is.

COTTAGE CHEESE is made from low-fat pasteurized milk that has been treated with a bacterial starter that increases its acidity and precipitates the milk proteins and fats from the whey. The resulting curds are drained to produce the loose solid we know as cottage cheese, available with a variety of fat contents, but none greater than that of whole milk. If the cheese is drained longer, the result is firmer and called pot cheese. Pressed of the remaining moisture, so it becomes drier and crumbly, it's called farmer cheese. There is also a version of this that is aged and thus more flavorful.

RICOTTA, an Italian cheese, was traditionally made from the whey separated from the curds of sheep's milk (used in the production of pecorino cheese). Whey contains a protein that can be coagulated by heating it. These "curds" are collected, placed in shallow conical baskets (fiscelle), and left to drain for 12 to 14 hours. This is the low-fat version. There are now richer ricottas available that have been fortified with more milk and butterfat. Ricotta can be used very much the way cottage cheese is used, and it can also be smoothed in a blender to make a cream cheese substitute. In Italy, it is used in fillings for pastas, pizzas, and cannoli. And it can be the major ingredient in delicious cheesecakes.

AMERICAN CREAM CHEESE is made from cream with at least 33% butterfat that's inoculated with a live culture to separate the curds from the whey. Once the whey has been removed, the resulting cheese is 90% fat in terms of calories. In some brands, other ingredients are added to stabilize it and increase its shelf life. There is a "light" cream cheese version that has about half the amount of calories as standard cream cheese. Blends of cream cheese and Greek yogurt are becoming more popular. There is also a whipped version of cream cheese that can't be substituted for the original because it contains a large percentage of air. Neufchatel cheese, which comes in the traditional cream cheese block, is made from a lighter cream with about 25% butterfat. Nonfat cream cheese is a final option and is a better choice to use as a topping on a baked good rather than in it.

ITALIAN MASCARPONE is made from a combination of cream and milk. It is treated with an acidic ingredient to separate the curds from the whey and, because there are no added stabilizers, tends to be softer than cream cheese. The two can be used fairly interchangeably, although you may want to add a few tablespoons of cream and/or sour cream to cream cheese to loosen it and make the texture a bit lighter. For a lower calorie version, you can use ricotta or cottage cheese whipped until smooth.

YOGURT Americans first experienced yogurt only in the later part of the last century. The first brands were often sweetened and promoted as health food. It is available as almost a liquid, or as thick as pudding, and can be substituted for sour cream in many recipes. When drained of its whey it becomes a spreadable yogurt cheese. You can use yogurt cheese in just about any way you'd use cream cheese. It's a lower fat, tart substitute. Liquid yogurts can be substituted for sour milk or buttermilk.

Yogurt is easy to make at home. If you want a thick yogurt, use whole milk. Scald it in a nonreactive saucepan, then let it cool to room temperature. Remove about a half cup and stir in a couple of tablespoons of yogurt that contains active cultures. Stir this back into the main body of milk, cover, keep warm, and let sit for about six hours without stirring, then chill.

GREEK YOGURT starts the same way conventional yogurt does, with milk and bacterial cultures; it's strained an extra time to remove more whey, yielding a thicker product with a higher concentration of protein and stronger taste than conventional yogurt. Greek yogurt can be found in nonfat and full-fat versions. Full-fat Greek yogurt can stand in for sour cream in baked goods.

CRÈME FRAÎCHE is a delicious French version of sour cream. It is a naturally cultured cream (containing active cultures) that becomes thick and develops a wonderful flavor, delicious on fresh fruit as it's used in France. It is also called for in some cream pie recipes. Although these days, it's usually available at the market, crème fraîche is easy to make at home. Pour 2 cups (454g) of heavy cream (not ultrapasteurized works best) in a jar and add 2 tablespoons (28g) of buttermilk. Cover loosely with foil or waxed paper and set aside at room temperature (60°F to 85°F) for 24 to 48 hours, until the mixture thickens a bit and becomes pleasantly tangy. Store in the refrigerator for up to one week.

SOUR CREAM was traditionally made by allowing the bacteria present in the cream to do their own work naturally. Because there is some risk in this (sometimes a bacteria will grow that is not pleasant tasting or is unsafe to eat), commercial sour cream is first pasteurized and then re-inoculated with a culture that will allow it to sour safely. Then it is often re-pasteurized to stop the process so there are no active cultures in many commercial sour creams. This makes it quite stable at refrigerator temperatures. Most of them also contain thickening agents such as guar gum and modified food starch. If you have access to a local dairy that makes sour cream, or an organic sour cream, you may find a version that has much better flavor. It can be used as you would crème fraîche.

Baking with Eggs

Eggs are called for in many recipes for baked goods; they're often essential for creating structure and stability, as well as for adding moisture and for thickening batters and sauces. Muffins, quick breads, and cakes made with only egg whites are usually tough, rubbery, chewy, and potentially dry. Egg whites form wonderfully stable foams, especially when whipped with a bit of acid and sugar. Whipped eggs are the primary leavening and structural component of foam cakes. Genoise and angel food are two familiar examples.

If want a very yellow, rich, tender cake, you can substitute 2 egg yolks for each whole egg called for, a practice that works particularly well with that cake at the other end of the spectrum, the pound cake.

Egg Size, Storage, and Handling

Our recipes call for large eggs, which weigh just over 56g apiece. Five eggs will yield just about 1 cup by volume measurement. If you use medium-size eggs, you'll need almost 1½ eggs for each large egg called for. If you need half an egg, beat the egg then measure out about 2 tablespoons.

Use only clean, uncracked grade-A eggs. Store eggs in their original container in the refrigerator; it's a good insulator and will prevent the porous-shelled eggs from picking up off-flavors. Don't wash eggs, as eggs have a thin coating on the shell that helps protect them from drying out and bacteria from getting in.

As with butter, eggs need to be at room temperature when you begin to put a recipe together. If you add cold eggs to butter that you've just beaten until light, the butter cells will turn solid and actually break, releasing all of the air that you've just beaten into them. If a recipe calls for separated eggs, separate the yolks and whites as soon as you take the eggs out of the refrigerator. If you try to separate a room-temperature egg, you're likely to end up with egg yolk in the whites.

SALMONELLA

The FDA discourages eating eggs that haven't either been pasteurized or completely cooked; eggs aren't considered cooked unless they've been brought to 140°F and held at that temperature for 3 minutes, or brought to 160°F and held for 1 minute. This can be a problem when making meringues that include uncooked egg whites. If in doubt, check your warm meringue with a digital thermometer before you add it to your recipe.

Even though most experts will tell you that the incidence of getting salmonella directly from contaminated eggs is low and that cross-contamination or bad food handling can be equally a problem, eating raw eggs is still a hazard, especially for the very old, very young, or those with any auto-immune disease. If you buy your eggs from a small, independent farmer whose flock is healthy, the eggs are probably free from contamination; but there are no guarantees. We've successfully used powdered whites in the meringues and frostings used in the recipes in this book.

Eggs in a Dough or Batter

So let's look at what each part of the egg contributes. The egg white is a stabilizer and, because you can incorporate so much air into it (it has the ability to increase in volume six to eight times), it opens and lightens the texture of whatever you're baking. The air that's beaten into them also is a primary leavener in sponge and angel food cakes. The yolk is an emulsifier and tenderizer. Taken altogether, an egg colors, binds, leavens, lightens, tenderizes, and, in recipes where the gluten in the flour is not developed (such as quick breads, cakes, muffins, or certain cookies), eggs become an integral part of the structure.

Some recipes call for adding beaten eggs to butter that has been creamed with sugar. As you dribble in the eggs, the batter may start to separate and curdle. Stop adding the eggs for a few moments and keep beating until the batter has re-emulsified. You can also reestablish the emulsion by adding a tablespoon or two of the flour from the recipe before adding more egg.

Eggs in Yeast Bread

In yeast breads, eggs also bring the same attributes as described above. But because they interfere somewhat with gluten development, the resulting texture of an egg bread is more cake-like. If you are looking for a chewy, artisan-style hearth bread, don't include eggs.

Eggs in Pie Crust

Whole eggs add protein, water, and fat to pie crust dough, along with color and flavor. Adding a lightly beaten egg will enhance browning and texture. If you use just the yolk, you add mostly fat, which will enhance tenderness and color.

Eggs in Custard

Quiche, flan, *crème anglaise*, and caramel custard all use eggs as a primary ingredient and also as a binder or thickener. One large egg (or 2 yolks) will soft-set or gel 1 cup (227g) of milk or cream. Custards can either be baked in the oven or cooked on the stovetop. The difference between a custard that's baked and one that's cooked on the stovetop while being stirred is that the stovetop version will never coalesce further than the sauce stage; it can't gel as solidly as a baked custard, because the protein molecules, while they are being agitated by a spoon, aren't able to form as strong bonds as those baked in an oven.

To successfully make a custard on the stovetop, you need to cook it slowly over low heat. Once the proteins in an egg start to bind at a molecular level, the rate at which they bind increases geometrically with each degree the temperature rises. At high heat, the proteins are binding so quickly they're difficult to control, and you'll end up with a product that's been overcooked and "weeping" fluid. So keep the water at a simmer; don't let it boil.

To successfully bake a custard in a dish or cup, set it in a water bath with the water just at or below a simmer. The water will act as an insulator, keeping the temperature of the custard below 212°F as it cooks. If you're baking a quiche or custard pie, skip the water bath; the crust is insulation enough. A custard is done when a knife inserted 2″ from the edge comes out relatively clean. The center should be wobbly, as it will continue to cook as it cools. If you have an instant-read thermometer, make sure the internal temperature of the custard does not go above 165°F. This is the point at which those proteins will begin to bind too quickly and the custard will begin to curdle, separate, and become tough.

Curdling

When a custard becomes watery, it's a signal that the eggs have been overcooked. Egg protein has the capacity to hold only a specific amount of water. As it cooks, the proteins bind tighter together and hold less water. Think of a sponge; it can hold a lot of water, but when it's squeezed, the water is forced out. This is what happens when something curdles. The water that was bound between the protein molecules is forced out as the proteins pull more tightly together as they cook.

Egg Whites

Another incredible property of the egg is the white's ability to retain air and create stable foam. This is what allows you to make meringue (or lighter cake batter). It's important to beat egg whites to their full volume, but not beyond. Overwhipping causes the protein in the whites to bind too tightly together, squeezing out water to pool in the bottom, leaving a dry, sad foam on top. The easy way to eliminate this problem is to beat them in a copper bowl, or if that's not available, to add something acidic to accomplish the same thing. The rule of thumb is ⅛ teaspoon of cream of tartar per egg white. A half teaspoon of lemon juice also works. The acid keeps the outer layer of the egg-white cells flexible. Without it, the cell walls can be become "brittle" and when you try to fold them into a batter, they will "shatter" and release all that air you beat into them.

When beating egg whites, make sure your bowl is clean and that there's absolutely no yolk attached to the whites. Just the tiniest amount of fat in the yolk will prevent the whites from expanding fully. For this reason it's best not to use a plastic bowl to whip egg whites; they often have traces of fat or oil on them. Egg whites at room temperature will beat up more quickly, so you save a bit of time.

Leavens

The word *leaven*, as applied to baking, means to lighten dough (i.e., cause it to rise), either physically or chemically, or biologically. There are three types of leavening in baking. First, the unsung leavens: These are the leavening agents inherent in the ingredients themselves, and in how they maximize trapped air when they're combined. Next are the biological leavens: yeast, both wild (sourdough), and domesticated. Finally, chemical leavens include baking powder, baking soda, and their chemical siblings.

The Unsung Leavens

The most basic leaven is simply the air that is captured in a dough or batter. This air is created and trapped by a number of different processes while dough is being mixed.

BEATING AND CREAMING: Don't minimize the importance of these steps; give them the time that's required. Electric mixers have greatly simplified the task of beating sugar, butter, and eggs into a light and creamy emulsion for cake, or of making egg whites into meringue.

FLOUR: Fluff up your flour before sprinkling it into a measuring cup. Aerated flour will get whatever you're baking off to a much lighter start. (One of the first things a King Arthur employee learns when taking our basic bread-baking class is to take a flour scoop and fluff up the first several inches of flour in its container.)

FATS: The way you incorporate fat into a dough or batter also increases the amount of air you add. Creaming butter and sugar together incorporates air, both through the action of the beaters and because jagged sugar crystals "grab" air as they come to the surface. Vegetable oil will produce a heavier product because it simply can't capture and hold as much air as butter. Also, the water in butter, when heated in the oven, expands and turns to steam; this also helps create a lighter baked good.

EGGS: Recipes that depend on eggs for leavening call for beating them (usually combined with sugar) until they're light and lemon-colored; that's the signal that they've incorporated an appropriate amount of air. Egg whites can be beaten until they've ballooned with air and become a stable foam. And if you beat eggs together with fat (e.g., creaming eggs and butter), you produce an emulsion that can hold more air than either alone.

SWEETENERS: Dry sugars will capture more air in a batter or dough than liquid sweeteners. This isn't to say you shouldn't use honey or molasses or maple syrup; when liquid sweeteners are used, the recipe calls for another type of leavening (usually baking soda in the case of these three liquids, since they're acidic) to raise the batter sufficiently.

Biological Leavens

WILD YEAST is a ubiquitous part of nature; a small, one-celled plant, it lives on many growing things, including grapes (where it manifests itself as the powdery sheen on a ripe grape) and whole grains. See the Sourdough chapter for more complete information on wild yeast and how to use it in bread baking.

Domestic Yeast

Domestic yeast is wild yeast that's been captured and "domesticated" by a yeast manufacturer. Each yeast manufacturer works with basically the same strain of yeast, *Saccharomyces cerevisiae*, but how each cultivates the yeast to produce a final product is what differentiates the different yeasts produced by different companies.

Manufacturers identify certain characteristics that they decide are desirable, isolate them, and then replicate them. The resulting yeast is given a "training" diet to make it replicate, then the cells, now in high density, are filtered, dried, ground, measured into appropriate sizes, packaged, and sent off to the market.

There are several types of yeast available to home bakers today. Here's how to make sense of the ones most of us have probably heard of.

CAKE OR COMPRESSED YEAST: This was the original "domestic yeast": moist, mushroom-colored, claylike in texture, and reasonably perishable. It's what our mothers and grandmothers used, and what most commercial bakers use today. Cake yeast will keep, refrigerated, in an airtight container for about a week. If your recipe calls for cake or compressed yeast, you may substitute 7g (2¼ teaspoons) of dry yeast for every 28g of compressed yeast. Cake yeast is typically crumbled into the recipe's liquid to dissolve it before being added to the other ingredients.

ACTIVE DRY YEAST: Yeast in this form was developed just before World War II to provide fresh bread for American troops: Fresh yeast wouldn't survive long-distance shipping and remain viable. Active dry yeast is much more stable than cake yeast and will keep, in an airtight container, almost indefinitely in the freezer (above 0°F), or for several weeks refrigerated. It is most often found in packets in the dairy products section at your grocery store. One packet = 7g = 2¼ teaspoons. To substitute active dry yeast for cake yeast, use about 40% by weight. In older recipes, this yeast was "proofed" to dissolve and activate it before adding it to the recipe. Dramatic improvements in manufacturing technology have made this step unnecessary, but if it's reassuring to you to see your yeast bubbly and expanding before proceeding, there's no harm in doing so.

INSTANT YEAST: This is a different strain of live yeast, but it's been dried at a much lower temperature, and uses a different process. It is typically added to a recipe with the dry ingredients and has a slightly quicker growth arc than active dry yeast (although active dry yeast will eventually catch up over the course of the dough's fermentation).

INSTANT YEAST FOR HIGH-SUGAR BREADS: This strain was developed to deal with sweet and more acidic doughs; SAF's Gold yeast is an example. It's more circumspect about its eating habits and will grow in these situations at a slower, more even rate.

RAPID RISE YEAST: This yeast is designed to work fast and die fast. It was created more as a marketing device for bakers in a hurry than to make good bread. We get a lot of questions from bewildered bakers as to why their bread had a tremendous first rise, only to peter out on the second. Usually it's because they unknowingly reached for a rapid rise yeast. As bread develops its wonderful flavor over a long, slow period of fermentation, we don't recommend short-circuiting the process by using this type of yeast.

Chemical Leavens

Most chemical leavens are fairly modern, having been developed in the past two hundred years. They were seen as a more "controllable" substitute for yeast, and it was originally thought that chemical leavens would completely replace yeast. Instead, they've created a baking category of their own, leaving yeast to continue the good work it's been doing for so long.

Chemical leavens work by first being mixed into the batter, where it dissolves and begins its work. Triggered by moisture, heat, or both, the leaven begins to release carbon dioxide, which then dissolves in the batter's liquid. Once dispersed in liquid, it begins to devolve into the bubbles of air captured in the batter. The carbon dioxide inside the air bubbles causes them to expand and, as they heat in the oven, they continue to expand until the batter around them bakes into a firm structure. That's how chemically leavened baked goods rise.

Each of the following commonly used chemical leaveners has its own characteristics, some desirable, some not.

BAKING SODA: Sodium bicarbonate, or sodium acid carbonate, is a natural alkaline ingredient derived from an ore called trona. The bulk of it is mined in the Green River Basin in Wyoming by Church and Dwight Co., makers of Arm & Hammer Baking Soda.

Finished products made with baking soda usually are associated with a slightly coarse or shaggy texture; often they will be slightly darker at the edges. Baking soda works by reacting with the naturally acidic ingredients in a dough or batter (e.g., buttermilk, sour cream, whey, citrus juice, and less obvious, brown sugar, chocolate, and molasses). It releases most of its gas immediately when combined with an acid and moisture, and a bit more when heated. Try to get a baking soda dough into the oven as quickly as you can, as it begins losing its leavening ability as soon as it's mixed. If all the baking soda isn't neutralized, meaning there's not enough acid to balance it, the final baked product will have a slightly soapy taste and a brownish-yellow cast. To balance baking soda, use ½ teaspoon baking soda with the following: 1 cup yogurt, buttermilk, whey, sour milk, or citrus juice; or ¾ cup honey or brown sugar or ½ cup natural cocoa.

DOUBLE-ACTING BAKING POWDER: Most baking powder on the market today is double-acting, meaning that its reaction occurs in two stages, using two different acids. One acid reacts very quickly and, when combined with a liquid, helps to aerate the batter. The second acid is slower acting, and begins to release carbon dioxide only when heated. This one-two kick is an advantage for several reasons. It gives the baker more timing flexibility; items such as baking powder biscuits may be made ahead, then refrigerated before being baked, and still have some chemical kick left by the time they go into the oven. Since double-acting baking powder includes a perfectly balanced amount of acid and soda, you don't need to worry about a soapy aftertaste (as long as the baking powder is evenly distributed).

CREAM OF TARTAR: Another natural ingredient, this fruit acid that accumulates on the inside of wine casks as the wine matures. It's one of the ingredients that, along with baking soda, goes into baking powder. Cream of tartar is often used to stabilize meringue, as its acid helps strengthen the proteins in the egg white, allowing them to trap more air as they're beaten.

AMMONIUM CARBONATE OR AMMONIUM BICARBONATE: We know this as baker's ammonia, which is an old-fashioned leavener not usually available in stores, although it can be found in some pharmacies, baking supply companies, or catalogues. The positive attribute of baker's ammonia is that, unlike modern baking powders, it leaves absolutely no chemical residue in finished baked goods, in neither smell, taste, nor color. It has a fast reaction time and while the release of gases (as a result of the chemical itself, plus heat, plus liquid) produces a telltale ammonia smell, this odor disappears once baking is complete, producing wonderfully crisp cookies and crackers. Baker's ammonia is used mainly in thin cookies and crackers, and sometimes in cream puffs and éclairs. It shouldn't be used in cakes or thick and/or moist cookies, as the ammonia won't have time to evaporate. Due to the unfamiliarity most bakers have with it, and its somewhat tricky nature, baker's ammonia should be used only in recipes calling for it.

Substitutions

When a recipe calls for baking soda, you can always choose to use baking powder instead. However, since the baking powder possesses an inherent acid-base balance, any acidic ingredient in the dough won't be neutralized, and will therefore have a more prominent flavor. If you like the slightly acidic flavor of buttermilk, and your recipe calls for baking soda to neutralize it, try using baking powder instead, which will allow the flavor of the buttermilk to be more assertive.

In general terms, up to 1 teaspoon of baking powder or ¼ teaspoon of baking soda is sufficient to leaven 1 cup (120g) of flour in any given recipe. If you want to use baking powder as a substitute for baking soda, you'll need about four times the amount of baking powder as baking soda called for in the recipe: for example, ½ teaspoon baking soda = 2 teaspoons baking powder, plus an acidic ingredient in the recipe.

Substituting baking soda for baking powder is a bit trickier. You can make the substitution successfully only if there's enough acid present to react with it; don't substitute baking soda for baking powder in a recipe without some clearly acidic ingredients.

To make your own self-rising flour, add 1½ teaspoons baking powder and ¼ teaspoon salt to 1 cup (120g) of all-purpose flour. This equals 1 cup (120g) of self-rising flour.

Fats

Let's start off on the right foot and think of fat as a baker's ally.

Fat is understood to be that which "shortens" or tenderizes. The term "shortening" refers to any fat used in baking: butter, margarine, vegetable oil, lard, and shortening. Shortening takes its name from the fact that fat coats the protein molecules in flour, making it difficult for them to combine and create that stretchy material called gluten. Any gluten strands that do form are shortened (rather than lengthened, as is the goal with fat-free hearth breads). When you use fats with flour in a recipe, you have the tender, fine-grained texture of a cake, rather than the chewy, open texture of low-fat hearth breads.

There are other ingredients that can do some of this work that fall under the dairy category, ingredients such as milk, cream, and eggs. And in discussing fats, you have more options for those that you put "on" your baked goods as opposed to "in." In other words, there are some types of fat substitutes that are fine as spreads, but can't be substituted for "real" fats in baking without damage to your recipe.

Fat is nature's clever way to store energy. Animals have it; so do plants. Most animal fats are solid at room temperature; most vegetable fats are liquid. Fat is a more compact storage unit than is a carbohydrate. A gram of fat provides more energy (9 calories per gram) than a gram of carbohydrates or protein (7 calories per gram).

Fats in Baking

Certain baked goods, such as most pie crusts and cookies, have to be made with a solid fat to attain their distinctive texture. Even solid fats vary in their melting points enough that you'll see a difference in texture between cookies made with shortening and those made with butter; since butter has a lower melting point, it will produce a softer, flatter cookie than shortening. Lard will produce a different result in a pie crust than will butter.

So why use vegetable shortening instead of butter? Each has a slightly different melting point and taste, and each will yield a slightly different final product. The following information should help you decide which fat to use or how to substitute one for another.

The Solid Fats

BUTTER, a byproduct of milk, is 80% fat with the remainder water and milk solids. Butter can be salted or sweet (meaning without salt).

We call for unsalted butter in most of our recipes when the amount called for is over 4 tablespoons (any amount smaller won't be affected by which type you use). The amount of salt added to salted butters isn't regulated, making it impossible to know exactly how much is being added. Using unsalted butter and adding salt separately yields more consistent results. Like other dairy products, and unlike most other fats, butter contains a significant natural nutritional boost in the form of vitamin A. Although whipped butter is still butter, it's had air beaten into it so it is expanded and can't be used successfully in most recipes with volume measurements.

Butter is made up of several types of fats; slightly more than half is saturated, a bit more than a quarter is monounsaturated, and the remainder is polyunsaturated. It also contains some cholesterol, some calcium, potassium, and lots of vitamin A.

The melting point of butter is just about at body temperature, which is why it has such a wonderful "mouth feel." Because of the milk solids in it, it begins to burn at a lower temperature than vegetable oil.

Butter has another attribute that is key in baking—it tastes wonderful. When you do use it in baking, buy the best. All butter is not the same. Good butter is very firm, which means it will hold more air in creaming that will help to leaven cakes, and it will create a flakier result in a pastry.

Butter, with its lower melting point, is often used in conjunction with vegetable shortening in making pie crusts, providing wonderful flavor and enhancing browning of the crust. It is a more brittle fat than lard or shortening, harder when cold, and softer when warmed to room temperature. When working with butter in pie crusts, biscuits, laminated doughs, anything where butter must be rubbed into the flour, everything must be kept cool. If the butter is overworked and warm, too much will melt into the flour, changing the texture of whatever you're baking. Since it is also about 80% fat, with the rest mostly water, you may need to use more butter and less water if substituting butter for lard or vegetable shortening.

Salted butter will keep almost six months if stored where it is dark and not subject to a lot of temperature fluctuation, say in the freezer, or a backup refrigerator. Unsalted butter has a shorter shelf life, about three months. It's what our recipes are written for and the one we prefer; unsalted butter allows us to better identify and adjust the salt in our formulas. But either way, it's best to buy what you need and use it up fairly quickly.

EUROPEAN-STYLE "CULTURED" BUTTERS are higher in butterfat, anywhere from 84% to 88%, and are traditionally made from cream that has been allowed to develop some flavor through the activity of its inherent bacteria before being churned into butter. Their flavors are more complex and intense. In baked goods where butter is a primary ingredient, such as shortbread or butter cookies, this butter not only adds its flavor but it also will make these baked goods more crisp.

CLARIFIED BUTTER is butter that has had the water and milk solids removed so it is 100% fat. As a result, it has a much longer shelf life and a higher smoke point than regular butter. While it can be used to fry things without smoking, it is missing the flavor components that the milk solids provide. But it does have its uses. Clarified butter is wonderful for sautéing, in sauces such as hollandaise and béarnaise, and in baked goods where you don't need to cream the butter (such as genoise).

MARGARINE has been around for well over a century. It was first developed in 1869 by a French food research chemist, responding to a directive by Napoleon to find a substitute for butter, presumably because it would be cheaper to make than the original. The original margarine contained a lot of animal fats combined with some vegetable oils. As we acquired the ability to hydrogenate liquid vegetable

CLARIFYING BUTTER

It's easy to clarify butter. Remember that the result will be between 20% and 25% less than the original amount. First, melt a pound of unsalted butter in a saucepan. Keep it over medium heat until the milk solids on the bottom just begin to brown (this adds a delicious nutty flavor). Remove the butter from the heat, skim any remaining foam off the top, and chill. After it has become solid, loosen the butter from the pot by placing it on the heat just momentarily. Turn it out onto a shallow dish upside down. Scrape off the milk solids that will have settled to the bottom (now the top). The remaining butter is now clarified and, if stored properly covered, will keep for many months in the refrigerator.

oils to make them solid, the percentage of vegetable fats increased as the animal fats decreased.

For many years, margarine was considered a healthy substitute for butter because of its lower percentage of saturated fats; then its reputation began to deteriorate because of the discovery of the negative health implications of transfatty acids, a byproduct of hydrogenation.

Most margarines are made almost entirely from vegetable oils, with added skim milk or whey solids (derived from milk) in some brands. And, like butter, they must be, as mandated by the USDA, at least 80% fat to mimic butter. They also must be fortified with vitamin A. "Diet" or "light" margarine is simply margarine that has had air and/or water whipped into it. Like whipped butter, it can't be used successfully as a solid-fat substitute in baking. Vegan butters are basically dairy-free margarines.

COCONUT OIL: One of the few plant-based fats that is solid at room temperature, coconut oil is composed mainly of saturated fat. In its "virgin" form, it smells and tastes of coconut. Many brands on supermarket shelves are refined (bleached and deodorized) and more neutral. It has a lower melting point than shortening.

LARD was the primary baking fat available to our ancestors. It is significantly lower in saturated fat and cholesterol than butter, made up of about 40% saturated, 50% monounsaturated, and 10% polyunsaturated fatty acids. The best lard is known as "leaf" lard, which comes from the fat around the kidneys of a pig. But most commercial lard is rendered (melted and clarified) from pork trimmings. Most grocery store lard is hydrogenated, so it's best to read labels carefully. It tends to be milder in flavor and more homogeneous in texture. Both are 100% fat and are softer and oilier than other solid fats. Because of its large crystalline structure, it works exceptionally well in biscuits and pie crusts, but won't create as fine a grain in cakes as butter, margarine, or vegetable shortening.

Lard is somewhat soft even when cold, so when making a pie dough, some of the fat coats the flour, inhibiting much of the gluten development. The remaining fat, which stays in larger flakes, melts at a slightly higher temperature than butter, keeping the layers of flour and water separate. This also allows what little water is in the dough to turn to steam and separate the layers further, which is what creates a pie crust's flakiness.

SHORTENING is made from vegetable oils and is thus 100% fat. To make this fat solid at room temperature, these oils are partially hydrogenated, chemically treated to change some of their polyunsaturated fatty acids to saturated fatty acids. This also gives it baking qualities necessary for many recipes as well as to prolong its shelf life. Unfortunately, partially hydrogenating the vegetable oils transforms something that was nutritionally a "good" fat into one that's not (what we now call trans fats). Vegetable shortening was reformulated in the mid-aughts to reduce trans fats to trace amounts (less than .5 grams per serving).

Unlike the vegetable oil it was made from, and as with butter, it can be creamed (i.e., because it's a solid, it can be beaten until it's malleable to capture air, which helps with leavening). As a result it can be used for such things as buttercream icings. Because it is all fat, this makes these icings more stable than those made with butter, which can begin to separate at warm temperatures. But you trade stability for flavor.

Shortening makes pie crusts that are almost as flaky as those made with lard. In a pie crust dough in which the pieces of fat are layered into the flour, shortening serves as a buffer between flour and any liquid that is added to hold it all together. As the crust bakes, the water turns to steam, forcing the flour-shortening layers apart and holding them apart until it melts, by which time the crust is set. This produces the classic tender, flaky pie crust.

High-sugar cookies tend to spread as they bake, but if you use shortening rather than butter, its higher melting point will help the cookies keep their structure long enough for the other ingredients to set, thus preventing spreading.

FRUIT PURÉES can be used to replace a portion of fats in recipes, such as muffins and cookies, but they won't produce a crisp cookie (the texture will be more cake-like). Because fat carries flavors in baking, a fruit purée just isn't going to help here either.

LECITHIN is a fatty substance naturally found in soybeans, egg yolks, and wheat. It's a very good emulsifier, meaning it's expert at bringing together disparate ingredients in a recipe. In its easy-to-use granular form, which we prefer, lecithin contains about 4 grams of fat per tablespoon.

In baking bread, lecithin may be used in place of fat in recipes calling for 1 to 2 tablespoons of fat per 3 to 4 cups of flour. The lecithin will help the bread stay soft and tender. In recipes calling for large amounts of fat, substituting 1 or 2 tablespoons of lecithin for an equal amount of fat is fine; you can't, however, use a cup of lecithin in place of a cup of butter—the texture and taste of the final product will suffer.

The Liquid Fats

These are oils that come primarily from plants: seeds, nuts, and vegetables. They all contain the same amount of total fat per tablespoon, but they vary greatly in percentage of saturated fat, with coconut oil checking in at 92% saturated fat, while canola oil contains only 7.6% saturated fat. Choose an oil that has a high percentage of polyunsaturated and/or monounsaturated fats (olive oil is the highest in monounsaturated fat, but its flavor usually isn't suitable for baking, except in the case of bread). They are used in baking where you don't need to cream or beat air into a fat. They moisten, tenderize, and help retain freshness. Liquid fats won't provide any structure in your cookie, cake, or pie, but it does a good job of "shortening" gluten strands, so it's fine for enhancing the texture of sandwich breads, muffins, quick breads, and other baked goods that don't depend on solid shortening for their structure. The type of oil best suited for most baking should have a light and unobtrusive flavor. Stronger flavored oils, such as extra virgin olive, peanut, or sesame, are best used for other purposes. It's important to store them in an airtight container where it's dark and cool to prevent rancidity.

Melting Points and Smoke Points

Knowing the points at which a fat becomes liquid and when it will begin to smoke as you heat it on the stove are of value in deciding which types of fat are best for any given purpose. Listed below are some of the fats you will most likely be using in baking and, where appropriate, their melting points and their smoke points. The melting points of most oils are not present as they are liquid at room temperature. And the smoke points of those fats you would not use for high-heat cooking are also not included. The presence of salt lowers the melting point of butter.

	SMOKE POINT	MELTING POINT
BUTTER	up to 350°F	98.6°F
CLARIFIED BUTTER	350°F to 365°F	
SHORTENING	325°F to 375°F	115°F to 119°F
COCOA BUTTER		96.8°F
CANOLA OIL	460°F	
CORN OIL	450°F to 460°F	
OLIVE OIL	375°F to 400°F	
PEANUT OIL	440°F to 450°F	
SAFFLOWER OIL	510°F	
VEGETABLE OIL BLENDS	428°F	

Weighty Conclusions

There's a lot of magic in fat. Animals have it. Plants have it. It's the most efficient container of calories (that measure of those fuels that allow us to live) in nature's emporium of nutrients. For human beings, at the dawn of civilization, fat in our bodies was a storage of fuel that helped us to seek yet more fuel, and it was a hedge against hard times. On our bodies, it kept us warm. But now in the age of easy access to fat calories, and overindulgence in the same, the magic has paled a bit—as does the value of anything when available in excess. But fat still has a critical place in our diets; we just need to know how to use it. And in most baked goods, it's invaluable. The venerable baguette is perhaps the most obvious exception. But even then, we tend to anoint it with some kind of fat when we eat it.

In baked goods, solid fats can be persuaded to contain a lot of air to lighten a recipe; it can be a buffer to tenderize; it can be incorporated in small or large sheets to create flakiness; it moisturizes; and it crisps. All fats can transmit more heat than water and are thus an efficient cooking medium. Some fats add flavor components of their own. And some just provide the assist for other flavors. Unfortunately, the English word for "fat" is difficult. It doesn't roll off the tongue easily; it stops dead and just sits there right in the middle of the mouth. Perhaps if we could use the French (*grasse*) or Italian (*grasso*), it would flow more easily and allow us to live with it more comfortably, as they seem to do.

Sweeteners

Sugar, in its many forms, is a critical component of most baked goods. It flavors both directly and indirectly, and it exacts its own chemistry on the other ingredients with which it's partnering. There are many myths about various forms of sugar, including the argument that some forms of sugar are better for you than others; that, as with grains, less refining means more nutrition. But all sweeteners are equal as far as energy is concerned; they contain about 4 calories of energy per gram. Although there are arguments that some sweeteners are better for you because they contain trace minerals and vitamins, or come from organic sources, all of them, with insignificant exceptions, are essentially empty nutritionally aside from the energy they produce.

Our bodies break down all carbohydrates, the simple kind (sugars) and the complex kind (fruits, vegetables, and grains) into glucose molecules so we can metabolize them to create energy. Your body can't tell whether the broken down glucose came from fruit, vegetable, bread, straight from the hive, a maple tree, or from a bowl of sugar.

Dry Sugars

Granulated white sugar is the most common sugar, the least expensive, the easiest to use, and imparts the least amount of flavor (other than sweetness). This is the sugar most commonly used in baking and on the table. It's the one we use as a benchmark for measuring the sweetness and baking characteristics of other sugars. Because it's the least assertive sweetener, it allows flavors of other ingredients to dominate. Some combinations:

CINNAMON SUGAR: 1 cup (198g) of granulated sugar combined with 2 tablespoons of cinnamon.

CITRUS SUGAR: 1 cup (198g) of granulated sugar blended with 1 tablespoon of lemon or orange zest, or ¼ teaspoon of lemon or orange oil.

VANILLA SUGAR: 1 cup (198g) of granulated sugar infused for several days with 1 or 2 chopped vanilla beans.

SUPERFINE, ULTRAFINE, OR BAR SUGAR is the finest of the granulated sugars. It's ideal for extra-fine-textured cakes and meringues and it dissolves easily, making it perfect for sweetening beverages. It's known as castor sugar in England, for the silver shaker (castor) it is kept and served in.

CONFECTIONERS' OR ICING SUGAR is a powdered white sugar with about 3% cornstarch added to prevent clumping. Because of its added cornstarch, don't bake with it unless the recipe calls for it. In this country there are three grades of confectioners' sugar, with only the finest (10X) available in supermarkets; the other coarser grades are used by institutional bakeries. Confectioners' sugar is used in icings, confections, and whipped cream. Glazing sugar is finer than confectioners' sugar, with maltodextrin added as an anticaking agent. It can be directly substituted for confectioners' sugar.

COARSE AND SANDING SUGARS are white sugars in large crystals. They're more stable than granulated sugar at baking temperatures, and thus can be used to decorate cookies or other pastries before baking. Since they don't melt at the same temperature as granulated sugar, they shouldn't be used as a substitute.

BROWN SUGAR is granulated sugar with some molasses mixed in to darken and deepen its flavor and texture. Light brown sugar has less added molasses (and less assertive flavor) than dark brown sugar; they can be used interchangeably, depending on personal preference. Dark brown sugar can be substituted for white granulated sugar measure for measure; it will alter the flavor just as you would expect and create a moister end product. If you're out of brown sugar and want to substitute white sugar, add a bit of molasses to approximate the flavor, 1 tablespoon (21g) of molasses per cup (198g) for light brown sugar and 2 tablespoons (42g) for dark.

Brownulated sugar is granulated brown sugar and can be substituted for either white or traditional brown sugars, with the same kinds of differences as you would discern between white and brown sugars.

RESCUING ROCK-HARD SUGAR

If your brown sugar has gotten rock hard, place it in a plastic bag with a slice of apple. It will soften in a day. For a quick fix, heat the sugar in a 250°F oven for a few minutes, or microwave on low for one to two minutes. Use it immediately before it seizes up. Better yet, store your brown sugar with a sugar softener or sugar bear (see Tools, page 549) to keep it moist all the time.

TURBINADO SUGAR is what most people imagine brown sugar is: granulated sugar that hasn't yet been refined. Unrefined sugar still has molasses in it. While brown sugar has molasses added back in, turbinado never had it taken out; it's a less-processed form of granulated sugar. Turbinado behaves the way brown sugar does, but at a higher price.

DEMERARA SUGAR, an English version of turbinado sugar, has larger crystals; it's often used in tea or on hot cereals, and can be used like coarse sugar to decorate pastries. The name denotes where this sugar originally came from, the Demerara district of British Guyana on the South American mainland.

RAW SUGAR isn't legally available in the United States because, like unpasteurized milk, it can contain bacteria and other foreign matter. "Sugar in the Raw" is a version of turbinado sugar.

COCONUT OR PALM SUGAR is derived from the nectar of flower buds of the coconut palm; it has butterscotch and brown sugar notes in its flavor. Palm sugar comes from the trunk sap of sugar palm species, and is equally as sweet as sugar.

DATE SUGAR is made of ground dried dates, thus it has a significant amount of fiber. It doesn't dissolve the way sugar does, is less sweet than sugar, and tastes like dates.

MAPLE SUGAR is maple syrup cooked down and then beaten into a crystallized form. Maple sugar has flavor overtones that result from its unique mineral content and the fact that the maple flavor is developed as the sap boils and the sugar caramelizes. This is not a good substitute for any other sugar; it is best appreciated in recipes designed for it.

MALT is a powder made from barley that has been sprouted and dried. Not long ago there was interest in sprouting grains to add an inexpensive nutritional wallop to one's diet. Malting takes this one step further. There are two types of dry malt: diastatic and non-diastatic.

As barley (or any grain berry) gets closer and closer to sprouting, it develops diastatic enzymes that will break down its starch into the simple sugars, maltose and dextrin, that become the food source for an emerging seedling. This is the food it uses while it develops its own independent feeding system. We can capture those enzymes by allowing barley or other grain berries to sprout. When their activity is at its greatest, the berries are dried at a relatively low temperature (not over 170°F) that doesn't damage the enzymes. They are then ground into a slightly sweet flour.

If you read the ingredient statement on most bags of all-purpose flour in this country, you'll find that a small amount of malted barley flour has been added as a natural yeast food. It has also long been used as a yeast food in Europe. When a tiny amount of malted barley flour is added to wheat flour in a dough, it breaks the wheat starch into sugars for yeast to feed on, and gives the dough a real boost.

Non-diastatic malt is made the same way, but dried at higher temperatures that destroy the ability of the enzymes to act on the starch.

Malt is an unsung health food that has been around for years. Diastatic malt, used in small amounts, enhances the appearance, flavor, and texture of bread; non-diastatic malt, in larger amounts, adds a familiar malt flavor, but is only one-third as sweet as granulated sugar.

Liquid Sugars

There are several liquid sweeteners (syrups) that are made from sources that define their flavor, color, and some baking characteristics. Some pure syrups include molasses (sugarcane), honey (bees), maple syrup (the sugar maple tree), and sorghum (sweet sorghum grass). There are others that are blends, in some cases with other flavors added. The base for several of these is corn syrup (or high-fructose corn syrup) because it has little flavor of its own and combines well with stronger flavored syrups. Dark corn syrup is an example of this. The most commonly used syrups are listed first.

CORN SYRUP is a sweetener that's become increasingly important, as corn is a relatively inexpensive and easy crop to grow. Corn syrup, the kind available in the grocery for the home baker, is about 25% water. The remainder is glucose, salt, and vanilla. Glucose is hygroscopic, or moisture retaining; baked goods made with corn syrup will stay moist longer.

DARK CORN SYRUP is a mixture of dark corn syrup, refiner's (cane) syrup, caramel flavor, salt, caramel color, and a preservative. Its flavor is stronger than light corn syrup; it can stand in for molasses in a pinch.

HONEY is probably our oldest sweetener. It's unique as a sweetener because it only needs to be removed from the hive. Once out and strained of bits of comb, it's ready to eat. It was used extensively by the Greeks and Romans and was the primary sweetener in Europe until the sixteenth century, when cane sugar became more easily available.

It's perceived as sweeter than sugar and it has different browning characteristics so you need to bake with it at a lower temperature. Honey is more hygroscopic than table sugar and will help keep baked goods moist. It also has a unique flavor that's an important part of many traditional baked goods, such as lebkuchen and baklava.

MAPLE SYRUP is another sweetener that, in its natural state, is as pure a source for sugar as is honey (unlike cane syrup, which has a lot of undesirable stuff in it that needs to be removed).

There are very few areas in the world where the sugar maple grows well and, fortunately for us, one of them is the northeastern United States (and Canada). Native Americans were making syrup long before Europeans came on the scene, but with Europeans came equipment and technology that has made the process somewhat easier.

Maple sugar and syrup were the sweeteners of choice for early colonial cooks. Before the Revolution, sugar from the West Indies was heavily taxed so it was too expensive for general use. Later on as our distaste for slavery grew, our distaste for sugar produced by slave labor grew as well. So maple sugar managed to sustain our needs for sweetening for quite some time. By the end of the nineteenth century, sugar from sugar beets began to be available and that, plus the fact that cane sugar had become much less expensive, meant that the maple was no longer used as a major sugar source. Maple syrup is still produced by hardy Northeasterners who can't yet get into their fields to plant and who somehow can't let the sugar season go by without a "go at it."

Maple sap tastes like water with a faint echo of sweetness. The sugar season begins in early spring when nights are still below freezing but days soar to heady temperatures of 45° to 50°F, preferably with no wind and lots of sun. Then the trees are tapped to release the sap (a slow, drip, drip, drip kind of process). After the sap is collected, it is poured into an evaporator placed over a wood- or oil-fired "arch."

To make a gallon of syrup, you need to boil down 35 to 50 gallons of sap. Early season sap is lighter flavored than later season sap, when bacterial activity begins to work on the sucrose and break it down into a larger glucose/fructose component. Thus early season sap makes lighter syrup, while darker syrup comes from the later sap. The labeling and grading system for maple syrup was changed in 2015, with all US maple syrups being labeled Grade A, then given a set of descriptions for the various iterations. The terms range from "amber color" (formerly Grade A) to "dark color and robust flavor" (formerly Grade B) to "very dark and strong" (formerly Grade C). Some people prefer dark syrup for its assertiveness in baking. Others love the ethereal taste of the first-run syrup as a condiment, on pancakes, waffles, and hot cereal.

MOLASSES is what's left after the juice of the sugarcane has been boiled and concentrated and all the available sucrose has crystallized. Because molasses making is done in three stages, there are three resulting grades. "First" molasses is lighter in color and flavor than "second" and "third" (blackstrap) molasses. With each boiling and extraction, the remaining liquid becomes more and more caramelized (darker), the minerals and other "impurities" become more and more concentrated, and the sugar content lowers. Blackstrap molasses contains only about 50% sugar components, with the result that its flavor is too strong to use in any but small amounts. In baking, use it in combination with other, lighter flavored sweeteners. "First" molasses produces the most pleasing flavor. It has a signature flavor that combines well with ginger and other spices in cookies and cakes, particularly gingerbread.

Molasses and maple syrup usually are interchangeable in a recipe, especially if small amounts are called for. Most other liquid sugars can be substituted for each other too, except barley malt syrup, corn syrup, and rice syrup. These are much less sweet than their counterparts. Be aware that some have a higher water content than others and they all behave slightly differently. Experiment with them, but not when you've got special guests arriving.

GOLDEN SYRUP is an English sweetener (the Australians and New Zealanders have their versions, too). An ultrathick, smooth syrup that tastes like a caramelized version of our corn syrup, golden syrup has much more flavor and is much more interesting. It's often drizzled onto scones or hot cereal, or into tea.

MALT SYRUP (barley malt syrup) is made from malted barley that is ground and then briefly treated with an acid to dissolve the enzymes, sugars, and vitamins. It is then heated with water to form the mildly sweet, concentrated liquid we know as malt syrup. Although dark-colored like molasses, its flavor is much milder. To create a moist and chewy bagel with a shiny shell, commercial bagel bakers add a small amount of malted barley syrup in place of ordinary sweetener.

SORGHUM is a classic Southern and Midwestern American sweetener extracted from an Old World grass. Its slightly molasses flavor complements a range of muffins, pancakes, cereals, and quick breads.

AGAVE SYRUP is extracted from the core of the agave cactus. It's slightly thinner and contains more water than honey. Its sweetness comes mostly from fructose (50% to 60%) and some glucose (20%). It's about 1.5 times sweeter than sugar.

Substitutions

We don't recommend substituting liquid sweeteners for granulated or brown sugars in recipes in which the fat is creamed with the sweetener. Liquid sweeteners can't induce fats to contain air because they don't have a crystalline structure. The result will be a dense, heavy product.

One potential substitution, honey for table sugar, can be done with some adjustments. It is sweeter than table sugar, so for 1 cup (198g) of sugar, use a generous ¾ cup (252g) of honey and decrease the liquid in the recipe by 3 to 4 tablespoons (42 to 56g). If the recipe contains no additional liquid, increase the flour by 3 tablespoons (23g). Don't use honey in recipes that need to be cooked at over 350°F because it scorches.

If a recipe calls for 1 cup (333g) of honey and you're out, you can substitute 1¼ cups (248g) of granulated sugar or brown sugar plus ¼ cup (57g) of water.

How Sugars Affect What We Bake

Certain breads are definitely superior with no added sweetener, but can you imagine a cake, cookie, quick bread, or pie without any sweetening? Sugar's most important attribute is easy to understand. It's sweet and we just like it.

But sugar's chemistry in baking is a more important consideration. Because it's hygroscopic (it attracts and absorbs water), it competes with the protein (gluten) in flour for liquids in a batter. By not allowing the flour to have all the liquid, it slows down the development of the gluten, which means that your cakes, quick breads, and cookies will be tender. And by slowing down the rate at which the flour can absorb the liquid in a batter, it allows a cake or quick bread to expand (rise) for a longer time. The same cake made without sugar not only will taste pretty bad, but will be tough as well as flat. This is why, when you make quick breads or biscuits that contain small amounts of sugar (or none at all), it's really important to do minimal mixing (20 seconds) because there's no sugar there to interfere with the development of the gluten. When you cream granulated sugar (remember it is in crystals so it has a lot of edges and sides) with butter in making a cake, air gets trapped on its surface to make this combination light and fluffy. When the rest of the ingredients are mixed in and the resulting batter is baked, the air bubbles expand and make the cake rise.

In angel food cakes, sugar, along with cream of tartar, helps stiffen and stabilize the egg white (protein), which means it can trap air and carbon dioxide bubbles. This makes these cakes bake up almost lighter than air. Another way in which sugar makes these cakes light is by interfering with the egg white protein's ability to coagulate and set. Because they take longer to cook, the egg foam can continue to expand for longer, giving the cake more height. It also makes the cake tender.

At 350°F to 375°F, granulated sugar caramelizes or, really, begins to burn slightly. It becomes golden in color and develops a flavor that most of us find very pleasing. This helps the surface of cakes and cookies to brown and become a bit crisp. The bonds that caramelized sugar form on the surface keep moisture inside your baked good. The higher the sugar content, the more browning will occur.

This caramelizing on the surface of cookies creates a "cracked" surface, golden brown color, and great flavor. Sugar is at work on the inside of the cookie, too; after a cookie dough is mixed, about half the sugar is still undissolved. As the cookie bakes, the sugar finally dissolves and allows the cookie to spread. The less sugar, the less spread.

All sugars are hygroscopic. But it's good to remember some are more hygroscopic than others; when you bake with honey, corn syrup, or another liquid sweetener, you'll have a moister end product. Cookies made with granulated sugar will be hard and crisp when they cool. Cookies made with corn syrup or honey will brown more easily and will become soft when they cool.

In a pie crust dough, sugar also will interfere with gluten formation, making a more tender crust. Pie crusts with a lot of sugar will have a sandy texture and not enough gluten development to be easily rolled out. There are some recipes where this is a good thing and some where it's not. For more information, see the Pies and Tarts chapter.

Even when no sugar is added to a bread recipe, sugar is at work. When a bread dough is rising, yeast is growing by converting the wheat starch into sugars. These sugars create that lovely golden surface on a well-baked loaf of bread.

Each sweetener has its own signature flavor that can create or change the personality of whatever you're baking. We don't recommend substituting one for another, as substituting sweeteners often changes the chemical balance in a recipe enough that it won't work right. Use your common sense; it's OK to substitute golden syrup for corn syrup, or light brown sugar for dark brown, but don't stray too far from the recipe's original sweetener or you may find yourself in trouble.

Sugar Substitutes

Refined sugar is 99% sucrose and a simple carbohydrate. Many additional types of sugars have "natural" sources. You'll recognize some of them on product labels because their chemical names also end in "-ose." Included are glucose (also called dextrose), fructose (also called levulose), lactose, and maltose. Additionally there are sugar alcohols, which are actually neither sugar nor alcohol. They are mostly found in candies and processed foods. You can identify them because most of them end in "-ol": maltitol, sorbitol, xylitol, and mannitol.

GRANULATED FRUCTOSE is a sucrose look-alike and can be found often with traditional sugars in the grocery store. It has the same caloric value as regular sugar, but is perceived as sweeter; therefore you can use about one-third less of it and thus decrease your intake of calories. But beware, it doesn't behave exactly like granulated sugar in baking. Because fructose is more hygroscopic than sucrose, fructose-sweetened products tend to be moister and darker than if they were made with white sugar.

FRUIT JUICE CONCENTRATES (apple, orange, or white grape) also can be substituted for sugar. To use them in baking, use ¾ cup (169g) for every cup (198g) of white sugar and decrease the amount of liquid by 3 tablespoons (42g). Start by substituting for only half the sugar called for in a recipe.

Artificial Sweeteners

Artificial sweeteners provide sweetness but not the other characteristics one expects from sugar, such as bulk and flavor. If you are going to use these, we recommend using them as a substitute for only some of the sugar in a recipe.

ASPARTAME was discovered in 1965 and is 160 to 220 times sweeter than sucrose. The FDA approved aspartame in 1981, making it the first low-calorie sweetener approved by the FDA in more than 25 years (since Saccharin). It is sold under trade names such as NutraSweet and Equal.

Aspartame sweeteners are heat-sensitive. They are not appropriate for recipes that are cooked more than 20 minutes because the chemical compounds break down and lose their sweetening power. Thus they aren't recommended for use in sweet yeast breads, quick breads, or cakes. You might want to experiment with short-bake cookies. It is best added to noncooked items such as fillings for no-bake pies or to puddings after they have been removed from the heat and are partially cooled. It is also marketed as "Equal for Recipes" and "Equal Spoonfuls," but while the packaging states that they can be used in "practically any recipe where sugar functions primarily as a sweetener," the label goes on to say, "In recipes where sugar also provides structure and volume [and other baking characteristics], some modifications may be required for best results." It takes 7¼ teaspoons of Equal to equal 1 cup (198g) of granulated sugar.

People with a rare condition called phenylketonuria (PKU) should avoid aspartame.

ACESULFAME POTASSIUM OR "ACESULFAME K" was discovered in 1967 and was brought to market in 1988. It is about 200 times sweeter than table sugar and sold under the brand names Sunett and Sweet One. It is heat stable so it can be used in baking and cooking, and it's suggested that you use acesulfame K in combination with granulated sugar when baking. Substitute 6 (1g) packets for each ¼ cup (50g) of sugar.

SACCHARIN, up to 700 times sweeter than sugar, is named after the Latin word for sugar (*saccharum*) and has the longest history of all the sugar substitutes. It was discovered in 1879 and was used during both World Wars to compensate for sugar shortages and rationing. Saccharin is sold under the trade names of Sweet'N Low, Sucaryl, Sugar Twin, Sweet Magic, and Zero-Cal. It has a long shelf life and is stable at high temperatures, so it is appropriate for use in baked goods. But as is stated on the Sweet'N Low container, "Many recipes require some sugar for proper volume, texture, and browning. We suggest replacing half the sugar your recipe calls for with an equivalent amount of Sweet'N Low." Some people with sensitive palates can detect an aftertaste. Because saccharin can pass from a mother to an unborn child, pregnant women may want to check with their obstetricians about the use of saccharin.

SUCRALOSE is the only noncaloric sweetener actually made from sucrose (table sugar) and was approved for public use by the FDA in 1998. To create it, three atoms of chlorine are substituted for three hydroxyl groups on the sugar molecule, a change that produces a sweetener that has no effective calories. It is 600 times sweeter than the sugar from which it was created, yet still tastes like it. Unlike aspartame-based sweeteners, it does not deteriorate at high temperatures so it can be used in cooking and baking. It measures and pours like sugar. It is sold under the brand name Splenda.

Splenda can be used whenever you use sugar in cooking and baking. However, it works best in recipes where sugar is used primarily for sweetening, such as fruit fillings, custards, sauces, and marinades. It also works well in quick breads, muffins, cookies, and pies. In recipes where sugar provides bulk structure to the product, such as yellow or chocolate cakes, you'll need to make a few changes in your recipe for best results. In recipes where the amount of sugar is quite high, such as meringues, caramel, pecan pies, and angel food or pound cakes, complete substitution for the entire sweetener called for may not yield the best results.

SUGAR'S COLORFUL PAST

The production of granulated white sugar, the most common baking sugar, is a complex and labor intensive job. Although the juice of sugarcane is almost 13% sucrose, it contains a lot of other stuff that makes it unpalatable in its natural state. This has to be removed (no easy task), and the remainder has to undergo a number of other processes to leave a crystalline structure that can be used for food consumption.

Sugarcane presumably originated in the South Pacific and then, with human migration, traveled west to Asia. It had reached the Indian subcontinent sometime before the Christian era and was used there to make a kind of raw sugar for sweetening. It continued traveling west with the Persians and then with the Arabians who conquered them. The Crusades made the connection between the Middle East and Europe during the Middle Ages. Venice was to become the conduit for Eastern sugar flowing to Europe during that period, although it didn't reach England until early in the fourteenth century.

Over the next several hundred years, as Europeans developed a real taste for cane sugar, it was clear that the potential market for this sweetener was vast. So, in spite of the obstacles, the sugar industry was aggressively developed. This precipitated one of the ugliest periods in European and American history and had an enormous impact on how the Western Hemisphere was colonized and exploited, as well as how Africa was exploited and de-colonized.

In their search for an appropriate climate to grow sugarcane and to break their dependence on Middle Eastern sugar, Europeans found their way to the West Indies. To facilitate the production of sugar, hundreds of thousands of slaves were brought there from Africa. Thus began that infamous trade of slaves, molasses and sugar, and rum that created enormous fortunes, new and thriving ports, and a social blight that eventually led to our own Civil War.

The hideous conditions that sugar-producing slaves had to endure finally induced the European countries to outlaw the importation of West Indian sugar. As a result, this eventually allowed the development of another sugar source, the sugar beet. Because sugar beets can be grown in cooler climates than sugarcane, it has become a thriving crop in the United States, Europe, and Russia. The world's sugar consumption is now divided pretty evenly between cane and beet sugars, although the United States is now using a form of corn sugar, fructose, in many manufactured products such as soft drinks.

Up until the early part of the twentieth century, some cane sugar still arrived in Europe and North America in "loaves." In the early years of West Indian sugar production the loaves were cones that were approximately a foot or more in diameter at the base and 3 feet high. A cone of sugar this size weighed about 30 pounds and lasted a very long time. As time went on, smaller and more manageable "loaves" became available in 14-pound and 8- or 9-pound sizes. To remove usable sugar from these loaves, the housewife had a special sugar cutter to cut off chunks that were kept in sugar drawers or boxes. When one wanted sugar for cooking, it was then pounded into granules.

The conical shape of the sugar helps explain molasses production. To make granulated or crystallized sugar, the cane was first crushed, then cleared of impurities and finally cooked until almost all the water had boiled off. It was then poured into cone-shaped clay molds to crystallize and harden. There was a hole in the tip so during this crystallization period, which lasted several days, any liquid residue (molasses) ran out the hole into a collection vessel. Often this meant that there were several grades of sugar in the cone. It was clearest and whitest at the wide (top) end and grew increasingly dark and more like what we think of as brown sugar toward the tip.

Europe's first reaction to sugar was to use it as a spice and a flavoring. This perhaps explains the medieval taste for dishes that were both savory and sweet, the remnants of which we have today in plum puddings and mincemeat pies, which were originally composed of much meat and some fruit. One of the earliest confections that could be considered simply a candy were almonds coated with sugar. These evolved into marzipan, a paste made of almonds and sugar ground together, which has become an integral part of European confection making and baking.

Other Ingredients

Flour, sugar, butter, water, milk, yeast—these are the workhorses of the baking world. But other key ingredients add such wonderful finesse to baked goods. What would the world be without chocolate? Without vanilla? How these and other baking accoutrements are chosen and used can be the defining element in your finished good.

Chocolate

Chocolate, *theobroma cacao*, "food of the gods," is one of those significant discoveries from the New World that has changed the lives (for better and worse) of all those who have come in contact with it. The cacao tree originated in the river valleys of South America. Sometime in the fifth century, the tree's seeds, or beans, were carried into what is now Mexico by the Mayas. When Columbus arrived in the New World he took seeds from the cacao tree back to Spain. As with many things ahead of their time, so was chocolate, at least in Europe. Spain wasn't interested. So it took another generation and another explorer to make the chocolate connection between new world and old. The rest, as they say, is history (see pages 509–510). It became such a prized ingredient that we still think of it as special.

Cocoa

NATURAL COCOA: Cocoa sold in the United States contains between 11% and 24% cocoa butter, with most supermarket cocoas falling in the 12% to 16% range. In Britain, cocoa must contain a minimum of 20% fat (the British know and like their fats). But they may know something else as well. Because fats are carriers of flavor, cocoa that has had most of the cocoa butter removed from it loses its flavor fairly quickly. Natural cocoa is light brown and has, because of its acidity, a slight edge to it. Because natural cocoa is acidic, you most often use baking soda, rather than baking powder, when you bake with it. The chemical reaction between the two creates carbon dioxide bubbles, which leaven the batter. At the same time, the baking soda neutralizes the acidity of the cocoa and the cocoa color darkens. Because of its lighter color and unique flavor, natural cocoa is used to make the beverage itself, as well as frosting, chocolate sauce, and fudge.

DUTCH-PROCESS (DUTCHED) COCOA: Dutch-process cocoa is either neutral or slightly alkaline. When you bake with it, you'll most often use baking powder rather than baking soda. Baking powder contains the acid that's needed for leavening that's been removed from the cocoa. Dutched cocoas are best in cakes and cookies.

If you have some cocoa and don't know whether it's natural or Dutch-process, stir some into a little warm water. Add a pinch of baking soda. If the cocoa fizzes and becomes a deeper color, you have natural cocoa. If it doesn't fizz, it's been Dutched.

BLACK COCOA: This is cocoa that has been severely Dutched, which intensifies the darkening and also the flavor. Use 1 or 2 tablespoons in conjunction with regular Dutch-process cocoa. This is the cocoa that makes Oreo cookies so dark.

Solid Chocolate

BITTER (UNSWEETENED) BAKING CHOCOLATE: Baking chocolate is essentially pure chocolate liquor—the ground cacao bean itself, plus chocolate solids and cocoa butter. It contains no sugar. This is the only chocolate that's fairly straightforward.

SWEET CHOCOLATE: This ranges from bittersweet to semisweet. There are different varieties and grades but in the United States they must contain a minimum of 35% chocolate liquor. The best bittersweet varieties contain 65% to 70%; in general, the higher the percentage of chocolate liquor, the darker and stronger the chocolate. Also included is sugar, additional cocoa butter, and such flavorings as vanilla beans (the whole bean), vanillin, salt, and/or spices (cinnamon, cloves, etc.). If a chocolate contains 70% chocolate liquor, what is the rest? Ideally, just sugar, vanilla,

FROM TREE TO TABLE

For the past 25 years, most of the chocolate that's consumed worldwide, more than half a million tons a year, comes from Ghana. But the world's "chocolate belt" encircles the globe, located in those tropical countries within about 20 degrees south and north of the equator (the areas known as the Tropic of Capricorn and Tropic of Cancer, respectively). Some of the finest varieties come from this hemisphere.

The cacao tree produces buds, blossoms, and fruit on an ongoing basis. The pods (fruit), which are 9″ or 10″ in length and 4″ or 5″ in diameter, look a bit like large acorn squash, with ridges more rounded than sharp. As the pods become ripe, they're gathered, split open with a machete, and allowed to dry for 24 hours. The seeds within the pulp are then removed and thrown into boxes, where they begin to ferment. This is called "sweating," which goes on for several days. During fermentation, the juice of the pulp in which the seeds (or beans) are embedded drains away, the germ within the bean dies, the beans themselves develop a reddish tint, their bitterness is tempered, and their flavor developed.

After the fermenting period, the beans are spread out in the sun or a kiln, where their moisture is reduced from about 33% to 6% or 7%. The flavor continues to develop and become less acidic. At this point the beans are bagged (it takes 20 to 30 beans to make a pound) and sent to a chocolate-processing plant.

The bean itself consists of the husk or shell (14%) and the interior kernel or "nib" (86%). The nibs are about 50% fat (the cocoa butter), 17% protein, and 30% various types of complex carbohydrates. They're particularly rich in potassium, calcium, phosphorus, and, of course, caffeine (although not as much as one might think—certainly less than coffee or even tea).

At the processing plant the beans are cleaned and roasted, allowing the chocolate flavor and color to emerge. The nibs pull away from the shells, making them easier to remove. Once the shells have been cracked open and winnowed away, just the nibs are left, and the process of making chocolate can begin. The nibs are screened by size, then mixed with others from other plantations to create blends that will suit different needs and tastes. Then they're ground. During the grinding process, the beans are heated, melting the fatty part (the cocoa butter) and creating a fairly liquid mass that we know as "chocolate liquor" (which has nothing at all to do with alcohol). Chocolate liquor is a combination of about 47% chocolate solids and 53% cocoa butter.

Chocolate liquor is processed in three ways. If it's to be made into bitter (or unsweetened baking) chocolate, the pure liquor itself is molded into cakes and chilled. If it's to be made into eating chocolate, additional cocoa butter and sugar are added and then it's conched, a kneading or rolling process taking 4 to 24 hours, which aerates, mellows, and creates that famous silky consistency of the best chocolate. After conching, it's molded into bars or blocks and cooled.

If it's to be made into cocoa, the liquor is pressed hydraulically to remove a certain percent of the fat or cocoa butter (which goes into eating chocolate or is made into "white" chocolate). The remaining solids are pulverized into a powder or "cocoa."

and milk powder if it's a milk chocolate. Because cocoa butter is expensive, some eating chocolates contain other vegetable fats to keep their price down.

BITTERSWEET CHOCOLATE: Used often in baking, bittersweet chocolate has a stronger chocolate flavor than semisweet chocolate because it contains less sugar. But because the amount of sugar is not regulated, what one manufacturer calls bittersweet may be called semisweet by another manufacturer, so what you use is a matter of choice and taste.

MILK CHOCOLATE: This contains 15% to 20% milk solids substituted for a portion of the chocolate liquor. Although this is America's favorite eating chocolate, it's not used often in baking.

"WHITE" CHOCOLATE: We all know there's no such thing; to be "chocolate" there must be chocolate solids present. The best white chocolate is made from cocoa butter, with sugar and milk solids added.

COATING CHOCOLATE (COUVERTURE): The best contains no other fat than cocoa butter, which is tempered to behave in a certain way. Because tempering is a bit tricky, other coating chocolates exist that contain other vegetable fats that aren't so heat-sensitive and don't require tempering. But these lack the texture, shine, and flavor of chocolate made solely with cocoa butter. Coating chocolate is not the same as chocolate coating.

HYBRID CHOCOLATE: Hybrid chocolates are those that contain fats in addition to cocoa butter. Due to the difference in melting points, some hybrid chocolates can have a waxy texture as a result. Brands that contain only cocoa butter are regarded as higher quality. But even the "best" need to be judged based on personal taste and inclination.

CHOCOLATE CHIPS: Most are usually hybrid chocolate and should be used where they are called for. For example, they should not be substituted for other baking chocolate made only with cocoa butter, because they won't behave the same way.

TEMPERING CHOCOLATE

Cocoa butter, also known as theobroma oil, is a very stable fat. It contains natural antioxidants that discourage rancidity and allow chocolate to be stored for two to five years. For chocolate aficionados, it's most valued for the way it behaves in the mouth. While it remains brittle at room temperature or lower, it begins to melt just below body temperature, which creates the silky, sensuous "mouth feel" of high-quality chocolate.

You can only temper chocolate that contains cocoa butter—no other kind of fat. Cocoa butter is actually not just one fat, but a variety of structurally different components. Some of them melt at a higher temperature than others. When chocolate has been heated and begins to cool, the high-melt-point fats solidify first. These are the ones that give high-quality chocolate its shine and snap.

The object of tempering is to create an evenly distributed, very fine fat-crystal structure, which will yield chocolate that remains shiny as it hardens. Because the high-melt-point fats solidify (crystallize) first, you're trying to "seed" the chocolate with these crystals, so the other fats will build their structure upon them as they cool and begin to set.

The easiest way to temper chocolate is with a chocolate tempering machine, available to the home baker through some catalogues, or at gourmet stores. To temper chocolate without a machine, place it in a double boiler (rather than over direct heat, because it can burn so easily). Heat dark or semisweet chocolate to 122°F; for milk or white chocolate, 105°F.

It's important not to let any moisture infiltrate the chocolate, or it will seize (become grainy). Allow the chocolate to melt uncovered to allow any steam generated to dissipate. Seizing is essentially a chaotic crystallization of all the fats around the point where the water entered; it's characterized by chocolate that has turned into a lumpy, grainy, unfortunate mass.

Once the chocolate is melted, remove two-thirds of it from the heat, set it in a cool place, and stir constantly until it reaches a temperature of 78°F. At this point, fine fat crystals have formed and the chocolate is thick and pasty. Many chocolate manufacturers recommend slow cooling with constant stirring in order to produce the best texture, but there are a number of pastry chefs who prefer to speed things up by stirring the chocolate over cold water or by pouring it onto a marble slab and working it with a bench knife until it's cool. When the chocolate has reached 78°F, stir it back into the hot chocolate. The temperature should then be about 88°F. At this point, the chocolate is tempered.

After the tempered chocolate has cooled and crystallized appropriately, it's too thick for dipping, molding, or anything else and must be warmed slightly before it can be used. Again, using a double boiler, it should be reheated to 88°F (for milk or white chocolate) to 90°F (for dark chocolate), where it's liquid enough to use. Don't let it get warmer than this, or the fat crystals will melt and come "out of temper." If that happens, it will take a long time to set and when it finally does, the texture won't be as good; it can remain tacky to the touch or become streaky when it sets. In addition, some of the cocoa butter can migrate to the surface, causing the chocolate to "bloom."

(continued)

There are two types of chocolate bloom, both the result of storage conditions. Fat bloom happens when chocolate has been stored where it's too warm. The low-melt-point fat crystals melt and recrystallize in larger crystals, which migrate to the surface of the chocolate. This makes the chocolate look as if it had been dusted with a gray or white powder. While it might look moldy, it's not; it can still be used for baking and/or the crystals can be recrystallized to assume their original form by tempering.

Sugar bloom happens when chocolate has been stored where it's damp. Because sugar is hygroscopic, moisture can condense on the surface of the chocolate and will slowly dissolve the sugars it comes in contact with. As it evaporates, it will leave small sugar crystals on the surface, which we experience as roughness.

Some chips, made for the professional baker, are made just with cocoa butter. Make sure you check the label.

CHOCOLATE EXTRACT: This is a natural extract from a special blend of cocoa beans that enhances the chocolate flavoring in baked goods. It's available through specialty shops and catalogues.

Vanilla

This is a "new world" flavor from an orchid that grew only in Central America until the middle of the nineteenth century. The Aztecs used it for flavor in conjunction with cacao. From here it made its way to the Philippines and, in 1846, to Tahiti. But the orchid wouldn't produce a bean just anywhere. In Mexico, a specific type of bee and hummingbird were responsible for its pollination and the subsequent bean. Finally, in Madagascar, in what used to be known as the Bourbon Islands (from the name of the royal French family) off the southeast coast of Africa, it was discovered that the flowers could be pollinated by hand. Thus began the successful pursuit of the commercial growing of vanilla beans, the "Bourbon vanilla" which is about 75% of the vanilla that we use today.

The process of creating vanilla is intensive and long so it is still an expensive flavoring. After the flowers are pollinated, bean pods begin to form, and take about a month and a half to reach full size, somewhere between 6˝ and 10˝ in length. They are picked before they are ripe, heated quickly to stop the ripening process, and then placed in the sun to dry. For several days, they dry in the sun during the day and are wrapped up to sweat at night. Then they are laid out to dry completely in the shade. Finally they are sorted and placed in containers to continue to age for as long as 9 months, during which time flavor and character are developed.

Today, Mexican vanilla is relatively scarce because its habitat has been reduced. But Mexican vanilla is considered by some to be the best in the world because of

A BIT OF CHOCOLATE HISTORY

For early Meso-Americans, the cacao tree played an important role. The beans were precious enough to be used as currency. The beans were also the source of an unsweetened drink, xocoatl, made by pounding them and mixing them with boiling water. Xocoatl was drunk and cacao beans offered to the deities that presided over every important ritual during their lives.

At court, Spanish explorer Hernán Cortés was ceremoniously served xocoatl, this beverage of the gods, the name coming from an Aztec word meaning "bitter water." Bitter it was. Not long after this congenial welcome, Cortés, in the name of Spain, took Montezuma prisoner and slaughtered hundreds of his people. Montezuma died while in captivity and the ascendancy of the Aztec nation came to a halt. Two years later, the Aztec capital, Tenochtitlán (now Mexico City), was under Spanish control.

Cortés returned to Spain by way of Africa, planting some of his Mexican cacao beans there. This agrarian impulse enabled Spain, which ultimately acknowledged the value of the cacao bean, to monopolize the trade in chocolate for the next century. Today the bulk of the world's chocolate is supplied by trees that are the descendants of those that Cortés took to Africa.

The Spanish treated chocolate differently than had the Meso-Americans. They sweetened it with honey and flavored it with cinnamon and vanilla. Served hot as a restorative, this new incarnation of the cacao tree remained a Spanish secret for close to a century before it found its way over the border to France. The French acquired chocolate when Jews were expelled from Spain and subsequently settled in the region of Bayonne, just over the Spanish border. The French initially considered the bitter paste made from the cacao bean to be noxious, so its production was forced outside the town limits. As many perceptions are changed from the top down, Spanish nobility who married into the French court helped illuminate their countrymen about the virtues of chocolate. Ultimately, Bayonne chocolate was celebrated by its citizens.

Once chocolate became the darling of the aristocrats, its movement into other markets began to happen more quickly. In the early seventeenth century a recipe found its way into Italy. In 1657, a Frenchman opened a shop in London called the Coffee Mill and Tobacco Roll, from which he sold this bitter chocolate paste to be used for beverage making. This initial appearance of chocolate in England was so expensive (it cost more than half its weight in gold because of excessively high import duties on cacao beans) that again, only the wealthy could afford to buy and use it.

Wherever it went, people experimented with flavorings. Vanilla, the one favored by the Aztecs, has survived to become the flavor most frequently paired with chocolate, although many others have been tried. Chocolate flavored with cloves was popular in the seventeenth century. Anise, ginger, pepper, and chilies have also been used. Today you'll find chocolate flavored with honey, as well as coffee, almond, hazelnuts, and, in Spain and Mexico, almost always, cinnamon. And in today's desserts, chocolate is paired with oranges, raspberries, strawberries, and other fruits.

Because so much ritual grows up around those things we perceive to be valuable and

(continued)

available only to a select few, there appeared in London, Amsterdam, and other European capitals fashionable chocolate houses where the wealthy would gather to savor this esoteric "restorative" drink. It wasn't until the mid-nineteenth century, when the duty on cacao beans was lowered to a rate of a penny a pound, that chocolate ceased being a luxury and began its ascendancy into popular culture.

In 1828, a Dutchman, C. J. Van Houten, found that by treating the cacao nibs with an alkali, he could make them release their fat (cocoa butter) more easily; the flavor was improved and the color darkened. This process has come to be known as "Dutching." Once chocolate liquor could be separated into its constituents, a great many opportunities for the evolution of chocolate presented themselves. The flavor of the chocolate was not contained in the fat, but in the separated solids. These solids, pulverized into a powder we now know as cocoa, were much more intensely flavored and the ability to handle cocoa butter separately made possible the next important incarnation of chocolate.

As time went on, many of the names that we now associate with chocolate began building on each other's discoveries. In England, first Fry and Sons and then Cadbury found that by adding sugar and additional cocoa butter to chocolate liquor, they could create a solid chocolate. Although we think of the Swiss as the originators of some the most successful recipes for making chocolate, they were actually slow to get to it. The Italians dominated in the eighteenth century. At the end of the eighteenth century, the Swiss began to become serious about chocolate. In 1819, the first Swiss chocolate factory was opened by François-Louis Cailler. Jean Tobler, of Toblerone fame, didn't make his appearance until the beginning of the twentieth century.

Because we also associate dairy products with the Swiss, it wasn't an accident that the Swiss developed another chocolate incarnation: milk chocolate. Earlier in the century, Henri Nestlé, a Swiss chemist, developed a process to make what we now know as condensed milk. In 1875, a Swiss chocolate manufacturer named Daniel Peter (who married into the Cailler chocolate dynasty) combined Henri Nestlé's condensed milk with his chocolate product. And so milk chocolate was born. Another significant contribution made by the Swiss was that of Rodolphe Lindt, who developed "conching," a kneading/rolling process that both improved flavor and removed the grittiness that had been associated with solid chocolate.

Chocolate finally made its way back across the Atlantic, north of its original origins, to the American colonies in the eighteenth century. Because the colonists were entranced by it, New England sea captains began bringing home cacao beans from their trading voyages to the West Indies. So Americans became seriously involved in the story of chocolate at just about the same time as the Europeans.

The manufacture of chocolate started in the United States in 1765 in Milton Lower Falls, near Dorchester, Massachusetts. James Baker financed the first water-powered chocolate mill. Since then, other US companies have become involved in the manufacture of chocolate. Although there's a sense that the best chocolate comes from Europe, there are today a number of US manufacturers that produce extremely high-quality chocolate, as well as a booming scene for small-batch, artisanal bars.

its complex and desirable flavor. Make sure you buy Mexican vanilla from a reliable source, as sometimes it's cut with other (potentially dangerous) ingredients. Tahitian vanilla is preferred by some for its flowery mellow aroma and flavor. Indonesian vanilla has the simplest flavor. Madagascar vanilla is the most widely used and is also preferred by many.

Vanilla is available as a whole bean (from which you can flavor any number of things, including sugar). It is also available ground to a powder, which is wonderful in custard, cookies, ice cream, and whipped cream—anywhere that you want an intense vanilla flavor and the visibility of bean flecks. Because the flavor of the powder doesn't evaporate when heated (vanilla extract loses some of its flavor in heating), it's well suited for baked goods. Vanilla extract, the essential oil of the vanilla bean dissolved in alcohol, is more widely available. There are double- and triple-strength vanilla extracts, as well as a vanilla essence so strong that only a drop or two is needed. These are available through special suppliers by mail order. To minimize the evaporation of vanilla extract when making cookies or cakes, always add it to the butter and sugar when you cream them. The butter acts as a buffer and protects it from the heat, resulting in more flavor. Vanilla paste can be used measure-for-measure in place of vanilla extract but with the addition of flecks of vanilla bean that are evident in the end product. One tablespoon of vanilla paste equals one vanilla bean.

MAKE YOUR OWN VANILLA

You can make your own vanilla extract by combining a vanilla bean, slit lengthwise and cut into 3 pieces, with 1 cup unflavored vodka or brandy. Put the mixture in a nonreactive container (glass is ideal) and let it steep for 2 to 8 weeks, or longer. The longer it steeps, the stronger the vanilla will be. Although this won't have the complexity of flavor of professionally manufactured vanilla extract, it's eminently suitable for recipes where vanilla plays a minor, rather than starring, role.

Almonds and Almond Flavoring

Next to vanilla, almond extract is probably the baker's most frequently used flavoring. Almonds, too, are an important ingredient in many baked goods. Almonds grow on flowering 20- to 30-foot-tall trees, beautiful enough that in some areas they are grown just for their aesthetic characteristics. The almond belongs to the same genus as apricots, cherries, plums, and peaches, but its fruit is not equivalently succulent; what we eat is the seed.

Trees that are grown for the almonds they produce are found in a fairly narrow band around the world where conditions are frost-free but not tropical. Although you will find producing almond trees in most Mediterranean countries, today California supplies more than half of the world's supply.

There are two types of almond: bitter and sweet.

SWEET ALMONDS are the ones we eat, with or without skins, unblanched or blanched. The skins are edible but can sometimes be bitter. If they're not too bitter (the taste test will determine this), don't bother blanching them because the skin adds positive flavor notes to whatever you're making.

Almonds have a mild flavor. You can find them in most groceries whole, sliced, slivered, and as meal or flour. Almond paste and marzipan are made of blanched sweet almonds that have been ground with sugar and almond extract to sweeten and intensify the flavor. Almond paste has less sugar than marzipan and is more coarsely ground; it's mostly used as a filling, while marzipan is rolled out to cover cakes, or colored and often shaped for decorations.

BITTER ALMONDS, cousins of the sweet almond, contain prussic acid, which is highly toxic. It makes the nuts so unpleasant to taste that it is unlikely that anyone would eat enough (50 or so can be lethal) to do any harm. It is these almonds from which oil is extracted—the prussic acid is destroyed during processing—and blended with ethyl alcohol to make almond extract, probably the most common baking extract after vanilla. Bitter almond oil is also sold without the addition of alcohol; it's extremely strong and should be used by the drop rather than by the teaspoon.

Like any nuts that contain oil, almonds will eventually become rancid. Packaged natural almonds can be stored in unopened packages in a cool dark place for up to two years. Unopened roasted almonds can be stored under the same conditions up to one year.

Almond flour and nuts that are blanched, slivered, and chopped should be stored in an airtight container in the pantry for no more than one year. Both will last even longer if refrigerated. Almond paste can be stored in the refrigerator up to two years. A hot pantry will hasten rancidity.

Other Extracts, Oils, and Flavors

EXTRACTS are made from the essential oils and/or flavoring components of natural ingredients dissolved in alcohol. There is a great array available, including those from fruit, nuts, and seeds and such things as mint and coffee. If you don't want to use an alcohol-based extract, which is the most common form, there are also glycerin-based extracts available from specialty shops and catalogues that perform the same way and with the same intensity of flavor.

OTHER ESSENTIAL OILS available include orange, lemon, and lime. These are very powerful and very little is needed to add flavor to any baked good. The oil comes from the skin of the fruit (the zest), where there is an intensity of flavor. Zest from both oranges and lemons is available although it's easy to create your own.

FLOWER WATERS are other flavoring agents. The ones most commonly available are made from the essential oils of rose petals and orange flower petals. They are more subtle than oils but add lovely overtones to lightly flavored confections, whipped cream, ice cream, sponge cake, and angel food cake.

BUTTERSCOTCH AND CARAMEL are often confused with each other. Today it is usually accepted that the flavor of butterscotch is that of brown sugar cooked with butter. To make butterscotch candy, according to F. Marian McNeill in *The Scots Kitchen*, you cook a combination of 1 pound of brown sugar with ¼ pound of butter to the soft-crack stage. Then you remove it from the heat, flavor it with a touch of ginger and a bit of lemon zest, beat it with a fork for a few minutes, and pour it on a slab to cool. Crack off pieces with the back of a knife.

CARAMEL is produced by cooking granulated sugar in a heavy pan until it melts and caramelizes; that is, it becomes liquid, then undergoes the Maillard reaction, which creates a cascade of complex and delicious flavors. Caramel can range in color from light to deep brown by cooking it somewhere between 320°F to 350°F. You'll also find caramelized sugar on crème brulée, which is done with a small culinary blowtorch or with a caramelizing iron. If caramel is cooked until it's very dark, it can be used as coloring in a variety of things from breads (usually rye) to gravy.

Spices and Herbs

ALLSPICE: This New World spice is from a tree in the myrtle family and was thought by Columbus to be pepper, which he was hoping to find at the end of his voyage, and which the allspice berry resembles. Today, most of the world's supply is grown in Jamaica and Jamaican allspice is coveted. Although it has its own personality, allspice is suggestive of a combination of other aromatic spices, particularly cinnamon and cloves but with a hint of nutmeg and black pepper. Allspice berries can be used whole in marinades or pickling. Ground allspice is available in most groceries or you can grind your own. A touch is wonderful in applesauce and it can also be used with other spices in fruit desserts, steamed puddings, pies, and cakes. As a substitute, try ground cloves, about one-quarter the amount of allspice called for, and a touch of nutmeg.

ANISE: This self-seeding annual, related to parsley, dill, and caraway, comes from countries bordering the eastern Mediterranean. It tastes like a sweet licorice and is used, as a seed, to flavor a variety of European breads, but it is also used to flavor other baked goods and desserts. As a substitute, try fennel.

STAR ANISE: This has some of the same flavor components and can also be used in baked goods. It is native to China and comes from an evergreen related to the magnolia.

CARAWAY: This plant is related to anise (their aromas are faintly similar), parsley, and dill. It is most frequently used as a seed rather than ground into a powder and, as such, is used to flavor many German and northern European breads as well as some Irish soda breads. You will also find it in some cheeses. Caraway is used most frequently in savory goods, but it can also be an interesting counterpoint in sweet goods, particularly paired with citrus or, in the case of soda breads, raisins. Caraway is not easily substituted. A caraway-flavored thyme comes close but is not easily available unless you grow your own. Fennel is another option.

CARDAMOM: A member of the ginger family, cardamom, after vanilla and saffron, is the third most expensive spice in the world. It grows as a perennial herb in South India and Sri Lanka, and also in Guatemala. The pods, which are about the size of a plump raisin, encapsulate three small compartments that contain tiny seeds. The pods should be either green or white (not brown or black, which is not true cardamom and of less interest to the baker). It is used to flavor teas and certain traditional baked goods from Germany and Scandinavia. The crushed seeds (a rolling pin does this nicely) produce the strongest flavor, although they can be bought already ground. If you have no cardamom, try substituting ginger.

CINNAMON: This spice comes from the dried bark of a tree native to Sri Lanka. It grows only there and in India and is the only true cinnamon recognized in Britain. But there are two types of "cinnamon" acknowledged in the United States and a number of other countries as well. The second is the one with which we are probably most familiar. This is cassia cinnamon, which is a member of the same family as true cinnamon, a type of laurel. This cinnamon is native to Southeast Asia, southern China, northern Vietnam, and Indonesia. Both are harvested from the bark of a tree. You can tell the difference between sticks of the former and the latter by the way they roll. Sticks of the Ceylon cinnamon—the sort grown in Sri Lanka—curl just in one direction, looking like rolled up paper. Sticks of cassia curl inward from both sides to resemble a scroll. Both types are available ground as well. The color as well as the flavor of Ceylon cinnamon is lighter. Cassia cinnamon is darker, redder, and more intense; one subset of cassia cinnamon is known as Vietnamese or Saigon cinnamon—it has an extra-strong strong and "spicy" flavor. Most of the cinnamon we buy at the grocery store is cassia cinnamon. But there are commercial cinnamons that are a blend of the two. If you buy ground cinnamon, buy it in small quantities as the flavor deteriorates with time. If you are out of cinnamon, you can substitute allspice with maybe a touch of ginger and nutmeg, but use about a quarter as much. Try sprinkling some cinnamon on French toast as you cook it before you turn it over.

CLOVES: This perennial evergreen shrub native to the Moluccas in East Indonesia belongs to the myrtle family. The unopened flower bud, picked by hand and then dried, becomes the little nail-like seed container that we know as cloves. In fact, the name "clove" evolved through a number of Latin-based languages and was ultimately incorporated into Middle English as "clowe," meaning nail shaped. Cloves are used commonly to flavor both savory and sweet foods. But, as has been stated by an astute culinarian, "The flavor is best when kept below the level of recognition." Cloves are available whole or ground. The most appropriate substitute is allspice.

GINGER: Not known as a wild plant, ginger probably originally came from Southeast Asia. It's been in use for several thousand years both for culinary as well as medicinal purposes. It reached Europe via Rome. When Rome fell, it was reintroduced to the West by Marco Polo. In medieval times, ginger as a flavoring became very common in England, and in fact, ginger and pepper were two of the most frequently used spices. It was at that point that gingerbread became part of culinary history. Ginger and gingerbread were for medieval England what chocolate is for us today. In pre-twentieth-century cookbooks, you'll find numerous "receipts" for ginger-based cakes.

Today half the world's ginger comes from India, but it is also grown in China, Hawaii, Africa, and some parts of the Middle East. Australia has become a new player and is the source of some of the best crystallized ginger. In the Eastern Hemisphere, ginger is used widely to flavor savory foods. In Europe and the United States, it is used most frequently in sweet baked goods. But we also experience it in ginger ale. For the baker, ginger is available as the whole root, the mature root dried and powdered, the young root crystallized, and in ginger syrup or extract. Powdered ginger is quite different from fresh or crystallized ginger and isn't an appropriate substitute when the former are called for. If you are out of powdered ginger, you might try allspice with a little cinnamon or mace.

LAVENDER: Historically, lavender was used by the Greeks and Romans as a bath perfume. It was introduced into Britain in 1568, and English gardeners started an immediate love affair with the plant. Pillows and sachets were stuffed with dried lavender flowers, and lavender "washing water" came into use. The culinary use of the flower was noted as early as the reign of Queen Elizabeth I. Powdered lavender was served as a condiment, and the queen so enjoyed conserve of lavender that it was always on her table. In this country, the Shakers used lavender in cooking, in their famous lemon pies and lemon breads. Its penetrating, sunny taste marries surprisingly well with the flavors of both butter and vanilla. Long overlooked as an edible flower, lavender makes a delightful contribution to baked goods. The pleasures of lavender transcend the garden when the flower is dried and used in baking. Anticipate the essence of summer by using lavender in pound cakes, cookies, and bread.

MACE AND NUTMEG: These spices come from the same tree, native to the Moluccas in Indonesia, although it's grown today in Grenada. After the fruit is removed (the fruit itself is dried with palm sugar and eaten as a snack food in Indonesia), you'll find a thin, lacy, leathery reddish tissue on the outside of the pit. This is called mace, and is removed, dried, and then sold either whole, as "blade mace," or ground. Mace has a faint aroma of nutmeg, but you'll also smell undertones of cinnamon, maybe cloves and ginger. You can substitute any or a combination of those if you don't have any on hand.

After the mace has been removed and the nutmeg pit dried, the shell is cracked and the nutmeg is removed to be sold whole or as powder. Nutmeg has a flavor all its own, which belongs in eggnog, but you'll also find a touch in savory dishes as well, such as quiche and béchamel sauce. Nutmeg's flavor makes it difficult to find a substitute, but try a little cinnamon, ginger, or mace.

MINT: A great addition to a baker's kitchen, mint comes in a wide array of flavors. Apple, chocolate, orange, peppermint, spearmint, and pineapple all can be used to flavor syrups, frostings, candy, and chocolate.

PEPPER: True pepper, or *piper nigrum*, grows on a tropical vine native to the Kingdom of Travancore and Malabar Coast of India (the southwestern tip). Although one of the finest kinds still comes from that part of India, it is now cultivated near the equator around the globe.

Like many other spices, pepper has played an important role in the power struggles throughout our history. It was valued so highly that it spurred new trade routes between the East and West. Like salt, it was used during the Middle Ages as money.

Black pepper is dried from still green but-about-to-be-ripe peppercorns. White peppercorns are dried from the hulled version of the same fruit after it has reached maturity. By changing the time of picking and drying, you can make black, white, red, and green pepper from the same plant. Tellicherry (a district on the Malabar Coast of India) pepper is dried from peppercorns that have been allowed to ripen beyond green to a yellow-orange. Because pickers wait until just this point to harvest them, this pepper has particularly rich flavor. This method is used only in India. Tellicherry peppercorns are larger than typical black peppercorns and their color is a dark, warm brown. They are slightly more expensive than regular black pepper because it's riskier to wait to pick until that precise point of ripeness. Another equally good type is the Lampong pepper (from the Lampong district of southeastern Sumatra, the second largest of the Indonesian islands). These two are considered the best varieties of black pepper.

Black pepper enhances savory dishes but it can also be used to enhance and give a little extra "spice" to sweet goods such as gingerbread, steamed puddings, and spice cakes. White pepper is missing the outer skin of black pepper, which contains some of the flavor components. Although it's more expensive than black pepper because it takes more work to produce, white pepper is used primarily where the black flecks of black pepper are not wanted.

SAFFRON: The costliest of all the spices, real saffron is the dried stigma of a crocus flower that originated probably in Persia but today is grown from Spain to

Kashmir. It was of great importance in medieval Europe where it was used as both a flavoring and a dye.

The dried stigmas look like red threads and, when soaked in a liquid, emit a bright yellow color. One hundred fifty thousand flowers are needed for one kilogram of dried saffron. Less expensive varieties are often adulterated with the yellow stamen of the flower, which has the right color but no flavor of its own. Spain and Iran are the largest producers, accounting for more than 80% of the world's production.

Saffron has long flavored a cake unique to the west country of England, called Saffron Cake. It's also important in a Swedish bread (*Lussekatter* or St. Lucia cats) that is made for the festival of Santa Lucia. You'll find it also as a dominant flavor in *Provençal bouillabaisse*. The flavor of saffron is not easily duplicated, although turmeric is an option for producing a yellow color.

Spice Blends

APPLE PIE SPICE can be any number of combinations, including whatever you decide you like. Here are a couple of commercial ones: cinnamon with a touch of cloves and nutmeg; or a more ambitious version is a blend of cinnamon, fenugreek (an herb that has the aroma of curry and is used in same), lemon peel, ginger, cloves, and nutmeg.

PUMPKIN PIE SPICE is multiple combinations, but usually includes cinnamon, ginger, cloves, and nutmeg.

You can use these spice blends to season any apple or pumpkin (or squash) dish, or any other dish you think would benefit from these particular blends of spices. Simply substitute the spice blend for the same amount, combined, of other spices called for in the recipe (excluding salt). For example, if a recipe calls for 1 teaspoon of cinnamon, ¼ teaspoon of cloves, and ¼ teaspoon of allspice, substitute 1½ teaspoons of apple pie spice. Use pumpkin pie spice in a similar manner. You can also sprinkle a little pumpkin pie spice over a dish of baked or mashed squash; or try a dash of apple pie spice on ice cream, or over hot applesauce.

CHAI SPICE, like curry powder, chai seasonings can be any blend of spices to an individual's taste, but most blends include ginger, cinnamon, cardamom, allspice, anise, and black pepper. Besides flavoring beverages, it makes compelling shortbread and is good in glazes for scones or muffins.

Salt

Salt has become fashionable and fun. Like bed linens that used to be white, salt now comes in a variety of shapes and colors, from white to gray to red, and physically as small solid cubes to lovely pyramid-shaped crystals. There are some that are less refined with more minerals in them creating, as many are convinced, subtle and unique flavors. And, of course, there are now the flavored "boutique" salts: smoked, garlic, chili, lavender, rosemary, and so on.

In baking, when any of these salts are allowed to dissolve, their impact in a baked product will be hard to differentiate (aside from the flavored ones). But when you use them as accoutrements, there may be flavor differentiations that are more discernible. And there are some that physically will "stick" better and melt more quickly (or not so quickly) on your tongue.

Most fascinating are the cultures and histories that they evoke. All salt comes from the sea, mined from old seabeds deep in the earth, or from salt deposits on the surface, or actively evaporated from the sea.

Salt intensifies and enhances flavors in all baked goods. Because it is hygroscopic, it attracts moisture. This is good in some situations, and not in others (bread crusts for instance). In yeast baking, salt strengthens dough and tightens its structure, which increases the time needed to sufficiently develop the gluten. It also slows fermentation. Bread without salt is insipid. Even the Tuscans' bread, which is traditionally unsalted, is eaten with salty foods. One of the most appealing ways to eat bread is to spread a slice of pain de campagne with sweet butter and sprinkle it with a bit of fleur de sel, a French sea salt.

There isn't anything that you can substitute for salt. In most baked goods it's there in quantities that are small enough not to be a problem. But if you need to reduce your salt intake, try cutting it in half before you eliminate it entirely.

Herbs

These flavorful little leaves are usually used fresh and are delightful in all manner of breads. Some actually have flavors that blend well with sweet goods, such as lemon thyme and caraway.

BASIL has an almost licorice or anise-like flavor when it is fresh, which is when it should be used. It is best used on top of flatbreads such as pizza or focaccia, and of course it is the linchpin in pesto or *Provençal pistou*, both of which are delicious on bread.

DILL FLAVOR can be found in its flowers, fronds, or seeds. Dill seeds are wonderful in breads, particularly soda breads, where you can substitute them for caraway.

GARLIC is also best on, rather than in, a bread. Minced raw, it can flavor butter or olive oil, or you can bake it until it is soft and sweet and use it as a condiment. To bake garlic, break a head into individual cloves, spread on a baking sheet, sprinkle with olive oil and a bit of salt, and bake for about 30 minutes. Then squeeze the cloves out of their skins with your fingers and mash.

OREGANO AND MARJORAM are similar in aroma and flavor, with oregano being the more assertive of the two. They can be used in savory quick or yeast breads along with, or in place of, thyme.

ROSEMARY has a very appealing and assertive flavor that is wonderful with roasted potatoes and lamb, in potato and cheese breads, and paired with ginger in some sweet goods. Unless it's being cooked in liquid, fresh rosemary is always better in baked goods than dried. Rosemary has antiseptic characteristics and can inhibit yeast growth if more than a tablespoon of the chopped fresh herb is used in a single loaf of bread.

TARRAGON is also anise-flavored but different from anise and fennel. You can infuse milk with it to use in sweet breads, or use it in a savory quick bread.

THYME, like mint, comes in many flavors: lemon, oregano, caraway, and traditional English. Lemon thyme can flavor sweet baked goods, but some of the others are wonderful in savory quick or yeast breads. Thyme is fun to grow and is probably the best way to come by some of the less common versions.

Nuts

Nuts are a wonderful addition to baked goods, adding flavor and texture. Almonds, pecans, and walnuts all seem to have a sweeter and deeper flavor if they are lightly toasted. Because nuts contain a significant amount of oil, you need to buy them fresh. If you buy them in bulk, keep them in the freezer. They'll keep nicely for up to a year.

To toast, spread nuts on a baking sheet and bake them at 325°F for 8 to 10 minutes or until fragrant. Keep an eye on them because they can burn quickly.

The easiest, fastest way to chop nuts is to put the required amount in a plastic bag, close the bag loosely, and whack nuts with the flat end of a meat mallet or the barrel of a rolling pin. A few whacks will give you coarsely chopped nuts; more whacks, and you'll get finely chopped, almost ground nuts. To make nut meal, pulse them in a food processor until they are as fine as you want.

ALMONDS (see page 511).

CHESTNUTS have had a long history in Europe as a food staple. Chestnut flour was even used to make bread and was the basis of Italian polenta before cornmeal, or maize, was introduced from the Americas. Nowadays it is more of a condiment. Chestnuts are often eaten roasted but chestnut flour, ground from dried chestnuts, can be used in many baked goods.

COCONUT, from the coconut palm tree, is almost always used flaked or shredded by bakers. Sometimes it is sweetened as well. It is used to flavor baked goods and sprinkled on top of frosted cakes as decoration, flavor, and for texture.

HAZELNUTS, or filberts, are grown in Oregon and farther north, in British Columbia. They are delicious buttery nuts that are wonderful alone, but are particularly wonderful with chocolate. They have a light, crunchy texture and can be used in cakes, breads, cookies, quick breads, and candy—anywhere you want the flavor and texture of nuts. Hazelnuts can also be purchased as a flour.

Here's an easy way to skin them. Most methods call for you to toast whole hazelnuts, and then to rub them between two towels to release their skins. We've found an easier method is to toast the hazelnuts for about 10 minutes (until they begin to brown) in a 325°F oven. Remove the nuts from the oven and let cool for 2 minutes. Put the nuts into a food processor equipped with the plastic dough blade and pulse until the nuts have shed most of their skins. Some of the nuts will crack, but this is quick and very effective. Pick the nuts out of the pile of skins, and you're ready to roll.

PECANS are a North American nut and probably one of the more frequently used, particularly in the South, where they are native. They are delicious raw and even more so toasted. You can purchase them whole, in pieces, or as meal, although it's easy to chop your own. You can easily create pecan meal in a food processor. Because of their oil content, they can become bitter fairly quickly, so use them up or keep them in the freezer. They can be used anywhere walnuts (or most other nuts) are called for.

PINE NUTS, or pignoli, are the rich, sweet, small seeds from the pinecones of certain pine trees, which are found in several parts of the world, including the American Southwest. These trees are not easily cultivated and are happier living wild where all kinds of creatures vie for the nuts. The Hopi, Navajo, and other Southwestern tribes have used them as a staple for thousands of years, eaten in every form: whole, ground, and baked into cakes, or pounded into a paste. Today, the most common pine nuts in our groceries are from a tree on the northern coastline of the Mediterranean, from Portugal and Spain in the west to Lebanon in the east. Pine nuts are essential in pesto, but after you've nibbled a few, you'll find you'll want to put them in other baked goods from quick breads to cookies.

PISTACHIOS, those lovely pale green nuts that are hard to stop eating, have been enjoyed by Middle Easterners for several thousand years. They grow on a small tree native to Turkey and the area around the Caspian Sea. There were formerly forests of pistachio trees from Lebanon, across Syria and eastward through and beyond northern Iraq. There is a variety raised in California. Pistachios are wonderful in ice cream, but you can use them in almost any baked good where you want the texture and flavor of nuts.

WALNUTS come from a tree that grows in temperate climates found wild from southeastern Europe all the way to China. Today they grow in abundance in California, especially in the Sacramento Valley, making the United States the largest walnut producer in the world.

Walnuts are related to the pecan, the American butternut (or American white walnut), and the black walnut, all of which grow in the east and whose nuts have a slightly stronger flavor. In baking, they can all be used interchangeably although there are some flavor differences.

Seeds

Seeds add flavor and texture to baked goods. Because, as with nuts, they contain a lot of oil, they are subject to rancidity. Freezing will extend the life of many seeds, but they're best when fresh.

CHIA SEEDS are a South American native and botanical member of the mint family. They can absorb 12 times their weight in liquid, creating a gelatinous mixture that is sometimes used as an egg substitute in baking.

FLAX SEED, the slightly larger bronze brothers of sesame seeds, can be sprinkled on the outside of bread. But because they are almost useless nutritionally unless the seed coat is cracked, it's best to use cracked or milled flax seeds in bread. They add a pleasing nutty flavor and their oil makes adding additional fat or oil unnecessary. Buy them often and use them fresh, as they will become rancid over time.

POPPY SEEDS are sprinkled on top of many baked goods and add a delicious flavor to coffeecakes and other quick breads. They can also be crushed and used with almonds, sugar, and a touch of lemon in pastry fillings. Toasting can bring out their flavor quite nicely. Buy just enough to use, or freeze what you don't use.

PUMPKIN SEEDS, or pepitas, are too large to be used on rolls or breads, but they can certainly be used in them, or in cookies or quick breads. They are enhanced with a bit of toasting.

SESAME SEEDS, also called benne seeds, are found in Southern cookies called Benne wafers (see page 113). They have a lovely, nutty flavor that toasting will bring out. You can use them on breads, rolls, and other baked goods, as well as in them. Sesame seeds are also ground into a paste called tahini or sesame butter. Tahini has a nutty flavor that can be used as a dip on its own or mixed with chickpeas, lemon juice, and garlic to make hummus. Sesame seeds mixed with honey are used to make halvah, a Middle Eastern confection.

SUNFLOWER SEEDS are our own native seeds. Unhulled they make wonderful bird food (because birds can do their own hulling). Hulled, they taste great plain and, as with small nuts, can be used in many baked goods as well as on them. They are very tasty raw or toasted. And sunflowers are enough to make anyone smile.

CHAPTER TWELVE

Tools

___

BAKING CAN BE A SIMPLE MATTER OF using your imagination, a spoon, and a bowl to create everything from brownies to bread. On the other hand, the journey from recipe to oven-hot goodies can involve any number of specialized tools and pans. There is almost no end to the array of tools (some say "toys") that a baker can accumulate. But knowing how to select the best tools for your baking, and also what attributes those tools should have, can save you a lot of time and money. Our test kitchens work with hundreds of tools every year, poking, dropping, and trying to scratch, break, or otherwise abuse just about every tool in the marketplace. Here's what we've learned from using all those funny whisks, trying every shape and surface imaginable for a mixing bowl, and baking in every pan—assessing it for size, durability, and ease of release—that comes our way.

Pans

Baking pans are typically made from aluminum (an excellent heat conductor), or an aluminum-steel combination. Less common are stainless steel pans; while easy to clean and nonreactive, they don't conduct heat as well as aluminum. A wonderful hybrid pan combines a core of aluminum between thin top and bottom layers of stainless steel, giving the baker the best of both worlds—good heat conduction and easy cleanup. Some newer pans are made from soft silicone, a naturally nonstick material whose flexibility assists the baker in getting baked goods out of the pan undamaged. We've found silicone pans to be best for sweet baked goods, whose sugar helps them to brown; baked goods low in sugar or fat (e.g., hearth breads) baked in a silicone pan don't brown well.

Other common materials for baking pans include glass, ceramic, and stoneware. On the plus side, these pans are often lovely to look at, and a clear glass pan allows you to see how well the crust is browning as the product bakes. On the minus side, ceramic and stoneware don't conduct heat as quickly as metal pans. If you're baking something where precise temperature isn't critical (bread pudding or pie), they're a perfectly acceptable choice. Because clear glass conducts heat almost too quickly compared to aluminum, it's recommended that you reduce the oven temperature 25°F when using a glass pan.

Baking pans are often coated with a nonstick surface. This is usually helpful, but also means you shouldn't cut baked goods in the pan unless you use a special nonstick-safe knife or server. Angel food pans should not have a nonstick surface, as the baking batter actually needs to climb up the wall of the pan in order for the cake to rise.

Look for pans that are sturdy, but not so heavy that they're hard to handle. When a recipe calls for a 9″ round pan, it means the top inside measurement should be 9″. Many manufacturers cut corners and make their pans 9″ from edge to edge, but only 8¾″ (or less) inside. This makes a difference, particularly with pies, in whether the pan can hold a recipe comfortably.

Quick Bread Pans

QUICK BREAD LOAF PANS: Most quick bread recipes (banana bread, zucchini bread) are written for 9″ × 5″ × 2¾″ pans, a traditionally shaped loaf pan that's just slightly larger than a yeast bread loaf pan. Caveat emptor: Using a yeast loaf pan for a quick bread recipe may result in batter overflowing the pan. Likewise, using a quick bread pan for a yeast loaf recipe may result in a loaf that doesn't dome. These pans, although similar in size and shape, are not interchangeable. Quick breads also can be baked in a longer, narrower pan called a tea loaf pan (about $12'' \times 4'' \times 2\frac{1}{2}''$). Recipes baked in this pan take less time to bake and yield a greater number of slightly smaller slices.

SCONE PANS: While scones are often made free-form by cutting a circular round of dough into wedges, or cut with a biscuit cutter, the scone pan, with its 8 wedge-shaped wells, forms beautifully shaped scones. Unless scones are very sweet (not generally the case), a dark pan will give them a lovely brown crust during the very short time they spend in the oven.

POPOVER PANS: Popovers do well in a pan with straight-sided cups in order to attain their full height. Sized in regular (to make 6 large popovers) or mini (to make 12 smaller ones), popover pans feature deep, narrow wells, which force the baking batter to rise up and then out, producing the typical popover shape. Popover pans made of dark metal will produce the best crust.

MUFFIN PANS: Muffins range from mini to maxi, and pans come in a variety of shapes and sizes. A standard muffin pan has 12 wells, each measuring about $2\frac{1}{2}''$ wide at the top and $1\frac{1}{2}''$ deep. A pan with wells significantly smaller than that won't hold a standard-size muffin recipe. A mini-muffin pan includes 24 wells, each about $1\frac{3}{4}''$ wide and $1''$ deep; it will hold a standard muffin recipe, as will a jumbo muffin pan, with 6 wells about $3\frac{3}{4}'' \times 2''$ deep.

Muffin pans are traditionally made of metal, most commonly aluminum, but also can be found in stoneware and cast iron. We don't recommend silicone pans for muffins; it's an insulator, and can burn the bottoms of the muffins before the centers have a chance to bake through.

CRÊPE PANS: A shallow, low-sided sauté pan is helpful in making crêpes. Most crêpe pans are made of carbon steel, cast iron, or heavy aluminum, as these metals heat evenly and quickly without hot spots. Crêpe pans can be nonstick, but it isn't crucial; crêpes cook in a film of butter and slide out of whichever pan you choose. Sizes range from about $4''$ to $10''$, with the smaller crêpes suitable for dessert, the larger ones perfect for entrées.

Quick bread loaf pans

Mini popover pan

Silicone muffin pans

Yeast Bread Pans

LOAF PANS: Just as the baguette is France's signature loaf, pan bread—the familiar sandwich loaf—must surely be America's. To make a sandwich loaf using a recipe calling for 3 to 3½ cups flour, use a pan that measures 8½″ × 4½″ × 2½″. For a recipe calling for 4 cups flour, use a 9″ × 5″ × 2½″ pan. Using the proper size pan will give you a nicely domed loaf; using a pan that's too big will yield a loaf that's flat across the top.

A pain de mie or Pullman pan, usually 13″ × 4″ × 4″, is a straight-sided loaf pan with a flat sliding cover. Holding a recipe made with about 4½ cups flour, it will produce a very fine-textured, flat-topped bread, perfect for sandwiches. There's a smaller pain de mie pan available that's 9″ × 4″ × 4″; its straight sides and square loaf shape are particularly well suited for better-looking gluten-free loaves. Its capacity is the same as a 9″ × 5″ pan.

When making sweet breads, use a light-colored pan to keep the bread's crust from burning. When making bread without a significant amount of sugar (1½ tablespoons of sugar or less per cup of flour), use a dark-colored pan to promote good browning.

Standard loaf pan

Pain de mie pan

COVERED STONE BAKERS: For extra-crisp hearth-style loaves, choose a covered stone baker. Shaped to hold round or baguette loaves, a covered stone baker will draw moisture from the bread as it bakes, producing a crunchy bottom crust. In addition, while that moisture is drawn off during the initial part of baking, it collects as steam inside the covered pan, keeping the bread's upper crust soft, so that it can rise to its fullest. Once the steam has dissipated into the oven, the upper crust becomes crisp as well.

DUTCH OVENS/BREAD POTS: The popularity and ease of no-knead breads has created a new bread-baking hero in the world of equipment: the Dutch oven, or a large, sturdy bread-baking pot. Their covers provide a closed environment that captures the dough's moisture to let the bread steam as it bakes. This creates a good rise and a

Stoneware

chewy crust. The lid is taken off for the last portion of the bake time to allow the bread to brown and the crust to become crisp.

CAST IRON SKILLETS: These can be used for baking pizza, pies, tarte tatin, or even dry-frying tortillas or flatbread. They retain and radiate heat, so they're ideal for creating crisp crusts or caramelizing sugar, as for upside down cakes or sticky buns. We find a 10″ skillet to be a real workhorse in the kitchen.

SHAPED PANS: There are a variety of pans on the market designed to shape and hold particular loaves. Included in this group are pans for baguettes (double and triple), Italian loaves (usually double), traditional rye loaves, breadsticks, and Italian sandwich rolls (4 to 5 rolls). These pans are usually perforated, allowing for air circulation to make a crisp crust. Other shapes include pans for hot dog and hamburger buns, brioche, panettone, and sticky buns or cinnamon rolls. These pans aren't perforated, as the goal is a soft crust and, in the case of sticky buns, no leaks!

PIZZA PANS: Whether your choice is Sicilian-style (rectangular thick-crust), Neapolitan (round thin-crust), deep-dish, or free-form, there's a pizza pan to fill your need. Pizza pans are usually made of dark metal, either anodized aluminum or, less common, blue steel. Both of these materials transfer heat quickly and thoroughly, and if there's one thing every pizza needs, it's high heat delivered quickly. An exception to this is porous (unglazed) stoneware pans. Because of their ability to draw moisture from the dough, they'll make pizza crust every bit as crisp as a dark metal pan, with less chance of burning the crust. Another alternative is to cook pizza directly on a preheated baking stone or steel.

Brioche pans

Pizza pans are available in various round sizes, both deep-dish and thin-crust versions; in individual deep-dish pans (about 6½″ wide, usually sold in a set of four); and in 13″ × 18″ rectangular. You can find them with perforated or solid bottoms; we prefer a perforated pan, which we set directly on a preheated baking stone. Don't purchase a nonstick pizza pan; you're sure to injure the finish eventually by cutting in the pan. Instead, make sure there's a good film of olive oil in the bottom of the pan before you add the dough.

Unless you're making a Chicago-style deep-dish pizza, which requires a 12″ to 14″ round pan at least 2″ deep, your pizza pan doesn't need to be very deep. In fact, a flat, rimless, perforated pizza disk is the top choice for some, as it allows the oven's heat to reach all parts of the pizza.

A typical pizza crust recipe calling for 3 cups of flour will make two thin-crust 12″ pizzas; or a thick-crust 14″ round or 13″ × 18″ (half-sheet pan) rectangular pizza; or four medium-crust 6½″ to 8″ individual pizzas.

Cookie Pans

COOKIE SHEETS: Flat metal sheets designed to hold rows of baking cookies come in a variety of sizes and finishes. Purchase a cookie sheet that optimizes the size of your oven. For best heat circulation, it should have a 2″ clearance on all sides when set on the oven rack. Make sure the sheet is substantial enough that it won't warp or buckle at high heat, or develop hot spots.

Cookie sheet (above)
Silicone lining (below)

Light-colored shiny cookie sheets will produce cookies much less likely to burn. Nonstick sheets are often black, and for this reason we don't recommend nonstick cookie sheets, unless their coating is no darker than light gray to gray. (If you already have a dark-colored nonstick cookie sheet and it tends to burn the bottoms of your cookies, reduce the oven temperature by 25°F.) If you have trouble with cookies sticking (and many cookies don't stick even on an ungreased pan, due to their high fat content), we recommend using parchment or a pan liner (see page 536).

Insulated cookie pans make it very hard to burn the bottom of your cookies. However, since they are very poor heat conductors, they also make it hard to bake your cookies at all; cookies baked on insulated pans tend to bake so long before browning that they dry out.

SHAPED COOKIE MOLDS: Many traditional European cookies, including shortbread, require molds. Molds to make shortbread, a simple butter, sugar, and flour cookie, are made of stoneware, 7″ to 8″ square, or octagonal; their insides feature a raised design that will be transferred to the cookies as they bake. Baked cookies are turned out of the pan and cut along the marks left by the pan prior to serving.

There is a pan made specifically for biscotti's first bake, a shallow aluminum loaf pan, 12″ × 5½″ × 2″. While not entirely necessary, it helps shape the dough into a uniform log, prior to cutting it into slices and baking it again.

Shortbread pan

Cake Pans

Nearly all cake pans are made from light-colored aluminum, as cakes need quick, steady heat to rise correctly. Some cakes (pineapple upside-down cake, cobbler) were traditionally baked in a cast iron "spider," a round, medium-depth skillet. Cast iron is still a useful way to make any type of cake that includes a melted or cooked layer atop which batter is poured; cast iron is very happy to go from stovetop to oven, unlike many types of cookware.

LAYER CAKE PANS: You'll want a set of round layer cake pans if you're baking a birthday or wedding cake. Our material of choice is light-colored aluminum. Layer cake recipes nearly always call for 8″ or 9″ pans; to assure batter won't overflow, choose pans that are at least 2″ deep and fill them no more than two-thirds full.

SHEET CAKE PANS: When you choose to bake a single layer sheet cake, you'll nearly always use a 9″ × 13″ pan. Some smaller cake recipes call for a 9″ × 9″, both should be at least 2″ deep. A 9″ × 13″ × 2″ pan shouldn't be filled with any more than 12 cups of batter; 10 cups is safer, although you can go to 12 cups with dense cakes that don't rise much.

A typical cake recipe is about 6 cups in volume. This will fill two 9″ round pans for two thick layers, or three 8″ pans for a three-layer cake. It will also fill a 9″ × 13″ pan, or make 24 standard-size cupcakes. If you've got a collection of odd-size pans and don't know how they match up to these standards, just do your math. A 7″ × 11″ pan (77 square inches) or 10″ round pan (79 square inches) are both roughly equivalent to a 9″ × 9″ pan (81 square inches), assuming all are the same depth.

SPRINGFORM PANS: For delicate tortes and cheesecakes, streusel-topped cakes, or any time you want to remove a cake from its pan to serve (but not upend it in the process), the springform pan is your best solution. They are usually round and available in lots of sizes, from about 4½″ in diameter to 12″. The flat bottom is surrounded by a 2½″ to 3″ tall removable locking sidewall. Less expensive spring-form pans are prone to leaks. When purchasing one, examine how tightly the walls lock onto the base when fastened into position.

BUNDT, TUBE, AND ANGEL FOOD PANS: These pans are the choice for angel food cake, or to bake a cake that looks fancier than a layer or sheet cake. Generally 8½″ to 10″ in diameter and featuring an 8- to 12-cup capacity, Bundt pans are usually nonstick aluminum or aluminum-steel, with the occasional glass or tinned steel pan available as well. For single-serving cakes, plaques featuring 4 or 6 small Bundt wells are available. The similarly sized tube pan has plain (rather than embossed) slightly flaring sides.

An angel food pan is a tube pan with some special features: It should not be nonstick; and it should include either "feet" (small posts attached to the top rim; be sure they're at least 2″ long), or a tube wide enough to fit comfortably over the top of a glass bottle, such as a wine bottle. Angel food cakes attain their maximum height by cooling upside down, either on the shoulders of a bottle or resting on the pan's feet. While not as intricately shaped as Bundt pans, these pans come in various shapes, including round, square, and flower. Choose one that's at least 4″ deep, 9″ to 10″ wide, and has a minimum 10-cup capacity.

Pie and Tart Pans

For variations in size, shape, and composition in the world of baking pans, there's not much that beats the pie pan. From tiny tartlets to mega-pies (think four and twenty blackbirds), from aluminum, tinned steel, or hand-painted ceramic to unglazed stoneware or clear glass, pie pans cover a lot of ground.

TRADITIONAL PIE PANS: Most pie recipes are written to fit a 9″ or 10″ wide, 1½″ deep pie pan. Beware of pie pans that are much shallower than 1½″; while 1¼″ is barely acceptable, a 1″ deep pie pan will not hold a typical pie filling. For deep-dish pies, choose a pan that's 1½″ to 2″ deep, with 2″ the preferred depth. A 9″ pie pan should hold 4 to 10 cups of filling. Why the wide variation? Because while 4 cups of pumpkin filling will expand just a bit, 10 cups of raspberries will shrink enormously. Both amounts (or anything in between) can make a nice-looking pie.

Dark-colored metal pie pans tend to become hotter, and transfer heat better, than ceramic pans, and for that reason to brown crust more quickly, a plus in pie-baking (where a pale, soggy bottom crust is the inexperienced baker's nemesis). However, most pie pans will brown a crust thoroughly, given enough time; and in the case of many pies (e.g., fruit pies), extending baking time beyond what the recipe says isn't a problem, so long as you cover the pie's exposed edges with a crust shield to prevent burning. We've forgotten pies in the oven sometimes, and even after 2 hours they've emerged happily bubbling and beautifully browned.

The advantage of stoneware or ceramic dishes (pans) is their beauty. Thanksgiving, a dinner party,

Deep-dish ceramic pie pan (above); metal pie pan (below)

Large round tart pan

or anytime you're seeking a fancier touch, choose a handsome colored or painted ceramic pie dish instead of utilitarian metal. It's likely these pans will take longer to cook your pie, depending on the formula of the clay used in their construction. Clear glass dishes allow you to see when the bottom crust is sufficiently browned.

TART PANS AND QUICHE DISHES: Tart pans, usually fluted, shiny tinplate, shaped round, square, or rectangular, and often feature a removable bottom, which is very handy for removing the tart from the pan without harming the appearance of the crust. Because they're usually only 1″ deep, tarts will have a greater ratio of crust to filling, an appropriate balance considering tart fillings often include pastry cream or some other very rich confection.

The classic French quiche dish is usually round, ceramic, and 10″ to 11″ in diameter, 1″ to 1½″ deep. Most quiche dishes have fluted sides, and unlike pie pans, the sides are straight, not slanted.

Yeast Bread Tools

While you can make yeast bread dough using nothing more than a bowl, measuring cup, and your hands, there are a number of tools to make your life much easier. Choose the ones you feel will help you the most.

KNEADING MAT: The nonstick surface of a silicone kneading mat makes dough-kneading easy and cleanup a snap. Mats range from 8″ × 11″ to about 16″ × 24″; the larger the mat, the more room you have to let the flour fly. Be sure to use only a plastic dough scraper on these mats as metal will cut their surface.

BAKER'S BENCH KNIFE: Use a bench knife, usually a 6″ × 4″ rect-angle of stainless steel with a handle across the top, to divide dough into pieces, or to scrape bits of dried dough from your countertop. They're also very handy for chopping nuts in a pinch.

Bench knife

SHAPING BASKETS AND COUCHE: European-style hearth loaves are traditionally given their second rise in shaping bas-kets, before being turned out onto a hot oven stone to bake. The French *banneton*, a willow basket lined with linen or canvas, comes in the same shapes as French breads, including boule, batard, and baguette. The cloth lining, which is floured before use, draws moisture from the dough as it rises, making the baked bread's crust chewy. Most times, when making baguettes, French bakers let their shaped loaves rise in a linen couche, a rectangular piece of cloth that can cradle multiple rising baguettes in its folds.

The German *brotform*, made of a coil of wood, gives German bread its classic beehive shape; the basket is heavily floured, and when the risen loaf is turned out onto a stone or pan, it retains the circular marks of the flour.

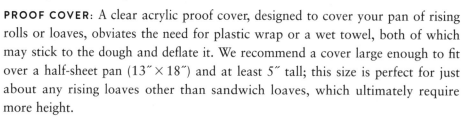

Brotform

Banneton

RISING BUCKETS: Often bakers let dough rise in a lidded rising bucket, a 2- to 6-quart acrylic or plastic bucket with measurements on the side, making it easy to judge when the dough has doubled or tripled in size. The lid keeps the dough moist, allowing it to rise fully.

PROOF COVER: A clear acrylic proof cover, designed to cover your pan of rising rolls or loaves, obviates the need for plastic wrap or a wet towel, both of which may stick to the dough and deflate it. We recommend a cover large enough to fit over a half-sheet pan (13″ × 18″) and at least 5″ tall; this size is perfect for just about any rising loaves other than sandwich loaves, which ultimately require more height.

LAME: A curved razor blade set into a handle is called a lame ("lahm"), and French bakers use it to slash the top crust of risen country loaves (most famously, baguettes). The slash allows the bread to expand fully to its proper shape as it bakes. A small, very sharp paring or serrated knife can be substituted.

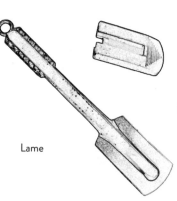

Lame

BAKER'S PEEL: Also known as a pizza peel, this beveled-edge square of flat wood or aluminum with a handle transfers large, flat loaves or pizzas from work surface to hot baking stone. If your dough sticks to the peel, put a piece of parchment on the peel, place the dough on the parchment, then slide both parchment and dough onto the stone; the parchment won't undermine the stone's ability to produce a crisp crust.

BAKING STONE: A baking stone, placed on the bottom shelf of your oven, is a wonderful surface for baking pizzas and hearth breads. The porous stone draws moisture away from the crust as it bakes, yielding a crisp, crunchy crust. The immediate contact between dough and hot surface helps bread with its oven spring. Select a baking stone that's at least ½″ thick; thinner stones may crack. The stone's dimensions should mirror your oven racks, leaving 2″ of clearance on all sides for heat circulation.

BAKING STEEL: Rectangular slabs of recycled steel ¼″ thick, baking steels are a lighter weight baking option than masonry baking stones. They're very efficient at transferring quick heat to dough, and can't crack or chip. They're used in the same way as baking stones, going into a low shelf in the oven to preheat to high temperatures.

Gadgets, Utensils, and Tools

PIZZA WHEEL: Also known as a rolling pizza cutter, this sharp wheel, with handle, makes short work of cutting bread sticks from a rectangle of unbaked dough. It's also useful for cutting crackers, the strips of pastry for a lattice pie crust, fettuccine from fresh pasta dough, or, of course, slices of pizza.

Pizza wheel

TONGS: Choose heat-safe metal tongs, with a heatproof handle that lock closed, so they're easier to store. If you're turning bagels or doughnuts in boiling water or hot oil, choose tongs with a flat, smooth underside; many tongs are manufactured in a folding process that leaves a perfect channel for water or oil to funnel through. When you lift this type of tongs, boiling oil or water is delivered directly to your wrist.

Tongs

FLOUR TOOLS: Sifting aerates flour, giving many types of cake a head start, and making the measuring process more accurate. When a recipe calls for "sifted flour," it's important to sift the flour before measuring it. When "flour, sifted" is called for, the flour should be measured first, then sifted.

Canister flour sifters, the most familiar kind, come in a variety of types and materials, including crank, shake, and electric, and aluminum, stainless steel, and plastic. Since sifters don't need to be washed—any spills or smears on the outside can be easily wiped off—there's no need to worry about dishwasher safeness. Choose a flour sifter that holds at least 3 cups; any less than that and all but the smallest amount of flour will tend to overflow when you start to sift it.

Another type of sifter, called a tamis or drum sieve, consists of a 2″ to 3″ deep round frame, usually about 9″ in diameter, with a metal or nylon mesh screen stretched across the bottom. Flour is simply shaken through the screen to sift it. The advantage of a tamis is its large capacity and speed, but the disadvantage is its lack of focus—you need to sift into a large bowl (at least 12″ in diameter), or onto a large sheet of parchment.

Many bakers no longer bother to sift flour. But even though the flour bag

Flour scoop

says "pre-sifted," that doesn't mean the flour shouldn't be aerated before using. Flour in the bag has settled during shipment, and to measure correctly, it needs to be fluffed up. A flour scoop—cast aluminum, wood, stainless steel, or plastic—is used to stir and fluff the flour, then gently sprinkle it into a measuring cup. Choose a flour scoop with a straight edge long enough to sweep the excess flour off the top of your dry measuring cup in one even motion.

POTHOLDERS AND OVEN MITTS: When you're pulling hot cookie sheets and cake pans out of the oven, it's critical to protect your hands. Don't rely on a handy dishtowel, because at some point you'll pick up a wet towel, grab a hot pan, and drop the pan on the floor as soon as the water in the towel turns to scalding steam.

Many bakers find long baker's mitts—mitts that cover your hands and part of your arms—useful in preventing burns on the tender under part of your forearms. However, if you're careful to stay away from the hot oven rack when loading and unloading pans, shorter mitts are sufficient. Potholders are fine if you're adept enough to use them successfully with your own collection of pans. Pans lacking good grabbing spots are more easily handled with mitts.

Potholders or mitts are made from quilted cotton (least protection), suede, or thick terrycloth (better protection), or a pricey combination of heatproof fabrics, with or without steam-proof liners (best protection). Flexible silicone mitts and holders are also available; they're a snap to wash and their protection is comparable to that of terrycloth. But don't think because they're waterproof you can plunge your hand into boiling water and leave it there; it's OK to snatch a simmering bagel or steaming ear of corn out of the pot, but prolonged exposure to boiling liquid will heat the silicone (and your hand) to uncomfortable levels.

HEAT DIFFUSERS: For simmering soup, cooking custard, melting chocolate, or any time even your burner's lowest flame isn't low enough (or, with gas stoves, if the flame keeps going out), a cast aluminum heat diffuser is a good solution. Heat diffusers (burner covers) with a lip on the underside are sized to cover your burners (6″ or 8″); or choose a large, flat diffuser that simply sits atop the burner.

SPATULAS: Spatulas are used to scrape cake batter off the sides of the mixing bowl, spread filling onto cinnamon bun dough, or any number of baking tasks. They are made of heat-resistant silicone so they also can be used to stir custard, scramble eggs, or turn doughnuts in a deep-fat fryer. Spatulas come in a variety of sizes; our favorite features a flat blade that's about 2″ wide and 3½″ long. Some spatulas are a solid piece of silicone; some feature a silicone blade attached to a wooden, plastic, or stainless steel handle. If you choose a spatula that's not all one piece, try to pull the blade off the handle; if it comes off without using a gargantuan amount of effort, choose another type. Eventually a blade that's not well fastened will fall off, usually just as you're scraping cake batter into a pan.

DOUGH OR BOWL SCRAPER: With one straight edge and one curved (it looks like a squared-off circle), a flexible plastic bowl scraper is useful for everything from sweeping all the batter out of the bowl in one scoop or cutting cinnamon bun dough to scraping bits of pie crust off the counter, crumbs into the wastebasket—or ice off your car windshield. Choose one that's flexible enough to curve easily to the shape of your bowl.

Spatulas

Bowl scraper

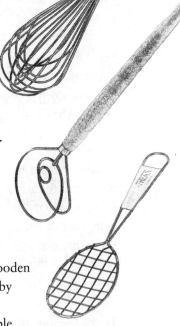

WHISKS: One way to aerate flour, besides sifting or fluffing, is to beat it gently with a wire whisk, a series of looped wires fastened into a handle. Whisks come in various sizes; we have whisks as small as 3″ and as large as a small person. They're most commonly made of stainless steel, although copper, plastic, and wooden whisks are also available; we find stainless to be the easiest to clean.

Whisks are distinguished by their size, the strength of their wires (the stronger the wires, the heavier the task the whisk can perform), and the shape those wires form. A balloon whisk, whose wires form a nearly round ball, is the choice for whipping egg whites and cream, as it whips more air into a mixture than any other design. A standard whisk has a more elongated head and can be used to whip batter and combine eggs and milk in place of a mixer. A flat or roux whisk is shaped particularly for making consistent contact with the bottom and corners of a saucepan, which is ideal for custard, white sauce, and other thickened sauces.

A dough whisk, also known as a *brodpisker*, is a long, wooden handled, stainless steel whisk ideal for mixing bread dough by hand, from sticky to stiff ones.

Whisks are like spoons: Choose one that feels comfortable in your hand. Our favorite all-purpose whisk is a standard one 10″ to 12″ long, with thin, flexible (rather than thick, stiff) wires.

From top to bottom: All-purpose whisk, Danish dough whisk, cake whisk

PASTRY BRUSHES: These are essential for brushing a loaf of hot bread with crust-softening butter, egg wash onto breadsticks or bagels, egg white onto the edges of turnovers, or milk onto a pie crust. Choose a silicone or natural bristle brush; natural (boar) bristles are much less likely to become spiky and bent with use. The bristles should be sealed into the handle with a plastic sealant; the brush will be easier to clean and the bristles won't fall out.

Our favorite all-purpose pastry brushes are 1″ to 1½″ wide with fairly long, flexible bristles; the more flexible the bristles, the gentler you can be, a major point when brushing risen bread dough.

PARCHMENT AND PAN LINERS: To avoid the aggravation of cookies glued to the cookie sheet or cakes that stick to the pan and crumble, use a pan liner. Pan liners negate the need to grease your baking pan; however, in recipes calling for a pan to be both greased and floured, if you use parchment, you should grease the pan, then add the parchment, then grease the parchment (no flour necessary).

Parchment is our preferred pan liner. Made of silicone or vegetable-oil coated paper, it's greaseproof and nonstick. It can be used more than once, but isn't as long-lasting as silicone or flexible fiberglass pan liners, which can be washed and reused hundreds of times (see illustration on page 528). Parchment comes in sheets sized for half-sheet (13″ × 18″) and full-sheet (18″ × 26″) baking pans; in rolls; and in sizes and shapes for particular pans, such as 9″ rounds for layer cake pans, or rectangles for loaf pans. Pan liners come in fewer sizes and shapes.

Parchment also comes precut in triangles to make pastry cones, used for piping decorations onto cakes.

COOLING RACKS: If fresh-from-the-oven baked goods are cooled on or in a pan, their crust can become soggy, due to condensation. Racks prevent this and are also helpful when you're drizzling icing or chocolate atop pastries and don't want them to end up in a sweet puddle.

Racks are available round (various diameters), perfect for layer cakes; and square or rectangular, also in varying sizes, good for cookies and pastries. Our favorite racks feature a grid design, rather than just parallel strips of wire; the grid supports soft pastries and keeps them from drooping. Nonstick racks are available, but not necessary. If something is so sticky it'll stick to a regular rack, it also sticks to a nonstick rack.

Handy innovations include racks that fold for storage and tiered racks, set atop one another, which save counter space.

BOWLS: The baker's most constant friend is a bowl. Bowls range from tiny, 1-tablespoon ingredient bowls to 2-gallon (or larger) bowls perfect for mixing up a triple yeast bread recipe or holiday fruitcakes.

Consider a variety of factors when choosing bowls. If you'll be melting butter or warming milk in a microwave, choose a microwave-safe bowl. Whipping cream in a chilled bowl? Choose stainless steel or copper (copper is especially good for whipping egg whites into meringue). Making a lot of yeast bread? Choose a crockery bowl, which will stay warm as the dough rises.

Another factor to consider is bowl shape. Sure, they're almost all round, but deep, narrow bowls are best for beating batters, whipped cream, and other loose mixtures that splatter. Wider bowls are best for mixing solid ingredients, such as the fruits for a fruitcake or apples for a pie. A bowl that's neither particularly narrow nor wide is ideal for dough, such as biscuits or pie crust, as it keeps the ingredients confined (and thus promotes cohesion), but also lets you get your hands into the bowl to work.

Some bowls come with a nonskid ring or coating on the bottom to keep them from slipping on the counter as you beat. This is a nice option, but not necessary, unless you do some fairly physical, vigorous mixing. Some bowls come with a spout (batter bowls), which makes them a good choice for pancake batter, melted chocolate, or anything else you'll be pouring.

A final factor to consider is weight. Extra-large crockery bowls are very attractive and are usually oven-safe (lovely for baking a stew), but before purchasing, decide whether you're strong enough and have a good enough grip to maneuver them around the kitchen. Acrylic and melamine bowls come in fun colors and they're lightweight and easy to handle, but some aren't microwave-safe. Stainless steel bowls are a good all-around choice, but if they're lightweight enough to handle easily, they'll also dent just as easily. Whichever material you choose, a set of bowls—approximately 2-, 4-, and 6-quart—is most useful. Add a larger bowl, if you like, for the occasional big baking job.

KNIVES AND SLICING GUIDES: A good bread knife should be a part of every bread baker's arsenal of tools. A bread knife should be serrated, preferably with a "wave" serration, as this is the most versatile style, and will work best on anything from a chewy-crusted hearth loaf to soft white sandwich bread. The blade should be 8″ to 10″ long, made of high-carbon stainless steel (which sharpens better than regular stainless steel), and feel balanced and comfortable in your hand. To preserve the knife's blade, hand-washing is a good choice, particularly if the knife has a wooden handle; drying it after washing is also good practice.

An offset bread knife, shaped like an offset spatula with the blade set below rather than even with the handle, allows you to slice all the way to the bottom of the loaf without rapping your knuckles on the breadboard. While not critical, it's a handy design feature.

A bread slicing guide, consisting of two rows of upright wooden or plastic posts on opposite sides of a breadboard, is a useful tool for cutting even slices of bread. If you bake bread in a bread machine, be sure to get a slicing guide that's wide enough to fit the loaf size you bake. The loaf is inserted between the posts and they're used as a guide for the knife as the bread is cut.

Offset bread knife

To cut pie, cake, or other pastries, a triangular-blade cake or pie server, serrated on one edge for cutting, combines two tools in one. The serrations for cake or pie knives are generally smaller than those on a bread knife to better deal with those pastries' tender crusts.

If you have nonstick bakeware and you bake things that are cut right in the pan, you'll need an acrylic or plastic serrated knife. These work well; even though they won't cut your hand or bakeware, they do a fine job slicing through brownies or a pizza. So put your prejudices about plastic aside and buy one.

A rigid plastic dough divider (it looks like a smaller plastic version of a bench knife) is excellent for cutting brownies and bar cookies in their pans, as well as for portioning dough.

CAKE TESTER: Remember Mom pulling a straw out of the kitchen broom to poke into the center of her baking cake? If the straw came out clean, the cake was ready. That old-fashioned tool hasn't changed much; now you can buy a small "broom" made just for plucking cake-testing straws from, or sharpened wooden testers about the diameter of cooked spaghetti, or thin metal cake testers. Choose one thick enough that you can easily see whether it's coated with batter after withdrawing it from the cake, but not so thick it leaves a noticeable hole.

Cake tester

PARING KNIFE: The most reliable test for a quick bread or pound cake is to insert a paring knife into the center when you think it's done. Thick batters can be deceptive, and the paring knife's increased surface area is more trustworthy for picking up raw batter for you to see when you examine it.

TURNERS: For flipping flapjacks or transferring cookies from pan to cooling rack, a good turner is essential. Choose one with a wide enough blade to handle your favorite size pancake on the griddle, but not so wide that it's not maneuverable around cookies lined up on a cookie sheet; around 3″ is a good compromise. A turner that's safe on nonstick surfaces is useful if you have a lot of nonstick pans. A bevel on the end of the blade is useful for getting underneath thin cookies. Press the turner down on the counter to flex the blade; it should flex willingly, but not be so flimsy that it can't do the hard work of getting the first brownie out of the pan.

Spice grinder

MORTAR AND PESTLE: The easiest way to crush cardamom or any type of seeds is with a mortar and pestle, a heavy bowl (mortar) and round-headed crusher with handle (pestle) that fits inside the bowl. Marble is a common material for both mortar and pestle; the heaviness of the stone does much of the

Mortar and pestle

work for you. Make sure the pestle and inside of the mortar are unglazed; a rough surface is essential for best crushing.

Some mortars and pestles, called spice grinders, are shaped specifically for crushing whole spices and seeds; the mortar has a much shallower bowl (more surface area), and the pestle a head that fits the bowl exactly, so no spices can escape as you work.

GRATERS: Looking very much like a wood rasp (in fact, that's the design they're based on), the plane grater does an excellent all-around job on cheese, chocolate, garlic, citrus peel, and anything else you can grip and grate. Ranging from long, thin, fine-blade graters to wider graters with blades ranging from extra-fine to coarse, these graters are easy to use, sharp and efficient, and easy to clean. We prefer them to the standard box grater.

ZESTER: When you need just a teaspoon or two of fresh citrus zest, use a zester, a simple stainless steel rod with a series of sharpened holes across one end. Simply scrape the zester across the orange or lemon with the same motion you'd use with a paring knife, removing thin strips of just the outer citrus peel.

Plane grater

Measuring

Baking, while considered an art, is equal parts science. Accurate measuring is always important, and sometimes essential, to baking success. Thus it's important that you invest in some good-quality (accurate) measuring tools.

MEASURING SPOONS: It used to be measuring spoons came in a simple set of four round spoons: ¼ and ½ teaspoon, 1 teaspoon, and 1 tablespoon. Now, that basic set has expanded to include ⅛, ¾, and 1½ teaspoon measures; and the spoons themselves may be oblong-shaped, to fit easily into spice cans, or given a handle with a bent end, to balance them securely on the counter when filled with salt or vanilla.

While it's difficult to ascertain the accuracy of measuring spoons, one check you can make is that the parts add up to the whole: 3 teaspoons should equal 1 tablespoon, two ½ teaspoons 1 teaspoon, and so on. If these measurements don't add up, the overall accuracy of the spoons should be questioned.

A small luxury and a real-time saver is to have more than one set of measuring spoons; one for wet ingredients, another for dry. Our favorite measuring spoons are stainless steel, with the size of each imprinted on its handle. They hold their shape through the heat of the dishwasher, unlike some plastic spoons. If you're willing to wash plastic spoons by hand, however, they're a good low-cost alternative. And, if they're color-coded (red = 1 teaspoon, etc.), they're ideal for those dealing with vision problems.

MEASURING CUPS: There are two basic types of measuring cup: liquid and dry. A liquid measure should have a pouring spout and be made of clear glass or plastic, with clear markings on the side; markings should include as many in-between volumes as possible (e.g., ⅔, ¾, etc.).

Some newer measuring cups allow you to look straight down into the cup at its markings; this is handy, as leaving the cup on the counter steadies the liquid, making it easy to measure.

Our favorite liquid measure size is 2 cups; we also appreciate a measure that's microwave-safe, for warming milk and melting butter.

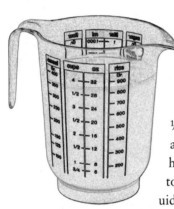

Liquid measure

To accurately read a traditional measuring cup, set it on a flat surface and crouch down to where you can see the top of the liquid at eye level. You'll see two very thin lines atop the surface of the liquid. This is the meniscus—you learned this in high school physics, right? Read the level at the base (bottom) of the meniscus.

Dry measures come in sets; a complete set will include ⅛-, ¼-, ⅓-, ½-, ⅔-, ¾-, and 1-cup measures. Add 1½-, 2-, and 3-cup measures, if you like. These measures shouldn't have spouts; a dry measure needs to be filled right up to the top to be accurate and shouldn't be used for measuring liquids. It's important to note that there's no enforced standard for measuring cups to be accurate; they can vary wildly from one manufacturer to the next. Be sure all the dry measuring cups you're using are from the same set; if you mix and match, the volumes they measure won't be in proportion to each other. While usually made of stainless steel, they also come in plastic. Each cup's size should be imprinted on its handle; some measuring cups also print the size on the outside base of the cup, so you can read it when the cup is hanging on a pegboard, a handy feature. It's also useful if the cups nest nicely, so you can stow them in a drawer if you don't want to hang them.

If you have what you believe to be an accurate scale, you can check the accuracy of your measuring cups by measuring out 1 cup of water and weighing it; it should weigh 227g (if you live close to sea level). Check smaller and larger amounts, as well.

THERMOMETERS: Digital thermometers (those that register a final temperature within 15 seconds or so) are an essential baking tool. Rather than guessing, it's nice to know the temperature of a fully cooked custard pie (165°F), a loaf of baked bread (190°F to 210°F), and yeast dough at its optimum rising temperature (76°F to 78°F). Why choose digital, rather than standard? Because standing with the oven

Instant-read thermometer

Probe
thermometer

door open waiting for a dial thermometer to work is unpleasant for you, and not helpful to your baked goods.

Thermometers are made of a sharpened, stainless steel probe attached to a measuring dial or window. The better thermometers will read temperatures in the final ⅛″ of the probe; lower-quality thermometers need to be inserted deeper in order to work, which is not helpful when you're trying to take the temperature of a shallow custard-based tart. The greater the temperature range of the thermometer, the more expensive it will be. It's helpful to have a thermometer that reads to at least 370°F, as that's the oil temperature required by many fried doughs. At the other end, yeast does well dissolved in water that's about 105°F, so choose a thermometer that goes that low.

A nice innovation is a thermometer whose probe is attached to the measuring dial via a long, thin metal cord. The probe can be inserted into your partially baked loaf of bread, the oven door closed, and when the bread's reached 190°F (or whichever temperature you program it for), the thermometer will beep to let you know.

Instant-read thermometers come in both digital and mechanical versions.

Digital thermometers are generally easier to read and may be more accurate; however, they also require a battery. Mechanical thermometers are less expensive.

An oven thermometer is also useful. One that can both hang from the oven rack, or stand on its own is handy; move it around the oven to check for any hot spots. Oven thermometers are always mechanical, never digital; while mercury oven thermometers are a bit more accurate, we hesitate to use them due to the slight possibility they could break and spill their mercury in the oven.

SCALES: You'll notice that all of the recipes in this book include weight as well as volume measurements; this is because weight measurements are more accurate, and it's usually easier to scale a recipe up or down (i.e., increase or decrease the yield) dealing with weight, not volume.

The two main types of scale are digital and mechanical. Digital scales are much more accurate, and, unless expense is a real issue, we suggest spending the money for a battery-powered digital scale. Here are some things to consider when purchasing a digital scale. First, make sure the measuring platform fits your favorite bowls; we suggest buying a scale with a flat platform rather than a detachable bowl. Second, ascertain that it measures in both American pounds and ounces, and metric grams, and that it's easy to switch from one to the other; the switch should be located on the front of the scale, not its bottom.

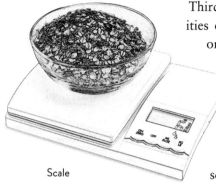

Scale

Third, assess the scale's capacity. In general, scales have capacities of between 4 pounds to about 11 pounds, in ¼-ounce or 5g (sometimes 2g) increments; or a combination (the smaller increments at the lower weights). For most usefulness, we recommend the higher capacity units. Fourth, make sure the scale has a "tare" feature—this allows you to measure one ingredient into your mixing bowl, then reset the scale to zero in order to measure the next ingredient. Finally, check the scale's automatic shut-off; our favorite scales will remain on during at least 5 minutes of inactivity (something that happens frequently when we're distracted by the phone ringing, the dog barking to be let out, or kids asking questions). A scale that shuts off after 1 minute is annoying; if you were partway through measuring flour into the bowl, you need to start over (unless you can remember how much was in the bowl before it shut off).

TIMERS: As with scales and thermometers, timers come in both mechanical and battery-powered digital versions. We prefer digital timers; not just because they're more accurate, but because we've never found a mechanical timer with a ring longer than about 8 seconds, and that's not long enough for the busy baker who might have stepped out of the kitchen for 10 seconds. Yes, you could use your phone, but a dedicated timer assigned to whatever's in the oven is more secure (and simpler to clean if you're operating it with messy hands).

A popular digital timer is a small, lightweight version that hangs around your neck; there's never a chance of burning your cookies because you're out in the garden or upstairs reading. Most digital timers are magnetized to attach to your refrigerator or oven; some also include a fold-out stand and/or clip to attach to a belt or pocket. Important features to assess include loudness and length of ring (1 minute is a good standard); size of numerals (¾˝ is helpful for keeping track of progress from across the kitchen); and range. Some timers count down by seconds, and their range is up to 9 hours, 99 minutes, 99 seconds. Some timers don't count by seconds, but their range is much higher. If you don't need second-by-second timing, choose the timer with the greater range; we prefer timers that measure by seconds, as often we're beating whipped cream or doing some other chore we like to measure in 30- or 90-second intervals.

Storage

BREAD BAGS: Storing bread at room temperature is best; refrigeration stales bread quickly. A plastic bag sized to fit your loaf is most efficient and works best. For bread with a crisp crust, try to purchase perforated plastic bags; they protect the bread while letting it breathe. Plastic-lined cloth bread bags are attractive and reusable.

INGREDIENT STORAGE: Flour and sugar are usually stored in lidded canisters. While flour and sugar canisters—made of ceramic, stainless steel, or clear glass—don't need to be airtight, that's an option if you're particularly troubled by moth infestations or ants. Choose canisters with an opening wide enough to dip a scoop into, and to hold a cup over to sweep off the excess.

Yeast canister with spoon

Other ingredients do best in containers with tighter lids, as they gradually deteriorate when exposed to air. Yeast, baking powder, and baking soda, the big three of leavening, do well in gasketed canisters with snap-tight lids. Olive oil and liquid flavors and extracts deteriorate in light, as well as air and heat, so keep them in dark or opaque, tightly closed containers, away from the stove.

Whole grains should be stored in the freezer for best shelf life. Plastic jars with screw-on lids are a good option here; be sure to mark the jar with what's inside and the date it was put in the freezer, or someday you'll find yourself trying to identify something brown and grainy by looks alone.

Flour canister

Cutters

COOKIE CUTTERS, STAMPS, AND MOLDS: Christmas and, increasingly, holidays such as Thanksgiving, Halloween, and July Fourth are marked by shaped cookies ranging from angels and trees to shooting stars, turkeys, and black cats. These cookies are made by rolling out cookie dough (sugar or gingerbread are the traditional flavors), then cutting it with a shaped cutter.

Most cookie cutters are made of tin, plastic, copper, or copper-plated aluminum. All work equally well, although the tin ones, if particularly flimsy, will bend out of shape easily. Many bakers keep their copper cutters on display in the kitchen when not in use. Be sure any cutters you purchase are at least ½˝ deep, and that they have a sharp side (for cutting) and a dull side (for holding).

Pastry cutters are similar to cookie cutters in all respects except one: They're usually very small, ranging from ¾″ to 2″ in size. They're used to cut shapes from pie crust (leaves and stars are typical) to decorate the top and edges of a pie.

Cookie stamps, often made of terra-cotta, are used to stamp designs into the top of shortbread-type cookies. The dough is rolled into a ball, then flattened with the stamp, whose impression remains after the cookie is baked. One caveat: You must choose a recipe without leavening, as stamped cookies won't hold their design if the cookie rises.

Ceramic cookie molds are a combination cookie stamp and cookie cutter. Cookie dough (again, unleavened is best) is pressed into the mold, where it acquires its shape and design; it's turned out of the mold onto a pan and baked. Springerle molds, native to Germany, were traditionally made of wood, but now are usually made of a wood-and-resin composite. Very intricately carved, these molds (or a springerle rolling pin) shape a traditional anise-scented dough that's turned onto baking sheets and dried overnight before baking—producing one tough cookie! Some folks enjoy springerle, but many feel they're better as Christmas tree ornaments than something you'd eat.

COOKIE PRESS: A cookie press, either manual or electric, is a necessity when making all manner of extruded cookies. Cookie dough is loaded into a hollow cylinder and pressed out through a shaped opening to create various fanciful designs. A key point to ensure cookie press success is to use the right cookie recipe; too stiff, and the press is difficult to work; too soft, and the cookies won't hold their shape. Also, pay attention to the temperature of the dough as mentioned in the recipe.

BISCUIT CUTTERS: Biscuit cutters are key to producing high-rising biscuits; biscuits cut with a dull cutter won't rise well as their sidewalls have been compacted rather than cleanly cut. Round biscuit cutters, made of tin, stainless steel, or plastic, usually come in nesting sets ranging from 1½″ to 2¾″ in diameter. Be sure they're at least 1″ deep, in order to cut through your thickest biscuit dough. Biscuit cutters (which also come in linked hexagons) can double as cookie cutters. In addition, we like to use biscuit cutters to cut small rounds out of a sheet cake, which we then ice and decorate to make tiny individual cakes.

Biscuit cutters

DOUGHNUT OR BAGEL CUTTER: A circular cutter with a smaller cutter in the center, the doughnut (bagel) cutter is used

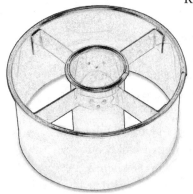

Doughnut cutter

to cut standard-size (3½″) doughnuts or bagels. Make sure the cutters are aligned; when you press the cutter down on the dough, both should cut all the way through. Less expensive cutters may be out of alignment, making them frustrating to use.

CAKE SLICER: When you want to cut a cake layer through the middle to make two thinner layers, try a cake slicer. A cake slicer has an adjustable height, and thin wire stretched tautly between two posts (similar to a jigsaw). Gently saw the wire back and forth through the cake; if you keep the metal feet at the bottom of the posts flush with the counter, you'll make a nice, straight, even cut.

Pastry Tools

CAKE COMB: The distinctive thin, parallel lines decorating the sides of a fancy iced layer cake are made with a cake comb, which features numerous thin, sharp sawlike teeth. The baker holds the comb in place against the side of the cake, then turns the cake turntable (below) to make lines in the frosting.

CAKE TURNTABLE: For easiest cake decorating, invest in a turntable (akin to a lazy susan). Turntables come in expensive cast aluminum or less expensive plastic. Some are elevated, some nearly flush with the counter; the elevated turntable raises the cake so it's easier to work with. An important thing to check before purchasing a turntable is whether it turns without wobbling. Crouch down so you're eye level with the top of the turntable and give it a spin; it should spin smoothly, without moving out of line at all.

COOKIE SCOOPS: Also known as a disher or depositor, the cookie scoop is simply an ice cream scoop sized to deposit a traditional (1-teaspoon or 1-tablespoon) ball of dough onto a cookie sheet, quickly and cleanly. While neither the 1-teaspoon nor 1-tablespoon scoop portions out that exact measurement of dough, the amount it scoops is what recipes have traditionally called for: the amount a rounded teaspoon or tablespoon—the kind you eat with, not the measuring kind—would spoon out. The teaspoon scoop will make cookies that are about 1½″ in diameter; the tablespoon scoop will make 2½″ cookies.

Cookie
scoops

Choose a scoop that's easy for you to squeeze; it will keep your hand and wrist from tiring when you're making lots of cookies. If dough starts to stick in the scoop, simply wipe the interior clean, spray with a nonstick baking spray, and continue.

MUFFIN SCOOP: Big brother to the cookie or ice cream scoop, a muffin scoop dishes out ¼ cup of muffin, cupcake, or pancake batter—easily, evenly, and quickly. Cupcakes or muffins will have smoother, rounder tops (and pancakes will be evenly sized) when they're deposited into the pan with a muffin scoop.

DOUGH DOCKER: Looking like a very small (3″ to 4″) spiked rolling pin, the dough docker cuts even rows of holes into cracker dough, or thoroughly pricks the bottom of a tart or pie shell in a few easy swipes. Unless you're very particular about how your pastry looks, or you're doing lots of pastry that needs docking, a fork can easily substitute for the docker.

Dough docker

FLOUR WAND OR SHAKER: This old-fashioned tool is used to dust a work surface (or the top of pastry or bread dough) with flour. A ball of coiled metal is filled with flour, then the handle is squeezed to let just a bit of the flour sift out, exactly where you direct it. It's perfect when you want just a dusting, rather than scattered handfuls, of flour.

Flour wand

GIANT SPATULA: This 11¾″ × 10½″ aluminum blade, affixed in a plastic handle, easily moves a rolled-out pie crust into its pan, transfers a small pizza or risen loaf of bread onto a hot baking stone, shovels crackers onto a baking sheet in two easy swipes, moves fragile cake layers from counter to top of the stack, and moves cookies from cookie sheet to cooling rack. Two used in tandem will move even the biggest, most fragile filled braid with ease.

OFFSET SPATULAS: These are one of the most useful tools in our test kitchen. The smaller size (4½″) is ideal for smoothing batter to be level inside the rim of a layer cake pan, sweeping extra frosting off the surface of a cookie, and putting just the right swirl on top of a cupcake. Larger versions (7½″ to 10″) are indispensable for frosting layer cakes and leveling batters inside 9″ × 13″ or half sheet pans.

Offset spatula

ICING SPATULA: For icing cakes, use an icing spatula, a long, narrow, flexible stainless steel turner, one that follows the curve of the cake as it smooths frosting around the sides and can bend to create artful swirls on top. Icing spatulas are available straight or offset, in an array of lengths; rounded on the end or tapering to a narrow point (for fine work). Choose a medium spatula that feels comfortable in your hand.

CAKE STRIPS: These 30″ strips of heat-resistant coated cotton are first soaked in water, then fastened around the circumference of a round layer cake pan to insulate its sides, preventing the edges from setting before the center of the cake, and thus keeping the cake's top surface flat.

PASTRY BAG AND TIPS: To shape the dough for éclairs or cream puffs, or to decorate a cake, use a pastry bag, a cone made of plastic-lined canvas, or single-use parchment or plastic. Batter or icing is spooned into the bag, then squeezed out through a decorative chrome-plated or stainless steel metal tip. Tips come in a huge array of designs and sizes; the beginning cake decorator does well to purchase a basic kit, which will include a bag and about a dozen different tips and accompanying paraphernalia (couplers, cleaners, etc.).

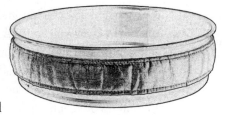

Cake strip

PASTRY BLENDER OR FORK: To combine flour and fat quickly and evenly when making pie crust, use a pastry blender, a series of parallel stainless steel wires or thin stainless blades, shaped in a half-moon with a handle on top. The baker gently chops down on the fat and flour (think of mashing potatoes with a hand masher) until the fat chunks are the desired size—large for flaky pastry, small for crisp pastry. A pastry fork, which resembles an oversized dinner fork with larger, thicker, wider-spaced tines, performs the same function.

Pastry blender and fork

PASTRY WHEEL: A pastry wheel is used to cut strips of pie pastry for a lattice-top crust, cut circles of turnover dough, or for any kind of dough-cutting chore. A standard pastry wheel resembles a miniature pizza wheel, with a circular blade that's only 1½″ to 2″ in diameter. A deckle-edge wheel lends a zigzag pattern to the edges of cut pastry dough. A sealing pastry wheel (also called a ravioli cutter) is designed to both seal and cut dough in one motion, useful for making ravioli or turnovers.

Pastry wheel

PIE CHAIN AND PIE WEIGHTS: When blind baking a pie crust (baking it prior to adding the filling), it's necessary to prevent it puffing up by adding weight. The old-fashioned solution, and one that still works, is to line the crust with parchment or waxed paper, then fill it with dried beans or uncooked rice, although these days we prefer to use sugar, which can be reused afterward for baking, or pie weights, which are designed for exactly this purpose.

The stainless steel pie chain, a beaded chain designed to be coiled onto the crust, is an easy solution. When crust is baked, simply lift the chain out with a pair of tongs; no worrying about hot beans or pie weights spilling all over the counter. While most pie chains on the market are 6 feet long, that's not really long enough to cover the crust; the 10-foot version is preferable.

PIE CRUST SHIELD: The bottom and top crusts of your baking pie are insulated by the filling, and are nigh impossible to overbake. The edge of the crust, however, is a different story—thin and unprotected by steamy filling, it's liable to burn if left in the oven too long. A pie crust shield—a round, flat piece of lightweight aluminum—replaces the crumpled strips of foil our mothers used to shield their pie crusts. Sized to fit a standard 9″ pie, the shield sits very gently atop any fancy fluted edges; just be sure not to put it on until the edge has had a chance to set, 20 minutes or so into the baking time. Also, don't wait until the edge of the crust is perfectly browned before adding the shield; even with the shield it will continue to brown, albeit slowly, so add the shield while the crust is still a light golden brown.

ROLLING PINS: The rolling pin is a critical tool for shaping all kinds of baked goods, so it's important to have one that works well and that you enjoy using. Some folks scoff at the need for a rolling pin, saying they get along just fine using an empty bottle. Yes, a bottle will work; so does a washboard, so why bother to buy a washing machine? The efficient, effective, easy way a rolling pin flattens dough is unmatched by any substitute.

Rolling pins come in a variety of types, ranging from 20″, one-piece hardwood pins tapered at both ends (a "French pastry pin"), to 2″ long pastry rollers, with lots of styles and sizes in between.

A good all-around size for rolling dough on a counter or board is a pin with a 10″ barrel. The wider the diameter of the barrel, the fewer strokes you'll need to take, and the more tender your pastry will be, as the gluten won't become overworked. Larger pins are fine, but anything smaller than a 10″ barrel is inefficient for most tasks.

Long pins, such as the aforementioned French pastry pin, are useful for rolling strudel or pasta dough, or other large sheets of dough; in addition, some bakers claim they have a better "feel" for the dough with this narrow-diameter pin. But if you're simply making standard recipes, an all-purpose pin is a better choice.

The most important part of a rolling pin is its barrel. Barrels are made from stainless steel, marble, nonstick aluminum, nylon, wood, composite, or even glass (an empty glass pin is designed to be filled with chilled water). Our favorites are heavy wood or stainless steel; the weight of either takes much of the effort out of rolling.

A pin that can be chilled before using (e.g., a marble or metal pin) will help keep the fat in pie crust and puff pastry from melting as you roll.

Another factor to consider is the pin's rolling mechanism. In some pins, the barrel simply rotates on a thin rod inserted through the center; on others, ball bearings help the rolling motion along.

When you've decided on the style and composition of your rolling pin, see if you can find a few to test before buying. Some will feel great under your hands; others, you just won't connect with. Roll the pin across a flat surface to make sure it rolls smoothly, with no catches; see if it's the best weight for your strength. A good rolling pin should last you a lifetime, so it's worth it to take some time to find the right one.

ROLLING PIN RINGS: Made of silicone in pairs of graduated widths, they slip over the barrel of your rolling pin, giving it a uniform height above the work surface. They're a simple way to make accurate, consistent thickness cookies or pastry.

SUGAR SOFTENER: Also known as a sugar bear for its traditional shape, this small (2″ to 3″), flat piece of porous terra-cotta is soaked in water, then added to a bag or canister of hard brown sugar. Within a day or two (depending on the quantity of sugar), the sugar will be soft again.

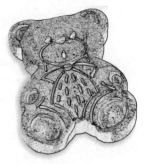

Sugar softener

Appliances

BREAD MACHINE: For kneading bread dough, nothing beats the efficiency and skill of a good bread machine. In side-by-side tests we've done, dough kneaded in a bread machine produced a higher-rising loaf of bread than dough kneaded by hand, electric mixer, or food processor. Look for a machine whose pan is a nice loaf shape, for those times you want to bake in the machine; and if you're a seasoned bread baker, you'll appreciate a programmable machine, one into which you can program your own kneading and rising times. There are a lot of bread machines on the market and many share the same features, so quality is what distinguishes one from another. Keep in mind that the lower the price, the less likely it is to be a quality machine.

MIXERS AND BEATERS: Unless you're really committed to doing everything the old-fashioned way, an electric mixer—either hand or stand—is a tool you should own.

When purchasing an electric hand mixer, look for one whose beaters are made from rounded wires (such as the type found in a whisk), rather than flat metal bars. The whisk-type beaters do a better job and are easier to clean. When shopping for one, pick up the mixer and hold it as if you were using it. Is it comfortable? Not too heavy? Can you reach the controls easily with one hand? Some hand mixers aren't sized for smaller hands. Is the cord long enough to let you maneuver around the counter a bit? Does the mixer have an extra-slow first speed, so flour and cocoa won't fly out of the mixing bowl? Check out which attachments come with the mixer. Does it have dough hooks? Perhaps a balloon whisk, for egg whites and whipped cream? What size is its motor compared to other mixers? The higher power the motor, the more and stiffer dough the mixer will be able to handle.

The stand mixer—an electric mixer attached to a stand, with a removable bowl—should go through an examination similar to that given a hand mixer. Are the controls conveniently located? Are the bowl and/or beating attachments easy to take off and put back on? Does the bowl have a handle? (This is a real selling point when you're trying to spoon a double batch of brownie batter out of a heavy, often greasy bowl.) What's the bowl's capacity? (We prefer 5 quarts or greater.) Check the lowest speed; is it sufficiently slow to allow dry ingredients to be added without poofing? Which attachments come with the mixer? (A dough hook or hooks, flat beater, and whisk should all be included.) What about extras, such as a pouring shield, extra bowl, a cover, or an interesting recipe book? What kinds of attachments would you be interested in purchasing in the future (pasta extruder? juicer?), and are they available for the model you're examining? How powerful is the motor? Does the machine appear sturdy enough to remain steady on the counter, even while dealing with a double batch of stiff bagel dough? If you take the time to answer all these questions to your satisfaction before purchasing, you'll be much more pleased with the mixer you choose.

IMMERSION OR STICK BLENDER: For the money, this is one of the most useful tools around for making emulsions (such as that ganache that's taking forever to smooth out), puréeing warm liquids or fillings while still in the saucepan, or fixing a broken mayonnaise. Look for one that has variable speeds, is comfortable in your hand, and has a chopping bowl or grinder accessory to make swift work of grinding nuts or bread crumbs without making a big food processor bowl dirty.

FOOD PROCESSOR: Most food processors include instructions for kneading bread dough. While it's not our favorite method to knead dough—we feel a food processor overheats and "beats up" the dough more than necessary—it does a satisfactory job. The processor does well with cookie dough or muffin batter, but you do need to watch carefully when adding chocolate chips, dried fruit, or other ingredients, so that you don't accidentally purée them. The processor's best baking uses, in our opinion, are chopping nuts (anything from a coarse dice to nut flour); chopping chocolate; whipping ganache; making pie crust; shredding cheese and slicing vegetables, for pizza or focaccia; making bread crumbs from a stale loaf; or slicing fruit for pies.

When choosing a food processor, make sure the feed tube is conveniently located and sufficiently large that you don't need to do too much pre-chopping of ingredients. We prefer a machine with a medium (11- to 14-cup capacity) work bowl. The machine should be heavy enough to sit securely on the counter.

WHERE TO FIND IT

Most of the ingredients in the recipes in this book are available from King Arthur Baking Company. Our *Baker's Catalogue* is the prime source of fine tools, ingredients, and recipes for the home baker. Many are also available in grocery and gourmet stores throughout the United States. Some of the tools mentioned in this section are available at quality kitchen accessory stores; all can be purchased from *The Baker's Catalogue*, or online (where you'll also find many more recipes and resources) at www.kingarthurbaking.com. When you're in Vermont, stop by The Baker's Store here in Norwich, which carries everything in the catalogue and more. Feel free to ask an employee-owner to sign your book!

Acknowledgments

This book is the realization of a decade-long dream by baking visionary P.J. Hamel, a longtime writer and editor at the King Arthur Baking Company. This book, these recipes, the patiently described techniques, and the friendly take-you-by-the-hand tone are in large part her handiwork. P.J. was ably accompanied by her team of bakers and writers in Norwich, Vermont, and by Brinna Sands, another visionary, inveterate baker, and prolific writer on all things baking. Brinna has been a part of the King Arthur family since 1976, and in 1990 she authored the company's first book, *The King Arthur Flour 200th Anniversary Cookbook*. P.J. and Brinna's dedication to the gentle art of making someone a homemade loaf of bread, a batch of cookies, brownies, muffins, a pie or cake, or other piece of love, is a true inspiration.

The book you hold in your hands was a true company-wide project, and recipes flowed from all corners. It's a testament to the hard work and contributions of all of King Arthur's employee-owners. After the recipes were chosen, baker/writer Susan Reid, with the assistance of Robby Kuit and Teresa Griffith, tested (and tested and tested), tweaked, massaged, and refined the recipes until they were just right. Susan picked up the slack all along the way, doing whatever needed doing—from writing headnotes to compiling lists of ingredients and checking weights, she smoothed what often seemed a bumpy road. Publications manager Toni Apgar coordinated this yearlong effort and, in the process, gently guided our team of bakers and writers.

In addition, the following people made invaluable contributions: longtime recipe developer and head of King Arthur's R&D team Sue Gray; artisan bakers Richard and Stephanie Miscovich, Michael Jubinsky, and Master Baker Jeffrey Hamelman; Susan Miller, founder of our King Arthur Baking School; and Cindy Fountain, Judy Ulinski, Shannon Zappala, Janet Matz, Robyn Sargent, Ali Scheier, Jen Korhonen, Starr Kilgore, Emmy Zietz, Jane Korhonen, Robin Rice, Brenda Hickory, and Steve Voigt.

We thank our original editor at The Countryman Press, Kermit Hummel, for his enthusiasm for this project from day one. He always believed this would be the wonderful book it is, and we now count him as a friend as well as an editor. We appreciate the sage advice of W. W. Norton editor Maria Guarnaschelli, who assisted us in developing this book's outline. And we're grateful to editor Ann Treistman at The Countryman Press for encouraging us in 2019 to embark on the journey of breathing new life into this book and for believing tirelessly in its future.

The new edition of this award-winning book wouldn't have been possible without the able guiding hand of Chris McLeod; writer Posie Brien, who painstakingly sifted through every recipe in the book, updating any that had changed over the past nearly 20 years; and King Arthur creative director Ruth Perkins, responsible for the book's fresh new look. Without them, this edition you now hold in your hands wouldn't have been possible.

We wish you all warm bread from the oven whenever you want it.

THE KING ARTHUR BAKING COMPANY

Index